4.a5

PURITANISM AND LIBERTY

PURITANISM AND LIBERTY

Being the Army Debates (1647–9)
from the
CLARKE MANUSCRIPTS
with Supplementary Documents

SELECTED AND EDITED WITH
AN INTRODUCTION BY

A. S. P. WOODHOUSE

PREFACE BY

IVAN ROOTS
Professor of History, University of Exeter

J. M. DENT & SONS LTD LONDON

Introduction and selection,
Copyright J. M. Dent & Sons Ltd., 1938
© Preface, J. M. Dent & Sons Ltd., 1974

All rights reserved
Printed in Great Britain
by Biddles Limited, Guildford, Surrey
for J. M. Dent & Sons Ltd.
Aldine House · Albemarle Street · London
and
The University of Chicago Press, Chicago 60637

First published 1938
Reprinted 1951, 1965, 1966
Second edition 1974

Dent edition
Hardback ISBN 0-460-10057-2
Paperback ISBN 0-460-11057-8

University of Chicago Press edition
Hardback ISBN 0-226-90703-1

(3|5|95)

134402

PREFACE

Interest in themes taken up in *Puritanism and Liberty* has grown enormously since its publication in 1938 and the book remains in constant demand. A. S. P. Woodhouse's interpretations in the Introduction have been modified, even rejected by some, but it is still so thought-provoking that to exclude it from this edition would have been unthinkable. As for the documents themselves there are none that can be dismissed as trivial. The unique value of the Putney and Whitehall debates in particular is increasingly appreciated. Even so, though the text has been copiously drawn upon, it has not been fully exploited. More than pamphlets and manifestoes, letters and memoirs which abound for this period, the debates are vital, alive. Here is material not filtered through a diarist's or commentator's prejudice or faulty recollection but almost verbatim what was said by men unaware of or at least indifferent to the fact that their spontaneous words were being taken down. Buffcoat and the Bedfordshire man are recorded with the same respect as Generals Cromwell and Ireton. It is a salutary exercise to read what was said in the order in which it was said, to make a sort of play-reading of the debates. There is then a growing realization that they not only illustrate the notions of the Levellers, of Cromwell, Rich and the rest, but that they reveal them in the process of development under stress. There is a war going on, not of words on paper—though a specific document, *The Agreement of the People*, set the thing off—but of ideas and aspirations, character and personality. The reader is swept along in the surge of battle.

Work on the Levellers has proliferated since 1938. Collections of Leveller propaganda have been made by W. Haller and G. Davies and by D. M. Wolfe.[1] There has been a substantial general survey by Joseph Frank, more dispassionate than H. N. Brailsford's massive *The Levellers and the English Revolution*.[2] D. B. Robertson examined the religious foundations of Leveller democracy in 1951,[3] an aspect which has been revived in an essay by J. C. Davis, 'The Levellers and Christianity'.[4] This stresses the impact of antinomianism on Levellers and denies Woodhouse's principle of the segregation of the orders of nature and of grace. The study most fruitful of controversy has been that of the marxist C. B. Macpherson in *The Political Theory of Possessive Individualism*.[5] Reading the Putney Debates (one may suspect) rather cursorily, he sets the Levellers in too rigid a frame. He sees them putting a natural property right firmly and centrally in their programme and thereby providing a basis for the political theory of John Locke. In particular, Macpherson repudiates a Leveller advocacy of manhood suffrage. His thesis, which almost became a new orthodoxy, has lately been criticised in general and in detail in a number of articles, not all of which are negative in their conclusions.[6] Of prime importance is Keith Thomas's 'The Levellers and the Franchise'[7] which by concentrating on this specific issue ('only one part of the Leveller programme, not necessarily the most important part at that') shows that 'the intellectual consistency' Professor Macpherson attempted to impart to their manifestoes is simply not there. In the process Dr Thomas finds the Levellers 'implausible as prophets of a new age of capitalism and wage labour'; 'however advanced their constitutional notions, their economic ideas were backward looking'—a view put forward earlier and in a rather different context by W. Schenk.[8] Thomas and Schenk like Macpherson and most other writers on the Levellers perhaps do not emphasize sufficiently what an eclectic lot they were. Some of them may have been even more radical in outlook, more lowly in social status even than the True Levellers or Diggers associated chiefly with Gerrard Winstanley. Responding to circumstances, Leveller groups not only realigned themselves but changed their order of priorities. The role of personality is important, too. There are two persuasive biographies of John Lilburne by M. A. Gibb and Pauline Gregg respectively.[9] John Wildman, for whom being a Leveller was perhaps only an episode in a picaresque career, has been written up by M. P. Ashley.[10] William Walwyn has been dealt with sympathetically—he was that kind of a man—by W. Schenk in the work cited above (note 8) and (more substantially) by A. L. Morton, whose *The World of the Ranters* examines a bunch of interconnexions of puritanism and liberty. H. Ross Williamson has provided a well-documented sketch of Col. Thomas Rainsborough.[11]

D. W. Petegorsky's *Left-Wing Democracy in the English Civil War* (1940) was largely about Winstanley, whose works appeared in an almost complete edition in New York in 1941, edited by G. Sabine, and in London in a selection by L. D. Hamilton (1944).[12] Much has been written about the Diggers since by Christopher Hill and others. In 1973 a substantial collection of Winstanley's writings appeared as a paperback Pelican classic—a striking indication of changes since the Second World War in attitude towards 'the English revolution'.[13] Woodhouse did not ignore the Diggers nor other strands of puritan thinking which have lately attracted more attention and respect—millenarianism and the privileges of the Saints.[14] Work here has brought the notion of an imminent second coming of Christ out of some 'lunatic fringe' of English theology almost into the main pattern. William Haller's *Foxe's Book of Martyrs and the Elect Nation* (1963) pointed to a long continuing and hallowed tradition. Others have gone back even further into medieval origins, as in N. Cohn's *The Pursuit of the*

Millenium (1957) and M. Reeves's *The Influence of Prophecy in the late Middle Ages* (1969).[15] The 'irrationality' of millenarianism is not taken for granted. As Christopher Hill has put it in his *Anti-Christ in Seventeenth-Century England* (Oxford, 1971) 'history must include much which seems irrational to the historian, too obsessed perhaps by the standards of irrationality fashionable in his own age and society.'[16] W. M. Lamont goes so far as to assert that 'millenarianism meant not alienation from the spirit of the age but a total involvement with it'.[17] A more modest but still large claim is made by the most detailed analyst of the Fifth Monarchists, Bernard Capp, who sees them as developing 'a potent and dangerous synthesis in which [millenarian] ideas become the justification for violent political action and sweeping social changes.'[18]

What all these writers show is that puritanism, given the conditions of early seventeenth-century English politics, religion and society, could not avoid being involved in them. Our knowledge of these things has improved since 1938. Puritanism has—or can be made to have—connexions with so many aspects of life that some doubts have been expressed as to the value of the concept at all. 'Puritan political thought is almost as non-existent as puritan theology' argues C. H. George,[19] who goes on to say that 'puritanism cannot be considered an entity'. 'An analytical concept which obscures the realities and significances of differences in ideas, ideals, programmes and class affinities is a bad concept. Puritanism is such a concept and should be abandoned.' Are things quite as bad as that? Is a concept which does accept differences quite impossible? Readers of the material in *Puritanism and Liberty* may or may not think so.

The University of Exeter   Ivan Roots

NOTES

Place of publication London unless otherwise stated.

1 *The Leveller Tracts 1647–1653*, ed William Haller and Godfrey Davies, New York, 1964, reprinted Gloucester, Mass., 1964; *Leveller Manifestoes of the Puritan Revolution*, ed Don M. Wolfe, New York, 1944, reprinted 1967. See also *Tracts on Liberty in the Puritan Revolution*, 3 vols, ed William Haller, New York, 1933–4, reprinted London, 1965, and D. M. Wolfe, *Milton in the Puritan Revolution*, New York, 1941.

2 Joseph Frank, *The Levellers, a History of the Writings of Three Seventeenth-Century Social Democrats: John Lilburne, Richard Overton and William Walwyn*, Cambridge, Mass., 1955; H. M. Brailsford, *The Levellers and the English Revolution*, ed Christopher Hill, 1961. See also Howard Shaw, *The Levellers*, 1968, a much briefer account, and chapters II and III in Perez Zagorin, *History of Political Thought in the English Revolution*, 1954, reprinted New York, 1966.

3 D. B. Robertson, *The Religious Foundations of Leveller Democracy*, New York, 1951.

4 In *Politics, Religion and the English Civil War*, ed Brian Manning, 1973. See also G. Huehns, *Antinomianism in English History*, 1951, and D. M. Himbury, 'The Religious Beliefs of the Levellers', *Baptist Quarterly*, xxxiii, 1954.

5 C. B. Macpherson, *The Political Theory of Possessive Individualism*, Oxford, 1962. See also C. Hill, 'Pottage for Freeborn Englishmen: Attitudes to Wage Labour in the 16th and 17th Centuries' in *Socialism, Capitalism and Economic Growth*, ed C. H. Feinstein, Cambridge, 1967.

6 See Isaiah Berlin, 'Hobbes, Locke and Professor Macpherson', *Political Quarterly*, xxxv, 1964; Alan Ryan, 'Locke and the Dictatorship of the Bourgeoisie', *Political Studies*, 1966; A. L. Merson, 'Problems of the English Bourgeois Revolution', *Marxism Today*, vii, 1963; Peter Laslett, 'Market Society and Political Theory', *Historical Journal*, vii, 1964; J. C. Davis, 'The Levellers and Democracy', *Past and Present*, xl, 1968; Roger|Howell, Jr., and David E. Brewster, 'Reconsidering the Levellers: The Evidence of *The*

Moderate', *ibid*, xlvi, 1970; B. S. Manning, 'The Levellers' in *The English Revolution 1600–1660*, ed. E. W. Ives, 1968; A. L. Morton, 'Leveller Democracy—Fact or Myth':in his *The World of\the\Ranters*, 1970.

7 In *The Interregnum: The Quest for Settlement 1646–60*, ed G. E. Aylmer, 1973.

8 Thomas, *op. cit.*, p 77; W. Schenk, *The Concern for Social Justice in the Puritan Revolution*, 1948.

9 M. A. Gibb, *John Lilburne the Christian Democrat*, 1947; Pauline Gregg, *Freeborn John: A Biography of John Lilburne*, 1961 (with a valuable bibliography).

10 M. P. Ashley, *John Wildman, Plotter and Postmaster*, 1947.

11 H. Ross Williamson, *Four Stuart Portraits*, 1948. Christopher Hill has written extensively on the Levellers, notably in his *Puritanism and Revolution*, 1958, and *The World Turned Upside Down*, 1972. See also G. E. Aylmer, 'Gentlemen Levellers', *Past and Present*, xlix, 1970.

12 *The Works of Gerrard Winstanley*, ed G. H. Sabine, New York, 1941, and *Selected Writings of Gerrard Winstanley*, ed L. D. Hamilton, 1944.

13 *Winstanley: The Law of Freedom and Other Writings*, ed (with a substantial introduction) C. Hill, 1973.

14 Leo Solt, *Saints in Arms: Puritanism and Democracy in Cromwell's Army*, Oxford, 1969, stresses 'authoritarian strains in puritanism' and looks askance at the notion of the New Model Army as 'the nursery school of radical ideas'. (See also John F. H. New, *Anglican and Puritan: The Basis of their Opposition, 1558–1640*, 1964.) On the other hand Michael Walzer, *The Revolution of the Saints*, 1965, considers 'puritanism as a revolutionary ideology'.

15 See also Keith Thomas, *Religion and the Decline of Magic*, 1971; *Puritans, the Millennium and the Future of Israel*, ed P. Toon, Cambridge, 1970.

16 p 177.

17 W. M. Lamont, *Godly Rule: Politics and Religion 1603–60*, 1969, p 14.

18 B. S. Capp, *The Fifth Monarchy Men: A Study in Seventeenth-Century English Millenarianism*, 1972, p 20. See also his 'Godly Rule and English Millenarianism', *Past and Present*, lii, 1971, and W. M. Lamont, 'Richard Baxter, the Apocalypse and the Mad Major', *ibid*, lv, 1972.

19 C. H. George, 'Puritanism as History and Historiography', *Past and Present*, xli, 1968, pp 103–4. (Apart from its stimulating arguments this article provides comprehensive bibliographical references.) See also I. Roots, *The Late Troubles in England*, Exeter, 1969.

CONTENTS

CONTENTS

[8]

CONTENTS

CONTENTS

INTRODUCTION

I

THE object of this volume is to exhibit, in certain aspects, the political thought of the Puritan revolution. Its attention is focused on the Army Debates about the constitutional settlement, commenced in the autumn of 1647, interrupted by the suppression of the General Council of the Army and the preoccupations of the Second Civil War, and resumed on the eve of Charles' trial and execution. But it looks before and after in order to illustrate and supplement what they yield.

The Debates have a special value, even beyond the pamphlet literature of the day, in giving us a spontaneous and unconscious revelation of the Puritan mind as it wrestles with its problems, practical and theoretic, in an effort not merely to justify a policy and battle down opposition, but to arrive at truth and agreement. There are the sharpest cleavages of opinion between the Independents and their allies to the Left, and they sometimes develop an acrimony in debate that suggests outlooks absolutely alien from each other. But even where they differ most markedly, they talk a common language very foreign to our ears; and all their differences are at last reducible to one: the point at which a revolutionary ideal must compromise with the demands of actual life, including those of order, tradition, sentiment, and vested interest. If the leaders on both sides came to the debate with a policy to advance, and with their minds largely closed, the other participants (who also reveal the Puritan temper and ideology) came both to convince and to be convinced; their presence and intervention are the necessary links between the opponents.

To provide an easily accessible text of these Debates was the first aim of the present volume, the only existing text (the late Sir Charles Firth's in his *Clarke Papers*[1]) having been long out of print and increasingly difficult to procure. On other grounds a new edition, based on a careful collation of Firth's text with the manuscript, seemed desirable, especially for the general reader. The debates were taken down in shorthand, presumably by

[1] Camden Society, 4 vols., 1891–1901.

INTRODUCTION

William Clarke (then assistant to John Rushworth, the secretary to the General and the Council of War), and were probably not deciphered and copied in a fair hand [1] till after the Restoration. The original notes were doubtless very defective. At some points the manuscript appears to be relatively correct and complete. At others it presents little more than a series of isolated phrases. Occasionally the order of the speeches is confused, owing (as Firth plausibly suggests) to the pages of the shorthand notes having got into the wrong order. What is less easy to explain is how sentences and clauses within a single speech have been wrested from their correct positions: we can only assume that it was due to a frenzied effort on the part of the stenographer to catch up with the speaker. But by far the commonest type of error is precisely the one that would be expected when an unskilful reporter is trying to copy verbatim the speeches in an excited argument: namely, the omission of words and phrases and the telescoping of sentences. No speech of any length is wholly free from this defect, and what appears at first sight to be an error in order sometimes turns out to be more easily explicable and remediable as an error of omission. The punctuation, which consists mainly of commas, serves in many instances rather to obscure than to clarify the sense. I have adopted modern punctuation,[2] spelling, and capitalization, since those of the original merely set an obstacle between the reader and the idea. Every other departure from the manuscript I have recorded in 'Notes on Text' (pp. 479 ff.), so that the student may at any given point check the text with the manuscript's reading if he chooses, in a way impossible in Firth's edition. Wherever feasible, I have restored the order of the manuscript. Finally I have tried (at the cost of a great deal of time and labour) to leave no speech and no sentence unintelligible. Assuming the presence of an error of omission wherever the manuscript gave no clear sense, I have added *in square brackets* such words as seemed necessary to link up the broken fragments and to present in an intelligible form the argument deducible from the speech itself and from the answers that it received. The result is a text which yields the speaker's sense much more readily than does that printed in the Camden Society's volumes. Nor do I think that it can justly be described as a less conservative text. It adopts many of Firth's emendations; it rejects some of his deviations from the original, especially his transpositions and omissions; its new departures consist almost

---

[1] In vol. 67 of the Clarke MSS., Worcester College, Oxford.
[2] With some latitude, however; see p. 479.

INTRODUCTION

wholly in additions, set in square brackets, which have only to be passed over in order to exhibit the reading of the manuscript (unless a letter indicates some further departure, precisely recorded in the notes). The general reader who is willing to accept my judgment, can ignore square brackets and letters; the special student has before him the materials with which to construct at any moment his own reading. Firth has spoken of the extraordinary difficulties presented to an editor of these reports by the state of the original. I can only in my own excuse emphasize these difficulties once more, and then record my constant debt to —for it would be impertinence to praise—his editorial labours: his many valuable emendations, and, where he has not ventured to emend, his luminous footnotes on the argument.[1]

It is singularly fortunate that the debates reported (or those whose reports have survived) deal with two of the most significant issues of Puritan political thought: democracy, or the proposed reform of the constitution in the direction of liberty and equality, with its attendant break with the past; and the question of religious liberty. Thus they form an ideal point of departure for studying these two major and closely related themes, to whose illustration I have devoted Part III of the volume. The selections there presented are not the sources, but representative analogues, of the arguments advanced in the Debates. As such they often serve to clarify the meaning of those arguments, and at the same time to illustrate the habit of mind from which the arguments spring. Less intimate in their revelation than the Debates, they have their own value in exhibiting the Puritan temper and ideology, and are worthy of inclusion on their independent merits since many of them are available to the modern reader only in the largest or most highly specialized library. Finally the Debates refer to some other documents, intrinsically less interesting perhaps, but essential to an understanding of what is said. These I have placed in an Appendix, together with some evidence on the religious and political enthusiasms of the New Model, and some material, from the Clarke MSS. and other sources, on the activities of the Agitators and the Council of the Army.[2]

[1] It has not been found possible to record which emendations have been adopted, what rejected, and what added, or, except in one or two cases, the grounds on which my decision has been reached. Nor would any useful purpose for the reader have been served had it been possible. The limited space available for notes must go to recording *all* deviations from the MS. in the present edition, whether in origin Firth's or my own.

[2] Of the documents from which I present (in Part III and the Appendix) selections more or less extensive, only one, the Large Petition of the Levellers (pp. 318–23) is already available in Professor William

INTRODUCTION

The chief interest of the Debates, and of the Supplementary Documents, is the light they throw on the Puritan mind. But if they are not to be misinterpreted they must be studied in connection with the situation in which the Puritans find themselves.

II

Among the victors in the First Civil War (with their history of conflicting principles and interests temporarily controlled by the necessity of defeating the enemy) only one point was held in common: the restored King must be so bound that he could never again exercise the arbitrary rule, civil and ecclesiastical, for whose overthrow the war had been fought. Beyond this general principle, disagreements at once emerged: first, as to the means of achieving the desired end, and what constituted satisfactory guarantees of its endurance; secondly, and more fundamentally, as to the disposition of the effectual sovereignty, taken from the King. Had that sovereignty been civil alone the problem would have presented enormous difficulties, but it was also ecclesiastical. In the Puritan revolution the religious problem may not have been—was not, in fact—more important than the civil, but in itself it was certainly the more difficult of solution, and it so combined with the civil problem as to render it, too, well-nigh insoluble.

Among the victors four main groups may be roughly distinguished. Each has a particular set of principles to advance, and a particular set of interests to guard, in the proposed religious settlement; and each is not only influenced in its whole policy by the interests, but, in varying degrees, takes the colour of its political thinking from the principles. Three of the groups fall under the general designation of *Puritan*; the fourth stands apart, for its guiding principle is secular, not religious, and its interest in the ecclesiastical settlement, while lively, is negative. This

---

Haller's admirable collection, *Tracts on Liberty in the Puritan Revolution*, New York 1934, which reproduces nineteen important pamphlets in full and in facsimile. To these pamphlets, and to Professor Haller's learned introduction and notes, I refer the reader. Two or three of my other selections are from material elsewhere reprinted, but not very readily accessible. The rest have never been reprinted.

These selections have been edited on principles similar to those employed in editing the Debates. The object has been to present a text at once accurate and intelligible to the modern reader. Omissions have been indicated: three dots (. . .) for omissions of less than a sentence; three asterisks (* * *) for longer omissions. See also 'Notes on Text' under the different titles.

INTRODUCTION

fourth group, known in the Long Parliament as the Erastians, is ineffectual in so far as it lacks the party organization which the two main Puritan groups possess, but influential through its power to combine with either of them and because it fully expresses the secular and anti-clerical spirit of the nation, the spirit which will accept passively any settlement in the church so long as that settlement is powerless to tyrannize or to endanger the peace.

The first of the three religious groups, the Presbyterian, had led the attack on absolutism and dominated the earlier phases of the struggle with Charles. Though it had lost the military ascendancy it once possessed, it could still generally command a majority in Parliament, and it hoped (with or without Scottish aid) to effect a settlement of the kingdom in its own interests. It stood for adherence to the Covenant, the establishment of Presbyterianism on the general lines laid down by the Westminster Assembly, and the suppression of every other doctrine and order. It was opposed to toleration, and was in general less interested in liberty than in reform. Its alliance with the Scots was its potential military strength and its actual political weakness, for in moments when national feeling ran high its majority in Parliament became a minority. But English Presbyterianism is not to be confounded with Scottish. Few indeed wished to see the Scottish church duplicated in England. Not only did the Presbyterian Party in Parliament rely on the Erastians to make its majority effective; its own adherents (as Baillie and his fellow Commissioners had lamented) were tainted with Erastianism. They would have a national Presbyterian church, and would suppress its rivals, but the church should be controlled by the state. In civil matters the Party was the most conservative of the revolutionaries (agreeing well enough with the Erastians herein); it was the Party of the Right in the Puritan coalition, finding its chief support among the aristocrats who had adhered to the Parliamentary cause, and the wealthy merchants of London, and fearing and hating the Parties of the Left for their civil, quite as much as their religious principles. The Presbyterians wished to limit the objectives of the revolution: to assert the effectual sovereignty not of the people but of Parliament, and to preserve at all costs the sanctity of property, whether real, personal, or political (the historic rights of the Crown and the material possessions of the Church alone excepted). The monarchy, shorn of its power, they would cherish in the interests of a lasting settlement—an assurance that the revolution had not been so very revolutionary after all, and a guarantee that it should go no further. (Had not God given the Israelites kings, and whenever they could do so with impunity, had not that model people knocked them about?) The King was indeed essential to their scheme, and the time was to come when they would sacrifice almost anything but the church settlement to gain him. He refused their terms and ruined himself and them. The Party of the Right is unrepresented in the Army Debates except in so far as the Independent officers agree with its civil policy or regard its opinion as something to be opposed only with caution.

To the spirit of this civil policy, the Independents, or the Party of the Centre, as we may call them,[1] did not at first demur. But they were alarmed at its conjunction with an ecclesiastical ideal at variance with their own. The Independents were the heirs of the Presbyterians' former military ascendancy, and between winning victories and opposing the hated Scots, they were sometimes able to gain a majority in Parliament. A common distrust of Presbyterian clericalism also enabled them to rely up to a point on the support of the Erastians.[2] But even more than the Presbyterians', their majority, when achieved, was highly precarious. Being astute politicians they knew that Parliament (or at all events this Parliament) would never settle the religion of the nation on their plan. Accordingly they were (or pretended to be) satisfied with a state-controlled Presbyterian establishment, so long as a toleration, of the general kind demanded by the Dissenting Brethren in the Assembly, were assured; and even for this they seemed content to wait, evidently sharing to some extent Cromwell's comfortable assurance that heaven was on their side and would presently afford them an opportunity of taking what they wanted. Thus, partly through force of circumstances, but partly through a logical development of their own basic doctrines, the Independents became the party of toleration. This fact gave them an immense advantage outside Parliament; for it enabled

---

[1] That is, in relation to the other Puritan groups and with care not to be confused by Cromwell's term 'the middle party' (p. 419), which he applies to the Erastians with other loosely attached elements in the House of Commons.

[2] In principle, Independency, with its ideal of an exclusive and divinely appointed church, was of course opposed to Erastianism; and there were Independent attacks on the Erastianism of the Presbyterian Prynne (see *Certain Brief Observations on Master Prynne's Twelve Questions*, 1644; and *Calumny Arraigned and Cast*, 1645). On the other hand, the separation of church and state, in proportion as the Independents were willing to make it absolute, would have the effect of rendering impossible the religious tyranny that the Erastians dreaded.

them to draw support from the Parties of the Left, almost unrepresented in the House of Commons, but strong in the Army, on which in the last analysis the Independents relied. As time went on an increasing rift between Independents and Presbyterians became apparent in the matter of the civil settlement. Like the Presbyterians (and Erastians), the leaders retained their respect for property, real, personal, and political. This is the burden of Ireton's impassioned argument at Putney: 'All the main thing that I speak for, is because I would have an eye to property' (p. 57). But they grew progressively less attached to the notion of the effectual sovereignty of Parliament, progressively more sensible of its tyranny; and, while loath to break with the existing Parliament, they sought a settlement which should put a definite limit to its life, and provide securely not only against the power of the restored King but also against the self-perpetuating tyranny of Parliaments in future. They discovered that if new presbyter was but old priest writ large, new Parliament also bore a striking resemblance to old King. To the monarchy itself they were certainly prepared to be not less generous than the Presbyterians, provided the King could be brought to their policy of discountenancing ecclesiastical tyranny, of ending the present Parliament, and of accepting the principle of biennial Parliaments—from whose power (as also from the King's) certain fundamental matters should be reserved, and whose institution should be preceded by certain electoral reforms. These are some of the provisions of the Independents' scheme of settlement, the *Heads of the Proposals* (pp. 422–6). But their attachment to monarchy was, like their attachment to Parliament, less deeply grounded than the Presbyterians'; it was more a matter of policy than of principle. The Independents could divest themselves of it when the moment came—when heaven (to adopt their own language) held forth the opportunity of other things; the Presbyterians could not. Independency is inherently the more radical creed. This does not mean that it is necessarily more democratic. In drawing support from the Parties of the Left, Independency allied itself with the one genuinely democratic party thrown up by the Puritan revolution, the Levellers, and temporarily even adopted some of their principles. But its immediate purpose served, the alliance dissolved, leaving the Levellers sadder and (as regards the Independents at least) wiser men. To gauge the cleavage between the Independents and their allies one has only to read the Putney Debates.

The Parties of the Left, the sectaries, religious and political,

were a heterogeneous company among whom the winds of doctrine
assumed the proportions of a tempest. They were descended
from the Separatists and Anabaptists, as the Independents were
from the more sedate Congregationalists, and were, so to speak,
the Independents' poor relations.[1] Among themselves they
agreed in little save the belief in a total separation of church and
state and the demand for liberty of conscience, both which tenets
are logical developments of parts of the Independents' own creed,
and the latter of them a main ground of the alliance between the
sects and the Independent Party. Two significant types of
opinion emerge among the sectaries. The one is recognizable as
predominantly democratic in tendency, and ultimately secular in
aim, though it maintains its emphasis on liberty of conscience and
at times adopts the language of religious enthusiasm. This is
the opinion of the Levellers (already mentioned), the political
doctrinaires, led by Lilburne, Overton, Wildman, and others. It
appealed more or less definitely to many of the rank-and-file in
the New Model, to the Agitators (old and new), and even to some
of the higher officers such as Colonel Rainborough. The second
type of opinion is at bottom neither democratic in tendency nor
secular in aim. It emphasizes not the rights of the people, but
the privileges of the Saints, and it looks forward to the millennium
(which always seems to be just around the corner) when the Saints
shall inherit the earth and rule it with, or on behalf of, Christ
(pp. 232-47, 390-6). This is the type of opinion held by the
Fifth Monarchy Men, the religious doctrinaires (if the title may
be awarded to one group when there are so many highly qualified
claimants). Much less effectively organized in 1647-9 than the
Levellers, this party had an advantage in the experience of victorious warfare through which the Army had passed, and in the
Army's susceptibility to religious enthusiasm. One cannot gauge
the precise extent of its influence in the lower ranks. Probably
that influence was very considerable, for up to a point it could

[1] It would be a mistake to exaggerate the sharpness of the line separating
parties, or to overlook the fact that a logical development of certain Independent principles would easily carry one over the line. Progressive
movement towards the Left is illustrated by Milton and Roger Williams:
it is another source of the sects. Thomas Edwards affected to think a
pure Independent a *rara avis*, a mistake in the other direction. Space
does not permit me to speak of the relation of parties before the meeting
of the Long Parliament, when the principles to be expressed after 1640
were taking shape. Much light on this subject may be expected from
forthcoming works by Professor M. M. Knappen and Professor William
Haller. See also the admirable account in Perry Miller, *Orthodoxy in
Massachusetts* (1934), pp. 1-101.

coalesce with democratic opinion. Among the higher officers Colonel Harrison and Lieutenant-Colonel Goffe are definite adherents, and others, including Cromwell himself, are not untouched by its spell.

Such, in brief, are the main groups into which the Puritans fall. As political forces these parties operate in three corporate but not homogeneous bodies, the Parliament, the City, and the Army;[1] and membership in each of these bodies partially, though only partially, cuts across party alignments and loyalties. (1) The Presbyterians' majority in Parliament (even after they were relieved of the odium of a Scottish army on English soil) was always insecure. Yet in a less overt way the Presbyterian Party dominated Parliament up to the very moment of Pride's purge; for they, with the Erastians, were in a special sense the Parliamentary party, insistent on the sovereignty of Parliament, determined that the regal powers and functions should be transferred to it, and that there should be no dissolution of the existing Parliament till all was settled and the kingdom safe—if ever. In these views the Parliament as a whole acquiesced, and even the Independent Party in Parliament (as distinct from the Independents of the Army and their allies) were influenced by the 'interest' of Parliament and of themselves as members of that august body: they could be induced to submit to Pride's purge, but nothing could persuade the resulting Independent House of Commons to dissolve. Equally instructive to contemplate is the long struggle in Cromwell between the leader of the Army and the member of the House of Commons. (2) In the oligarchy which ruled the City the power of the Presbyterians was far more secure than in the House of Commons,[2] and it was therefore a special object of the Army's distrust. It generally acted in collusion with the Presbyterian leaders in Parliament. But the City, like the Parliament, was jealous of its independence and had its own special interests, material and political, to guard, and on occasion these interests

---

[1] In an early Declaration [E. 390 (26)] the Army significantly speaks of the City and itself as 'bodies': why should the Army's petitions 'be apprehended as a putting of conditions upon Parliament more than all other petitions have been, from counties, from corporations, and especially from the City of London, being a body more numerous, more closely compacted, more near to the Parliament, and more plentifully furnished with money and all things else to back and carry on their desires than the Army is . . . ?' (p. 5).

[2] Among the citizens Presbyterian sympathies also prevailed, tinged, like the oligarchy's, with Erastianism. But in the City and surrounding municipalities, there was a vigorous minority whose allegiance was divided between the Independents and the Parties of the Left.

conflicted ·with the needs of the Parliamentary party and the Presbyterian cause. (3) The Army was a corporate body in a sense somewhat different from Parliament and City, but no less real. Its *ethos* was as pronounced as theirs. All that it lacked was appropriate organs of expression, and these, with a remarkable initiative, it proceeded to create. The Army became, indeed, at once a sort of fourth estate in the realm, and a body not less representative than the (not very representative) Parliament at Westminster. It contained men of every shade of Puritan opinion, and no doubt a substantial number quite indifferent to the special ideals of the various Puritan parties and intent only on the soldiers' material needs and grievances. But the political activities of the Army were dominated by two groups working in uneasy co-operation, the Independents, including many of the higher officers, and the Parties of the Left, finding their chief strength in the lower officers and the common troopers. These, and especially the leading Independents (Cromwell and Ireton, with a group of loyal colonels) shaped for the Army a policy which was in general harmony, but certainly not identical, with the policy of the Independent Party in Parliament. The Army had its own sense of corporate being and its own special needs and interests, in which officers and men of no close party affiliations could share. At the head of the Army, a symbol of its existence as a separate entity, stood Fairfax, of whom Gardiner remarks: 'Most likely no one in England—probably not Fairfax himself—knew whether he was a Presbyterian or an Independent.'

A Parliament insecurely, but until Pride's purge fairly constantly, dominated by the Presbyterians; an Army increasingly dominated by the Independents; the City where the Presbyterian interest prevailed; at a distance the Scots, and at home a vast but relatively unorganized mass of Royalist and Anglican discontent, and a smaller but more articulate body of popular and radical discontent; and finally, the endless and futile machinations of Charles—this (with a brief interruption, of the Second Civil War) is the general scene presented by the two years between February 1647 and January 1649. With this general scene in mind, our attention must turn more definitely to the activities of the New Model.

The plan of Parliament to rid itself of the New Model was highly alarming to the leading Independent officers, to the sectaries in the ranks, indeed to the whole Army. It was proposed to disband the force piecemeal, with, as an alternative, enlistment for service in Ireland under different commanders; and the plan did not include any adequate guarantees for long arrears of pay, for an Act of Indemnity covering deeds in the past war, or against being pressed for service outside England. On these defects, and the Parliament's angry and threatening rejection of the soldiers' protests, the whole scheme broke down; for the manifest injustice and ingratitude welded the Army into a unity of resentment, placed its disbanding completely beyond the Parliament's power to effect, prepared it to become the political force which the Presbyterians dreaded, and fostered revolutionary propaganda in its ranks to the embarrassment of its commanders as well as to the danger of Parliament and nation. The soldiers looked to their officers for guidance, and towards the end of March these drew up a petition to Parliament, which confined itself to demanding guarantees for the soldiers' material welfare and scrupulously avoided all reference to larger issues, political and ecclesiastical.[1] But the men were also ready to organize in their own behalf. 'Though the Army differ in religion,' wrote an observer of Ireton's regiment, 'they all agree in their discontented speeches of the Parliament. . . . As for the petition, they now speak it openly that they will send it up with two out of every troop.' [2] Here is the first hint we have of the plan of appointing Agitators.

By the end of the month it had been carried into effect by eight regiments of horse, to be followed by the remaining horse and by the foot. Thus the rank-and-file created their own leaders, and opened a channel of communication with the high command, the

[1] *Clarke Papers*, 1. x–xi.
[2] Letter from Suffolk, 20th April, Duke of Portland's MSS., quoted, Gardiner 3. 236–7. Already on 26th March, Thomason had acquired a sheet, which Gardiner and Firth overlook, and which prints what purports to be *An Apology of the Soldiers to all their Commission Officers* [E. 381 (18)]. This *Apology* justifies the actions of the Army in the Civil War by an appeal to 'the law of nature and the necessity of the land.' It declares that the soldiers, believing the Parliament's declarations, fought for 'the utter extirpation of all ungodliness and illegal proceedings . . .; for the preservation of the Gospel, the liberty of the subject, and the just right and privileges of Parliament.' It warns the officers of the danger of being led to abandon the cause of their soldiers, and concludes:

'Now these and many other such like reasons being taken into your serious considerations, we hope, will be just cause for you to go along with us in this business, or at the least to let us quietly alone in this our design, we desiring no more than what is just and right, according to all their declarations and protestations to the whole world, that being one witness. Thus leaving you to the powerful wisdom of God, which is only able to make you wise in all things, we rest so praying,
Your servants so far as we may.'
[unsigned].

Parliament, and public opinion in the country. It is a more striking achievement of democratic organization than the forming of the General Council of the Army early in June. For the latter was prompted by the higher officers and would never have been adopted had not the regiments elected their Agitators first; and the Agitators remained in fact a more potent force outside the Council than they ever became in it. Some of them were men of undoubted energy and ability. Sexby, Allen, and Lockyer figure in the debates at Reading and Putney. Allen describes them as young in statecraft (p. 421), but they show a natural aptitude for politics. Questioned at the Commons' bar, on 30th April, for their first official act, the presentation of the soldiers' grievances, Sexby, Allen, and Shepherd answer with all the astuteness of Lilburne himself.[1] The scope of the Agitators' plans is best realized from 'Advertisements for managing the counsels of the Army,' dated from Saffron Walden, 4th May (p. 398). They aim at the penetration and effective guidance of the whole Army. They know the power of the press and propose to utilize it in their meditated struggle for public favour. They grasp the need of circumspection and an orderly procedure: in their pleas for liberty and reform they will invoke 'the declarations of Parliament put forth to engage us in blood,' and when they 'call for public justice . . . upon all offenders' (or in other words the Presbyterian leaders in Parliament), it shall be 'according to the Covenant'! The immediate needs of the soldiers (arrears and indemnity) are still emphasized, but the minds of the Agitators run on to the settlement of the kingdom upon principles of justice and common right.

Next to arrears and indemnity, the question most likely to move numbers in the Army was liberty of conscience. Here, too, the Presbyterian Party seemed determined to alarm and exasperate the soldiers by attacks on heterodoxy and threats of suppression. The extension of the soldiers' demands to include, above all, liberty of conscience, but also other reforms, is evident in the grievances forwarded from various regiments to be presented to the Parliamentary Commissioners at Saffron Walden, on 13th–14th May (p. 399). Thus the principles of the Levellers (who stood, among other things, for complete religious toleration) made progress in the ranks. No doubt the Agitators were in their debt for doctrine and method, and advanced their cause; but it is also probable that the first movement to elect Agitators was itself a

[1] Tanner MSS. (Bodleian) 58. f. 84: quoted by Firth, *Clarke Papers*, I. 430–1.

result of the infiltration of Leveller principles. We hear of their presence in April: 'Some of the soldiers do not stick to call the Parliament-men tyrants; Lilburne's books are quoted by them as statute laws'; and again (with patent exaggeration), the whole Army 'is one Lilburne throughout, and more likely to give than to receive laws.'[1]

Be this as it may, the hotter spirits were preparing to take the law into their own hands. By the middle of May an elaborate organization (complete with theatrical properties—secret agents and code numbers) had been developed by the Agitators and their friends (p. 400). It was soon to be put to the test; and if we cannot restrain a smile at the evident enjoyment of No. 102 ('Now, my lads, if we work like men we shall do well. . . . Yours till death, 102'), we must admit that in one instance it achieved a *coup* which left a mark on all future happenings. In the first days of June Cornet Joyce, acting in close collusion with the Agitators, and under (though perhaps also beyond) the secret orders of Cromwell and Ireton, seized the person of the King. This is not the place to tell again the familiar though problematical story, but we recall the significance of the hard-pressed cornet's answer to Charles' demand for a sight of his commission: 'Here is my commission' (pointing to his five hundred troopers). The Army had assumed the direction of events; its duel with a hostile majority in Parliament had entered on a new phase which was to culminate in Pride's purge; and beyond that a dozen years of military rule were heralded in Joyce's reply. But so far the soldiers' action was unofficial, agreeable in this instance to the real commanders of the Army, Cromwell and Ireton, but not satisfactorily subject to their control. And a pressing problem faced them: to devise some means of preserving discipline and unity of action in face of the dubious (though at present friendly and potentially useful) forces emerging from the ranks. The solution of the problem—or more strictly the first step in its solution—was taken with the drawing up of the *Solemn Engagement of the Army*, and the organization of the General Council which it created.

The *Solemn Engagement of the Army* (pp. 401–3), accepted at a general rendezvous at Newmarket on 5th June, was a sort of military covenant made among the soldiers and with the kingdom.

[1] Letter from Suffolk, 20th April (Duke of Portland's MSS.); Letter of intelligence from Saffron Walden, 26th April (Clarendon MSS. 2502): Gardiner 3. 237, 245. Baxter speaks of the diffusion of Overton's and Lilburne's pamphlets as already widespread in the ranks (p. 389).

It set forth the soldiers' grievances and the conditions on which they would disband, or enlist for service in Ireland, binding them to do neither until a council (called into existence for that purpose) should declare the conditions to have been fulfilled. It also demanded the exclusion from power of the Presbyterian leaders (the eleven members soon to be impeached in the name of the Army) who had sought to destroy the New Model and kindle the flames of a fresh war. The *Engagement* disavowed all intention of serving the ends of any particular persons or party, of attempting to set up Independency in the place of Presbyterianism, of introducing 'a general licentiousness under pretence of liberty of conscience,' or of seeking to undermine the principle of magistracy; it glanced at the settlement, the securing of the liberties of citizen as well as soldier, the 'establishment of common and equal right, freedom, and safety' for all 'that do not by denying the same to others render themselves incapable thereof'; and it invoked God's blessing on the Army's covenant and effort. The General Council, which the *Engagement* called into being, accepted the election of Agitators as an accomplished fact, balanced them with two commissioned officers from each regiment, and tipped the scale in favour of authority by associating them with the General, with the other general officers, and (though the document does not mention this) with the commanders of regiments.[1] Thus was secured that precarious unity of the Army, which Cromwell was determined at all costs to preserve. Thus too was established what we may perhaps describe as the Putney Debating Society.

The *Solemn Engagement*, according to its promise, was followed, on 14th June, by a more detailed statement of the Army's principles and its desires for the settlement of the kingdom. *A Representation from Sir Thomas Fairfax and the Army under his command* (pp. 403–9) is an able document, probably, like the *Engagement*, the work of Ireton. After setting forth once more the soldiers' grievances and demands, it justifies the Army's concern in larger issues and its right to resist, if need be, the orders of the Parliament, 'considering that we were not a mere mercenary army hired to serve an arbitrary power, but called forth and conjured by the several declarations of Parliament to the defence of our own and the people's just rights and liberties, and so we took up arms in judgment and conscience to those ends.'

---

[1] The Levellers afterwards complained (*Second Part of England's New Chains*, 1649, p. 3) that 'the General Councils . . . were . . . overgrown with colonels, lieutenant-colonels, majors, and others not chosen, and many of them dissenters from the . . . *Engagement*.'

This appeal to the declarations of Parliament is reinforced by one to 'the law of nature and nations' as manifested in Scottish and foreign precedent, and to the final and highest test: 'Nor is that supreme end, the glory of God, wanting . . . to 'set a price upon all such proceedings of righteousness and justice, it being one witness of God in the world to carry on a testimony against the injustice and unrighteousness of men and against the miscarriages of governments when corrupted or declining from their primitive and original glory.' And so, on to the settlement of the kingdom: the termination of the present House of Commons, biennial Parliaments, and more equal representation (later to be elaborated in the *Heads of the Proposals*); the right of free petition, the right of speedy trial, toleration for those unable to accept the religious settlement imposed by the Parliament (here the influence of the Parties of the Left); these things guaranteed, a willingness 'freely and cheerfully [to] commit our stock or share of interest in this kingdom into this common bottom of Parliaments,' and finally the promise to restore the King to his rights 'so far as may consist with the right and freedom of the subject and with the security of the same for the future.' The *Representation of the Army*, and especially this last-named clause, is one of the prior engagements so earnestly debated at Putney four months later.

Documents like the *Representation* were very well, but the more radical elements in the Army, while passionately addicted to declarations, were also eager for a march on London as the swiftest way of bringing Parliament and the City to their senses. On 24th–25th June the commanders, already at St. Albans, tried the experiment of advancing to Uxbridge (where they could easily cut off the City's supplies) with a view to securing effective measures against the eleven members, and the cessation of the attempts to break down the *Engagement* by bribing desertion with the payment of arrears, and to provide forces that could, if necessary, be used to oppose the New Model. The voluntary withdrawal of the eleven members, and the submissive attitude of the City, satisfied the commanders, and the Army retired to Reading. Thus was demonstrated the power of the New Model to coerce Parliament and City. But the retirement was perhaps premature. While commissioners were engaged on a treaty between Parliament and Army, and Ireton was busy on the *Heads of the Proposals*, the Presbyterians continued their machinations. The purging of Independents from the London militia (contemplated by an ordinance passed in May) was effected. In the process a mystified lieutenant-colonel was ordered 'to take notice he must fight against all malignants, sects, and sectaries, and *all godly persons* that shall come to oppose the City. To which the lieutenant-colonel replied: "Gentlemen, I had thought you all of you professed godliness. For my part I do, and therefore I shall not engage against any godly man. Whereupon Mr. Alderman Gibbs . . . answered that their meaning was . . .: if any, out of pretence of godliness, should come to oppose them, that he should fight against such. . . .'" [1] Nothing could better reveal the state of parties, or the notorious religiosity of the Army. News of these doings reached Reading. To the Agitators it appeared that Parliament and City had relapsed into their old wicked ways and were preparing for a fresh appeal to arms. They drew up new demands, and urged an immediate march on London. The policy of the Army's commanders, to avoid an open break with the Parliament and the sacrifice of its commission (the Army's only legal ground of existence), was being assailed on two sides, by the recalcitrance of the Presbyterian Party and by the impatience of the soldiers. On 16th July the Agitators' proposal was the subject of a great debate in the Council of the Army, the first to be reported in the Clarke MSS. Much less interesting in subject than the later debates, it is still highly significant of tempers and policies, and an excellent example of the sort of discussion that must frequently have arisen in the Council. Accordingly, I have prepared for the Appendix a summary of the arguments, with all the more striking passages quoted in full (pp. 409–20). [2] In the debate Cromwell and Ireton, careful of appearances, as the extremists never were, insisted that the occasion offered for a show of force was insufficient. Heaven would provide a better opportunity. It did, before the month was out. With the Army at a distance, renewed pressure from the London mob forced the Speakers of both Houses, and the leading Independent members, to flee. To restore them to their places, and Parliament to its liberty, the Army entered London on 6th August. But so short-lived was the effect of this demonstration that by 14th August the Agitators were petitioning Fairfax for a purging of the House of Commons, and a new march on London for that purpose. The question was debated, and this time Cromwell was on the side of the Agitators. The calculated procrastination of Fairfax prevented the desired march; but Cromwell, not to be

---

[1] 'Certain Informations,' *Clarke Papers*, I. 152.
[2] For 17th July, there is a fragmentary account of a debate on the *Heads of the Proposals*, from which I have extracted two significant speeches (p. 421).

INTRODUCTION

thwarted, made a show of force with his cavalry, and the leading Presbyterians retreated, leaving the Independents for the time masters of a small majority in the House.[1]

Soon, however, a new danger threatened, a widening rift between the Independent leaders and their allies of the Left. The leaders hoped for a speedy settlement of the kingdom on the basis of the *Heads of the Proposals*. The method they advocated was a series of bills securing the liberties of the subject, the privileges of Parliament, and the settlement of the militia, to be followed, when these had received the royal assent, by others securing the rights of the King. On 16th September, the Council of the Army met at Putney after a sermon by Hugh Peter, and Cromwell was able to get this plan accepted, but in the teeth of a vigorous opposition led by Rainborough.[2] The theoretic republicans found their opportunity in the growing impatience with the disingenuousness of Charles, and exploited it to the full. In Parliament too the rift appeared. On 22nd September, Marten moved for no further addresses to the King. He was easily defeated by aid of the Presbyterian vote, but it is significant that the Centre Party had to call upon the Right in order to correct the exuberance of its allies. Discontent in the ranks of the Army could think of no better expedient than to elect new Agitators. There were dark hints that those formerly appointed 'did [now] more consult their own advancement than the public interest'; and they were supplemented in five regiments of horse (later in four more of horse and seven of foot) by new Agents. Whether or not this action was inspired by Levellers outside the Army, Ireton credits Wildman with composing the manifesto of the new Agitators, *The Case of the Army Truly Stated* (pp. 92, 95, 429–36), and the Proposals submitted by them are for an Agreement of the People (pp. 443–5). This, then, is the immediate background of the Putney Debates, with the documents that furnished their point of departure.

The debates reported took place on 28th and 29th October, and 1st November. It is unnecessary to summarize them since I print the text in full (pp. 1–124). Here for the first time the Levellers are represented, and the Agitators supported, by civilians whose presence has been invited. At the first debate Cromwell urged 'that they should not meet as two contrary parties, but as some desirous to satisfy or convince each other.' The wish was not fulfilled. The relative harmony of 5th June, or even of

[1] Gardiner 3. 335–40, 343–52; *The Humble Address of the Agitators* [E. 402 (8)].
[2] Gardiner 3. 364–5; Rushworth 7. 815.

[*27*]

16th July, was gone beyond recall, destroyed by the increasing rift between the Independent leaders and the Parties of the Left.

Though greatly superior in general interest to the discussion of 16th July, these debates are much less impressive as an example of truth and agreement reached through free discussion. They open with a personal attack on Cromwell and Ireton, and a frank commentary on their blasted reputations, which reflects the distrust of them coming to be entertained by Lilburne and his friends, and also suggests that as a means of preserving unity and discipline in the Army the Council has not been an unqualified success. Their defence leads into a discussion of the Army's engagements. And here a new difference emerges: Cromwell and Ireton hold that, though the situation may have altered, the principles set forth in the declarations of the Army are binding; the radicals, that nothing is binding if it conflicts with reason, justice, and the safety of the people. 'Rationalizations' the arguments of both parties may be—what arguments are not?—but they are rationalizations which employ the deepest convictions, the most characteristic ideas, of those who adopt them. What the Independents are contending for on the practical level is, first, the settlement of the nation by treaty with the King; secondly, the preservation of unity and discipline in the Army: both alike forbid the acceptance of an Agreement of the People. In one respect, Cromwell and Ireton's insistence on engagements is an example of what we may call the lower tactics of debate. Part of their object (Cromwell's rather ingenuous disclaimers notwithstanding) is to kill time and prevent an irrevocable decision; they have discovered that the Council of the Army, however defective it may be as an organ of truth and agreement, is a thoroughly reliable instrument of delay, and in a select committee truth and agreement may have a better chance (pp. 13, 17). Even the seizing on Lieutenant-Colonel Goffe's motion for a prayer-meeting is not quite free from suspicion, and, the prayer-meeting over, Cromwell and Ireton return to 'engagements,' to relinquish the subject only when it is patently exhausted and they must pass on to a new one, the provisions of the *Agreement of the People*. Here the same problem of interpretation arises: to distinguish clearly between profound convictions and the lower tactics of debate. Indeed the whole thing parallels closely the previous discussion of engagements, with the Levellers cutting through all obstacles to reason, justice, and natural right, and the Independents insisting on the claims of precedent and established interests. In two ways the Putney

INTRODUCTION

Debates mark the gulf that is widening between the Independents and their allies of the Left: first, in the frank irreconcilability of the principles advanced; secondly, in the atmosphere of tension, and in the necessity for the tactics which Cromwell and Ireton use. Yet the spirit of a lost unity reasserts itself at moments. Cromwell may reprobate the policy and arguments of the Left, but he is not wholly unsympathetic to their aspirations and ideals; and up to a point they share his conviction that to divide is to perish, and are frightened by his threat (skilfully concealed as an offer) to withdraw and leave them to their own devices. The last fully reported debate closes on a curious blend of acquiescence and irony. 'It will be thought boldness in me not to agree with you,' says Wildman to Ireton, and goes on to wish that provision might be made for the safety of the people and their champions when the King is restored. 'But if not, I am but a single man; *I shall venture myself and my share in the common bottom.*' The words are adapted from Ireton's own *Representation of the Army.* The 'common bottom' had sprung a good many leaks since they were written.

But this was not the end. In the meetings of the Council on 4th and 5th November, and of its committee on 4th November (none of them, unfortunately, reported by Clarke), the Levellers would seem from the brief account available (pp. 452-4) to have defeated the Independent leaders, and carried a resolution in favour of manhood suffrage, a letter to the House of Commons virtually disclaiming any desire for further addresses to the King, and a demand for a general rendezvous (at which they intended to appeal from the officers to the Army and from Parliament to the people). But Cromwell had not played his last card. By 8th November he decided that the Council of the Army must be made to undo its recent work and then be placed beyond the possibility of further mischief (pp. 454-5). Somehow he managed to obtain from the Council a second letter to the Parliament explaining away that of the fifth, the dismissal of the representatives (Agitators and officers) to their regiments on the pretext of preparing for the forthcoming rendezvous, and a fresh committee of officers to examine the engagements of the Army and the *Agreement of the People*, whose findings were to be reported to 'the several regiments at their *respective* rendezvous' (ominous phrase). Simultaneously Fairfax sought from Parliament a further provision for the troops, 'that so your care of the Army may appear, and myself and my officers be thereby enabled to let the soldiers see we take such consideration of them as

becomes us and [as we] have engaged ourselves unto.'[1]   Three
separate rendezvous were substituted for the general rendezvous
demanded by the Council of the Army.   At that of the first
brigade, on 15th November, Rainborough presented a petition in
favour of the *Agreement of the People*, and some copies of the
Agreement were distributed among the soldiers, with incitements
to stand by it and defy their commanders.   Only two regiments
gave any trouble (and that easily quelled by the prompt action of
Cromwell), Colonel Harrison's, which had assembled against
orders, wearing papers inscribed 'England's Freedom; Soldiers'
Rights,' and Colonel Robert Lilburne's, which had mutinied
against its higher officers and driven them away.   The rest
readily accepted a new engagement to unite for the prosecution
of specified aims and to yield obedience to the orders of the
General (sent forth with the advice of the Council of the Army
as regarded these aims, but of the Council of War as regarded all
other matters).[2]   Thus discipline (which had been threatened by
the very device created to sustain it) was once again restored, but
at the price of the Independents' alliance with the Parties of the
Left.   That this was possible offers a strong indication that while
the Army as a whole was insistent on 'soldiers' rights,' only a
minority cared for 'England's freedom' as the Levellers interpreted that phrase.   The Levellers' discontent with Cromwell
and Ireton is voiced in Wildman's *Putney Projects* and other
pamphlets.   Soon, however, the breach was partially healed by
the Independents' decision to terminate negotiations with the
King.

Between 25th November and 8th January the Council of the
Army met at Windsor to arrange with Parliamentary Commissioners the final settlement of the Army's demands for arrears,
indemnity, and a present and future provision.   This business
concluded, 'the agreement was sweet and comfortable, the whole
matter of the kingdom being left with the Parliament.'   On one
practical issue the Centre Party was moving rapidly towards the
Left.   Charles's rejection of the Four Bills confirmed the fear of
a renewed intrigue for restoration by means of a Scottish invasion,
and at last convinced the Independent leaders in Parliament and
Army of the probable necessity of settling the kingdom without
him, a conviction which was embodied in the Commons' vote of

[1] Fairfax to the House of Commons, 9th November: Rushworth
7. 867.
[2] *Clarke Papers*, 1. liv–lv; Gardiner 4. 22–3; Rushworth 7. 875; *A
Full Relation of the Proceedings at the Rendezvous in Corbush Field*;
A Remonstrance from Fairfax concerning the late Discontent.

no addresses on 3rd January. In the Council of the Army there were 'many exhortations to unity and affinity, and motions made for passing by offences that had, through weakness, come from brethren': the Leveller mutineers were tried, but, on submission, immediately restored to their places. The recaptured unity was signalized by a fast and a feast: Cromwell, Ireton, and others 'prayed very fervently and pathetically,' and Fairfax entertained the Council at dinner on the eve of its dispersal. At its final meeting the Council declared its unanimous approval of the vote of no addresses and its determination to support the Parliament in its effort to settle the kingdom without, and if need be, against the King.[1] This unanimous declaration was possible because on one issue the Independents had come into line with the Parties of the Left. But it represents the triumph not of their principles but of Cromwell's policy: the achievement of at least a sufficient unity in the Army and the restoration of discipline; the adoption, furthermore, of a plan for settling the kingdom in harmony with the Independents' wishes, and through the forms of Parliamentary action, not by the intervention of the Army (as the extremists had been always too ready to urge) or on the basis of an Agreement of the People (as one group of them had hoped). The triumph was temporary. Before all was done the Independents of the Army, under stress of circumstances, had to move much further to the Left in practical policy if not in principle.

When the work of settling the kingdom was resumed after the Second Civil War, it was without the Council of the Army, a Council of Officers having taken its place. But Ireton and other Independent leaders had moved sensibly nearer to the policy of the Left. They lost thereby the wholehearted support of part of the Independent following in both the Council of Officers and the Parliament, but were able to outweigh the loss, and capture the control of events, by a new alliance with the Left. Their policy was set forth in the *Remonstrance of the Army* (pp. 456–65). This was submitted to the Council of Officers at St. Albans on 10th November 1648, and finally accepted for forwarding to Parliament on 18th November; but Parliament evidently determined to postpone its discussion—if possible until the kingdom had been settled without it. Once more the Parliament was ranged against the Army, and once more membership in either body cut in some degree across party loyalties. Once more an alliance with the Parties of the Left became essential to the Independent leaders in

[1] *Clarke Papers*, I. lvi–lviii; Rushworth 7. 922–61 (*passim*), from which latter are the above quotations.

the Army if they were to impose their will on Parliament. While the Council of Officers was hesitating to accept the *Remonstrance*, Ireton, already working in somewhat uneasy alliance with Harrison and his Millenarian group, entered into conference with the Levellers. The first result was the influence of Lilburne in the final revision of the *Remonstrance*; the second, Ireton's reluctant acceptance of the Levellers' most cherished principle, settlement by means of an Agreement of the People, in return for the Levellers' reluctant acceptance of the immediate steps proposed by Ireton and Harrison. These steps were, to put an end to the existing Parliament and bridge the interval till the new constitution could be framed, and the new Parliament elected, by creating their supporters in the House of Commons a committee to administer the kingdom. Meanwhile a committee of sixteen (four from each of the Army, the Parliament, the Levellers, and the Independents unconnected with any of these bodies) [1] was to draw up the proposed Agreement of the People (see pp. 342–9). The new alliance, however insecure, gave Ireton and his supporters effective control of the Army, which, in addition to the radicalism in its ranks, had an incentive to intervention in the withholding by Parliament and City of its promised pay. On 30th November, the Council of Officers issued a declaration calling upon the Parliament voluntarily to dissolve, and, in case the majority remained obdurate, upon the honest party to dissociate themselves from the rest, when the Army would support them in an effort to establish a just and lasting settlement by means of a constitution guaranteeing a succession of free Parliaments and ratified by an agreement and subscription of the people. To further that end, the Army was marching towards the capital, 'there to follow Providence as God shall clear our way' (p. 467). On 2nd December, it entered London, only to encounter opposition from the Independent Party in the House, which would consent to a purge, but not to a dissolution. The result was Pride's purge on 6th December. [2]

Four days later the work of Lilburne's committee was finished and the *Agreement* ready for presentation to the Council of Officers. This body had no intention of adopting it without due consideration. On its civil provisions there seems to have been little disagreement. Not so on the reserve in matters of religion.

[1] Of this committee Lilburne managed to collect all but three. Save Marten the Parliamentary members refused to act, disapproving of the forcible dissolution of the Parliament. The *Agreement* was actually drawn up by Lilburne, the three other Levellers, and Marten (p. 349).

[2] Gardiner 4. 233–43, 260–70.

INTRODUCTION

When that question was debated, on 14th December (for the full text see pp. 125–69), all the differences among the Independents and their allies came to light. Clerical advice was not wanting. Philip Nye supported the Independent belief in the Christian magistrates' carefully delimited powers in matters of religion; John Goodwin supported the claim of the Parties of the Left that the magistrates' functions and responsibilities were purely secular; Sprigge and others declared for the privileges of the Saints, and, as essential to their realization, for the withholding from magistrates of all power to tyrannize. The religious (we have said) may not have been the most important problem in the Puritan revolution, but it was certainly the problem most difficult of solution. The fact is important for understanding the Puritan mind, and it is amply confirmed and illustrated by this long and heated argument. No final decision could be reached. The question was referred to a committee, and the officers turned to less controversial matters. But discontent with the suggested compromise flared up in the final discussion of the Agreement (pp. 175–8). There was nothing that the Parties of the Left held with more tenacity than liberty of conscience.

Their dissatisfaction with the Agreement as modified by the Independent officers, is plain to read. It was no great matter: the radicals had served their turn. From the final debates Lilburne was certainly, and the other Levellers presumably, absent. They could not approve either of the officers' interference or of their leaving the final settlement in the hands of the now quite unrepresentative Parliament. They had always desired a direct appeal to the people. For such an appeal Lilburne had in some degree provided by publishing the original text of the Agreement in his *Foundations of Freedom* (pp. 356–64). The Millenarians and their sympathizers brought forward different grounds of complaint: (1) What was needed was not a new constitution and a new Parliament, but a dozen or two conscientious and able men who would set about the reform of existing abuses; (2) the Agreement, professing to set men free, in reality imposed new restrictions upon them by extending, and grounding more firmly, the magistrates' powers; (3) God had providentially put the settlement into the hands of the Army for the nation's good and they had no right to surrender their power and abandon the task. Nothing is more remarkable than Ireton's answer to the second objection—unless it be Harrison's to the third. Ireton declares that magistracy will continue to exist until God, by the breaking forth of his power among men, shall render all government needless, that meanwhile the chief object should be to restrain the magistrates' power within fixed limits, and that this end the Agreement (so far from extending the scope of magistracy) clearly serves. Harrison has ceased to expect much good from the Agreement. It must be presented to Parliament and people because the Army stands pledged to that course. It will establish some measure of liberty for the people of God, but not enough effectively to safeguard them. *God intends its failure*: for it is not the final Agreement which shall establish the kingdom of heaven on earth. That will come from God, and in God's good time. One may suspect a touch of disingenuousness in both officers. But their arguments prevailed.

The Whitehall debate on the reserve in religion has its own special background in the divergent views of the Puritans regarding the power and duty of the magistrate, and in the history of toleration; and these, in turn, clarify the division into Right, Centre, and Left. The Presbyterians (unrepresented in the debate save in so far as Ireton and Nye agree with their view of the magistrate's power and duty or wish to leave a door open for compromise with them) expect a reform of the whole ecclesiastical polity, by the magistrate and in accordance with the scriptural model as they interpret it. On the other hand, the sectaries, however much they differ among themselves, agree in demanding the total separation of church and state (in the interests of the former) and the establishment of liberty of conscience—though the Millenarians of course intend the ultimate rule of the state itself by the Saints. The Centre Party occupied the whole interval between these opposed positions. It does so in virtue partly of its own composite character, partly of the historical situation in which it is placed. The party embraces both non-separating Congregationalists (who differ from the Presbyterians on but two points, though these are fundamental: the character of the scriptural model, and the question of a limited toleration) and separating Congregationalists, who are, indeed, sectaries of a kind, and approximate fairly closely to the Parties of the Left. The former group is represented in the debate by Ireton and Nye; the latter, by John Goodwin. At least a limited toleration had been rendered necessary for the Independent Party, first by the imminence of a Presbyterian settlement, secondly as a means of contenting its own left wing and of drawing in the Parties of the Left. In the Whitehall debate one must neither exaggerate nor minimize the divergence of opinion. Ireton and Nye say no word in defence of toleration, but in the *Apologetical Narration* (1644) Nye had

[34]

pleaded for a limited toleration, and in Ireton's manifestos of the Army the demand had been put forward in no uncertain terms. Now they are faced to meet the arguments not of the Right, but of the Left, and, without inconsistency, they speak for the right wing of the Centre Party. The divergence between that right wing and the exponents of the separation of church and state and of a thorough-going liberty of conscience, is nevertheless emphatic. The ground that is fought over had been mapped out in 1644, when Roger Williams [1] repudiated the *Apologetical Narration* because it allowed the magistrate's interference in religion and demanded at most a strictly limited toleration. But the considerable advance towards liberty of conscience which could be made from the fundamental position of Ireton and Nye is attested by the anonymous *Ancient Bounds* a year later (pp. 247–265), and by the practice of Cromwell's state church. Less thorough-going, and above all less logical, than the great Separatist and Baptist pleas for liberty of conscience—those of Milton, *The Bloody Tenent* (pp. 266–92), Robinson's *Liberty of Conscience*,[2] *John the Baptist*, *The Compassionate Samaritan*, *A Paraenetic for not loose but Christian Liberty*, *The Arraignment of Persecution*, and Richardson's *Necessity of Toleration*—they still ensure a large measure of practical freedom.

III

These divergences of opinion may be allowed to raise here a question of definition. Can such divergences be profitably embraced under a single term? What does one mean by Puritanism?

Puritanism is an entity.[3] It is to be understood neither as a resurgence of medieval thought (though there is some force in Acton's description, 'the middle ages of Protestantism') nor simply as a harbinger of the modern world, of naturalism and democracy (though it actually advanced them both). It is to be studied in itself—and the penalty of disregarding this counsel is to misunderstand not only the movement, but its relation to past and future. One's definition must be eclectic and must ignore no fact that is prominent in the period under consideration.

It is possible to extend the term *Puritan* to cover all the varied forces generated by the Protestant Reformation, and given their

[1] *Queries of Highest Consideration* (1644).
[2] This, with *The Compassionate Samaritan* and *The Arraignment of Persecution*, reproduced in *Tracts*, edited Haller.
[3] The subject of an interesting paper by Professor M. M. Knappen, read before the American Historical Association in December 1936.

opportunity of expression and action by the revolt against the Crown and the Church in the first half of the seventeenth century; and this is probably still its commonest use.[1] Again, it is possible to subdivide these forces and relegate the term *Puritan* to the more conservative, to those that remain strictly Calvinistic, adhering not only to the doctrine of predestination but also to the Genevan pattern in church and state, and opposing religious, while setting severe limits to political, liberty—or in other words to make *Puritan* practically synonymous with *Presbyterian*; this practice has some historical foundation and has been adopted by one or two modern historians.[2] The cleavage between the Presbyterians and the sectaries is indeed marked; and it is tempting to adopt and enforce Troeltsch's distinction between the church-ideal and the sect-ideal. But the problem is the Centre Party, the Independents, who increasingly dominate the situation in and after 1647. They occupy (as we have observed) the whole interval between the Right, where the Puritan church-type is dominant, and the Left, where the Puritan sect-type is not less supreme. No fact is more prominent than the existence of the two types side by side, or than their mutual influence particularly in the Centre Party, where indeed they merge.

The reason is this: Calvinism itself, the main seed-ground of the Puritan movement, is (as Troeltsch has made clear) deeply influenced by the 'sect ideal.' In especial, Calvin adopted the ideal of the 'holy community.' And as a result, Calvinism 'was obliged to make the bold attempt of constituting its national church as a church of professing believers, and of constituting its unity of church and state as a Christian society in the strict sense of the personal faith and character of each individual member.'[3] In some form the ideal of the 'holy community' remains constant among all the Puritan groups. And the Calvinistic, or Presbyterian, is but one of the possible inferences therefrom. If the primary effort is to erect the holy community among the Saints (as the sect ideal in its simplest form demands), one of two inferences may be drawn: the world may be left to perish in its own fashion, which means temporarily to live and order itself by its own standards; or the Saints, constituted as a holy community, may seek to impose their will upon the world and to inaugurate

---

[1] See *Writings and Speeches of Oliver Cromwell*, edited W. C. Abbott (1937), especially 1. 752.
[2] See Perry Miller, *Orthodoxy in Massachusetts*; W. K. Jordan, *The Development of Religious Toleration in England* (2 vols., 1932–6).
[3] Ernst Troeltsch, *The Social Teaching of the Christian Churches*, translated Olive Wyon (1931), pp. 622–3; cf. pp. 578, 593–8.

an outward conformity to their standards—a result which approximates to the course taken by Calvinism as a church-type, but must still be distinguished from it. The active presence of this ideal of the 'holy community' (however divergent the inferences in theory and practice therefrom) appears to me to furnish the only satisfactory basis for a working definition of Puritanism in its social and political aspects. Puritanism means a determined and varied effort to erect the holy community and to meet, with different degrees of compromise and adjustment, the problem of its conflict with the world. The acceptance of the ideal bespeaks a common element in all Puritan thought. The rival modes of application denote wide differences. One's definition of Puritanism must be broad enough to include them both, with the specific ideas and the habits of mind from which they spring. Nor must one forget that the differences, inherent in the creeds of Presbyterian and Congregationalist, of Separatist and Anabaptist, from the beginning, are brought in our period into sharp relief by the pressure of swiftly moving events, or that the interval between the extreme positions is always occupied by the composite Centre Party. It is unnecessary to posit a *unity* in all Puritan thought; it is sufficient to recognize a *continuity*. Such a continuity is apparent in the documents here collected, even where the divergences of interest and opinion are most acute.

For the purposes, then, of the present volume, I have adopted the popular definition of Puritanism. But I have tried to render the divergences within Puritanism thus conceived, at once clearcut and intelligible by discriminating between the Parties of the Right, the Centre, and the Left—and where necessary, still further between the components of these large divisions. And in my effort to isolate the elements in Puritan thought which bear, positively or negatively, upon the problem of liberty, I have been careful to set down nothing which cannot be found in the Debates and illustrated abundantly from other documents in the period. It is scarcely necessary to observe that all the generalizations are not equally applicable to all sections of Puritanism, but the difference (unless attention is specifically called to it) is usually one of emphasis only. As is natural, the stage is mainly occupied by the Parties of the Centre and the Left. The Right, which is unrepresented in the Debates, receives only occasional reference. But it has some share in the discussion and illustration of principles of resistance; and extracts not only from Prynne and Rutherford, but from Calvin and Luther (in the form in which the Puritans read them), are included in order to remind the reader of the

[37]

continuity of Puritan thought. Beyond the Puritan Left, as it appears in the Debates and in the Supplementary Documents, there lie reaches to which again we can afford only occasional references: they are marked by the break-down of traditional dogma and the emergerce of habits of mind which belong rather to Quakerism than to Puritanism proper. To penetrate farther into this subject would be to forsake the centre afforded by the Debates; but one must not ignore in Puritans like Saltmarsh and Dell, Collier and Erbury, Lilburne and Winstanley, trains of thought and feeling which finally led some of them into association with the despised followers of George Fox.[1]

There are certain defects in analysis, considered as a method, which cannot be escaped. In one sense it is possible too successfully to *isolate* the elements in the Puritan mind which bear upon the problem of liberty: we murder to dissect. But the documents may be relied upon to correct the deficiencies of the Introduction, and to restore to their proper complexity and animation the elements which we have isolated in order to explain. The Puritans (though in different degrees) were men who had undergone a religious experience, whose effect was to bestow a new unity of feeling upon their thoughts. Thus (to take a single example) it will be necessary for us to distinguish between the emphasis upon dogma and scripture and the emphasis upon experiential religion; but in very many cases these are not two things, but one, dogma furnishing the framework within which the experience is enjoyed, and scripture confirming the experience by the record of Moses, of Elijah, of St. Paul. 'This,' says Thomas Collier, preaching to the Army at Putney, 'I shall for your satisfaction confirm unto you from scripture, *although I trust I shall deliver nothing unto you but experimental truth*' (p. 390).

The first feature of the Puritan mind to strike a reader of the Debates is the dominant place held in it by dogmatic religion, and the tendency to carry inferences from dogma into secular life. It is true that this character is peculiar to the Puritan rather in degree than kind. Grotius observed the addiction of the English as a nation to theology; and, with certain notable exceptions (Hobbes, Harrington, Selden), the cast of its political thinking in the first half of the seventeenth century is definitely theological. Yet, despite some common ground, the distinction between the Anglican and the Puritan mind is valid; for Anglican dogmatism

---

[1] It has been felt desirable, while observing this emphasis in our discussion, to afford one example of Digger thought (pp. 379–85) together with some reference to it (pp. [56], [99]).

INTRODUCTION

was continually moderated by the tradition of Hooker, with his
appeal to philosophy and history to supplement and correct
a reliance on the bare letter of the scripture. More important
as qualifying our generalization is the evident beginning of a
movement among the Puritans of the Left, away from dogma and
towards humanitarianism. This is the Puritan counterpart of
the Latitudinarian current already becoming apparent in Anglican
thought, the Puritan premonition of that general secularizing of
the English temper, the date of whose beginning is conventionally
placed in 1660. But even in his movement away from dogma
the Puritan retains his identity and carries with him the lessons
learned in the conventicle. Almost to our own day the difference
of the Anglican and the Nonconformist outlooks was a fact to be
reckoned with in English life. To the growth of a secular spirit
which leaves the Puritan identity still easily recognizable, we shall
return. Our present interest is in the more obvious features of Puritanism during the decade of the Debates; and of these the dominance
of dogmatic religion is easily the most obvious, together with the
tendency to carry the implications of dogma into secular life, into
the fighting of civil wars and the subsequent reform of institutions.

The Puritan turned to the theological aspects of a question as
naturally as the modern man turns to the economic; and his first
instinct was to seek guidance within the covers of his Bible—or
was it rather to seek there justification for a policy already determined on other, on political and economic, grounds? Our own
answer to the query has been suggested above in discussing the
tactics of Cromwell at Putney, and need not be repeated here.
Granted the theological mode of argument is in some sort a
'rationalization,' granted even the disingenuousness with which it
is often pursued; that does not dispose of the matter. The terms
in which the Puritan insists that the argument shall be carried on,
are real to him, and of first-rate historical importance because
they are the terms in which he views his world. Ignore the terms,
or misunderstand them, and the Puritan mind has eluded you.
The Puritan viewed the world as a twofold system, a scheme of
nature and a scheme of *grace*. The two were interrelated: because
God was the creator and supreme ruler of them both, and because
they had a common subject-matter in man, and a common
object, the good. Man *as man* belonged to the natural order; the
elect belonged also to the order of grace. The author of *The
Ancient Bounds* writes (pp. 247-8):

Christ Jesus, whose is the kingdom, the power, and the glory, both
in nature and in grace, hath given several maps and schemes of his

B*   [39]

dominions . . .: both of his great kingdom, the world, his dominions at large which he hath committed to men to be administered in truth and righteousness, in a various form as they please; . . . and also his special and peculiar kingdom, the kingdom of grace. Which kingdoms though they differ essentially or formally, yet they agree in one common subject-matter (man and societies of men) though under a diverse consideration. And not only man in society, but every man individually, is an epitome, either of one only or of both these dominions: of one only, so every natural man (who in a natural consideration is called *microcosmus*, an epitome of the world), in whose conscience God hath his throne, ruling him by the light of nature to a civil outward good and end; of both, so every believer who, besides this natural conscience and rule, hath an enlightened conscience carrying a more bright and lively stamp of the kingly place and power of the Lord Jesus, swaying him by the light of faith or scripture, and such a man may be called *microchristus*, the epitome of Christ mystical.

There was a goodness appropriate to the natural order; and there was a goodness appropriate to the order of grace, which, while it included the natural goodness, also (because spiritual) transcended it. The views taken of the precise relation of these separate, yet interrelated orders, colour the Puritans' thought, and condition the terms—and perhaps more than the terms—of their particular and practical demands, as, for instance, that of Roger Williams for the absolute separation of church and state (the social organs of grace and nature) with complete liberty of conscience, or again the demand of others for the subjection of the natural man, and his institutions, to the church—or the Saints (pp. 241–7). God was the lawgiver of the two orders. Israel was a model (so ran the simpler view), and in the Bible might be read the precepts by which all men ought to be governed: 'Though the laws be few and brief, yet they are perfect and sufficient, and so large as the wisdom of God judged needful for regulating judgment in all ages and nations. For no action or case doth, or possibly can, fall out in this or other nations . . . but the like did, or possibly might, fall out in Israel.' [1] If one was to escape the conclusion which the Old Testament enforced in a particular issue (as, for example, in the question of the magistrate's power in religion), it could be only by an appeal to the New Testament, with an elaborate argument tending to prove that Israel was 'typical,' that its law (or some part of its law) was abrogated by the appearance of Christ, who was the 'antitype,' and that Israel

[1] William Aspinwal, *Description of the Fifth Monarchy* (1653), p. 10. Presbyterians appealed with like confidence to the Old Testament.

furnished, therefore, no literal model for life under the Gospel. Beside precept and model, there was prophecy. Daniel and Revelation afforded a key to events, past and present, and a vision of the future. From these books the Millenarians derived a view of history and a motive of revolution. And the pattern exhibited coloured the thought of many who could not be described as active adherents, so that one may speak of Millenarian doctrine as in a sense typical.

The cultural and disciplinary value to the Puritan mind, of all this biblical study, formal theological reasoning, and eager and disputatious searching into the purposes of God, is rarely, I think, appreciated to the full. It was on such studies that the logical faculty of Roger Williams was formed. Narrow and one-sided as the Puritan mind is apt to be, it is never flaccid. In their attitude toward reason the Puritans differed widely among themselves, ranging from the extremes of voluntarism and obscurantism to almost pure rationalism; but whatever the avowed attitude, their tacit reliance in the exposition of dogma and text was on logical thought: no one was ever more insistent on hearing a reason for the faith that was in you. That is why Puritanism carried its own special mental discipline. The Debates furnish abundant illustration of the dominance of dogmatic religion and scriptural reference; it appears in connection with every subject discussed, and (though in varying degrees) in all the participants. Unbelievably remote as the argument often seems, its general level attests the bracing effect of the Puritan discipline on ordinary minds. Nor must the limits which it set to inquiry be exaggerated. Dogma, brought into hourly relation with life, led men beyond dogma. Especially is this true of the group who separated most sharply the two orders of nature and grace. But this is to anticipate.

According to the Puritan notion, God spoke in the first instance through his word—the dominance of dogmatic religion means Puritan scripturism; but there were two other modes of learning his will. There was the mode of immediate religious experience. If dogmatic religion is heavily represented in the Debates, so is experiential. There are moments when one could hardly parallel the atmosphere at Putney outside the walls of Little Bethel. Yet to the Puritans it seems perfectly natural. They listen to each others' experiences and are duly edified and impressed. Even the hard-headed Ireton is strangely moved (pp. 21–2). The exposition of dogma and text make their claim upon reason, but in these experiences imagination and emotion have their play: the

[41]

Puritan imagination is fired, and the passions necessary to great, and sometimes desperate enterprises, are kindled. And there is a community of feeling not less important than intellectual agreement; this, too, religious experience, enjoyed in common, fosters. But the thing has its dangers. Cromwell finds that he is without anything to report 'as in the name of the Lord' (p. 102), and is a little fearful lest 'carnal imaginations' may pass themselves off as promptings from heaven (p. 104). He prefers, because it seems more objective, the testimony of events. That is God's third mode of revealing his will. The Puritan lives in a world of particular providences. God has 'owned' the Army by the success he has vouchsafed.[1] Let the Army pursue its course, but let it not outrun its commission or seize an opportunity before God has given one; and guidance will not fail. We have seen the Army on its momentous march to London, 'there to follow Providence as God shall clear our way.' The way was cleared to Pride's purge and the judicial murder of the King.

The sense of special insight into, and co-operation with, the purposes of God, is a distinguishing mark of the Puritan, and it sets him at a distance from other men. It is both a strength and a weakness. At its worst it issues in self-righteousness. (All the publicans and sinners were on one side, said Chillingworth, *all the scribes and Pharisees* on the other.) But it nerved the arm and brought an access of courage, which on any other premise, would have been reckless. Like everything else in the Puritan's outlook, the separation from his fellows rested on a dogmatic basis: the doctrine of predestination taught him that it was from the beginning. The Saint alone belonged to the order of grace, with its special equipment, its privileges, and its duties. The possible inferences from this fact were various, but so long as the dogma remained unimpaired, or uncircumvented, the attitude towards the natural man was constant. 'Men as men,' said Ireton, 'are corrupt and will be so' (p. 174).

If this account of the dominant place held by religion in the Puritan mind is even approximately correct, no wonder the religious issue bulked so large in the Civil War and the subsequent settlement. 'The interest of England is religion,' said Hugh Peter (p. 138). 'Kings, and Armies, and Parliaments,' said another speaker, 'might have been quiet at this day if they would have let Israel alone' (p. 147). And the religious issue is not

[1] Not all the Puritans are satisfied with such reasoning. 'But success alone is not a rule for wise men to go by . . .' (*The Ancient Bounds*, p. 55).

isolated. It complicates, and is complicated by, the civil.[1] Nor does the connection depend merely on the fact observed above, that each section of the Puritan Party has both religious and civil interests to guard, and religious and civil aims to secure. There is perpetual interaction between the two struggles. Passion generated in the one is available for the prosecution of the other. And here the primacy of the religious struggle appears: in it Puritan idealism burns with its steadiest flame, and religion exercises its influence not only directly by intrusion into the civil sphere, but indirectly by analogy. Milton speaks of 'the best part of our liberty, which is our religion'; and the Puritan's whole conception of liberty is (as we shall see) deeply coloured by his religious thought, while the second and partially incompatible object of his concern, positive reformation, is equally so coloured.

The zeal for positive reform [2] is one of the most constant and indisputable notes of Puritanism. 'Reform the universities. . . . Reform the cities . . . the countries, . . . the sabbath, . . . the ordinances, the worship of God. . . . *Every plant which my heavenly Father hath not planted shall be rooted up.*' [3] Alike in Presbyterians, Congregationalists, and the sects, the ideal of the 'holy community,' pure in doctrine and exemplary in life, is dominant; but with very different effects upon political thought and action. By the strictest and most logical of the Separatists the ideal is recognized as applicable to, and attainable by, the elect alone; and it operates within the limits of a voluntary religious community made up of visible Saints, with no attempt to influence the state save by exhortation and example. Wherever, on the other hand, the ideal is combined with that of a national church, an attempt will be made to bring the nation into outward conformity with the standard of the godly. The non-elect and the unbelievers are (as Troeltsch puts it) disciplined for the glory of God and the peace and welfare of the church. Thus the effect of what is at bottom the same motive would appear to be totally different in the Puritans of the Right and of the Left, with those of the Centre

[1] A different account of the priority of the religious struggle is given in *An Answer to Mr. William Prynne's Twelve Questions* (1644): the needed civil reforms might have been effected without an appeal to arms had not Episcopalian fears and Presbyterian ambitions complicated and forced the issue.

[2] It is necessary to distinguish between positive and negative reforms. The latter term may designate the reforms whose object is merely the removal of abuses and of restrictions upon the individual; the former may designate new interference with the individual for his or the community's benefit or in the interests of righteousness or efficiency.

[3] Thomas Case, *Two Sermons to the Commons*, 1641, pp. 21-2.

occupying the interval between them. But this does not exhaust the possibilities. A further distinction has to be drawn among the Puritans of the Left, where the idea of a national church, at least in its Presbyterian form, has no place. It is among some of the sectaries, whose church organization is Separatist and who (for their own purposes) join in the plea for liberty of conscience, that the ideal of the 'holy community' assumes its most menacing aspect, the doctrine of the rule of the Saints. And the rule of the Saints means the enforcement of the standards of the 'holy community' upon the nation at large, as the Millenarians frankly avow. If the idea of toleration is one ground of alliance between the Parties of the Centre and Left, this opposing idea is certainly another. Puritanism was not only committed in all sections to the ideal of the 'holy community,' but, in most of them, strongly drawn to the establishment of its reign outside the body of the elect, where, since persuasion could be of no avail, reform must be by coercion.

Its zeal for reformation results in part from the fact that the Puritan temper is in general active rather than contemplative. Though its official creed repudiates works as a *means* of salvation, it emphasizes them as a *sign*; and the Puritan has an overwhelming sense of one's responsibility to use every effort for advancing the kingdom of God. 'It is action,' says Baxter, 'that God is most served and honoured by.' [1] And the predilection comes out repeatedly in different forms. There is a vein—even here it is not .he dominant vein—of pure contemplation in Anglican literature. The Puritans on the other hand, despite their addiction to experiential religion, seem very often deficient in the higher and more disinterested kinds of mysticism. Milton is the least mystical of all great religious poets. And in his hands spiritual concepts like 'Christian liberty' are capable of being wrested from the contemplative to the active sphere. This is not to deny an element of mysticism in some of the Puritans. Cromwell can remind the Council of the Army, eager to dictate the settlement of the kingdom, that the best government 'is but a moral thing; . . . it is but dross and dung in comparison of Christ' (p. 97). They appear to disagree with him—and when the time comes Cromwell too will act. In Roger Williams a more unfaltering sense of the mystical quality of religious experience tends to set it apart, thus assigning religion to the contemplative spirit, but to the active reserving all the rest of life. Where no such separation occurs the strong Puritan impulse to action results in the constant

[1] *Christian Directory* (1678), 1. 336.

intrusion of religion into the secular sphere in an effort to enforce the standards of the holy community upon the world, and in a marked tendency to press on, in the name of that ideal, from the quest for religious liberty to the quest for political power.

Within limits the spirit of Puritanism is not only active, but experimental. Naturally the experimental spirit will be operative only in those sections of the party which conceive that the necessary point of compromise between the ideal and the demands of actual life has not yet been reached. For the rest, and notably for the Presbyterians, the period of its operation is already past. For the Independents, and much more markedly for the sects, the point is not yet reached.[1] The Bible embodies a revelation complete and unalterable; but there is still room for progressive comprehension, progressive interpretation;[2] and it is here that free discussion can (as Milton maintains in the *Areopagitica*) minister to the discovery of the truth and to agreement in the truth. 'I am verily persuaded,' said John Robinson to the departing Pilgrims, 'the Lord hath more truth yet to break forth out of his holy word. . . . I beseech you remember it is an article of your church covenant that you be ready to receive whatever truth shall be made known to you from the written word of God. . . . It is not possible that the Christian world should come so lately out of such thick Antichristian darkness and that perfection of knowledge should break forth at once.'[3] The Apologetical Narrators, the most moderate of Congregationalists, resolve 'not to make our present judgment and practice a binding law unto ourselves for the future' and could wish that this principle 'were (next to that most supreme, namely to be in all things guided by the perfect will of God) enacted as the most sacred law of all other . . . in

[1] The effort of Independency to replace Presbyterianism as the latter was replacing Episcopacy could be best rationalized in terms of progressive comprehension: '[D]oth Master Prynne think we have no more light discovered in these days about church-government than the godly had in former days? Or must all the Saints be regulated by former patterns? Then should Episcopacy be more followed than Presbytery' (*Certain Brief Observations*, 1644, p. 7).

[2] *The Independent Catechism* (1647) associates progressive comprehension of truth with an approaching millennium. The companion *Presbyterian Catechism*, issued by the same publisher, but a fair presentation of Presbyterian beliefs, is significantly silent on both progressive knowledge and the millennium. According to Williams, however, even the Presbyterians 'profess to want more light' (*Queries of Highest Consideration*, 1644).

[3] Neal's *History of the Puritans* (1822) 2. 110–11; cf. Edward Winslow, *Hypocrisy Unmasked* (1646), p. 97.

Christian states and churches throughout the world.'[1] The Christian, Henry Robinson urged, ought continually to grow not only from grace to grace, but from knowledge to knowledge.[2] 'The true temper and proper employment of a Christian is always to be working like the sea, and purging ignorance out of his understanding and exchanging notions and apprehensions imperfect for more perfect, and forgetting things behind to press forward' (p. 259). 'To be still searching what we know not, by what we know,' said Milton, 'still closing up truth to truth as we find it . . . .: this is the golden rule in theology as well as in arithmetic.'[3] The exponents of toleration, says another writer, 'count not themselves perfect but stand ready to receive further light, yea though from the meanest of the brethren.'[4] This experimental spirit, this eager quest of truth (whether adequately or inadequately conceived), with the attendant confidence in truth's power to guard itself and to prevail if given an open field, is the deepest and most abiding element in the Puritan campaign for liberty of conscience. There it joins hands with other traditions of free inquiry coming down from the Renaissance, as appears in quotations from Charron (pp. 260–1), and in John Goodwin's argument:

If so great and considerable a part of the world as America is . . . was yet unknown to all the world besides for so many generations together, well may it be conceived . . . that . . . many truths, yea and those of main concernment and importance, may be yet unborn and not come forth out of their mother's womb—I mean the secrets of the scripture to see the light of the sun. . . . [No] man is completely furnished for the ministry of the Gospel . . . who is not as well able to make some new discovery, and to bring forth something of himself

---

[1] *Apologetical Narration* (1644), p. 10. The tentative and experimental spirit of Independency is one of the reproaches levelled against it by the Presbyterian ministers, irritated by the Dissenting Brethren's demand for toleration coupled with a wary and largely politic refusal to set forth a counter-scheme of settlement: '[T]hey profess reservations and new lights for which they will no doubt expect the like toleration and so *in infinitum*' (*Letter of the Ministers of London, to the Assembly, against Toleration*, 1646, pp. 2–3). A clever satire makes the ministers complain: 'The Independents will ever be looking for further light, and go on still in reformation, and would carry the people along with them "to grow in grace and in the knowledge of Jesus Christ" . . .; by which means things will never be settled perfectly whilst the Church is militant. Therefore Independency is a mischief to the Church' (*Certain Additional Reasons to Those in A Letter by the Ministers of London to the Assembly*, 1646, p. 6).
[2] *Liberty of Conscience* (1644), p. 50.
[3] *Areopagitica, Prose Works*, 2. 90.
[4] *A Paraenetic for Christian Liberty* (1644), p. 34.

in the things of God in one kind or other, as to preach the common and received truths. . . . That is neither new nor unjustifiable by the practice of wise men, to examine, yea and to impugn, received opinions. He that will please to peruse the first book of Doctor Hakewell's learned *Apology of the Power and Providence of God &c.*, shall meet with great variety of instances . . . in divinity, philosophy, in ecclesiastical history, in civil or national history, in natural history, of opinions which had a long time been received, and yet were at last suspected, yea and many of them evicted and rejected upon due examination. . . . There are many errors (erroneously so called) in the Christian world which are made of the greatest and choicest truths; yea and which doubtless will be redeemed from their captivity and restored to their thrones and kingdoms by diligence, gifts and faithfulness of the approaching generation.[1]

Transferred to the political field, the experimental spirit manifests itself chiefly in the Levellers. But it is shared in some degree by the official body of the Independents and underlies the idea of the Debates.

An attitude tentative, yet confident and expectant, was further fostered by the rapid march of events. The break in the ordered procession of the traditional in church and state seemed to the more visionary to place the ideal within their reach. 'God,' wrote the Leveller leaders, 'hath so blessed that which has been done as thereby . . . to afford an opportunity which these six hundred years has been desired, but could never be attained, of making this a truly happy and wholly free nation.' [2] 'God's people, as well as worldlings,' said Henry Robinson, 'have their times to fish in troubled waters.' [3] The circumstances of the period fostered in those whose minds already contained the germs, both utopianism and the iconoclasm which, for the active temper, is inseparable from it.

Already in the *Grand Remonstrance* there is a suggestion of the utopian spirit in the programme of reforms which its framers outline;[4] Charles, indeed, specifically complains of 'that new Utopia of religion and government into which they endeavour to transform this kingdom.' [5] Here again Puritanism met other currents of thought: the still-living tradition of Renaissance utopianism (always more academic than the Puritan), embodied in the work of a More and a Campanella; the teaching of Bacon,

[1] *Imputatio Fidei* (1642), preface.
[2] *Manifestation*, 14th April 1649, p. 3.
[3] *Liberty of Conscience* (1644), preface.
[4] Husband's *Exact Collection* (1643), pp. 15–16, 19–20.
[5] Ibid., p. 315.

now commencing to find eager disciples and to shape its own august memorial, the Royal Society (a dream of the New Atlantis come true); the cult of Comenius, assiduously fostered by Samuel Hartlib, who had plans for the reform of everything from bee-hives to the state, not to mention a scheme, the special department of his friend John Dury, for the reunion of Protestant Christendom. Whatever the intentions of the Long Parliament, there were plenty of persons ready to point the way to Utopia: in education (to mention only the most important examples), Hartlib, Dury, Milton, Petty, John Webster, and William Dell; in the organization of society and the state, Hartlib, Harrington, Milton, Vane, Baxter, Hugh Peter, Henry Robinson, the Levellers in general, and Richard Overton in particular (see pp. 335-8), the Millenarians with their vision of rule by the Saints, and Gerrard Winstanley with his communist *Law of Freedom in a Platform*. All these writers, with the exception of Harrington and Petty, definitely belong to the Puritan parties (and even they have connections with the Puritans). Up to a point the outcropping of utopianism may further illustrate the beginnings of a trend away from dogmatic and towards humanitarian religion, or, in the case of the Levellers, Harrington, and Petty, a definite process of secularization; but Baxter, Vane, Dell, and the Millenarians certainly manifest no drift from dogma, on whose acceptance, indeed, their utopias depend. And all exhibit qualities recognized elsewhere in the products of the Puritan mind—above all the Puritan impulse to action; for these are not utopias in the sense of Sir Thomas More, but somewhat visionary schemes of reform to be actually attempted, utopias in the sense of Charles I's indignant protest. They may, like the *Areopagitica*, even repudiate 'Atlantic and utopian politics.' Typical is John Cook's *Unum Necessarium*, which pleads for the control of the drink trade and the relief of the poor (including free medical service): 'I am not of their opinion that drive at a parity, to have all men alike. *'Tis but a utopian fiction.* The scripture holds forth no such thing: *the poor ye shall have always with you.* But there ought to be no beggar in England, for they live rather like beasts than men.' [1] Fostered by the unsettled state of English institutions, and supplemented by various intellectual influences, this utopianism takes its rise in the Puritan mind and temper, and constitutes an important element in the Army Debates.

Hand in hand with utopianism goes iconoclasm. The common effort to destroy religious institutions of a thousand years had

[1] *Unum Necessarium* (1648), p. 36.

confirmed this trait in the Puritan mind, even when the purpose
was to replace them with a sterner rule and 'not to loose the
golden reins of discipline and government in the church.' [1] 'And
for the extirpation of prelacy,' wrote John Saltmarsh, 'though it
be a government riveted into our laws and usages . . . yet let
us not like the Jews lose our Gospel with holding our Laws too
fast. I know this kingdom hath ever been a retentive nation of
customs and old constitutions. . . . And hence it is that reformation . . . hath been with such little power and duration. . . .' [2]
Though fostered by the revolution in the church the triumph of
iconoclasm was but partial in the end; for some of the deepest
instincts of the national temper (as Saltmarsh hints) were ranged
against it, and these kept cropping up—in the Puritans themselves.
Only in the Parties of the Left is iconoclasm willingly adopted
and unhesitatingly pursued. Beyond a certain point, the Independents are drawn into it not by choice, but by the force of
circumstances. In November 1647, Ireton defends 'the fundamental constitution' from Leveller attacks. By November 1648,
he has had to retreat from this position: 'the fundamental constitution' gives too little ground for beheading monarchs and
establishing republics in their place.[3] The subject leads into a

[1] *Grand Remonstrance.*
[2] *A Solemn Discourse upon the Covenant* (1644), p. 6.
[3] Ireton is forced to execute a partial retreat on the related subject of
the binding character of engagements. At Putney he declares them to be
inescapable. A year later in the *Remonstrance of the Army* (p. 460) he
does not reverse the decision, but he provides a very pretty example of
Puritan casuistry by indicating how, without doing so, he can set the
Covenant aside. The Covenant indeed constituted a recurrent stumb-
ling-block to the Independents and the Parties of the Left. Hugh
Peter chose simply to ignore it: he had it administered to him, 'as he
thought, twenty times, and saw nothing in it that men should make such
a stir about' (Thomas Edwards, *Gangraena*, part 3, p. 123). The
spokesmen of the Left at Putney take up the position that no engagement is binding if, and when, it conflicts with the claims of justice and
right, or with the safety of the people (which is the supreme law). They
are merely giving reasoned expression to a rather obscure tendency in
the Puritan mind to regard no bargain as binding once it has ceased to
be advantageous — especially to the children of grace. This form of
iconoclasm is fairly widespread (cf. Milton's treatment of the marriage
contract in *The Doctrine and Discipline of Divorce*). The same idea could
be expressed in the language of religious enthusiasm. Buff-Coat remarks ecstatically: 'Whatsoever obligation I should be bound unto, if
afterwards God should reveal himself, I would break it, if it were an
hundred a day' (p. 34). Though the principle had been invoked by
the Independents in their struggle for religious liberty, and by the
Parliament in its struggle with Charles, Ireton voices the alarm of
the Centre Party: 'When I hear men speak of laying aside all engagements, to consider only that wild or vast notion of what in every man's

INTRODUCTION

consideration of the appeal to natural rights, which must be
reserved for our consideration of liberty; but we may glance at
the Puritan attitude to custom, precedent, and history, taking
Milton as our example.[1] No sooner has he attacked the problem
of religious liberty and reform than he decides that change cannot
be too 'swift and sudden provided still it be from worse to better.'
Custom, he discovers, is 'a natural tyrant' in religion and in the
state, a tyrant which has an ally in man's fallen nature—'a double
tyranny of custom from without and blind affections within.'
Custom, it is assumed as self-evident, always enters into alliance
with error, never with truth: '. . . Error supports custom, custom
countenances error, and these two between them would persecute
and chase away all truth and solid wisdom out of human life,
were it not that God, rather than man, once in many ages calls
together the prudent and religious counsels of men, deputed to
repress the encroachments and to work off the inveterate blots
and obscurities wrought upon our minds by the subtle insinuating
of custom and error.' In this passage is implied the Puritan
view of history (the view which informs Adam's vision in *Paradise
Lost*): deterioration is its note, but deterioration relieved by
sudden interventions of God in behalf of truth and righteousness,
as seen in the prophets of old, pre-eminently in the earthly ministry
of Christ, and recently, after twelve hundred years of increasing
darkness, in the Reformation, whose work England was called on
to complete, 'even unto the reformation of reformation.' The
view can best be characterized as the direct antithesis of Burke's:
history is not 'the known march of the ordinary providence of
God'; it is a protracted wandering from the way, relieved by
sudden interventions of God's *extraordinary* providence. The
common elements of theism and idealism in the two thinkers
make the comparison legitimate and significant. For Milton
theism does not validate the actual, does not dispose him to seek
for evidences of the ideal in the actual, or in history which is the
record of the actual. Though other influences contribute to form
his mind, there is strong indication that in this he speaks for
Puritanism: and he is at one with the Independent John Cook,
who repudiates 'the puddles of history,'[2] and with the Levellers,

---

conception is just or unjust, I am afraid and do tremble at the boundless
and endless consequences of it' (p. 27).

[1] *Of Reformation, Reason of Church Government, Tenure of Kings and
Magistrates, Doctrine and Discipline of Divorce: Prose Works*, 2. 410, 503,
2; 3. 171–2; 2. 485.

[2] G. P. Gooch, *English Democratic Ideas in the Seventeenth Century*
(1927) p. 159.

who dismiss the past as vicious and irrelevant: '. . . Whatever our forefathers were, or whatever they did or suffered, or were enforced to yield unto, we are men of the present age and ought to be absolutely free from all kinds of exorbitancies, molestations, and arbitrary power.' [1] It is in connection with the plea for liberty that Puritan iconoclasm most frequently appears; but the attitude was learned in connection with church reform. 'Let them chant while they will of prerogatives,' said Milton, 'we shall tell them of scripture; of custom, we of scripture; of acts and statutes, still of scripture.'

With the Puritan concern for liberty we come to a trait immensely important in itself and for our purposes, but also problematical as those previously enumerated are not. It is the subject of the concluding section of this essay, but the question of its status must be broached at this point. The problem is raised by two facts: that a concern for liberty does not appear to be a constant feature of the Puritan mind, and that it runs counter to another and the most universally recognized of traits, the passionate zeal for positive reform, with the will, if necessary, to dragoon men into righteousness—or the semblance of righteousness. If we confine our attention to the Puritans of the Right we shall find as time goes on little enthusiasm for liberty as an ideal, and many hard sayings regarding it. Preaching before the House of Commons on 26th May 1647, Thomas Case denounced liberty of conscience as opening the floodgates of anarchy. Publish liberty of conscience as one of the people's rights, he said, 'and see . . . how long your civil peace will secure you when religion is destroyed. . . . For no doubt if this once be granted them . . . they may in good time come to know also—there be them that are instructing them even in these principles, too—that it is their birthright to be freed from the power of parliaments and . . . kings. . . . Liberty of conscience (falsely so called) may in time improve itself into liberty of estates and . . . houses and . . . wives, and in a word liberty of perdition of souls and bodies.' [2] Here speaks the outraged Puritan ideal of righteousness, reinforced by a sense that the moment of a necessary compromise between the impulse towards liberty and the demands of actual life is long overdue. The protest is thoroughly typical and could be paralleled by dozens of others. If, on the contrary, we turn to the Puritans of the Centre, and more particularly of the Left, we find

[1] *Remonstrance of Many Thousand Citizens*, 7th July 1646, p. 5.
[2] Thomas Case, *Spiritual Whoredom Discovered in a sermon before the House of Commons, 26th May 1647*, p. 34.

not only the utterances of the Levellers, but the official declarations of the Army, exalting liberty to the position of the main motive in the Puritan revolution, and Overton (typical in this at least) championing the ideal of liberty against what he chooses to regard as the pseudo-ideal of reform.[1] The conflict between the two ideals is, or may become, real enough. But the contrast between the Puritans of the Right and the Left is apt to be misleading. The desire for liberty was not (or rather had not always been) absent as a motive from the Party of the Right. In the hour of oppression it had been a main plea of every group. In the matter of liberty of conscience, one of the chief indictments against the Presbyterians was that they withheld from others what they had demanded for themselves. Nor can one fail to recognize in such a document as Rutherford's *Lex Rex* (pp. 199–212) a genuine (if limited) passion for liberty and a host of arguments in its behalf. Again the concern for liberty is by no means equally manifested in the different groups which form the Puritan Left. The ideal of reform in the interests of righteousness is certainly not less dominant in the Millenarians than in the Presbyterians. Finally, in seeking to determine which of the two constitutes the authentic Puritan ideal, it is an error to concentrate on the Right and Left to the exclusion of the Centre. In the Independents the two ideals are constantly present, and the conflict between them is unmistakable. The principal Whitehall debate is very largely a record of that conflict. So much for the attitude towards liberty and reform manifested by different Puritan groups. There is another way of viewing the problem. One may ask what bearing the basic theological dogmas adopted by Puritanism have upon these issues. Of the reforming spirit, the zeal for righteousness, and the willingness to coerce if need be, the theological foundations have been sufficiently explored above. These things, there is no denying, are of the essence of Puritanism. In the case of the concern for liberty, the theological foundations, which have not perhaps been so fully understood, will be discussed in some detail below. For the moment it is enough to indicate their existence by a single sentence from Milton (p. 228), who is pleading for liberty of conscience but is ever ready to extend the demand from religion to politics: 'Ill was our condition changed from legal to evangelical and small advantage gotten by the Gospel, if for the

---

[1] *The Arraignment of Persecution* (reproduced in *Tracts*, edited Haller, 3. 203–56). Cf. Samuel Richardson, *The Necessity of Toleration* (pp. 17–18), which condemns the Presbyterian reformation as sinful, foolish, carnal, cruel, and deceitful.

spirit of adoption to freedom, promised us, we receive again the
spirit of bondage to fear. . . .' Basic Puritan theology and the
history of the revolution suggest the same answer to our problem.
The motives are equally authentic: the passionate concern for
liberty and the passionate zeal for reform in the interests of
righteousness. Capable of co-operation up to a certain point,
they finally remain, somewhere near the heart of Puritanism, in a
state of potential and unresolved conflict.

More or less closely connected with the feeling for liberty are
Puritan individualism and Puritan equalitarianism, each with
its appropriate dogmatic basis, whose fuller discussion may also
be postponed. Here one must recognize, however, counter-
tendencies and counter-associations in the Puritan mind. Puritan
individualism speaks most significantly of all in the voice of conscience. The Puritan asserts the right and duty of thinking for
himself. Those in authority (the Agents observe to Fairfax) may
demand an unquestioning obedience, but a man is finally answerable to his own conscience (p. 436 n.)—that is (in Ireton's phrase) to
'conscience obliging above or against human and outward constitutions' (p. 459). The consciences of common men were a new
phenomenon in politics, and one that has never since disappeared.
Ideally, to assert one's right of private judgment should be to
concede the same right to every one else. But it is not always
thus that the celebrated Nonconformist conscience has reasoned
—and we understand the Puritan conscience the better if we give
it its later name. Some of its associations are with liberty, but
not all. For it can argue that all it pleads for is the autonomy of
the illuminated conscience and that this it denies to no man.
Again, in regard to Puritan equalitarianism it is sufficient to
observe that the equality of believers implies their superiority to
unregenerate men. And this superiority, so long as dogma is
unimpaired, or in the secular field uncircumvented, will continue
to oppose an effective barrier against a wider equalitarianism.

The two processes, the impairing of dogma and its circumvention,
must be clearly distinguished. Both are present in Puritanism of
the Left, and each has its place in the history of liberty and equality.

Of the forces counteracting, and ultimately impairing, the dogmatic attitude we have noticed one, the principle of the progressive
interpretation of truth. With its operation (as also with the
ineptitude of amateur theologians) may be associated the rapid
multiplication of sects and heresies which Thomas Edwards de-
plores.[1] Standing in varying relations to the Puritan movement,

[1] *Gangraena* (3 parts, 1645–6).

the new opinions consist either in some exaggeration of the dominant Calvinistic creed (a repudiation of some compromise which it had sanctioned) or in a reaction, theological or ethical, against some part of that creed and its inferences. For our present purpose the latter type alone is directly important, though the very multiplication of opinions, whatever their character, would do something to weaken the authority of dogma as such. Most significant of all is the reaction against the Calvinistic dogma of predestination as that dogma is set forth by Prynne (pp. 232–3) and others. The reaction, which extends far beyond the ranks of the Puritans, represents a shift towards a rational theology and a humanistic, even a humanitarian, religion. As the Cambridge Platonists were to demonstrate, Arminianism was pre-eminently the doctrine of Christian rationalism [1] and Christian humanism, re-reading the stern pronouncements of the Reformation in the mellow light of the Renaissance. The Calvinists were quick to point out its affinities with the Pelagian heresy, whose effect was to eliminate divine grace and substitute a gospel of self-help. This is a gospel comfortable to human nature (All men, said Culverwel, are naturally born Pelagians), and one whose role in the making of the modern mind is self-evident.[2] It is not surprising then to find some of the sectaries going far beyond the Arminian position proper, hinting the sufficiency and the natural goodness of human nature and calling in question the doctrine of original sin. But apart from these dubious inferences, and by its central attack on the extreme form of the Calvinistic doctrine of predestination, of absolute election and reprobation, Arminianism weakens the theological basis of Puritan *in*equalitarianism, of the conception of an aristocracy of the elect, and thus undermines the most formidable of the barriers separating Puritanism from democracy.

Other forces are at work among the sectaries to a similar end. Two may be distinguished, though not so as to exclude their mutual influence. For, as Chesterton observes, heterodoxies, often of the most opposite kinds, will flock together. In seventeenth-century England (as in the Europe of the Reformation)

---

[1] This is illuminatingly explained in Joseph Glanvill's 'Free Philosophy and Anti-fanatical Religion' (*Essays*, 1676). In Puritan pamphlets the term 'Arminian' is loosely used to designate the whole Laudian position, but usually with some reference to the attitude on predestination which was felt to be basic (see Godfrey Davies, 'Puritan *vs.* Arminian,' *Huntington Library Bulletin*, April 1934).

[2] See the suggestive analysis in T. E. Hulme's *Speculations* (1924), pp. 46–71.

INTRODUCTION

currents which in spirit belong to no religious tradition but rather to libertinism, seek a temporary alliance with radical Protestant thought. In Overton there is a militant naturalism and a thinly veiled hostility to dogmatic religion. He champions the mortalist heresy in the name of scripture and reason and advances a materialistic view of man and the world.[1] He claims to have attempted a proof of the main truths of revelation from nature and reason;[2] it is difficult to judge of his motives, but the method seems to link him with the beginnings of Deism. He is perfectly familiar with Puritan doctrine and can use it on occasion. He talks of the order of nature in terms reserved by the more orthodox for the order of grace, by the simple expedient of omitting all reference to the Fall (p. [69]). He seizes upon the radical plea for liberty of conscience put forward on religious grounds by Roger Williams and others, and gives it his own emphasis.[3] Wildman can also speak the language of the Saints:[4] on the most extreme Separatist ground, he argues against the magistrate's power in matters of religion, developing the doctrine of the two orders in a direction which might lead to either scepticism or fideism, and incidentally in one diametrically opposed to Overton's boasted effort to deduce the truths of revelation from nature (pp. 168–9). By Walwyn a subtler method is used. His aim is to inculcate a sentiment. He adapts (sometimes almost out of recognition) such parts of Puritan doctrine as he can use, while undermining, rather than openly assailing, the rest. The doctrine of Christian liberty, detached from its dogmatic basis, becomes an invitation to free oneself from the oppression of religious ordinances; Eden is approximated to the life of the golden age, and of Montaigne's happy savages; the Fall is thus interpreted as a forsaking of nature for human 'inventions,' and the rule of the Gospel as an injunction to return to a natural simplicity; the genuine (and at this time somewhat neglected) humanitarian element in Christianity is emphasized at the expense of every other, and, more dubiously, it is presented as a militant and revolutionary creed. It is not without significance that Walwyn here affects to be expounding the

[1] Cf. R[ichard] O[verton], *Man's Mortality* (1643; enlarged 1655).
[2] *Picture of the Council of State* (1649), p. 28 (quoted by Haller, *Tracts*, 1.96). Overton and Walwyn both sign the *Manifestation* (14th April 1649), in which the Leveller leaders protest their belief in God and the Bible.
[3] *Arraignment of Persecution*, pp. 14–17, 22–6.
[4] *Putney Projects* (1647; p. 1): 'God's present great design . . . is the shaking of the powers of the earth and marring the pride of all flesh. Isaiah 2. 11: *The lofty looks of man shall be humbled and the haughtines; of men shall be bowed down, and the Lord shall be exalted in that day.* . . . To-day is this scripture fulfilled. . . .'

doctrines of the Familists.[1] Such teaching carries us over from the sceptics to the mystics, who tend to undermine dogma in the act of reinterpreting it. This is the second force to which we referred above. The influential teaching of Winstanley may serve as an example, whose blend of the practical with the mystic points on to Quakerism. His method of interpreting the Bible is frankly allegorical. The unfallen state is one in which the in-dwelling God (variously described as Reason and as Universal Love) rules the life of man. The Fall means the intrusion of self-love, which is followed by the curse. This, however, can be but temporary; for Reason or Universal Love must triumph, and mankind be restored to its primal perfection (pp. 375–89).[2] By this and other such reinterpretations of the Christian scheme (in which some of the essential dogmas of Calvinism are omitted and the whole takes on a universalist colouring) Winstanley builds the theological foundations of his social teaching.

A fourth influence is less theoretic. Apart from the varying notes of naturalism and scepticism detected in some of their leaders, there was among the Levellers a marked transfer of interest from religion to the world. But even in the leaders the drift from Puritan belief and sentiment is by no means constant. There appears to have been no such drift in John Lilburne, the most in-fluential of them all. His earliest sufferings had been in the cause of liberty of conscience, and eight years later he published an account of his religious experience at this time.[3] Increasingly preoccupied with secular concerns, and thrown into association with Overton and Walwyn, he seems, nevertheless, to have

[1] I have tentatively adopted Professor Haller's ascription of *The Power of Love* (1643) to Walwyn (*Tracts* 1. 121–7; 2. 271–303).

[2] Cf. *The Mystery of God Concerning the Whole Creation : Mankind* (1648); *A New-Year's Gift for the Parliament and Army* (1650); L. H. Berens, *The Digger Movement* (1906), p. 44. The name for God, 'the Universal Love,' points to a connection with Familist teaching, the alternative name 'Reason,' points as clearly to rationalist thought (see further, below, p. [*94*]). The whole conception is coloured by opposition to Calvinism and by incipient naturalism. In his attack on the clergy in *The Law of Freedom in a Platform* (1652; p. 58) he declares: '. . . To know the works of God within the creation is to know God himself, for God dwells in every visible work or body. And indeed if you would know spiritual things, it is to know how the spirit or power of wisdom and life . . . dwells within and governs both the several bodies . . . in the heavens above, and . . . the earth below . . .; for to reach God beyond the creation . . . is a knowledge beyond the . . . capacity of man to attain. . . .'

[3] John Lilburne, *Innocency and Truth Justified* (1646). The account is dated 11th November 1638. We hear of his disagreement with Walwyn's views on religion (*England's Lamentable Slavery*, 1645, p. 1).

remained a religious enthusiast to the end. And wherever he deals with religion he appears as a rigorous Separatist who could readily subscribe to all the teachings of Williams's *Bloody Tenent*.[1] More significant still is the fact that all the Levellers, when arguing in favour of religious liberty, do so on the grounds set forth in that great book, which is as orthodox as it is radical.

For the undermining of dogma is not a necessary prelude to a contribution by Puritanism to liberty or even equality. While there are enemies to be encountered, an uncritical religious enthusiasm, not too careful of logical consequences, may do yeoman service. But before the contribution can be one of ideas, and unequivocal in its logical bearings, limits must be set to the drawing of inferences from religious dogma in the secular sphere. The way actually taken by true Puritans depends on no serious undermining of dogma itself, but on quite another process which leaves the reign of dogma in religion unimpaired. With this we come to the final characteristic of Puritan thought. If it is ignored, one cannot gauge correctly the relation of Puritanism to political liberty and secular progress. That characteristic is a tendency, already hinted, to distinguish sharply between religion and the rest of life, to segregate the spiritual from the secular, and to do this, in the first instance, for the sake of religion, though with momentous consequences for the life of the world. As in the case of the Puritan concern for liberty itself, the characteristic is of the utmost importance; and, once more, it is problematical because it manifests itself only in some of the Puritans, and those not the majority, and because it would seem to run counter to one of the characteristics already fully established: the tendency of the Puritan mind to carry the implications of dogma into secular life. Like the Puritan concern for liberty, it obviously requires to have its status examined and vindicated.

The groups in which the new characteristic appears are roughly identical with those already cited as exhibiting most clearly the Puritan concern for liberty and as setting limits to the Puritan zeal for positive reform. In the Party of the Right, the Presbyterians, the new characteristic is absent;[2] but so is it also in the

---

[1] Cf. Lilburne's *Nine Arguments* (1644), kindly lent to me by Professor Haller. Lilburne finally became a Quaker, and there is a hint of his repudiation of all church organization in his *Legal Fundamental Liberties* (1649, p. 39), in a contemptuous reference to 'their [Cromwell and Ireton's] champions in all their pretended churches of God, either Independent or Anabaptistical.'

[2] Save in so far as it is adumbrated in that limited doctrine of the two kingdoms common to Puritan and Jesuit theory (see J. N. Figgis, *Divine Right of Kings*).

Millenarians, and in the other groups (of the Centre and Left) who share in any appreciable degree their vision of the future. On the other hand, in those groups of the Left who are most deeply devoted to liberty of conscience and from whom proceeded the main Puritan argument and effort in behalf of political liberty, the new characteristic is very strongly marked. In the Independents, the Centre Party, it clearly emerges, but less decisively than in these. From the facts thus baldly set forth, one might predict a close relation between the new characteristic—the tendency to segregate the spiritual and the secular—and the effective emergence of the Puritan concern for liberty. The segregation of the spiritual and the secular is indeed the means by which the concern for liberty frees itself in the secular sphere from other and countervailing impulses, and disposes of all those particular inferences from dogma which are inimical to liberty. If the concern for liberty is an authentic characteristic of the Puritan mind, so also is this, the necessary mode of its transfer to the secular field. But the proof need not rest here. As in the case of the concern for liberty, the separation of the spiritual and the secular (or what we may for brevity call the *principle of segregation*) is traceable to the foundations of Puritan thought. In discussing the Puritan conception of man and the world, we observed as a constant feature, the recognition of a twofold system, an order of nature and an order of grace, and we remarked on the extent to which the different views taken of the precise relation subsisting between the two orders coloured Puritan thought. It is upon an extreme interpretation of this dogma of the two orders that the principle of segregation depends. The two orders are separate and opposed. God indeed is the creator and ruler of them both, but he rules them by different dispensations, and the goods which pertain to them are totally different (for, though spiritual goodness no doubt assumes all the natural virtues, it also transcends them). What God has thus divided, the Christian may not seek to join. He must not (for example), through mistaken zeal, try to bring the natural man under a rule meant only for the elect. In all his thinking, indeed, he must be mindful of the distinction of the two orders. This principle, thoroughly applied, imposes severe limits upon the intrusion of dogma into secular life. In other words, it completely secularizes one division of existence. But the principle is derived not from any conscious reaction against dogma as such, but from a confident and extreme appeal to one of the basic dogmas of the Puritan creed. The correctness of this interpretation is, I think, confirmed by the fact that for many who apply the principle of segregation the reign of dogma in the spiritual sphere remains (for a long time at least) unassailed.

The practical manifestations of this principle, and its less immediate results, are far-reaching indeed. The most obvious manifestation, the perfect example in action, is the insistence by Puritans of the Left on the absolute separation of church and state, the social organs of grace and nature respectively. That this insistence becomes the groundwork of a plea for complete liberty of conscience illustrates the close connection between the principle of segregation and the Puritan concern for liberty. But the alliance does not stop short with religious liberty; the reasoning which issues in a purely spiritual view of the church issues just as certainly in a purely secular view of the state. This in itself invites a reconsideration of the state's origin, function, and sanctions. It does not follow that the reconsideration will be democratic in tendency; but it may be so, and the invitation is the first service of the Puritan principle of segregation to the cause of liberty and equality. There is a second service. We have seen that Puritanism nourishes both a concern for liberty and a sentiment of equality (and this it does without reference to the principle of segregation). But both terms require to be qualified: it is *Christian* liberty, and it is the equality of *believers*. The natural man can claim no share in these privileges, which belong to a higher order, the order of grace. The sense of a fundamental *inequality* underlies both the concern for liberty and—the paradox is only seeming—the sentiment of equality itself. In other words: when the order of nature and the order of grace are considered together, the superiority of the latter will always assert itself. The principle of segregation enters to insist that they must be considered apart. That is its second service. But there is a third. Puritanism fosters the impulse to reform in the interests of righteousness, and this impulse (we have seen) runs, or may run, counter to a concern for liberty. Viewing Puritanism as a whole, we detected a potential and unresolved conflict between these two motives. The incentive to reform belongs to the order of grace, but it may be translated into action in the order of nature. To such a passage from one order to the other the principle of segregation once more opposes a barrier. At least it insists that the attempt to reform the world shall be in the terms appropriate to the world, the terms not of religion but of natural ethics. Indeed where the principle is carried to its logical conclusion, as it is in Roger Williams, it resolves the conflict between the two motives of liberty and reform. This is the third and final service.

But is not the principle of segregation a two-edged sword? Will it not, logically applied, cut off from the secular sphere the liberalizing as well as the reactionary influences of Puritanism, at least in so far as these are grounded in dogma? Theoretically it should. Indeed, in so far as the principle is anticipated by Luther it has precisely that result: Christian liberty, he reiterates, has no bearing on politics. Furthermore, Separatism in essence means separation from the world and its cares. But the predominantly active character of the Puritan temper—not to mention the instincts of human nature, even when sanctified—may be depended on to forestall that result. And the segregation of the spiritual and the secular cannot in practice mean that all influence of the one upon the other will cease. The lessons learned in the conventicle will not be forgotten in the forum. But we may look for a new mode of influence: not the direct influence of intrusion, but the indirect influence of *analogy*. There is a spiritual equality in the order of grace: is there not an analogous equality in the order of nature? This is but one of a dozen points at which analogically Puritanism could reinforce the cause of liberty and equality.

In briefest outline, and too abstractedly perhaps (but illustration will follow), we have suggested the importance of the principle of segregation in its bearing on liberty. The principle opened to the Puritan other developments in the secular field: it enabled him to adopt Baconian ideas in education as readily as democratic ideas in politics, and in the next century it contributed to make some of the Dissenting academies outposts of the Enlightment and of radical thought. With the true Puritan, religion remains the first concern: the principle—one might almost call it the device—of segregation prevents (or rather, as the subsequent history of Dissent seems to show, postpones) the repercussion upon his dogmatic creed, of radical and naturalistic ideas adopted in a secular sphere.

IV

The service of Puritanism to the cause of liberty is not bounded by its disinterested attachment to liberty as an ideal. If this attachment had been wholly absent, if Puritanism had advanced no theological doctrine of liberty, elaborated no theory of religious toleration, pointed no analogies between the economies of grace and nature or between a free church and a free state, it would still have been, in the circumstances, a potent engine of destruction

INTRODUCTION

and the most effective school of revolution then available. It is a
truism that the years between 1640 and 1649 saw the overthrow
of a system of absolutism in church and state, which if it had been
allowed to prevail, might radically have altered the whole subsequent course of English political development: in so far at least
the 'Whig view of history' is correct. Nor is it easy to conceive
of this overthrow without the powerful incentive and example of
Puritanism, not at one stage merely but at point after point of its
course. Nothing could dissipate the divinity that hedged a king
save the divinity of religion itself when religion was ranged against
him. The analogies between Puritan and Jesuit thought seized
on by the Royalists are not all fanciful: Puritanism effected in
Protestant England what even the Church could not (or would
not) effect in the Roman Catholic countries of Europe. . . .

It is true that in the twin sources of Protestant thought, Calvin
and Luther, there was impressive authority for passive obedience
even to ungodly magistrates. But the oracles were not altogether
consistent: Milton was able to quote from the Reformation divines
in order to round out a universal testimony against tyrants—and
if they sometimes spoke in another sense, so much the worse
for their authority![1] On the Puritans of the Right Calvin was
the dominant influence. Notably more reticent than Luther on
Christian liberty and the privileges of the Saints, Calvin does not,
like Luther, limit the application to the spiritual sphere; and he
writes between the lines of his injunction to passive obedience a
prescription of strictly limited *dis*obedience, which in the emphatic closing sentences of the *Institutes* becomes perfectly specific:

But in that obedience . . . due to . . . rulers we must always make
this exception . . .: that it be not incompatible with obedience to Him
to whose will . . . kings should be subject, to whose decrees their
commands must yield, to whose majesty their sceptres must bow.
And indeed how preposterous were it, in pleasing men, to incur the
offence of Him for whose sake you obey men! . . . If they command
anything against Him, let us not pay the least regard to it, nor be
moved by all the dignity which they possess as magistrates—a dignity
to which no injury is done when it is subordinated to the special and
truly supreme power of God.[2]

Calvin enjoins Christian obedience *and fixes its limits*. Nor does
he leave active resistance without recognition or a means of becoming effective: private citizens may not actively oppose their
prince; but the inferior magistrates may, and when godliness is

[1] *Tenure of Kings and Magistrates, Prose Works*, 2. 37–47.
[2] *Institutes*, 4. 20. 32 (translated Beveridge).

[61]

menaced, must (pp. 197–8). Here Calvin is at one with the more liberal thought of the Renaissance. His prescription might have been written for the Presbyterian Party of the First Civil War. Charles is cast for the role of prince, and Parliament for that of the inferior magistrates; they fight by the book. In practice Calvinism imposes little restraint upon the rebels: they are not to destroy monarchy, but they are to discipline it and render it wholly subservient to the higher ends of government. Once the inferior magistrates have declared against the prince, and freed opposition from the stigma of rebellion, so staunch a Calvinist as Rutherford can forge in *Lex Rex* almost every argument of revolution later to be employed by the Levellers, can invoke the law of nature and the ultimate sovereignty of the people (pp. 203–211).[1] It is thus that one side—on the face of it the more emphatic side—of Calvin's teaching is sunk in favour of the other, the revolutionary. 'We can pick and choose from a Reformer,' says Saltmarsh in another connection, 'what fits to the standard of our own light and reformation, and cast the other by. . . .'[2]

There was a point in action beyond which the Presbyterians would not go. With the end of the First Civil War the side of Calvin's teaching neglected in the heat of the struggle began to reassert itself. But by this time an increasing body of Puritans were quite ready, as we have seen, to run counter to Calvin's views on magistracy as also on church polity, while they held for the most part by his fundamental doctrine of predestination. The Presbyterians, not without chapter and verse in the *Institutes*, had sown the wind: the year 1647 marks the beginning of the whirlwind. On the basis of the doctrine of predestination had been erected the ideal of the rule of the Saints. With many this ideal swept away every other theory of government. For many others the belief in the sovereignty of the people no longer required such dubious underpinnings as Calvinistic theology could be made to yield. It appeared self-evident. One might even go so far as to secularize the Civil War—might decide that it was never legitimate to take up the sword for religion, but only for the gaining of civil rights:[3] the revolution could proceed under its own power.

---

[1] Unlike the Covenant, *Lex Rex* makes little pretence of differentiating between the King and his advisers, but frankly asserts the will of the people as against the King himself. As a result it was not obsolete in 1648, when it was reprinted with the title: *The Pre-eminence of the Election of Kings, or a Plea for the People's Rights.*

[2] John Saltmarsh, *Free-Grace* (1645), p. 210.

[3] Thus Hugh Peter (Thomas Edwards, *Gangraena*, part 3, p. 135). Roger Williams (who, despite his inveterate fundamentalism, treats the

INTRODUCTION

For others no authority was left but the sword: the conquerors should distribute the spoils whether in terms of the rights of the people or the privileges of the Saints—two standards which seemed less incompatible in practice than they now appear in theory. In this later period of conflicting doctrines, however, Puritanism is still—indeed more unconditionally than ever before—a mighty revolutionary agent; for its radical elements are liberated to act by themselves. If the Calvinistic view of the limits of Christian obedience is one of the chief impelling forces in the First Civil War, the confused ideals of Christian privileges and human rights then take its place, all but sweeping away the authority of Calvin's inferior magistrates, the Lords and Commons in Parliament assembled, and substituting the rule of the Army in its stead.

This fact raises an issue of fundamental importance. From the vantage ground of a later century no one will doubt that the most important political doctrine to emerge from the revolution was one temporarily defeated, but destined to ultimate triumph, the sovereignty of Parliament, a doctrine whose assertion altered the character of that body, and vastly extended its powers.[1] The direct debt of this doctrine to Puritanism does not appear to be great. Its indirect debt is, on the other hand, immense; for Parliament allied itself with the forces of Puritanism and asserted its own sovereignty by claiming its right to undertake the reform of religion. The doctrine of Parliamentary sovereignty is not necessarily a doctrine of liberty or of democracy. It is significant that we find arrayed against it, in the Debates, the most extreme forces of Puritanism, both democratic and anti-democratic. In order that the sovereignty of Parliament may become a doctrine of liberty and democracy, and their most effective safeguard, Parliament must be democratized and its general conformity to the will of the nation must be ensured. These are the hard-won achievements of a later day. But they are implicit in the Levellers' opposition to the sovereignty claimed by the existing Parliament; and that opposition draws sustenance from the Puritan belief in liberty of conscience and, more generally, from the habits of thought which directly and indirectly Puritanism inculcates.

It is not on particular issues, however fundamental, that the

---

Millenarian prophecies with reserve) roundly asserts that Christ has given no 'pattern, precept or promise for the undertaking of civil war for his sake' (*Queries of Highest Consideration*, pp. 26–9).

[1] C. H. McIlwain, *The High Court of Parliament* (1910).

influence of Puritanism in the revolution alone depends. The contemporary view is best given in such a retrospect as the *Declaration of the English Army now in Scotland* (pp. 474-8), which unhesitatingly assigns the chief place to religion, and exhibits Puritanism's marshalling of its forces as a continuous and divinely appointed process, extending from the outbreak of the Bishops' War to Cromwell's invasion of Scotland eleven years later. The constant operation of the ideal of godliness is also the burden of Ireton's masterly account of the revolution, written at the end of 1648: the object of the struggle was the establishment of 'common right and freedom'; but true religion alone can make men free, and godlessness and superstition are equally the allies of the tyrant (pp. 458-9). It is thus that Puritanism visualizes its role in the revolution and stakes its claim to have fought for emancipation.

In part that claim must be allowed, but without confusing the service of liberty with its *disinterested and unqualified service*. If the cause of emancipation had depended alone on disinterested and unqualified believers in liberty as an ideal, it would have made but a sorry showing in the world. For objectives in practical politics are always limited and generally selfish. But those who start revolutions build—and destroy—better than they know. The pressure of events bears them along and forces them to develop ever more extreme inferences from their original premises (witness the Presbyterian Rutherford and the Independent Ireton). And when they reach the point beyond which they will not go, the moment of imperative compromise, there are others who will complete the last syllogism—or finish the final furrow: Rutherford has declared the right, and Goodwin will acclaim the meeting of right with might (pp. 212-20); the Independents invoke the purposes of God and the duties of the Saints, and the Millenarians will define those purposes and duties with a terrifying literalness; or the Independents invoke the sovereign people, and the Levellers will demand the reforms to which the invocation points—and get them if they can. . . .

All or much of this might have been true even if Puritanism had not evolved from its theological consciousness ideas of liberty, of equality, of individualism, of government by consent and agreement, and of a species of privilege which had nothing to do with worldly possessions or existing class distinctions. But these very ideas Puritanism did evolve. They come into strongest relief in the struggle for religious freedom and reform, and thence, by processes already glanced at, are transferred to the political field.

INTRODUCTION

The foundation of each is some Protestant doctrine pushed to an extreme.

Most fundamental for our discussion is one which has received little attention—we might almost say none—from students of Puritanism: the doctrine of Christian liberty. Its sources in the New Testament, particularly in St. Paul, are rehearsed in Luther's exposition of Galatians (pp. 221-5) and in Milton's practical applications of the doctrine (pp. 226-8). In simplest terms, the Gospel frees men from the burden of the Law. The essence of the old dispensation is bondage: men were slaves of an outward law. The essence of the new dispensation is freedom: believers are sons of God and joint-heirs with Christ. Theirs is a voluntary service—and in the spirit, not to the letter.[1] *Deo parere libertas est.* The idea was familiar to every Protestant, and, with varying emphasis, was accepted by them all. Its revolutionary influence turns chiefly on two questions: (1) What portion of the Mosaic Law (Ceremonial, Judicial, and Moral) is abrogated by the coming of the Gospel? (2) How far is the liberty conferred a purely spiritual gift without applications beyond the religious experience of the individual? To the first question Luther and Milton return the same extreme answer: Not the Ceremonial Law merely, but the whole Mosaic Law is abrogated (p. 224).[2] Their answers to the second question differ widely: Luther limits the application to the spiritual life and experience of the believer, a decision characteristic of his theological radicalism and practical conservatism. Milton, on the contrary, makes Christian liberty the very corner-stone of his theory of toleration (pp. 226-8);[3]

[1] These aspects of Christian liberty are highly significant as inculcating a habit of thought which (1) insists on the importance of consent as opposed to conformity, and (2) presses beyond the institution to the end or reason of the institution. The sabbath was made for man, not man for the sabbath (as Milton reiterates); how much more is this true of merely human institutions!

[2] And for Milton, see *De Doctrina Christiana*, 1. 26-7. Unqualified, this answer would lead to Antinomianism, and apparently did so in some of the sects. Luther escapes this result by reinstating the Law as a useful instrument of self-examination, and by his answer to the second question. Milton escapes it by replacing the outward with an inward Law conceived as ethical and rational in character, and identified with the law of nature (of which indeed the Moral Law was itself a formulation); so that the essence of the Law is not abolished but accepted and obeyed in a new spirit of free and voluntary activity—a conception which, taken in conjunction with his answer to the second question, is of definite importance in the emancipation of the individual.

[3] To tamper with beliefs, and persecute for nonconformity, is 'crowding free consciences and Christian liberties into canons and precepts of men' (*Areopagitica ,Prose Works*, 2. 92).

[65]

INTRODUCTION

and from the ecclesiastical sphere he presses on boldly to the civil
(pp. 229–30). In many of his contemporaries the doctrine has its
influence even when it is not set forth in detail. Wherever in the
struggle for toleration one encounters the phrase *Christian liberty*
—and it is everywhere—this theological basis is implied.[1]

Christian liberty itself the Presbyterians do not deny; but they
seek to limit the inferences drawn from it and to counteract them
by an appeal to the Old Testament, to other theological doctrines,
and to common sense. Thomas Edwards would have the issue
squarely faced: 'Whether the commanding men by the power of
laws to do their duties, to do the things which God requires of
them, with the using outward means to work them to it when
unwilling, be unlawful for the magistrate, and against Christian
liberty, yea or no?'[2] George Gillespie states the Presbyterian
position in *Wholesome Severity Reconciled with Christian Liberty*
(1645); and the *Westminster Confession of Faith* significantly concludes its chapter (chiefly devoted, in the manner of Calvin,[3] to
explaining what the doctrine is not) with the declaration that
'they who, upon pretence of Christian liberty, shall oppose any
lawful power . . . whether . . . civil or ecclesiastical, resist the
ordinance of God,' while whoever disturbs the peace of the church
may be proceeded against not by ecclesiastical censures only,
but by 'the power of the civil magistrate.' With this view the
moderate Independents at Whitehall do not disagree in principle,
but rather in its application. They believe that it is a Congregational polity that the magistrate is authorized to set up and
defend, and they are willing to concede to allies, past and present,
a measure of toleration under the new system. No such compromise will satisfy their allies of the Left. They are for Christian
liberty in its widest range.

With those who emphasize Christian liberty and plead for freedom of conscience as the Christian's birthright, the doctrine is a
genuine and perennial source of emancipation. It is closely
associated with—is indeed an aspect of—that appeal from the Old
Testament to the New, which is a feature of liberal Puritan
thinking. In Milton's interpretation the note of the old dispensation in general is the note of bondage; that of the new, the

---

[1] In Milton himself it occurs from 1642 onwards. Accordingly I
have felt free to illustrate it (pp. 226–32) from Milton's clearest expositions, which happen to occur in the decade subsequent to the Debates.
[2] *Antapologia* (1644), p. 301. In *The Casting-down of the Last and
Strongest Hold of Satan* (1647) Edwards seeks to meet the affirmative
answer to this question.
[3] Cf. *Institutes*, 3. 19.

note of freedom: Christ came to set men free (p. 229). In Roger Williams the matter is put in another way. The Old Testament is prophetic and symbolic: it is the type of which the New Testament supplies the antitype, and its models and precepts are not, under the Gospel, to be taken literally. Israel's church-state does not countenance a church-state to-day, but merely foreshadows the true Church, God's mystical Israel; so the injunctions to purify Israel of idolater, heretic, and blasphemer, with the civil sword, prescribe no such duties to the Christian magistrate, but hold forth the purity of the true and voluntary church of Christ, and the spiritual censures by which that purity is maintained (pp. 288–92). Thus in their different manners Williams and Milton try to nullify the arguments from the Old Testament for the magistrate's power and responsibility in religion, the arguments which will be advanced so long as Christian liberty is interpreted as the abrogation merely of the Ceremonial Law, and which are actually advanced at Whitehall, and countered straight out of *The Bloody Tenent* (pp. 150–69). In both Milton and Williams there is really more than an appeal from the Old Testament to the New; there is an effective application of what I have called the principle of segregation. Like Luther, Williams, and in measure, also, Milton,[1] insist on the purely spiritual character of all that pertains to the Christian religion, but, unlike Luther, they do not infer from this that the organization of the church and the relation of church and state are things indifferent and at the discretion of the civil magistrate. On the contrary, they insist that by the Gospel these things are prescribed, and that, with the Separatists, one must interpret the autonomy of the spiritual sphere as including the freedom of the church.

Though this is the most notable achievement, and the clearest practical result to which it ministers, the doctrine of Christian liberty extends its influence on Puritan thought in various, and (it must be admitted) sometimes contrary directions; three of which may be briefly indicated at this point. (1) Despite the spiritual character of Christian liberty the doctrine was actually pressed into the service of revolution, as Milton, no doubt speaking the language of the military Saints whom he was defending, clearly illustrates; and for the Millenarians in particular it was obviously quite compatible with a rule of the elect won and exercised by the sword. (2) The very fact of grounding one's appeal for freedom on *Christian* liberty restricts the direct benefits of that appeal to the regenerate: Christian liberty freed you *for*, not *from*, the

[1] The force of this reservation will appear below (pp. [*92-3*]).

[67]

service of God. It is thus that the Millenarians conceive of freedom, and that Milton comes increasingly to conceive of it; and they are so far typical, at least, that the freedom of the regenerate is the primary concern of all genuine Puritans: here Presbyterians, Independents, and sectaries stand on common ground, differing only in their definition of the regenerate and their conception of the kind of liberty to be sought. But two forces counteract this restrictive emphasis: the first is the impossibility, recognized alike by Milton, Williams, and the Levellers, of guaranteeing the liberty of the regenerate without guaranteeing the liberty of all, and on this fact at last depends the direct contribution of Puritanism to general liberty; the second counteracting force is a consistent and thorough-going application of the principle of segregation, whereby the idea of Christian liberty is freed to operate by analogy in the natural order: Christian liberty for the regenerate, natural liberty for man. (3) There are other ways in which the doctrine of Christian liberty may operate by analogy. Christian liberty is conceived in terms of the abrogation of outward law, and the influence of this conception is apparent in one dominant Puritan attitude to the state and its enactments. But to these questions we shall return.

Not less clearly than the idea of liberty, that of equality rests on a theological foundation. The priesthood of the believer and the doctrine of election established an equality in the spiritual sphere. This equality is, strictly speaking, quite independent of worldly rank and possessions and has no bearing upon them. But it is susceptible of an extension precisely similar to that observed in the case of Christian liberty: the equality of believers may be thought of as a spiritual condition which carries certain definite implications for the church. The demand is not for a free church only, but for a church of equals. The equality of believers is used to assail first the ecclesiastical hierarchy and then the distinction between cleric and lay (pp. 312–13). It is a levelling principle of no little potency, and it may be extended outside the ecclesiastical sphere in one of two ways, and with results diametrically opposed. (1) It may give effect not to absolute equality but to a new species of privilege. The equality of believers is an equality in their superiority to other men. This is a view discernible in the thought of Presbyterians and Independents; and it reaches its logical consequences in the creed of the Millenarians, the full doctrine of the privileges of the Saints. But (2) where the principle of segregation is applied, this result is prevented, and the doctrine of the equality of believers operates in the

[68]

natural sphere by analogy alone. As in the order of grace all believers are equal, so in the order of nature all men are equal; as the church is composed of believers all equally privileged, so the state should be composed of men all equally privileged. The premise was the lesson taught by the sects; the conclusion was the inference drawn in politics by the Levellers and in economics by the Diggers.

Their position had its secular sources in the ideas of the law of nature and of natural rights; but these ideas were, for men bred in the conventicle, enormously reinforced, and given a sort of religious sanction, by the parallel presented between the order of nature and the order of grace, and between the ideals of liberty and equality as they appeared in state and in church. It is the sectaries whom Overton is really addressing when he writes:

For by natural birth all men are equal, . . . born to like propriety, liberty and freedom, and as we are delivered of God by the hand of nature into this world, every one with a natural innate freedom and propriety, . . . even so we are to live, every one equally . . . to enjoy his birthright and privilege, even all whereof God by nature hath made him free. . . . Every man by nature being a king, priest, prophet, in his own natural circuit and compass, whereof no second may partake but by deputation, commission, and free consent from him whose right and freedom it is.[1]

This is virtually a statement of the doctrines of Christian liberty and equality, with *man* written over the word 'believer,' and *nature* written over the word 'grace.' . . .

In close connection with its ideals of liberty and equality, Puritanism developed its own pronounced note of individualism. Once more the main theological basis is to be sought in the doctrines of election and of the priesthood of the believer, with their enormous emphasis on the value of the individual soul, chosen by God before time was. Beside that, the organized forces of society must seem a trivial thing. Moreover the priestly function included, with ever-increasing emphasis, the prophetic. Here the experiential side of Puritan religion—manifested in 'prophesyings,' disputations, and harangues such as Lilburne's from the pillory [2]—played its part in fostering and expressing individuality and perhaps an overweening sense of the individual's importance. There are, of course, considerations which limit the action of Puritan individualism. One is the element of stern repressiveness

[1] Richard Overton, *An Arrow Against All Tyrants* (1646), pp. 3–4. Cf. Overton (below, p. 327), and Lilburne (below, p. 317).
[2] *A Work of the Beast* (1638; *Tracts*, edited Haller, 2. 1–34).

in the Puritan creed, but this is mitigated wherever the doctrine of Christian liberty is emphasized, by some sense of having risen superior to all outward law. Another is the necessity (nowise peculiar to Puritanism) of subordinating the individual to a group and a cause: under pressure from without, the Puritans manifest remarkable powers of association and temporary cohesion, but the inherent individualism, with its disruptive fôrce, remains, and is written large in the history of the sects. A true church, said Milton, may consist of a single member.

In politics we have already noticed the force of individual judgment, or the Puritan conscience. It remains to observe another important result, in an attitude towards the state which anticipates the individualism of a later day. Burke remarked the similarity in language between the revolutionaries of 1649 and of 1789, with their talk of natural rights and the sovereignty of a free and equal people; and some historical connection can be traced, mainly through the leaders of American thought. Not less striking, and perhaps more significant, is the anticipation of Bentham and James Mill. Up to a point Independents and Levellers agree in advancing a *laisser-faire* ideal of the state. One tendency of all the Agreements of the People is clearly to circumscribe the activity of government as such. This they do by placing certain matters for ever beyond its power, by limiting the duration of Parliaments, and otherwise reducing to a minimum their possible independence of the nation's will. Like the famous essay *On Government*, they set forth a scheme of democratic reform whose motive was quite as much the provision of satisfactory guarantees against interference with the individual as any sentiment of abstract equality. Human nature being what it was, a measure of democracy was the best protection against tyranny. Economic motives mingle with political, and, as in Mill, the underlying philosophy is individualist, not socialist, in character. Recent history had done much to foster individualism. Under the absolutist system of Charles I, government had been everywhere; and under a self-perpetuating Parliament the old menace had assumed a new guise.

Though they differed as to the degree of institutional reform needed, many of the Independents were at first hardly less determined than the Levellers to end it. It is obvious that the reforms contemplated by the Independents (pp. 424-6) and by the Levellers (pp. 318-22, 335-42, 433-5) are in the main negative reforms, the removal of restrictions. An example is the effort to abolish state-granted monopolies and to establish what they called *free trade.* Their ingenuity runs much to the erection of political machinery to compass these ends; and in this they remind the modern reader of Bentham. Added to the practical motives were some more theoretic. Government, said Ireton, was a necessary evil, the result of man's fallen condition; it could not be abolished; but it could be restricted, and the individual safeguarded; the merit of the Agreement of the People was that it achieved these results. Milton, a little remote from the tumult of practical politics, formulates the position with perfect clarity: the function of the state is to preserve peace and order and to guarantee the freedom of the individual; a wise government will be more willing to repeal old laws than to enact new ones, for the intention of laws is to check the commission of vice, but liberty is the best school of virtue (p. 230). Here in the implied conceptions of both law and liberty, the supporting influence of the doctrine of Christian liberty can be seen. Outward laws are a mark of bondage, a burden to the good; and liberty is conceived in terms of their abrogation, whereby individuals are freed to follow the inner law, which, according to Milton, is the law of nature written in the heart.[1] The *ideal* condition is to be able to live without laws because 'our reason is our law.' [2] Too extreme to be wholly typical, this view is at least symptomatic.

For the safeguarding of the individual, the restriction of the state to its proper sphere, and the founding of necessary government on an equitable basis, the Levellers relied on an Agreement of the People whose simple philosophy must at this point be recalled. The social contract was, in the first instance, a voluntary covenant, based on, and expressive of, the fundamental law of nature. Custom had thwarted its intention and obscured its meaning. The Agreement would restore them. It would reserve to the individual his inalienable rights; it would give effect once more to the principle of government by the consent of the governed, and provide, through universal suffrage, for the renewal of the consent as each succeeding Parliament was elected. The elements of which the Agreement was compounded were none of them new. The fundamental law of nature, known to reason, conformity to which must furnish the final sanction of every positive law; the notion of inalienable rights embodied in Magna Charta and other

---

[1] The 'law of nature given originally to Adam, of which a certain remnant or imperfect illumination still dwells in the hearts of all mankind and which in the regenerate, under the influence of the Holy Spirit, is daily tending towards a renewal of its primitive brightness' (*De Doctrina Christiana, Prose Works*, 4. 378).

[2] *Paradise Lost*, 9. 654.

INTRODUCTION

:ablished in the courts of law; and even the idea of a
act originally voluntary in character—all these had
ed more or less familiar by the long struggle with the
ut an Agreement of the People turned on something
an elaboration and weaving together of these notions.
Behind ... idea of a free state lay the model of a free church.   In
the *Ready and Easy Way* Milton points the basic analogy.   Those
who would reform the state, he remarks, are

not bound by any statute of preceding Parliaments but by the law of
nature only, which is the only law of laws truly and properly to all mankind fundamental, the beginning and end of all government, to which
no Parliament or people that will thoroughly reform but may and
must have recourse, *as they had (and must yet have) in church reformation
. . . to evangelic rules,* not to ecclesiastical canons though never so
ancient, so ratified and established in the land by statutes which for
the most part are mere positive laws, neither natural nor moral. . . .[1]

The model of ecclesiastical excellence, says another writer, is
founded on the law of God set forth in the New Testament and
received by faith; that of civil excellence is 'founded on the law
of God engraven in nature and demonstrated by reason.'[2]   In
each case there is a fundamental law and a primitive model of excellence; and in each case the injunction is to depart from, and if
need be destroy, whatever conflicts with the law or fails to conform
to the model.   In the church Puritan scripturism is a mighty
agent of destruction and reform.   And whether operating directly
or, as in the case of the Levellers and of the writers cited above,
analogically, it is capable of having a similar effect in the state.
But the analogy can be carried further.   If the Leveller emphasizes the contract on which the authority of just government
depends, and insists on the principle of consent, he has had, in
his church, experience of a community organized on these very
principles.   Not the idea of the social contract, but the hold which
it took upon the Puritans of the Left, may with some confidence
be attributed to the covenanted and more or less democratic
Puritan churches.

The idea of a covenant, derived ultimately from the Old Testament, appears in different forms in the more extreme Protestantism
of the sixteenth and seventeenth centuries, where its vogue is
associated with that of 'covenant' theology in general.   First
found among the Anabaptists of Germany (in what was to be its
dominant 'congregational' form), the idea passes, about the middle

[1] *Prose Works*, 2. 111.   [2] *Regal Tyranny Discovered* (1647), p. 11.

[72]

of the sixteenth century, into Scotland; and there, characteristically, it adheres more closely to the Old Testament model and produces a series of *national* covenants, destined in a later day to be opposed to the congregational church covenant, but at the same time to reinforce the covenant idea. In England the first exponent of the congregational covenant is Robert Browne, whose *True and Short Declaration of the Gathering and Joining Together of Certain Persons* recounts:

A covenant was made and their mutual consent was given to hold together. There were certain chief points proved unto them by the scriptures; all of which being particularly rehearsed . . ., they agreed upon them, and pronounced their agreement to each thing particularly, saying, 'To this we give our consent.' First therefore they gave their consent to join themselves to the Lord in one covenant and fellowship together and to keep and seek agreement under his laws and government. . . . Further they agreed of those which should teach them . . . whom they allowed and did choose as able and meet for that charge. . . . So they prayed for their watchfulness and diligence and promised their obedience. Likewise an order was agreed on for their meetings together for their exercises . . . as for prayer . . . exhortation and edifying either by all men which had the gift or by those which had a special charge before others; and for the lawfulness of putting forth questions to learn the truth, as, if anything seemed doubtful and hard, to require some to show it more plainly, or for any to show it himself and cause the rest to understand it. . . . Again it was agreed that any might protest, appeal, complain, exhort, dispute, reprove, &c., as he had occasion, but yet in due order, which was then also declared. . . . Furthermore they particularly agreed of the manner how to watch to disorders and reform abuses, . . . for gathering and testifying voices in debating matters and propounding them in the name of the rest that agreed, for an order of choosing teachers, guides and relievers . . .; for separating clean from unclean, for receiving any into fellowship, for presenting the daily success of the church and the wants thereof, . . . for taking an order that none contend openly, nor persecute, nor trouble disorderly, nor bring false doctrine nor evil cause, after once or twice warning or rebuke.[1]

The basic ideas of agreement and covenant persist in English Separatism, whether in England or Holland, and are transferred to New England. The distinguishing mark of Congregationalism, Robert Baillie (who is not concerned with nice distinctions between separating and non-separating varieties) finds in 'an explicit covenant, wherein all and every one of the members by a voluntary association . . . do bind themselves under a solemn oath to

[1] Quoted by Champlin Burrage, *Church Covenant Idea* (1904), pp. 46-8.

walk in the ways of the Gospel.'[1] Among the non-separating Congregationalists, and among some of the Separatists, less power was conceded to the people than in Browne's scheme; and the former would allow of an implicit covenant when an explicit could not be achieved. But it remains broadly true that Congregationalism, in its different forms, by emphasizing the idea of the covenant, preserved the possibility of a free and democratic church order, and of its influence in the civil sphere, between which and the ecclesiastical there is constant interaction. The classic example of a social contract modelled on a church covenant is the civil covenant of the Pilgrims, and the charter and constitution of the Providence Plantation, with other colonial documents, furnish instances no less striking of the idea of agreement, and the principle of government by consent, transplanted into the civil life. On the other hand, the church covenant itself could be defended by a reference from the ecclesiastical sphere to the civil. 'All voluntary relations,' wrote Richard Mather in his *Apology for Church Covenant*, '[that is] all relations which are neither natural nor violent, are entered into by way of covenant' (p. 300). The ultimate consequence of such a theory had already been hinted by Robert Browne in his *Book Concerning True Christians*; he finds in church ministers, and in *civil magistrates*, an authority, derived from God, but bestowed on them respectively by the consent and agreement of the congregation and the *people*.[2]

In trying to estimate the influence of the church covenant on Puritan political thought, and especially on the ideals and practice of the Army, it must be made clear that among the sectaries the Baptists seem to have discarded the covenant. Hanserd Knollys speaks of churches gathered in London 'without urging or making any particular covenant with members upon admittance,' for their conditions were 'faith, repentance and baptism, and none other.'[3] And William Dell, manifesting the extreme Puritan tendency to approximate the Visible to the Invisible Church, and to discover new distinctions between the spiritual and the secular, repudiates the covenant as belonging to the light of nature merely, whereas the true Church has a higher and purely spiritual bond of union; the use of a covenant, then, is the mark not of the true Church, but of the churches of men (pp. 304–5). It would be a mistake, however, to exaggerate the importance of these facts. The

[1] *Dissuasive from the Errors of the Times* (1645), p. 23.
[2] Quoted by H. M. Dexter, *The Congregationalism of the Last Three Hundred Years* (1880), p. 106.
[3] *A Moderate Answer to Dr. Bastwick's . . . Independency Not God's Ordinance* (1645), pp. 19–20.

churches which retained the covenant idea embraced the Puritans of the Centre, and possibly the majority of the Puritans of the Left. And in the minds of those who came to repudiate the covenant as essential to the constitution of a church, the idea had already done its work and become firmly established as the *only* mode of association in civil things.   There is no reason to suppose that the Baptist churches were less democratic in their practices than the congregation described by Browne in the preceding century (see pp. 307–14).   If the absence of a covenant withdrew the formal dependence of the ministry on the laity, this was more than offset by the progressive disappearance of the distinction between the two orders.   Finally, all the churches remained in fact voluntary associations with power over the individual only after he had conceded it and only for so long as he continued to acquiesce in its exercise.   Thus the results of the church covenant were preserved even among the sectaries who had pressed beyond its formal employment.   Familiarity with the idea of the covenant, and with the principles that it embodied, gave a common ground for agreement—and for argument—among the Puritans of the Centre and the Left.   By analogy it had helped to establish in the civil sphere the doctrine of the social contract and government by consent.   And it provided in the covenanted churches models of organization in different degrees democratic.   Its influence is widespread and pervasive.

To that influence the beginning and the end of the General Council of the Army alike testify.   The *Solemn Engagement of the Army* was a contract of voluntary association, a · covenant among the soldiers, with the nation, and before God.   As such it suggests a linking of two forms of the covenant idea.   It is a simple and almost perfect example of the church covenant transposed to secular ends, based on and embodying the law of nature as the church covenant is based on and embodies the law of Christ, and elaborating, as do the early church covenants, its own organs of expression and administration.   At the same time it derives something from the Solemn League and Covenant, which it is in measure designed to offset; and in its quasi-national character, as in other respects, it marks a step on the way to the Agreements of the People.   But the covenant idea is potent in defeat as well as in victory.   When Fairfax is able to undo the work of the *Solemn Engagement* and insist on the Army's retirement from 'England's freedom' to 'soldiers' rights,' he can effect those purposes only by a new engagement (p. [*30*]).

It is, of course, the Agreements of the People that mark the apotheosis of the covenant idea and its complete and triumphant translation to the civil sphere. In the Agreements the covenant's every principle is represented: the recognition of a fundamental law (the law of nature for the law of Christ), which the terms of the contract must embody and by which alone they are conditioned; the ideas of voluntary association and government by consent; the reservation of the individual's inalienable rights, implicit in the church covenant and safeguarded by the power of withdrawal, but necessarily explicit in the Agreements (since the power of withdrawal is virtually non-existent in the civil state); the delegation of power, under due safeguards, to those who must act for the community; the elaboration of an 'order,' or the necessary machinery of administration and of popular expression; and the whole thing extended and raised to a national scope and level, thus assimilating, and subordinating to the principles of the church covenant, the model of its deadly rival from beyond the Scottish border. Such was the final object of the Agreements, but on the way to that object they exemplify yet another ideal recognized in some of the church covenants. The reader will recall what was said at an earlier point about the Puritan belief in the progressive interpretation of truth and will remember that this principle was written into the covenant of the Pilgrims' church (p. [45]). It is not written into the Agreements, but it is recognized in the fact that, as issued by the Levellers, and perhaps also by the Independents, they were designed to furnish a basis for discussion, and to serve as explorations leading to truth and consent. Behind the Agreements lies the belief in free and equal discussion which seems to have been nourished by the more liberal forms of Puritanism, and which dominates the proceedings of the General Council of the Army.

Considered in themselves those proceedings are sufficiently remarkable; and one would wish to know more, and with greater certainty, of their models. Mr. A. D. Lindsay [1] has suggested that the congregation was the school of democracy. There the humblest member might hear, and join in, the debate, might witness the discovery of the natural leader, and participate in that curious process by which there emerges from the clash of many minds a vision clearer and a determination wiser than any single mind could achieve. To the congregation we may look for the source and model of that democratic organization and practice of which the recorded proceedings of the General Council of the

[1] *The Essentials of Democracy* (1929), pp. 11–24. See further Charles Borgeaud, *The Rise of Modern Democracy in Old and New England* (1894).

Army are the most striking examples. To this suggestion may be added certain others, in no way incompatible with it. By the soldiers at large, the Council of the Army would be most naturally regarded as a sort of extension, to include their representatives, of a body already instituted by Fairfax: the Council of War,[1] in which the General placed his plans of campaign before the higher officers and sought their criticism and advice. And it is observable, in contrast with its later developments, that the first object of the General Council was also to reach decisions on particular and practical issues like those presented in the Reading debate (pp. 409–21). But the Council of War, as Fairfax used it, was itself an innovation whose origin has not been fully explained, a remoter product of the zeal for discussion and agreement whose more striking example is the General Council; so that we succeed merely in forcing the question one step back. There is, however, another parallel with the General Council which seems unescapable though it has never been noticed: the House of Commons itself. And actually the General Council is referred to as 'the Representative of the Army' (p. 48). Though it might be at odds with its masters, this was the Army of the Parliament, pledged at first to maintain the liberties of Parliament, on which those of the nation were supposed to depend. What more likely than that it should take the Parliament for its model? The parallel extends to details. Like the Parliament the Army bids for public support by issuing its declarations; like the Long Parliament the General Council makes extensive use of committees; nor is it fanciful to see in the added deliberations of Fairfax and the higher officers, the 'meeting in the inner room' to which Cromwell refers (p. 412), something which stands to the General Council in the double relation of executive and second chamber. But more important is the view taken by the Puritans of the object and method of Parliamentary debate. Two years before the founding of the General Council a pamphleteer wrote (p. 264):

And what reformation this kingdom had in the late days, it did consist in the . . . spontaneousness of it in the Parliament . . . as one reports of it: 'For in the senate . . . all had the opportunity to speak, nor was leave denied any kind of man to speak in opposition and utter his own belief, to argue and contend with free exchange of opinions; wherein shines forth greatly the justice and moderation of the rulers that have sought to allure, to lead, to persuade, and not to force, to drag, or

---

[1] On the Council of War see C. H. Firth, *Cromwell's Army* (1921), pp. 57–9.

[77]

to command. So that it is a shameless falsehood if any shall say that it was the power of authority that won the day, and not truth. . . .' I quote the words because if they had never been realized, yet the idea of such a carriage when men are seeking out the truth is lovely as being very equal and rational.

It would not be easy to find a better formulation of the ideal at which the Army Debates also aim than this (confessedly idealized) account of the proceedings in the Parliament. At the least, those proceedings supplement for the Puritan the lessons learned in the congregation.[1] The sum of the matter seems to be that a common ideal of truth and agreement through free debate comes into special prominence in the seventeenth century, and that it informs the proceedings of congregation, of Parliament, and of General Council alike, in part at least because it finds in the Puritan mind and temper a peculiarly congenial ground. But due recognition of the Parliamentary model brings one's understanding of the Council into line with another fact. The principles advanced in the Debates (as in the Agreements and other pamphlets of the Levellers) are not altogether new. They are the principles advanced by the Parliament in its struggle with the King, carried to their logical conclusion, and that conclusion is democratic. Repeatedly in support of their own contentions, the Independents and their allies of the Left turn to the declarations of Parliament. And so with the organization and practice of the Council itself, if the Parliament furnishes one of its models, it is the Parliament democratized.[2] To explain the impulse towards democracy is clearly the ultimate problem.

[1] As the debates in the Council developed, they further took on something of the character of arguments in a court of law. Wildman later acts as counsel for the popular cause before the Lord Mayor and Court of Aldermen (pp. 369–78). His presence at Putney (as also Petty's) is in much the same capacity. Nor is Ireton a less formidable opponent than Maynard, Hale, or Wilde.

[2] In theory the House of Commons was *representative of the democracy*. The 'true nature' of parliamentary power lies in 'public consent . . ., that being the proper foundation of all power.' Parliament is a device 'whereby the people may assume its own power to do itself right,' and whereby 'the whole community in its underived majesty shall convene to do justice, and that this convention may not be without intelligence certain times and places and forms shall be appointed for its regiment; and that the vastness of its own bulk may not breed confusion, by virtue of election and representation a few shall act for many, the wise shall consent for the simple, the virtue of all shall redound to some, and the prudence of some shall redound to all' (Henry Parker, *Observations upon Some of His Majesty's Late Answers and Expresses*, 1642, pp. 13, 15; the pamphlet is reproduced in *Tracts*, edited Haller, 2. 167–213). Such a theory in itself fosters democratic ideas. Sir Benjamin Rudyerd com-

It is widespread and can be seen working not only in the democratic idealism of the *Agreements of the People* and in the General Council of the Army, but less conspicuously, though with a curious exactness of parallel, in the London companies and in agitations for a reform of the City's government. Like the soldiers the commonalty of the companies assert their rights, demand to be heard in free debate, and carry the question back to first principles, not without allusions to the changes in the national government. In the Clothworkers' Company, for example, there were debates between representatives of the commonalty and of the Court of Assistants, whether by the letter of the charter the commonalty had not a voice in the election of officers; this the Court refused to concede, but was willing to discuss less drastic changes which might safeguard the interests (and, it was hoped, satisfy the demands) of the commonalty; but new popular leaders emerged, and the question had to be referred to the Parliament. The Saddlers trace their woes to that common source of tyranny, the Norman Conquest; and the commonalty of the Founders, admitting that 'men in all ages have, through their supine carelessness, degenerated from the righteousness of their first principles,' demanded the restoration of their 'primitive rights and privileges' in the name of 'the law of God, of nature, and of nations.' [1] The Leveller leadership which such language plainly attests, also appears in the agitations regarding the City's government. There the issues are complicated by the City's importance in national politics and by the dominance of the Presbyterian interest in the oligarchy; and Independents, as well as Levellers, raise their voice. Lilburne, who enjoyed some popularity in the Common Council, writes on *London's Liberty in Chains* (1646). *A Moderate Reply to the City Remonstrance* (1646) distinguishes between the 'city representative' and the 'city collective,' and anticipating the arguments to be used by the Army against the Parliament, maintains that the 'city collective' owes no obedience to commands of the 'city representative' which contravene 'the will and word of God,' 'the good of the kingdom,' 'the proper end' of the representative's being, *i.e.*, 'the city's welfare,' or the limits set to the representative's power.[2] And Wildman, with John Price, upholds

---

plained, in 1648, that the functions of Parliament were being usurped by the people: 'We have sat thus long, and we are come to a fine pass; for the whole kingdom has become parliament all over' (H. A. Glass, *The Barebone Parliament*, 1899, p. 49).

[1] Margaret James, *Social Problems and Policy during the Puritan Revolution* (1930), pp. 200–11.

[2] Ibid., pp. 223–31.

in debate the right of the citizens to elect the City's officers, quoting Parliament's declaration that 'the original of all just power under God proceeds from the people' (pp. 369–78).

Against this background of democratic agitation the Debates are to be read. The ideas advanced and the methods adopted are everywhere the same: a primitive model of excellence to which institutions, corrupted by custom, must be restored, or a fundamental law into conformity with which they must be brought; the possibility of arriving through discussion at truth, that is, at a free and unconstrained recognition of what model and law demand, and hence of agreement therein; government resting on a contract and on consent; and implicit in it all—becoming explicit when necessary—the idea of *equal* rights, which is the distinguishing idea of democracy. How do these things relate themselves to Puritan thought and experience? The materials for answering that question have been set forth above, and hints towards an answer have been given. It remains to bring them together, to bring together also what has been said of the obstacles to secular democracy which Puritanism presents, to suggest once more the way in which those obstacles were partially overcome, and to estimate the contribution of Puritanism to democracy. We need not further consider the Puritans of the Right, or the Puritans of the Centre in the points where they differ from those of the Left: on the Puritans of the Left we may concentrate our final attention.

In some of them the concern for liberty as an authentic feature of Puritanism most unequivocally appears. They emphasize the doctrine of Christian liberty, and (as one would expect from the active Puritan temper) they use it to support a campaign for religious liberty. But to demand liberty as the Christian's birthright is, strictly, to demand it only for Christians, or (as the Puritan would phrase it) for the Saints: it is the truth that makes you free, and only for the truth can liberty be challenged. This is the source of the reproach so often uttered against the Puritan (and in fact rather exaggerated), that he believes in liberty for himself but not for other people, and it is one source of the policy of partial toleration or toleration in indifferent things for those who are sound in essentials. In its extension beyond toleration to revolutionary politics Christian liberty may manifest the same limitation, may support an idea of the privileges of the Saints. But the fact that there *is* a Puritan doctrine of liberty, whatever its limitations, is immensely important. Repeatedly Puritanism brings the question of liberty up for discussion, and this is a major service. While operating within the prescribed bounds of 'Christian' liberty, Puritanism, further, does a great deal to foster the notion of individuality, and an individualistic outlook, with results partially, though not wholly, favourable to democracy.

Puritanism also fosters equality within the 'Christian' scheme: there is a Christian equality as well as a Christian liberty. In the more extreme sects truth may come from the meanest of the brethren (p. [46]), and, in the spirit of the Gospel, which weights the scales against the rich man, Williams finds that God has 'chosen a little flock out of the world, and those generally poor and mean' (p. 282). Within the sects, clearly, a levelling principle of great potency is at work. But what Christians enjoy is an equality of superiority to other men. To describe the congregation as a model democracy in little, is true of the congregation considered in itself. But considered in relation to the world in which it subsists, it is an aristocracy of grace. Liberty and equality for the privileged is the ideal of an aristocracy, though there is certainly some wider significance in the fact that Christian privilege has nothing to do with (or is even thought of in contrast to) privilege as the world understands it. In the Millenarians' view the Saints constitute an aristocracy of grace whose divinely appointed destiny is to conquer and rule the world. And they question whether the natural man has really any rights at all (p. 246).

A measure of practical equality was, however, forced upon the Puritans in the struggle for religious liberty. (In a careful discussion equality must be distinguished from liberty; but the distinction is always breaking down.) The Puritans of the Left discovered that you cannot effectually guarantee the liberty of the Saint without guaranteeing the liberty of all men—without adding, in this one department at least, equality to liberty. The Levellers, and also Cromwell, record their frank recognition of this fact when they make liberty of conscience not the birthright of the Christian, but one of the natural rights of man (p. 444).[1] The amazing importance of the struggle for religious liberty is due partly to the momentous issue with which it deals;[2] but

[1] Carlyle, *Cromwell's Letters and Speeches*, Speech III.

[2] Of toleration Roger Williams writes (*Queries of Highest Consideration*, pp. 34–5): 'We know the allegations against this counsel. The head of all is that from Moses (not Christ) his pattern in the typical land of Canaan, the kings of Israel and Judah, &c. We humbly desire it may be searched into, and we believe it will be found but one of Moses' shadows, vanished at the coming of the Lord Jesus: yet such a shadow as is directly opposite to the very Testament and coming of the Lord Jesus; opposite to the very nature of a Christian Church, the only holy

beyond that is the fact that it holds, as it were in solution, within itself all the rest of the struggle for liberty and equality. 'Where civil liberty is entire,' said Harrington, 'it includes liberty of conscience; where liberty of conscience is entire it includes civil liberty.' [1] It also includes equality. When the Puritans of the Left are forced by the hard logic of facts to champion liberty of conscience for others as well as for themselves, we see the thin end of the wedge. But until it becomes, with Williams and the Levellers, something more than a grudging concession to facts, the wedge will not get much further.[2]

Before turning to the Levellers, and considering again the process by which the forces of democracy, of liberty and equality, in Puritanism are released to operate in the secular sphere, it will be well to take a final view of the group, sometimes associated with them in action, in whom the release is not finally effected. The importance of the Millenarians resides in the fact that they carry to an extreme one set of principles found in the Independents of the Army, just as the Levellers carry to an extreme another set of principles. In their church order the Millenarians do not differ from other Puritans of the Left. Their churches are voluntary and democratic congregations (pp. 241, 245), though some form of national union may be necessary before they can rule the world (p. 245). Meanwhile they join in the demand for liberty, and above all for liberty of conscience (because without it the churches cannot exist and increase, as they must if they are ever to rule). The resort to violence, the effort to establish and exercise the rule of the Saints by force, is not perhaps an essential of the Millenarian creed, but rather a character impressed upon it

---

nation and Israel of God; opposite to the very tender bowels of humanity (how much more of Christianity!), abhorring to pour out the blood of men merely for their souls' belief and worship; opposite to the very essentials and fundamentals of the nature of a civil magistracy, a civil commonweal, or combination of men, which can only respect civil things; opposite to the Jews' conversion to Christ, by not permitting them a civil life or being; opposite to the civil peace, and the lives of millions, slaughtered upon this ground, in mutual persecuting each other's conscience, especially the protestant and the papist; opposite to the souls of all men, who by persecutions are ravished into a dissembled worship, which their hearts embrace not; opposite to the best of God's servants, who in all popish and protestant states have been commonly esteemed and persecuted, as the only schismatics, heretics, &c.; opposite to that light of scripture which is expected yet to shine, which must by that doctrine be suppressed as a new or old heresy or novelty. All this in all ages experience testifies, which never saw any long-lived fruit of peace or righteousness to grow upon that fatal tree.'

[1] *Political Aphorisms*, 23–4.   [2] See p. 143 and note.

by a revolutionary era. In the inevitability of the process by which the Saints shall inherit the earth they have a strong incentive to patience, but in the supposed plotting of that process in scripture, and in the definite role assigned to the Saints, they have a strong temptation to direct action. They are dimly conscious of the problem (pp. 39-42). In the result, they are like the Levellers, who should be willing to wait till reason has wrought conviction, but who actually seek to anticipate the triumph to come. Their reading of the Bible is at once fantastic and literal, but it is instructive to observe how much of spiritual religion can be woven into it (pp. 390-6). One should not exaggerate their difference from other Puritans of the Left. When all is said, however, they present a marked contrast with Williams and the Levellers. In all who share in any degree the Millenarian outlook, the doctrines emphasized by Puritanism—Christian liberty and equality, election (with final perseverance), the priesthood of the believer—issue in a theory of the special privileges of the Saints. The active Puritan temper carries this theory into the secular sphere and gives equal development to its converse side, the special *duties* of the Saints. And the Puritan tendency to draw literal inferences from scripture and dogma operates in connection not only with the theological doctrines mentioned above, but with prophecy and especially with the dazzling hope of Christ's kingdom on earth, which, in its turn, absorbs and directs the utopian and iconoclastic impulses. The latent impulses towards democracy are not merely thwarted; their motive power is appropriated and directed to other ends. At an earlier point, we recognized somewhere near the heart of Puritanism an unresolved conflict between the concern for liberty and the concern for reform, and we saw how in the Puritans of the Right the concern for reform was in the ascendant. The ideals of the Millenarians differ widely from the Presbyterian: theirs is a clericalism without clergy (the Saints having taken its place), an ecclesiasticism without a uniform church (the Puritan distrust of outward forms having destroyed the church in favour of the sect); for the rest, they may even have adopted some of the proposals of the Levellers. But with them the concern for reform, by coercion if need be, is once more in the ascendant; and at bottom they are indifferent or hostile to the liberty and equality for which the Levellers stand. This statement is borne out by a set of political ideas, much less fully organized than the Levellers', but clearly perceptible in the Debates: repudiation of, or at least indifference to, the democratic ideas of agreement, of representative institutions, of safeguards for the rights of the individual; emphasis, instead, on the monarchy of Christ as administered by the Saints, and (in conformity with this ideal) a reliance on good men rather than on a good constitution or a duly elected Parliament; willingness, finally, to regard victory in the field as the outward call of the Saints to rule the world. These ideas lead not to the democratic state but to junto and dictatorship; and though the Millenarians soon found that they had mistaken their man, and learned to speak of him in terms previously reserved for the Pope and Charles I, the prevalence of these ideas far beyond the ranks of the strict Millenarians was a foundation of Cromwell's power. There is in Puritanism a possibility of autocracy as well as a possibility of democracy. To that fact the Puritans of the Left, as well as those of the Right and Centre, bear undeniable testimony. Each possibility—which develops, of course, in relation to a set of particular circumstances, and within the limits imposed by the need of compromise when that need is felt—inheres in a group of theological doctrines; and they are, with some difference in emphasis, the same doctrines.

How are the inferences from dogma inimical to democracy avoided by the Levellers and by others who manage to avoid them? No doubt the weakening of dogma, where it occurred, ministered to that result. But we have seen some reason to believe that the weakening was not very widespread, and that Walwyn and Overton, while very influential, were less typical than a Leveller like Lilburne or a radical thinker like Roger Williams. And we have stated our conviction that the second and more important answer to the question is found in what we have called the *principle of segregation*, which means a clear-cut and consistent distinction between the order of grace and the order of nature. There are, as Roger Williams puts it, 'divers sorts of goodness,' and 'a subject, a magistrate, may be a good subject, a good magistrate, in respect of civil or moral goodness, . . . though godliness (which is infinitely more beautiful) be wanting' (pp. 282–3). That belongs to the order of grace; the others to the order of nature. The principle of segregation is momentous in its results; but it has another claim on our attention. It is the Puritan counterpart of a widespread principle in modern thought which Herr Ernst Cassirer runs back chiefly to Bacon,[1] and the Archbishop of York to a twofold source in

[1] *Die Platonische Renaissance in England und die Schule von Cambridge* (1932). Herr Cassirer recognizes its latent presence in Puritanism, but does not know Williams or the Levellers, in whom it is fully realized, or recognize its bearing on political thought.

INTRODUCTION

Luther and Descartes.[1] In the strict Puritan it springs from a sense of the superlative value of the order of grace and the uniqueness of the spiritual experience which seals one a member thereof, and from the accompanying determination to keep them untainted by anything of this world. The result as seen in Luther is to prevent the drawing of inferences from one order to the other. In a sense the basic result with those Puritans of whom Roger Williams may stand as our example, is the same—but with an important difference added: direct inference is banished, but analogy is instated in its place. The most obvious example of the principle of segregation is the absolute separation of church and state; and in Williams (as also in Henry Robinson and Milton) this does immediate service to the cause of liberty by becoming one of their chief supports in the argument for toleration. Further, if it destroys the idea of a state church, it also destroys the idea of a church-state; if it spiritualizes the church—and Dell's essay (pp. 203-16) indicates how eager is the Puritan for that result— it also secularizes the state and invites a new examination of its origin, function, and sanctions. The new examination does not necessarily issue in a democratic theory—it is the virtual, though not formal, secularizing of the state on other terms, that permits Hobbes's realistic defence of absolutism—but it may do so. The secularizing of the state is democracy's opportunity. The effectiveness of the principle of segregation as a barrier to direct dogmatic inference is seen when we contrast Williams' theory of a church with his theory of a state (pp. 283-4). His church is of the most rigorously restrictive kind, a church of visible Saints, which, viewed in relation to the world, could be regarded only as an aristocracy of the elect. But his state is a pure democracy— though the great majority of its members are, spiritually speaking, unregenerate and lost.[2] Viewed in relation to the world his church is an aristocracy; but it must not be so viewed, for they belong to two different orders. Viewed in itself the church too

[1] 'Back to Unity,' *University of Toronto Quarterly* (1934), 4. 1-10.

[2] Mr. J. W. Gough, in his useful history *The Social Contract* (1936), seriously misinterprets Williams's position when he writes (p. 86, n. 1; cf. pp. 85-6): '[Williams] seems . . . to *equate* a commission from the people with a commission from Christ; the basis of this, however, is not so much the crude maxim *vox populi vox Dei* as the *identification* of the people with a body of true believers (Protestant "Saints"), pledged to be guided in their lives by the will of Christ.' The position is that adopted by Puritans who conceal their undemocratic attitude in democratic language; that Williams could not adopt it, is sufficiently demonstrated by the passage on church and state cited above. The misunderstanding is due to a failure to recognize the principle of segregation and to take seriously Williams' distinction between the Law and the Gospel.

is a democracy, a voluntary association of equals, and as such may well furnish a model for the civil state as Williams conceives it. Behind the church covenant as it was elaborated by the first of the Separatists there lie (it has been suggested) the guilds and merchant companies.[1] It is significant that when Williams comes to describe the relation of the church to the civil state in which it exists, the terms are precisely those applicable to the guild or merchant company (p. 267). The church preserves the free form of community and finally enables (or at least aids) it to influence by analogy the theory of the state. First the principle of segregation; then, after that is enforced, the power of analogy: on these two things the democratic influence of Puritanism chiefly depends. Where they are applied but partially the result will be a limited and inconclusive acceptance of liberty and equality— the attitude illustrated by the leaders of the Independent Party, whose effort at compromise springs immediately from practical considerations, but nevertheless runs back from the particular issue to first principles. Where, on the contrary, segregation and analogy are fully applied, the result is more than a set of logical inferences; it is nothing less than a release of the forces of Puritanism to work in the natural order on the side of democracy, and these forces include its active and (within limits) experimental spirit, its utopianism and iconoclasm, and the libertarian, equalitarian, and humanitarian impulses, in precisely the degree in which they had manifested themselves within the limits of the Puritan church or sect.

The conclusions reached, or perhaps merely supported and rendered acceptable, by the principle of analogy, have been sufficiently indicated above: natural liberty and equality; a fundamental law of nature and a primitive model of civil excellence, alike known by reason; a social contract embodying that law and conforming to that model, safeguarding the individual's rights and applying the principle of government by consent; a democratic order of administration and expression with some provision for arriving at truth and agreement through free discussion. All this seems clear enough; but the parallel of a fundamental law for each of the economies, the law of Christ [2] and the law of nature, requires a little further elucidation.

It is a feature of their common scripturism that all the Puritans should affect (though with different degrees of rigour) to draw the

[1] Charles Borgeaud, *The Rise of Modern Democracy*, pp. 86–7, 129.
[2] On this subject, as on the origins of Leveller thought in general, see T. C. Pease's brilliant study, *The Leveller Movement* (1916).

prescriptions and models of church government from the Bible:
the Presbyterians, from the New Testament read in the light of
the Old and tempered by reference to the authoritative example of
Geneva and the demands of a national organization; the non-
separating Congregationalists, from the New Testament with a
simpler emphasis but not without some reference to Israel and to
the needs of a Christian state; the sectaries who most emphasize
the difference between the Law and the Gospel and most logically
apply the principle of segregation, from the New Testament alone,
the 'evangelic rules' to which Milton refers.   For these Puritans
of the Left, then, the fundamental law for a church is simply the
law revealed in the New Testament and received by faith.   But in
perfect consonance with that law (it is held) is the inward law in
the heart of the believer; and this inward law too must be included in the wider definition of the fundamental law spiritual.
Sometimes it is interpreted as the mystical indwelling of Christ;
sometimes, as the inward law given to Adam, restored by God to
its original brightness.

In the civil sphere Puritan scripturism (as we have seen) also
exercises its widespread influence.   The political thinking of
groups so divergent as the Presbyterian and the Millenarian
depends in no small measure on a direct appeal to the Bible; and,
with certain modifications, so too does the political thinking of
the Congregationalists, which sometimes approaches the scriptural ideal of the Presbyterians, and may sometimes even be
coloured by that of the Millenarians.   In the case of Presbyterians and Congregationalists alike the scriptural reference, in
addition to being tempered by the needs of a particular historical
situation, is accompanied by various degrees of attention to the
law of nature.   In those Puritans of the Left, however, with
whom we are at present chiefly concerned, the differentiation of
the Law and the Gospel logically implies the second result of
limiting the scriptural reference to the New Testament, and the
principle of segregation (seconded by the reticence of the Gospel
in matters political) operates to shift the reference altogether from
scripture to the law of nature.   The Leveller, by the principles
of his *religious* thinking, was thrown back wholly upon the law of
nature in the civil sphere.

The concept itself was no way peculiar to Puritan thought.
The law of nature was familiar to every one if only in the celebrated text-book, *Doctor and Student* [1] (where, however, the term

---

[1] Christopher St. German's dialogues on the Laws of England, repeatedly printed.

is said not to be in general use in English law) or in defences of the Parliament (where it often occupies only a subordinate place). But it is worth while to see what could be known of the law of nature from a Puritan source (pp. 187–91). For William Ames (1) God's law is of two kinds, natural and positive. (2) The law of nature consists of whatever rules of conduct can be immediately apprehended, or logically arrived at, by reason, 'out of the natural instinct of natural light, or . . . at least from that natural light by evident consequence.' (3) It is eternal 'in relation to God, as it is from eternity in him,' and 'natural as it is . . . imprinted in the nature of man by the God of nature.' (4) God's positive law is 'added to the natural by some special revelation of God,' and differs from the natural in two respects. Though it can be received, it cannot be arrived at, by reason. And it is not immutable, but 'mutable and various according to God's good pleasure; for that which was heretofore in the Judaical church is different from that which is in the Christian church.' (5) All the precepts of the moral law (as embodied in the Decalogue) are

out of the law of nature (except the determination of the sabbath-day . . . which is from the positive law). For . . . we meet with nothing in them which concerneth not all nations at all times, so that these precepts do not respect any particular sort of men, but even nature itself. . . . There is nothing in them . . . but what may be well enjoined from clear reason. . . . They all much conduce to the benefit of mankind in this present life, insomuch that if all these precepts were duly answered there would be no need of any other human laws or constitutions.

(6) The judicial and ceremonial laws of the Jews, as distinct from the moral, are positive, not natural; but some precepts of the so-called judicial law may be in reality moral, for 'where the special intrinsical and proper reason of the law is moral, there it always follows that the law itself must be moral.' (7) As has already been implied (above, 5), the 'worshipping of God . . . is a principle of the law of nature.' Hence the common formulation of that law ('To live honestly; not to hurt another; to give every man his due') is 'confused and imperfect.' (8) Much less can one admit the teaching of some Civilians, that 'the law of nature is that which nature hath taught all living creatures.' For though the brutes have their law it implies neither reason to distinguish, nor will or choice, nor justice. The law of nature is the law for man. (9) The civil law enacted by men for their city or society 'inasmuch as it is right is derived from the law of nature,' and receives its moral sanction from this fact. It falls short of the law of nature, how-

ever, because 'it hath no eye at all upon the inward affections but only upon outward actions' and 'doth not make good men but only good subjects or citizens,' and because even within these limits 'the reason of man can only imperfectly judge . . . and is often therein cozened.' For (10) it is fallen man of which we speak; and the full implication of this fact appears when the question is asked why, if it is identical with the natural law 'writ in the hearts of all men,' the Decalogue required to be promulgated by God. It is because

ever since the corruption of our nature such is the blindness of our understanding and perverseness of our will and disorder of our affections that there are only some relics of that law remaining in our hearts like to some dim aged picture, and therefore by the voice . . . of God it ought to be renewed as with a fresh pencil. Therefore is there nowhere found any true right practical reason, pure and complete in all parts, but in the written law of God (Psalm 119. 66).

One observes the exalting of the law of nature as the only moral law (5, 6); its clear distinction from the positive law of God (with the statement that this might vary between the Old Testament and the New) (4); the asserted dependence of all civil laws upon the law of nature (9); the recognition of the law as common to all men and of reason as the faculty by which it is cognizable (2, 3, 5); and the implication that a test of the law of nature is its conduciveness to civil welfare (5). These are the points on which democratic Puritanism fastens and which it develops; they are also adopted by the Party of the Centre, and furnish the common ground on which Ireton and Nye meet and argue with Goodwin and the Levellers at Whitehall (pp. 125–69). But they are accompanied by other propositions: that practically the whole Decalogue and even parts of the so-called judicial law are identical with the law of nature and unabrogated by the Gospel (5, 6); that not merely what is immediately perceptible to reason, but whatever may be logically derived therefrom, has the sanction of natural law (2), and particularly that the belief in the true God, commanded by the Decalogue, is a part of that law (7); that though civil laws can reach only to outward actions and make good subjects the law of nature is concerned with beliefs and motives, and not merely with good subjects but good (which, in contrast with Williams' use, implies religious) men (9, 7, 5); that, as a result of man's fallen condition, the natural law as reason can actually know it is inadequate and requires to be set in a brighter light by the written law of God (10). These propositions the Congregationalists at Whitehall would without reservations accept; but the Separatists and

[89]

Levellers reject them, or accept only with marked reservations. Agreeing enthusiastically with an appeal to the law of nature, and especially with the decision of all civil questions thereby (5), they insist on rigorous separation of the natural and civil from the religious sphere. There must be no overlapping, no cross-reference between the two that may furnish a pretext for the magistrate's interference in matters of conscience; his commission is purely civil and concerned with the outward man, and its terms are prescribed by natural law. The law of nature becomes then God's law for the natural order as distinct from the order of grace. It is (we repeat) in the interests of religious liberty that the principle of segregation is fully developed; but it has momentous consequences in the civil as well as in the religious field.

Once the principle is adopted, the idea that the natural law as it is known by reason in man's fallen state is necessarily imperfect, may be safely accepted. The restored illumination of the Saint is a spiritual gift, whose appropriate place of exercise is not the state but the church. In a sense the imperfection of the natural law is precisely its inadequacy to anything higher than civil or natural ends.[1] For these it is perfectly adequate, furnishing the only rule—and all the rule that is required. In an opinion of the practical adequacy of the law of nature *within its appointed sphere*, the Levellers were no doubt confirmed by the frequent appeals heard to it, and by the whole secular tradition of the law of nature, glanced at and condemned as inadequate by Ames (7, 8).

In opposing Ireton's effort to use the law of nature as a touchstone to distinguish between the merely typical portions of the Mosaic Law which are abrogated by the Gospel and the portions identical with the law of nature and hence of permanent and universal application, the Levellers (supported by Goodwin) give their clearest exposition of the principle of segregation as applied to the idea of a natural law. Scripture is the rule for the church; the law of nature, the only rule for the state. To attempt to introduce the Mosaic Law into the constitution of the state under the guise of natural law is sophistical. Nor are we left without strong indications of what the law of nature teaches in the civil sphere: it teaches that the people not only designate the persons of their governors, but bestow upon them all their power (pp. 157–9).[2]

[1] In Overton, who (as we have seen) studiously ignores the Fall, reason is, apparently, held to be perfectly adequate in all men and the law of nature to have retained its original brightness.

[2] In Israel the people designated the person and God bestowed the power. This was typical, just as was the combination of civil and ecclesiastical functions. It foreshadowed the practice not of the state, but

INTRODUCTION

The insistence on the law of nature as the only rule for the state and on its basic democracy is of the first importance. But to gauge the full bearing of the appeal to nature in politics one must turn to the Putney Debates (pp. 53–79) and to the pamphlets of the Levellers. At Putney Ireton declares that the Levellers can ground their demand for manhood suffrage only on some plea of natural rights as opposed to the historic rights held forth by the fundamental constitution of the English state. They do not deny the fact. To the law of nature they confidently appeal, and when Ireton further declares that the appeal to nature will destroy all property, they try to show that the right to property is guaranteed by the law of nature, and not, as Ireton maintains, merely by positive laws (pp. 61–2). It is the law of nature, furthermore, that teaches the individual his rights and their attendant duties: the right and duty of self-preservation, and the natural limits of obedience (or the right and duty of resistance to tyrannical rulers). It teaches him what are the ends of government; and it inculcates the basic principles of social life, the principles of natural justice and equity which dictate the political equality of all men within the state and issue in the maxim (also enshrined in the Gospel), 'to do unto others as you would have them do unto you.'

Behind the Levellers' appeals to the law of nature lie those of Parliamentarians against the King, and of the Army against both the King and Parliament. Already in 1642, Parliamentary apologists are declaring that the law of nature is paramount: by it all power is 'originally inherent in the people,' and (whatever was the case among the Jews, where God intervened by a direct revelation) the source of the magistrates' authority 'can be nothing else among Christians but the actions and agreements of such and such political corporations.' The 'paramount law that shall give law to all human laws whatsoever . . . is *salus populi*. . . . Neither can the right of conquest be pleaded to acquit princes of that which is due to the people . . .; for mere force cannot alter the course of nature or frustrate the tenor of law. . . .' 'The charter of nature entitles all subjects of all countries whatsoever to safety by its supreme law.' [1] Most striking of all the early pleas is that of Rutherford's *Lex Rex*, which, like the later appeals of the Army,

---

of the church under the Gospel. In nature, and under the Gospel (where civil magistracy is once more a purely natural office), God bestows power upon the people, who delegate it (under such safeguards as are deemed necessary) to the civil magistrate, designating the person *and bestowing the power*. Cf. pp. 212, 283.

[1] Henry Parker, *Observations upon Some of His Majesty's Late Answers and Expresses*, pp. 1–4.

is fully illustrated in the texts that follow (see Index *sub* 'Law of Nature'). Behind these again lies the long and complex tradition of the law of nature, as it comes down from classical times,[1] as it is adapted and formulated by the Civilians and Canonists, and as it influences the theory and practice of English law.[2] The law of nature comes to the Levellers with peculiar authority, even if they are ignorant of many of the stages in its august tradition; for is it not God's law for the natural order? And it comes to them with unexhausted potentialities; for it is unwritten (all formulations being but partial and approximate), and finally determinable only by reason. By resolutely applying the principle of segregation it can be freed from the trammels of its association with the written law of scripture. By the principle of analogy it can take its place as the fundamental law for the state not less certainly than does the law of Christ as the fundamental law for the church. With this vast authority, with these potentialities, and with a new freedom from reference to anything beyond itself, the law of nature becomes the foundation of the Levellers' political creed and their final court of appeal.

Where the principle of segregation is applied in its most radical form, the effect is to exalt the law of nature as known by the reason of fallen man into an absolute standard within, but not beyond, the natural order. There remains, however, the large body of Puritan thought, even of extreme Puritan thought, in which the principle of segregation is not rigorously applied. For it, the distinction between the law of nature in its primal brightness (a brightness restored in the regenerate) and the dim relic of that law known to fallen men (above, p. [*89*], (10)) retains its full effect, and with two results already indicated: the necessity of supplementing reason by scripture in the civil field, and the possibility of calling in the doctrine of the law of nature to support an enforcement upon the unregenerate of a standard whose full glory is hidden from them and known only to the Saints. Even in Milton (if he were our chief concern here) we could demonstrate something of these results, though in a more refined form. Despite his passion

---

[1] 'There is a law which is the same as true reason accordant with nature, a law which is constant and eternal. . . . This law is not one at Rome and another at Athens, but is : . . . immutable, the expression of the command and the sovereignty of God' (Cicero, *De Rep.* 3. 22, quoted by Lactantius, *Div. Inst.* 1. 6. 8). All civil law is but the expression and application of this law of nature, and derives its final authority from that fact (cf. Cicero, *De Leg.* 1. 6. 19–20, *et passim*).

[2] See A. J. Carlyle, *History of Mediaeval Political Theory in the West*; and Sir Frederick Pollock, 'The History of the Law of Nature' (*Essays in the Law*, 1922, pp. 31–79).

for liberty, and his partial application, in the interests of religious liberty, of the principle of segregation, he is, as Wordsworth rightly divined, radical but not democratic. For him the law of nature is not a law for the natural order merely, and sufficiently known to all men within that order. It is a law of liberty which the regenerate alone can fully know, and by which only they are adequately equipped to live. The most obvious inferences to be drawn in the political field are reactionary in character, and they appear in Milton's final disregard of the will of the majority. But this does not mean that the law of nature thus conceived is wholly without a liberating influence. It has some effect upon the provisions suggested for civil life; and, above all, nothing can prevent its exerting its influence *as an ideal*. Thus Milton's interpretation of liberty as the abrogation of outward law, while it applies only to the regenerate, has a pronounced effect on his conception of the state (if only because the state's highest purpose is to serve the regenerate); and it holds forth an *ideal* of liberty, individualist, and even anarchist, in character. So long as dogma remains unimpaired the ideal is, strictly, inaccessible to the ordinary man, but the use of the term *nature* in designating the ideal is a perpetual invitation to the unwary to extend its benefits to him. And sooner or later dogma is impaired. As this occurs there are two ways in which the identification of the law of nature with the rule of man's unfallen, or his regenerate, condition may tend to radical conclusions. To associate the natural with the unfallen state is to approach the general type of thought now described as primitivistic. To associate it with a regenerate condition presents, on the other hand, some affinity with the type of thought known as perfectibilitarian. In the eighteenth century these two types were to furnish, separately and together, the dominant modes of radical thinking. Discontent with the existing social order issued in the cry of 'back to nature,' or in the cry of 'onward to perfection.' Then the happy discovery was made that the two things were really identical: in order to go onward to perfection one had only to go back to nature for one's rule. But before this blessed state of confusion could be achieved dogma must have disappeared or have been interpreted so figuratively that nothing but the smudged outline of its pattern persisted. In some of the radicals of the Puritan revolution these processes are seen at work. Walwyn and Winstanley furnish examples. But in another way, and without any break-down of dogma, these primitivistic and perfectibilitarian tendencies can in measure be released to work in radical political thought: namely, by analogy. Grant that

[93]

natural reason is adequate *within the natural sphere*; then it can lead men to the perfect *natural* state; and this line of thought encounters strong support from the secular tradition of natural law to which Stoicism had bequeathed some primitivist and some perfectibilitarian elements.

Bound up with the conception of the law of nature, however it is defined, is the idea that it is known by reason (either by reason unaided or by right reason, which is reason illuminated from above [1]): the appeal to the law of nature is virtually an appeal to reason. The attitude of Puritanism towards reason, we have remarked, ranges all the way from the contempt of the voluntarist to the idolatry of the rationalist (see Index). Voluntarism, which seeks the final sanction of positive laws in the will of the law-giver, has for its natural outcome absolutism. Rationalism, whose final sanction is conformity to reason, is opposed to absolutism in so far as the latter is an expression of mere arbitrary will, and leads naturally to a doctrine of liberty.[2] But the principle of segregation can achieve the curious result of establishing a rationalist standard in the natural order while leaving the view of God purely voluntarist. Precisely this result is achieved in Lilburne's thinking, who can even turn the dichotomy to account by declaring that only God can act from arbitrary will, and the magistrate is not God! In the natural order the appeal must be to reason (p. 317). An observer of the General Council comments on 'a new sect sprung up among them, and these are the rationalists, and what their reason dictates to them in church and state stands to them for good, until they be convinced with better.' [3] But *reason*, like *nature*, is a term which always stands in urgent need of precise definition. In few of the Puritans does it receive that definition. In Winstanley it approximates to the Quaker notion of the 'inner light' and is used so loosely that it can be interchanged with the expression, the *universal love*. In Overton, *discursive reason* no doubt sets the tone of his use of the term. In most of the Puritans, as in Ames, it embraces both discourse and intuition. The fact of most importance is that in this volume its use is never, I think, 'intellectualist' or esoteric. Reason is

---

[1] Overton (cf. p. [90], n. 1) uses the term right reason without any such reference, or more in its classical than its Christian sense (pp. 323–4).

[2] This is obvious if one examines Milton's political thinking in connection with the true character, not the popular misconception, of his theology, or if one pauses to relate the feeling of the Cambridge Platonists for intellectual liberty to the tenets of their rational theology.

[3] *Clarendon State Papers*, vol. 2, App.; 14th October 1647. The word *church* signifies merely the relation of church to state.

thought of as something common to all men and independent of education. It is the light of nature, not of the schools: an equalitarian conception. Natural truth may be perceived by any man, just as spiritual truth may be perceived by the meanest of the brethren. And this furnishes the basis of the belief in free discussion, in which the humblest may be convinced (as is his right), and may in his turn convince if he can (as is his right also). The only distinction is that between reason operating unaided and reason illuminated from above; and we have gauged the significance of that distinction.

The appeal to reason in politics brings us once more to the attitude towards historical precedent. In the earlier opponents of absolutism the appeal was twofold, to precedent and to a paramount law known by reason (which might or might not be described as the law of nature). Positive laws finally claimed obedience as particular and approximate embodiments of that general law. To appeal to precedent was not to deny, but rather silently to assume, the paramount law. This too was the position of Lilburne,[1] who was for ever conning the Book of Statutes and citing Magna Charta and the other formularies of the Englishman's historic rights. But the struggle of Parliament with the Crown, and of the Army and people with Parliament, soon outran precedent; and this fact, combined with Puritan utopianism and the predominant Puritan view of custom and of history, resulted in a progressive shift of emphasis from precedent to the law of nature, or from historic to abstract rights. It is on this point that Ireton and the Levellers divide (pp. 52–62). The appeal to reason as opposed to history, whatever its weaknesses, has (as Mr. Laski observes) one great advantage: it permits an extension of rights, not merely a defence of rights already won. The fact did not escape the debaters at Putney. Already Walwyn had dissented from Lilburne: 'Magna Charta hath been more precious in your esteem than it deserveth; for it may be made good to the people and yet in many particulars they may remain under intolerable oppression.'[2] And Overton is equally dissatisfied with the appeal to existing laws:

Ye know the laws of this nation are unworthy a free people, and deserve from first to last to be considered and seriously debated and reduced to an agreement with common equity and right reason, which ought to be the form and life of every government. Magna Charta

[1] *London's Liberty in Chains* (1646), p. 41.
[2] *England's Lamentable Slavery* (1645), p. 5. (The pamphlet is reproduced in *Tracts*, edited Haller, 3. 311–18, and assigned to Walwyn.)

itself (being but a beggarly thing, containing many marks of intolerable bondage) and the laws that have been made since by Parliaments have in very many particulars made our government much more oppressive and intolerable.[1]

But even the most radical were loath to break entirely with the past. So they invented a new past more consonant with the demands of reason.

As the most primitive age of the church was that in which it embodied most purely the law of Christ, so in the most primitive era of English history did not the state embody most purely the law of nature? And here the rival theory of absolutism played into the hands of the radicals by asserting that the King's right rested not on contract but on conquest. It was an old contention assailed by Buchanan, revived by the Royalists, and attacked once more by Parker and Rutherford (pp. 204–5); and it was obviously a two-edged sword: 'There were more reason why the people might justify force to regain due liberty than the prince might to subvert the same.'[2] The effects of conquest could be reversed by victory. This was an idea highly congenial to a victorious Army, especially to those who held that there was now no power in England but the sword—there was no other power and since the Norman Conquest there never had been.[3] A wave of Anti-Normanism swept through the ranks, and Edward the Confessor became a Puritan hero.[4] The Normans had destroyed the primitive English state and enslaved a nation; all the long struggle with kings had been an effort to regain its lost rights; Magna Charta and the other concessions wrung from them were so many fragments of recovered freedom. Now the Army's victory had exchanged the roles of conqueror and conquered. It must be followed by a new constitution with the abrogation of all those positive laws which were a badge of slavery; and a restoration of their rights to the commons whom the Norman had despoiled. What were the barons but William the Conqueror's colonels? Their right fell with his: a convenient doctrine for those whose equalitarian sentiments or practical needs were demanding the abolition of the House of Lords and the end of all feudal privileges.

[1] *A Remonstrance of Many Thousand Citizens* (1646), p. 15 (ibid., 3. 351–70).
[2] Henry Parker, *Observations* (1642), p. 3.
[3] Francis White, *Copy of a Letter to Fairfax with an Account to the Officers of the General's Regiment* (11th November 1647).
[4] John Hare (in *St. Edward's Ghost* and other pamphlets) advanced the mad notion of the superiority of the Germanic race and declared war on all the French words in the English language.

INTRODUCTION

Not only the military Saints and the Levellers, but the Diggers too, could find their account in the attractive theory of Anti-Normanism (p. 383). It is, of course, no more tenable than the absolutist theory of conquest which first suggested it. Nathaniel Bacon found them the subject of excited debate and determined to examine the evidence on which they rested. His *Historical Discourse of the Uniformity of the Government of England* (1647) yields them little support. But this does not diminish the significance of Anti-Normanism as an effort of the imagination to accommodate history to the demands of reason, and (with the pattern of ecclesiastical history hovering in the background) to clothe abstract rights in a concrete and primitive form. It furnishes also a striking example of a theory on which divergent groups of the Puritan Left could temporarily combine.

To forget the fact of such combination is to misread the history of Puritanism, of the Army, and of their relations to democracy in the seventeenth century: a common enemy is almost as important as common principles—at times, more important. Though the main direction of the Levellers was democratic, while that of the military Saints was not, some alliance was possible—even some mutual influence. And the moment of inevitable conflict was forestalled by the practical politicians of the Centre who snatched all the fruits of victory from the busy and contradictory theorists of the Left. They did so by participating in and directing the precarious union of interests and ideals, which was the Army in politics, and a phenomenon of great, if temporary, importance. For the victorious Army combined, and in some sort reconciled, two divergent notions: it was a godly Army, in which the Saints were sufficiently numerous (and vocal) to satisfy the religious ideal; and it was a representative Army, a cross-section at least of Puritan England, which satisfied the democratic ideal and supported its pretence of speaking in the name of the nation. It deliberated in a council whose forms were democratic and whose language was quasi-religious. The deliberations could be turned into a debate on natural rights by Rainborough, or into a prayer-meeting by Goffe. They bore a general resemblance to those of the House of Commons—not least in the rather sinister fact that Cromwell could control them, and end them. The Council of the Army was, within limits, a genuine democratic assembly. Where else in 1647 could the common soldier urge his reasons upon his commanders, or grandees be told to their faces that 'the poorest he that is in England hath a life to live, as the greatest he'? It was democratic, also, in including among its members many who at bottom cared for democracy not at all. And it betrayed the weakness of the democratic assembly: it was the easy prey of political astuteness and of physical force. . . .

We must take its good meaning; and to do so is to see the Council as the very imperfect realization of the Levellers' hope,[1] and hearken chiefly to their utterances. They, at least, were passionately devoted to the democratic ideal: taking justice and equality as the foundation of their scheme; believing in truth and agreement through free discussion; in their hearts distrusting force even as a method of effecting beneficent ends and even when betrayed into acquiescing in its use; willing, when truest to themselves, to postpone victory till reason, and not the sword, could win it. They were often intolerably factious, and they were incurably rash and doctrinaire. But the ideals for which they stood were magnanimous. The position of the Centre Party is more equivocal. That they *used* the Council of the Army it is idle to deny—but no one (unless it were Mr. Belloc) could now be found to assert that it was for personal ends. Ireton, who was probably the ablest political thinker that the revolution produced, sympathized with many of the Levellers' pleas for practical reforms, as the *Heads of the Proposals* (pp. 422–6) makes abundantly clear; and the vigour and acuteness with which he debates are incompatible with a merely opportunist and cynical attitude towards free discussion. But his belief in democracy was much less thorough-going than the Levellers'. Indeed in the Centre Party in general Puritan democracy was crossed and finally defeated not only by practical considerations, but by anti-democratic elements in the Puritan creed. The Levellers remain the chief exponents of Puritan democracy; and even their limitations are significant.

They are at bottom individualists, distrusting the state and thinking in terms of safeguards: a character which is part of the Puritan inheritance and shared with the Independents, where,

---

[1] The plan of the General Council was probably in the first instance a concession to the Levellers' demand. And in the idea of the Council they never ceased to believe, however disillusioned they may have become with its control by Cromwell and his officers. The advisers of the new Agents (in contrast with Rainborough and the old Agitators) are somewhat suspicious and reserved at Putney, but are led into a series of animated debates. After the Council's suppression the Levellers urged its restoration (Gardiner, *History of Commonwealth*, 1. 33–4; *Clarke Papers*, edited Firth, 2. 194). Not less significant is the temporary conversion of the Council of Officers at Whitehall into a sort of facsimile of the Council of the Putney Debates (though without the Agitators) and Lilburne's eager plans for its effective discussion (p. 473).

however, it is at war with the zeal for making righteousness prevail. Only in the Diggers, who carry over from politics to economics the Levellers' feeling for justice and equality, is there an unmistakable shift to a philosophy predominantly socialist in character —and it is an idealistic socialism that has more in common with William Morris than with Karl Marx.[1] It does not follow,

[1] One highly typical document of the Diggers (pp. 379–85) is included for purposes of comparison. Numerically unimportant, they are the one proletarian group, as the Levellers are the one fully democratic group, in the Puritan revolution. They differ from the Levellers in the character of their social philosophy, belonging rather to the history of equality than of liberty, and to that of socialism rather than of democracy proper. They also differ in the processes connecting their social to their theological thought, and stand in a somewhat different relation to Puritanism. But there is some common ground, besides their effort to extend the Levellers' principles of justice and equality from politics to economics. They share the Puritan characteristics of activity, utopianism, and iconoclasm; and (as in the case of the Levellers) they come into prominence as a result of the revolution. There is nothing of communism in the Debates or in the *Agreements of the People*; but one occasionally catches a hint of the Diggers' mode of thought or the glimpse of a principle which fully developed might lead to their position. Broadly speaking, it remains true, however, that the affinity of the Diggers is not with the Levellers, whose concern is for liberty, but with the Millenarians, whose concern is for positive reform. In the Diggers the desire to establish the reign of righteousness, as they conceive it, obliterates every other motive. In them, as in the Millenarians, the principle of segregation is not invoked; the direct inferences from their religious thought are allowed to dominate their view of secular life, their interpretation of the past and their vision of the future; the ideal of the holy community, in the peculiar form which it takes in their minds, is not restricted to the order of grace but intrudes upon the order of nature. In what at first sight looks like the language of the Millenarians, they address Fairfax: 'The intent of writing to you is not to request your protection . . .; for truly we dare not cast off the Lord and make choice of . . . men to rule us. For the creation hath smarted deeply for such a thing since Israel chose Saul to be their king; and therefore we acknowledge before you in plain English that we have chosen the Lord God to be our king and protector' (*The Levellers' New Remonstrance*, 1649, p. 1). The Diggers are working for an economic millennium. And by them the liberty of the individual is perhaps as little regarded by the stern visionaries who hope immediately to usher in the rule of Christ and his Saints. But instead of taking scripture, dogma and prophecy with the terrifying literalness of Harrison and his fellows, Winstanley and his group subject them to a process of allegorical interpretation no less startling: the Fall and its curse mean the emergence of pride and covetousness and the introduction of private property; the whole history of Israel and the coming of Christ are re-read in the light of this assumption; and the millennium (which, wherever emphasized, always carries some promise of perfectibility) is interpreted as the defeat of covetousness, the abolition of private property, and the establishment of communism throughout the world. Thus does the dogmatic scheme furnish a pattern for their social and political thought, even though they undermine dogma in the very process of interpretation.

however, that the Diggers are better exponents of the democratic ideal than the Levellers. In that ideal individualism has its place, and if history teaches anything it is the permanent necessity of individualism as a corrective. Nor need it issue merely in distrust of the state, as the *Areopagitica* and the *Essay on Liberty* remind us. But even at its best, individualism requires to be balanced—not over-balanced—by a sense of the community, the sense that speaks in the noblest of all English definitions of the state: 'It is not a partnership in things subservient only to the gross animal existence, of a temporary and perishable nature. It is a partnership in all science, a partnership in all art, . . . in every virtue and in all perfection.' From no descendant of the Puritans, these words come; but from an Anglican and a conservative, from one for whom the state has not been completely secularized and by whom (with only the safeguards of the historic constitution) it can still be trusted. But that is another story. . . . In the Levellers an individualism which prompts an emphasis on reserves and new safeguards, is in fact balanced by a more limited, but still real, sense of the community. It finds no direct expression in the *Agreements of the People* and little enough in other pamphlets. But in their belief in the arrival at truth and agreement through free discussion a sense of the community is implied because the individual needs the help of his fellows—or, if not consciously implied, it is inevitably discovered in the process of translating the belief into action. And, unlike Burke's, it is a sense of 'the *democratic* community because it is realized in the experience of the democratic assembly. We have noticed how William Dell, in his *Way of True Peace*, repudiates the church covenant in favour of a spiritual bond between all believers, achieved in Christ. Here the analogy between the order of nature and the order of grace seems to fail—and does fail. But it is neither irreverent nor fanciful to detect in a sense of the community which cannot be written into constitutions, but can only be experienced, some dim and partial analogy of the spiritual bond.

PART I. THE PUTNEY DEBATES

At the General Council of Officers [1] at Putney, 28th October 1647.

The Officers being met, first said

Lieutenant-General Cromwell: That the meeting was for public businesses; those that had anything to say concerning the public business, they might have liberty to speak.

Mr. Edward Sexby: Mr. Allen, Mr. Lockyer, and myself are three. They have sent two soldiers, one of your own regiment and one of Colonel Whalley's, with two other gentlemen, Mr. Wildman and Mr. Petty.

Commissary-General Ireton [said]: That he had not the paper of what was done upon all of the [a] [matters discussed]. It was referred to the committee, that they should consider of the paper that was printed, *The Case of the Army Stated*,[2] and to examine the particulars in it, and to represent and offer something to this Council about it. They are likewise appointed to send for those persons concerned in the paper. The committee met, according to appointment, that night. It was only then resolved on, that there should be some sent in a friendly way (not by command or summons) to invite some of those gentlemen to come in with us, I think.

Sexby: I was desired by the Lieutenant-General to know the bottom of their desires. They gave us this answer, that they would willingly draw them up and represent them unto you. They are come at this time to tender them to your considerations, with their resolutions to maintain them.

We have been by Providence put upon strange things, such as the ancientest here doth scarce remember. The Army acting to these ends, Providence hath been with us, and yet we have found little [fruit] of our endeavours. The kingdom and Army

---

[1] i.e. the General Council of the Army, which also included representatives of the regiments.

[2] See Appendix, pp. 429–36. The committee referred to is one appointed at a meeting of the General Council of the Army on 22nd Oct.

calls for expedition.   And really I think all here, both great and small, both officers and soldiers, we may say we have leaned on,[a] and gone to Egypt for help.   The kingdom's cause requires expedition, and truly our miseries (with our fellow soldiers') cry out for present help.   I think, at this time, this is your business, and I think it is in all your hearts to relieve the one and satisfy the other.   You resolved if anything [reasonable] should be propounded to you, you would join and go along with us.

The cause of our misery [is] upon two things.   We sought to satisfy all men, and it was well; but in going [about] to do it we have dissatisfied all men.   We [b] have laboured to please a king, and I think, except we go about to cut all our throats, we shall not please him; and we have gone to support an house which will prove rotten studs [1]—I mean the Parliament, which consists of a company of rotten members.

And therefore we beseech you that you will take these things into your consideration.

I shall speak to the Lieutenant-General and Commissary-General concerning one thing.   Your credits and reputation have [c] been much blasted, upon these two considerations.   The one is for seeking to settle this kingdom in such a way wherein we thought to have satisfied all men, and we have dissatisfied them—I mean in relation to the King.   The other is in reference to a Parliamentary authority, which most here would lose their lives for—to see [d] those powers to which we will subject ourselves, loyally called.   These two things are, as I think conscientiously, the cause of all those blemishes that have been cast upon either the one or the other.   You are convinced God will have you to act on.   But only [e] consider how you shall act, and [take] those [ways] that will secure you and the whole kingdom.   I desire you will consider those things that shall be offered to you; and, if you see anything of reason, you will join with us, that the kingdom may be eased and our fellow soldiers may be quieted in spirit.[f]   These things I have represented as my thoughts. I desire your pardon.

Cromwell: I think it is good for us to proceed to our business in some order, and that will be if we consider some things that are lately past.   There hath been a book printed, called *The Case of the Army Stated,* and that hath been taken into consideration, and there hath been somewhat drawn up by way of exception to things contained in that book.   And I suppose there was an

---

[1] The uprights in a lath-and-plaster wall (FIRTH).

answer brought to that which was taken by way of exception, and yesterday the gentleman that brought the answer, he was dealt honestly and plainly withal, and he was told that there were new designs adriving, and nothing would be a clearer discovery of the sincerity of [their] intentions than [a] their willingness, that were active, to bring what they had to say to be judged of by the General Officers and by this General Council, that we might discern what the intentions were. Now it seems there be divers that are come hither to manifest those intentions, according to what was offered yesterday; and truly I think that the best way of our proceeding will be to receive what they have to offer. Only this, Mr. Sexby, you were speaking to us two—[I know not why], except you think that we have done somewhat, or acted somewhat, different from the sense and resolution of the General Council. Truly, that that you speak to, was the things that related to the King and things that related to the Parliament; and if there be a fault, I may say it (and I dare say), it hath been the fault of the General Council, and that which you do speak you speak to the General Council, I hope, though you name us two, both in relation to the one and to the other.[d] Therefore truly I think it sufficient for us to say, and 'tis that we say—I can speak for myself, let others speak for themselves—I dare maintain it, and I dare avow I have acted nothing but what I have done with the public consent and approbation and allowance of the General Council. That I dare say for myself, both in relation to the one and to the other. What I have acted in Parliament in the name of the Council or of the Army, I have had my warrant for it from hence. What I have spoken [b] in another capacity,[c] as a member of the House, that was free for me to do; and I am confident that I have not used the name of the Army, or interest of the Army, to anything but what I have had allowance from the General Council for, and [what they] thought it fit to move the House in. I do the rather give you this account, because I hear there are some slanderous reports going up and down upon somewhat that hath been offered to the House of Commons [by me] as being the sense and opinion of this Army, and in the name of this Army, which (I dare be confident to speak it) hath been as false and slanderous a report as could be raised of a man. And that was this: that I should say to the Parliament, and deliver it as the desire of this Army, and the sense of this Army, that there should be a second address to the King by way of propositions. I dare be confident to speak it. What I delivered there I delivered as my own sense, and what I delivered as my own sense I am not ashamed of. What I delivered as your sense, I never delivered but what I had as your sense.

Colonel [Thomas] Rainborough : [a] For this the Lieutenant-General was pleased to speak of last, it was moved that day the propositions were brought in. That [day] it was carried for making a second address to the King, it was when both the Lieutenant-General and myself were last here; [1] and when [b] we broke off here, and when we came upon the bill, it was told us that the House had carried it for a second address. And therefore the Lieutenant-General must needs be clear of it. But it *was* urged in the House that it was the sense of the Army that it should be so.

Ireton : I desire not to speak of these things, but only to put things into an orderly way, which would lead to what the occasion is that hath brought these gentlemen hither that are now called in. Yet I cannot but speak a word to that that was last touched upon. If I had told any man so (which I know I did not), if I did, I did tell him what I thought. And if I thought otherwise of the Army, I protest I should have been ashamed of the Army and detested it; that is, if I had thought the Army had been of that mind [that] they would let those propositions sent from both kingdoms [c] be the things which should be [final] whether [for] peace or no, without any further offers; and when I do find it, I shall be ashamed on 't, and detest any days' condescension with it. And yet for that which, Mr. Sexby tells us, hath been one of the great businesses [cast] upon the Lieutenant-General and myself, I do detest and defy the thought of that thing, of any endeavour or design or purpose or desire to set up the King; and I think I have demonstrated it, and I hope I shall do still, [that] it is the interest of the kingdom that I have suffered for. And as for the Parliament, too, I think those that know the beginnings of these principles that we [set forth] in our declarations of late [d] for clearing and vindicating the liberties of the people, even in relation to Parliament, will have reason [to acquit me. And] whoever do know how we were led to the declaring of that point, as we have [done], as one [fundamental], will be able to acquit me that I have been far from a design of setting up the persons of these men, or of any men whatsoever, to be our law-makers. And so likewise for the King: though I am clear, as from the other, from setting up the person of one or other, yet I shall declare it again that I do not seek, or would not seek, nor will

---

[1] i.e. 23rd September (FIRTH).

join with them that do seek, the destruction either of Parliament or King. Neither will I consent with those, or concur with them, who will not attempt all the ways that are possible to preserve both, and to make good use, and the best use that can be, of both for the kingdom. And I did not hear anything from that gentleman (Mr. Sexby) that could induce or incline me to [abandon] that resolution. To that point I stand clear, as I have expressed. But I shall not speak any more concerning myself.

The committee met at my lodgings as soon as they parted from hence. And the first thing they resolved [was this]. On hearing there was a meeting of the Agitators, though it was thought fit by the General Council here [that] they should be sent for to the regiment[s], yet it was thought fit [by the committee] to let them know what the General Council had done, and to go on in a way that might tend to unity; and [this] being resolved on, we were desired by one of those gentlemen that were desired to go, that lest they should mistake the matter they went about, it might be drawn in writing, and this is it:

That the General Council, [&c.] [a]

This is the substance of what was delivered. Mr. Allen, Mr. Lockyer, and Mr. Sexby were sent with it, and I think it is fit that the Council should be acquainted with the answer.

Mr. William Allen: As to the answer, it was short—truly I shall give it as short. We gave them the paper, and read it amongst them, and to my best remembrance they then told us that they were not all come together whom it did concern, and so were not in a capacity at the present to return us an answer, but that they would take it into consideration, and would send it as speedily as might be. I think it was near their sense.

(The answer of the Agitators read.[1])

Ireton: Whereas it was appointed by the Council, and we of the committee did accordingly desire, that these gentlemen,[b] being members of the Army and engaged with the Army, might have come to communicate with the General Council of the Army and those that were appointed by them for a mutual satisfaction: by this paper they seem to be of a fixed resolution —setting themselves to be a divided party or distinct council from the General Council of the Army [c]—that there was nothing

---

[1] Followed by blank in manuscript. The substance of the answer is probably contained in *Two Letters from the Agents of the Five Regiments of Horse* (28th October) and in the letters appended to the *Agreement of the People* (3rd November); see pp. 437–8, 445–9.

to be done as single persons to declare their dissatisfaction, or the grounds for informing themselves better or us better, but that they [would speak] as all the rest should concur, so that ª they seemed to hold together as a formed and settled party, distinct and divided from others; and withal [they] seemed to set down these resolutions [as things] to which they expect the compliance of ⁿ others, rather than their compliance with others to give satisfaction.

But it seems, upon something that the Lieutenant-General and some others of that committee did think fit ᵇ [to offer], the gentlemen that brought that paper ᶜ have been since induced to descend a little from the height, and ᵈ to send some of them to come ᵉ as agents particularly, or messengers from that meeting or from that council, to hear what we have to say to them, or to offer something to us relating to the matters in that paper. I believe there are gentlemen sent with them, that (though perhaps the persons of them that are members of the Army may ᶠ give the passages in) ᵍ they may be better able to observe them. And, therefore, if you please, I move that they may proceed.

Buff-Coat: [1] May it please your Honour: [I desired] to give you satisfaction in that there was such a willingness that we might have a conference. Whereupon I did engage that interest that was in me that I would procure some to come hither, both of the soldiers and of others for assistance. And in order thereunto, here are two soldiers sent from the Agents, and two of our friends also,ʰ to present this to your considerations, and desire ᶦ your advice. According to ʲ my expectations and your engagements,ᵏ you are resolved every one to purchase our inheritances which have been lost, and free this nation from the tyranny that lies upon us. I question not but that it is all your desires. And for that purpose we desire to do nothing but what we present to your consideration. And if you conceive ᵍ that it must be for us to be instruments, (that we might shelter ourselves like wise men before the storm comes) we desire that all carping upon words might be laid aside, and [that you may] fall directly upon the matter presented to you.

We have [here met on purpose], according to my engagement, that whatsoever may be thought to be necessary for our satisfaction, for the right understanding one of another,ᵐ [might be

---

[1] A trooper whose name was at this point unknown to Clarke, but was later discovered to be Everard; i.e. Robert Everard, Agent of Cromwell's Regiment.

done], that we might go on together. For, though our ends and aims be the same, if one thinks this way, another another way,[a] that way which is the best for the subject [is] that they [both] may be hearkened unto.

(The answer of the Agitators, the second time read.[1])

Buff-Coat : [For the privileges here demanded], I think it will be strange that we that are soldiers cannot have them [for] ourselves, if not for the whole kingdom; and therefore we beseech you consider of it.

Cromwell : These things that you have now offered, they are new to us: they are things that we have not at all (at least in this method and thus circumstantially) had any opportunity to consider of,[b] because they came to us but thus, as you see; this is the first time we had a view of them.

Truly this paper does contain in it very great alterations of the very government of the kingdom, alterations from that government that it hath been under, I believe I may almost say, since it was a nation—I say, I think I may almost say so. And what the consequences of such an alteration as this would be, if there were nothing else to be considered, wise men and godly men ought to consider. I say, *if* there were nothing else [to be considered] but the very weight and nature of the things contained in this paper.[c] Therefore, although the pretensions in it, and the expressions in it, are very plausible, and if we could leap out of one condition into another that had so specious things in it as this hath, I suppose there would not be much dispute—though perhaps some of these things may be very well disputed.[c] How do we know if, whilst we are disputing these things, another company of men shall [not] gather together, and[d] put out a paper as plausible perhaps as this? I do not know why it might not be done by that time you have agreed upon this, or got hands to it if that be the way. And not only another, and another, but many of this kind. And if so, what do you think the consequence of that would be? Would it not be confusion? Would it not be utter confusion? Would it not make England like the Switzerland country, one canton of the Swiss against another, and one

---

.[1] No blank follows in manuscript. This suggests that the answer read was the same as that read before, for which a blank was left. But the course of the debate suggests that what was here read was not an apology, but a set of proposals, probably those printed on 3rd and 4th November, as *An Agreement of the People* (see pp. 443–5).

county against another? I ask you whether it be not fit for every honest man seriously to lay that upon his heart? And if so, what would that produce but an absolute desolation—an absolute desolation to the nation—and we in the meantime tell the nation: 'It is for your liberty; 'tis for your privilege; 'tis for your good.' (Pray God it prove, so whatsoever course we run.) But truly, I think we are not only to consider what the consequences are if there were nothing else but this paper, but we are to consider the probability of the ways and means to accomplish [the thing proposed]: that is to say, whether,[a] according to reason and judgment, the spirits and temper of the people of this nation are prepared to receive and to go on along with it, and [whether] those great difficulties [that] lie in our way [are] in a likelihood to be either overcome or removed. Truly, to anything that's good, there's no doubt on it, objections may be made and framed; but let every honest man consider whether or no there be not very real objections [to this] in point of difficulty.[b] I know a man may answer all difficulties with faith, and faith will answer all difficulties really where it is, but [c] we are very apt, all of us, to call that faith, that perhaps may be but carnal imagination, and carnal reasonings. Give me leave to say this. There will be very great mountains in the way of this, if this were the thing in present consideration; and, therefore, we ought to consider the consequences, and God hath given us our reason that we may do this.[b] It is not enough to propose things that are good in the end,[e] but suppose this model were an excellent model, and fit for England and the kingdom to receive,[f] it is our duty as Christians and men to consider consequences, and to consider the way.

But really I shall speak to nothing but that that, as before the Lord I am persuaded in my heart, tends to uniting of us in one, [and] to that that God will manifest to us to be the thing that he would have us prosecute. And he that meets not here with that heart, and dares not say he will stand to that, I think he is a deceiver. I say it to you again, and I profess unto you, I shall offer nothing to you but that I think in my heart and conscience tends to the uniting of us, and to the begetting a right understanding among us; and therefore this is that I would insist upon, and have it cleared among us.

It is not enough for us to insist upon good things. That every one would do. There is not [one in] forty of us but [g] could prescribe many things exceeding plausible—and hardly anything worse than our present condition, take it with all the troubles that are upon us. It is not enough for us to propose good things, but it behoves honest men and Christians (that really will approve themselves so before God and men) to see whether or no they be in a condition—whether, taking all things into consideration, they may honestly endeavour and attempt that that is fairly and plausibly proposed. For my own part I know nothing that we are to consider first but that, before we would come to debate the evil or good of this [paper], or to add to it or subtract from it. And [a] if we should come to any [such] thing,[b] I am confident (if your hearts be upright as ours are—and God will be judge between you and us) you do not bring this paper with peremptoriness of mind, but to receive amendments, to have anything taken from it that may be made [c] apparent by clear reason to be inconvenient or unhonest.

But [first of all there is the question what obligations lie upon us and how far we are engaged].[d] This ought to be our consideration and yours, saving [that] in this you have the advantage of us—you that are the soldiers you have not, but you that are not [soldiers]—you reckon yourselves at a loose and at a liberty, as men that have no obligation upon you. Perhaps we conceive we have; and therefore this is that I may say [e]—both to those that come with you, and to my fellow officers and all others that hear me: that it concerns us as we would approve ourselves before God, and before men that are able to judge of us, if we do not make good [our] engagements, if we do not make good that that the world expects we should make good. I do not speak to determine what that is; but if I be not much mistaken, we have in the time of our danger issued out declarations; we have been required by the Parliament, because our declarations were general, to declare particularly what we meant. And (having done that) how far that obliges or not obliges [us], *that* is by us to be considered—if we mean honestly and sincerely and to [f] approve ourselves to God as honest men. And therefore, having heard this paper read, this remains to us: that we again review what we have engaged in, and what we have that lies upon us.[g] He that departs from that that is a real engagement and a real tie upon him, I think he transgresses without faith; for faith will bear up men in every honest obligation, and God does expect from men the performance of every honest obligation. And therefore I have no more to say but this: we having received your paper, we shall amongst ourselves consider what to do; and before we take this into consideration, it is fit for us to consider how far we are obliged, and how far we are free; and I hope we shall prove ourselves honest men where we are free to tender anything to the good of the public. And this is that I thought good to offer to you upon this paper.

Mr. [*John*] *Wildman:* Being yesterday at a meeting where divers country gentlemen and soldiers and others were, and amongst the rest the Agents of the five regiments, and having weighed their papers, I must freely confess I did declare my agreement with them. Upon that, they were pleased to declare their sense in most particulars of their proceedings, to me, and desired me that I would be their mouth, and in their names ᵃ represent their sense unto you. And upon that ground I shall speak something in answer to that which your Honour last spake.

I shall not reply anything at present, till it come to be further debated, either concerning the consequences of what is propounded, or [the contents] of this paper; but I conceive the chief weight of your Honour's speech lay in this, that you were first to consider what obligations lay upon you, and how far you were engaged, before you could consider what was just in this paper now propounded; adding that God would protect men in keeping honest promises. To that I must only offer this. That, according to the best knowledge [I have] of their apprehensions, they do apprehend that whatever obligation is past must afterwards be considered when it is urged whether [the engagement] ᵇ were honest and ᶜ just or no; and if it were not just it doth not oblige the persons, if it be an oath itself. But if, while there is not so clear a light, any person passes an engagement, it is judged by them (and I so judge it) to be an act of honesty for that man to recede from his former judgment, and to abhor it. And therefore I conceive the first thing is to consider the honesty of what is offered; otherwise it cannot be considered of any obligation that doth prepossess. By the consideration of the justice of what is offered, that obligation shall appear whether it was just or no. If it were not just, I cannot but be confident of the searings of your consciences. And I conceive this to be their sense; and upon this account, upon a more serious review of all declarations past, they see no obligations which are just, that they contradict by proceeding in this way.

Ireton: Sure this gentleman hath not been acquainted with our engagements. For he that will cry out of breach of engagement in slight and trivial things and things necessitated to—I can hardly think that man that is so tender of an engagement as to frame, or [at least] concur with, this book in their insisting upon

every punctilio of [the] *Engagement*,[1] can be of that principle that
no engagement is binding further than that he thinks it just or no.
For he [a] hints that,[b] if he that makes an engagement (be it what
it will be) have further light that this engagement was not good
or honest, then he is free from it. Truly, if the sense were put
thus, that a man finds he hath entered into an engagement and
thinks that it was not a just engagement, I confess something
might be said that [such] a man might declare himself for his part
[ready] to suffer some penalty [c] upon his person or upon his
party.[d] The question is, whether it be an engagement to another
party. Now if a man [1] venture into an engagement from him[self]
to another, and find [e] that engagement [not] just and honest, he
must apply himself to the other party and say: 'I cannot actively
perform it; I will make you amends as near as I can.' Upon the
same ground men are not obliged [to be obedient] to any authority
that is set up, though it were this authority that is proposed here—
I am not engaged to be so *actively* to that authority. Yet if I
have engaged that they shall bind me by law, though afterwards[f]
I find they do require me to a thing that is not just or honest,[j]
I am bound so far to my engagement that I must submit and
suffer, though I cannot act and do that which their laws do impose
upon me. If that caution were put in where a performance of
an engagement might be expected from another, and he could
not do it because he thought it was not honest to be performed—
if such a thing were put into the case, it is possible there might
be some reason for it. But to take it as it is delivered in general,
[that we are free to break, if it subsequently appear unjust],
whatever engagement we have entered into, though it be a promise
of something to another party, wherein that other party is concerned, wherein he hath a benefit if we make it good, wherein
he hath a prejudice if we [g] make it not good: this is a principle
that will take away all commonwealth[s], and will take away the
fruit of this [very] engagement if it were entered into; and men
of this principle would think themselves as little as may be
[obliged by any law] if in their apprehensions it be not a good
law. I think they would think themselves as little obliged to think
of standing to that authority [that is proposed in this paper].

Truly, sir, I have little to say at the present to that matter of
the paper that is tendered to us. I confess, there are plausible
things in it, and there are things really good in it.[h] There are
those things that I do with my heart desire; and there are those

[1] *Solemn Engagement of the Army* (pp. 401–3); see *Case of the Army
Truly Stated* (pp. 429–32).

things, for the most part of it, [that]—I shall be so free as to say—
if these gentlemen (and other gentlemen that will join with them)
can obtain, I would not oppose, I should rejoice to see obtained.
There are those things in it, divers [of them]. And if we were,
as hath been urged now, free; if we were first free from consideration of all the dangers and miseries that we may bring
upon this people, [the danger] that when we go to cry out for the
liberty of it we may not leave a being [in it], free from all [those]
engagements that do lie upon us, and that were honest when they
were entered into: I should concur with this paper further than,
as .the case doth stand, I can. But truly I do account we are
under engagements; and I suppose that whatsoever this gentleman that spoke last doth seem to deliver to us, holding himself
absolved from all engagements if he thinks it, yet those men that
came with him (that are in the case of the Army) hold themselves
more obliged; and therefore that they will not persuade us to
lay aside all our former engagements and declarations, if there
be anything in them, and to concur in this, if there be anything
in it that is contrary to those engagements which they call upon
us to confirm. Therefore I do wish that we may have a consideration of our former engagements, of things which are generally the engagements of the Army. Those we are to take notice
of; and sure we are not to recede from them till we are convinced [a]
that they are unjust. And when we are convinced of them, that
they are unjust, truly yet I must not fully concur with that
gentleman's principle, that presently [b] we are, as he says, absolved
from them, that we are not bound to them, or we are not bound
to make them good. Yet I should think, at least, if the breach
of that engagement be to the prejudice of another whom we have
persuaded to believe by our declaring such things, [so] that
we [c] led them to a confidence of it, to a dependence upon it,
to a disadvantage to themselves or the losing of advantages to
them; [I say, I think then that] though we were convinced they
were unjust, and satisfied in this gentleman's principle, and free
and disengaged from them, yet we who made that engagement
should not make it our act to break it. Though we were convinced that we are not bound to perform it, yet we should not
make it our act to break [it]. And so [d] I speak to enforce this
upon the whole matter.[e] As for [f] the particulars of this Agreement, [there are other questions]: whether they have that goodness
that they hold forth in show, or whether [there] are not some
defects in them which are not seen, [so] that, if we should rest in
this Agreement without something more, they would [g] deceive

us; and whether there be not some considerations that would tend [more] to union. But [a] withal [I wish] that we who are the Army and are engaged with [its] public declarations, may consider how far those public declarations, which we then thought to be just,[b] do oblige, that[f] we may either resolve to make them good if we can in honest ways, or at least not make it our work to break them. And for this purpose I wish—unless the Council please to meet from time to time, from day to day, and to consider it themselves, to go over our papers and declarations and take the heads of them—I wish there may be some specially appointed for it; and I shall be very glad if it may be so that I myself may be none of them.

Rainborough : I shall crave your pardon if I may speak something freely; and I think it will be the last time I shall speak here,[1] and from such a way that I never looked for. The consideration that I had in this Army and amongst honest men—not that it is an addition of honour and profit to me, but rather a detriment in both—is [c] the reason that I speak something by way of apology first. This paper I saw by chance, and had no resolution to have been at this Council, nor any other since I took this employment upon me, but to do my duty. I met with a letter (which truly was so strange to me that I have been a little troubled, and truly I have so many sparks of honour and honesty in me) to let me know that my regiment should be immediately disposed from me. I hope that none in the Army will say but that I have performed my duty, and that with some success, as well as others. I am loath to leave the Army,[d] with whom I will live and die, insomuch that rather than I will lose this regiment of mine the Parliament shall exclude me the House, [or] imprison me; for truly while I am [employed] abroad I will not be undone at home. This was it that called me hither, and not anything of this paper. But now I shall speak something of it.[e]

I shall speak my mind, that, whoever he be that hath done this, he hath done it with much respect to the good of his country. It is said, there are many plausible things in it. Truly, many things have engaged me, which, if I had not known they should have been nothing but good, I would not have engaged in. It hath been said, that if a man be engaged he must perform his engagements. I am wholly confident that every honest man is bound in duty to God and his conscience, let him be engaged in

---

[1] Rainborough refers to his having been transferred to naval service.

what he will, to decline it when [he sees it to be evil]: he is engaged, and [as] clearly convinced, to discharge his duty to God as ever he was for it. And that I shall make good out of the scripture, and clear it by that, if that be anything. There are two [further] objections are made against it.

The one is *division*. Truly I think we are utterly undone if we divide, but I hope that honest things have carried us on thus long, and will keep us together, and I hope that we shall not divide. Another thing is *difficulties*. Oh, unhappy men are we that ever began this war! If ever we [had] looked upon difficulties, I do not know that ever we should have looked an enemy in the face. Truly, I think the Parliament were very indiscreet to contest with the King if they did not consider first that they should go through difficulties; and I think there was no man that entered into this war, that did not engage [to go through difficulties]. And I shall humbly offer unto you—it may be the last time I shall offer, it may be so, but I shall discharge my conscience in it—it is this. That truly I think,[a] let the difficulties be round about you—have you death before you, the sea on each side of you and behind you—[and] are you convinced that the thing is just, I think you are bound in conscience to carry it on; and I think at the last day it can never be answered to God, that you did not do it. For I think it is a poor service to God and the kingdom, to take their pay and to decline the work.[b] I hear [it] said [that] it 's a huge alteration, it 's a bringing in of new laws, and that this kingdom hath been under this government ever since it was a kingdom. If writings be true there have[c] been many scufflings between the honest men of England and those that have tyrannized over them; and if it be [true what I have] read, there is none of those just and equitable laws that the people of England are born to, but[d] are entrenchment[s on the once enjoyed privileges of their rulers] altogether. But [even] if they were those which the people have been always under, if the people find that they are [not] suitable to freemen as they are, I know no reason [that] should deter me, either in what I must answer before God or the world, from[e] endeavouring by all means to gain anything that might be of more advantage to them than the government under which they live. I do not press that you should go on with this thing, for I think that every man that would speak to it will be less able till he hath some time to consider it. I do make it my motion: That two or three days' time may be set for every man to consider, and [that] all that is to be considered is the justness of the thing—and if that be considered

then all things are—[so] that there may be nothing to deter us
from it, but that we may do that which is just to the people.

Cromwell : Truly I am very glad that this gentleman that spoke
last is here, and not sorry for the occasion that brought him
hither, because it argues we shall enjoy his company longer than
I thought we should have done——

Rainborough : If I should not be kicked out——

Cromwell : And truly then, I think, it shall not be long enough.
But truly I do not know what the meaning of that expression is,
nor what the meaning of any hateful word is here.   For we are
all here with the same integrity to the public; and perhaps we
have all of us done our parts, not affrighted with difficulties, one
as well as another, and, I hope, have all purposes henceforward—
through the grace of God, not resolving in our own strength—
to do so still.   And therefore truly I think all the consideration
is that.   Amongst us we are almost all soldiers; all considerations
[of not fearing difficulties], or words of that kind, do wonderfully
please us; all words of courage animate us to carry on our business,
to do God's business, that which is the will of God.   And I say
it again, I do not think that any man here wants courage to do that
which becomes an honest man and an Englishman to do.   But we
speak as men that desire to have the fear of God before our eyes,
and men that may not resolve in the power of a fleshly strength
to do that which we do, but to lay this as the foundation of all our
actions, to do that which is the will of God.   And if any man
have a false conceit [a]—on the one hand, deceitfulness, [pretending]
that which he doth not intend, or a persuasion, on the other hand,
[to rely on fleshly strength]—I think he will not prosper.

But to that which was moved by Colonel Rainborough, of the
objections of difficulty and danger [and] of the consequences:
they are proposed not to any other end, but [as] things fitting
consideration, not forged to deter from the consideration of the
business.[b]   In the consideration of the thing that is new to us,
and of everything that shall be new, that is of such importance as
this is, I think that he that wishes the most serious advice to be
taken of such a change as this is—so evident and clear [a change]
—whoever offers that there may be most serious consideration,
I think he does not speak impertinently.   And truly it was offered
to no other end than what I speak.   I shall say no more to that.

But to the other, concerning engagements and breaking of them:
I do not think that it was at all offered by anybody, that though an

engagement were never so unrighteous it ought to be kept. No
man offered a syllable or tittle [to that purpose].   For certainly
it's an act of duty to break an unrighteous engagement; he that
keeps it does a double sin, in that he made an unrighteous engagement, and [in] that he goes about to keep it.   But this was only
offered, that before we can consider of this [paper] (and I know
not what can be more fitly [offered]) we labour to know where we
are, and where we stand.   Perhaps we are upon engagements
that we cannot with honesty break.   But let me tell you this, that
he that speaks to you of engagements here, is as free from engagements to the King as any man in all the world.   I know it, and [a]
if it were otherwise, I believe my future actions would provoke
some to declare it.   But, I thank God, I stand upon the bottom
of my own innocence in this particular; through the grace of God
I fear not the face of any man, I do not.   I say, we are to consider
what engagements we have made; and if our engagements have
been unrighteous, why should we not make it our endeavours to
break them?   Yet if [they be] unrighteous engagements it is
not [wise to hasten] a present breach of them unless there be a
consideration of circumstances.   Circumstances may be such as
I may not now break an unrighteous engagement, or else I may
do that which I do [b] scandalously, [even] if the thing [itself] be
good.   But if that be true concerning the breaking of an unrighteous engagement, it is much more verified concerning [c]
engagements disputable [d] whether they be righteous or unrighteous.   If so, I am sure it is fit we should dispute [them], and
if, when we have disputed them, we see the goodness of God
enlightening us to see our liberties, I think we are to do what we
can to give satisfaction to men. [e]   If it were so, [it ought to appear
that] as we made an engagement in judgment and knowledge, so
we go off from it in judgment and knowledge.   But there may be
just engagements upon us, such as perhaps it will be our duty to
keep; and if so, it is fit we should consider.   And all that I said
[was] that we should consider our engagements, and there is
nothing else offered, and therefore what need [that] anybody be
angry or offended?   Perhaps we have made such engagements
as may in the matter of them not bind us; [yet] in some
circumstances they may.   Our engagements are public engagements.   They are to the kingdom, and to every one in the kingdom
that could look upon what we did publicly declare, could read or
hear it read.   They are to the Parliament.   And it is a very fitting
thing that we do seriously consider of the things.   And [f] this is
what I shall shortly offer.   That because the kingdom is in the

danger it is in, because the kingdom is in that condition it is in, and time may be ill spent in debates, and it is necessary for things to be put to an issue (if ever it was necessary in the world it is now), I should desire this may be done. That this General Council may be appointed [to meet] against a very short time, two days—Thursday—if you would against Saturday, or at furthest against Monday; that there might be a committee out of this Council appointed to debate and consider with those two gentlemen, and with any others that are not of the Army, that they shall bring, and with the Agitators of those five regiments; that so there may be a liberal and free debate had amongst us, that we may understand really, as before God, the bottom of our desires, and that we may seek God together, and see if God will give us an uniting spirit.

And give me leave to tell it you again, I am confident there sits not a man in this place that cannot so freely act with you [that], if he sees that God hath shut up his way that he cannot do any service in that way as may be good for the kingdom,[a] he will be glad to withdraw himself, and wish you all prosperity. And if this heart be in us, as is known to God that searches our hearts and trieth the reins, God will discover whether our hearts be not clear in this business. And therefore I shall move that we may have a committee amongst ourselves [to consider] of the engagements, and this committee to dispute things with others, and a short day [to be appointed] for the General Council. And I doubt not but, if in sincerity we are willing to submit to that light that God shall cast in among us, God will unite us, and make us of one heart and one mind.[b] Do the plausiblest things you can do, do that which hath the most appearance of reason in it, that tends to change: at this conjuncture of time you will find difficulties. But if God satisfy our spirits this will be a ground of confidence to every good man; and he that goes upon other grounds, he shall fall like a beast. I shall desire this: that you, or any other of the Agitators or gentlemen that can be here, will be here, that we may have free discourses amongst ourselves of things, and you will be able to satisfy each other. And really, rather than I would have this kingdom break in pieces before some company of men be united together to a settlement, I will withdraw myself from the Army to-morrow, and lay down my commission. I will perish before I hinder it.

Bedfordshire Man: [1] May it please your Honour: I was desired by some of the Agents to accompany this paper,[c] having

¹ Perhaps the Agent from Whalley's Regiment.

manifested ᵃ my approbation of it after I had heard it read several times. And they desired that it might be offered to this Council, for the concurrence of the Council if it might be.ᶠ I find that the engagements of the Army are at present the things ᵉ which is insisted to be considered. I confess my ignorance in those engagements; but I apprehend, at least I hope, that those engagements have given away nothing from the people that is the people's right. It may be they have promised the King his right, or any other persons their right, but no more. If they have promised more than their right to any person or persons, and have given away anything from the people that is their right, then I conceive they are unjust. And if they are unjust [they should be broken], though I confess for my own part I am very tender of breaking an engagement when it concerns a particular person—I think that a particular person ought rather to set down and lose than to break an engagement. But if any men ᵇ have given away anything from another whose right it was ᶠ to one or more whose right it was not, I conceive these men may [break that engagement]— at least many of them think themselves bound not only to break this engagement, but to [re]place [it with another] to give every one his due. I conceive that for the substance of the paper, it is the people's due. And for the change of the government, which is so dangerous, I apprehend that there may be many dangers in it, and truly I apprehend there may be more dangers without it. For I conceive, if you keep the government as it is and bring in the King, there may be more dangers than in changing the government. But however, because (from those things that I heard of the Agents) they conceive that this conjuncture of time may almost destroy them, they have taken upon them a liberty of acting to higher things, as they hope, for the freedom of the nation, than yet this General Council have acted to. And therefore, as their ᶜ sense is,ᵈ I must make this motion. That all those that upon a due consideration of the thing do find it to be just and honest, and do find that if they have engaged anything to the contrary of this it is unjust and giving away the people's rights, I desire that they may, and all others [may], have a free liberty of acting to anything in this nature, or any other nature, that may be for the people's good, by petitioning or otherwise; whereby the fundamentals for a well-ordered government [and] for the people's rights may be established. And I shall desire that those that conceive them[selves] bound up would desist, and satisfy themselves in that, and be no hindrances in that to hinder the people in a more perfect way than hath been [yet] endeavoured.

Captain [Lewis] Audley : [a] I suppose you have not thought fit, that there should be a dispute concerning things [b] at this time.[c] I desire that other things may be taken into consideration, delays and debates. Delays have undone us, and it must be a great expedition that must further us; and therefore I desire that there may be a committee appointed.

Lieutenant-Colonel [William] Goffe : I shall but humbly take the boldness to put you in mind of one thing which you moved enow. The motion is, that there might be a seeking of God in the things that now lie before us.

I shall humbly desire that that motion may not die. It may be that there are [d] some particular opinions among us concerning the use of ordinances and of public seeking of God. No doubt forms [e] have been rested upon too much; but yet since there are so many of us that have had so many and so large experiences of an extraordinary manifestation of God's presence when we have been in such extraordinary ways met together, I shall desire that those who are that way [moved] will take the present opportunity to do it. For certainly those things that are now presented [f] are well accepted by most of us,[g] though I am not prepared to say anything either consenting or dissenting to the paper, as not thinking it wisdom to answer a matter before I have considered. Yet [I am troubled] when I do consider how much ground there is to conceive there hath been a withdrawing of the presence of God from us that have met in this place [h]—I do not say a total withdrawing; I hope God is with us and amongst us. It hath been our trouble night and day, that God hath not been with us as formerly, as many within us, so without us, [have told us], men that were sent from God in an extraordinary manner to us. I mean [that though] the ministers may take too much upon them, yet there have been those that have preached to us in this place, [in] several places, we know very well that they spake to our hearts and consciences, and told us of our wanderings from God, and told us in the name of the Lord that God would be with us no longer than we were with him. We have in some things wandered from God, and as we have heard this from them in this place, so have we had it very frequently pressed upon our spirits [elsewhere], pressed upon us in the City and the country. I speak this to this end, that our hearts may be deeply and thoroughly affected with this matter. For if God be departed from us, he is somewhere else. If we have not the will of God in these counsels, God may be found among some other counsels.

Therefore, I say, let us show the spirit of Christians, and let us not be ashamed to declare to all the world that our counsels and our wisdom and our ways, they are not altogether such as the world hath walked in; but that we have had a dependency upon God, and that our desires are to follow God, though never so much to our disadvantage in the world if God may have the glory by it.

And, I pray, let us consider this: God does seem evidently to be throwing down the glory of all flesh. The greatest powers in the kingdom have been shaken. God hath thrown down the glory of the King and that party; he hath thrown down a party in the City. I do not say that God will throw us down—I hope better things—but he will have the glory. Let us not stand upon our glory and reputation in the world. If we have done some things through ignorance or fear or unbelief, in the day of our straits, and could not give God that glory by believing as we ought to have done,[a] I hope God hath a way for to humble us for that, and to keep us as instruments in his hand still. There are two ways that God doth take upon those that walk obstinately against him: if they be obstinate and continue obstinate, he breaks them in pieces with a rod of iron; if they be his people and wander from him, he takes that glory from them and takes it to himself. (I speak it, I hope, from a divine impression.) If we would [b] continue to be instruments in his hand, let us seriously set ourselves before the Lord, and seek to him and wait upon him for conviction of spirits. It is not enough for us to say, 'If we have offended we will leave the world, we will go and confess to the Lord what we have done amiss, but we will do no more so.' Aaron went up to Hor and died; and Moses was favoured to see the land of Canaan—*he* did not voluntarily lay himself aside. I hope our strayings from God are not so great but that a conversion and true humiliation may recover us again; and I desire that we may be serious in this, and not despise any other instruments that God will use. God will have his work done; it may be, we think we are the only instruments that God hath in his hands. I shall only add these two things. First,[c] that we [should] be wary how we let forth anything·against his people, and that which is for the whole kingdom and nation. I would move that we may not let our spirits act too freely against them till we have thoroughly weighed the matter, and considered our own ways too.[a] The second is, to draw us up to a serious consideration of the weightiness of the work that lies before us, and seriously to set ourselves to seek the Lord; and I wish it might

be considered of a way and manner that it should be con-
veniently done, and I think to-morrow will be the [best] day.

Cromwell: I know not what [hour] Lieutenant-Colonel Goffe
means for to-morrow, for the time of seeking God. I think it
will be requisite that we do it speedily, and do it the first thing,
and that we do it as unitedly as we can, as many of us as well may
meet together. I think it would be good that to-morrow morning
may be spent in prayer, and the afternoon might be the time of
our business. I do not know whether [a] these gentlemen do
assent to it, that to-morrow in the afternoon might be the time? [b]
For my part I shall lay aside all business for this business, either
to convince or be convinced as God shall please.[c]

Goffe: I think we have a great deal of business to do, and we
have been doing of it these ten weeks. I say, go about what you
will, for my part I shall not think anything can prosper unless
God be first [publicly] sought.[d] It is an ordinance that God
hath blessed to this end.[e]

Cromwell:[f] If that be approved of, that to-morrow [morning]
shall be a time of seeking the Lord, and that the afternoon shall
be the time of business, if that doth agree with your opinion and
[the] general sense, let that be first ordered.

Ireton: That which Lieutenant-Colonel Goffe offered hath
[made] a very great impression upon me; and indeed I must
acknowledge to God, [and] to [g] him, that as he hath several times
spoke in this place (and elsewhere) to this purpose, he hath never
spoke but he hath touched my heart; and that especially in the
point [of] that one thing that he hints.[h] In the time of our
straits and difficulties, I think we none of us—I fear we none of us
—I am sure I have not—walked so closely with God, and kept so
close with him, [as] to trust wholly upon him, as not to be led
too much with considerations of danger and difficulty, and from
that consideration to waive some things, and perhaps to do some
things that otherwise I should not have thought fit to have done. [i]
Every one hath a spirit within him—especially [he] who has that
communion indeed with that Spirit that is the only searcher of
hearts—that can best search out and discover to him the errors
of his own ways and of the workings of his own heart. And
though I think that public actings [are necessary in relation to]
public departings from God, [which] are the fruits of unbelief

and distrust, and not honouring God [a] by sanctifying him [b] in our ways,[c] and [though], if there be any such thing in the Army, *that* is to be looked upon with a public eye in relation to the Army; [d] [yet] they do more publicly engage God to vindicate his honour by a departing from them, that do so. But I think the main thing is for every one to wait upon God, for the errors, deceits, and weaknesses of his own heart; and I pray God to be present with us in that. But withal I would not have that seasonable and good motion that hath come from Lieutenant-Colonel Goffe to be neglected, of a public seeking of God, and seeking to God, as for other things so especially for the discovery of any public deserting of God, or dishonouring of him, or declining from him, that does lie as the fault and blemish upon the Army.[e] Therefore I wish his motion may be pursued, that the thing may be done, and for point of time as was moved by him.[e] Only this to the way. I confess I think the best [way] is this, that it may be only taken notice of as a thing by the agreement of this Council resolved on, that to-morrow in the morning, the forenoon we do set apart, we do give up from other business, for every man to give himself up that way [f] in private by himself [if he so chooses] —though *not in public*,[g] I cannot say. For the public meeting at the church, it were not amiss that it may be thus taken notice of as a time given from other employments for that purpose, and [h] every one as God shall incline their hearts,[e] some in one place, and some another, to employ themselves that way.[1]

(*Agreed for the meeting for prayer to be at Mr. Chamberlain's.*)

Cromwell [urged]: That they should not meet as two contrary parties, but as some desirous to satisfy or convince each other.

Mr. [Maximilian] Petty: For my own part, I have done as to this business what was desired by the Agents that sent me hither. As for any further meeting to-morrow, or any other time, I cannot meet upon the same ground, to meet as for their sense, [but only] to give my own reason why I do assent to it.

---

[1] From this point to the next long speech (by Cromwell, p. 23) the report is fragmentary. Some arguments, presumably springing from the Puritan distrust of outward forms, resulted in removing the projected prayer-meeting from the church to the Quartermaster-General's lodgings. Probably also there were expressions of fear lest the officers should use the gathering to insinuate their own opinions in others. Cromwell protests against the spirit of antagonism, and later seems to reply to a specific charge.

Ireton: I should be sorry that they should be so sudden to stand upon themselves.

Petty: To procure three, four, or five (more or less) to meet, for my own part I am utterly unconcerned in the business.

Buff-Coat: I have hereat this day answered the expectations which I engaged to your Honours; which was, that if we would give a meeting you should take that as a symptom, or a remarkable testimony, of our fidelity. I have discharged that trust reposed in me. I could not [absolutely] engage for them. I shall go on still in that method: I shall engage my deepest interest, for any reasonable desires, to engage them to come to this.

Cromwell: I hope we know God better than to make appearances of religious meetings covers for designs or for insinuation amongst you. I desire that God, that hath given us some sincerity, will own us according to his own goodness and that sincerity that he hath given us. I dare be confident to speak it, that [design] that hath been amongst us hitherto is to seek the guidance of God, and to recover that presence of God that seems to withdraw from us. And to accomplish that work which may be for the good of the kingdom is our end. But [a] it seems as much to us in this as anything, we are not all of a mind.[b] And for our parts we do not desire or offer you to be with us in our seeking of God further than your own satisfactions lead you, but only [that] against to-morrow in the afternoon (which will be designed for the consideration of these businesses with you) you will do what you may to have so many as you shall think fit, to see what God will direct you to say to us, that whilst we are going one way, and you another, we be not both destroyed. This requires [guidance from the] Spirit. It may be too soon to say it, [yet 't]is my present apprehension: I had rather we should devolve our strength to you than that the kingdom for our division should suffer loss. For that 's in all our hearts, to profess above anything that 's worldly, the public good of the people; and if that be in our hearts truly and nakedly, I am confident it is a principle that will stand. Perhaps God may unite us and carry us both one way. And therefore I do desire you, that against to-morrow in the afternoon, if you judge it meet, you will come to us to the Quartermaster-General's quarters—where you will find us [at prayer] if you will come timely to join with us; at your liberty, if afterwards to speak with us.[c] There you will find us.

Wildman: I desire to return a little to the business in hand, that was the occasion of these other motions. I could not but take some notice of something that did reflect upon the Agents of the five regiments, in which I could not but give a little satisfaction [as] to them; and I shall desire to prosecute a motion or two that hath been already made. I observed that it was said,[a] that these gentlemen do insist upon engagements in *The Case of the Army*,[b] and therefore it was said [c] to be contrary to the principles of the Agents, that an engagement which was unjust could [d] lawfully be broken.[e] I shall only observe this: that though an unjust engagement, when it appears unjust, may be broken; yet when two parties engage [each that] the other party may have satisfaction,[j] because they are mutually engaged each to other one party that apprehends they are broken [is justified] to complain of them; and so it may be their case, with which, I confess, I made my concurrence.

The other [thing I would mention] is a principle much spreading, and much to my trouble, and that is this: that when persons once be engaged, though the engagement appear to be unjust, yet the person must sit down and suffer under it; and that therefore, in case a Parliament, as a true Parliament, doth anything unjustly, if we be engaged to submit to the laws that they shall make, though [f] they make an unjust law, though they make an unrighteous law, yet we must swear obedience. I confess, to me this principle [g] is very dangerous, and I speak it the rather because I see it spreading abroad in the Army again—whereas it is contrary to what the Army first declared: that they stood upon such principles of right and freedom, and the Laws of Nature and Nations, whereby men were to preserve themselves though the persons to whom [h] authority belonged should fail in it; and they urged the example of the Scots, and [argued that] the general that would destroy the army, they might hold his hands; and therefore if anything tends to the destruction of a people, because the thing is absolutely unjust that [i] tends to their destruction, [they may preserve themselves by opposing it].[1] I could not but speak a word to that.

The motion that I should make upon that account is this. That whereas [it is said] there must be a meeting [to examine differences and promote union], I could not find [but] that they were desirous to give all satisfaction, and they desire nothing but the union of the Army. Thus far it is their sense. [But they

[1] Wildman is paraphrasing the *Representation of the Army* (14th June 1647); see p. 404.

apprehend] that the necessity of the kingdom is such for present
actings, that two or three days may lose the kingdom. I desire
in the sight of God to speak—I mean plainly: there may be an
agreement between the King [and the Parliament] by propositions,
with a power to hinder the making of any laws that are good, and
the tendering of any good [laws]. ᵃ   And therefore,ᵇ because none
of the people's grievances are redressed,ᶜ they do apprehend that
thus a few days may be the loss of the kingdom. I know it is
their sense: that they desire to be excused, that it might not be
thought any arrogancy in them, but they are clearly satisfied that
the way they proceed in is just, and [they] desire to be excused
if they go on in it; and yet, notwithstanding, [they] will give all
satisfaction. And whereas it is desired that engagements may be
considered, I shall desire that only the justice of the thing that is
proposed may be considered. [I would know] whether the chief
thing in the Agreement,¹ the intent of it, be not this, to secure the
rights of the people in their Parliaments, which was declared by
this Army, in the declaration of the fourteenth of June, to be
absolutely insisted on. I shall make that motion to be the thing
considered: Whether the thing be just, or the people's due ? And
then there can be no engagement to bind from it.

Ireton : Truly, sir, by what Lieutenant-Colonel Goffe moved, I
confess, I was so taken off from all [other] thoughts in this business
that I did not think of speaking anything more. But what this
gentleman hath last said hath renewed the occasion, and indeed ᵈ
if I did think ᵉ all that he hath delivered [to] be truth and innocence—nay, if I did not think that it hath venom and poison in it.
—I would not speak it.
  First, I cannot but speak something unto the two particulars
that he holds forth as dangerous things—indeed he hath clearly
yoked them together, when before I was sensible of those principles and how far they would run together; that is that principle
of not being obliged, by not regarding ᶠ what engagements men
have entered into, if ᵍ in their future apprehensions ʰ the things they
engaged to are unjust; and that principle, on the other hand, of
not submitting passively to that authority we have engaged to for
peace' sake. For he does hold forth his opinion in those two points
to clear their way; and I must crave leave on my part to declare
[that] my opinion of that¹ distinction doth lie on the other way.
  I am far from holding that if a man have engaged himself to a

  ¹ By this title, a favourite with the Levellers, Wildman designates the
proposals submitted in the name of the Agents.

thing that is not just—to a thing that is evil, that is sin if he do it —that that man is still bound to perform what he hath promised; I am far from apprehending that. But when we talk of just, it is not so much of what is sinful before God (which, depends upon many circumstances of indignation to that man and the like), but it intends of that which is just according to the foundation of justice between man and man.[a] And for my part I account that the great foundation of justice,[b] [that we should keep covenant .one with another]; without which I know nothing of [justice] [c] betwixt man and man [d]—[in] particular matters I mean, nothing in particular things that can come under human engagement one way or other.[e] There is no other foundation of right I know, of right to [any] one thing from another man, no foundation of that [particular] justice or that [particular] righteousness, but this general justice, and this general ground of righteousness, that we should keep covenant one with another.[f] Covenants freely made, freely entered into, must be kept one with another. Take away that, I do not know what ground there is of anything you can call any man's right. I would very fain know what you gentlemen, or any other, do account the right you have to anything in England—anything of estate, land or goods, that you have, what ground, what right you have to it. What right hath any man to anything if you lay not [down] that principle, that we are to keep covenant? If you will resort only to the Law of Nature, by the Law of Nature you have no more right to this land, or anything else, than I have. I have as much right to take hold of anything that is for my sustenance, [to] take hold of anything that I have a desire to for my satisfaction, as you. But here comes the foundation of all right that I understand [g] to be [h] betwixt men, as to the enjoying of one thing or not enjoying of it: we are under a contract, we are under an agreement, and that agreement is what a man has for matter of land[i] that he[j] hath received by a traduction from his ancestors, which according to the law does fall upon him to be his right. That [agreement is] that he shall enjoy, he shall have the property of, the use of, the disposing of [the land], with[k] submission to that general authority which is agreed upon amongst us for the preserving of peace, and for the supporting of this law. This I take to be [the foundation of all right] for matter of land. For matter of goods, that which does fence me from that [right] which another man may claim by the Law of Nature, of taking my goods, that which makes it mine really and civilly, is the law. That which makes it unlawful originally and radically is only this: because that man is in covenant with me to live together in peace one with another, and not to meddle with that which another is possessed of, but that each of us should enjoy, and make use of, and dispose of, that which by the course of law is in his possession, and [another] shall not by violence take it away from him. This is the foundation of all the right any man has to anything but to his own person. This is the general thing: that we must keep covenant one with another when we have contracted one with another.[a] And if any difference arise among us, it shall be thus and thus: that I shall not go with violence to prejudice another, but with submission to this way. And therefore when I hear men speak of laying aside all engagements to [consider only] that wild or vast notion of what in every man's conception is just or unjust, I am afraid and do tremble at the boundless and endless consequences of it. What [are the principles] you apply to this paper? You say,[b] 'If these things in this paper, in this engagement, be just, then'—say you —'never talk of any [prior] engagement, for if anything in that engagement be against this, your engagement was unlawful; [c] consider singly this paper, whether it be just.'[d] In what sense do you think this is just? There is a great deal of equivocation [as to] what is just and unjust.

Wildman: I suppose you take away the substance of the question. Our [e] [sense] was, that an unjust engagement is rather to be broken than kept. The Agents think that to delay is to dispose their enemy into such a capacity as he may destroy them. [f] I make a question whether any engagement can be [binding] to an unjust thing. [If] a man may promise to do that which is never so much unjust, a man may promise to break all engagements and duties. But [I say] this: we must lay aside the consideration of engagements, so as not to take in that as one ground of what is just or unjust amongst men in this case. I do apply this to the case in hand: that it might be considered whether it be unjust to bring in the King in such a way as he may be in a capacity to destroy the people. This paper may be applied to [the solution of] it.

Ireton: You come to it more particularly than that paper leads. There is a great deal of equivocation (and that I am bound to declare) in the point of justice.

Audley: Mr. Wildman says,[g] if we tarry long,[h] if we stay but three days before you satisfy one another, the King will come and say who will be hanged first.

Ireton : Sir, I was saying this: we shall much deceive ourselves, and be apt to deceive others, if we do not consider that there are ᵃ two parts of justice. There may be a thing just that is negatively [so], it is not unjust, not unlawful—that which is not unlawful, that 's just to me to do if I be free. Again, there is another sense of just when we account such a thing to be a duty—not only a thing lawful, 'we ᵇ may do it,' but it 's a duty, 'you ought to do it.' And there is a great deal of mistake if you confound these two. If I engage myself to a thing that was in this sense just, that 's a thing lawful for me to do supposing me free, then I account my engagement stands good to this. On the other hand, if I engage myself against a thing which was a duty for me to do, which I was bound to do, or if I engaged myself to a thing which was not lawful for me to do, which I was bound not to do: in this sense I do account this [engagement] unjust. If I do engage myself to what was unlawful for me to engage to, I think I am not then to make good actively this engagement. But though this be true, yet the general end and equity of engagements I must regard, and that is the preserving right betwixt men, the not doing of wrong or hurt by ᶜ men, one to another. And therefore if [in] that which I engage to, though the thing be unlawful for me to do, [yet] another man be prejudiced [by my not doing it, I may not merely renounce my engagement]. Though it be a thing which was not lawful ᵈ for me to do, yet I did freely [engage to do it], and I did [engage] upon a consideration to me; and that man did believe me, and he suffered a prejudice by believing in case I did not perform it: [then], though I ᵉ be not bound by my engagement to perform it,ᶠ yet I am [bound] to regard that justice that lies in the matter of engagement, so as to repair that man by some just way as far as I can. And he that doth not hold this, I doubt whether he hath any principle of justice, or doing right to any, at all in him. That is: [if] he that did not think it lawful hath made another man believe it to his [possible] prejudice and hurt, and another man be [actually] prejudiced and hurt by that, he that does not hold that he is in this case to repair [it] to that man, and free him from [the prejudice of] it, I conceive there is no justice in him. And therefore I wish we may take notice of this distinction when we talk of being bound to make good [our] engagements, or not.

This I think I can make good in a larger dispute by reason. If the things engaged to were lawful to be done, or lawful for me to engage to, then [I] by my engagement am ᵍ bound to [perform] it. On the other hand, if the thing were not lawful for me to engage, or [if it were] a duty for me to have done to the contrary, then I am not bound positively and actively to perform it. Nay, I am bound not to perform it, because it was unlawful [and] unjust by another engagement. But when I engage to another man, and he hath a prejudice by believing,[a] I not performing it, I am bound to repair that man as much as may be, and let the prejudice fall upon myself and not upon any other. This I desire we may take notice of, on that part, to avoid fallacy. For there is [an] extremity [b] to say, on the one hand, that if a man engage what is not just he may act against it so as to regard no relation or prejudice; [as] there's an extremity [c] for a man to say, on the other hand, that whatsoever you engage, though it be never so unjust, you are to stand to it.

One word more to the other part which Mr. Wildman doth hold out as a dangerous principle acting amongst us, that we must be bound to active obedience to any power acting amongst men—

Wildman [interrupting]: You repeat not the principle right— 'To think that we are bound so absolutely to personal obedience to any magistrates or personal authority, that if they work to our destruction we may not oppose them.'

[*Ireton*:] That we may not deceive ourselves again [by arguments] that are fallacious in that kind, I am a little affected to speak in this, because I see that, [in] those things the Army hath declared, the abuse and misapplication of them hath led many men into a great and dangerous error and destructive to all human society. Because the Army hath declared, in those cases where the foundation of all that right and liberty of the people is (if they have any),[d] that in these cases [e] they will insist upon that right, and that they will not suffer that original and fundamental right to be taken away, and because the Army, when there hath been a command of that supreme authority, the Parliament, have not obeyed it, but stood upon it to have this fundamental right settled first, and [have] required a rectification of the supreme authority of the kingdom—therefore, for a man to infer [that] upon *any* particular [issue] you may dispute that authority by what is commanded, whether [f] [it] is just or unjust, [this would be the end of all government]. If in your apprehension [it is unjust, you are] not to obey (and so far it is well); and if it tend to your loss, [it is no doubt unjust, and you are] to oppose it!

Wildman [interrupting]: If it tend to my destruction—*that* was the word I spoke.

Ireton : Let us take heed that we do not maintain this principle [till *it*] leads to destruction. If the case were so visible as those cases the Army speaks of, of a general's turning the cannon against the army, the bulk and body of the army, or [of] a pilot that sees a rock [and] does by the advantage of the stern [1] put the ship upon 't; if you could propose cases as evident as these are, there is no man but would agree with you.[2] But when men will first put in those terms of destruction, they will imagine anything a destruction if there could be anything better [for them]; and so it is very easy and demonstrable that things are counted so abhorred and destructive, when [a] at the utmost [b] a man should make it out by reason, that men would be in a better condition if it be not done, than if it be done. And though I cannot but subscribe to [it], that in such a visible way I may hold the hands of those that are in authority as I may the hands of a madman; yet [c] that no man shall think himself [bound] to acquiesce particularly, and to suffer for quietness' sake, rather than to make a disturbance (or to raise a power, if he can, to make a disturbance) in the state —I do apprehend and appeal to all men whether there be not more folly or destructiveness in the spring of that principle than there can be in that other principle of holding passive obedience. Now whatsoever we have declared in the Army [declarations], it is no more but this. The Parliament hath commanded us [to do] this; we have said, no. First we have insisted upon [the] fundamental rights of the people. We have said, we desire [first] to have the constitution of the supreme authority of this kingdom reduced to that constitution which is due to the people of this kingdom, and, reducing the authority to this, we will submit to it, we will acquiesce, we will cast our share into this common bottom; and if it go ill with us at one time, it will go well at another.[3] The reducing of the supreme authority to that constitution, by successive [d] election, as near as may be,[e] we have insisted upon as an essential right of the kingdom; and no man can accuse the Army of disobedience, or holding forth a principle of disobedience, upon any other ground.

Cromwell : Let me speak a word to this business. We are now upon that business which we spake of consulting with God

---

[1] i.e., by his position there, to command and steer the ship.

[2] By citing Ireton's own arguments from the *Representation of the Army*, Wildman has forced him to agree to the *general* validity of what he says.

[3] Cf. pp. 407-8.

about,[a] and therefore for us to dispute the merit of those things, I judge it altogether unseasonable unless you will make it the subject of debate before you consider it among yourselves. The business of the *Engagement* lies upon us. They [claim that they] are free in a double respect: they made none; and if they did, then the way out is now, and [it is a way] which all the members of the Army, except they be sensible of it, [may take], and, at one jump, jump out of all [engagements]. And it *is* a very great jump, I will assure you. As we profess we intend to seek the Lord in the thing, the less we speak in it [now] the better, and the more we cast ourselves upon God the better.

I shall only speak two things to Mr. Wildman in order to our meeting. Methought he said, if there be delay he fears this business will be determined, the propositions will be sent from the Parliament, and the Parliament and King agree, and so those gentlemen that were in that mind to go on in their way, will be cut off in point of time to their own disadvantage. And the other thing he said was that these gentlemen who have chosen Mr. Wildman, and that other gentleman,[1] to be their mouth at this meeting to deliver their minds, they are, upon the matter, engaged by [b] what they have resolved upon, and they come as engaged men upon their own resolution. If that be so, I think there neither needs consideration of the former [nor the latter]. For you will not be anticipated. If that be so, you [can] work accordingly. And though you meet us, yet, having that resolution in your way, you cannot be prevented by any proposition, or any such thing; [even] though we should have come hither [with propositions] and we should [not] meet to-morrow as a company of men that really would be guided by God.

[But] if any come to us to-morrow only to instruct us and teach us,[c] I refer to every sober-spirited man to think of [d] and determine how far that will consist with the liberty of a free deliberation [e] or an end of satisfaction. I think it is such a pre-engagement that there is no need of talk of the thing. And I see then, if that be so, things are in such an irrevocable way—I will not call it desperate—as there is no hope of accommodation or union, except we receive the counsels—I will not call it the commands—of them that come to us. I desire that we may rightly understand this thing. If this be so, I do not understand what the end of the meeting will be. If this be not so, we [f] will [not] draw any men [g] from their engagements further than the light of God shall draw them from their engagements; and I

[1] Maximilian Petty.

think, according to your own principle, if you be upon any engagement you are liable to be convinced—unless you be infallible. If we may come to an honest and single debate, how we may all agree in one common way for public good; if we [may] meet so, we shall meet with a great deal the more comfort, and hopes of a good and happy issue, and understanding of the business. But if otherwise, I despair of the meeting; or at least I would have the meeting to be of another notion, a meeting that did represent the Agitators of five regiments to give rules to the Council of War. If it signify this, for my own part I shall be glad to submit to it under this notion. If it be a free debate what may be fit for us all to do, with clearness and openness before the Lord, and in that sincerity, let us understand [it], that we may come and meet so. Otherwise, I do verily believe, we shall meet with prejudice, and we shall meet to prejudice—really to the prejudice of the kingdom, and of the whole Army—if we be thus [a] absolutely resolved upon our way and engaged beforehand. The kingdom will see it is such a real actual division as admits of no reconciliation, and all those that are enemies to us, and friends to our enemies, will have the clearer advantage upon us to put us into inconveniency. And I desire if there be any fear of God among us, I desire that we may declare ourselves freely, that we do meet upon these terms.

Rainborough : I wish that the motion of Lieutenant-Colonel Goffe might have taken effect, not only to the time and place for meeting, [but without further preliminary] as he desired. But, sir, since it is gone thus far, and since I hear much of fallacy talked of, I fear it as much on the one side as the other.[h] It is made a [b] wonder of, that some gentlemen without should have principles [c] to break engagements, yet [no wonder of], that some gentlemen within should so much insist upon engagements. I do not consider myself as jumping, but yet I hope when I leap I shall take so much of God with me, and so much of just and right with me, as I shall jump sure. But I am more unsatisfied against [another of] those things that have been said, and that is as to another engagement. For all that hath been said hath been [as to engagements] between party and party: if two men should make an agreement and the like, and there were no living one with [d] another if those engagements were not made [good]. Yet I think under favour that some engagements may be broke. No man [e] takes a wife but there is an engagement,[f] and I think that a man ought to keep it; [g] yet if another man that had married her before claims her, he ought to let him have her and so break the engagement. But ª whereas it is told ᵇ [us that] this engagement is of another nature, that the party to whom we make the engagement relied upon [it], and becomes thereby prejudiced, [and so] we ought to take it rather upon ourselves than to leave it upon them—*this* may serve in a particular case: if any men ᶜ here will suffer they may. But if we will make ourselves a third party, and engage between King and Parliament, [it is not a particular case], and I am of that gentleman's mind that spoke: the King's party would have been about our ears if we had not made some concessions ᵈ as concerning them.ᵉ Here is the consideration now: do we not engage for the Parliament and for the liberties of the people of England, and do we not engage against ᶠ the King's party? ᵍ We have got the better of them in the field, but they shall be masters of our houses. Never were ʰ engagements broken more than [as] we do [break them]. We did take up arms ¹ with all that took part with the Parliament, and we engaged with them; [but now we are to be engaged to bring the King in]. For my part, it may be thought that I am against the King; I am against him or any power that would destroy God's people, and I will never be destroyed till I cannot help myself. Is it ʲ not an argument, if a pilot run his ship upon a rock, or [if] a general mount his cannon against his army, he is to be resisted? I think ᵏ that this [is] as clear[ly] the very case as anything in the world. For clearly the King and his party could not have come in upon those terms that he is [to] come in [on], if this very Army did not engage for him; and I verily think that the House had not made another address, if it had not been said that it was the desire of the Army and the Army were engaged to it.¹ Therefore, I say, I hope men will have charitable opinions of other men. For my part, I think I shall never do anything against conscience, and I shall have those hopes of others. That which is dear unto me is my freedom. It is that I would enjoy, and I will enjoy if I can. For my own part, I hope there is no such distance betwixt these gentlemen [and you] as is imagined, but they will hear reason that may convince them out of it. I do verily believe they are so far from a disunion that they will be advised by this Council in general, or by any honest man of this Council in particular. I have not the same apprehensions that two or three days will undo us, but I think a very little delay will undo us; and therefore I should only desire—it may be because I have spoken some other may answer me—the less we speak, it may be the better. And as this Agitator, whom I never saw before, says ¹ that he will use his interest, I hope that God will do something in that for our next meeting to-morrow, that when we do meet we shall have a very happy union.

Buff-Coat [said]: That he could break engagements in case they [were] proved unjust, and that it might [so] appear [a] to his conscience.[b] Whatsoever hopes or obligations I should be bound unto, if afterwards God should reveal himself, I would break it speedily, if it were an hundred a day; and in that sense we delivered our sense.

Wildman [*amending*]: Provided that what is done tends to destruction, either [to] self-destruction or to [the destruction of] my neighbour especially. Unlawful engagements [are] engagements against duty, and an engagement to any person to bring him in [in] such a way as he may be enabled to engage [us to his further designs], it is that which may tend to destruction.

Cromwell: I think [c] you were understood to put it upon an issue where there is clearly a case of destruction, public destruction and ruin. And I think this will bring it into consideration whether or no our engagements have really in them that that hath public destruction and ruin necessarily following; or whether or no we may not give too much way to our own doubts and fears. And whether it be lawful to break a covenant upon our own doubts and fears, will be the issue. And I think [it best] if we agree to defer the debate, [and] to nominate a committee.

Rainborough: One word. I am of another opinion. Not that the engagements of the Army are looked upon as destructive, but the not-performance of the engagements of the Army is that which is destructive.

Ireton: I think Mr. Wildman's conclusion is, that they are destructive because they are destructive to our neighbours.

Wildman: That if such an engagement were, it does not bind.

Ireton: Then if [d] such a meeting [e] were [for] a compliance, or [at least] not for a law [to us] but for [free debate, it might tend to mutual] satisfaction. But [f] whereas the only ground [on] which the thing seems to me to be represented [is] that these gentlemen think that their own Agreement is so clear, so infallibly just and right, that whosoever goes about to take it from them, or whoever does not agree to it, is [about] a thing unlawful,[a] *I* do think those gentlemen have not so much ground of confidence to each part of that Agreement as it lies there.[b] But something may be seen in that if you come—in the debating [c] of it. And therefore in that relation, and not [merely to enforce] your own principles, [I desire] that you would admit of so much conference as to question it.

Mr. [Nicholas] Lockyer: I have gathered from two men's mouths, that destruction is something near, and the cause of the destruction, as they understand, is the going of the proposals to the King. I think it were very necessary that, if it be true as is supposed, the proposals may be brought hither when they do go, that we may see what they are.

Cromwell: The question is whether the propositions will save us, or [whether they will] not destroy us. This discourse concludes nothing.

Captain [John] Merriman: One party fears that the King will rise by the proposals, another that he will lose. [But] I think that most men's eyes are open to see that they are like to prove a broken reed, and that your chariot wheels do move heavily, and that this Agreement,[d] which is the ground of most of your discourse,[e] [in] the fundamental business of it, is the desire of most of this Council.[f] You both desire a succession of Parliaments, to have this Parliament that it might not be perpetuated. And I think [g] that when [h] this Oedipus riddle is un-opened, and this Gordian knot untied, and the enemies of the same [unmasked, it will be found that the dictates of] [i] the Spirit of God are the same in both, and the principles of both are the same. You have both promised to free the people, which you may do by taking off tithes and other Antichristian yokes [from] upon them, and [to] give content [j] to the soldiers. And I hope that when you meet together it will be for good, and not for evil.

Buff-Coat: Whereas this gentleman that we have requested to come along with us hath declared some part of [k] our resolutions with them,[l] and we are resolved that we will have the peace of the kingdom if we can;[l] yet, notwithstanding, if a further [m] [guidance] for the manner of procuring of it is what God shall direct unto us, I would not have you judge that we will deny that

light, till that you know what we will do. No man can judge so
of any man. A man cannot be called to be [of] a peremptory will,
or self-willed, and [be judged to] come resolved *nolens volens*,
[till you know what he will do]. We desire that better thoughts
may be of us.

Lieutenant [Edmund] Chillenden: I hope that these gentlemen
of the five regiments, their ends are good, and [I] hope their
hearts do tend to peace; and I shall move this: that they would
willingly come to-morrow, and join with us in our counsels
together. And also I shall humbly move: that, after we have
sought God in the business,[a] God will make it out to us, to see
wherein we have failed, and that their being with us [will conduce
to that] and [to] our vigorous proceeding in it, and [that] these
gentlemen of the five regiments, they will manifest this [same
spirit] by a sweet compliance in communicating counsels.

Cromwell: That which this gentleman [1] hath moved I like
exceeding well; he hath fully declared himself concerning the
freedom of their spirit as to principles. In general they aim at
peace and safety, and really I am persuaded in my conscience it is
their aim [to act] as may be most for the good of the people; for
really if that be not the supreme good to us under God (the good
of the people), our principles fall. Now if that be in your spirits
and our spirits, it remains only that God show us the way, and
lead us [in] the way; which I hope he will. And give me leave
[to add] that there may be some prejudices upon some of your
spirits, and [upon] such men that do affect your way, that they
may have some jealousies and apprehensions that we are wedded
and glued to forms of government; so that, whatsoever we may
pretend, it is in vain for [you] to speak to us, or to hope for any
agreement from us to you. And I believe some [entertain] such
apprehensions as [that we are engaged to secure] some part of the
legislative power of the kingdom where it may rest besides in the
Commons of the kingdom. You will find that we are [b] far from
being [so] particularly engaged to anything to the prejudice of
this—further than the notorious engagement[s] that the world
takes notice of—that we should not concur with you that the
foundation and supremacy is in the people, radically in them, and
to be set down by them in their representations. And if we do
so [concur, we may also concur] how we may run to that end that
we all aim at, or that that does remain [within our power], and
therefore let us only name the committee.

[1] i.e., Everard (Buff-Coat).

Goffe: You were pleased to say that [there was] something that gave you another occasion of the meeting (if it were only designed to lie upon you, [I would not protest]): that which should be offered by these gentlemen. I hope that you did not conceive that any such ground did lie in my breast.[1] But [a] I would speak this word to the quickening of us to a good hope: [b] I am verily persuaded if God carry us out to meet sincerely, as with free spirits to open ourselves before the Lord, we may [not] be found going on according to our will. I desire such prejudices may be laid aside.

Allen: A meeting is intended to-morrow; but that we may fully end, I would humbly offer to you: whether these gentlemen have a power to debate; and if they have not, that they may have recourse to them that sent them, to see what [powers] they will give [them], that we may offer our reasons and judgment upon the thing, and [may] act upon that principle upon which we agree.[c] If we unite and agree to it, it will put on other things. [When we have] formally [d] made an agreement, we must be serious in it, and to that end [it is desired] that we may have a full debate in it. Otherwise it will be useless, and endless, our meeting.

Cromwell: That gentleman says he will do what he can to draw all or the most of them hither to be heard to-morrow; and I desire Mr. Wildman, that if they have any friends that are of a loving spirit, that would contribute to this business of a right understanding, [they would come with him]. And I say no more but this, I pray God judge between you and us when we do meet, whether we come with engaged spirits to uphold our own resolutions and opinions, or whether we shall lay down ourselves to be ruled [by God] and that which he shall communicate.

Rainborough: He did tell you he would improve his interest, which is as full satisfaction to what Mr. Allen says, as could be. If they shall come [though] not [with power] to do, yet [e] I hope they will come with [f] full power [g] to debate. I think there needs no more.[2]

[1] Goffe's purpose is to clear himself of the suspicion of having suggested the prayer-meeting with any ulterior object.

[2] The report of the meeting concludes with the names of the committee appointed (Cromwell, Ireton, Hammond, Deane; Colonels Rainborough, Rich, Scroope, Tomlinson, Overton, Okey, Tichborne, Sir Hardress Waller; Messrs. Sexby, Allen, Lockyer, Clarke, Stenson, Underwood), and with its terms of reference: 'To confer with the Agitators of the five

Putney, 29th October 1647

At the meeting of the officers for calling upon God, according to the appointment of the General Council, after some discourse of Commissary [Nicholas] Cowling, Major White, and others—

Captain [John] Clarke [said]: We have been here, as we say, seeking of God, though truly he is not far from every one of us; and we have said in the [a] presence of God (as out of his presence we cannot go) that we have none in heaven in comparison of him, nor none we have even in earth in comparison of him. I wish our hearts do [b] not give us the lie, for truly had that been a truth [c] —I mean a truth in our carriages—we should not have been so lost this day. Had we given ear to the inspiring word of Christ, and had [we] not given ourselves to the false prophet within us, certainly God would have kindled that light within us, and [we] should have gone [on] and submitted to his will, and should not have been troubled or harassed, as we are, with troubles and amazements, but must have gone with God as he hath allotted to us. The cause of every evil sought after, what is the reason that we find the light and glory of God eclipsed from our eyes this day? Truly we may find this silence within us, and let us but search our own spirits with patience, and look by the light [d] of God within us, and we shall find that we have submitted the Spirit of God unto the candle of reason, whereas reason should have been subservient unto the Spirit of God. We are troubled when our own reasons tell us that this is the way, and we are careless to seek the way, or that true light, Christ in us, which is the way. We are apt to say, all of us, that if we seek that first (the latter first) the light [e] will not be wanting. But truly, we have sought the first last, and therefore the first is wanting. And before this light can take place again that darkness must be removed—that candle of reason, and [g] first within us our lust, which doth seduce and entice us to wander from God, must be eaten out of us by the Spirit of God, and when there is no place for lust, there is place enough for the Spirit of God. If we shall with resolution [f] and humility of spirit not say, but do, as the children

regiments, and such gentlemen as shall come with them, about the "Engagement" now brought in, and their own declarations and engagements.' The Agitators, here mentioned, are the newly appointed Agents of the five regiments; the 'Engagement' is the set of proposals (otherwise referred to as the Agreement) handed in by the Agents. Here (and elsewhere) 'Engagement' is probably Clarke's mistake.

of Israel used to do many times when they were in distress—
many times they cried unto the Lord; if we shall do as we profess
before God this day, that is, lay down our reason, lay down our
goods, lay down all we have at the feet of God, and let God work
his will in us that we may be buried with God in our spirits; I
doubt not but the appearances of God will be more glorious, and
I doubt not but there will be that contentedness in spirit. We
should desire no way, but wait which way God will lead us. I
say, we should choose no way, but if the Spirit of God lead us, we
should be ready to submit to the will of God.[a] And therefore I
desire that, since this is in order to another meeting in the afternoon, we may lay down all at the feet of God, not following our
own reasons, but [b] submitting unto that light which is lighted [c] in
us by his Spirit.

(After this Captain Carter prayed.)

Adjutant-General [Richard] Deane: Motion for a meeting at
this place, the Quartermaster-General's quarters, to meet Monday,
the council day, from 8 till 11, to seek God, *&c.*

Goffe: That which I must now desire to express to you was
partly occasioned by the thoughts that I had the last night, as
being indeed kept awake with them a good while; and, hearing
something that did concur with it from one that spake since we
came together, I feel some weight upon my spirit to express it
to you. That which was spoken enow [was] concerning the
conjunction that is between Antichrist, or that mystery of iniquity
in the world carried on by men that call themselves the church,
that [d] certainly it is with the conjunction of men in places of power
or authority in the world, with kings and great men. And truly
my thoughts were much upon it this night, and it appears to me
very clearly from that which God hath set down in his word in
the Book of the Revelations—which is that word that we are bid
and commanded to study and to look into, being the word which
God sent by his angel to John, to declare as things shortly to be
done. Now certainly this work of Antichrist hath been a work
of great standing, and, as it was well observed, it hath been mixed
with the church, and men that call themselves the church, the
clergy, mixed with men of authority.[e] It is said in the Revelation,
that the kings of the earth should give up their power unto the
Beast, and the kings of the earth have given up their power to the
Pope. But some places that have seemed to deny the Pope's
supremacy, yet they have taken upon them that which hath been

equivalent to that which the Pope himself holds forth. Truly I
could bring it to this present kingdom wherein we are. 'Tis true
the kings have been instruments to cast off the Pope's supremacy,
but we may see if they have not put themselves into the same
state. We may see it in that title which the King hath, 'Defender
of the Faith,' but more especially in that canonical prayer which
the clergy used, 'In all causes, and over all persons, as well ecclesiastical as civil, [supreme].' Certainly, this is a mystery of
iniquity. Now Jesus Christ his work in the last days is to destroy
this mystery of iniquity; and because it is so interwoven and
entwisted in the interest of states, certainly in that overthrow of
the mystery of iniquity by Jesus Christ, there must be great
alterations of states. Now the word doth hold out in the Revelation, that in this work of Jesus Christ he shall have a company of
Saints to follow him, such as are chosen and called and faithful.
Now it is a scruple among the Saints, how far they should use the
sword; yet God hath made use of them in that work. Many of
them have been employed these five or six years. Yet whatsoevei
God shall employ us in, I could wish this were laid to heart by us:
whereas [a] we would be called the chosen and faithful that will
follow Christ wheresoever he goes, let us tremble at the thought [b]
that we should be standing in a direct opposition against Jesus
Christ in the work that he is about. Let us not be twisted amongst
such kind of compartings where there shall be a mystery of iniquity [c]
set up by outward power, lest [d] we should be the instruments of
giving any life or strength to that power. And I wish [we may
lay this to heart]—and I believe it may somewhat tend to the work
by the way—because we are to hold out the will of God for the
time to come, and to be humbled for what we have done against
it. Let us inquire whether some of the actions that we have
done of late, some of the things that we have propounded of late,
do not cross the work of God in these particulars; because in our
proposing things we do endeavour to set up that power which
God would not set up again—it hath been hinted already—I mean
in our compliance with that party which God hath engaged us to
destroy. We intended nothing but civility, but I wish they were
not in some measure compliances; and, if I mistake not, there are
ways which God hath laid open to us, whereby we may lay aside
that compliance.

But this is not all that I would speak, because God hath called
forth my spirit to unity. What we do according to the will of
God will not tend to division. This I speak concerning compliance; and [since] this may be thought to reflect upon some

particular persons more than other some, so on the other hand I
desire to speak something that may concern some persons that
may stand, or at least may seem to stand, in direct opposition to
us. And truly I wish we may be very wary what we do; and let
us take heed of rejecting any of the Saints of God before God
rejects them. If God be pleased to show any of his servants that
he hath made use of [them] as great instruments in his hand, [and
to show them], as [also] those that God hath blessed in them, that
God hath blessed them, and [that] this hath been the greatest
instrument of the ruin of sin and corruption in this Army, let us
be wary and consider what we have to do in that kind. And I
spake this the rather because I was sensible of some personal
reflections that did not argue the workings of God [so much] as
the workings of passions in us. Now the work of the Spirit is,
that we do pull down all works [that are not] of the Spirit whatsoever; and therefore I desire that, as in the presence of God, we
may take heed of all things which may tend to disunion, and that
we may not despise those who may have some things in their
hands to contribute for the work of God.

And there is another thing. If we have lost the opportunity of
appearing against [God's] enemies, let us take heed, when we be
sensible of God's displeasure, that we do not run before he bids
us go a second time. There is a place which is very remarkable,
Numbers 14, where the spies were sent to the land of Canaan;
and when they came back the hearts of the people were discouraged. God was displeased at this, and he discovered it in
some such way as he did this day. But upon a sudden there was
a party that would go up and fight against the Amalekites, and at
such a time when God would not have them go up. 'Though
you did sin against the Lord in not going at first,' says Moses,
'yet go not now up, for the Lord is not among you, that ye be not
smitten before your enemies.' Yet they did go up unto the hill-
top, and were discomfited. I think we have sinned in that we
did not show our courage and faithfulness to God. Let us not
now in a kind of heat run up and say, 'We will go now'; because
it may be there is a better opportunity that God will give us.
And that we may a little help us by our own experiences, let us
remember how God hath dealt with this Army in our late proceedings. There was some heaviness in our proceedings before
the City, as was thought by some; and it was said by many, 'Go
up, go up quickly, and do our work.' But let us remember that
God found a better season for us than if we had gone at first.
Let us consider whether this be the best juncture of time for us

[to press on the work of God. But let us, as well, be careful not] to declare [against], and to throw off, some of our friends when that they would have it discovered whether [a] God goes along with us. Let this be considered, that so we may be humbled, on the one hand, and break off all unlawful compliance with the enemies of God, so, on the other hand, we may stay, and take the company one of another, or rather the presence of God, [along with us]. And so for the work of the day, I wish there may be a day of union amongst us; for it may be it is the will of God that we should wait upon him therein, to see what will be the issue of a business that is now transacted; and if we can trust God in this strait we shall see him straight before us, if we can be of one mind. I wish this may be considered, and if there be anything of God in it, it may be received.

Mr. [Robert] Everard: This honourable Council hath given me great encouragement. Though I have many impediments in my speech, yet I thank you that you will hear me speak. I engaged myself yesterday to bring the men to have a debate,[1] and for that purpose I have prosecuted these my promises, and I have been with them—as many as I can find; but the most of them are dispersed, so that I lost that opportunity which I would have enjoyed. But, nevertheless, I hope you will take it kindly, that those that were there are come hither, and those two friends that were with me yesterday.[b] Our ends are that we desire, yet once more, a compliance in those things that we propounded to you, but if it shall please God to open our eyes that we can see it, we shall comply with you. For our desires are nothing but (according to our first declaration) to follow our work, to deliver the kingdom from that burden that lies upon us. For my part I am but a poor man, and unacquainted with the affairs of the kingdom; yet this message God hath sent me to you, that there is great expectation of sudden destruction—and I would be loath to fill up that with words. We desire your joint consent to seek out some speedy way for the relief of the kingdom.

Cromwell: I think it would not be amiss that those gentlemen that are come would draw nigher.

I must offer this to your consideration: whether or no we, having set apart this morning to seek God, and to get such a preparedness of heart and spirit as might receive that that God was minded to have imparted to us, and this having taken up all

[1] This identifies Everard as the 'Buff-Coat' of the previous debate.

our time all this day, and it having been so late this last night as indeed it was when we brake up, and we having appointed a committee to meet together to consider of that paper, and this committee having had no time or opportunity that I know of, not so much as a meeting; I make some scruple or doubt whether or no it is not better [to adjourn the debate. I know] that danger is imagined [near at hand], and indeed I think it is; but be the danger what it will, our agreement in the business is much more [pressing] than the pressing of any danger, so by that we do not delay too [long].[a] That which I have to offer [is]: whether or no we are [as] fit to take up such a consideration of these papers now as we might be to-morrow; and perhaps if these gentlemen, which are but few, and that committee should meet together, and spend their time together an hour or two the remainder of this afternoon, and all this company might meet about nine or ten o'clock at furthest,[a] they [might] understand one another so well that [c] we might be prepared for the general meeting, to have a more exact and particular consideration of things than [we can have] by a general loose debate of things which our committee, or at least many [d] of us, have [not] had any, or at least not many, thoughts about.

Rainborough: Sir: I am sorry that the ill disposition of my body caused me to go to London last night, and [e] [hindered me] from coming so soon this morning as to be with you in the duty you were about. But I hope that which hath been said at this time (which I hope is a truth and sent from God) will so work upon me that I shall endeavour at least to carry myself so that I may use all that interest I have, to a right and quick understanding between us. And truly, sir, to that present motion that hath been made, I confess I have nothing against it, but only the danger that lies upon us; which truly—if we may have leave to differ one from another—may in a moment overcome [us]. I hope we shall all take [to heart] one word that was spoken to us by Lieutenant-Colonel Goffe, and I think that nothing will conduce so much [to union as] that we may have no personal reflections.[a] I think it would have been well if the committee had met, but since all this company—or the greatest part of them [f]—have been here [and] have joined in that duty which was on the former part of the morning, I think there is not much inconveniency that they may spend the other part of the day with us. And if we were satisfied ourselves upon debate, and yet [g] there should be one party, or one sort of men, that are of a judgment [at] present contrary, or others that should come over to us, it would cost some time hereafter to know the reasons of their [contrary judgment or of their] coming over. And therefore I think it an advantage that it should be as public [as possible], and as many as may, be present at it.[a] The debating this thus publicly may be an advantage unto us; and [b] after the multitude of people that are here [c] have been spoken to, if we find that inconvenient, I do not doubt but the committee, when this company breaks up, may have two hours' time together. And therefore I should desire that, since the gentlemen and you are met together to such an end and purpose,[c] you will follow to that end.

Everard: [c] If is not [fit], as I conceive, to dispute anything touching particular [f] [persons], for all, as I conceive, do seek the kingdom's good. Much business will be [g] if we stand disputing the work! I desire this honourable Council — [if it] will pardon me—to make out some speedy way for the easing of us.[h] Let us go about the work;[i] no question but we shall go together. I beseech you that you will consider upon that. I believe we shall jump all in one with it, if we do not fall upon some extraordinary ways between. Some laws with us that will prick us to the heart, we must wink at them; [but] let us now [seek to reform such of them as we may], not that I desire that we should seek to ruinate any wholesome laws, but [only] such as will not stand with the wholesome peace of the kingdom.

Audley: I shall desire to second that gentleman's motion.[c] While we debate we do nothing. I am confident that whilst you are doing you will all agree together, for it is idleness that hath begot this rust and this gangrene amongst us.

Cromwell: I think it is true. Let us be doing, but let us be united in our doing. If there remain nothing else [needful] but present action,[k] [let us be doing]—I mean, doing in that kind, doing in that sort. I think we need not be in council here [if] such kind of action, action of that nature, [will serve].[l] But if we do not rightly and clearly understand one another before we come to act, if we do not lay a foundation of action before we do act, I doubt whether we shall act unanimously or no. And seriously, as before the Lord, I knew no such end of our speech the last night, and [our] appointing another meeting, but in order to a more perfect understanding of one another, what we should do, and that we might be agreed upon some principles of action. And truly if I remember rightly, [c] upon the delivery of the paper that was yesterday, this was offered, that the things [that] are now upon us [a] are things of difficulty, the things are things that do deserve therefore consideration, because there might be great weight in the consequences; and it was then offered, and I hope is still so in all our hearts, that we are not troubled with the consideration of the difficulty, nor with the consideration of anything but this: that if we do difficult things, we may see that the things we do, have the will of God in them, that they are not only plausible and good things, but seasonable and honest things, fit for us to do. And therefore it was desired that we might consider, [before] we could come to these papers,[1] in what condition we stood in respect of former engagements,[b] however some may be satisfied [c] that there lie none upon us, or none but such as it's duty to break, it's sin to keep. Therefore that was yesterday premised, [that] there may be a consideration had of them—and I may speak it as in the presence of God, that I know nothing of any engagements, but I would see liberty in any man as I would be free from bondage to anything that should hinder me from doing my duty—and therefore that was first in consideration. If our obligation be nothing, or if it be weak, I hope [d] we shall [e] receive satisfaction why it should be laid aside, [and be convinced] that the things that we speak of are not obliged. And therefore, if it please you, I think it will be good for us to frame our discourse to what we were, where we are, what we are bound to, what we are free to; and then I make no question but that this may conclude what is between [us and] these gentlemen, in one afternoon. I do not speak this to make obligations more than what they were before, but as before the Lord. You see what they are ([*producing the printed volume of Army Declarations*[1]]); and when we look upon them we shall see whether [f] we have been in a wrong way, and I hope it will call upon us for the more double diligence.[g]

Rainborough : I shall desire a word or two before that. I did exceedingly mistake myself the last night [h] upon what we say now was [then] determined. I looked upon the committee as a committee to look over this paper, to see whether it were a paper that did hold forth justice and righteousness, whether it were a paper that honest men could close with. But truly I am of opinion that if we should spend ten days' time in going over that book, and debate what engagements we have broke, or whether we have broke any or no, or whether we have kept our engagements, it would not come to the business; neither would it prevent

[1] *A Declaration of the Engagements, Remonstrances, Representations . . . of the Army*, London, 1647 [Oct. 2].

that evil that I think will overtake us (unless God in abundant
manner prevent).   Let us go the quickest way to work [and not
fear lest we start] before we fall into the right way.   And truly,
sir, I have thought that the wounds of the kingdom, and the
difficulties that we are fallen into, and our [need of] cure, is
become so great that we would be willing, all of us, to heal the
sore, and [not] to skin it over but leave it unwholesome and corrupt
at the bottom.   Therefore for my part I do [thus] conclude in
my spirit—and I could give you reasons for it, which this day I
have from very good hands, but ª which I think [it] is not ᵇ
prudent to declare so publicly as this is; for my own part I [did]
say this yesterday upon another occasion: I will not say positively
that we are to take the course prescribed in that paper at present,
but if we do not set upon the work [of settlement presently we
are undone].   Since in order to that there is a thing called an
Agreement which the people [must] have subscribed, and being
that is ready to our hands, I desire that you would read it and
debate it, whether it be a way to deliver us yet or no; and if it be,
[that you would accept it], and if not, that you would think of
some other way.

Cromwell: I shall but offer this to you.   Truly I hope that we
may speak our hearts freely here; and I hope that there is not
such an evil amongst us as that we could or would exercise our
wits, or our cunning, to veil over any doubleness of heart that
may possibly be in us.   I hope, having been in such a presence
as we have been [in] this day, we do not admit ᶜ such a thought
as this into our hearts.   And therefore if the speaking of that
we did speak before—and to which I shall speak again, with
submission to all that hear me; if the declining to consider this
paper may have with any man a working ᵈ upon his spirit through
any jealousy that it aims at delay; truly I can speak it as before
the Lord, it is not at all in my heart, but sincerely this is the
ground of it.   I know this paper doth contain many good things
in it, but this is the only thing that doth stick with me, the desiring
to know my freedom to this thing.   Though this [paper] doth
suggest that that may be the bottom of all our evils—and I will
not say against it because I do not think against it—though this
doth suggest the bottom of all our evils, yet for all to see ourselves
free to this, all of us, [so] as we may unanimously join upon this,
either to agree to this, or to add more to it, [or] to alter [it] as we
shall agree, [that is alone needful; but, lacking it,] this impedi-
ment lies in our way, [even] if every man be satisfied with it but

myself. [I repeat] that this is the first thing that is to be considered, that we should consider in what condition we stand to our former obligations, that if we be clear we may go off clear, if not we may not go on. If I be not come off [clear] with what obligations are made, if I be not free to act to whatsoever you shall agree upon, I think this is my duty: that I should not in the least study either to retard your work or hinder it, or to act against it, but wish you as much success as if I were free to act with you. I desire we may view over our obligations and engagements, that so we may be free [to act together] upon honest and clear grounds, if this be——

Rainborough (offering to speak): ª My desire ᵇ——

Cromwell: I have but one word to prevent you in, and that is for imminent danger. It may be possibly so [imminent] that [it] may not admit of an hour's debate, nor nothing of delay. If that be so, I think that 's above all law and rule to us.

Rainborough: I would offer one word, for I think this will bring us to no issue at all. Both yesterday and to-day, and divers times, we have had cautions given us to have care of divisions. I do speak it to avoid division: that we may not at this time consider the engagements. If you, or any other gentlemen, are of opinion that you have not broke them, and then some others are of opinion that you have broke them, we may fall into contest[s] which may occasion division. But if you read this, and find it not against the *Engagement*,¹ that will be the work. If it be not against the *Engagement*, you will find that in it which you will find from your engagements. And I have something to say to the particulars in it.

Cowling: I shall only offer this, the necessity of expedition if the people shall consider the necessities that they and we are in. We live now upon free-quarter, and we have that against our wills. Those that know what belongs to armies well know, none are to quarter soldiers but those that are within so many miles. And if so be too that the owner of the house should refuse to open his doors, we are prevented to pay our quarters by those that might have supplied us. I have seen this paper, and upon second reading of it I set my hand to it, that we may not lie as drones to

¹ The *Solemn Engagement of the Army*, 5th June 1647; see pp. 401–3.

devour their families. I am ready where I am called by my superiors. If not, the Lord be merciful to me.

Major White: [1] I should offer one word to this Council: I think it is in all our minds to deliver the kingdom; if there be particular engagements we must lay them aside [a] to lay down [something for the] public good.

Cromwell: I desire to know what the gentleman means concerning particular engagements: whether [b] he means those that are in this book? If those that are in this book [they are the engagements of the Army]. But if he means engagements personal from particular persons, let every man speak for himself. I speak for myself, I disavow all, and I am free to act, free from any such——

White: I conceive that [if] they be such as are passed by the Representative of the Army, I think the Army is bound in conscience to go on with them.

Colonel [John] Hewson: All the engagements that have been declared for have [not] been by the Representative of the Army. And whether or no that hath not been the cause of this cloud that hangs over our heads, I think if we lay our hands over our hearts we may not much mistake it.

Petty: [c] According to your Honours' desire yesterday, I am come [d] here to give in my reasons why I do approve of this paper, this Agreement, [and] to receive reasons why it should not be agreed to.[e] For the particular engagements of the Army, I am ignorant of them, but if it please this Council [I would move them] to let this [paper] be read,[e] that either the matter or manner of it may be debated; and when any of the matter shall come to touch upon any engagement [so as] to break any engagement, that then the engagement may be shown; and if that engagement shall prove just, and this unjust, this must be rejected, or if this just, and these engagements unjust, [then they must be rejected]. I desire all those that are free from it in their spirits may act farther; and those that think themselves bound up so [f] to acquiesce in it, that they would be pleased to rest satisfied in the actions of other men that are at liberty to act for the peace and freedom of the kingdom.

Ireton: Truly I would, if I did know of any personal, particular engagements, if I were personally or particularly engaged myself,

[1] Perhaps an error. Major Francis White had been expelled from the Council.

which I profess, as in the presence of God, I know not for ᵃ myself.
I myself am not under any engagement in relation to that business
that the great question lies upon—I need not name it—more
than what all men know that have seen and read, and in the Army
consented to, those things that were published. But if I were
under any particular engagement, it should not at all stand in any
other man's way. If I were under ᵇ [any particular engagement],
I say, that I could be convinced ᶜ was ill and unlawful for me to
enter into, my engagement should not stand in any other man's
way that would do anything that I could be convinced of to be
better. And till God hath brought us all to that temper of spirit
that we can be contented to be nothing in our reputations, [in
our] esteems, in our power—truly I may go a little higher and say,
till the reputation and honour of the Army, and such things,
become nothing to us, [at least] not so as to stand at all in the way,
[or allow] the consideration of them to stand at all in the way, to
hinder us from what we see God calling us to, or to prompt us
on to what we have not a clear call from him [to undertake]—we
are not brought to that temper wherein I can expect any renewing
of that presence of God that we have sought. And therefore, for
my part, I profess first, I desire no [particular] engagements [may
be considered]. If there were particular engagements of any
particular man whatsoever, I desire they may not be considered
[so] as to [influence] the leading of the Army one way or other, but
let that man look to himself for what justice lies upon him, and
what justice will follow him. Neither do I care for the engagements of the Army so much for the engagements' ᵈ sake, but I look
upon this Army as having carried with it hitherto the name of
God, and having carried with it hitherto the interest of the people
of God, and the interest which is God's interest, the honour of his
name, the good and freedom and safety and happiness of his
people. And for my part I think that it is that that is the only
thing for which God hath appeared with us, and led us, and gone
before us, and honoured us, and taken delight to work by us.
I say, that very thing: that we have carried the name of God
(and I hope not in show, but in reality), professing to act, and to
work, as we have thought,ᵉ in our judgments and consciences,
God to lead us; professing to act to those ends that we have
thought to be answerable and suitable to the mind of God, so far
as it hath been known to us.ᶠ We have professed to endeavour
to follow the counsels of God, and to have him president in our
councils; and I hope it hath been so in our hearts. [We have
professed] that we have been ready to follow his guidance; and

I know it hath been so in many things against our own reasons, where we have seen evidently God calling us. And [I know] that we have been carried on with a confidence in him: we have made him our trust, and we have held forth his name, and we have owned his hand towards us. These are the things, I say, which God hath in some degree and measure wrought his people in this Army up to, in some degree of sincerity. And this it is (as I said before) that I account hath been [the thing] that God hath taken delight in, amongst us, to dwell with us, to be with us, and to appear with us, and [the reason why he] will manifest his presence to us. And therefore by this means, and by that appearance of God amongst us, the name and honour of God, the name and reputation of the people of God, and of that Gospel that they profess, is deeply and dearly and nearly concerned in the good or ill manage of this Army, in their good or ill carriage; and therefore, for my part I profess it, that 's the only thing to me. [It is] not to me so much as the vainest or lightest thing you can imagine, whether there be a king in England or no, whether there be lords in England or no. For whatever I find the work of God tending to, I should desire quietly to submit to. If God saw it good to destroy, not only King and Lords, but all distinctions of degrees—nay if it go further, to destroy all property, that there 's no such thing left, that there be nothing at all of civil constitution left in the kingdom—if I see the hand of God in it I hope I shall with quietness acquiesce, and submit to it, and not resist it. But still I think that God certainly will so lead those that are his, and I hope too he will so lead this Army,[a] that they may not incur sin, or bring scandal upon the name of God, and the name of the people of God, that are both so nearly concerned in what this Army does.[b] And [therefore] it is my wish, upon those grounds that I before declared, which made the consideration of this Army dear and tender to me,[c] [that] we may take heed, [that] we may consider first engagements,[d] so far as they are engagements publicly of the Army. I do not speak of particular [engagements]; I would not have them considered, if there be any. And secondly, I would have us consider of this: that our ways and workings and actings, and the actings of the Army, so far as the counsels of those prevail in it who have anything of the spirit of Jesus Christ, may appear suitable to that spirit. And [as] I would [not] have this Army in relation to those great concernments (as I said before: the honour of God, and the honour and good name of his people and of religion),[e] as I would not have it to incur the scandal of neglecting engagements, and laying aside all consideration of engagements, and [the scandal] of juggling, and deceiving, and deluding the world, making them believe things in times of extremity which they never meant; so I would [not] have us [a] give the world occasion to think that we are the disturbers of the peace of mankind. I say, I would not give them just occasion to think so; nay, I would have them have just cause to think that we seek peace with all men, and [b] the good of all men, and [that] we seek the destruction of none—that we can say. And in general I would wish and study, and that my heart is bent to, that the counsels of this Army may appear acted [1] by that wisdom that is from above, which we know how it is charactered.[2] It is first pure, and then peaceable, and then gentle, and easy to be entreated, and we find many characters of the same wisdom, and all other fruits of the same spirit, that still run clearly that way. Therefore, I say, I wish that we may have no otherwise a consideration of engagements or anything of that nature. That which makes me press it, is chiefly that consideration of the concernment of the honour of God and his people in the Army; and as I prize them so I press [e] [that in] all [things] whatsoever,[f] though we were free and had no engagements,[g] we do act as Christians, as men guided by the Spirit of God, as men having that wisdom [that is] from above, and [is] so characterized.

To the method of our proceeding. Having expressed what I desire may be all our cares, I cannot but think that this will be clearest, because I see it is so much pressed and insisted upon: not [h] to read what our engagements are, but [to] read the paper that is presented here, and consider upon it, what good and what matter of justice and righteousness there is in it, and whether there be anything of injustice or unrighteousness, either in itself or in reference to our engagements. And so far, I think our engagements ought to be taken into consideration:[i] that so far as we are engaged to a thing that was not unlawful to engage to [j] (and I should be sad to think them so), we should think ourselves bound not to act contrary to those engagements. And first that we may consider of the particulars of this paper,[k] whether they be good and just (that is [not ill], not unjust); and then further to consider whether they be so essentially due and right as that they should be contended for, for then that is some kind of check to less engagements,[l] and for such things, if we find any, light engagements [may] be cast off and not considered.[m] But if we find any matter in them that, though it be just, though it be good [n] (that is not ill, not unjust),[o] is not [p] probable to be so beneficial and advantageous (not to few, but to many), that [q] withal we may

---

[1] Actuated.   [2] Characterized.

consider whether it be so much a duty, and we be so much bound to it by the thing itself, as that no engagement can take us from it. And [a] if we find any thing[s] that, if they be just or good, [are] yet not so obligatory or of [such] necessity to the kingdom [but that] the kingdom may stand without them, then I think, it being [so, it is] not absolutely lawful [for us] to act for them.

Major [William] Rainborough: I desire we may come to that end we all strive after. I humbly desire you will fall upon that which is the engagement of all, which is the rights and freedoms of the people, and let us see how far we have made sure to them a right and freedom, and if anything be tendered as to that [in this paper]. And when that engagement is gone through, then, let us consider of those [things only] that are of greater weight.

(The paper called the Agreement read. Afterwards the first article read by itself.) [1]

Ireton: The exception that lies in it is this. It is said, they are to be distributed according to the number of the inhabitants: 'The people of England,' *&c.* And this doth make me think that the meaning is, that every man that is an inhabitant is to be equally considered, and to have an equal voice in the election of those representers, the persons that are for the general Representative; and if that be the meaning, then I have something to say against it. But if it be only that those people that by the civil constitution of this kingdom, which is original and fundamental, and beyond which I am sure no memory of record does go——

[Cowling, interrupting]: [b] Not before the Conquest. [c]

[Ireton]: But before the Conquest it was so. If it be intended that those that by that constitution that was before the Conquest, that hath been beyond memory, such persons that have been before [by] that constitution [the electors], should be [still] the electors, I have no more to say against it.

Colonel Rainborough objected: [d] That others might have given their hands to it.

Captain Denne denied that those that were set of their regiment [e] were their hands.

[1] See pp. 443–5.

Ireton [asked]: Whether those men whose hands are to it, or those that brought it, do know so much of the matter as [to know] whether [a] they mean that all that had a former right of election [are to be electors], or [that] those that had no right before are to come in.

Cowling: In the time before the Conquest.[b] Since the Conquest the greatest part of the kingdom was in vassalage.

Petty: We judge that all inhabitants that have not lost their birthright should have an equal voice in elections.

Rainborough: [b] I desired that those that had engaged in it [might be included]. For really I think that the poorest he that is in England hath a life to live, as the greatest he; and therefore truly, sir, I think it's clear, that every man that is to live under a government ought first by his own consent to put himself under that government; and I do think that the poorest man in England is not at all bound in a strict sense to that government that he hath not had a voice to put himself under; and I am confident that, when I have heard the reasons against it,[d] something will be said to answer those reasons, insomuch that I should doubt whether he [e] was an Englishman or no, that should doubt of these things.

Ireton: That's [the meaning of] this, ['according to the number of the inhabitants']?
Give me leave to tell you, that if you make this the rule I think you must fly for refuge to an absolute natural right, and you must deny all civil right; and I am sure it will come to that in the consequence. This, I perceive, is pressed as that which is so essential and due: the right of the people of this kingdom, and as they are the people of this kingdom, distinct and divided from other people, and [f] that we must for this right lay aside all other considerations; this is so just, this is so due, this is so right to them.[g] And that those that they do thus choose must have such a power of binding all, and loosing all, according to those limitations, this is pressed as so due, and so just, as [it] is argued, that it is an engagement paramount [to] all others: and you must for it lay aside all others; if you have engaged any otherwise,[h] you must break it. [We must] so look upon these as thus held out to us; so it was held out by the gentleman that brought it yesterday. For my part, I think it is no right at all. I think that no

person hath a right to an interest or share in the disposing of the
affairs of the kingdom, and in determining or choosing those that
shall determine what laws we shall be ruled by here—no person
hath a right to this, that hath not a permanent fixed interest in
this kingdom, and those persons together are properly the represented of this kingdom,[a] and consequently are [also] to make up
the representers of this kingdom,[b] who taken together do comprehend whatsoever is of real or permanent interest in the kingdom.
And I am sure [1] otherwise I cannot tell what [c] any man can say why
a foreigner coming in amongst us—or as many as will coming in
amongst us, or by force or otherwise settling themselves here, or
at least by our permission having a being here—why they should
not as well lay claim to it as any·other.　We talk of birthright.
Truly [by] birthright there is thus much claim.　Men may justly
have by birthright, by their very being born in England, that we
should not seclude them out of England, that we should not
refuse to give them air and place and ground, and the freedom of
the highways and other things, to live amongst us—not any
man that is born here, though [d] by his birth there come nothing
at all (that is part of the permanent interest of this kingdom) to
him.　That I think is due to a man by birth.　But that by a man's
being born here he shall have a share in that power that shall
dispose of the lands here, and of all things here, I do not think
it a sufficient ground.[e]　I am sure if we look upon that which is
the utmost (within [any] man's view) of what was originally the
constitution of this kingdom,[f] upon that which is most radical
and fundamental, and which if you take away, there is no man
hath any land, any goods,[g] [or] any civil interest,[h] that is this:
that those that choose the representers for the making of laws by
which this state and kingdom are to be governed, are the persons
who, taken together, do comprehend the local interest of this
kingdom; that is, the persons in whom all land lies, and those in
corporations in whom all trading lies.　This is the most fundamental constitution of this kingdom and [that] which if you do not
allow, you allow none at all.　This constitution hath limited and
determined it that only those shall have voices in elections.　It is
true, as was said by a gentleman near me, the meanest man in
England ought to have [a voice in the election of the government
he lives under—but only if he has some local interest].　I say this:
that those that have the meanest local interest—that man that hath
but forty shillings a year, he *hath* as great voice in the election of
a knight for the shire as he that hath ten thousand a year, or more
if he had never so much; and therefore there is that regard had

to it. But this [local interest], still the constitution of this government hath had an eye to (and what other government hath not an eye to this?). It doth not relate to the interest of the kingdom if it do not lay the foundation of the power that 's given to [a] the representers, in those who have a permanent and a local interest in the kingdom, and who taken all together do comprehend the whole [interest of the kingdom]. There is all the reason and justice that can be, [in this]: if I will come to live in a kingdom, being a foreigner to it, or live in a kingdom, having no permanent interest in it, [and] if I will desire as a stranger, or claim as one freeborn here, the air, the free passage of highways, the protection of laws, and all such things [b]—if I will either desire them or claim them, [then] I (if I have no permanent interest in that kingdom) must submit to those laws and those rules [which they shall choose], who, taken together, do comprehend the whole interest of the kingdom.[c] And if we shall go to take away this, we shall plainly go to take away all property and interest that any man hath either in land by inheritance, or in estate by possession, or anything else—[I say], if you take away this fundamental part of the civil constitution.[d]

Rainborough: Truly, sir, I am of the same opinion I was, and am resolved to keep it till I know reason why I should not. I confess my memory is bad, and therefore I am fain to make use of my pen. I remember that, in a former speech [which] this gentleman brought before this [meeting], he was saying that in some cases he should not value whether [there were] a king or no king, whether lords or no lords, whether a property or no property. For my part I differ in that. I do very much care whether [there be] a king or no king, lords or no lords, property or no property; and I think, if we do not all take care, we shall all have none of these very shortly. But as to this present business. I do hear nothing at all that can convince me, why any man that is born in England ought not to have his voice in election of burgesses. It is said that if a man have not a permanent interest, he can have no claim; and [that] we must be no freer than the laws will let us [e] be, and that there is no [law in any] chronicle will let us be freer than that we [now] enjoy. Something was said to this yesterday.[b] I do think that the main cause why Almighty God gave men reason, it was that they should make use of that reason, and that they should improve it for that end and purpose that God gave it them. And truly, I think that half a loaf is better than none if a man be anhungry: [this gift of reason without other property may seem a small thing], yet I think there is nothing that God hath given a man that any [one] else can take from him. And therefore I say, that either it must be the Law of God or the law of man that must prohibit the meanest man in the kingdom to have this benefit as well as the greatest. I do not find anything in the Law of God, that a lord shall choose twenty burgesses, and a gentleman but two, or a poor man shall choose none: I find no such thing in the Law of Nature, nor in the Law of Nations. But I do find that all Englishmen must be subject to English laws, and I do verily believe that there is no man but will say that the foundation of all law lies in the people, and if [it lie] in the people, I am to seek for this exemption.

And truly I have thought something [else]: in what a miserable distressed condition would many a man that hath fought for the Parliament in this quarrel, be! I will be bound to say that many a man whose zeal and affection to God and this kingdom hath carried him forth in this cause, hath so spent his estate that, in the way the state [and] the Army are going,[a] he shall not hold up his head, if [b] when his estate is lost, and not worth forty shillings a year, a man shall not have any interest. And there are many other ways by which [the] estates [c] men have (if that be the rule which God in his providence does use) do fall to decay. A man, when he hath an estate,[f] hath an interest in making laws, [but] when he hath none, he hath no power in it; so that a man cannot lose that which he hath for the maintenance of his family but he must [also] lose that which God and nature hath given him! And therefore I do [think], and am still of the same opinion, that every man born in England cannot, ought not, neither by the Law of God nor the Law of Nature, to be exempted from the choice of those who are to make laws [g] for him to live under, and for him, for aught I know, to lose his life under. And therefore I think there can be no great stick in this.

Truly I think that there is not this day reigning in England a greater fruit or effect of tyranny than this very thing would produce.[d] Truly I know nothing free but only the knight of the shire, nor do I know anything in a parliamentary way that is clear from the height and fulness of tyranny, but only [that]. As for this of corporations [which you also mentioned], it is as contrary to freedom as may be.[e] For, sir, what is it? The King he grants a patent under the Broad Seal of England to such a corporation to send burgesses, he grants to [such] a city to send burgesses. When a poor base corporation from the King['s grant] shall send two burgesses, when five hundred men of estate

shall not send one, when those that are to make their laws are
called by the King, or cannot act [but] by such a call, truly I think
that the people of England have little freedom.

Ireton: I think there was nothing that I said to give you
occasion to think that I did contend for this, that such a corporation [as that] should have the electing of a man to the Parliament. I think I agreed to this matter, that all should be equally
distributed. But the question is, whether it should be distributed
to all persons, or whether the same persons that are the electors
[now] should be the electors still, and it [be] equally distributed
amongst *them*. I do not see anybody else that makes this objection; and if nobody else be sensible of it I shall soon have done.
Only I shall a little crave your leave to represent the consequences
of it, and clear myself from one [a] thing that was misrepresented
by the gentleman that sat next me. I think, if the gentleman
remember himself, he cannot but remember that what I said was
to this effect: that if I saw the hand of God leading so far as to
destroy King, and destroy Lords, and destroy property, and [leave]
no such thing at all amongst us, I should acquiesce in it; and so I
did not care, if no king, no lords, or no property [should] be,[b] in
comparison of the tender care that I have of the honour of God,
and of the people of God, whose [good] name is so much concerned in this Army. This I did deliver [so], and not absolutely.
All the main thing that I speak for, is because I would have an
eye to property. I hope we do not come to contend for victory
—but let every man consider with himself that he do not go that
way to take away all property. For here is the case of the most
fundamental part of the constitution of the kingdom, which if
you take away, you take away all by that. Here [c] men of this
and this quality are determined to be the electors of men to the
Parliament, and they are all those who have any permanent
interest in the kingdom, and who, taken together, do comprehend
the whole [permanent, local] interest of the kingdom. I mean by
permanent [and] local, that [it] is not [able to be removed] anywhere else. As for instance, he that hath a freehold, and that
freehold cannot be removed out of the kingdom; and so there's a
[freeman of a] corporation, a place which hath the privilege of a
market and trading, which if you should allow to all places
equally, I do not see how you could preserve any peace in the
kingdom, and that is the reason why in the constitution we have
but some few market towns. Now those people [that have free-
holds] [d] and those [that] are the freemen of corporations,[e] were

looked upon [a] by the former constitution [b] to comprehend the permanent interest of the kingdom. For [first], he that hath his livelihood by his trade, and by his freedom of trading in such a corporation, which he cannot exercise in another, he is tied to that place, [for] his livelihood depends upon it. And secondly, that man hath an interest, hath a permanent interest there, upon which he may live, and live a freeman without dependence. These [things the] constitution [c] [of] this kingdom hath looked at. Now I wish we may all consider of what right you will challenge that all the people should have right to elections. Is it by the right of nature? If you will hold forth that as your ground, then I think you must deny all property too, and this is my reason. For thus: by that same right of nature (whatever it be) that you pretend, by which you can say, one [d] man hath an equal right with another to the choosing of him that shall govern him—by the same right of nature, he hath the same [equal] right in any goods he sees—meat, drink, clothes—to take and use them for his sustenance. He hath a freedom to the land, [to take] the ground, to exercise it, till it; he hath the [same] freedom to anything that any one doth account himself to have any propriety in. Why now I say then, if you,[g] against the most fundamental part of [the] civil constitution (which I have now declared), will plead the Law of Nature, that a man should (paramount [to] this, and contrary to this) have a power of choosing those men that shall determine what shall be law in this state, though he himself have no permanent interest in the state, [but] whatever interest he hath he may carry about with him—if this be allowed, [because by the right of nature] we are free, we are equal, one man must have as much voice as another, then show me what step or difference [there is], why [I may not] by the same right [take your property, though not] of necessity to sustain nature. It is for my better being, and [the better settlement of the kingdom]? Possibly not for it, neither: possibly I may not have so real a regard to the peace of the kingdom as that man who hath a permanent interest in it.[e] He that [f] is here to-day, and gone to-morrow, I do not see that he hath such a permanent interest. Since you cannot plead to it by anything but the Law of Nature, [or for anything] but for the end of better being, and [since] that better being is not certain, and [what is] more, destructive to another; upon these grounds, if you do, paramount [to] all constitutions, hold up this Law of Nature, I would fain have any man show me their bounds, where you will end, and [why you should not] take away all property.

Rainborough : I shall now be a little more free and open with you than I was before. I wish we were all true-hearted, and that we did all carry ourselves with integrity. If I did mistrust you I would [not] use such asseverations. I think it doth go on mistrust, and things are thought too [readily] matters of reflection, that were never intended. For my part, as I think, *you* forgot something that was in *my* speech,[a] and you do not only yourselves believe that [some] men are inclining to anarchy, but you would make all men believe that. And, sir, to say because a man pleads that every man hath a voice [by right of nature], that therefore it destroys [by] the same [argument all property—this is to forget the Law of God]. That there 's a property, the Law of God says it; else why [hath] God made that law, *Thou shalt not steal*? I am a poor man, therefore I must be [op]pressed: if I have no interest in the kingdom, I must suffer by all their laws be they right or wrong. Nay thus: a gentleman lives in a country and hath three or four lordships, as some men have (God knows how they got them); and when a Parliament is called he must be a Parliament-man; and it may be he sees some poor men, they live near this man, he can crush them—I have known an invasion [b] to make sure he hath turned the poor men [c] out of doors; and I would fain know whether the potency of [rich] men do not this, and so keep them under the greatest tyranny that was [ever] thought of in the world. And therefore I think that to that it is fully answered: God hath set down that thing as to propriety with this law of his, *Thou shalt not steal*. And for my part I am against any such thought, and,[d] as for yourselves,[e] I wish you would not make the world believe that we are for anarchy.

Cromwell : I know nothing but this, that they that are the most yielding have the greatest wisdom; but really, sir, this is not right as it should be. No man says that you have a mind to anarchy, but [that] the consequence of this rule tends to anarchy, must end in anarchy; for where is there any bound or limit set if you take away this [limit], that men that have no interest but the interest of breathing [shall have no voice in elections]? Therefore I am confident on 't, we should not be so hot one with another.

Rainborough : I know that some particular men we debate with [believe we] are for anarchy.

Ireton :[f] I profess I must clear myself as to that point.[g] I would not desire,[h] I cannot allow myself, to lay the least scandal upon anybody. And truly, for that gentleman that did take so much offence, I do not know why he should take it so. We speak to the paper—not to persons—and to the matter of the paper. And I hope that no man is so much engaged to the matter of the paper—I hope [that] our persons, and our hearts and judgments, are not [so] pinned to papers but that we are ready to hear what good or ill consequence will flow from it.[a]

I have, with as much plainness and clearness of reason as I could, showed you how I did conceive the doing of this [that the paper advocates] takes away that which is the most original, the most fundamental civil constitution of this kingdom, and which is, above all, that constitution by which I have any property.[b] If you will take away that and set up,[c] as a thing paramount,[d] whatever a man may claim by the Law of Nature, though it be not a thing of necessity to him for the sustenance of nature; if you do make this your rule, I desire clearly to understand where then remains property.

Now then [e] — I would misrepresent nothing — the [f] answer which had anything of matter in it,[g] the great and main answer upon which that which hath been said against this [objection] rests, seemed to be that it will not make a breach of property,[h] [for this reason]: that there is a law, *Thou shalt not steal.* [But] the same law says, *Honour thy father and [thy] mother*, and that law doth likewise hold out that it doth extend to all that (in that place where we are in) are our governors; so that by that there is a forbidding of breaking a civil law when we may live quietly under it, and [that by] a divine law.[b] Again it is said—indeed [was said] before—that there is no law, no divine law, that tells us that such a corporation must have the election of burgesses,[i] such a shire [of knights], or the like. Divine law extends not to particular things. And so, on the other side, if a man were to demonstrate his [right to] property by divine law, it would be very remote.[j] Our [right to] property descends from other things, as well as our right of sending burgesses. That divine law doth not determine particulars but generals in relation to man and man, and to property, and all things else: and we should be as far to seek if we should go to prove a property in [a thing by] divine law, as to prove that I have an interest in choosing burgesses of the Parliament by divine law. And truly, under favour, I refer it to all, whether there be anything of solution to that objection that I made, if it be understood—I submit it to any man's judgment.

Rainborough: To the thing itself—property [in the franchise]. I would fain know how it comes to be the property [of some men,

and not of others]. As for estates and those kind of things, and
other things that belong to men, it will be granted that ª they are ᵇ
property; but I deny that that is a property, to a lord, to a gentleman, to any man more than another in the kingdom of England.
If it be a property, it is a property by a law—neither do I think
that there is very little property in this thing by the law of the
land, because I think that the law of the land in that thing is the
most tyrannical law under heaven. And I would fain know what
we have fought for. [For our laws and liberties?] And this is
the old law of England—and that which enslaves the people of
England—that they should be bound by laws in which they have
no voice at all! ᶜ [With respect to the divine law which says
Honour thy father and thy mother] the great dispute is, who is a
right father and a right mother? I am bound to know who is my
father and mother; and—I take it in the same sense you do—I
would have a distinction, a character whereby God commands
me to honour [them]. And for my part I look upon the people
of England so, that wherein they have not voices in the choosing
of their [governors—their civil] fathers and mothers—they are
not bound to that commandment.

Petty : I desire to add one word concerning the word *property*.
It is for something that anarchy is so much talked of. For my own
part I cannot believe in the least that it can be clearly derived from
that paper. 'Tis true, that somewhat may be derived in the paper
against the King, the power of the King, and somewhat against
the power of the Lords; and the truth is when I shall see God
going about to throw down King and Lords and property, then I
shall be contented. But I hope that they may live to see the power
of the King and the Lords thrown down, that yet may live to see
property preserved. And for this of changing the Representative
of the nation, of changing those that choose the Representative,
making of them more full, taking more into the number than
formerly, I had verily thought we had all agreed in it that more
should have chosen—all that had desired a more equal representation than we now have. For now those only choose who have
forty shillings freehold. A man may have a lease for one hundred
pounds a year, a man may have a lease for three lives, [but he has
no voice]. But [as] for this [argument], that it destroys all right
[to property] that every Englishman that is an inhabitant of
England should choose and have a voice ᵈ in the representatives,
I suppose it is, [on the contrary], the only means to preserve all
property. For I judge every man is naturally free; and I judge

the reason why [a] men [chose representatives] when they were [h] in so great numbers that every man could not give his voice [directly], was [b] that they who were chosen might preserve property [for all]; and therefore men agreed to come into some form of government that they might preserve property, and I would fain know, if we were to begin a government, [whether you would say], 'You have not forty shillings a year, therefore you shall not have a voice.' Whereas before there was a government every man had such a voice,[1] and afterwards, and for this very cause, they did choose representatives, and put themselves into forms of government that they may preserve property, and therefore it is not to destroy it, [to give every man a voice].

Ireton : I think we shall not be so apt to come to a right understanding in this business, if one man, and another man, and another man do speak their several thoughts and conceptions to the same purpose, as if we do consider [c] where the objection lies, and what the answer is which is made to it; [d] and therefore I desire we may do so. To that which this gentleman spake last. The main thing that he seemed to answer was this: that he would make it appear that the going about to establish this government, [or] such a government, is not a destruction of property, nor does not tend to the destruction of property, because the people's falling into a government is for the preservation of property. What weight there [is in it] lies in this: since there is a falling into a government, and government is to preserve property, therefore this cannot be against property. The objection does not lie in that, the making of [e] the representation [f] more equal, but [in] the introducing of men into an equality of interest in this government, who have no property in this kingdom, or who have no local permanent interest in it. For if I had said that I would not wish at all that we should have any enlargement of the bounds of those that are to be the electors, then you might have excepted against it. But [what I said was] that I would not go to enlarge it beyond all bounds, so that upon the same ground you may admit of so many men from foreign states as would outvote you. The objection lies still in this.[g] I do not mean that I would have it restrained to that proportion [that now obtains], but to restrain it still to men who have a local, a permanent interest in the kingdom, who have such an interest that they may live upon it as freeman, and who have such an interest as is fixed upon a place, and is not the same equally everywhere. If a man be an inhabitant upon a rack rent for a year, for two years, or twenty years, you cannot think that man hath any fixed or permanent interest. That man, if he pay the rent that his land is worth, and [a] hath no advantage but what he hath by his land,[b] is as good a man, may have as much interest, in another kingdom as [c] here. I do not speak of not [d] enlarging this [representation] at all, but of keeping this to the most fundamental constitution in this kingdom, that is, that no person that hath not a local and permanent interest in the kingdom should have an equal dependence in election [with those that have]. But if you go beyond this law, if you admit any man that hath a breath and being, I did show you how this will destroy property. It may come to destroy property thus. You may have [e] such men chosen, or at least the major part of them, [as have no local and permanent interest]. Why [f] may not [g] those men vote against all property? [Again] you may admit strangers by this rule, if you admit them once to inhabit, and those that have interest in the land may be voted out of their land. It may destroy property that way. But here is the rule that you go by.[h] You infer this to be the right of the people, of every inhabitant, [1] because [j] man hath such a right in nature, though it be not of necessity for the preserving of his being; [and] therefore you are to overthrow the most fundamental constitution for this. By the same rule, show me why you will not, by the same right of nature, make use of anything that any man hath, [though it be not] for the necessary sustenance of men.[k] Show me what you will stop at; wherein you will fence any man in a property by this rule.

Rainborough : I desire to know how this comes to be a property in some men, and not in others.

Colonel [Nathaniel] Rich : I confess [there is weight in] that objection that the Commissary-General last insisted upon; for you have five to one in this kingdom that have no permanent interest. Some men [have] ten, some twenty servants, some more, some less. If the master and servant shall be equal electors, then clearly those that have no interest in the kingdom will make it their interest to choose those that have no interest. It may happen, that the majority may by law, not in a confusion, [1] destroy property; there may be a law enacted, that there shall be an equality of goods and estate.[1] I think that either of the extremes may be urged to inconveniency; that is, [that] men that have no interest as to estate should have no interest as to election [and

---

[1] Possibly someone interrupts to object that *now* only the rich are chosen; see Rainborough, p. 67.

that they should have an equal interest]. But there may be a more equitable [g] division and distribution than that he that hath nothing should have an equal voice; and certainly there may be some other way thought of, that there may be a representative of the poor as well as the rich, and not to exclude all. I remember there were many workings and revolutions, as we have heard, in the Roman Senate; and there was never a confusion that did appear (and that indeed *was* come to) till the state came to know this kind of distribution of election. That is how [a] the people's voices were bought and sold, and that by the poor; and thence it came that he that was the richest man, and [a man] of some considerable power among the soldiers,[b] and one they resolved on,[c] made himself a perpetual dictator. And if we strain too far to avoid monarchy in kings [let us take heed] that we do not call for emperors to deliver us from more than one tyrant.

Rainborough: I should not have spoken again. I think it is a fine gilded pill. But there is much danger, and it may seem to some that there is some kind of remedy [possible]. I think that we are better as we are [if it can be really proved] that the poor shall choose many [and] still the people be [d] in the same case, be [d] over-voted still. [But of this, and much else, I am unsatisfied], and therefore truly, sir, I should desire to go close to the business; and the [first] thing that I am unsatisfied in is how it comes about that there is such a propriety in some freeborn Englishmen, and not [in] others.

Cowling [demanded]: Whether the younger son have not as much right to the inheritance as the eldest.

Ireton: Will you decide it by the light of nature?

Cowling: Why election was [given] only [to those with freeholds of] forty shillings a year (which was [then worth] more than forty pounds a year now), the reason was: that the Commons of England were overpowered by the Lords, who had abundance of vassals, but that still they might make their laws good against encroaching prerogatives [by this means]; [e] therefore they did exclude all slaves. Now the case is not so: all slaves have bought their freedoms, [and] they are more free that in the commonwealth are more beneficial. [Yet] there are men [of substance] in the country [c] [with no voice in elections]. There is a tanner in Staines worth three thousand pounds, and another in Reading worth three horseskins. [The second has a voice; the first, none.]

Ireton: In the beginning of your speech you seem to acknowledge [that] by law, by civil constitution, the propriety of having voices in election was fixed in certain persons. So then your exception of your argument does not prove that by civil constitution they have no such propriety, but your argument does acknowledge [that] by civil [constitution they have such] propriety. You argue against this law [only] that this law is not good.

Wildman: Unless I be very much mistaken we are very much deviated from the first question.[a] Instead of following the first proposition to inquire what is just, I conceive we look to prophecies, and look to what may be the event, and judge of the justness of a thing by the consequence. I desire we may recall [ourselves to the question] whether it be right or no. I conceive all that hath been said against it will be reduced to this [question of consequences], and [to] [b] another reason [c]—that it is against a fundamental law, that every person [choosing] ought to have a permanent interest, because it is not fit that those should choose Parliaments that have no lands to be disposed of by Parliament.

Ireton: If you will take it by the way, it is not fit that the representees should choose [as] the representers, or the persons who shall make the law in the kingdom, [those] who have not a permanent fixed interest in the kingdom. [The reason is the same in the two cases.]

Wildman: Sir, I do so take it; and I conceive that that is brought in for the same reason: that foreigners might [otherwise not only] come to have a voice in our elections as well as the native inhabitants, [but to be elected].

Ireton: That is upon supposition that these [foreigners] should be all inhabitants.

Wildman: I shall begin with the last first. The case is different with [d] the native inhabitant and [the] foreigner. If a foreigner shall be admitted to be an inhabitant in the nation,[e] so he will submit to that form of government as the natives do, he hath the same right as the natives but in this particular. Our case is to be considered thus, that we have been under slavery. That's acknowledged by all. Our very laws were made by our conquerors; and whereas it's spoken much of chronicles, I conceive there is no credit to be given to any of them; and the reason is because those that were our lords, and made us their vassals, would suffer nothing else to be chronicled. We are now engaged for our freedom. That's the end of Parliaments: not to constitute what is already [established, but to act] according to the just rules of government. Every person in England hath as clear a right to elect his representative as the greatest person in England. I conceive that's the undeniable maxim of government: that all government is in the free consent of the people. If [so], then upon that account there is no person that is under a just government, or hath justly his own, unless he by his own free consent be put under that government. This he cannot be unless he be consenting to it, and therefore, according to this maxim, there is never a person in England [but ought to have a voice in elections]. If [this], as that gentleman says, be true, there are no laws that in this strictness and rigour of justice [any man is bound to], that are not made by those who[m] he doth consent to. And therefore I should humbly move, that if the question be stated—which would soonest bring things to an issue—it might rather be thus: Whether any person can justly be bound by law,[a] who doth not give his consent that such persons shall make laws for him?

Ireton : Let the question be so: Whether a man can be bound to any law that he doth not consent to? And I shall tell you, that he may and ought to be [bound to a law] that he doth not give a consent to, nor doth not choose any [to consent to]; and I will make it clear. If a foreigner come within this kingdom, if that stranger will have liberty [to dwell here] who hath no local interest here, he, as [b] a man, it's true, hath air, [the passage of highways, the protection of laws,[c] and all] that by nature; we must not expel [him] our coasts, give him no being amongst us, nor kill him because he comes upon our land, comes up our stream, arrives at our shore. It is a piece of hospitality, of humanity, to receive that man amongst us. But if that man be received to a being amongst us, I think that man may very well be content to submit himself to the law of the land; that is, the law that is made by those people that have a property, a fixed property, in the land. I think, if any man will receive protection from this people though [neither] he nor his ancestors, not any betwixt him and Adam, did ever give concurrence to this constitution, I think this man ought to be subject to those laws, and to be bound by those laws, so long as he continues amongst them. That is my opinion. A man ought to be subject to a law, that did not give his consent, but with this reservation, that if this man do think himself unsatisfied to be subject to this law he may go into another kingdom. And so the same reason doth extend, in my understanding, [to] that [a] man that hath no permanent interest in the kingdom. If he hath money, his money is as good in another place as here; he hath nothing that doth locally fix him to this kingdom. If that [b] man will live in this kingdom, or trade amongst us, that man ought to subject himself to the law made by the people who have the interest of this kingdom in them.[c] And yet I do acknowledge that which you take to be so general a maxim, that in every kingdom, within every land, the original of power of making laws, of determining what shall be law in the land, does lie in the people—[but by the people is meant those] that are possessed of [d] the permanent interest in the land. But whoever is extraneous to this, that is, as good a man in another land, that man ought to give such a respect to the property of men that live in the land. They do not determine [that I shall live in this land]. Why should I have any interest in [e] determining [f] what shall be the law of this land?

Major [William] Rainborough : I think if it can be made to appear that it is a just and reasonable thing, and that it is for the preservation of all the [native] freeborn men, [that they should have an equal voice in election]—I think it ought to be made good unto them. And the reason is: that the chief end of this government is to preserve persons as well as estates, and if any law shall take hold of my person it is more dear than my estate.

Colonel Rainborough : I do very well remember that the gentleman in the window [1] [said] that, if it were so, there were no propriety to be had, because [h] five parts [i] of [the nation], the poor people, are now excluded and would then come in. So [j] one on the other side said [that], if [it were] otherwise, then rich men [only] shall be chosen. Then, I say, the one part shall make hewers of wood and drawers of water of the other five, and so the greatest part of the nation be enslaved.[k] Truly I think we are still [l] where we were; and I do not hear any argument given but only that it is the present law of the kingdom. I say still,[m] what shall become of those many [men] that have laid out themselves for the Parliament of England in this present war, that have ruined themselves by fighting, by hazarding all they had? They are Englishmen. They have now nothing to say for themselves.

[1] Colonel Rich, p. 63.

Rich: I should be very sorry to speak anything here that should give offence, or that may occasion personal reflection[s] that we spoke against just now. I did not urge anything so far as was represented, and I did not at all urge ᵃ that there should be a consideration [had of rich men], and that [a] man that is [poor] shall be without consideration, [or that] he deserves to be made poore[r] and not to live [in independence] at all. But all that I urged was this: that I think it worthy consideration, whether they should have an equality in their interest.ᵇ However, I think we have been a great while upon this point, and if we be as long upon all the rest, it were well if there were no greater difference than this.

Mr. [Hugh] Peter: I think that this [matter of the franchise] may be easily agreed on—that is, there may be a way thought of. I think you would do well to set up all night [if thereby you could effect it], but I think that three or four might be thought of in this company [to form a committee]. You will be forced [only] to put characters upon electors or elected; therefore I do suppose that if there be any here that can make up a Representative to your mind, the thing is gained.ᶜ But I would fain know whether that will answer the work of your meeting.ᵈ The question is, whether you can state any one question for [removing] the present danger of the kingdom, whether ᵉ any one question or no will dispatch the work.

Sir, I desire, [if it be possible], that some question may be stated to finish the present work, to cement us [in the points] wherein lies the distance; and if the thoughts [be] of the commonwealth [and] the people's freedom, I think that's soon cured.ᵇ I desire that all manner of plainness may be used, that we may not go on with the lapwing and carry one another off the nest. There is something else ᶠ that must cement us where the awkwardness of our spirits lies.

Rainborough: For my part, I think we cannot engage one way or other in the Army if we do not think of the people's liberties. If we can agree where the liberty and freedom of the people lies, that will do all.

Ireton: I cannot consent so far.ᵍ As I said before: when I see the hand of God destroying King, and Lords, and Commons too, [or] any foundation of human constitution, when I see God hath done it, I shall, I hope, comfortably acquiesce in it. But first, I cannot give my consent to it, because it is not good. And secondly, as I desire that this Army should have regard to engagements wherever they are lawful, so I would have them have regard to this [as well]: that they should not bring that scandal upon the name of God [and the Saints], that those that call themselves by that name, those whom God hath owned and appeared with— that we should ᵃ represent ourselves to the world as men so far from being of that peaceable spirit which is suitable to the Gospel, as we should have bought peace of the world upon such terms— [as] we would not have peace in the world but upon such terms— as should destroy all property. If the principle upon which you move this alteration, or the ground upon which you press that we should make this alteration, do destroy all kind of property or whatsoever a man hath by human constitution, [I cannot consent to it]. The Law of God doth not give me property, nor the Law of Nature, but property is of human constitution. I have a property and this I shall enjoy. Constitution founds property. If either the thing itself that you press or the consequence [of] that you press [do destroy property], though I shall acquiesce in having no property, yet I cannot give my heart or hand to it; because it is a thing evil in itself and scandalous to the world, and I desire this Army may be free from both.

Sexby: I see that though liberty ᵇ were our end,ᶜ there is a degeneration from it. We have engaged in this kingdom and ventured our lives, and it was all for this: to recover our birthrights and privileges as Englishmen; and by the arguments urged there is none. There are many thousands of us soldiers that have ventured our lives; we have had little propriety in the kingdom as to our estates, yet we have had a birthright. But it seems now, except a man hath a fixed estate in this kingdom, he hath no right in this kingdom. I wonder we were so much deceived. If we had not a right to the kingdom, we were mere mercenary soldiers. There are many in my condition, that have as good a condition [as I have]; it may be little estate they have at present, and yet they have as much a [birth]right as those two ¹ who are their law-givers, as any in this place. I shall tell you in a word my resolution. I am resolved to give my birthright to none. Whatsoever may come in the way, and [whatsoever may] be thought,ᵈ I will give it to none. If this thing [be denied the poor], that with so much pressing after [they have sought, it will be the greatest scandal]. There was one thing spoken to this effect: that if the poor and

¹ MS. *too*; but reference was probably to Cromwell and Ireton.

those in low condition [were given their birthright it would be the destruction of this kingdom]. I think this was but a distrust of Providence. I do think the poor and meaner of this kingdom— I speak as in [a] relation [to the condition of soldiers], in which we are—have been the means of the preservation of this kingdom. I say, in their stations, and really I think [a] to their utmost possibility; and their lives have not been [held] dear for purchasing the good of the kingdom.[b] [And now they demand the birthright for which they fought.] Those that act to this end are as free from anarchy or confusion as those that oppose it, and they have the Law of God and the law of their conscience [with them]. But truly I shall only sum up [in] this.[c] I desire that we may not spend so much time upon these things. We must be plain. When men come to understand these things, they will not lose that which they have contended for. That which I shall beseech you is to come to a determination of this question.

Ireton: I am very sorry we are come to this point, that from reasoning one to another we should come to express our resolutions. I profess for my part, what I see is good for the kingdom, and becoming a Christian to contend for, I hope through God I shall have strength and resolution to do my part towards it. And yet I will profess direct contrary in some kind to what that gentleman said. For my part, rather than I will make a disturbance to a good constitution of a kingdom wherein I may live in godliness and honesty, and peace and quietness, I will part with a great deal of my birthright. I will part with my own property rather than I will be the man that shall make a disturbance in the kingdom for my property; and therefore if all the people in this kingdom, or [the] representative[s] of them all together, should meet and should give away my property I would submit to it, I would give it away. But that gentleman, and I think every Christian, ought to bear that spirit,[d] to carry that in him, that he will not make a public disturbance upon a private prejudice.

Now let us consider where our difference lies. We all agree that you should have a Representative to govern, and[e] this Representative to be as equal as you can [make it]. But the question is, whether this distribution can be made to all persons equally, or whether [only] amongst those equals that have the interest of England in them. That which I have declared [is] my opinion [still]. I think we ought to keep to that [constitution which we have now], both because it is a civil constitution—it is the most fundamental constitution that we have—and [because] there is so much justice and reason and prudence [in it]—as I dare confidently undertake to demonstrate [a]—that there are many more evils that will follow in case you do alter [it] than there can [be] in the standing of it.   But I say but this in the general, that I do wish that they that talk of birthrights—we any of us when we talk of birthrights [b]—would consider what really our birthright is.

   If a man mean [c] by birthright, whatsoever I [d] can challenge by the Law of Nature (suppose there were no constitution at all,[e] no civil law and [no] civil constitution), [and] that *that* I am to contend for against constitution; [then] you leave no property, nor no foundation for any man to enjoy anything.   But if you call that your birthright which is [1] the most fundamental part of your constitution, then let him perish that goes about to hinder you or any man of the least part of your birthright, or will [desire to] do it.   But if you will lay aside the most fundamental constitution, which is as good, for aught you can discern, as anything you can propose—at least it is a constitution,[f] and I will give you consequence for consequence of good upon [that] constitution as you [can give] upon [g] your birthright [without it] [h]—and if you merely upon pretence of a birthright, of the right of nature, which is only true as for [your being, and not for] your better being; if you will upon that ground pretend that this constitution, the most fundamental constitution, the thing that hath reason and equity in it, shall not stand in your way, [it] is the same principle to me, say I, [as if] but for your better satisfaction you shall take hold of anything that a[nother] man calls his own.

   Rainborough : Sir, I see that it is impossible to have liberty but all property must be taken away.   If it be laid down for a rule, and if you will say it, it must be so.   But I would fain know what [i] the soldier hath [j] fought for all this while ?   He hath fought to enslave himself, to give power to men of riches, men of estates, to make him a perpetual slave.   We do find in all presses that go forth none must be pressed that are freehold men.   When these gentlemen fall out among themselves they shall press the poor scrubs [k] to come and kill [one another for] them.

   Ireton : I confess I see so much right in the business that I am not easily satisfied with flourishes.   If you will [not] lay the stress of the business upon the consideration of reason, or right relating to anything of human constitution, or anything of that nature, but will put it upon consequences, I will show you greater ill consequences—I see enough to say that, to my apprehensions, I can show you greater ill consequences to follow upon that alteration which you would have, by extending [voices] to all that have a being in this kingdom, than [any] that [can come] by this [present constitution], a great deal. That ª [that you urge of the present constitution] is a particular ill consequence. This [that I object against your proposal] is a general ill consequence, and this ᵇ is as great as that ᶜ or any [ill consequence] else [whatsoever], though I think you will see that the validity of that argument must be ᵈ that for one ill [that] lies upon that which now is,ᵉ I cᴀn show you a thousand upon this [that you propose].

Give me leave [to say] but this one word. I [will] tell you what the soldier of the kingdom hath fought for. First, the danger that we stood in was that one man's will must be a law. The people of the kingdom must have this right at least, that they should not be concluded [but] by the Representative of those that had the interest of the kingdom. So[m]e men fought in this, because they were immediately concerned and engaged in it. Other men who had no other interest in the kingdom but this, that they should have the benefit of those laws made by the Representative, yet [fought] that they should have the benefit of this Representative. They thought it was better to be concluded by the common consent of those that were fixed men, and settled men, that had the interest of this kingdom [in them]. 'And from that way,' [said they], 'I shall know a law and have a certainty.' ᵉ Every man that was born [in the country, that] ᶠ is a denizen ᵍ in it, that hath a freedom, he was capable of trading to get money,ᵉ to get estates by; and therefore this man, I think, had a great deal of reason to build up such a foundation of interest to himself: that is, that the will of one man should not be a law, but that the law of this kingdom should be by a choice of persons to represent, and that choice to be made by, the generality of the kingdom. Here was a right that induced men to fight, and those men that had ʰ this interest,ᵉ though this be not the utmost interest that other men have, yet they had *some* interest. Now [tell me] why we should go to plead whatsoever we can challenge by the right of nature against whatsoever any man can challenge by constitution. I do not see where that man will stop, as to point of property, [so] that he shall not use [against other property] that right he hath [claimed] by the Law of Nature against that constitution. I desire any man to show me where there is a difference. I have been answered, 'Now we see liberty cannot stand without [destroying] property.' Liberty may be had and property not be destroyed. First, the liberty of all those that have the permanent interest in the kingdom, *that* is provided for [by the constitution]. And [a] [secondly, by an appeal to the Law of Nature] liberty cannot be provided for in a general sense, if property be preserved. For if property be preserved [by acknowledging a natural right in the possessor, so] that I am not to meddle with such a man's estate, his meat, his drink, his apparel, or other goods, then the right of nature destroys liberty. By the right of nature I am to have sustenance rather than perish; yet property destroys it for a man to have [this] by the right [b] of nature, [even] suppose there be no human constitution.

Peter: [c] I do say still, under favour, there is a way to cure all this debate. I will mind you of one thing: that upon the will of one man abusing us, [we reached agreement], and if the safety of the Army be in danger [so we may again]. I hope, it is not denied by any man that any wise, discreet man that hath preserved England [is worthy of a voice] in [d] the government of it. So that, I profess to you, for my part I am clear the point of election should be amended [in that sense]. I think, they will desire no more liberty. If there were time to dispute it, I think they [e] would be satisfied, and all *will* be satisfied.

Cromwell: I confess I was most dissatisfied with that I heard Mr. Sexby speak, of any man here, because it did savour so much of will. But I desire that all of us may decline that, and if we meet here really to agree to that which is [f] for the safety of the kingdom, let us not spend so much time in such debates as these are, but let us apply ourselves to such things as are conclusive, and that shall be this. Everybody here would be willing that the Representative might be mended, that is, [that] it might be [made] better than it is. Perhaps it may be offered in that [other] paper [1] too lamely. If the thing [there] insisted upon be [g] too limited, why perhaps there are a very considerable part of copyholders by inheritance that ought to have a voice; and there may be somewhat [in that paper] too [that] reflects upon the generality of the people [in denying them a voice]. I know our debates are endless if we think to bring it to an issue this way. If we may but resolve upon a committee, [things may be done]. If I cannot be satisfied to go so far as these gentlemen that bring this paper,[2] I say it again [and] I profess it, I shall freely and willingly withdraw myself, and I hope to do it in such a manner that the Army shall see that I shall by my withdrawing satisfy [h] the interest of the Army, the public

---

[1] *Heads of the Proposals.*   [2] The Agreement.

interest of the kingdom, and those ends these men aim at.   And
I think if you do bring this to a result it were well.

Rainborough : If these men must be advanced, and other men set
under foot, I am not satisfied.   If their rules must be observed, and
other men, that are [not] in authority, [be silenced, I] do not know
how this can stand together [with the idea of a free debate].   I
wonder how that should be thought wilfulness in one man that is
reason in another; for I confess I have not heard anything that
doth satisfy me, and though I have not so much wisdom, or [so
many] notions in my head,[a] I have so many [apprehensions] that
I could tell an hundred [such] of [b] the ruin of the people.   I am
not at all against a committee's meeting; and as you say—and I
think every Christian ought to do the same—for my part I shall
be ready, if I see the way that I am going, and the thing that I
would insist on, will destroy the kingdom, I shall withdraw [from]
it as soon as any.   And therefore, till I see that, I shall use all the
means [I can], and I think it is no fault in any man [to refuse] to
sell that which is his birthright.

Sexby : I desire to speak a few words.   I am sorry that my zeal
to what I apprehend is good should be so ill resented.   I am not
sorry to see that which I apprehend is truth [disputed], but I am
sorry the Lord hath darkened some so much as not to see it, and
that is in short [this].   Do you [not] think it were a sad and
miserable condition, that we have fought all this time for nothing?
All here, both great and small, do think that we fought for something.   I confess, many of us fought for those ends which, we
since saw,[c] were not those [d] which caused us to go through difficulties and straits [and] to venture all in the ship with you.   It
had been good in you to have advertised us of it, and I believe you
would have [had] fewer under your command to have commanded.
But if this be the business, that an estate doth make men capable
—it is no matter which way they get it, they are capable—to
choose those that shall represent them,[a] I think there are many
that have not estates that in honesty have as much right in the
freedom [of] their choice [e] as any that have great estates.   Truly,
sir, [as for] your putting off this question and coming to some
other, I dare say, and I dare appeal to all of them, that they cannot
settle upon any other until this be done.   It was the ground that
we took up arms [on], and it is the ground which we shall maintain.   Concerning my making rents and divisions in this way.
As[f] a particular, if I were but so, I could lie down and be trodden

there; [but] truly I am sent by a regiment, [and] if I should not speak, guilt shall lie upon me, and I [should] think I were a covenant-breaker.[a]   I do not know how we have [been] answered in our arguments, and [as for our engagements], I conceive we shall not accomplish them to the kingdom when we deny them to ourselves.[b]   I shall be loath to make a rent and division, but, for my own part, unless I see this put to a question, I despair of an issue.

Clarke : The first thing that I should [c] desire was, and is, this: that there might be a temperature and moderation of spirit within us; that we should speak with moderation, not with such reflection as was boulted one from another, but so speak and so hear as that which [is said] may be the droppings of love from one to another's hearts.   Another word I have to say is [that] the grand question of all is, whether or no it be the property of every individual person in the kingdom to have a vote in election[s]; and the ground [on which it is claimed] is the Law of Nature, which, for my part, I think to be that law which is the ground of all constitutions. Yet really properties are the foundation of constitutions, [and not constitutions of property].   For if so be there were no constitutions,[d] yet [e] the Law of Nature does give a principle [for every man] to have a property of what he has, or may have, which is not another man's.   This [natural right to] property is the ground of *meum* and *tuum*.   Now there may be inconveniencies on both hands, but not so great freedom [on either as is supposed —not] the greater freedom, as I conceive, that all may have whatsoever [they have a mind to].   And if it come to pass that there be a difference, and that the one [claimant] doth oppose the other, then nothing can decide it but the sword, which is the wrath of God.

Audley : I see you have a long dispute [and] that you do intend to dispute here till the tenth of March.   You have brought us into a fair pass, and the kingdom into a fair pass, for if your reasons are not satisfied, and we do not fetch all our waters from your wells, you threaten to withdraw yourselves.   I could wish, according to our several protestations, we might sit down quietly, and there throw down ourselves where we see reason.   I could wish we might all rise, and go to our duties, and set [f] our work in hand.   I see both [parties] at a stand; and if we dispute here, both are lost.

Cromwell : Really for my own part I must needs say, whilst we say we would not make reflections we do make reflections; and if I had not come hither with a free heart to do that that I was persuaded in my conscience is my duty, I should a thousand times rather have kept myself away. For I do think I had brought upon myself the greatest sin that I was [ever] guilty of, if I should have come to have stood before God in that former duty,[a] and if [I did retreat from] that my saying—which I did say, and shall persevere to say—that I shall not, I cannot, against my conscience do anything. They that have stood so much for liberty of conscience, if they will not grant that liberty to every man, but say it is a deserting I know not what—if that [liberty] be denied me, I think there is not that equality that is [b] professed to be amongst us.[c] Though we should be satisfied in our consciences in what we do, we are told we purpose to leave the Army, or to leave our commands, as if we took upon us to do it as [d] [a] matter of will. I did hear some gentlemen speak more of will than anything that was spoken this way, for more was spoken by way of will than of satisfaction, and if there be not [k] more equality in our minds I can but grieve for it, I must do no more.[e] I said this (and I say no more): that [if you would] make your businesses as well as you can, we might bring things to an understanding; [for] it was [in order] to be brought to a fair composure [that we met]. And when you have said [what you can for the paper and have heard our objections], if [then] you should put this paper to the question without any qualifications, I doubt whether it would pass so freely. If we would have no difference we ought to put it [with due qualifications]. And let me speak clearly and freely —I have heard other gentlemen do the like: I have not heard the Commissary-General answered, not in one [f] part, to my knowledge, not in a tittle. If, therefore, when I see there is an extremity of difference between you, [I move for a committee] to the end it may be brought nearer to a general satisfaction [g]—if this [too] be thought a deserting of that interest, [I know not] if there can be anything more sharply said; I will not give it an ill word.

Ireton : I should not speak [again], but reflections do necessitate [it], do call upon us to vindicate ourselves. As if we, who have led men into engagements and services,[h] had divided [from them] because we did not concur with them! I will ask that gentleman [i] that spoke [j] (whom I love in my heart): whether when they drew out to serve the Parliament in the beginning, whether when they engaged with the Army at Newmarket, whether *then* they thought of any more interest or right in the kingdom than this; whether they did think that they should have as great interest in Parliament-men as freeholders had, or whether from the beginning we did not engage for the liberty of Parliaments, and that we should be concluded by the laws that such did make. Unless somebody did make you believe before now that you should have an equal interest in the kingdom, unless somebody did ᵃ make that to be believed, there is no reason to blame men for leading [you] so far as they have done; and if any man was far enough from such an apprehension, that man hath not been deceived. And truly, I shall say but this word more for myself in this business, because the whole objection seems to be pressed to me, and maintained against ᵇ me. I will not arrogate that I was the first man that put the Army upon the thought either of successive Parliaments or more equal Parliaments; yet there are some here that know who they were [that] put us upon that foundation of liberty of putting a period to this Parliament, [in order] that we might have successive Parliaments, and that there might be a more equal distribution of elections. There are many here that know who were the first movers of that business in the Army. I shall not arrogate that [to myself], but I can argue this with a clear conscience: that no man hath prosecuted that with more earnestness, and ᶠ will stand to that interest more than I do, of having Parliaments successive and not perpetual, and the ᶜ distribution of elections ᵈ [more equal]. But, notwithstanding, my opinion stands good, that it ought to be a distribution amongst the fixed and settled people of this nation. It's more prudent and safe, and more upon this ground of right for it [to be so]. Now it is the fundamental constitution of this kingdom; and that which you take away [you take away] for matter of wilfulness. Notwithstanding, [as for] this universal conclusion, that all inhabitants [shall have voices], as it stands [in the Agreement], I must declare that though ᵉ I cannot yet be satisfied, yet for my part I shall acquiesce. I will not make a distraction in this Army. Though I have a property in being one of those that should be an elector, though I have an interest in the birthright, yet I will rather lose that birthright and that interest than I will make it my business [to oppose them], if I see but the generality of those whom I have reason to think honest men and conscientious men and godly men, to carry them[selves] another way. I will not oppose, though I be not satisfied to join with them. And I desire [to say this]. I am agreed with you if you insist upon a more equal distribution of elections; I will agree with you, not only to dispute for it, but to fight for it and contend for it. Thus far I shall agree with you. On the other hand, [to] those who differ

[in] their terms [and say], 'I will not agree with *you* except you go farther,' [I make answer], 'Thus far I can go with you: I will go with you as far as I can.' If you will appoint a committee [a] of some [b] [few] to consider of that, so as you preserve the equitable part of that constitution [that now is, securing a voice ·to those] who are like to be free men,[c] men not given up to the wills of others, [and thereby] keeping to the latitude which is the equity of constitutions, I will go with you as far as I can. [And where I cannot] I will sit down, I will not make any disturbance among you.

Rainborough: If I do [d] speak my soul and conscience I do think that there is not an objection made but that it hath been answered; but the speeches are so long. I am sorry for some passion and some reflections, and I could wish where it is most taken [amiss] the cause had not been given. It is a fundamental [of the] constitution of the kingdom, [that] there [be parliamentary boroughs]; I would fain know whether the choice of burgesses in corporations should not be altered. [But] the end wherefore I speak is only this. You think we shall be worse than we are, if we come to a conclusion by a [sudden] vote. If it be put to the question we shall [at least] all know one another's mind. If it be determined, and the [common] resolutions known, we shall take such a course as to put it in execution. This gentleman says, if he cannot go he will sit still. He thinks he hath a full liberty [to do so]; we think we have not. There is a great deal of difference between us two. If a man hath all he doth desire, [he may wish to sit still]; but [if] I think I have nothing at all of what I fought for, I do not think the argument holds that I must desist as well as he.

Petty: The rich would very unwillingly be concluded by the poor. And there is as much reason that the rich should conclude the poor as the poor the rich [e]—and indeed [that is] no reason [at all].[f] There should be an equal share in both. I understood your engagement was that you would use all your endeavours for the liberties of the people, that they should be secured. If there is [such] a constitution that the people are not free, that [constitution] should be annulled. That constitution which is now set up is a constitution of forty shillings a year, but this constitution doth not make [the] people free.

Cromwell: Here's the mistake: [you make the whole question to be] whether that's the better constitution in that paper, or that which [now] is. But if you will go upon such a ground as that,[a] although a better constitution was [really] offered for the removing of the worse, yet some gentlemen are resolved to stick to the worse [and] there might be a great deal of prejudice upon such an apprehension. I think you are by this time satisfied that it is a clear mistake; for it is a dispute whether or no this [proposed constitution] be [f] better—nay, whether it be not destructive to the kingdom.

Petty: I desire to speak one word to this business, because I do not know whether my occasions will suffer me to attend it any longer. The great reason that I have heard [urged] is, 'the constitution of the kingdom, the *utmost* constitution of it'; and 'if we destroy this constitution there is no property.' I suppose that if constitutions should tie up all men in this nature it were very dangerous.

Ireton: First, the thing itself were dangerous if it were settled [so as] to destroy propriety. But I say the principle that leads to this [proposed change] *is* destructive to property. For by the same reason that you will alter this constitution, merely that [b] there 's a greater [liberty] by nature [than this] constitution [c] [gives]—by the same reason, by the Law of Nature, there is a greater liberty to the use of other men's goods, which that property bars you of. And I would fain have any man show me why I should destroy that liberty which the freeholders, and burghers in corporations, have in choosing [knights and] burgesses (that which if [d] you take away, you leave no constitution), and this because there is a greater freedom due to me [e] by the Law of Nature—[why I should do this] more than that I should take another man's goods because the Law of Nature does allow me.

Rainborough: I would grant something that the Commissary-General says. But [I would have the question stated]: Whether this be a just propriety, the propriety [that] says that forty shillings a year enables a man to elect? If it were stated to that [effect], nothing would conduce so much [to determine] whether some men do agree or no.

Captain [Edmund] Rolfe: I conceive that, as we are met here, there are one or two things mainly to be prosecuted by us; that is especially unity, [the] preservation of unity in the Army, and so likewise to put ourselves into a capacity thereby to do good to the kingdom.[a]   Therefore I shall desire that there may be a tender consideration had of that which is so much urged, in that of an equal, as well as of a free, Representative.   I shall desire that a medium, or some thoughts of a composure, [may be had] in relation to servants or to foreigners, or such others as shall be agreed upon.   I say, then, I conceive, excepting those, there may be a very equitable sense [p]resented to us from that offer in our own declarations wherein we do offer the common good of all, unless they have made any shipwreck or loss of it.

Clarke : [b] I presume that the great stick here is this: that if every one shall have his [natural] propriety [of election] it does bereave the kingdom of its principal fundamental constitution, that it [now] hath.   I presume that all people, and all nations whatsoever, have a liberty and power to alter and change their constitutions if they find them to be weak and infirm.   Now if the people of England shall find this weakness in their constitution, they may change it if they please.   Another thing is this: [it is feared that] if the light of nature be only [followed] in this, it may destroy the propriety which every man can call his own. [But it will not, and] the reason is this, because this principle and light of nature doth give all men their own—as, for example, the clothes upon my back because they are not another man's. [Finally] if every man hath this propriety of election to choose those who [shall make the laws], you fear [it] may beget inconveniencies.   I do not conceive that anything may be so nicely and precisely done but that it may admit of inconveniency.   If it be [that there is inconveniency] in that [form of the constitution] wherein it is now, there may [some of] those inconveniencies rise [from the changes, that are apprehended] from them.   For my part I know nothing [of fatal consequence in the relation of men] but the want of love in it, and [then, if difference arises], the sword must decide it.

I [too] shall desire [that] before the question be stated it may be moderated as for foreigners.

Chillenden : In the beginning of this discourse there were overtures made of imminent danger.   This way we have taken this afternoon is not the way to prevent it.   I would [c] humbly move that we should put a speedy end to this business, and that not only to this main question of the paper, but also according to the Lieutenant-General's motion, that a committee may be chosen seriously to consider the things in that paper, and compare them

with divers things in our declarations and engagements, that so
[we may show ourselves ready], as we have all professed, to lay
down ourselves before God. If we take this course of debating
upon one question a whole afternoon, [and] if the danger be so
near as it is supposed, it were the ready way to bring us into it.
[I desire] that things may be put into a speedy dispatch.

Sir Hardress Waller : This was that I was [desirous of] saying.
(I confess I have not spoken yet, and I was willing to be silent,
having heard so many speak, that I might learn).ᵃ It is not easy
for us to say when this dispute will have an end; but I think it is
easy to say when the kingdom will have an end.ᵇ If we do not
breathe out ourselves, we shall be kicked and spurned of all the
world. I would fain know how far the question will decide it; for
certainly we must not expect, while we have tabernacles here, to be
all of one mind. If it be to be decided by a question, and ᶜ all
parties are satisfied in that, I think the sooner you hasten to it the
better. If otherwise, we shall needlessly discover our dividing
opinion, which as long as it may be avoided I desire it may. Therefore I desire to have a period [put to this debate].

Audley : I chanced to speak a word or two. Truly there was
more offence taken at it. For my part I spoke against every man
living, not only against yourself and the Commissary, but [against]
every man that would dispute till we have our throats cut,ᵈ and
therefore I desire I may not lie in any prejudice before your
persons.ᵉ I profess, if so be there were none but you and the
Commissary-General alone to maintain that argument, I would
die in any place in England, in asserting that it is the right of
every free-born man to elect, according to the rule, *Quod omnibus
spectat, ab omnibus*ᶠ *tractari debet,* that which concerns all ought
to be debated by all. [*He continued :* That] he knew no reason
why that law should oblige [him] when he himself had no finger
in appointing the law-giver.

Captain Bishop : You have met here this day to see if God
would show you any way wherein you might jointly preserve the
kingdom from its destruction, which you all apprehend to be at
the door. God is pleased not to come in to you. There is a
gentleman, Mr. Saltmarsh, did desire what he has wrote may be
read to the General Council.[1] If God do manifest anything by
him I think it ought to be heard.

¹ See letter of John Saltmarsh, Appendix, pp. 438–9.

Ireton: [I have declared] that you will alter that constitution from a better to a worse, from a just to a thing that is less just in my apprehension; and I will not repeat the reasons of that, but refer to what I have declared before. To me, if there were nothing but this, that there is a constitution, and that constitution which is the very last constitution, which if you take away you leave nothing of constitution, and consequently nothing of right or property, [it would be enough]. I would not go to alter this,[a] though a man could propound that which in some respects might be better, unless it could be demonstrated to me that this were unlawful, or that this were destructive. Truly, therefore, I say for my part, to go on a sudden to make such a limitation as that [to inhabitants] in general, [is to make no limitation at all]. If you do extend the latitude [of the constitution so far] that any man shall have a voice in election who has not that interest in this kingdom that is permanent and fixed, who hath not that interest upon which he may [b] have his [c] freedom in this kingdom without dependence, you will put it into the hands of men to choose, [not] of men [desirous] to preserve their liberty, [but of men] who will give it away.

[d] I am confident, our discontent and dissatisfaction [e] if ever they do well, they do in this. If there be anything at all that is a foundation of liberty it is this, that those who shall choose the law-makers shall be men freed from dependence upon others.[f] I have a thing put into my heart which I cannot but speak. I profess I am afraid that if we, from such apprehensions as these are of an imaginable right of nature opposite to constitution, if we will contend and hazard the breaking of peace upon [g] this business of that enlargement,[h] I think if we, from imaginations and conceits, will go about to hazard the peace of the kingdom, to alter the constitution in such a point, I am afraid we shall find the hand of God will follow it [and] we shall see that that liberty which we so much talk of, and [have so much] contended for, shall be nothing at all by this our contending for it, by [our] putting it into the hands of those men that will give it away when they have it.

Cromwell: If we should go about to alter these things, I do not think that we are bound to fight for every particular proposition. Servants, while servants, are not included. Then you agree that he that receives alms is to be excluded?

Lieutenant-Colonel [Thomas] Reade: I suppose it's concluded by all, that the choosing of representatives is a privilege; now I see

no reason why any [a] man that is a native ought to be excluded that
privilege, unless from voluntary servitude.

Petty : I conceive the reason why we would exclude apprentices,
or servants, or those that take alms,[b] is because they depend upon
the will of other men and should be afraid to displease [them].
For servants and apprentices, they are included in their masters,
and so for those that receive alms from door to door; but if there
be any general way taken for those that are not [so] bound [to the
will of other men], it would be [c] well.

Everard : I being sent from the Agents of [the] five regiments
with an answer unto a writing, the committee was very desirous
to inquire into the depth of our intentions.   Those things that
they had there manifested in the paper,[d] and what I did understand as a particular person, I did declare.[e]   It was the Lieutenant-General's desire for an understanding with us,[f] presuming
those things I did declare did tend to unity. 'And if so,' [said he],
'you will let it appear by coming unto us.'   We have gone thus
far: we have had two or three meetings to declare and hold forth
what it is we stand upon, the principles of unity and freedom.
We have declared in what we conceive these principles do lie—
I shall not name them all because they are known unto you.   Now
in the progress of these disputes and debates we find that the time
spends, and no question but our adversaries are harder at work
than we are.   I heard [g] (but I had no such testimony as I could
take hold of) that there are meetings daily and contrivances against
us.   Now for our parts we [h] hope you will not say all [the desire
for unity] is yours, but [will acknowledge that] we have nakedly
and freely unbosomed ourselves unto you.   Though those things
[in the paper] have startled many at the first view, yet we find
there is [still] good hopes.   We have fixed our resolutions, and
we are determined, and we want nothing but that only God will
direct us to what is just and right.   But I understand that [in]
all these debates if we shall agree upon any one thing, [to say],
'This is our freedom; this is our liberty; this liberty and freedom
we are debarred of, and we are bereaved of all those comforts,'
[that even] in case we should find out half an hundred of these, yet
the main business is [first] how we should find them, and [then]
how we should come by them.   Is there any liberty [1] that we
find ourselves deprived of?   If we have grievances let us see who
are the hindrances [that oppose the best way of removing them][j]
when we have pitched upon that way.   I conceive—I speak

humbly in this one thing as a particular person ᵃ—I conceive,
myself, that these delays, these disputes, will prove little en-
couragement.ᵇ It was told me by [one of] these gentlemen,
that he had great jealousies that we would not come to the trial
of our spirits and that perhaps there might happen [to be]
another design in hand. I said to his Honour again, if they
would not come to the light I would judge they had the works of
darkness in hand. Now as they told me again on the other hand,
when it was questioned by Colonel Hewson: ᶜ 'These gentlemen,'
[said they], not naming any particular persons, 'they will hold
you in hand, and keep you in debate and dispute till you and we
[shall] come all to ruin.' Now I stood as a moderator between
[the asserters of] these things. When I heard the Lieutenant-
General speak I was marvellously taken up with the plainness of
the carriage. I said, 'I will bring them to you. You shall see if
their hearts be so. For my part I [shall expect to] see nothing
but plainness and uprightness of heart made manifest unto you.'
I will not judge, nor draw any long discourse upon, our disputes
this day. We may differ in one thing: that you conceive this
debating and disputation ᵈ will do the work; [while we conceive]
we must [without delay] put ourselves into the former privileges
which we want.

Waller : I think this gentleman hath dealt very ingenuously ᵉ
and plainly with us. I pray God we may do so too, and, for one, I
will do it. I think our disputings will not do the thing. I think
[we shall do well] if we do make it our resolution that we do hold
it forth to all powers—Parliament or King, or whoever they are
—to let them know that these are our rights, and if we have them
not we must get them the best way we can.

Cromwell : I think you say very well; and my friend at my
back, he tells me that [there] are great fears abroad; and they
[that bring the paper] talk of some things such as are not only
specious to take a great many people with, but real and substantial, and such as are comprehensive of that that hath the good
of the kingdom in it. ᶠ Truly if there be never so much desire of
carrying on these things [together], never so much desire of
conjunction, yet if there be not liberty of speech to come to a right
understanding of things, I think it shall be all one as if there were
no desire at all to meet. ᶠ I may say it with truth, that I verily
believe there is as much reality and heartiness amongst us [as
amongst you], to come to a right understanding, and to accord
with that that hath the settlement of the kingdom in it. Though

when it comes to particulars we may differ in the way, yet I know nothing but that every honest man will go as far as his conscience will let him; and he that will go farther, I think he will fall back. And I think, when that principle is written in the hearts of us, and when there is not hypocrisy in our dealings, we must all of us resolve upon this, that 'tis God that persuades the heart. If there be a doubt of sincerity, it 's the devil that created that effect; and 'tis God that gives uprightness [of heart]. And I hope that [a] with such an heart we have all met withal. If we have not, God find him out that came without it; for my part I do [come with] it.

Ireton : [b] I would have us fall to something that is 'practicable, with as little pains and dissatisfaction as may be. [c] [As for the distribution of representatives], when you have done this according to the number of inhabitants, do you think it is not very variable, [d] for the number will change every day ? [e] I remember that in the proposals that went out in the name of the Army, [1] it is propounded as a rule [for the seats] to be distributed according to the rates that the counties bear in the [burdens of the] kingdom. And remember then you have a rule, and though this be not a rule of exactness [either], yet there was something of equality in it, and it was a *certain* rule, where all are agreed; and therefore [by adopting it] we should come to some settling. Now I do not understand wherein the advantage does lie, [if] from a sudden [apprehension of] danger, [we should rashly fix] upon a thing that will continue so long, and will continue so uncertain as this is.

Waller : 'Tis thought there 's imminent danger; I hope to God we shall be so ready to agree for the future that we shall all agree for the present to rise as one man if the danger be such, for it is an impossibility to have a remedy in this. The paper says that this [present] Parliament is to continue a year, but will the great burden of the people be ever satisfied with papers [whilst] you eat and feed upon them ? I shall be glad that, [if] there be not any present danger, [f] you will think of some way to ease the burden, that we may take a course [to do it]; and when we have satisfied the people that we do really intend the good of the kingdom [they will believe us]. Otherwise, if the four Evangelists were here, and lay [at] free-quarter upon them, they [g] would not believe them. [h]

Colonel Rainborough moved : That the Army might be called

---
[1] *Heads of the Proposals*; see p. 422.

to a rendezvous, and things settled [as promised in its printed engagements].

Ireton : We are called back to engagements. I think the engagements [a] we have made and published, and all the engagements of all sorts, have been better kept by those that did not so much cry out for it than by those that do, and—if you will [have it] in plain terms—better kept than by those that have brought this paper. Give me leave to tell you, in that one point, in the engagement of the Army not to divide,[1] I am sure that he that understands the engagement of the Army not to divide or disband [b] [as meaning] that we are not to divide for quarters, for the ease of the country, or the satisfaction of service—he that does understand it in that sense, I am not capable of his understanding.[c] There was another sense in it, and that is, that we should not suffer ourselves to be torn into pieces. Such a dividing as [that] is really a disbanding, and for my part I do not know what disbanding is if not that dividing. [I say] that [d] the subscribers of this paper, the authors [e] of that book that is called *The Case of the Army*, I say that *they* have gone the way of disbanding.[f] Disbanding of an army is not parting in a place, for if that be so, did we not at that night disband to several quarters? Did we not then send several regiments: Colonel Scroope's regiment into the West — we know where it was first; Colonel Horton's regiment into Wales for preventing of insurrection there; Colonel Lambert's [and] Colonel Lilburne's regiment[s] then sent down for strengthening such a place as York?[g] And yet the authors of that paper and the subscribers of it [h]—for I cannot think the authors and subscribers all one [i]—know, and [well] they may know it, that there is not one part of the Army is divided [in body] farther than the outcries of the authors of it [are in spirit].[j] [For] they go [about] to scandalize [us as breakers of] an engagement [not to disperse] or divide; [yet they know that] there 's no part of the Army is dispersed to quarters further than that [I have stated]. Whereupon [all] that outcry is [made]! But he that will go to understand this to be a dividing that we engaged against, he looks at the name, and not at the thing. That dividing which is a disbanding [is] that dividing which makes no army, and [k] that dissolving of that order and government which is as essential to an army as life is to a man—which if it be taken away I think that such a company are no more an army than a rotten carcass is a man; and [it is] those [who have done this] that have gone [about] to divide the

[1] See p. 430.

Army. And what else is there in this paper [but] that we have acted so vigorously for [already]? We proposed that this Parliament should end within a year at most]; they do not propose that this [present] Parliament should end till the beginning of September.[a] When all comes [to be considered] upon the matter, it is but a critical difference and the very substance of that we have declared [for] before.[b] And let it be judged whether [c] this way [d] we have taken and [e] that [way] they have taken be not the same as to the matter [of it].[f] For my part I profess it seriously, that we shall find [g] in the issue that the principle of that division [which they seek to raise on the question] of disbanding is no more than this: whether such [men] or such shall have the managing of the business.[h] I say plainly, the way [they have taken] hath been the way of disunion and division, and [i] [the dissolution] of that order and government by which we shall be enabled to act [at all]. And I shall appeal to all men: [whether] the dividing from that General Council [and from the resolution] wherein we have all engaged [that] we would be concluded by [the decisions of] that [Council], and [whether likewise] the endeavouring to draw the soldiers to run this way [with them—whether this is not the real dividing of the Army]. I shall appeal [to them]: whether there can be any breach of the Army higher than that breach we have now spoke of, [any truer sense in which] that word 'dividing the Army' [j] [can be taken]; whether that dividing were not more truly and properly [such, which is] in every man's heart, [than] this dividing [which they do accuse us of incurring], wherein we do go apart one from another [but remain united in heart], and [whether it does not follow] consequently, [that] those that have gone this way have not broke the *Engagement*, [but that] the other dividing [k] [cannot be] a keeping of the *Engagement*. And those that do [so] judge the one [and the other, will concur with me when I say], I do not think that we have been fairly dealt with.

Rainborough : I do not make any great wonder that this gentleman hath sense above all men in the world. But for these things, he is the man that hath undertaken [the drawing-up of] them all. I say, this gentleman hath the advantage of us [on the question of engagements]: he hath drawn up the most part of them; and why [l] may he[m] not keep a sense that we do not know of? If this gentleman had declared to us at first that this was the sense of the Army in dividing, and it was meant that men should not divide in opinions! To me that is a mystery.[n] It is a huge reflection, a taxing of persons,[o] and because I will avoid further reflections, I shall say no more.

[*An*] *Agitator :* Whereas you say the Agents did it, [it was] the soldiers did put the Agents upon these meetings. It was the dissatisfactions that were in the Army which provoked, which occasioned, those meetings, which you suppose tends so much to dividing; and the reason[s] of such dissatisfactions are because those whom they had to trust to act for them were not true to them.

[*Ireton*] : If this be all the effect of your meetings to agree upon this paper, there is but one thing in this that hath not been insisted upon and propounded by the Army heretofore, [in the *Heads of the Proposals*, and] all along. Here it is put according to the number of inhabitants; [a] there according to the taxes. This says a period at such a day, the last of September; the other says a period within a year at most. [The Agreement says] that these have the power of making law, and determining what is law, without the consent of another. 'Tis true the *Proposals* said not that [but would restore the consent of the King]. And for my part, if any man will put that to the question whether we shall concur with it, I am in the same mind [still, especially] if [by your franchise] you put it in any other hands than [of] those that are free men. But [even] if you shall put the question [b] with that limitation [to free men] that hath been all along acknowledged by the Parliament, till we can acquit ourselves justly from any engagement, old or new, that we stand in, to preserve the person of the King, the persons of Lords, and their rights, so far as they are consistent with the common right [and the safety of the kingdom] —till *that* be done, I think there is reason [that] that exception [in their favour] should continue, [but with the proviso] which hath been all along, that is, where the safety of the kingdom is concerned. This the *Proposals* [c] seem to hold out. I would hold to positive constitution where I [see things] would not do real mischief.[d] I would neither be thought to be a wrong-doer or disturber; so long as I can with safety continue a constitution I will do it.[e] And therefore where I find that the safety of the kingdom is not concerned, I would not for every trifling [cause] make that this shall be a law, though neither the Lords, who have a claim to it, nor the King, who hath a claim to it, will consent. But where this [safety] is concerned [I think that particular rights cannot stand]. Upon the whole matter let men but consider [whether] those that have thus gone away to divide from the Army [will not destroy the constitution upon a fancied right and advantage of the people]. Admit that this Agreement of the People be the advantage, it may be.[f] Shall we [g] [then] agree to that without any limitation? I do agree that the King is bound by his oath at his coronation [a] to agree to the law that the Commons shall choose without Lords or anybody else.[d] [But] if I can agree any further, that if the King do not confirm with his authority the laws that the people shall choose [those laws require not his authority], we know what will follow.

Petty: I had the happiness sometimes to be at the debate of the *Proposals*, and my opinion was then as it is now, against the King's vote and the Lords'. But [I did] not [then] so [definitely desire the abolition of these votes] as I do [now] desire [it; for] since [that time] it hath pleased God to raise a company of men that do stand up for the power of the House of Commons, which is the Representative of the people, and deny the negative voice of King and Lords. For my part I was much unknown to any of them, but [e] I heard their principles; and hearing[1] their principles I cannot but join with them in my judgment, for I think it is reasonable that all laws are made by their[1] consent [alone]. Whereas you seem to make the King and Lords so light a thing as that it may be [f] without prejudice [g] [to keep them, though] to the destruction of the kingdom to throw them out;[j] for my part I cannot but think that both the power of King and Lords was ever a branch of tyranny. And if ever a people shall free themselves from tyranny, certainly it is after seven years' war and fighting for their liberty. For my part [I think that] if the constitution of this kingdom shall be established as formerly, it might rivet tyranny into this kingdom more strongly than before. For when the people shall hear that for seven years together the people were plundered, and [that] after they had overcome the King and kept the King under restraint,[j] at last the King comes in again,[h] then it will rivet the King's interest; and so when any men shall endeavour to free themselves from tyranny we may do them mischief and no good. I think it 's most just and equal, since a number of men have declared against it, [that] they should be encouraged in it, and not discouraged. And I find by the Council that their thoughts are the same against the King and Lords, and if so be that a power may be raised to do that, it would do well.

Wildman: Truly, sir, I being desired by the Agents yesterday to appear at council or committees either, at that time [in their behalf], I suppose I may be bold to make known what I know of their sense, and a little to vindicate them in their way of

---

[1] i.e. the people's.

proceeding, and to show the necessity of this way of proceeding that they have entered upon. Truly, sir, as to breaking of engagements, the Agents do declare their principle, that whenever any engagement cannot be kept justly [a] they must break that engagement. Now though it 's urged they ought to condescend to what the General Council do [resolve], I conceive it 's true [only] so long as it is for their safety. I conceive [it 's] just and righteous for them to stand up for some more speedy vigorous actings. I conceive it 's no more than what the Army did when the Parliament did not only delay deliverance, but opposed it. And I conceive this way of their appearing hath not been [b] in the least way anything tending to division, since they proceed to clear the rights of the people; and so long as they proceed upon those righteous principles [for which we first engaged], I suppose it cannot be laid to their charge that they are dividers. And though it be declared [that they ought to stand only as soldiers and not as Englishmen], yet [c] the malice of the enemies would have bereaved you of your liberties as Englishmen, [and] therefore as Englishmen they are deeply concerned to regard the due observation of their rights, [and have the same right to declare their apprehensions] as I, or any commoner, have right to propound to the kingdom my conceptions [of] what is fit for the good of the kingdom. Whereas it is objected, 'How will it appear that their proceedings shall tend for the good of the kingdom?' that [d] matter is different [from the point of justice they would propound]. Whereas it was said before, it was propounded [in the Council, that] there must be an end to the [present] Parliament [and] an equality as to elections, I find it to be their minds [also; but] when they came there, they found many aversions from matters that they ought to stand to as soldiers and [e] as Englishmen, and therefore, I find, it [was discovered that there was a difference] concerning the matter of the thing, [and] I conceive it to be a very vast difference in the whole matter of [the] *Proposals*. [By it] the foundation of slavery was riveted more strongly than before—as where the militia is instated in the King and Lords, and not in the Commons, [and] there [too] is a foundation of a future quarrel constantly laid. However, the main thing was that the right of the militia was acknowledged [f] to be in the King, [g] [as] they found in the *Proposals* propounded, [h] before any redress of any one of the people's grievances [or] any one of their burdens; and [the King was] so to be brought in as with a negative voice, whereby the people and Army that have fought against him when *he* had propounded such things, [would be at his mercy]. And finding [this], they perceived they were, as they thought, in a sad case; for they thought, he coming in thus with a negative [voice], the Parliament are but as so many ciphers, so many round O's, for if the King would not do it, he might choose, *Sic volo, sic jubeo, &c.*, and so the corrupt party of the kingdom must be so settled in the King. The godly people are turned over and trampled upon already in the most places of the kingdom.[a] I speak but the words of the Agents,[b] and I find this to be their thoughts. But whereas it is said, 'How will this paper provide for anything for that purpose?' I shall say that this paper doth lay down the foundations of freedom for all manner of people. It doth lay the foundations of soldiers' [freedom], whereas they found a great uncertainty in the *Proposals*, [which implied] that they should go to the King for an Act of Indemnity, and thus the King might command his judges to hang them up for what they did in the wars, because, the present constitution being left as it was, nothing was law but what the King signed, and not any ordinance of Parliament [without his consent]. And considering this,[c] they thought it should be by an Agreement with the people, whereby a rule between the Parliament and the people might be set, that so they might be destroyed neither by the King's prerogative nor Parliament's privileges ([including those of the Lords, for] they are not bound to be subject to the laws as other men, [and that is] why men cannot recover their estates). They thought there must be a necessity of a rule between the Parliament and the people, so that the Parliament should know what they were entrusted with,[d] and what they were not; and that there might be no doubt of[k] the Parliament's power, to lay foundations of future quarrels. The Parliament shall not meddle with a soldier after indemnity [if] it is [so] agreed amongst the people; whereas between a parliament and [a] king [the soldier may lose his indemnity]. If the King were not under restraint [his assent might be made to bind him. But if the present Parliament] should make an Act of Indemnity, who[e] [shall say that] another Parliament cannot alter this? [An Agreement of the People would be necessary], that these foundations might be established, that there might be no dispute between Lords and Commons, and[f] [that], these things being settled, there should be no more disputes [at all], but that the Parliament should redress the people's grievances. Whereas now almost[g] all are troubled with [the] King's interests, if this were settled the Parliament should be free from these temptations.[h] And besides[i]—which for my own part I do suppose to be a truth[j]—this very Parliament, by the King's voice in this very Parliament, may destroy [us], whereas [then] they shall be free from temptations and the King cannot have an influence upon them [such] as he now ª hath.

Ireton: Gentlemen, I think there is no man is able to give a better account of the sense of the Agents, and so readily; he hath spoke so much as they have in their book, and therefore I say ᵇ he is very well able to give their sense.ᶜ I wish their sense ᵈ had [not only] not been prejudicial to other men's senses, but, as ᵉ I fear it will prove, really prejudicial to the kingdom [as well], how plausibly ᶠ soever it seems to be carried.   That paper of *The Case of the Army* ᵍ doth so abuse the General and General Council of the Army, [stating] that such and such things have been done that made them do thus and thus,ᶜ [that I cannot leave it unanswered]. First as to the material points of the paper.   You know as to the business of the Lords, the way we were then in admitted no other [course].   This gentleman that speaks here, and the other gentleman that spake before, when we were at Reading framing the *Proposals* [they] did not think of this way. I am sure they did not think of this way; and according to the best judgments of those that were entrusted by the General Council to draw up the *Proposals*, it was carried by a question clearly, that we should not [adopt such a way].   In these *Proposals* our business was to set forth particulars; we had set forth general declarations, which did come to as much in effect as this; the thing then proposed was that we should not take away the power of the Lords in this kingdom, and it was [so] concluded ᵍ in the *Proposals*. But as to the King we were clear.   There is not one thing in the *Proposals*, nor in what was declared, that doth give the King any negative [voice].   And therefore that 's part of the scandal amongst others: we do not give the King any negative voice; we do but take the King as a man with whom we have been at a difference; we propound terms of peace. We do not demand that he shall have no negative, but we do not say that he shall have any.   There 's another thing: ᵍ we have, as they say, gone from our engagements in our declarations in that we go in the *Proposals* to establish the King's rights before [taking away] the people's grievances.   In our general declarations ¹ we first desire a purging of this Parliament, a period [to be set] for ʰ this Parliament, and provision for the certainty of future Parliaments; and if the King shall agree in these things and what [things] else the Parliament shall propound,

¹ See the *Representation of the Army*; see also *Heads of the Proposals* and Wildman's *Putney Projects* (pp. 403-9, 422-6, 426-9).

that are necessary for the safety of the kingdom, then we desire
his rights may be considered so far as may consist with the rights
of the people. We did so [speak] in the declarations, and you
shall see what we did in the *Proposals*. In the *Proposals*, [we put
first] things that are essential to peace, and it distinguishes those
from the things that conduce to our better being, and things
that lay foundations of an hopeful constitution in the future.
When those are passed, then we [1] say that, 'these things having
the King's concurrence, we desire that his right may be considered.' There were many other grievances and particular
matters [of] which we did not think [it] so necessary that they
should precede the settling of a peace, [the lack of] which is the
greatest grievance of the kingdom. Our way was to take away
that [first]. Then we say there, [after] propounding what things
we thought in our judgments [a] to be essential and necessary as
to peace,[b] 'Yet we desire that the Parliament would lose no time
from the consideration of them.' These gentlemen would say
now [that] we have gone from our declarations, that we propose
the settling of the King [first, because] it stands before those
grievances. We say, those grievances are not so necessary [to
be remedied] as that the remedying of them should be before the
settling of the peace of the kingdom. What we thought in our
consciences to be essential to the peace of the kingdom we did
put [j] preceding to the consideration of the King's personal right;
and the concurrence of [the King to] those is a condition without
which we cannot have any right at all, and without [which] there
can be no peace, and [we] have named [it] before [c] the consideration of the King's rights in the settling of a peace, as a thing
necessary to the constitution of a peace. That, therefore, [to
say] we should prefer the King's rights before a general good, was
as unworthy and as unchristian an injury as ever was done [by
any] to men that were in society with them, and [d] merely equivocation. But it was told you, that the General Council hath
seemed to do so and so, to put the soldiers out of the way.[e] It is
suggested that the *Engagement* is broken by our dividing to
quarters; and whether that be broken or not [f] in other things,[g]
it is said that the General Council hath broken the *Engagement* in
this: that whereas before we were not a mercenary army, now we
are. Let any man but speak what hath given the occasion of that.
It hath been pressed by some men that we should [not] have
subjected [our propositions] to the Parliament, and we should [h]
stand to the propositions whatever they were; but the sense of the
General Council was this: that, as they had sent their propositions

to the Parliament,[g] they would see what the Parliament would do
before they would conclude what themselves would do; and that
there was respect [to be had] to that which we have hitherto
accounted the fundamental council of the kingdom. If all the
people to a man had subscribed to this [Agreement], then there
would be some security to it, because no man would oppose [it];
but otherwise our concurrence amongst ourselves is no more than
our saying [that] ourselves we will be indemnified.[a] Our indemnity must be [owed] to something that at least we will uphold,
and we see we cannot hold [the Army] to be a conclusive authority
of the kingdom.[b] For that [charge] of going to the King for
indemnity, we propose[d] an Act of Oblivion only for the King's
party; we propose[d] for ourselves an Act of Indemnity and
Justification. Is this the asking of a pardon? [c] Let us resort to
the first petition of the Army, wherein we all were engaged once,
which we made the basis of all our proceedings. In that we say,
that [we wish] an ordinance might be passed, to which the royal
assent might be desired; but we have [since] declared that, if the
royal assent could not be had, we should account the authority
of the Parliament valid without it. We have desired, in the
General Council, that for security for arrears we might have the
royal assent. And let me tell you (though I shall be content to
lose my arrears to see the kingdom have its liberty [b]—if any man
can do it—unless it be by putting our liberty into the hands of
those that will give it away when they have done [with it]; but I say
what [f] I do think [g] true in this): Whoever talks either of [arrears
gained by] the endeavours of the soldiers or of any other indemnity [won] by the sword in their hands, is [for] the perpetuating
of combustions; so that word cannot take place [of], and does not
suppose, the settling of a peace [b] by that authority which hath
been here [1] the legislative power of the kingdom, and he that
expects to have the arrears of the soldiers so, I think he does but
deceive himself. For my own part I would give up my arrears,
and [j] lose my arrears, if we have not [first a] settlement; no
arrears [n]or [any] want of indemnity, nor anything in the world,
shall satisfy me to have a peace upon any terms wherein that which
is really the right of this nation is not as far provided for as can
be provided for by men. I could tell you many other particulars
wherein there are divers gross injuries done to the General and
[the] General Council, and such a wrong [done them] as is not fit
to be done among Christians, and so wrong and so false [a design
imputed to them] that I cannot think that they have gone so
far in it.

Wildman : I do not know what reason you have to suppose I should be so well acquainted with *The Case of the Army*, and the things proposed [in it]. I conceive them to be very good and just. But for that which I give as their sense, which you are pleased to say are scandals cast upon the Army. The legislative power had been acknowledged [hitherto] to be in the King with [the] Lords and Commons; and ᵃ considering that, and what [indeed] you said before was a[nother] scandal [laid upon you], that you propounded to bring in the King with his negative voice, [you seem to restore him to his controlling part in the legislative power. For] I do humbly propound to your consideration [that] when you restrain the King's negative in one particular [only], which is in [your] restraining unequal distributing,ᵇ you do ᶜ say the legislative power to be now partly in him. And [indeed you] say directly, in these very words, [that he] 'shall be restored to his personal rights.' And therefore I conceive (if I have any reason) [that] the King *is* proposed to be brought in with his negative voice. And whereas you say it is a scandal for [us to assert that you would have] the King to come in with his personal rights [before the grievances of the people are redressed, it is said in the *Proposals*] that, the King consenting to those things, the King [is] to be restored to all his personal rights. There 's his restoration. Not a bare consideration what his rights are before the people's grievances [are considered], but a restoration to his personal rights, these things being done. Is the Parliament not to lose their rights [by such a provision]? And for that of [asking the King's consent to an Act of] Indemnity, I do not say [that] it was an asking of the King['s] pardon; [but] it is rendering us up [without promise of future security, for the King is under constraint], and therefore it is null in law.ᵈ

.   .   .   .   .   .

Putney, 1st November 1647

At the General Council of the Army

The Lieutenant-General first moved, that every one might speak their experiences as the issue of what God had given in, in answer to their prayers.

Captain [Francis] Allen made a speech, expressing what experiences he had received from himself and from divers other godly people: that the work that was before them was to take away the negative voice of the King and Lords.

Captain [John] Carter expressed his experiences: that he found not any inclination in his heart (as formerly) to pray for the King, that God would make him yet a blessing to the kingdom.

Cowling made a speech expressing that the sword was the only thing that had from time to time recovered our right[s], and which he ever read in the word of God had recovered the rights of the people; that our ancestors had still recovered from the Danes and Normans their liberties, by the sword, when they were under such a slavery that an Englishman was as hateful then as an Irishman is now, and what an honour those that were noblemen thought it to marry their daughters to, or to marry the daughters of, any cooks or bakers of the Normans.

Lieutenant-Colonel [Henry] Lilburne [said]: That he never observed that the recovery of our liberties which we had before the Normans was the occasion of our taking up arms, or the main quarrel; and that the Norman laws were [a] not slavery introduced upon us, but an augmentation of our slavery before. Therefore what was by some offered, I doubt, for those reasons I have given you, was not of God.[1]

A report from Colonel Lambert's regiment that two horsemen, Agitators, came and persuaded them to send new Agitators, for that the officers had broken their engagements.[2]

Cromwell: [As] to that which hath been [heretofore] moved concerning the negative vote, or things which have been delivered [on that matter], in papers and otherwise, [some] may [indeed] present a real pleasing [of the King; but] I do not say that they have all pleased; for I think [it hath been made clear] that the King is king by contract; and I shall say, as Christ said, 'Let him that is without sin cast the first stone,' and mind [you of] that word of bearing one with another—it was taught us to-day. If we had carried it on in the Parliament, and by our power, without any things [b] laid on [us of] that kind, so that we could say that

---

[1] Possibly this sentence is a detached fragment (or an echo) of an unreported speech of Cromwell's; see Goffe, p. 100.

[2] This detached note is transposed from after Captain Allen's speech, above. The debate then, apparently, turned to engagements, the legitimacy of the Army's interference, and the treatment of the King.

we were without transgression, I should then say it were just to cut off transgressors; but considering that we are in our own actions failing in many particulars, I think there is much necessity of pardoning of transgressors.

For the actions that are [now] to be done, and those that must do them, I think it is their proper place to conform to the Parliament, that first gave them their being; and I think it is considerable whether they do contrive to suppress the power [of the King and his party] by that power or no, if they do continue [their endeavour] to suppress them. And [indeed] how they can take the determination of commanding men, conducting men, quartering men, keeping guards, without an authority otherwise than from themselves, I am ignorant.[a] And therefore I think there is much [need] in the Army to conform to those things that are within their sphere. For those things that have been done in the Army, as this of [issuing] *The Case of the Army Truly Stated*, there is much in it useful, and to be condescended to; but I am not satisfied how far we shall [do well to] press [it]. Either they are a Parliament or no Parliament. If they be no Parliament they are nothing, and we are nothing likewise. If they be a Parliament, we are [not to proceed without them in our plan for settlement, but] to offer it to them.[b] If I could see a visible presence of the people, either by subscriptions or number, [I should be satisfied with it]; for in the government of nations that which is to be looked after is the affections of the people. And that, [if] I find [it],[c] would satisfy [d] my conscience in the present thing.

[Consider the case of the Jews.] They were first [divided into] families where they lived, and had heads of families [to govern them], and they were next [e] under judges, and [then] they were under kings. When they came to desire a king they had a king, first elective, and secondly by succession. In all these kinds of government they were happy [f] and contented.[g] If you make the best of it, if you should change the government to the best of it, it is but a moral thing. It is but, as Paul says, 'dross and dung in comparison of Christ'; [1] and [I ask] why we shall so far contest for temporal things, that [h] if we cannot have this freedom [peacefully] we will venture life and livelihood for it. When every man shall come to this condition [of mind], I think the state will come to desolation.[1]

Therefore the considering of what is fit for the kingdom does belong to the Parliament, [provided they be] well composed in their creation and election. How far I shall [think we ought to]

[1] Philippians 3. 8.

leave it to the [present] Parliament to offer it, [will depend on their willingness to do so]. There may be care [had to secure a proper representation]. That the elections, or forms of [choosing the] Parliament, are very unequal [a] [is evident], as I could name but one for a corporation to choose two. I shall desire that there may be a [common] form for the electing of Parliaments. And another thing [is] [b] the perpetuity of the Parliament; [c] that there is no assurance to the people but that it is [to be] perpetual, which does [not] satisfy the kingdom.[d] And for other things that are [subject] to the King's negative vote [so] as [he thereby] may cast you off wholly, it hath been the resolution of the Parliament and of the Army [to safeguard these things]. If there be a possibility [then] of the Parliament's offering those things unto the King, that may secure us, I think there is much may be said for the[ir] doing of it.

As for the present condition of the Army, I shall speak something of it. For the conduct of the Army, I perceive there are several declarations from the Army [e] calling rendezvous and otherwise [1] [containing] disobligations to the General's orders. I must confess I have a commission from the General, and I understand that I am to do by it. I shall conform to him according to the rules and discipline of war, and according to those rules I ought to be conformable [to no orders but his]. And therefore I conceive it is not in the power of any particular men to call a rendezvous of a troop or regiment, or in [f] [the] least to disoblige the Army from those commands of the General; which must be destructive to us in general or [to] every [g] particular man in the Army.[h] This way is destructive to the Army, [I say], and to every particular man in the Army. I have been informed by some of the King's party, that if they give us rope enough we will hang ourselves. [We shall hang ourselves] if we do not conform to the rules of war. And therefore I shall move [that] what we shall centre upon [must be the rules of war and our authority from the Parliament. We must not let go of that] if it have but the face of authority. [We are like a drowning man]: if it be but an hare swimming over the Thames, he will take hold of it rather than let it go.

Chillenden [observed]: That God hitherto hath been pleased to show us many mercies, [and proceeded to] the relation of God's providence in bringing us from our march to London.

[*William*] *Allen:* On Friday was a day for to seek God for direction in this work, and upon Saturday many were giving in their thoughts concerning what God had given in to them to speak, as to a cure for a dying kingdom. Truly amongst the rest my thoughts were at work. Providentially, my thoughts were cast upon one thing which I had often seen before, [which] yet, if prosecuted, may be the means of an happy union amongst us. That which I hint at, and which I ª would speak to, is ᵇ *The Case of the Army Stated.* I do perceive that there is either a real or an apprehensive disunion amongst us, or rather a misapprehensive; and truly in my heart there was something providentially laid for a uniting, and that in that passage that those Agents—at that very time of dissenting from us, and when they were ripping up our faults to open view—in the issue came to lay us down [as] a rule, and that was [a thing] which before had been laid down as a rule, and we and they were to act according to it; but being laid down by them again, I think it is a twofold cord that cannot easily be broken. They do refer us to our three declarations,ᵈ of [the] fourteenth [of] June,[1] [the] twenty-first of June, [the] eighteenth of August; and their desires are that those might be looked upon, and adhered unto; and if they be our desires, and theirs with them, and [if it be] their desire ᵉ that we should walk up to them, I think this will put the business to a very fair issue. I did look over for my part all [the] things [contained] in those three declarations. There, [I find], is [set forth] whatsoever we should persist in. And therefore I humbly desire that whatsoever [there] is in those declarations we may intend and pursue, as tending to that end we all aim at, namely the kingdom's good.

Lieutenant-Colonel [John] Jubbes: Truly I do not know how to distinguish whether the Spirit of God lives in me or no, but by mercy, love, and peace; and on the contrary whether the spirit of Antichrist lives in me, but by envy, malice, and war.ᶜ I am altogether against a war if there may be a composure [possible, so] that the Englishman may have his privileges. I have a commission ready to deliver up whensoever I shall be called.

Queries wherein Lieutenant-Colonel Jubbes desireth satisfaction for the preventing of the effusion of blood:
  1. Whether or no the Parliament may yet be purged of all such members as assented to the late insurrections and treason of the City, and still continue a House?
  2. If it may be purged, and an House still remaining,ᶠ whether the major part of the remainder be such persons as are desirous of giving satisfaction to our, or the kingdom's, just desires?

[1] See Appendix, pp. 403–9.

3. If the second be assented unto, that they are such persons, whether then they may not satisfy our just desires, and declare the King guilty of all the bloodshed, vast expense of treasure, and ruin that hath been occasioned by all the wars both of England and Ireland, and then, for that he is the King of Scotland, and also of Ireland, as well as England, [whether they should not agree, after] that, therefore to receive him as King again for avoiding further wars?

4. Whether, if the Parliament may adjourn and dissolve when in their discretions they shall find cause (or not before), as at this present, even by law, God hath ordered it, they may not then reject the King's Act of Oblivion, and take unto themselves that godly resolution to do that justice unto the kingdom which now they dare not do?

Rainborough moved that the papers of the committee might be read.

Goffe : I think that motion which was made by the Lieutenant-General should not die, but that it should have some issue. I think it is a vain thing to seek God if we do not hearken after his answer, and something that was spoken by the Lieutenant-General moves me to speak at this time, and [a] upon this ground. Upon what was spoken by one here, it was concluded by the Lieutenant-General that that was not the mind of God that was spoken by him. I could wish we might be wary of such expressions. 'There was a lying spirit in the mouth of Ahab's prophets. He speaks falsely to us in the name of the Lord.' [1] I do not speak this, that this [particular] was the mind of the Lord in anything; yet we may not break abruptly off,[b] [concluding] that what one spoke was [not] the mind of the Lord : [c] we must consider whether something was not spoken by others which may be the mind of the Lord. Truly I am very tender in this thing: if we shall wait for God, and if God shall speak to us [and we not hearken], we shall bring much evil upon ourselves. God hath spoken in several ages in sundry ways. [Of old] when [d] they sent to a prophet and he comes and tells them upon his bare word,[e] he tells them that he received such a message from the Lord. But God hath put us upon such a course which I cannot but reverence, and God does not now speak by one particular man, but in every one of our hearts; and certainly if it were a dangerous thing to refuse a message that came from one man to many,[f] it is a more dangerous

[1] 1 Kings 22. 22; Jer. 43. 2.

thing to refuse what comes from God, being spoke by many to us. I shall add this: that it seems to me evident and clear that this hath been a voice from heaven to us, that we have sinned against the Lord in tampering with his enemies. And it hath so wrought with me that [though] I cannot run precipitately to work, yet I dare not open my mouth for the benefit or upholding [of] that [kingly] power.[a] I think that hath been the voice of God, and whatsoever was contradicted [by events] was [only] our precipitate running on, our taking hold of an opportunity before it was given. And therefore I desire we may not precipitately run on, but wait upon God,[a] that in the issue we may not see that God hath [not] spoken to us; and if the Lord hath spoken to us I pray God keep us from that sin that we do not hearken to the voice of the Lord.

Cromwell: I shall not be unwilling to hear God speaking in any [man]; but I think that God may [as well] be heard speaking in that which is to be read, as otherwise.

But I shall speak a word in that which Lieutenant-Colonel Goffe said, because it seems to come as a reproof to me, and I shall be willing to receive a reproof when it shall be in love, and shall be [so] given, but [not otherwise]. That which he speaks was, that at such a meeting as this we should wait upon God, and [hearken to] the voice of God speaking in any of us. I confess it is an high duty, but when anything is spoken [as from God] I think the rule [1] is, Let the rest judge![b] It is left to me to judge for my own satisfaction, and the satisfaction of others, whether it be of the Lord or not, and I do no more.[a] I do not judge conclusively, negatively, that it was not of the Lord, but I do desire to submit it to all your judgments, whether it was of the Lord or no. [a] I did offer some reasons which did satisfy me—I know not whether they [c] did others.[d] If in those things we do speak, and pretend to speak from God, there be mistakes of fact, if there be a mistake in the thing [or] in the reason of the thing, truly I think it is free for me to show both the one and the other, if I can. Nay, I think it is my duty to do it; for no man receives anything in the name of the Lord further than [to] the light of his conscience appears. I can say in the next place—and I can say it heartily and freely: as to the matter [of which] he speaks I must confess I have no prejudice, not the least thought of prejudice, upon that ground—I speak it truly as before the Lord. But this I think: that it is no evil advertisement, to wish us in our speeches of righteousness and justice to refer us to any engagements that

[1] 1 Cor. 14. 29.

are upon us, and [it is] that which I have learned [1] in all [our] debates. I have still desired we should ^a consider where we are, and what engagements are upon us, and how we ought to go off as becomes Christians.^b This is all that I aimed at and I do aim at. And I must confess I had a marvellous reverence and awe upon my spirit when we came to speak. [We said], let us speak one to another what God hath spoken to us; and, as I said before, I cannot say that I have received anything that I can speak as in the name of the Lord—not that I can say that anybody did speak that which was untrue in the name of the Lord, but upon this ground, that when we say we speak in the name of the Lord it is of an high nature.

Lieutenant-Colonel Goffe made an apology for what he had said before.

William Allen: My desire is to see things put to an issue. Men have been declaring their thoughts, and truly I would crave liberty to declare mine. The difference between us, I think, is in the interest of King and Lords, some declaring against the name and title of King and Lords, [others preferring to retain them]. For my part [I think], clearly, according to what we have engaged we stand bound; and I think we should be looked upon as persons not fit to be called Christians, if we do not work up to them. As first, concerning the King. You say you will set up the King as far as may be consistent with, and not prejudicial to, the liberties of the kingdom; and really I am of that mind [too]. If the setting up of him be not consistent with them, and prejudicial to them, then down with him; but if he may be so set up —which I think he may—[then set him up], and it is not our judgment only, but of [all save] those that set forth *The Case of the Army*.

Rainborough took occasion to take notice as if what Mr. Allen spoke did reflect upon himself or some other there, as if [it were asserted that] they were against the name of King and Lords.

Sexby: Truly I must be bold to offer this one word unto you.^c Here was somewhat spoke of the workings and actings of God within us;^d I shall speak a word of that. The Lord hath put you into a state, or at least [suffered you] to run you[rselves] into such a one, that you know not where you are. You are in a wilderness condition. Some actings among us singly and jointly ^e are the

[1] i.e. taught (FIRTH).

cause of it. Truly I would entreat you to weigh that.[a] We find in the word of God, 'I would heal Babylon, but she would not be healed.'[1] I think that we have gone about to heal Babylon when she would not. We have gone about to wash a blackamoor, to wash him white, which he will not. We are going about to set up that power which God will destroy: I think we are going about to set up the power of kings, some part of it, which God will destroy; and which will be but as a burdensome stone[2] that whosoever shall fall upon it, it will destroy him.[c] I think this is the reason of the straits that are in hand.[d] I shall propose this to your Honours, to weigh the grounds, whether they be right, and then you shall be led in pleasant paths by still waters, and shall not be offended.[f]

Cromwell: I think we should not let go that motion which Lieutenant-Colonel Goffe made, and so I cannot but renew that caution that we should take heed what we speak in the name of the Lord.[e] As for what that gentleman spoke last, but [that] it was with too much confidence, I cannot conceive that he altogether meant it.[e] I would we should all take heed of mentioning our own thoughts and conceptions with that which is of God. What this gentleman told us [was] that which [he conceived] was our great fault. He alludes to such a place of scripture: 'We would have healed Babylon, but she would not.' The gentleman applied it to us, as that we [g] had been men that [h] would have healed Babylon, and God would not have had her healed. Truly, though that be not the intent of that scripture, yet I think it is true that whosoever would have gone about to heal Babylon when God hath determined [to destroy her], he does fight against God, because God will not have her healed. And yet certainly in general to desire an healing, it is not evil, [though] indeed when we are convinced that it is Babylon we are going about to heal I think it 's fit we should then give over our healing.

But I shall desire to speak a word or two since I hear no man offering anything[1] as a particular dictate from God [that he would] speak to us, [and] I should desire to draw to some conclusion of that expectation of ours. Truly, as Lieutenant-Colonel Goffe said, God hath in several ages used several dispensations, and yet some dispensations more eminently in one age than another. I am one of those whose heart God hath drawn out to wait for some extra-ordinary [j] dispensations, according to those promises that he hath held forth of things to be accomplished in the later times, and I

[1] Jer. 51. 9; 13. 23.   [2] Zech. 12. 3; Matt. 21. 44.

cannot but think that God is beginning of them.[a] Yet certainly [we do well to take heed], upon the same ground that we find in the Epistle of Peter, where he speaks of the scriptures, to which, says he, you do well to take heed [as] 'a more sure word of prophecy' than their testimonies were,[b] as a light shining in a dark place.[1] If, when we want particular and extraordinary impressions, we shall either altogether sit still because we have them not, and not follow that light that we have, or shall go against, or short of, that light that we have, upon the imaginary apprehension of such divine impressions and divine discoveries in particular things—which are not so divine as to carry their evidence with them to the conviction of those that have the Spirit of God within them—I think we shall be justly under a condemnation. Truly we have heard many speaking to us; and I cannot but think that in many of those things God hath spoke to us. I cannot but think that in most that have spoke there hath been something of God laid [c] forth to us; and yet there have [d] been several contradictions in what hath been spoken. But certainly God is not the author of contradictions. The contradictions are not so much in the end as in the way. I cannot see but that we all speak to the same end, and the mistakes are only in the way. The end is to deliver this nation from oppression and slavery, to accomplish that work that God hath carried us on in, to establish our hopes of an end of justice and righteousness in it. We agree thus far. Further too: that we all apprehend danger from the person of the King and from the Lords—I think we may go thus far farther, that all that have spoke have agreed in this too, though the gentleman in the window [2] [seemed to deny it] when he spoke [of] sett[ing] up, [but he], if he would [e] declare it, did not mean all that that word might import. I think that seems to be general among us all, [that] there is not any intention of any in the Army, of any of us, to set up the one [or the other].[f] If it were free before us whether we should set up one or [the] other, I do to my best observation find an unanimity amongst us all, that we would set up neither. Thus far I find us to be agreed; and thus far as we are agreed, I think it is of God. But there are circumstances in which we differ as in relation to this. Then I must further tell you that as we do not make it our business or intention to set up the one or the other, so neither is it [our intention] to preserve the one or the other, with a visible danger and destruction to the people and the public

---

[1] 2 Pet. I. 19.
[2] Reference is to Allen (p. 102), or to someone whose speech is unrecorded.

interest. So that that part of difference that seems to be among us is whether there can be a preservation [of them with safety to the kingdom]. First of all, on the one part, there is this apprehension: that we cannot with justice and righteousness at the present destroy, or go about to destroy, or take away, or [altogether] lay aside, both, or all the interest they have in the public affairs of the kingdom; and those that do so apprehend would strain something in point of security, would rather leave some hazard—or at least, if they see that they may consist without any *considerable* hazard to the interest of the kingdom,[a] do so far [wish] to preserve them. On the other hand, those who differ from this, I do take it (in the most candid apprehension) that they seem to run thus: that there is not any safety or security to the liberty of the kingdom, and to [the] public interest, if you do retain these at all; and therefore they think this is a consideration to them paramount [to] the consideration of particular obligations of justice, or matter of right or due towards King or Lords. Truly I think it hath pleased God to lead me to a true and clear stating [of] our agreement and our difference. And if this be so, we are the better prepared to go [on]. If this be not so, I shall desire that any one that hath heard me [will] declare [it], if he do think that the thing is misstated as to our agreement or difference.[b]

I shall go on, only in a word or two, to conclude that we have been about. As to the dispensations of God, it was more particular in the time of the Law [of Moses than in the time of the law] written in our hearts, that word within us, the mind of Christ;[1] and truly when we have no other more particular impression of the power of God going forth with us,[c] I think that this law and this [word] speaking [within us], which truly is in every man who hath the Spirit of God, we are to have a regard to. And this to me seems to be very clear, how[d] we are to judge of the apprehension[e] of men [as] to particular cases, whether it be of God or no. When it doth not carry its evidence with it, of the power of God to convince us clearly, our best way is to judge the conformity or disformity of [it with] the law written within us, which is the law of the Spirit of God, the mind of God, the mind of Christ. And as was well said by Lieutenant-Colonel Jubbes, for my part I do not know any outward evidence of what proceeds from the Spirit of God more clear than this, the appearance of meekness and gentleness and mercy and patience and forbearance and love, and a desire to do good to all, and to destroy none that can be saved. And for my part I say, where I do see this, where

[1] Heb. 8. 10; 1 Cor. 2. 16.

I do see men speaking according to this law which I am sure is the law of the Spirit of Life [I am satisfied. But] I cannot but take that to be contrary to this law, [which is], as he said, of the spirit of malice and envy, and things of that nature. And I think there is this radically in that heart where there is such a law as leads us *against all opposition.* On the other hand, I think that he that would decline the doing of justice where there is no place for mercy, and the exercise of the ways of force, for the safety of the kingdom, where there is no other way to save it, and would decline these out of the apprehensions of danger and difficulties in it, he that leads that way, on the other hand, doth [also] truly lead us from that which is the law of the Spirit of Life, the law written in our hearts. And truly having thus declared what we may apprehend of all that hath been said, I shall wish that we may go on to our business; and I shall only add several cautions on the one hand, and the other.ᵃ

I could wish that none of those whose apprehensions run on the other hand, that there can be no safety in a consistency with the person of the King or the Lords, or [in] their having the least interest in the public affairs of the kingdom—I do wish ᵇ that they will take heed of that which some men are apt to be carried away by, [namely] apprehensions that God will destroy these persons or that power; for, that they may mistake in. And though [I] myself do concur with them,¹ and perhaps concur with them upon some ground that God will do so, yet let us [not] make those things to be our rule which we cannot so clearly know to be the mind of God. I mean in particular things let us not make those our rules: that 'this [is] to be done; [this] is the mind of God; ᶜ we must work to it.' But at least [let] those to whom this is not made clear, though they do ᵈ think it probable that God will destroy them, yet let them make this [a] rule to themselves: 'Though God have a purpose to destroy them, and though I should find a desire to destroy them—though a Christian spirit can hardly find it for itself—yet God can do it without necessitating us to do a thing which is scandalous, or sin, or which would bring a dishonour to his name.' And therefore those that are of that mind, let them wait upon God for such a way when the thing may be done without sin, and ᵉ without scandal too. Surely what

---

¹ I have not ventured to alter the text in a point so crucial. But the statement does not entirely harmonize with the tenor of Cromwell's utterances in the Debates, and I suspect that what he said was: 'And though [I] myself do concur with them, perhaps, upon some ground [of hope] that God will do so.' The repetition of such a phrase as 'concur with them' is very common in the MS.

God would have us do, he does not desire we should step out of the way for it. This is the caution, on the one hand, that we do no wrong to one or other, and that we abstain from all appearance of wrong, and for that purpose avoid the bringing of a scandal to the name of God, and to his people upon whom his name is bestowed.[a] On the other hand, I have but this to say: that those who do apprehend obligations lying upon them—either by a general duty or particularly in relation to the things that we have declared, a duty of justice, or a duty in regard of the [b] *Engagement* —that they would clearly come to this resolution, that if they found in their judgments and consciences that those engagements led to anything which really cannot consist with the liberty and safety and public interest of this nation,[c] they would account the general [duty] paramount [to] the other, so far as not to oppose any other that would do better for the nation than they will do.[h] If we do act according to that mind and that spirit and that law which I have before spoken of, and in these particular cases do [d] take these two cautions, God will lead us to what shall be his way, and [first] as many of us as [e] shall incline their minds to [him], and the rest in their way in a due time.

Bishop: I shall desire to speak one word, and that briefly.[f] After many inquiries in my spirit what 's the reason that we are distracted in counsel, and that we cannot, as formerly, preserve the kingdom from that dying condition in which it is, I find this answer,[h] the answer which is [vouchsafed] to many Christians besides, amongst us. I say [it] not in respect of any particular persons, [but] I say [that the reason is] a compliance to preserve that man of blood, and those principles of tyranny, which God from heaven by his many successes [given] hath manifestly declared against, and which, I am confident, may [yet] be our destruction [if they be preserved]. I only speak this [as] what is upon my spirit, because I see you are upon inquiry what God hath given in to any one, which may tend to the preservation of the kingdom.

Wildman: I observe that the work hath been to inquire what hath been the mind of God, and every one speaks what is given in to his spirit. I desire as much as is possible to reverence whatsoever hath the Spirit or Image of God upon it. Whatever another man hath received from the Spirit, that man cannot demonstrate [it] to me but by some other way than merely relating to me that which he conceives to be the mind of God. [In spiritual matters he must show its conformity with scripture,

though indeed] it is beyond the power of the reason of all the men
on earth to demonstrate the scriptures to be the scriptures written
by the Spirit of God, and [a] it must be the spirit of faith [in a man
himself] that must [finally] make him believe whatsoever may be
spoken in spiritual matters. [The case is] yet [more difficult] in
civil matters; [for] we cannot find anything in the word of God
[of] what is fit to be done in civil matters. But I conceive that
only is of God that does appear to be like unto God—[to practise]
justice and mercy, to be meek and peaceable. I should desire
therefore that we might proceed only in that way, if it please this
honourable Council, to consider what is justice and what is mercy,
and what is good, and I cannot but conclude that that is of God.
Otherwise I cannot think that any one doth speak from God when
he says what he speaks is of God.

But to the matter in hand. I am clearly of opinion with that
gentleman that spake last save one, that it is not of God [to
decline the doing of justice] where there is no way left of mercy;
and I could much concur that it is very questionable whether
there be a way left for mercy upon that person that we now insist
upon. [I would know] [b] whether it is demonstrable by reason or
justice, [c] [that it is right] to punish with death those that according
to his command do make war, or those that do but hold compliance
with them, and then [to say] that there is a way left for mercy for
him who was the great actor of this, and who was the great contriver of all? But I confess because it is in civil matters I would
much decline that, and rather look to what is safety, what the mind
doth dictate from safety. . What is [for] the safety [of the people],
I know it cannot be the mind of God to go contrary to [that].
But for what particulars that gentleman speaks, of the difference[s]
between us, I think they are so many as not easily to be reckoned
up.[d] That which he instanced was that some did desire to preserve
the person of the King and person[s] of the Lords, so far as it was
[consistent] with [the] safety or the good of the kingdom, and
other persons do conceive that the preservation of the King or
Lords was [e] inconsistent with the people's safety, and that law to
be paramount [to] all [considerations].

Ireton: [1] Sir, I [think he] did not speak of the destroying of
the King and Lords—I have not heard any man charge all the

[1] Wildman has been criticizing a speech ascribed by MS. to Cromwell.
Ireton evidently intervenes to explain Cromwell's meaning. Wildman
in reply addresses Cromwell, but Ireton, perhaps at a sign from Cromwell, continues to answer for him. This is the only assumption that
does not make some change in the ascription of speeches necessary.

Lords so as to deserve a punishment—but [of] a reserving to them any interest at all in the public affairs of the kingdom.

Wildman [addressing Cromwell]: Then, sir, as I conceive, you were saying the difference was this: that some persons were of opinion that [they stood engaged to] the preservation of the power of King and Lords, [while others held that the safety of the people] was paramount to all considerations, and might keep them from any giving them what was [their] due and right.

Ireton: I [think it was] said that [while] some men did apprehend that there might be an interest given to them with safety to the kingdom, others do think that no part of their interest could be given without destruction to the kingdom.

Wildman [addressing Ireton]: For the matter of stating the thing in difference, I think that the person of King and Lords are not so joined together by any; for as yourself said, none have any exception against the persons of the Lords or name of Lords. But the difference is whether we should alter the old foundations of our government so as to give to King and Lords that which they could never claim before. Whereas it's said that those that dissent[1] look after alteration of government, I do rather think that those that do assent [a] do endeavour to alter the foundations of our government, and that I shall demonstrate thus. According to the King's oath he is to grant such laws as the people shall choose,[b] and therefore I conceive they are called laws before they come to him. They are called laws that he must confirm, and so they are laws before they come to him.[c] To give the King a legislative power is contrary to his own oath at his coronation, and it is the like to give a power to the King by his negative voice to deny all laws.[d] And for the Lords, seeing the foundation of all justice is the election of the people, it is unjust that they should have that power. And therefore I conceive the difference only is this: whether this power should be given to the King and Lords or no.

For the later part of that noble gentleman's words, this may be said to them: whether this consideration may [not] be paramount to all engagements, to give [e] the people [f] what is their due right.

Ireton: The question is not, whether this should be given to King and Lords, or no; but the question is: whether that interest that they have in this (if they have any), whether it should be now positively insisted upon to be clearly taken away.

[1] i.e. to giving King and Lords a negative voice.

Wildman: Sir, I suppose that the interest they have, *if* they have any—if (for that supposition is very well put in)—for (as I said before) I conceive that neither King nor Lords according to the foundation of government ever had a right——

Ireton [interrupting]: I spake it to you, and those that are of your mind, if you were [not] satisfied not to have an exception.

Wildman: Then, I say, the whole tenor of the propositions or proposals must be altered, if anything be in them [allowing the King a negative voice]. I conceive, thus not to express it, because it hath been usurped, is to confirm his usurpation of it. For many years this hath been usurped. Now, if after God hath given us the victory over them we shall not declare against them, we give no security for the people's liberty.

Ireton: You speak part to the point of justice and part to the point of safety. To the point of justice you seem to speak this: that by the fundamental constitutions of this kingdom, neither King nor Lords have rightfully a negative voice; and therefore to take it away, or to clear it that they have none, is but justice. I think that is it: that [by] the fundamental constitution [a] [neither of them can claim a voice, and so it should be given to] neither of them.[b]

You seem to argue only from the King's oath. And then you conclude: if, as it appears by that, they had it not before, though we all be satisfied [that] we would say nothing to give them it, yet if we do not expressly take it away—nay, if we do send [c] a proposal [d] to any of them [to know their opinion]—we do leave to them a power to assent or dissent, and give them that which we had before——

[Wildman, interrupting]: Sir,[e] you well remember that that which you argue of the King's oath [f]——

[Ireton]: And I know for my own part no other [evidence] than an old statute or two cited in the declaration wherein the Commons declare, [with reference to the coronation oath, the form of the King's withholding of assent, and the custom of Parliament, the extent of their own, and the limits of his, legislative power].[1]

I remember I spoke it, and I speak it again, and [g] that this [h] is the intent, I do verily believe: that the original sense and intention

---

[1] Presumably Ireton refers to Parliament's Third Remonstrance, 26th May 1642 (Husband's *Exact Collection of All Remonstrances*, London, 1643, pp. 266 ff.). The words added pretend to be no more than a plausible completion of the sentence.

of the oath of the King's which is published in that declaration of
the Commons was, and is, and ought to be, that the King ought
to confirm those laws that the Commons choose. Now whether
this King be so bound by his oath as that he breaks his oath if he
do not confirm every law that they seek, I conceive that depends
upon what he did verily at his coronation make his oath; but I
think that in the sense and intention of the people of the kingdom,[a]
their intention was that he should confirm all the laws that they
should choose. But you must take notice that the oath doth
take them [as] laws before he should make them: it calls them
laws, the laws in election, *quas vulgus elegerit.* The King promises
that he will by his authority confirm those laws that the people
shall choose, so that this shows clearly what use, in the constitution
of the kingdom, they made of the King in the commonwealth.
The Commons are to choose the laws and the King to confirm.
They had this [to] trust to: the King would confirm what they
should choose, and, he confirming them, they were firm laws. I
do really believe that this was the agreement that the people of
England made with their Kings; that is, they would have him
give his consent to what laws they should choose, and so to have
that implicit use [of him]. But this is most apparent, both by the
oath itself, and by all the practice since [b]—the sending of laws
to the King [c]—that they had some [g] relation to the King and to his
consent [d] in the making of a law.[e] This I am sure: if it were never
so clear in the constitution that they were good laws without it,
yet this is clear—if that were true in the original constitution of
this kingdom this is clear—that they have [been] sent still to him
to be confirmed; as the word was to be confirmed or corroborated,
Leges [quas vulgus elegerit] cor[roborandas].[1]

And I think: if we do [take into] account all the sending of laws
heretofore to be corroborated by him, and if his denying of some
of them—not absolutely denying but advising—if these have not
at all prejudiced [the right of] the people against his negative
voice, so the sending of propositions now for his assent cannot
prejudice the right of the people more than all their sending [laws
to him] before. If we should put it to the King as his act, [yet]
the Parliament have declared it and asserted it, that it is their
right that the King ought not to deny any [laws they offer to
him]; it is his oath. They have gone thus much farther, that if
he did not confirm them they were laws without him. Upon this
there hath been a war made. They have gone [so far as] to make
all laws and ordinances that were needful for the management of
the affairs of the kingdom, without the King. It is now come to a

period.   So that *de facto* it is thus they have made laws, and held them forth to the kingdom [as laws].   Now if the King by his act do confirm what the Parliament have done, and condemn all that hath [a] been [done] against the Parliament, [I ask] whether he do not acknowledge to all posterity, that in case of safety, when the Parliament doth adjudge the safety of the kingdom to be concerned, they are to make [b] a law without him.   For my part I think there can be nothing more clear than this is.   For my own particular, I do apprehend that there is that general right [in the Parliament], that the laws [it shall pass] ought to be confirmed [by the King]; and that is my thought, [c] that without anything of the King's declaration to that purpose, [d] [and] though [e] they cannot dispense with the suspending [power] of the King, [f] they are, [g] in point of safety, [h] a law without him.   This the Parliament hath declared, and this is asserted in all the declarations that have been sent out, and [this is] the ground that I have proceeded [on] in those *Proposals* of the Army.   That [1] 'in a case of safety' was provided for, in those matters that I have spoke of.   I account them materially and essentially provided for in those; and if I had not, for my part I should never have rested or been satisfied in that point, and in other points [where] there might have been a dispensing [j] with a suspending [power], notwithstanding [that] the liberty of the kingdom hath been provided for in this, that there should not be anything done, or laws made, without the consent of the people.

Audley: I think if so be that this business of the negative voice be all the dispute, we shall all agree in it; for [k] it appeared by what you spake the other night, that he ought to have his negative voice taken away.

Hewson: The Scots have made provision that he should have no negative voice among them, and why should not we make the same provision with them?

Ireton: Those things that the committee did propose, and [that] they proceeded in last night, [l] will almost end us this dispute. [l] Whereas it was desired that we should take into consideration [m] the several heads to be insisted upon as fundamental laws that we must stand [to] for the establishing of the

---

[1] There are no records of the meeting of the committee on Sunday, 31st October. Apparently it was concerned with completing the proposals now about to be read. See p. 113, note 1.

kingdom, [we were also to consider the previous declarations of
the Army, how far] they are still [binding, and adequate] in
relation to the security of the kingdom.

The Proposal[s of the Committee] read [1] *[by Ireton, with numerous
interruptions by Wildman, some of which, with Ireton's rebuke, are
reported]* : [2]

a *Wildman :* b I conceive [that in] this concerning the succession
of Parliaments [it] is proposed positively that it shall be as triennial
Parliaments were.

Ireton : [Tell me whether] you did in your way propose a
certainty or not. If you did not propose it, the Act for Triennial
Parliaments [which in its general purport] says the same [thing,
supplies the defect. Observe] how far that which you propose is
[from certainty]: the people shall meet, [but] you neither say
where nor when. We say, [with such provision] for the certainty
of it [as] in [the late Act made for Triennial Parliaments]; that
Act tells you particularly. But because you must make a new

[1] Unfortunately these proposals are not copied into the report. Their
nature may be fairly accurately deduced: (1) from what is said in the
debate; (2) from the resolutions adopted by the committee on 2nd
November, which presumably embody these proposals as modified
by the debate and perhaps by subsequent discussion in the committee
(see pp. 450-2). The question is complicated, however, by the fact
that some of the ground covered in the resolutions reached by the
committee on 30th October (see pp. 449-50) again comes up for debate
here on lines different from those of the resolutions. It seems possible
that the resolutions should all be recorded as of 2nd November, and
that the earlier meetings were given over wholly to preparing the
proposals here debated, some of which were dropped from the final
resolutions owing to the opposition which they aroused. The proposals
appear to have differed from the resolutions in the following points:
(1) in more specifically exempting the Lords from the operation of laws
to which they had not consented; (2) in the tentative proposal to make
them eligible for election to the House of Commons (unless this was
'offered' not in the proposals, but in an unrecorded speech in the debate);
(3) in adopting from the *Heads of the Proposals*, I. 1 (p. 422), a partial
acceptance of the provisions of the Triennial Act (no word of this in
Resolution 2 of 30th October, p. 449); (4) in suggesting a property
qualification of £20 per annum for members of the House of Commons
(absent from Resolution 5, of 30th October, pp. 449-50).
[2] The speeches, which obviously constitute a selection from the
objections and replies made during the reading of the proposals, have
somehow got themselves embedded in a later part of the report. The
clue to their correct position is given by Ireton's request to be allowed
to proceed with the reading without interruption. For details regarding
my transpositions, see 'Notes on Text.'

provision for it, since you must make a new division and distribution of the kingdom, and a new circuit,ᵃ therefore it says, 'with
such further provision as shall be made for reducement [of it]
to a certainty.'

Rainborough [stated]: That he does take exception at [the
proposal] that no man should be chosen [as a representative] that
hath not twenty pounds a year.

[*Wildman, interrupting the proposals regarding the negative
voice*]: ᵇ Though I protest I would not widen a difference, yet I
conceive the difference is as wide as ever.   In what 's there provided for,ᶜ [the interest of the people] is laid aside, [and] the
interest of the King and Lords, which the Lord by a judgment
from heaven hath given away, [is restored].ᵈ

Ireton: If Mr. Wildman think fit to [let me] go on without
taking an advantage [to object] to every particular as it is read, [he
may show afterwards] what [things] they are that do render these
propositions so destructive and [that] give the King and Lords
such an interest as they never had before—if he will take them
upon his memory and [not] by the way.

Wildman: I only affirm that it doth establish the King's and
Lords' interest surer than before.

Ireton: ᵉ I hope Mr. Wildman will not offer such an assertion
but he hath arguments to make it good.ᶠ

[*Wildman*]: ᵍ I would proceed to the things in hand.ʰ

Rainborough [observed, the reading concluded]: That some
things in the Agreement were granted there.   [He moved]: To
debate whether or no, when the Commons' Representative do
declare a law, it ought not to pass without the King's [or the
Lords'] consent.

Ireton: Truly this is all [that question amounts to]: whether,
honour, title, estate, liberty, or life, [if] the Commons have a
mind to take it away by a law, [they may do so]; so that to say
you are contented to leave ⁱ King and Lords ʲ all, this [negative]
being taken away, is as much as to say you are to allow them
nothing.   Consider how much of this dispute is saved [by] this

that is read to you. It gives the negative voice to the people, that no laws can be made without their consent. And secondly, it takes away the negative voice of the Lords and of the King too, as to what concerns the people; for it says that the Commons of England shall be bound by what judgments and also [by] what orders, ordinances, or laws, shall be made for that purpose by their [a] [representatives]; and all that follows for the King or Lords is this, that the Lords or King are not bound by that law they pass, unless they consent to it for their own persons or estates, as the Commons are. Therefore what [more] is there wanting for the good or safety of the Commons of England?

Rainborough: [b] If the negative voice be taken away [on these terms], then if the King or Lords were taking courses destructive, how should they be prevented?

Ireton: It is further provided, if they will meddle in any other offices, as[1] officers of justice or ministers of state in this kingdom, then they likewise are so far subject to the judgment of the House of Commons. If they only stand as single men, their personal interest and the like [is secured], and the right of being only judged by their peers, and [c] their individual persons [are not bound] by any law that they do not consent to.

Rainborough [objected]: If the Lords should join together by their interest in the kingdom, and should act against the Commons, then the Commons had no way to help themselves.

Ireton: If it comes to a breach of the peace it will come to break some law. The Lords heretofore,[d] [as] to the breaches of peace, have been subject to the common law; only [as] to the matter of fact, whether guilty or not guilty, they must be tried by their peers. We have stood very much for ourselves, that we should be judged by our peers,[e] by our fellow Commoners; I would fain know this: [since] that a Lord is subject to the common law, how we can take away that right of peers to [f] be for the matter of fact, whether guilty or not guilty of the breach of such a law,[g] tried by their peers, when that it is a point of right for the Commons to be tried by *their* peers.

Rainborough: [It seems then] that the laws that bind the Commons are exclusive of [h] the Lords.

Ireton : I would fain know this: whether the high sheriff in every county of the kingdom [may not apprehend a Lord who shall break the peace]. And I am sure the law hath [thereby] provided for the keeping of the peace. I know that there is no law but [that] the chief justice of the King's Bench, nay the sheriff of a county, nay the constable of any town, may seize upon him.

Rainborough : If a petty constable or sheriff shall apprehend a peer of the kingdom, [I would know] whether he can answer it?

Ireton : [a] If a Lord shall be accused, and by a jury found guilty, he will expect to be tried by his peers.[b]
We do agree that all the Commons of England are bound [by whatever laws the House of Commons shall pass], but the King and Lords as to their persons are not bound; but if any of them be an officer or minister of state [—and the King is—] then he is to be subject [to the judgment of the House of Commons].

Rainborough : How does it reach the King, and not a Lord?

Ireton : Every Lord is not a minister of justice [to be accountable to the Commons for his official acts], but if there be any other difference they are tried by their peers.

Rainborough : It is offered to make them capable of being chosen.

Ireton : Every Baron, [not disqualified] by the other exception[s], may be chosen.[1]

Rainborough : Is it not so in Scotland?

Ireton : In Scotland every Lord hath his place as burgess.

[c] *Rainborough :* [I ask], why the Lords should not have the same privilege [to sit as a body with the Commons].

Ireton : I should think [of] that as the directest [way to make their] interest [dangerous] to the kingdom, in the world; for that, for so many persons to be a permanent interest in the House, every two years [d]—

---

[1] Lacking the proposals, one can only surmise the provision referred to. Possibly the 'other exceptions' are those listed as disqualifying persons to be electors or elected, in the committee's fifth resolution (p. 450).

Colonel [Robert] Tichborne: I was speaking to this of the negative, I do remember, on Saturday last. We were [then] at this pitch and there I did leave it, [for] it did concur with my sense—and that was this. That all the power of making laws should be in those that the people should choose; only the King and Lords should serve to this end, that laws should be presented to them, that if they would do the Commons that right as to confirm those laws, they should do it; but if they should not think fit to sign them, it should beget a review of that by the House of Commons; and if after a review the House of Commons did declare that was for the safety of the people, though neither King nor Lords did subscribe, yet it was a standing and binding law; [a] and therefore we shall not need to fear [and] to take [off] a shadow when they can do us [so] little hurt.[b] This was what I did then suppose agreed upon.

Ireton: 'Tis true, Saturday night we were thinking of that, but we had an eye to that of safety, that is provided for by the Commons. No money can be raised, no war raised, but by those that the Commons shall choose. And so we thought to put it to consideration, that the Commons should make so much use of the Lords in all affairs [that] they might occasion a review, but if the Commons should upon that review think it fit, it should be looked upon as a law. But instead of that the committee voted last night that (whether the Commons of England should be bound by all the laws passed in the House of Commons, or whether it should be valid, in the case of safety, [that] that which you speak of should [c] follow) if there do but continue such a thing as Lords, and they do not sit jointly with the House of Commons, then the Lords shall [c] agree [to the laws that the Commons propose] or otherwise the Commons shall [c] do it presently themselves.[d] But that which [was then proposed] was questioned in the name [of] the safety [of the Lords themselves], and [the] securing of [their] safety, [by those] that t¹ ɔught it fit that they should have a liberty to preserve one another.[e]

Rainborough: [Otherwise] if they be injured they have not a remedy.

Ireton: That's all that can be said. The question is, whether there be so much need of giving them a power to preserve themselves against the injuries of the Commons. They are not capable of judgment as to their persons unless it be as they are

officers of state. Only the truth of it is, there is this seems
to be taken away [by taking away their judicial power]: if
a man do come and violently fall upon them in the court,
or do any such thing, they have no power to preserve themselves, and all their way will be to complain to the House of
Commons.

Wildman : I conceive that whilst we thus run into such particulars there is very little probability of coming to satisfaction.
The case, as there it is stated in the Agreement, is general; and it
will never satisfy the godly people in the kingdom unless that all
government be in the Commons, and freely. Truly, I conceive
that according to what is there propounded the power of the
House of Commons is much lessened—from what it is of right,
not [from] what it is now by usurpation of King and Lords.
Whereas it 's said that no law shall be made without the consent
of the Commons, it doth suppose some other law-makers besides
the Representative of the Commons. Whereas it is said that the
Lords in some cases should sit as an House of Parliament to
consent to laws, [this] doth give them that power which they never
had before the wars; for as yourself said of the King's oath, it
says that the King shall consent to such laws as the people shall
choose, but the Lords have no power.[a] If there be a liberty to
the King to give them a title of honour, they ought to be under all
laws, and so they ought to concern them as well as all others;
which I conceive is diminished in those particulars. Besides,
the general current of the whole offer runs that nothing shall be
declared against that usurpation in the King formerly, nor in the
Lords formerly, and so it remains perpetually dubious. They
shall say, 'Though it does not concern me in my private [capacity],
yet it does in my politic'; and no law can be made but it must be
sent to the King and Lords, and that must occasion a review; and
so they must have recourse [to the King for their laws], to the
unrighteous for righteousness, and so long as it is not clearly
declared that he hath no power to deny it, and that they need not
address themselves to him,[b] the kingdom cannot be in safety, but
his own party may get up and do what he will.

Ireton : This business is much heightened. Yet[c] I do not
know, by all that hath been said, that the King or Lords are more
fastened [on us] than before. We hear talk of laws by ancient
constitution, and by usurpation, and yet I do not find that the
gentleman that speaks of them doth show [any evidence] what

was the ancient constitution, nor of [that] usurpation, but only [the evidence] of the King's oath; and [from] that is drawn, as taking it for granted, that by ancient constitution there were laws without the King's consent. For that [question of the oath], I did before clear [it] sufficiently by comparing that with other evidence; for if we could look upon that as an evidence paramount to all [other], that needed not [to] be so much insisted upon. But if this gentleman can find no law in being in this kingdom, which hath not Lords to it, and King to it, and expressly,[a] 'Be it ordained by the King, Lords, and Commons'—if it always have gone so, and no interruption and no memory of any kind of proceeding to the contrary, but that all laws passed by the Commons have been sent to the Lords for their concurrence—[if] the Lords have [made amendments and] sent down [to the Commons] for their concurrence, they have had conferences, and [when they] could not agree, the Commons have let it rest and not insisted upon it: we must look upon these as evidences of what is constitution, together with that testimony of the King's oath. [But] whereas those other things that are numerous and clear evidences do [e] in express terms relate to the Lords,[j] when I do consider the consequences of that oath, I do conclude either that the word *vulgus* is concluded [b] to comprehend all Lords and Commons; or else it is thus, that the two great powers of this kingdom are divided betwixt the Lords and Commons, and it is most probable to me that it was so: that the judicial power was in the Lords principally, and the House of Commons yet to have their concurrences, the legislative power principally in the Commons, and the Lords' concurrences in practice to be desired. It is a clear and known thing that the House of Commons [c] cannot give [d] an oath, by the constitution of the kingdom, but they must resort to the Lords if they will have an oath given. And then, besides, all the judges of [the] Common Law in the kingdom [c] sit as assistants to the Lords. Upon this the practice hath been in any private cause wherein unjust sentence hath been given—it is beyond all record or memory—that [by] a writ of error that [which] hath been passed in another court may be judged here. So that these two powers, of the legislative power and the judicial, have been exercised between both Lords and Commons, and neither [f] of them to exercise the one or the other without mutual consent.[g] I desire this gentleman, or any other that argues upon the other part [than] that we are upon—unless they will produce some kind of evidence of history upon record by law—that they will forbear arguments of that nature,[h] calling such things usurpations[i] from constitution or from right, and [rather] insist upon things of common safety as supposing no constitution at all.

Cowling : Contrary to resolution I must now speak—whether it be from the Lord or no, I know not. What foundation had the Commons of England to sitting (being a four hundred b years in sitting)? For in King Henry the Third's time, when Magna Charta was finished (which by computation was four hundred c years [ago]),d this was granted to the Lords Spiritual and Temporal, and Edward, the son, was called to be a witness. But when the Lords saw that they were not strong enough to sit in that magnificence, the Commons were drawn in, and [it was contrived] that in that law [of] the King's oath [they] should [also] come in. Now had it not been a fundamental law [before the Conquest] the Commons should not have been drawn up, but that they did drive up [now to support the Lords] is clear. And what will become of us if we drive up to no other purpose but to support a Norman prerogative? The Lord knoweth, not I.

Ireton : I thought this gentleman had had some answer to this matter of history as to the Norman Conquest before, so as we should not seem to derive all our tyranny from the Norman Conquest. If subjection to a King be a tyranny, [we had a King before the Norman Conquest]; the question was between him and the Conqueror who had the right to e the crown. But I cannot but wonder at the strange inferences that are made. He tells us that there is no memory of the Commons' having any interest in the legislative power till Edward the First's time, and then [that] the Lords Spiritual and Temporal f found themselves not strong enough in King Henry the Third's time, and therefore they brought them in, and yet [he] would certainly have us to believe that the Commons had all the right before [the Conquest].

Cowling : In Alfred's time,f the Commons had all the power, and the King, before the Conquest, hanged forty-three [of the Lords Justices] in one year.[1]

Rainborough : [I observe] that the Commissary-General is willing to lay that of constitution aside, and that of custom aside, and [I think it well for us] to consider the equality and reason-

---

[1] Alfred's hanging of forty-four justices (which has nothing to do with the Commons' power) is cited (from Andrew Horne's *Mirror of Justice*), in connection with the subject's liberties, in *Vox Plebis* (1646).

ableness of the thing, and not to stand upon [a] constitution which we have broken again and again. I do not find in all the reading that I have done—I do not know that ever the Commons made war with the King [till now, though] the Barons did. Yet,[a] besides the oath he found, [I would add] that one of the main articles against Richard the Second [was] that he did not concur with, and agree upon, those wholesome laws [which] were offered him by the Commons for the safety of the people. If that were so great a right as did depose him, it is in the kingdom [still], and therefore let us go to the justice of the thing. That justice and reason doth not give to the major part——

Ireton: You would have us lay aside arguments of constitution, and yet you have brought the strongest that may be. I have seen the Articles of Richard the Second, and it is strange that the Parliament should not insist upon that.

Rainborough: That is not the thing that I would consider of.

Ireton: I suppose no man will make a question that that may be justice and equity upon no constitution, which is not justice and equity upon a constitution. As 'for instance in the matter of a common, &c.

I wish but this, that we may have a regard to safety—safety to our persons, safety to our estates, safety to our liberty. Let's have that as the law paramount, and then let us regard [the] positive constitution as far as it can stand with safety to these. Now therefore—thus for my part I confess it—if I should have ever given a consent in my heart to propound anything that did not consist with this, with regard to any constitution whatsoever, [I revoke it]; but for my part I cannot see that anything but safety is provided for.[b] Mr. Wildman says that many godly men would not be satisfied with this that we have read, which amounts to this: that the Commons have power to make laws for all the Commons of England, [and] that only the person of the King and [the] persons of the Lords [c] as persons,[d] with their estates, are freed from them. [If this be so], I do not see [that] they are satisfied with anything without having a power over other men's liberties.

Wildman: Whereas you are pleased to say I produced no other evidence, Colonel Rainborough brought another. Because you did confess the Lords had no other power in making laws——

Ireton [interrupting]: I never confessed it in my life, [otherwise] than [by] the recitation of that oath: 'which the people shall choose.'

Wildman: I could wish we should have recourse to principles and maxims of just government, [instead of arguments of safety] which are as loose as can be. [By these principles, government by King and Lords is seen to be unjust.]

Ireton: The government of Kings,[a] or of Lords,[b] is as just as any in the world, is the justest government in the world. *Volenti non fit injuria.* Men cannot wrong themselves willingly, and if they will agree to make a King, and his heirs, [their ruler], there's no injustice. They may either make it hereditary or elective. They may give him an absolute power or a limited power. Here hath been agreements of the people that have agreed with this. There hath been such an agreement when the people have fought for their liberty, and have established the King again.

[c] *Wildman:* 'Twas their superstition, to have such an opinion of a great man.[d]

Ireton: Any man that makes a bargain, and does find afterwards 'tis for the worse, yet is bound to stand to it.

[e] *Wildman:* They were cozened, as we are like to be.[f]

Ireton: I would not have you talk of principles of just government when you hold that all governments that are set up by consent are just. [Argue instead that] such or such a way, *that* can consist with the liberty of the people. Then we shall go to clear reason. That's one maxim, that all government must be for the safety of the people.

Tichborne: Let us keep to that business of safety. 'Tis upon the matter [of safety that the real power of making laws is vested] solely in the people [by] what hath been proposed. In that I give King and Lords [no more than an opportunity] to do me a courtesy if they will——

Wildman [interrupting]: No courtesy.

Tichborne : It is only an opportunity—and [to] show themselves as willing as the Commons. Let us not fight with shadows.

[*Wildman*] : [a] We do not know what opportunity God will give us.[b]

Ireton : If God will destroy King or Lords he can do it without our or your wrong-doing. If you [not only] take away all power from them, which this clearly does, but [do also] take away all kind of distinction of them from other men, then you do them wrong.[c] Their having [such] a distinction from other men cannot do us wrong. That you can do to the utmost for the[ir] safety is this: that a Lord or King may preserve his own person or estate free from the Commons. Now [I would know] whether this can be destructive to the Commons, that so few men should be distinct from a law made by the Commons, especially when we have laws made as to the preserving of the peace of the king-dom and preserving every man in his right. The King and Lords are suable, impleadable, in any court. The King may be sued, and tried by a jury, and a Lord may be sued, and tried *per pares* only, [as] a knight by esquires. What needs more, where there are such laws already that the King and Lords are so bound?

Wildman : I conceive that the difference does not lie here, but whether the King shall so come in that the Parliament must make their addresses themselves unto him for [the confirmation of] everything they pass. Whether it be a shadow or no, I think it is a substance when nothing shall be made but by address to the King. This will be very shameful in future chronicles, that after so much blood there should be no better an issue for the Commons.

Ireton : Do you think we have not laws good enough for the securing of [the] rights [of the Commons]?

Wildman : I think [that] according to the letter of the law, if the King will, [he may] kill me by law.[d] Ask any lawyers of it: by the letter of the present law he may kill me, and forty more, and no law call him to account for it.

Ireton : I think no man will think it.[e] When the King stands thus bound with so many laws[f] about him, and all the Commons of England bound to obey what law they [by their representatives] do make, let any man guess whether the King, as he is a single person, will hazard himself to kill this, or that, or any other man.

Wildman: It will be thought boldness in me [not] to agree. If God will open your hearts to provide so that the King may not do me injury, I shall be glad of it. If not, I am but a single man, I shall venture myself and [my] share in the common bottom.[1]

[1] Report concludes: 'Resolved, that the Council be adjourned till to-morrow, and so from day to day till the Proposals be all debated, and the same committee to meet again.' The remaining debates are not reported in detail. The fragmentary reports are reprinted in the Appendix, where they are supplemented by the account given in *A Letter from Several Agitators to their Regiments* (11th November); see pp. 452–5.

PART II. THE WHITEHALL DEBATES [a]

General Council [1] at Whitehall, 14th December 1648 [b]

[SUMMARY OF QUESTIONS DEBATED AND METHODS TO BE USED]

Question debated: Whether the magistrate have, or ought to have, any compulsive and restrictive power in matters of religion ? [c]

Question: Whether to have [in the Agreement of the People] any reserve to except religious things, or only to give power in natural and civil things and to say nothing of religion ? [2]

Orders for the discussing of this question: (1) That those who are of opinion in the affirmative begin (if they will) to lay down the grounds; (2) That the discussion be alternate, *viz.*, that when one hath reasoned for the affirmative, the next admitted to speak be such as will speak for the negative, and after one hath spoke for the negative, the next admitted to speak be for the affirmative; (3) That if none arguing in the affirmative give grounds for a compulsive power, then none in the negative to speak against any other than the restrictive power.

[Meeting of a committee with divines ordered]: [3] Col. Rich, Col. Deane, Mr. Wildman, Mr. Stapleton, [d] Mr. John Goodwin, Mr. Taylor, Mr. Collier, Capt. Clarke, to meet at Col. Tichborne's to-morrow, at four of the clock in the afternoon, with Mr. Calamy, Mr. Ashe, Mr. Seaman, Mr. Burgess, Mr. Cordwell, Mr. Marshall, Mr. Nye, Mr. Russell, Mr. Ayres, Mr. Brinsley, about the particulars this day debated. [e]

[THE DEBATE] [f]

The first reserve as in relation to matters of religion read. [4]

[1] i.e. the Council of Officers, not the General Council of the Army, which held its last meeting on 8th January 1648 (see Introduction, pp. [*30–1*]).

[2] Debated below. Decided at meeting of 21st December; see pp. 467–8.

[3] Search has failed to discover the minutes of the debate of this committee. They would be of great interest.

[4] The first reserve attached to Article VII of the draft *Agreement of the People.* See pp. 361–2.

The question [*stated*] : [1] Whether the civil magistrate had a power given him from God [in matters of religion] ?

Tichborne [amended]: *How far* the civil magistrate had power from God ?

Deane [said: That] the law is, that what a man would have done to himself he may do to another, and that according to that rule he did not understand the magistrate to have power.

Mr. Jo[*hn*] *Goodwin* offered ᵃ to consideration: That God hath not invested any power in a civil magistrate in matters of religion. And I think if he had he might more properly be called an ecclesiastical or church officer than a civil; for denominations are given from those [things] that are most considerable in an office. There is no difference [between the two] in that [case]. That the magistrate hath [not] in any way a concession from God for punishing any man for going along with his conscience, I conceive that is not necessary to be argued upon.

That [which], I suppose, is [necessary to be argued upon, is]: whether it be proper or conducing to your ends, whether it be like to be of good resentment of the wisest, or [even the] generality, of the people, [or whether it will not be held] but a subjecting of them, that a business of this nature should be of your cognizance [at all], it being that which hath taken up the best wits to determine, whether the magistrate hath power in matter of religion or no. [And if in policy you may proceed], yet it being a matter of that profound and deep disputation as men have made it, [I question] whether it will be a matter appropriate to the cognizance of you to interpose [in] to determine, and to decide a question which hath been the great exercise of the learning and wits and judgment of the world. And I conceive, though there be reasons upon reasons of very great weight, commanding why it should be inserted [in the Agreement, that the magistrate has no coercive power in matters of religion, that yet your competence to decide the matter may be questioned]. Certainly if so be the inserting of it could carry it, if it could obtain [support] and be likely to prevail in the kingdom, I think it would bless the nation with abundance of peace, and [be] the preventing of many inconveniencies and troubles and heart-burnings, that are [otherwise] like to arise. But inasmuch as I do not apprehend that it is a matter proper for you to take notice of, to intermeddle in, [I recommend you not to insert it, or at least not here. For it is either a question

---

[1] Presumably by Ireton (see below, p. 129).

of conscience or of civil right]. It being a matter of conscience and matter of religion, whether you will [or no], you must, [if you insert it], do it ᵃ as [a sort of] magistrates, and then you go against your own principles, [for] you do assume and interpose in matters of religion. [On the other hand], if it be no matter of conscience, but only matter of civil right, it will fall into those articles which concern the civil power of the magistrate.

Mr. Hewitt: Every poor man [that] does understand what he does, and is willing that the commonwealth should flourish, hath as real an hand here as the greatest divine, and [for] all [the] divinity [you] have had from reading, if you had as many degrees [as there are hours] of time since the creation, learning is but the tradition of men.[1] He is [as] properly concerned ᵇ as [any] one [man] of England, and therefore [is as likely] to know, whether you give him any power or no.

Those men that are [most truly] religious, they are those men that have ᶜ the greatest spirits and fittest for public service, and to have religion given under the hand of a magistrate or two, and [for] all the noble spirits of the poor, to turn them out of the commonwealth [is tyranny to them and robbery of the commonwealth].ᵇ Therefore if we do honour the commonwealth of England, it is best to let them be free, that they be not banished or injured for matters of conscience, but that they may enjoy [and serve] the commonwealth.

Wildman: I suppose the difference is concerning the stating of the question. For what that learned gentleman was pleased to say, [that he doubted] whether it were proper for this Council [to judge of the question, I am unable] to conceive [that it should be so], whether it were matter of conscience [or of civil right]. Through the judgment of God upon the nation all authority hath been broken to pieces, or at least it hath been our misery that it hath been uncertain whether ᵈ the supreme authority hath been [here or there], [so] that none have known where the

---

[1] Firth quotes from *Mercurius Pragmaticus*, 12th–19th December: 'On Saturday the two politic pulpit-drivers of Independency, by name Nye and Goodwin, were at the debate of settling the kingdom, in the mechanic council at Whitehall, and one main question was concerning the extent of magistracy, which Nye and Goodwin requested them not to determine before advice had with some learned divines. Which saying of theirs turned the debate into a quarrel; for the mechanics took snuff, told them they thought themselves as divine as any divines in the kingdom, which a brother standing by undertook to prove, and pretended a sudden revelation for the purpose, by which means both Nye and Goodwin were once again made silenced ministers.'

authority of the magistrate is, or [how far] his office [extends]. For the remedy of this your Excellency hath thought fit to propound a new way of settling this nation, which is a new constitution. Your Excellency thinks it [evident] that there [a] can þe no other way for to govern the people than this way.

And though this Agreement were resolved [upon] here, [yet it must be submitted to the people]. And therefore the question is now what power the people will agree to give to the magistrates that they will set over them to be their governors. Now the great misery of our nation hath been the magistrates' trust not being known.[b] We being about settling the supreme power, I think it is [necessary] clearly to declare what this power is; and therefore I think the question will be: [first], whether we shall entrust the magistrate [with power] in matters of religion or not; [and secondly], whether it be necessary to express [c] it or not.[d] Then the question must be thus: whether it be [not] necessary,[e] after we have had a war for the power, to show what power we do give them, and what not. And I desire that the question may be stated: Whether it is [not] necessary clearly to determine [f] in this constitution whether to entrust the magistrate [with any power] in matters of religion or not; [and] whether it be necessary to express it or not?

Hewson : No man hath said that in this Agreement nothing hath been [granted to the magistrate, save that which hath been] expressed. The main thing is not whether he should be entrusted, but what should be reserved. I think that's sufficient. For to trust him,[h] if they have a power in themselves either to bind or not to bind, I think that will be a thing questionable still.[1] But[1] that's doubted by many, whether the people can tie up themselves to any particular measure of their obedience. Now if so, if they have not this power in themselves, then for them to say they reserve it from others, which they have not themselves——

Rich : I think the greatest cause of the lengthening of the debate is the mistake of the question in hand, and I have heard difference[s] in opinion, several, about the question. As to that the gentleman that spoke last asserted, that if we did not give him this power expressly, impliedly he has it not, I refer it to your Excellency [e] whether or no the [not] empowering the civil magistrate does [g] reserve it, and therefore to consider whether it be

[1] Report appears defective. Probably what follows belongs to another speaker, and was followed in turn by the unreported speech to which Rich refers.

[not] a necessary reserve. If it be a reserve that concerns the conscience of any of those faithful friends that have gone along with your Excellency—and this is a reserve that does not concern us but them—[they have a right to expect it]. Even for that I refer it to your Excellency, whether it ought not to be inserted.

But as to the equity and reason of the thing, whether he hath this [power over consciences] from God, or whether he can have it, that is so clear that no man will argue for it. [But there is another question.] That is, whether the civil magistrate hath a power to be exercised upon the outward man for [other than] civil things. It has been said: we may entrust the civil magistrate with our lives and our estates, but to entrust the civil magistrate with a compulsive power for religious ends, this does implicitly signify that we will submit [our consciences] to such a power. Now the question is [not] whether we can empower him over our consciences; it's impossible. But this is that which sticks with me: whether we ought to countenance the magistrate, much less give him a power over the persons of men, for doing or not doing religious things according to his judgment.

Lieutenant-Colonel [*John*] *Lilburne:* To my understanding, [in] all that hath been said to reach [an end of] this business, that which hath been principally aimed at [is] to state the question. According to [the] Commissary-General's first stating of it, [it] is this: [Whether the civil magistrate hath a power given him from God]?ᵃ Seeing there hath been a great war about breach of trust (and that unlimited trust), and seeing we are now about to [seek a way to] avoid those miseries that hitherto have happened, I conceive the substance of the question will be this: Whether it be [not] necessary to represent [in the Agreement] the trust that is reposed in the magistrates—that I conceive, that is the principal thing that will reach our end, whether it be requisite to express their trust positively in this Agreement, yea or no?

Ireton: I have heard so many things, and so many mistakes, that it makes me think of some other method, and that is to find out the persons of [those adhering to] the several opinions that are started amongst us, that [they] may apply themselves to answer [each other]: not many to speak together of one part, and ᵃ that which they have said ᵇ go without answer, but immediately, as one hath spoken anything of one part, that it may be answered of the other part. Otherwise we shall, as far as my reason goes, perplex ourselves and all that hear us.

My memory is not able to reach to those many mistakes that I have found in the debate hitherto, but I 'll speak a word to the last because it is very material. I perceive by this gentleman that the foundation of the necessity—the ground of the necessity —of the determination of this point now, is fixed upon this: that we have had wars and troubles in the nation, and that hath been for want of ascertaining the power in which men should have acquiesced in the nation, and for that men have not known where to acquiesce. If the meaning of this be that it hath been for want of knowing what power magistracy hath had, I must needs say that it hath been a clear mistake, [to say] that this was the ground of the wars.[a] The grounds have been these. That whereas it is well and generally known what is the matter of the supreme trust (that is all things necessary for the preserving of peace), [it is not so well known] what is the end of civil society and commonwealths. If I did look [chiefly] at liberty, I would mind no such thing [as a commonwealth]; for then I am most free when I have nobody to mind me. Nor do I find anything else that 's immediately necessary, not [as the cause] of making any power amongst men, but [c] [only] the preserving of human society in peace. But withal to look at such a trust.[d] You commit the trust to persons for the preserving of peace in such a way as may be most suitable in civil society. [And they are persons] that are most probable and hopeful for [preserving] liberty, and not [like] to make us slaves. [For] as it may be most hopeful for common and equal right among us, so [e] may [it] be most hopeful to provide for the prosperity and flourishing state of the nation. But [f] the necessary thing, that which *necessarily* leads all men into civil agreements or contracts, or to make commonwealths, is the necessity of it for preserving peace. Because otherwise, if there were no such thing, but every man [were] left to his own will, men's contrary wills, lusts, and passions would lead every one to the destruction of another, and [every one] to seek all the ways of fencing himself against the jealousies of another.

And [g] that which hath occasioned the controversies [in this nation] heretofore hath been this, [the placing of the supreme power, in which men must acquiesce for peace' sake].[d] All civil power whatsoever, either [h] in natural or civil things,[i] is not [able] to bind men's judgments, [but only their actions]. The judgment of the Parliament, [which] is the supremest council in the world, cannot bind my judgment in anything. [Whatever power you give the magistrate], and whether you limit it to civil things

or natural things, the effect of that power is that he hath not power
to conclude your inward, but [only] your outward man; the effect
of all is but the placing of a power in which we would acquiesce
for peace' sake.[a] This being taken for granted,[b] that which hath
occasioned the war in this nation is not the not knowing what the
limitations [of that power] are, or of what [nature] is the supreme
trust, but [only] that we have not known in what persons, or what
parties, or what council, the trust hath lain. The King he hath
claimed it as his right, as in the case of ship-money, but the people
thought they had another right then. There was a Parliament
called, and it was then clear and undenied; the King could not
deny it—that it was the right of the kingdom, that they should
not be bound and concluded but by common consent of their
deputies or representatives in Parliament. It [not] being thus
far made clear where the supreme trust did lie,[c] [nevertheless]
thus much was clear, that the King could not do anything alone.
Then he insists upon it, that the Parliament could not do anything
without him; this was the [next] difference, because they did
assume to do something without him, which they thought necessary for the safety of the kingdom. So that the ground of the
war was not what difference [might arise regarding the extent of
power] in the supreme magistracy, [but only] whether [it was]
in the King alone. Now we are, all that are here, I suppose,
unanimous that this bone of contention should be taken away,
that it should be determined in what persons, or succession of
persons, the supreme trust doth lie.

[But] the [other] question is [also] with us: what kind of power
we should commit with those that have the supreme trust. Since
it is clear in this question [that] it is not intended [to determine]
whether we shall commit [to them] a trust of our judgments or
consciences,[c] the question is: whether we should give a trust to
them for the outward man, and [the extent of that trust], with
acquiescence but for peace' sake. Take that for granted then.
To come [now] to consider whether as to the [magistrate's] proceeding to the outward man, and our acquiescence unto him for
peace' sake, it be fit for us to commit a trust to the civil magistrate,
for this purpose,[d] concerning spiritual things as concerning civil
things.

Now the ground [of the dispute] is this. There are two pretences of conscience [involved]. There are [e] many men who do
claim a right to the civil commonwealth with you, and have not
forfeited that right. They say: 'We think, though it be in your
power to determine who shall be the supreme magistrate, that,[f]

that being determined, there is something of divine institution
that does tell him what is his duty to do,ᵃ [and] gives him rules.
[of right] in point of acting between man and man in civil things,
[and that] he ought to have regard to that right.' Secondly,
they say that that same word or witness of God left to us, which
gives him directions in this case in civil things, [which tells him]
what is right and what is wrong, and so must be the guide of his
judgment—that same [word or witness] does tell him that in
some things [that concern religion] he ought to restrain. This
is truly the pretence of conscience on one· part. That which is
said against this. First, many men do not believe that there is
by the word of God, by the scripture, any such direction or
power or duty laid upon the magistrate, that he should exercise
any such power in things that concern religion. They differ in
that point. And secondly, they say:ᵇ 'Though it were so, to your
satisfaction that are of that opinion, yet we being not satisfied in
it, that we ought to think so, it is not fit for us to commit a power
to him, which God hath not entrusted him withal.' That 's the
[counter-]argument; for otherwise it would follow,ᵇ if there be
a pretence of conscience, and some probable grounds and reasons
on the one side, that the magistrate should not be bound in matters
of religion, but that he may exercise this power in this case.
When we are upon the business [of settlement], or upon agreement, it will be necessary [that] we should leave this out. Let
us go on to make an agreement for our civil rights upon those
things wherein we are agreed, and let us not make such a thing
necessary to the agreement as will inevitably exclude one of us
from the agreement, but let us make such a distribution of the
public trust in such hands as shall give every one an equal share,
an equal interest and possibility; and let us submit ourselves to
these future Representatives, and if we ᶜ be not satisfied in one
Representative, it may be [we shall be] satisfied in the next. This
would certainly be the most reasonable way in all those that have
not admitted this Agreement, [and might satisfy all men], seeing ᵈ
that [as] it 's alleged on one hand, 'If you put this [reserve] into the
Agreement you necessarily exclude me from it, as my conscience
[is that the magistrate should have that power]'; so says the other,
'If you have not this in the Agreement you do exclude me from
the Agreement for my conscience' sake, for my conscience is that
the magistrate should not have that power.

   Then, sir—for ᵇ truly I think it has been offered to the end we
may come to the nearest possibility, that I can see, of ᵉ an agreement—this ᶠ hath been offered: that you cannot conscientiously

entrust the magistrate with a power which by the rule of God he ought not to exercise, but if you find it is alleged to give him a power to all things but those that are reserved, and [if we do] not reserve this from him, then we give him the power of that. To that it hath been [further] offered: that, in your general clause concerning the power of the supreme magistracy of the people's Representative,[a] we should [make it] extend [only] to all civil and natural things. Then [the magistrate], if [b] having [in his own opinion] right to [such] a power from him[self],[c] will exercise his power without claiming it from somebody else, [but, if not having right to such a power in himself, he cannot claim it from the Agreement]. If he have it in him of God, then your Agreement cannot take it from him; if he have it not [of God], then it is not [given him] in the Agreement.

For that, for a settling of the power, there are no rightful foundations of this trust [save] either divine institution or designation of the person, or else an human placing of them.[1] Now though it be in man (where God doth not designate [d]) rightfully to elect and designate [d] the persons, yet when the persons are elected and instituted, what is their duty to do in point of justice, and what is their duty in point of those things of religion whereof they are to judge, [those are things] that are not to be determined by those that commit the trust to them. Certainly [by] the same reason as we in only making our choice of the persons and of the time of their continuance (that are clearly in our power) do [f] leave it to them [g] according to their [h] judgment to determine and proceed in matters of civil right and civil things—we may upon the same ground, without further prejudice to the inward [i] man, refer to them [g] a power of determining as to the outward man what they [m] will allow or suffer in matter of religion.

And thus I have endeavoured as clearly as I can to state the question and the several questions that are in this business.

Colonel [Edward] Whalley: My Lord, we are about preparing an Agreement for the people and truly, my Lord, it is high time that we did agree. If we now vary, it is a ready way to common ruin and destruction. My Lord, I do perceive in this paper which is prepared for the people to be [adopted] by agreement, there is one article [j] which hath been so much spoken [k] of, to [l] the great stumbling of many. It causes a great difference amongst us. If so, we cannot but expect that it will cause a greater in the kingdom, and so great as doubtless will occasion a new commotion. Since it is so

[1] i.e. the power *and* trust.

apparent to us, I must think it were a very necessary question to put: Whether this ought not to be left out of this paper, yea or no? For how can we term that to be an *Agreement of the People* which is neither an agreement of the major part of the people, and truly for anything I can perceive—I speak out of my own judgment and conscience—not [an agreement of] the major part of the honest party of the kingdom? If the question were whether the magistrate should have coercive power over men's consciences, I think it is a very necessary thing to put. We have been necessitated to force the Parliament, and I should be very unwilling we should force the people to an agreement.

Lilburne: I agree to that motion of the Commissary-General, that there might be some of contrary principles or parties chosen out to agree upon the stating of our question, that we may not spend so much time in [determining] that which we are to debate upon.

Mr. [Joshua] Sprigge: My Lord, I should be loath to tax any here with mistakes, though I have not a better word to call it by, and it hath been used oft already. I conceive there are many mistakes have passed in bringing forth the state of the question. There has been a mistake, I conceive, of the true subject that is to be entitled to this business, and a mistake of the capacity that you are in to act in this business, and a mistake of the opportunity that lies before you, and of the fruit and end of your actions. I conceive, my Lord, that he hath not been entitled to this thing who ought to be entitled, and that is our Lord Jesus Christ, who is heir of all things; and as he was God's delight before the world was made, why, so God did bring forth all things by him in a proportion and conformity to him, to that image of his delight and content, his Son; and so retaining this proportion, and acting in this conformity to him, have all states and kingdoms stood that have stood, and expect to stand; and declining from this proportion, it hath been the ruin of all governments [that have done so]. It is God's design, I say, to bring forth the civil government, and all things here below, in the image and resemblance of things above; and whenas those things that are but of [a temporary] and representative nature have clashed with that which hath been their end, and have either set up themselves, or set up things that are of this world like themselves, as their end, and so have made all things (I mean the things of the other world) to stoop and vail to these ends, and have measured religion and the appearances of God according to rules and ends of policy, it hath been the ruin of all states.ᵍ I conceive that that is the account that is to be given of the condition that this kingdom is brought into at this time.

Now, my Lord, God having thus taken us apieces, and that righteously, because our government did not stand in God in its pattern, why, he hath only by his providence now brought forth the government of the sword, being that which we are only capable of, and which we have brought ourselves into a condition of needing ᵃ and acquiring. Now, my Lord, I conceive that this same goodwill which is in your Excellency and in the Army ᵇ to promote the spiritual liberties of the Saints, as well as the civil liberties of men, it cannot but be taken well. It is that which certainly you shall not fare the worse for at the hands of God, who will award unto you according to your doings, and according to your intentions. But this we must also profess, that the kingdom of Christ does not stand in [need of help from] any power of man; and that Christ will grow up in the world, let all powers whatsoever combine never so much against him. So that I conceive the question is not so much to be put in the interest of Christ and of the truth—I mean in the interest of the need of Christ of your restraining of the magistrate, of your providing against such coercion. But ᶜ if it should be, now that the magistrate is despoiled of all power to oppose the Saints, that ᵈ you should go to lay an opportunity before him again, and offer such a thing to him, certainly that were to lay a great snare before magistrates,ᵉ and, by thrusting them on, to [have them] break their own necks the faster. For thus ᶠ I look upon [it], that magistrates and all the powers of the world, unless they were in the immediate hand and guidance of God, unless he does superact, they will dash against this stone. And it is natural to them not to retain themselves in that subordination wherein they are, unto God and unto Christ, who are but to represent [him] in this sphere of theirs in a lower way, and to be subservient to him. But there is an enmity in all these, there is an enmity in the powers of the world [against God], and therefore Christ must be put down [by them], as we have it at this day. God is in the kingdom, and he is growing up, and men shall not be able to hinder him. So that here's all the question that I conceive can be made, and all that is concerned in it: whether you will declare your goodwill or no to Jesus Christ. For I say, Christ depends not either upon this or that, or the truth upon it, as if it should suffer or die if such a power do not appear for it, but whether you will hinder the magistrate [from persecuting Christ and the truth] or as much as you can [a] [further him therein, they shall prevail. Yet] there may be something else concerned than [the truth, namely] the flesh of the Saints, which God is tender of; for he is tender of all of us in our several administrations and under our several dispensations; and if so be that [the] Saints are not prepared so [b] to suffer, or enabled to commit themselves to him in well-doing without such defence [g] as your sword [or] your arm, to restrain and keep back persecutors, it may be God may in mercy put this into your hearts to accommodate the weakness of his people so. But I conceive, my Lord, that this thing is not at all essential unto your work; for the power [h] of the sword, and all other power whatsoever, being extinct righteously because it stood not and did not act in God, I conceive that which you have to do is to wait upon God until he shall show you some way, and not to be too forward to settle.[c] I perceive by this Agreement of the People there is a going on to settle presently, and [to] make a new constitution, which I think we are not in such a capacity [as] to do. God will bring forth a New Heaven and a New Earth. In the meantime your work is to restrain [all], indeed to restrain the magistrate, from such a power [to persecute; for it is evident] that the people of God, and that [other] men too, that all men that are, ought to live within such bounds as may be made manifest to them to be such bounds [d] that they may not suffer wrong by might. And certainly, if so be you shall so manage your opportunity, I conceive you shall fully answer your end, waiting upon God until he shall [direct you], who certainly is growing up amongst us; and if we could have but patience to wait upon him, we should see he would bring us out of this labyrinth wherein we are.

Waller : My Lord, that that I was [e] about to say was only this. I shall not take upon me to dispute the question, [but] only tell you, I fear I shall go away with the same opinion [that] I came [with]: that it was the question, it is the question, and it will be the question to the ending of the world, whether the magistrate have any power at all [in matters of religion], and what that[1] power is. And, my Lord, I offer it to yourself and everybody, whether your affairs will admit of so much delay as to determine the question, whether [yea] or no.[f] This that is termed the Agreement of the People, [I would know] whether you do always expect to uphold it by the power of the sword. Otherwise you must have something suitable to the affections of the people, something to correspond with [their will, in] it.

Truly, my Lord, I should be glad [that] all men might be satisfied, and I think, if I know my heart, I could suffer for their satisfaction. But since it is upon these terms [we must act], that we cannot go together in all things, I desire we may be so good-natured as to go [together] as far as we can, and I hope, before that [time for parting] comes, God will find out a way to keep us together.   [I think, we may go on together] if the other things which are civil may so be termed the *Agreement* by us, [and] if they may be gone through withal.   And if we can express anything to let the world know we do not go about to give the magistrate power in that [in] which he hath no power, truly, my Lord, this will show that we go not about to give him more than [in right] he has, [and yet] if he have it [in right] at all, we take it not away.   Certainly what we do here does not conclude against right, [for] we may be mistaken.   If we give it not, certainly we restrain [not from the power, but] from that usurpation [of power] hitherto [experienced]. Though I could think it a great deal of happiness that every man had as much liberty as I desire I may have, not to be restrained [in matters of conscience; yet I will venture something for unity], and [the more readily] since I venture nothing but a persecution of the flesh.   And [if we preserve not unity], instead of bringing ease to the kingdom [by the Agreement] I should [think we shall] lay it out [for the kingdom's destruction], and to that which lies upon us of destroying Kings and Parliaments and all that, we shall [add that we] destroy a people of our own; we shall not be thought agreers, but disturbers of the peace.[a]   Therefore I shall desire we may go on to other things and leave this till that time [when God shall give us further guidance].   And truly it is something to me that the Spirit of God has not [yet] thought fit to determine [for us the power of the magistrate over matters of religion] in this world, as we are to live upon such incomings [b] from God; and though it be a very pleasing thing to have God appear in power to us in it, yet God hath been as much glorified in the suffering of Saints as in their doing.   And therefore I desire we may go on to other things and not stick at this.

Peter: May it please your Lordship.   I think we have [c] hardly time enough to spend about those things that are very essentially and certainly before us to be done out of hand.

First of all, I do not find anything at all is put to the question; so [d] we do not know any one's mind.[e]   For if any one of these three or four [propositions] were put to the question we might [at least] have no question [on that score].   I know without all

controversy, there hath been dispute, and will be a great while,
[about this], and I know not in what country this will be first
decided.   Not that God and nature have [a] left it so [doubtful],
but from Diotrephes [1] to this day there hath been a spirit of
dominating.   There are two things upon which I will raise the
conclusion.   (1) I am marvellous tender that there shall be nothing done about religion in England (and I am only tender in
England; if I were in another country I would not say so) because
the interest of England is religion.   I say it looks like the interest
of the kingdom; and I believe you will find that [religion is the
cause of] those contests that have been in the kingdom.   And
though that gentleman and others are enabled to know if [it be]
so [better than I am, I ask], why do we march with our swords by
our sides ?   From first to the last we might have suffered under
Kings, or Bishops, or Parliament or anybody, and we that [speak]
know what it is to suffer and to be banished a thousand miles.
You shall know, all the disputes all along have been upon this
very point.[b]   It was the old question in Pharaoh's days, whether
the people should worship or no.   Yet [though] I think, in
truth, [that] though we all sat still, yet the work of God will go
on,[c] I am not in the mind we should put our hands in our pockets
and wait what will come.[c]   We have been drawn to this work;
we have not been persuading ourselves [to it].   I should spit
him out that would look for any plantations of his own from the
other side; let that be cursed from heaven, to mind the things of
that [worldly] kingdom.   I only offer these two thoughts.   First,
God seems to call for something at our hands about religion, and
that only because we are Englishmen.   [(2)] And then the second
thing is this: that I think we should not be too much perplexed
about it.   And therefore my thought is this, if I find it move upon
other spirits that it is a matter of great intricacy or trouble among
Christians: Do but tame that old spirit of domination, of trampling
upon your [d] brethren, and giving law, and the like; [and all may
be well].   Witness the country next from us, that hath all the
marks of a flourishing state upon it—I mean the Low Countries:
they [e] are not so against, or afraid of, this toleration.   And I
am not so against [or afraid of it as some] on the other side that
are [wont] to fear some [damage to religion by] suffering [f] [it].
That which I would hint is, that now we are come here to settle
something for magistrates [we may settle something for the
Church too].   'If she be a wall,' says [Solomon, of] the Church,
'we will build a silver palace upon her, and if she be a door we

¹ 3 John 9.

will have her of boards of cedar.' [1] For the present case I think this: that that last motion made by that noble friend and some others [should be agreed to]. I wish we would do as all other republics would do when we come to such a rub as this is, I wish that this thought about this reserve may be hung forth in every market town. If men will write or speak about it, give it a time [for that]—it may have a month or two [a]—before you [attempt to settle it. Meanwhile] go on with your other work, and those things that can be agreed to, and the affairs of the kingdom [shall benefit, for] from such time they may not [need to] have long debates.. And so you have my thoughts.

Captain Spencer: We are now about an Agreement of the People, and I perceive one clause in it is, that if we have this Agreement we will acquiesce. I conceive, if you leave this [power to the magistrate] I can never comfortably [acquiesce in it], nor any man breathing, and this surely will be [a cause of disagreement], if he be not restrained in his power.

Mr. [*Richard Overton*]: [2] That gentleman hath mentioned it three or four times as if it might be taken for granted, [that] the magistrate hath power over the outward man [but none over the inward man]. In some case it may be done. [But] if he hath power over my body, he hath power to keep me at home when I should go abroad to serve God. And concerning [yourselves] one word I would speak. God has pleased by your means [to give us what liberty we have], which we look at as from himself, by whom we have had all the comforts we enjoy—I say God hath made you instruments of liberty. In matters of religion that's preferred by us before life. Let's have that or nothing. Now God hath by your means trodden upon that power which should [otherwise] have trodden upon us. [Let us agree] to prevent any [new] authority from coming upon us. If you never agree in your judgments, it's no matter, [if you] keep but authority from beating of us and killing of us, and the like. And whereas that gentleman spake of [leaving] this concerning [their own powers to] a Representative, concerning what power they should have hereafter, we have this to say. If you your own selves cannot help us [to freedom] in matters of opinion, we do not look for it

[1] Song of Solomon, 8. 9.

[2] The speaker is, clearly, a layman, a Leveller, not a member of the Army, and one whose name the reporter does not at the moment know. Of those recorded as being present only Overton can fulfil all these requirements (for Wildman has already had speeches ascribed to him).

while we breathe. The Lord hath been pleased to inform you as [well as] many other men. If you cannot agree upon it, then I [a] shall conclude, for my part, never to expect freedom whiles I live.

Colonel [Thomas] Harrison: May it please your Excellency. I would not trouble you save that [b] it may save you trouble. I do wish that which was offered at first might be entertained to save time, that you would put the business in such a way [as] to have [us proceed immediately to] the stating [c] of the question.[d] If it be so long before you come to the question, it will be longer before you come to a resolution in it. I offer this [b] (because this is that which sticks upon the consciences of [so many] men, [and] I would not have it taken notice of by any that you would so slight them as not to do that now): [g] that some of all interests may have the consideration of this, and therein you may have confidence that God will bless the issue.[e]. For what expedient there may be found in it, *that* may be left to their consideration, and the blessing of God upon their endeavours.[d] Whether they should have assistance from some out of London, or those that would be willing to meet [them from] elsewhere upon it, [I know not, but I think it] would be an happy thing to guide them to the right of it. [And I move]: That then you would please to go [on] with the rest of the things that, I think, you may more generally concur in.

Deane: I should make this motion: Whether we might not find something at this time might satisfy all, and whether in that foregoing clause, 'That in all civil things,' [&c.],[f] we might not [by the words 'civil and natural'] satisfy all interests ?[1]

Harrison: That will lead you to a consideration of the merit of the thing, and will spend much time in debate *pro* and *con*; and if it please God to guide the hearts of some few [gathered in a committee], it may be a satisfaction.

Captain Clarke: I shall take the boldness to offer one word or two. That gentleman that spoke last [but one] was pleased to offer this as an expedient to satisfy all: that if the word[s] 'civil and natural' [were inserted, it] might suffice to satisfy all. I

---

[1] The final form of the Agreement (Article VIII) adopted this suggestion, conceding to the people's Representative 'the highest and final judgment concerning all natural or civil things, but not concerning things spiritual or evangelical.' (See p. 361, n. 25.)

suppose [they will] not [satisfy all], because that all punishments, though for matters of religion, are merely civil for the punishment of the body, and whatsoever the sentence of the church [may be], if they do sentence any person, they send him to the secular power. So that will [hardly] be as himself has spoken.

But I shall add one word. This Army by the blessing of God hath done very great things for the nation, and it's the honour of the nation that it hath been a shelter to honest people that had otherwise been hammered to dust, and as long as God makes us a shelter to them [it will be an honour to us]. We are now closing up the day, and I think every one here is willing to see an end of the day, yea, [the] years [of his life], were it to see that freedom so often spoken of, and that common right so often desired, clearly brought forth to the people. Your Lordship, and the Army under your command, hath taken upon you to interpose in those times of straits, to see if you could find out such a way as might settle the people in forms of common right and freedom. You have remonstrated this to the world; and to that end you have hinted unto a petition of [the] eleventh of September,[1] wherein (if your Lordship please to look upon that it doth aim at) the thing principally spoken of [is] that there may not be a restriction to the opinions of men for matters of religion, [or] to the[ir] consciences [therein]. We all conclude, men cannot master [their opinions as they should their] passions. I refer this to be considered: whether [a] this be not our common right and our common freedom, to live under a civil magistrate, to live by our neighbours, but as touching religion [to be free from the interference of either, and] why any people should [then for their religion] be punished. I think, my Lord, that every one here, when he speaks his conscience, will say plainly [that they should not]. And [I ask] now, whether we for prudence or policy should [not] protest. Let us do that which is right, and trust God with the rest. No man or magistrate on the earth hath power to meddle in these cases. As for *meum* and *tuum*, and right between man and man, he hath right [to interfere], but as between God and man he hath not. And therefore I desire [that] though all agree [b] that the magistrate hath no power to do so, and we have no power to give him, yet seeing he hath in all ages usurped it, and in these late years, and in this last age (almost as [fresh as ever] in the remembrance of [all]), he, under pretence of] errors and blasphemies, had made most of them here to fall to the ground—that [c] since that is so, we have great reason

[1] See pp. 338–42.

to reserve it so. We might be willing to reserve it [hereafter], when we cannot.

Ireton : Truly, my Lord, I should not trouble you again, but that I see we are fallen upon an argument; and from the convincing of one another with light and reason we are fallen to an eager catching at that which is our own opinion, and dictating that which is our apprehension, as if it were the mind of all, and indeed of God himself, and a studying to preconclude one another by consequence, as especially the gentleman did that spoke last. He tells us that we are bound by the *Remonstrance* [1] to do this thing that now we are questioning about, whether we should do [it] or no; and one ground is because in [1] our *Remonstrance* we had referred so to a petition c of the eleventh of September, d that we had desired all things [in it] to be granted. But if so, it had been an ill use of it; if there had been generally good things in it, and one thing prejudicial, though we did stand upon all things [good] that were in it we were false to our engagement. When we had desired the whole we did not insist upon every particle of it. And I desire we may not proceed upon mistakes of this kind. This conduces [not to foster agreement, but] only to stifle it, and I wish we may not go about to set such things upon men's minds. For I must clearly mind that gentleman, that all that is said in the *Remonstrance* concerning the [petition of the] eleventh of September j is but this. When we have prosecuted our desire concerning justice, and our desires to a general settlement, and amongst the rest, a dissolving of this [present] Parliament, [we then desire] that this Parliament would apply themselves for the remainder of the[ir] time to such things as are of public consideration, and lay aside particular matters that have interrupted them hitherto, e and [we urge them] for the further time they shall sit, not meddling with private matters, k to consider those things that are proper for Parliaments. f And [this is all we say] in g relation to laws in that kind and for providing better for the well-government of the nation; and we move this as to advice [in regard] to matters of justice and of the [settlement of the] kingdom, h [that they ought] to hearken to what hath been offered to them by persons well-affected for the public good; and amongst the rest [we mention] that petition of the eleventh of September. Now because we saw very many and great dream[s] of good things, and therefore have desired they would take [1] into consideration with this Agreement, and [in the] settlement,

[1] See pp. 456–65, especially p. 464.

things of that nature, and [that petition] amongst the rest—that therefore it ᵃ should be concluded because of that, that we should not now have anything in this Agreement that shall not provide for that which the petition does [demand, is unreasonable].

Another thing we have declared [for]: to have a settlement upon grounds of common right and freedom.   It is [in] the title of the Agreement.   'Tis true, but I do not altogether remember that it is in our declaration.   Let it be so that it is a common right— it is dictated to us by that gentleman to be a common right and freedom—[that any man] submitting to the civil government of the nation should have liberty to serve God according to his conscience.   This is a right, I will agree to that.   That is not the question amongst us.   For if that were the question, I should be sure to give my *no* to the allowance of any man [to be punished] for his conscience, and if I had a thousand noes [in one] I should give it, and that as loud as any man.

Here's a[nother] gentleman that does speak for what is to be done in this business, [as being] a matter that is not necessary to God and Jesus Christ, but a thing wherein we must show our goodwill to him, in preserving his people from sufferings for that which is his work, his act.   If that were the thing in question, I should think that we of this Army, above all others, should walk most unworthy of the mercies we have found, if we should not endeavour [it].

But here's the case.   The question is now: Whether you shall make such a provision for men that are conscientious, [in order] that they may serve God according to their light and conscience, as shall necessarily debar any kind of restraint on ᵇ anything that any man will call religion?   That's the very question; truly, it is so, or else you will make no question.   If you could bring it to such a restraint for [the power of] the magistrate to punish, only [in the case of] men that are members and servants of Jesus Christ, all that are here would give an *ay* ᶜ to it.[1]   But whether, admitting that to be never so good, as I think it is, [and] our great duty and our great interest to endeavour [to secure it]—yet whether we shall make our provision for that in such a way as shall give to all men their latitude, without any power to restrain them, [though they were] to practise idolatry, to practise atheism, and anything that is against the light of God?   [That is the question.]

---

[1] This is the point beyond which the official Independent Party, and its clerical representatives, the Dissenting Brethren, were loath to go, whereas the more advanced advocates of toleration saw that to gain this end you must establish liberty for all.   See Introduction, pp. [*81–2*].

Lilburne interrupts: [a] It is *not* the question; but [whether] that clause may be in the Agreement or not?

Ireton: [I ask] whether this be not the question [really at issue]: that [all that] will join with you in civil things [shall be free from any restraint in spiritual things]? Now I come to tell you of what kind those things are that conscientious men do think the magistrate ought to restrain. I do not think any man conscientious [that says] that the magistrate ought to restrain a man from that which Jesus Christ does teach him; but men have consciences to say that there are many things that men may own and practise under pretence of religion, that there may, nay there ought to be the restraint of them in; and that is the ground of our question. But if I have mistaken this, I shall willingly be mistaken. However, I am sure of this in general, that there is no exception to the putting of this in this Agreement but this: that you cannot so provide for such a reserve as this is for men really conscientious, that they shall not be persecuted, but you will by that debar the magistrate of a power that he ought to have to restrain.

Sprigge: There is something offered in that which I made bold to speak of. The question that I conceived to be canvassed was: Whether your Excellency should improve this opportunity to restrain any power whatsoever from oppressing or vexing any man for the things that he does conscientiously?

Ireton: That's *not* the question.

Sprigge: I suppose it will be resolved in this,[b] though the terms may be different.

Ireton: Do you make that [clear], that they shall [do right] not [to] punish for anything but that [which is against conscience], and we shall stand to it.

Sprigge: I conceive that there is a supposition, all along, of a provision to be made to prevent heresies in the world, besides that same which is (as I conceive) the only means of suppressing them and eradicating them, and that is the breaking forth of him who is the Truth, the breaking forth of Christ, in the minds and spirits of men. This is that which does only root up and destroy those heresies, those false conceptions and imaginations; and I conceive that this same is altogether omitted and forgotten in the discourse [of the Commissary-General]. For this is the extremity that we are reduced to ^a look upon: how we shall avoid, say you, but that the kingdom may be over-run with such things as idolatry, and the grossest things that are. I conceive that it is not proper for magistracy to be applied unto this [task at all]; and therefore if you do reserve ^b [from the magistrate] this power to apply himself this way to the restraint of these [evils], you do not reserve [from] him that which is his right, that to which he bears any proportion, neither do you withhold any means that is proper for the suppressing and preventing of these things. And [to look to the magistrate for] it, is ^c showing a great diffidence in the Spirit of God, and in Christ, as if he would not provide for the maintaining his own truth in the world.

Harrison : I will only trouble you in a word. We are not yet resolved upon a question. [The Commissary-General] and the gentleman that spoke last there [differ] which ought to be the question;^d though in the issue it will be this: Whether this clause concerning religion ought to be in [the Agreement, or no]? Yet to the end that you may come to such a period, [I desire] that you would first take this into consideration: whether the magistrate, in matters of religion, hath any inspection at all. And when you have concluded that, it will fall under your consideration how much [power] will be needful for you, upon any considerations, to give to him. And therefore, if you will fall into the debate of the business, I do humbly offer this to your Excellency as the first question: Whether the magistrate hath any power or no?

Doctor Parker : I would not have spoken in this kind, but that I have heard divers men speaking, and yet in my own sense they do not come to that which I apprehend concerning the thing. The gentleman that spoke last spoke well: that he would have a question [stated: Whether the magistrate hath any power or no?]^e All that I would add [is, that the question be]: Whether they have any power to restrain men in their own consciences acting to civil peace and civil honesty? Whether Jesus Christ under the New Testament hath given any power to the civil magistrate to restrain men professing their consciences before God, while they walk orderly according to civil peace and civil honesty?

Ireton : It is good to keep to the question which was first drawn; and, as it is last, it is a catching question: Whether Jesus Christ hath given such power? It was not the business of Jesus Christ, when he came into the world, to erect kingdoms of the

world, and magistracy or monarchy, or to give the rule of them,
positive or negative. And therefore if you would consider this
question, whether the magistrate have anything to do in anything
which men will *call* religion (for you must go so large), you must
not confine it [to the inquiry] whether Jesus Christ have under
the Gospel given it, but you must look to the whole scripture.
As there is much in the Old Testament which hath lost much,
yet there are some things of perpetual and natural right, that the
scripture of the Old Testament doth hold forth, wherein it does
bear a clear witness to that light that every man hath left in him
by nature, if he were not depraved by lust. There are some things
of perpetual right in the Old Testament, that the magistrate had
a power in before the coming of Jesus Christ in the flesh. And
unless you can show us that those things are not a perpetual right,
nor had not their perpetual end, but had only their temporary [a]
end, so as to determinate by his coming in the flesh, you must
give us leave to think that the magistrate ought according to the
old institution to follow that right.

Hewson : I desire your Excellency to consider whether it tends
[not to give to magistrates an unlimited power]. If it be a question
tending to that, then consider what you do in putting it to the
question. Either you resolve [b] that they have a power [and
trust] or not. I would fain learn, if it be resolved [that they have],
whether that trust be infallible. If it be liable to a mistake, then
we may build a very great foundation [of future mischief].

Lo[rd] General [Fairfax] : Now is only to dispute the question.

Mr. [Philip] Nye : My Lord, [I desire] that your Lordship
would be pleased to state the question. There is one thing that
I have observed, that words of a near significancy [sometimes
lead to confusion], and I conceive these two words do. It is one
word of 'matters of religion,' and another 'matters of conscience.'
'Matters of conscience' is larger than 'matters [c] of religion.'
It concerns that of the Second Table [as well]. Now if it be the
power of the civil magistrate over consciences [that is denied,
the consequences are dangerous], for a man may make conscience
of some things [that are contrary to common morality]. There
was a gentleman cast into Newgate,[d] to be executed for having
two wives,[e] and he had this case of conscience. He sent for
several divines, and amongst the rest I had this dispute. All the
arguments [he advanced were] about persecution for conscience:

'Those that were of nearest affinity, to set them farthest off,' [&c.]. [Say], such matters [of conscience] as concern the First Table; then you come to distinct terms.

Mr. [Edward] Walford: As a servant to your Excellency I desire to speak a word. There is none concerned more in liberty than the Lord himself. I know nothing but that Kings and Armies and Parliaments might have been quiet at this day if they would have let Israel alone. For men to give away God, how well they will answer it I do not know. The Lord is a transcendent thing. There is a seed gone forth from God ª ['which is Christ' ¹]. It was not the Saints [only], but God himself, [that the world persecuted. Christ can say (and the Saints with him)]: 'Whiles I am in bonds here you will punish me, [but] when I shall come to return in [the glory of] my Spirit, [I shall rule the earth.' For he alone is Lord.] ᵇ And therefore all that I shall say to [the question is] this: if you can make by your power a magistrate a Lord,ᶜ let him be set up as soon as you will. I have no more to say.

Waller: I should desire the question if I thought the question would do the business.ᶜ I am afraid we are gotten into the ocean again. I should desire that [you] might be minded to save the time. It was moved awhile since, and that by the way, to put it to [the question as the only way to discover] such a thing as may be satisfactory; for I do not think that words can satisfy the hearts of men. But if your Lordship shall take such a course that men of all interests shall ᵈ be [thereby brought] together, let the world know you will bring them into their civil quiet. We do not know but that they will be all agreed in this; and when it is declared to the world [nothing more may be necessary, and] all God's people may be free.

Major [Nathaniel] Barton: An't please your Lordship, for aught I perceive there are many presumptions [in what has been offered against the reserve]. Many think there are great presumptions. I desire there may be tenderness had [of all different opinions amongst us], but (and that is first) that justice may be executed. I fear stating this [question of the magistrate's power] so high ᵉ does something put a demur upon that; and upon what ground [we can proceed against the King if we do so], I do not know. I shall desire that the merit of the *Remonstrance* may be

¹ Gal. 3. 16.

considered, and no other thing offered that may intermingle [other arguments therewith], and [I] desire that as it is of that tender consideration as to blood or peace, [so you will seek to give it effect]. I hear of something that hath been spoken here, that there have been divers invited that as yet do not appear; and [I move] what was by one gentleman offered to your Lordship, [that] the place and time may be so determined, as to this particular [matter of the reserve], that they may have a further invitation, and so be invited that they may come. I shall desire that we do not lay a foundation of distractions [by acting without them].

Tichborne : I shall desire to move this. That when we do put it to the question, first,[a] you would propose here what shall be the questions in the debate, and then [take steps] to refer it to some [select] persons [for debate], and [finally set] some time wherein you may take the concurrence of all persons that do concur; and in the meantime that the rest may be [busied] in the matters [b] that concern the whole.

Overton : I have observed that there hath been much controversy about this point, and several motions concerning the matters [of procedure]. One thing [has been] offered by Colonel Harrison,[c] and some others might be offered, that some of all parties might be chosen. [But] I humbly conceive the same thing hath been already done; for there hath been four of several parties chosen for the drawing up of this Agreement,[1] which they have done to try who will agree, and who will not agree. For it is a thing not of force, but of agreement. And I presume that there is no man here but is satisfied in his own judgment what to agree to, and what not to agree to. I desire [therefore], it may pass to the question, [yea] or no.

Ireton : I should be as free as any man to have a catch of his own Agreement. There was little difference in those that drew this up.

(*All calling for the question.*)

Ireton :[d] My Lord, the question that men do call for is not as to [what shall be stated in] the Agreement, but [what is] to be debated in relation to our judgments. [The question was not]:

---
[1] On the drawing up of the draft Agreement see pp. 347-9.

Whether that clause may be fitly in or no, or anything to that purpose. The question was: Whether the magistrate have any power in matters of religion, that is, those things concerned under the First Table?

Rich: I shall offer one word to the question——

Ireton [*interrupting him to repeat the question*] *:* Whether the magistrate have, or ought to have, any power in matters of religion,[e] by which we understand the things concerned under the First Table?

Rich: My Lord, I find that there is a general agreement by every person that hath spoken, that it is not his desire that the civil magistrate should exercise a[f] power to persecute any honest man that walks according to his conscience in those things that are really religious, and not pretended so. And what is represented in opposition to this is: that we cannot find out any way to discriminate this from that [a] exorbitant liberty which those that are not religious, but would pretend to be so, would take. If you please I should offer my sense to the question [moved by Dr. Parker]: Whether or no the civil magistrate is to exercise any power, restrictive or compulsive, upon the persons of men in matters of religion, they walking inoffensive to the civil peace?

Ireton: My Lord, I still say that whoever is eager to catch advantages for his own opinion does not further agreement. That which is propounded, I did offer it [with no such intention]. That there may be an advantage gained on the other hand, that men under pretence of religion may break the peace [and do] things that are civilly evil, [that may be considered in due course; but] now, my Lord, I suppose that that is not at all necessary to be considered in this which is the first and main question. Whether[b] a man do walk civilly and inoffensively or no, yet it may still be [necessary to decide] the question that is here propounded: Whether in some things which he may call religion [c] the magistrate [d] may [not] have a restrictive power? But if you will have it put, whether [a] compulsive or restrictive power, you may take it [after the main question]: Whether you will [concede him any power at all]?

Parker: One word more I added, that word 'civil peace' or 'civil honesty.'

Ireton: Make it what you will, according to 'civil peace' or 'civil honesty'; yet still it remains to be debated: Whether [the magistrate is to exercise any power] whatsoever [in matters of religion]?

Barton: My Lord, I do perceive—as I judge, and speak it with submission—that there are some here that are too inclinable to follow the course of corrupt committees formerly, that were forward to. put the question before there be satisfaction given.

Captain [Richard] Hodden: Here have been very many disputes [as to] what should ᵃ be the question. And if these words be not further explained, in those terms the question is still, and hath been,ᵇ I think most men's spirits here have from the beginning [been] satisfied to [have it] be: Whether you will restrain magistrates from that tyranny of compelling or enforcing men, and persecuting men for doing those things they do out of conscience,ᶜ as to the worship of God?

Ireton reads the question: Whether ᵈ [the magistrate have, or ought to have, any power in matters of religion, by which we understand the things concerned under the First Table]?

[*Someone interposing:* Any *restrictive* power.] ¹

Harrison: I desire the word 'compulsive' may be [also] added, for 'restrictive' will not be large enough. If [the words] 'any power' be not precise ᵉ enough, [I desire that] then you will take both 'compulsive' and 'restrictive.'

Ireton: My Lord, I perceive it's every man's opinion, that the magistrate hath a protective power; and if you will apply 'matters of religion' [only] to the First Table, it will be granted [that he should also have a] compulsive. 'Thou shalt have no other Gods but me.' 'Thou shalt make no graven image,' *&c.*; 'Thou shalt not take the name of the Lord in vain.' And then for the fourth, 'Thou shalt not do any manner of work [on the sabbath day].' [*Repeating the question*]: Whether the magistrate have or ought to have any power in matters of religion?

¹ This is the minimum addition necessary to preserve continuity; for Harrison clearly does not reply to Ireton's reading of the question, but to a suggested addition of the word 'restrictive.' Indeed there is some suggestion in the speeches which immediately follow Harrison's, that several speeches have been omitted from the report.

Mr. Bacon: I do apprehend [h] there hath been much time taken up about the restrictive power and [a] the compulsive power; that is, concerning the power of the magistrate in matters appertaining to the Kingdom of Heaven, and the Kingdom of God. And they have been debated: first,[b] whether he have power;[c] and secondly,[d] what is that power that he hath;[a] and so whether the power that he hath be either compulsive or restrictive? Now I do conceive that any other power [than that] which is purely protective he hath not; and I do give this account [why] the other question, [which] is whether his power be restrictive or compulsive, [is not necessary to be debated at all]. The whole power of the magistrate is said to be the power of the sword, an outward power. I do apprehend [that] really all matters relating to the Kingdom of God [f] are purely and altogether spiritual; and therefore I conceive [that] to allow the magistrate any other power than that which is purely protective of men to live quietly, is to put a power into the hands of the magistrate which [g] is not at all given him by God. I speak something as a man, and [now] I crave leave to speak a word only as a Christian, as touching affairs of this nature, which I do confess is a matter to be acknowledged as the great and wonderful work of God. To wit, that there is a time [of] coming forth of captives, according as the scripture speaks, 'I will take off every yoke and remove every heavy burden from off the people, because of the anointing,' [1] that is, because of Christ. Now, sir—give me leave in this thing—the great matter is [that we still conform ourselves to this wonderful work of God], and [that] the care of the honourable Council and all the good people of the nation [be directed to that end].[h] It is the glory of the nation [1] that we have lived to [see so much of] it [accomplished; and our care must be] how we are [to] secure the people of the nation from [ever coming again into] the like thraldom they have been in in times past. I will lay down only this one position as the ground of all that enmity that hath been of men one against another, and of the universal enmity that hath been in all sorts of men against God: I conceive this hath been [due to] the state of ignorance, and darkness, and pretence of religion, that hath been amongst us, [j] so that,[k] not having [had] the faith itself which we have pretended to, we have [had] rather the form of godliness than the power of it. And [yet] God hath been pleased to bring forth [his work of deliverance], as we have heard. There are certain men in the Army, that, having tasted of the good work of God and the powers of the world to come, [1] have been in the

---

[1] Isa. 10. 27.

land, in such a scattered time, [a] [witnesses of God's working. Now]
we all, having [some] light come [to us, should take example by
them], that the land may have her sabbath in a good sense after
six or seven years' disturbance or trouble now taken away. And
therefore the Lord fill the nation with men of [such] upright
spirits! [But to return to the question], whatsoever you do appoint
for the restraining of men [gives] the magistrate [a power]; his
hands will not be bound,[b] but he will [be able to] keep up his power
against that religion that is contrary to himself. And therefore
that's to be prevented at this time [only by limiting him to a
protective capacity, which may be safely conceded] as long as we
go no further.

Ireton: [I would hint] a caution, that you would use [only]
such words as concern a *restrictive* power. [The question is]:
Whether the magistrate have or ought to have any compulsive
or restrictive power in matters of religion? [And our procedure
should be]:
   1. That those who are of the opinion in the affirmative,[c] begin
to lay down their grounds, and that the discussion be alternate;
   2. That if no man give grounds for a compulsive power, then[g]
those that do speak against the power of the magistrate will
speak only to the restrictive power.

Mr. [*Gilbert*] : [1] If there be no man here to speak [d] [for a compulsive power, I would speak for a restrictive, and] that I should
offer to consideration is this. When Israel had renewed their
Covenant with God so that God accepted them, [they] having
been [e] at a loss a long time,[f] he was pleased to deliver his mind
to them (and not only to them but to all the sons of men) in those
ten words, commonly called the Ten Commandments. Now
as your good Apostle saith, they consist of two Tables, and the
commands of the First Table are all negatives. Now God never
gave any rules to the sons of men but he gave them to be in force.
For my own part I apprehend that they are moral, and so a rule
to all the sons of men as well as to Israel, but especially to those
who are zealous for their God. That there is a compulsive power
left to the magistrate, that I cannot allege; but that there is a
restrictive [power from the very] nature of the Commandments,
that I do hold necessary. Neither did Israel itself go about to
compel any man, but were very watchful and shy whom they did

   [1] In view of the argument advanced, no other name (of one known
to have taken part in the debate) seems possible.

admit into communion with them; but we have observed that they have restrained, as it concerns every magistrate [to do]. We must not look to [a] pagans and heathens that are revolted from their duties to God, and yet God hath left those impressions upon the sons of men that you shall not find any people but they worship some God. Now the command of God in that kind is that they should worship no other God but him.[b] This is that which I think lies upon all powers, to suffer no other God to be worshipped but Jehovah. And so the Second Commandment[c] does restrain idolatry. But as he is pure in himself, so he will have such a worship as himself hath instituted and appointed; he will not have the sacred name taken in vain. Now, any that shall break the Second or Third Commandment comes under the cognizance of the civil magistrate. And so for the Fourth: though there be a prologue leading to it, yet it is restrictive. So that though I have nothing to say for compulsive power, yet thus much I have to say, that [the magistrate ought to have a restrictive power].[d] God delivered these things to Moses, that was a prince in Israel, and it is a rule to this day, and it is a rule [also] by the light of nature; and therefore it properly concerns the princes of the people, especially those that know God, to restrain corrupt worship.

Nye: I speak to this.[e] There is no ground from the nature of the meeting to conclude every man [as agreeing] that says nothing. If your end be, by the suffrage of silence, to second your own judgments, to stamp your own judgments [upon the meeting],[f] these have [surely] a better foundation than silence. But lest silence should be so far thought of [as unqualified assent, I will tell you to what I assent]. Truly as the question is stated I think a man may assent to it, [that the magistrate ought not to have any power in matters of religion] if you will take the words [to mean] [g] 'those things that are truly religious.' [h] If the contest [i] that is between us and [the] Bishops were by way [either] of compulsion [or restriction], they have assumed so much as this, that even in that which is truly religious, the worship and service of God, they have put such restrictions [j] as these are: that men shall not preach though they be called of God; and so likewise [of] compulsion, that such a form of prayer [should be be used], that was [a matter] truly religious. In this sense your question ought to be understood; and so [it is, if one is] to take [in their correct meaning] the words in your proper speech, and that is ['matters of] religion.' For if you say 'religion' simply, by it you understand true religion; and if you speak of any other thing you will give its adjunct, 'false' religion; and so a man may easily stand to it, and yet not come to what is the [second] drift of the question: Whether a false religion, or such matters as these, are [matters which] the magistrate hath to do withal? If it be understood in that strict sense, I must stand with you in it.[a] I do not think that the civil magistrate hath anything to do determinatively to enforce anything that is matter [b] of religion; to enforce the thing [a] is that I do extremely question. But for the other [question], whether the magistrate have anything to do [with religion] under any notion or consideration whatsoever, either of setting up the false God, which is no religion indeed, [or of other practices contrary to God's Commandments],[a] for my own part I must profess that I do think the magistrate may have something to do in that. And so I shall deliver my judgment, that no man [may] shipwreck himself in this thing.

Mr. Wildman's Question: Whether the magistrate have any restrictive or compulsive power in the time or manner of God's worship, or [as to] faith or opinion concerning him?

Ireton: Whether the magistrate have or ought to have any power of restraining men, by penalties or otherwise, from the profession or practice of anything the evil or good whereof relates to God only?

Harrison: [a] You will leave [thereby] the judgment to the civil magistrate [to decide] whether the doing of such a thing be [relating] to God [only] or no. [I would know] whether, [when the magistrate punishes] error or heresy, he do not [always profess to] punish it [f] as it relates to the neighbour; and whether, if so, we [g] do not leave them to be punished [by using those words].

Ireton: [h] I take it for granted, whether there be any here that assent [i] [or not, that] in those words which we call the four first Commandments [j] are matters of religion, the fault or non-performance whereof relates to God only, the duty and satisfaction if a man do observe them relates to God only. I speak concerning such things. As to them I give my ground thus, that as to those things the magistrate hath a power to restrain men, and ought to do it; and I argue first from the possibility of the thing.[a] Those are things against which there is a testimony in the light of nature, and consequently they are things that men as men are in some capacity [to judge of], unless they are perverted—

indeed a man perverted in his own lusts cannot judge of anything, even matters of common honesty. Secondly, those who are subject[s] and not the judges, they are likewise in [a] capacity to judge of the evil of those things even by the light of nature. And in that respect I account it proper and not unsuitable to the judgment of men as men, and of magistrates as magistrates, because—if anybody will take notes of it in writing he [a] may— because [h] in such things the magistrate, by the light that he hath as a man, may judge, and the subject may, by that light that he hath as a man, [i] be convinced.

In the next place I go to grounds of scripture, and show that this is the magistrate's duty. And first I will take it for granted, till somebody give me reason to the contrary, [b] that 'tis the injunction [of the Old Testament], and likewise it hath been the practice of magistrates in all the time of the Old Testament till the coming of Christ in the flesh, to restrain such things. If any doubt it they shall have proofs: [first], that the magistrates of the Jews as magistrates were commanded to restrain such things; secondly, that they were commended when they did it; thirdly, that they were reproved when they did [it] not. This is clear through the current of the Old Testament.

And first, because I see the answer[s] to these are obvious, I shall speak to the two chief [answers], and show you what is objected. [c] That is first, [that] what the magistrates of the Jews might or ought to do is no rule to others, for they were to do it as [ecclesiastical] magistrates, church matters concerning them; [that by] the punishment of death, or such other punishments, they did but allude to excommunication in [d] the time of the Gospel; and that you can make no [such] inference from what they ought to do as to conclude a perpetual duty of magistrates, but [only] a duty allegorically answered in the duty of ecclesiastical [officers in ecclesiastical] things. This I have heard to be one answer; and to this I shall but apply one reason to show the inconveniency of this answer [to] those grounds that we give from scripture, and that is thus. If it do appear that those that were the magistrates among the Jews, whether they were ecclesiastical or civil magistrates, [e] were to exercise this power, [f] not only [g] to persons within the church, but [to persons] without the church [and] professedly no way within the compass of the church, then that objection is taken away. But I think [it is clear that] they were to extend this power to those that were out of the church. They were commanded to beat down the idols and groves and images of the land whither they went; they were commanded

that they should not suffer the stranger that was within the gate
to work on the sabbath, [and not] to suffer swearers or idolaters
of any kind.   And if any man doubt that, it is an easy matter to
produce scripture for that purpose.   So that it is clear to me,
they did [it], considered [a] as civil magistrates, as magistrates having
an authority civil or natural, and not as [ecclesiastical] magistrates
or as persons signifying [b] or typifying the power of ecclesiastical
officers under the Gospel; and therefore what was a rule of duty
to them (unless men can show me a ground of change) [should]
be [c] a rule and duty of magistrates now.

And that rule or duty to them leads me to the next evasion:
that what was a rule to them under the Law as magistrates does
not hold under the Gospel.   Now to this I answer—and I do
these things because I would give men grounds against the next
meeting to consider of some things—I say that I will acknowledge
as to those things enjoined, the practice whereof was commanded,
the neglect whereof was reproved in the magistrates of the Jews,
whose end was typical and determinative, to end at the coming
of Christ—to all those [things] the duty of the magistrate doth
cease either as to restriction or compulsion.   [It] doth cease
because it relates [not] to the things themselves.   But for those
things themselves for which they had a perpetual ground in relation of the duty to God, a perpetual rule by the law written in
men's hearts, and a [perpetual] testimony left in man by nature,
and so consequently for those things whereof the ground of duty
towards God is not changed—for those things I account that
what was sin before is sin still, what was sin to practise [before]
remains sin still, what was the duty of a magistrate to restrain
before remains his duty to restrain still.

And thus I have given my grounds why we ought [not] to bind
the hands of the magistrate[s so] that they shall not restrain men
from evils, though against God only, that are given as breaches
of the First Table.[d]

Goodwin : I shall crave leave to speak a few words to what the
Commissary-General hath said.[e]

You were pleased to lay this for your ground, that the magistrate ought to have a restrictive power in matters of religion,
because [f] matters of false worship (or at least of idolatry) are
matters comprehended within the light of nature, such as may be
perceived by natural men.   I conceive, first, that it is not whatsoever may be made out, may be drawn [g] out by much meditation
or discourse or inference, [that is said to be known] by the light

of nature. You will not call these [a] matters of the light of nature, [but at most matters of inference therefrom].[b] There are abundance of things that may be made out by the light of nature, which are not [fit to be assumed in] laws or constitutions; for then every man that is to obey your laws ought to be a student and by contemplation [c] find [out] those things that lie [k] remote from men's first apprehensions.[1] All law[s] ought to be [based, not upon such] things [as may be derived perhaps] by [inference from] the light of nature, but [upon] such things as ought to be known by the light of nature without inquiry, without meditation. So, [let me ask, what] things [can be known by the light of nature] as to the being [of God, or] as to the creation of the world? It is an hard thing for any man to come to frame a notion [even] by [d] meditation of such a being as is in God. You must put in infiniteness of wisdom, &c. It will require much of a man's time to frame such a notion as [e] will [at all] answer the being of God. For this is not [to know God]: to believe that there is a God, to say [that] there is a being which is more than men [and] from above that which is of men. But to know God is to believe that there is a true God. 'This is life eternal, to believe thee the only true God.'[1] That was [said] for that [very] thing, that though it be [possible] by the light of nature to make out [that there is a God, that though] men are capable by the light of nature to conceive that there is a God, yet to conceive this in a right and true manner, it is in the profundities, in the remotest part, amongst those conclusions which lie farthest off from the presence of men, [even] though it should be [admitted to be grounded] in the light of nature.

And then again, [with regard to] what you were pleased to observe concerning the Old Testament [2] and the power of the magistrate, I shall desire to suggest these two things by way of answer.[f] My ground is: that there is not the same reason for the power,[g] and the exercise of power, [under the] Gospel [as there was] under the Law.[h] My first reason is this:[i] we know that the magistracy of the Old Testament was appointed, instituted, and directed by God himself. The magistracy under the Gospel [j] is chosen [by men], and they are vested with that power which they have from men. Now God, he may be his own carver: if he will create and set up magistrates, he may give them

---

[1] 'This is life eternal, that they might know thee the only true God' (John 17. 3).
[2] On the distinction drawn between the Law and the Gospel, and related questions, see Introduction, pp. [40-1], [65-7].

what power he pleases, and give them in charge to exercise such
a power as he shall confer upon them. And then further there is
this: that there is a peculiar and special reason why [a] magistrates
under the Law should be invested with such a power in matters
of religion, and that reason being changed under the New Testament, the consideration will not hold; it will not parallel here.
The reason is this. We know the land of Canaan, and indeed
all things in it, not only those that were [described poetically], [b]
but the land and nation and people, was typical of churches and
[typical] of the Churches of Christ under the Gospel, of the
the purity of them and holiness of them. Canaan is the Kingdom
of Heaven, as we all generally know. There was a necessity, that
land being a type of perfect holiness and of the Kingdom of
Heaven, that there should be laws and ordinances of that nature
which should keep all things as pure and [as] free [from corruption
as] to worship, as possibly might be. Otherwise the visage, the
loveliness of the type, would have been defaced. It would not
have answered God's design in it. Now unless we shall suppose
[that] the lands and state[s] under the Gospel [c] are typical also,
there is no reason that we should think to reduce them to those
terms, for matter of freeness [from corruption, that obtained in
the land of Canaan], or by such ways; that is by forcible means,
by [a] strong hand, as God did then order and then use for the
clearing of that land, [and the shaping] of that naked piece which
he intended should be a type of that whole estate of things in his
Kingdom and his Church. And there's [d] another thing. Inasmuch as [all] magistrates, now in [being under] the Gospel,
[are instituted by man (as) they are from the first, and so consequently [from the highest] to the lowest—for they have all
their descent from him): if so be we shall conceive [that] they
have [their] power [solely] from man, [e] it should be [by virtue]
of that power which is put into him [by God], and [f] vested in [g]
him, who [in turn] made them and set [them] up in the place of
magistrates. [The magistrates' power is bestowed by man, by
the people.] For that you were pleased to suggest in another
part of your discourse, that there is a certain power [inherent]
in magistrates—for man [but] makes the case and God puts in
the jewel, men present and God empowers—I do not conceive
there is any such thing in it. For then there were [h] a necessity
that the extent of the magistratical power should be the same
throughout the world; whereas if you look into the state of all
nations, [you will see] that the power that is put into the hands
of kings and princes is moulded and fashioned by the people,

and there is scarce any two places in the world where the power[s]
of the rulers are the same.[a] Magistrates, [I say], have so much
power as the people are willing to give them. If [it be] so,[b]
then if a body of people, as the commonalty of this land,[c] have
not a power in themselves to restrain such and such things, [as]
matters concerning false worship, amongst themselves, certain
it is that they cannot derive any such power to the magistrate;[d]
but he does act it, [if at all], of himself, and by an assuming unto
[himself of] that which was never given unto him. There is
much more to be spoken in this point.

Nye:[e] I should [not] have made bold to suggest my thoughts
this way before. But now I shall do it [because I disagree] upon
a ground or two [with the last speaker's reasons against what was
previously urged, though][f] I do not [thereby] profess *it* to be
[wholly conformable with] my opinion.[g] Under favour, I think
your resolution at first was to propose some objections [and
counter-objections] now and leave them to consideration, [and
therefore I speak].[h]

The arguments [advanced] to abate what the Commissary-
General said are many. I shall speak but to one branch, and
[that] the last thing mentioned: that the magistrate hath no other
power but what is conveyed to him by the people; for that truly,[i]
I think, is the [great] consideration. [I am not satisfied with the
rebuttal] of what the Commissary was pleased to say as in relation
to the Jews. We do not believe that all that was there was but[j]
typical; much [was] rather moral [and] judicial; but[k] such a
thing was then in practice as [seemed] to put a power in the
magistrate to have something to do about religion, about matters
of God. [I] will [not] take up this consideration [however, but
will assume] that that [is a] fundamental principle of a commonwealth, [for the people] to act what they are pleased to act, in
[the most as in] the least. [Freedom of action] does not lie
[then] in the ministerial power but in the legislative power. And
if it lie[s] in the people,[l] then [I would ask] whether it do not
lie in the power of the people to consider anything that may tend
to the public weal and public good, and make a law for it, or give
a power [for it]. Whatsoever a company of people gathered
together may judge tending to the public good, or the common
weal, [that] they have a liberty [to do], so long as it is not sinful,
[and] they may put this into the ministerial power, to attend [to]
it. Now, sir, [this argument extends to matters of religion;
for] suppose this be laid down as another principle, that [religion]

(the things of our God), it is *that* which is of [greatest] public good and public concernment, or [a] [even that] among all the other comforts of life I look upon this as one, as well as my house and food and raiment. Then [b] may not a company conclude together and sit down in a commonwealth to do what may be done in a lawful way for the preserving [f] [of their religion as well as for the] feeding of the[ir] bodies, to their [own] good?

A second consideration may be this: that there may be such [and such] sins of [c] which God will take account and [for which he will] make miserable this commonwealth, those [who compose it] being Christians, or [even] if they have the light of nature [only]. By the light of nature we are able to say [that] for such things God will plague a nation, and judge a nation. A company of men, met together to consult for common good, do pitch upon such things as do concern the commonwealth.[d] They would do what they can to prevent such sins or provocations as may [make judgments] come down upon their heads. In this case I do not go about to say [e] that a magistrate, as if he had an edict from heaven, should oppose this [or that sin], but that the people, [in whose power lies the] making of [laws, should oppose] them. If it be lawful for them to make such conclusions [f] or constitutions [g] to avoid such evils, that which they may lawfully make the magistrate may lawfully exercise. And therefore I say [of the magistrate's power in matters of religion now, that it may be as lawfully exercised as] it was once exercised under the Jewish commonwealth. [f]

Then [if the end of a commonwealth be to provide] for common good, and if the things of God, [and blessings] appertaining to them, be a good to be wished; if they do not [only] tend to that [common good], but prevent [h] evil and [the attendant] judgments of God, I know nothing but in conclusion there may be some power made up in the magistrate as may [at]tend to it.

Wildman: I suppose the gentleman that spoke last mistakes the question. He seems to speak as in relation to the people's giving [the magistrate] that [very] power [that] the gentleman [who] spoke before [proved they could not lawfully give]. But to that which he spoke this may be answered, [and indeed was answered] *de futuro*.[d] It is not lawful to entrust the magistrate with such a power. [You cannot deduce that power from the Jewish magistrate unless you can prove] that it was not merely typical. The question was whether it were [also] moral. If it were not moral, it were [not] perpetual. If it were moral, it must go to all magis-

trates in the world. That the magistrate should act to his conscience [might mean that he would] destroy and kill all men that
would not come to such a worship as he had. [Accordingly]
God hath not given a command to all magistrates to destroy
idolatry, for in consequence it would destroy the world. But
to that which the gentleman said, that the people might confer
such a power upon the magistrate in relation to a common good,
to that I answer: that matters of religion or the worship of God
are not a thing trustable, so that either a restrictive or a compulsive power should make a man to sin. To the second thing,
that [there might be such a power] not only in relation to a common
good, but to the prevention of evil, because by the magistrate's
preventing such things as are contrary to the light of nature
[punishment might be turned aside, and] to that end there might
be such a power—to that I answer, it is not easily determinable
what is sin by the light of nature.[a] If the gentleman speak of
things between man and man, of things that tend to [destroy]
human society, he is beside [b] the question; if concerning matters
of the worship of God, it is an hard thing to determine [by the
light of nature]. It is not easy by the light of nature to determine [more than that] there is a God. The sun may be that
God. The moon may be that God. To frame a right conception or notion of the First Being, wherein all other things
had their being, is not [possible] by the light of nature [alone].
Indeed, if a man consider there is a will of the Supreme Cause,
it is an hard thing for [him by] the light of nature to conceive
how there can be any sin committed. And therefore the magistrate cannot easily determine what sins are against the light of
nature, and what not. And to both of those considerations
together it may be said: [c] Supposing both [d] these things were
[satisfactorily proved to be] thus, yet [to give him this power] [e]
is but to put the magistrate in a probable condition to do good,
or in a capacity probably to prevent the sin; [but] because the
magistrate must be conceived to be as erroneous as the people [f]
whom he is to restrain,[g] and more probable to err than the people
that have no power in their hands, the probability is greater that
he will destroy what is good than [that he will] prevent what is
evil. So that [it is sufficient reply] to both of them, [that] they
do not put the commonwealth into so much as a probability of
any good [from magistrates] by such a trust committed to them.

Ireton : I shall desire but a word or two. Truly I did endeavour,
when I began, to go in the way that men might judge whether

there was weight in what was said in the reply; and I perceive there was no other ground laid than what I said, [or] than what Mr. Nye did add further as a rational satisfaction to men, why such a thing might be entrusted. But I suppose, [since this is so], the grounds [which we urged] of this [power] are such as to lay a ground why [a] upon conscience it is or should be the duty of magistrates in a commonwealth to use what power they have for the restraining of such things as [b] sins against the First Table, [as are] practices forbidden in the First Table; and I would very fain once hear somebody to answer to these grounds that I lay to that. I have heard an answer to one of those grounds: that [such] things are subject to men's judgments,[c] to the judgment of the magistrates and to the conviction of the subject, [and that hence they cannot in reason or with safety be made matter of compulsion]. But I have heard none upon the scripture ground, and I would hear something of that. [I argued] [d] that in the state of the Jews [e] the magistrate there as a magistrate, and as a magistrate not of a church only but as a magistrate of a nation,[f] had [the] power and [the] right [to restrain such things]—nay, it was a duty upon him; he was enjoined to it, and when he did it he was commended for it, and when he neglected it he was condemned and brought to ruin for it [g]—and [it was] to be exercised to others than to those that were members of the church only.[h] This, therefore, which was the rule then, is a rule to a magistrate as a magistrate [now], and as the magistrate of a kingdom or a nation: that [which] was then a rule to them that were then [magistrates], to deserve this commendation if they did it, and reproof if they did it not, is a rule to magistrates under the Gospel, unless in such things the evil or good whereof as then was taken away [by the coming of Christ]. If the thing which he had a power to restrain [were temporarily or typically evil], then I agree that by the coming of Christ in the flesh it was taken away. But if the thing were morally and perpetually evil, and so that which was the ground of the duty [then] will remain the ground of the duty still, then I conceive the duty as to such things remains the same still. I would I could express it shorter—but men may take it shorter. But I would have some [persons] answer [these grounds]; that is, to deny that the magistrates had [i] power to restrain, or [to assert that they exercised it not] as civil magistrates [j] of a civil society,[k] and [that it] extended only over the members of an [l] ecclesiastical society; [m] and if it were a duty then, to show me some grounds why it should be altered now, and be [n] subject to men to [be] judge[d] of.

Deane : The business, [as] you seem to state [it], is thus: that in the state of the Jews there was a magistrate, and that magistrate did this and that [to them] that did not act according to the Jewish religion ?

Ireton : I will agree [that] all that was in the Jewish religion,[a] the good and evil whereof [b] did tend to typical institution, is not a rule of our practice.

Deane : Why should not the civil magistrate in this time punish any man for walking contrary to those rules for [walking contrary to] which the Jews were punished ?

Ireton : Those things which the magistrates of the Jews did punish as evil, if they be of the grounds and evil as they were then——

Deane : Why will you not destroy the Turk and the Jews, and all others as they did the Canaanites ?

Parker : I would offer this to the consideration of our worthy friends that are here. You say that which was commanded to the civil magistrates of the Jews, that is of [moral] right, [and] that is also to be continued amongst us. I shall offer this objection as to that.[a] Those things that are of moral right as you [c] conceive, and that they did practise in their religion,[d] were commanded immediately from God [and that was the ground why they were to be practised]. If they were commanded to them immediately from God,[e] with an [f] injunction [that they were] to be practised by their successors and that they should practise the same thing, then your argument holds good; otherwise not.[g] My meaning is this. We know it was of moral right, that no man should kill his own son. Abraham had an injunction to the contrary. God may give out injunctions to his own will and pleasure, face to face, to any particular person, and to be obeyed by that particular person, [even if contrary to] those things that are of moral right.[h] It is of moral right, [that] I should preserve my child and do him all the good I can do. Yet because God did command a contrary thing it was practised, [but not by others not so commanded]. So on the other side, if God will command things to be done [by particular magistrates], they do not conclude all successors of [those] magistrates, that are in the same power or [1] not.

Gilbert : The Doctor says, if we can show that those commands are now binding upon magistrates he'll grant us the question as for his part. Truly I have this to offer. It will be much in compliance with what [a] the Commissary-General [said]. There were three laws among the Jews, the Ceremonial, Judicial, and Moral Laws. I suppose the Judicial Law, as to the pains [b] of it, was a fence [c] and guard to the Ceremonial and Moral Law. [In the first place] the [Judicial] Law doth aim at obedience to it, and in the second place [at] a punishment to its disobedience. I conceive [d] the punishment [for infringement] of the Ceremonial Law was not [part] of the Law itself, but [a fence] of the purity of the Jews, [and] the punishment [for infringement] of the Moral Law was not [part] of the Moral Law, [but a fence to it].[e] So far as the Judicial [Law] was a fence and outwork to the Ceremonial Law [it] is fallen with the Ceremonial [f] Law. So far as it was a fence and outwork to the Moral Law it stands with the Moral Law, and that still binds upon men. So [that part of] the Judicial Law that was a fence to that, is still the duty of magistrates.

Mr [Thomas] Collier : As far as I remember, the Commissary-General offered two things. And the first was: whether [1] [the commands of] this Judicial Law for the magistrate to punish things which were sin, sin against God, those things in the Old Testament mentioned, are not commanded by God? And the second: whether they are taken away, and so have no relation to the magistrates under the Gospel? Now to the first, I shall give you the ground why those laws or commands and that Judicial Law, given under the time of the Law, have [g] no reference to us under the Gospel. And I might give you particular grounds; but one principal ground [of] that I shall give you, [and it] is this, as one ground of that which is given already. If [h] it is moral, it should have been given to all states as well as to the Jews. But the ground [I would now urge] is this: that the law of the Jews is not binding to us under the Gospel; [for] if it be, I shall then thus infer, that the magistrate hath his power from Divine institution, and so hath his power from God and not from the Agreement of the People, and if so, then he [i] must come to have [by] the same claim [all his power] from God.[j] If he have his commission from God let him show it—so say I; if he have his commission from God we have nothing to do to limit him.[k]

The second thing that I would mind you then—it is that we generally agree in, [as we have been] often minded this day, but [1]

I shall offer [it] in the second place—is that the Judicial Law to the Jews is abrogated to us in the Gospel; I mean in respect of the circumstances of it, though in respect of the truth of it there is a judicial law to be executed upon the people not in the way the Jews did. I shall give you the grounds of it. One ground is this: that there are some things mentioned with which magistrates [a] in the New Testament [b] have nothing to do, [and] yet [c] [it] was given as command [d] to magistrates in the Judicial Law to punish [them]; and I shall mind [you of] two in particular. The first is that [sin] of idolatry, which was punished with death in the Old [e] Testament: idolaters are to be put to death. Yet [f] under the Gospel, the Gospel is so far from denying [g] [even to] that [a] liberty or toleration (much less [giving] power unto a magistrate to punish an idolater with death), that if a man or woman had a wife or husband that was an idolater, they were to live with them and not to punish them according to the law of the Jews.[h] To me it 's very clear in these words of the Apostle in [1] 1 Corinthians 7.[j] The second thing I shall mind to you is that of adultery. Adultery was to be punished with death, [and] if we look to the Judicial Law we must be exact as to every particular of it. [But] we shall find that this law was done away. The woman that was taken in adultery, I look upon it to be mystical. The woman [k] was taken in adultery and was brought to Christ, and they told him that Moses' law was to put her to death. Christ answers: 'He that is without sin, let him throw the first stone at her.' Now to me it was this: that the Gospel would admit of no such thing as this [judicial law], but that there was a new law; and in the Epistles, there were [l] rules given for the excommunication of adulterers, and [persons guilty of] incest, and the like [offences]; which gives me ground to judge that the appointing of death under the Old Testament [to these] and the like [sins] doth relate to excommunication [m] [of] those which commit such offences.

Hewson: I am not satisfied as to the thing, and therefore I shall not use any argument as from myself; but having heard some [use an] argument that is not answered, I shall desire to hint it again. I shall gather it up in few words. That which in the Moral Law is enjoined unto the Jews is still of perpetual use amongst us under the Gospel. But restriction in the Moral Law is enjoined unto the Jews, as in the Fourth Commandment. Therefore restriction is in perpetual use now under the Gospel. This I conceive to be the sum of what you have from the Fourth Commandment. To me it seems to be of some force. There is something hinted of that which was typical, and the like, but nothing as to this argument from the Moral Law.

Ireton : Because this gentleman doth relate an argument from me, I 'll tell you how I put it. That which was evil in the time of the Jews, and remains as evil now, and hath the same ground of evil now that it had then—and especially if such a thing ᵃ was evil ᶠ even before that law [was] given; for such a thing, what was the duty of a magistrate to restrain then [remains his duty to restrain now], though I cannot say to restrain it with the same penalty. For the imposing of a penalty was judicial, but the imposing of a restriction was not judicial but perpetual. This I take for granted. That [which] was evil then and remains upon the same ground equally evil now,ᵇ if the Jewish magistrate ought to restrain that even in persons not under the ecclesiastical jurisdiction, so ought Christian magistrates to restrain it, if they be Christians, even in those that are not under the ecclesiastical jurisdiction.

Goodwin : Though it be supposed and granted, that the same things, [which] are evil now as they were under the Law, [are] to be punished now as they were [then], but if God hath ordained new kind of punishments [for them] to be punished with,ᶜ we cannot suppose that they are punishable with both punishments. The latter does disannul the former. If he that blasphemes is to be cast out to Satan that he may learn not to blaspheme, it is impossible that this commandment of God should be put in execution if a blasphemer should be put to death.

Ireton : I think if we were now upon the question of what an ecclesiastical judicature or church magistrate should do, it would very well be ᵈ that that should be the rule that Mr. Goodwin says: that such punishments should be used by the ecclesiastical officers (and only such) as are warranted by the Gospel, upon which the outward calling of the church hath its ground; but it is concerning a civil magistrate, or a magistrate of a mere civil constitution. I say this. If any man do but consider,ᵇ in the Gospel there is nothing that is to be called and taken as a positive institution, but that [which is expressly so designated]. I will desire that it may not ᵉ be taken any advantage of. But [for] the Gospel, the parts of it are either historical, expressing what Christ did when he was in the flesh and how he was brought to death, as the four Evangelists, and the Acts of the Apostles; or else they are exhortatory, written by way of advice to the churches of the Saints in the several parts of the world; and they are written to them, [partly] as applied to what was in general to be the condition of all Saints in all ages to the world's end, and partly [as applied to] what things were the condition of all the Saints to whom these Epistles were written.[a] As for the historical part of the Gospel—or [the] prophetical, that 's the Revelation— I suppose no man from the historical part will go to make it necessary that in the historical part there should be anything of [the] institution of ecclesiastical or other magistrates. In the epistolary part, if we first consider that all the Saints or churches to whom these Epistles were written were all under a condition of persecution under heathen magistrates, rather [b] than having a power of magistracy in their own hands, we have no reason to think that the Epistles written to them should be intended as to give the rules concerning magistracy. But since there was a rule concerning magistracy, that is [a rule] by which [c] the magistrate [d] might judge what was evil and what was good—first, [a rule] had from the light of nature, [and] secondly, [a rule which] had a more clear foundation in the Moral Law (as they call it), that gave grounds which way the magistrate[s] might go—[e] the Epistles [f] do as well leave the magistrate[s free] in the punishment of those things that are in the First Table, upon prudential grounds,[a] not tying them up to the judicial grounds of the Jewish commonwealth, but, when there should be any magistrates Christian[s], leaving them to those foundations and rules of their proceeding which they had a ground for in nature, leaving [to their decision] that which was good or evil, to restrain or not. I conceive the whole drift of the Gospel hath been to apply [restraint] in that kind either [g] to what things are [un]fit to be used amongst men in society as Christians, or else [to] things that [it] were the common duty of men, not [merely of Christian] magistrates, [to restrain]—though [indeed] it says something of that, and if any will say [that he will seek the ground of this action in the Gospel itself], I shall think it to be very good. But this I shall wish to be considered: whether in relation to what is said in the Gospel, if the penalty does cease, then the punishment of it at all does cease. Then I would fain know whether, by the same ground that idolatry should [not] be punished [with death],[h] murder [also] should not be punished with death. And what should exempt the magistrate under the Gospel from [i] punishing idolaters—what you can *imagine* should excuse the magistrate under the Gospel, or should deter him from punishing them,

with death or other punishment, which under the Judicial Law
are ^a punishable with death—[I would know] whether the same
thing will not serve to this [end]: that now even for murder, for
theft, for all those things that are evils against men, which in
that law had their particulars [of punishment] prescribed—
whether it would not hold as well for these,^b that now there ought
to be a liberty under the Gospel, [for] it is a time of mercy, and
that we ought not to punish those things.

Goodwin : Those punishments of murder by death, and the
like, the[ir] original is [a. rule of] the equity and justice [which]
was not [given] to the Jews [alone], but [to all men]. They are
from the Law of Nature. [The Old Testament says]: 'By whom
man's blood is shed,' [&c.].. [But] long before this [murder was
punished by death].

Ireton : We shall desire no more [than this]: that if the ground
of that which made it sin, and the ground of the punishment, do
remain the same now, then the sin is to be restrained as it was
then, and that which was sin then is sin now.

Nye : Blasphemy may be punished with two punishments, if ^c a
sin may be punished with two punishments; as for example, theft:
if a man were a church member he might be excommunicated
first, and hanged afterwards. That was not a fallacy.
There were two places that Mr. Collier had [alleged]. They
must not punish idolaters ^d then because the magistrate was so.[1]
But for the woman taken in adultery, this was the reason that
Christ did not judge her, because he would not meddle with
magistratical matters. All the while Christ lived no Jewish rite
was abolished.

Wildman : I humbly conceive that, while there is a new-seeming
question [made], whether such things be nulled by the Gospel,
the ground [of your argument is still that] which the Commissary-
General says: that which was sin then is sin now.^e This is your
argument: that what was sin then, and is sin now, and ought to
be punished then, it ought to be punished now. I suppose there

---

[1] i.e. the magistrate was himself an idolater. Collier (in a part of his
speech unreported) had probably urged the example of Gallio, who
refused to interfere in matters of religion and gratify the Jews by punishing St. Paul (Acts 18. 12–16)—a favourite example with the exponents
of toleration. Nye scornfully replies that Gallio, a pagan, is no model
for the Christian magistrate.

is no consequence at all [in this argument],[a] if it were punished
then, it ought to be punished now; because it was [punished then]
upon a judicial law which was [indeed] [b] moral, but not naturally
moral, and [you] yourself said that the [ground of] punishment
was not [alone] naturally [moral].[c] If so, I would desire to know
how we should distinguish what [d] part of it was naturally moral
and what was not. The Decalogue contains the whole Law. If
you will extend it beyond that,[e] I would know where you will
terminate it. Besides, if it were [true that the Judicial Law was]
naturally moral, you should find [the whole of] it [in] natural [law].
If it had been given as a thing naturally moral, and [to the magis-
trate] as a magistrate, then it must belong to every magistrate
that was in the world;[f] and then you must hold that God had
ordained such a power to them [all, such a power] in every
magistrate.[g] I must confess [my conviction] that what was
given to them was as Jewish magistrates, but not *quatenus* magistrates. Not determining what a magistrate shall be, you leave
us to an uncertainty. We find no such power at all in any
magistrate.

Goodwin : [h] If this power should have been destinated in all
magistrates, then every magistrate in the world had been bound [i]
to have put all his subjects to death.

Ireton : If I should reply to what was said, and then adjourn
the court, it would be thought not fair; and therefore I shall say
nothing in the world to answer to this, but leave men to judge
whether that which hath been said be an answer [to my argument]
or no.

[FINAL DEBATES ON SETTLEMENT OF RELIGION] [1]

Mr [2] *[William] Erbury :* [j] Every man believes his God [to be the
God] of all nations.

Ireton : Those that do not own Jesus Christ as a second Person
from the Father, yet, if you ask them [k] whether they have

---

[1] Of the three debates (8th, 10th, 11th January 1649) fragments only
are reported. Their subject is the four clauses of Article IX of the
final Agreement (for text, see p. 361, n. 26); the article was substituted
for Article VII, clause 1, of the Agreement as originally drawn (pp. 361-2),
which had been rejected (pp. 467-8). Of the debates on the civil settlement (16th December—6th January) little is reported save the votes.
For a summary, and for an account of the examination of Elizabeth
Poole (29th December and 5th January), see Appendix, pp. 467-71.
[2] On Clause 3 (8th January). I omit headings of these fragments.

[fulfilled] this [condition of faith in God] through faith in Jesus Christ,[a] [declare that they have], acknowledging the man Jesus Christ as the person through whom God hath revealed himself.[b]

Erbury : If any man do offend in relation to the civil injury of others, he is punishable by the laws.[c]

To [1] what purpose will you give that liberty to the Jews and others to come in unless you grant them the exercise of their religion?

Captain [2] [William] Butler : Truth and light and knowledge have [d] still gone under the name of errors and heresies, and still they have put these Esau's garments upon Jacob's back. And in that regard (that for the most part truth and light go [e] under the name of error and heresy) we shall give occasion to our adversaries to rail against us in every pulpit; and [they will] make it their work not to discover truth and preach sound doctrine, but to rail against honest men.

Ireton : You agree [to allow them to preach against beliefs], if you do but say they must instruct the people as well concerning what is truth as what is false. I would know what latitude you give them to rail [against persons] by this, or that.

[There is] a use for satisfaction of conscientious men in those words.[f] By our denying [the magistrate] compulsive power or restrictive power to [suppress] errors and heresies, we do allow they should be opposed with spiritual weapons.

Captain Spencer : We are now about an agreement, and as if the power were in our own hands, but if we labour for liberty [for ourselves], let us give it to others that are as dear to Christ as we are. [For an official ministry], let them preach what they will, they cannot touch me; only they touch me in my purse.

Erbury [3] :[g] [I would know] whether they do by that go about to set up a state religion. Men should be called before they can teach publicly.

[1] On Clause 4. Firth quotes *Mercurius Pragmaticus* (19th–26th December): ' . . . the Council of Mechanics at Whitehall . . . voted a toleration of all religions whatsoever, not excepting Turks nor Papists nor Jews.' The Jews were seeking readmission to England on the terms which they enjoyed in the Netherlands.

[2] On Clauses 1 and 2 (10th January).

[3] 11th January.

[On the Agreement as a Whole]

Whitehall, 13th January 1649

General Council [1] [a]

Erbury made a long speech declaring his dissent to the Agreement: setting forth that whilst we were in a way of putting down of authority we had the power of God going along with us; but as it was with the Parliament in [imposing] the Covenant, that which they looked for to be for agreement proved to be a great disagreement amongst the nation, so [with us] this [Agreement would prove] to be an hellish thing, and altogether tending to disagreement; and though he likes the greatest part of that Agreement, yet the last [article], as in relation to religion, is that which will do much hurt.

Ireton [made] answer to it: That [2] it was not to advance themselves [they offered this Agreement to the nation], but [as] such a settlement as might be equally good for all. And when we do [b] hold this forth without any enforcement upon any, merely tendering [it] to them as our utmost essay in this kind, then it hath surely its proper effect of its testimony to the kingdom of our endeavours in that kind; and that effect I cannot but expect from it, because it is a duty we are led to, for avoiding a just offence, and the preventing those evils amongst men that may ensue upon that offence. But indeed if ever we shall come to use forcible impulsions to bind men up in this Agreement, and shall so set it up as the necessary thing without which the kingdom cannot be, or so set it up as that from which we would promise good things to the kingdom, with a neglect or denial or diminution of God, or of his power, then I think we shall incur (when we do come to that end) the same blame as hath been in the enforcement of the Covenant.

But truly, I shall not trouble your Lordship to speak [of] the vast differences both in religious and civil respects that are between covenants of that kind that was, and such as this is; [c] I shall say this only in general: that this business of this Agreement is more of the destructive nature to all covenants and to all authorities [d] than it is of the confirming nature to any—except it be in that last clause of the non-resistancy of the people's future

[1] i.e. the Council of Officers.
[2] Ireton sets forth the explanation to be embodied in the 'Humble Petition of the Army,' and presented to Parliament with the Agreement.

Representatives by force of arms. It is then contrary to [that: rather] the throwing down of all despotic ^a power than the erecting of any. [Its final overthrow], that will [not] be till God destroy it. Nay, I am confident that it is not the hand of men that will take away the power of monarchy in the earth, but if ever it be destroyed, it will be by the breaking forth of the power of God amongst men, to make such forms needless. But the nature of this [Agreement] is that, [and] upon that ground, [that I shall now tell you]. Till God do so break it there will be some power exercised [by magistrates], either by a voluntary dispensation of the power from the people, or by the sword, [and] since in the meantime there will be some [power yielded] ^b to them,^c all the effect of this Agreement is no more but as restrictions upon that power. [We agree, as to that power], that it shall not be in the hands of a King; it shall not be in the hands of Kings or Peers, or in the hands of [the present House of] Commons, but [in the hands] of such as are chosen [by the people]; and not in their hands [perpetually], but [only] for so many months as they are chosen; and that there shall be a new election of another [Representative once in two years]; and for elections, that they shall not be in corporations, but [in] more equal [divisions]. And for the power [given to the magistrate], it gives [him] no power but what the supposition of a magistracy or a commonwealth doth imply in itself. But the business of this Agreement is rather a limiting [of] his power [and that of the Representative]. In time, they shall not sit so long. In the matter, they shall not have power to do in those things that we reserve from them; and one thing is a reservation of all other things that are in this Agreement, which are foundations of liberty. And truly if any man will justly find fault with this Agreement—as it is passing from us to deliver the nation from oppression, and to settle such a government, as there must be such a government ^d—if any man will take any just exception to this, it will [only] be by ^e showing ^f that we did not take away enough of power, [not that we are setting up new powers]. The whole Agreement is the taking away of any [undue power]; it is not a setting up of power where there is none, but it is taking off of power, a paring off of those unnecessary advantages which power in this kingdom formerly had, and is still apt to have, whereby it may oppress. Now if it be blamable in anything, it is in that it does not take away [more]. And if we be unanimous to take away thus far, [and] if there were [yet] something else wherein power should be abridged, we may have patience one towards another till God satisfy us in that also.

Under that notion upon which, in my understanding, this Agreement doth pass from this Council, I do not understand that it does come under that sense that Mr. Erbury hath given of it; and to that purpose it will be best to consider the terms upon which we put it forth, and to that purpose there was a declaration to be drawn, to publish to the kingdom.

Erbury: One word, that I might not be mistaken [as to] the destruction that I speak of. It is not minded, or thought in my heart, to destroy any man's person, no, not to destroy the person of the King, so his power be down. I do not look upon men's persons or destroying of that magisterial power,[a] that power of the magistrate that is now. The Parliament[b] are a power by whom men may act according to the appearance of God in them. I do not look upon it [as a power to be destroyed], neither do I speak anything of that kind; but [I speak of] the destroying of those oppressive principles both in powers and persons, and in courts and laws. Those [are] things that have been complained of and petitioned [against] by the poor country to the Parliament. The Parliament would never hear them. Many thousand petitioners have petitioned [first] the Parliament, then the Lord General, that they would please to rectify them; cries against unjust laws, against tithes, [against] many unrighteous things crept up amongst us here, among committees, receivers of moneys. God was with you to take away the oppressions of men, and not the powers of men—not to take away magistracy, but to take away those oppressions that lay before you and in your view, to remove them in the power of God.

I conceive the settlement of the nation is properly to remove those things that are [the cause the nation is] unsettled. The things that trouble the nation are these.[b] I do not find they are any ways unsettled about government, but they are unsettled about those oppressions that lie upon them. I conceive the removing of these is a settling of[c] the people;[d] but I conceive this [Agreement] will be a means to unsettle them, [this en]acting [for] the nation, that should be settled by the word of God. Now if God would so work and act by his people of this Army as to remove those things that unsettle them, they would agree; but this will[e] unsettle them, to see all things put into this frame. For my part I do think that a dozen or twenty-four may in a short time do the kingdom as much good as four hundred[f] that sit in the Parliament[g] in seven years may do, and therefore that which I would have is to [remove those burdens that] unsettle them.

Ireton : I think not that burdens are the causes of unsettlement, or the beginnings of unsettlement, but [that] the beginnings of unsettlement are the controversies about power, where the power was.g We find this, that all the fixing of power to persons hath clearly tended to unsettlement—to the increasing of jealousies amongst men, and so to unsettlement, because that men as men are corrupt and will be so. And therefore there is probably a nothing more like to tend to a settlement than the clearing of power, which formerly hath been so much in dispute, and the b taking away [of] that controversy c concerning d [the rights] of those several competitors to the legislative power of the kingdom, King, Lords, and Commons. If it please God to dispose the hearts of the people to [the] Agreement, in it e they may take away [that disputed power]; and so taking away power from men to oppress the people, and not leaving power hereditary in [any] men, is some means of settlement. But if we think merely that burdens to the nations are beginners, and are the continuers, of unsettlement, or f think to take away burdens without something of settlement of another nature, that is of clearing of things that are in controversy, [we are mistaken]. We cannot limit God to this, or that, or [an]other way; but certainly if we take the most probable way according to the light we have, God gives those things [their success]. e If it please God these things should take, and be received in the kingdom: things that do tend to these effects, to the clearing of the controversies that have been about power and the like, are [things] tending to settlement, and this [Agreement] is a probable way to bring it to that. But h whether God will bring it to pass that or the other way, is a secret in his will, and is further than what is revealed to me; i let him [to whom it has been revealed] speak it.

Spencer : Mr Erbury speak[s] of taking off burdens. This Agreement doth tend to [confirm] the power, either the power that is now in the Parliament or [in] the Army, and [so] this Agreement doth lead us to that power to take away those j [burdens].

Erbury : There is as just a power now [in this Army], by which you may act, in appearance, as in other following Representatives. This [Army] is called now from a just power to remove oppressions. I do not speak of armies and such things [in themselves], but there are oppressions hidden in [the nation], and corrupt things, that may be removed [by armies, through] the power of God if it appear in them.

Waller: [a] All that put[s] [b] it off to your hand does a great [dis]service. Sure there is at this time a very great disagreement in the world and in this kingdom, and if there be not need of an Agreement now, there never was since the sons of men were upon earth. And [for the articles of the Agreement], if all of them be liked except some particulars, and if, [because] they are not liked, the whole must be left out, I think it will be hard. It hath been already said, it must be offered to the House before it comes from them as their act. I am sure there needs something to go out from you. You promised it in your *Remonstrance.* We are now got into the midst of January. You have lost two months. It is not only necessary that you pass this from you in regard of time, but that the Agreement [may help men to agreement. For I would know] [c] whether every man does not see that, [left to themselves], thousands and ten thousands of men are senseless.[d] I shall desire it may be put to the question: Whether it shall go out or no?

Captain [George] Joyce: I desire a word or two for satisfaction, having been at a distance for three months, because it is desired it may be put to the question. I beg [to be heard] concerning two things which are very much debated in the Agreement: concerning the magistrates' power over men conscientiously fearing God,[e] whether or no they ought to have anything to do in that thing; and the other, whether the magistrate shall have power to punish any man contrary to a law, or without a law.

I have something to speak further: this concerning the contending about the power, which was the cause of the controversy. I believe it is so still, and I am sure it is the [cause of the] jealousy that is begotten in God's people. God's people they are that have jealousy now at this time over the power.[1] Some say, the power is in your Excellency and the Council; and some in the Council,[f] when they are there,[g] go to put it off to others, namely the men at Westminster, or the Parliament so called—which for my part I can hardly so call it. Therefore I must entreat your Excellency, whom the Lord hath clearly called unto the greatest work of righteousness that ever was amongst men, that your Excellency and the Council go not to shift off that [power] which the Lord hath called you to. For my part, I do verily believe that, if there were not a spirit of fear upon your Excellency and the Council,[h] he would make you instruments of the things that he hath set before you, to the people. It is that confidence I have, and [have] it upon sufficient ground; because God hath said he will do those things by his people, when they believe in him: they by belief [shall] remove mountains, [and do] such things as were never yet done by men on earth. And certainly if I mistake not, the Spirit is now [about] to break [a] forth; and so, if it were not [for] fear in us, we should not be disputing among ourselves. Some are studying to please men. I shall instance [b] [our attempt to satisfy] that party of men called Presbyterians. I dare not lay it [upon us] as a [general] charge, that we do not so much study to fear the Lord our God, who is able to satisfy them [c] though in an higher and [more] glorious way [d]—and God hath so far satisfied some [e] better than we can. [But, I say, some of us are studying to please men, through fear, whereas] we [ought only to] hold forth the lives of Christians as being filled with the spirit of Jesus Christ. So I say that all that we now seem to be jealous over [in regard to] each other, is about [worldly] power, and truly it is for want of the power of God [in us] that we are jealous over [this thing], one [of] another.

For the other [thing as to which] I have not received satisfaction. As Mr. Sprigge said once at this question, if we should not out of goodwill tell the magistrate plainly that he had no power in the things of God, [either] compulsive or restrictive, I believe that God will yet visit us[m] once more. [And] though I believe [nothing but] that shall [k] keep it away, [yet it is not for that that I urge it]; but let us be children unto God, showing our love unto the Father. I beg that in the name of him; I do not beg it [f] in my own name, and in my own strength. Not but that I can trust the Lord. I believe [that] he is about to turn some of our swords into ploughshares, and to [bid us] sit still and behold his works amongst men, and [that] this is the day wherein he is answering unto that great work, and that we should not so much endeavour to give away a power that God hath called us unto, or to contend about it, but to put that into their[n] hearts which is in our hearts.

Harrison: I think that it [g] would be in order to the gentleman's satisfaction that spoke last,[1] that this [letter] that is in question before your Excellency be read; [and also] because there are many that have not read it since some alterations be made in it.[h]

I do believe, there are few here can say in every particular [i] that it is to the satisfaction of their heart, that it is as they would have it; but yet that there are few here but can say there is [j] much in one or other kind [that is so].

I think, that gentleman that spoke last speaks the mind of

others; but we find Jesus Christ himself spoke as men were able
to bear. It is not a giving [of] power to men, [to permit such
provision for a public ministry as the Agreement contemplates,
with due guarantees for liberty of conscience]. Only, while we
are pleading [for] a liberty of conscience there is a liberty [to be]
given to other men [who perhaps believe upon conscience that
such a provision should be made]. This is all the liberty that is
given.[1] If the best magistrate[s] were chosen that ever were, or
the most able men [to preach], it is but such a liberty given that
such a magistrate can give authority [a] to one [of them] to dispense [publicly] the things of God,[b] [to preach] from the word
of God [such doctrine as it] gives the ground of.[c] Only it [d] is
feared that we may not have such magistrates because we have
not had them, nor [perhaps] have them now,[e] nor the men to
preach. Now if the magistrates [and ministers] be not such as
we [would] have dispensing the things of edification,[f] which
should be true, [yet] it is not [proved] to me to be [destruc-
tive of true religion, the specified limits of their power being
observed]. Though [g] I look upon it as the truth of God, that the
magistrate should not have [any] power in these cases; yet,[h]
since it is my liberty [that is in question], it is my liberty [if I
choose] to part with that which is my right for a weak brother,
and [his burden], I can bear it as my own.

For the Agreement in the whole,[1] I think it hath been acting
upon the hearts of many of us, that it is not [such] an agreement
amongst men that must overcome the hearts of men; it shall not
be by might, nor by strength, but by His Spirit. Now this
Agreement doth seem to me to be a fruit of that Spirit [in this
respect].[1] Since God hath cast very much upon your Excellency
and those that waited upon you in the Army,[i] [it seemed, if] we
would hold forth [to the nation] those things [which tended to]
a settling of that, or anything which might be of concern to others,
that we [must make it appear that we] would not make use of
any opportunity of this kind [to perpetuate our own power; and
for our opponents], that we would not serve them as we [b] have
been served, or as they would serve us, but that there might be
some conviction that God is in us (for it is not a principle of man,
when we have brought down such men that would have kept us
under, to give them a liberty, but it is more of God, to put them
into such a condition). [And so we have determined],[j] especially
as to things of civil concernment,[k] that we need not seek ourselves

[1] Like Ireton's first speech, this of Harrison's in some degree parallels
the 'Humble Petition of the Army.'

[at all, but] that we will trust God and give them up in a common current again. And that hath been an argument [of] very much [weight] with many, why things of this kind might be proposed— though this hath stuck: that the word of God doth take notice that the powers of this world shall be given into the hands of the Lord and his Saints, that this is the day, God's own day, wherein he is coming forth in glory in the world, and [that] he doth put forth himself very much by his people, and he says, in that day wherein he will thresh the mountains, he will make use of Jacob as that threshing instrument.

Now by this [Agreement] we seem to put power into the hands of the men of the world when God doth wrest it out of their hands; but that having been my own objection, as well as [the objection of] others, it had this answer in my heart.[a] When that time shall be, the Spirit of God will be working to it, and he will work us on so far [b] that we are [to be] made able in wisdom and power to carry through things in a way extraordinary,[c] that the works [d] of men shall be answerable to his works [e]; and finding that there is not such a spirit in men [we know that the time is not yet].[f] Some that fear God, and are against us upon other grounds, they think that our business is to establish ourselves:[g] it is only to get power into our own hands, that we may reign over them; it is to satisfy our lusts, to answer the lusts within us. But [we know] rather that it was in our hearts to hold forth something that may be suitable to [the minds of] men. That present reproach upon us doth call upon us to hold forth something to the kingdom. And this was all of argument that did come down to it: first to answer that objection, and secondly, to take away that reproach.[h] So that that objection was answered.[i]

Now [we send forth the Agreement], hoping there will appear [so] much of God in it,[j] that by this we do very much hold forth a liberty to all the people of God—though yet it may so fall out that it may go hardly with the people of God. And I judge [indeed] it will do so, and that this Agreement will fall short [of its end]. I think that God doth purposely design it shall fall short of that end we look for, because he would have us know our peace, [that] our agreement shall be from God, and not from men. And yet I think the hand of God doth call for us to hold forth [something] to this nation, and to all the world, to vindicate the profession that we have all along made to God, [and] that we should let them know that [what] we seek [is] not for ourselves,[1] but for [all] men.

[1] His actual phrase was possibly: 'that we seek not ourselves' (cf. pp. 177, 334).

PART III. PURITAN VIEWS OF LIBERTY [a]

I. SOME PRINCIPLES OF THE PURITAN PARTIES

From John Saltmarsh, *Smoke in the Temple* (1646) [b]

[PRINCIPLES OF THE PARTIES] [c]

Presbytery so called: what it is, and what they hold

The Presbytery is set up by an alleged pattern of the eldership and presbytery of the Apostles and Elders in the first churches of the Gospel, strengthened by such scriptures as are in the margin,[1] and by allusion to the Jewish government and to appeals in nature. Their churches are parochial, or parishes, as they are divided at first by the Romish prelates and the statute-laws of the state. Which parishes and congregations are made up of such believers as were made Christians first by baptism in infancy, and not by the Word; and all the parishes or congregations are under them as they are a classical, provincial, and national Presbytery. And over those parishes they do exercise all church power and government [2] which may be called the Power of the Keys. * * *

Independency so called: what it is, and what they hold

The people of God are only a church [3] when called by the Word and Spirit into consent or covenant and [when] Saints by profession, and all church-power is laid here and given out from hence into pastorship and elders, &c.; and a just distribution of interest betwixt elders and people.[4] All spiritual government is here and not in any power foreign or extrinsical to the congregation, or authoritative. Their children are made Christians first by infant baptism and after by the Word; and they are baptized by a federal or covenant-holiness, or birth-privileges as under the

[1] Matt. 18. 15; Acts 15. 19, 28, 31; Acts 16. 4; 1 Tim. 4. 14; Tit. 1. 5; 1 Tim. 1. 2; Tit. 1. 6; Acts 13. 1; 1 Cor. 12. 17.
[2] Acts 6. 6; 2 Tim. 2. 2; 1 Tim. 4. 14; Eph. 4. 11–12; Heb. 13. 17; Acts 20. 28–9; Rev. 2. 14, 20.
[3] 1 Pet. 2. 5; 1 Cor. 1. 2, 9; Col. 1. 2; 2 Cor. 6. 16–17; Acts 2. 41–2; Rev. 3. 1, 17; Acts 9. 26.
[4] Matt. 18. 15–20; Matt. 16. 18–19; 1 Cor. 12. 28; Eph. 4. 11; Acts 6. 3, 5; Acts 15. 22; 1 Tim. 3. 15.

Law.[1] They may enjoy all ordinances in this estate, and some may prophesy.[2] * * *

Anabaptism so called : what it is, and what they hold

The Church of Christ are a company of baptized believers,[3] and whatsoever disciple can teach the Word or make out Christ, may baptize or administer other ordinances.[4] That the church or body, though but of two or three, yet may enjoy the Word and ordinances by way of an administrator, or one deputed to administer, though no pastor.[5] That none are to be baptized but believers.[6] That those commonly called church-officers as pastors, &c., are such as the church or body may be without.[7] That none are to be called brethren but baptized believers. All administration of ordinances were given to the Apostles as disciples; not so under the notion of church-power as is pretended.[8] That none ought to communicate in the ordinances of Christ till first baptized.[9] * * *

Seeking or Seekers so called : what their way is, and what they hold

That there is no church nor ordinances yet. That if they did not end with the primitive or Apostles' times, yet they are to begin as in the primitive times with gifts and miracles,[10] and that there is as much reason for the like gifts to make out the truth of any of the Gospel now to an Antichristian estate, as formerly to a Jewish or heathenish. That such a believer as can dispense ordinances must be qualified as the believers in Mark 16, and as the former disciples were.[11] That there is a time and fulness for the Spirit[12] and for the later pure spiritual dispensations, as there was formerly for the first dispensations. And [they query] whether this shall be while the Angels are but pouring out their vials or not, or when Babylon is fallen; and whether there is not

[1] 1 Cor. 7. 14; Acts 2. 39; Rom. 11. 16.
[2] Acts 2. 42; 1 Tim. 3. 15; 1 Cor. 14. 22, 6, 11, 4.
[3] Heb. 12. 22; Acts 10. 48; Acts 2. 41; Acts 16. 32–3.
[4] Matt. 10. 1 compared with Matt. 28. 18; John 4. 1; John 8. 31; Isa. 1. 16; Acts 9. 10; Acts 1. 15.
[5] 1 Cor. 12. 5.
[6] Acts 2. 38; Acts 10. 48; Matt. 28. 18; Mark 16. 16; Acts 8. 37.
[7] Acts 1. 15; Acts 2. 42.
[8] Matt. 10. 1 compared with Matt. 28. 18; Isa. 8. 16; Acts 9. 10.
[9] Acts 2. 41–2, and Acts 16. 31.
[10] Matt. 10. 1; Mark 16. 16; 1 Cor. 12.
[11] Acts 8. 6, and Acts 9. 17.
[12] Rev. 15. 8, and Rev. 18. 1.

as much need for new tongues [1] to reveal the pure original to us, it being conveyed with corruptions and additionals in translations, by which truth may be more purely discovered and the waters of life that now run muddily may flow more clear and crystal-like from the throne of God.[2] * * *

A WAY OF PEACE OR A DESIGN OF RECONCILIATION [a] * * *

Liberty for printing and speaking

Let there be liberty of the press for printing, to those that are not allowed pulpits for preaching. Let that light come in at the window which cannot come in at the door, that all may speak and write one way, that cannot another. Let the waters of the sanctuary have issue and spring up valleys as well as mountains. * * *

Let all that preach or print affix their names that we may know from whom. The contrary is a kind of unwarrantable modesty at the best. If it be truth they write, why do they not own it? If untruth, why do they write? Some such must either suppress themselves for shame or fear, and they that dare not own what they do, they suspect the magistrate or themselves. * * *

Let all that teach or print be accountable, yet in a several way. If it be matter of immediate disturbance and trouble to the state, let them account for it to the magistrate *under whom we are to live a peaceable and quiet life* (1 Tim. 2. 2); if matter of doctrine, *&c.*, let them be accountable to the believers and brethren who are offended, by conference, where there may be mutual conviction and satisfaction (Gal. 2. 11).

Free debates and open conferences

Let there be free debates and open conferences and communication, for all and of all sorts that will, concerning difference in spirituals; [b] still allowing the state to secure all tumults or disturbances. [c] Where doors are not shut, there will be no breaking them open. So where debates are free there is a way of vent and evacuation, the stopping of which hath caused more troubles in states than anything; for where there is much new wine in old bottles the working will be such as the parable speaks on. * * *

No assuming infallibility over each other

Let us not, being under no further degree of the revelation of truth and coming out of Babylon, assume any power of infallibility

[1] Acts 2. 4; Mark 16. 17; Acts 19. 6; 1 Cor. 14. 22, 39.   [2] Rev. 22. 1.

to each other, so as to soar up all to our light or degree of knowing or practising; for there lies as much on one side for compulsion as on another, respectively to one another, for another's evidence is as dark to me as mine to him, and mine to him as his to me, till the Lord enlighten us both for discerning alike. So ª when there is no power in us to make that appear to another which appears to us, there can be no reasonable equity for any enforcing or compelling in spirituals. The first great rent betwixt the Eastern and Western kingdoms began when the Bishop of Rome would needs excommunicate the East for not believing as they believed.

No civil power drawn into advantages

Let not those believers who have the advantage of the magistrate strive to make any unwarrantable use of it one against another, because scripture principles are not so clear for it; and because they know not the revolution of Providence, and we are to do as we would be done to. * * *

No despising for too much learning, or too little

Let not one despise another for gifts, parts, learning. Let the Spirit be heard speak in the meanest; let not the scribe or disputer of the law despise the fishermen, nor they despise them because scribes and disputers. The Spirit is in Paul as well as Peter, in both as well as one.

We may be in one Christ, though divers

Consider that we may be one in one Christ though we think diversely, and we may be friends though not brethren, and let us attain to union though not to unity.

The spiritual persecution to be forborne

Consider there is a twofold persecution; there is a spiritual or that of believers, and a mixed persecution or civilly ecclesiastical. The spiritual persecution is that of the spirit merely, and this kind of persecution little thought on and studied. This is when we cannot bear one another's several opinions or soul-belief[s] in the same spiritual society or fellowship, but [they] must either be of us or out of us; and surely this kind of persecution is as unreasonable as any other. For what is this but soul-compulsion, when another must only believe as we believe and not wait till the Lord reveal even this. This kind of spiritual compulsion will in time break and dissolve the visible communion of Saints and body of

Christ exceedingly, if taken up or continued, and it will be amongst Christians as amongst the Antichristians, where they divide and subdivide and some cast themselves into a monkery from all the rest. Jerusalem and Antioch were not of this way to cast out one another upon such grounds, but to meet, reason and counsel, and hear. And surely the churches can ill complain of a mixed persecution from without if they persecute one another from within. The magistrate may as justly whip them both as they whip one another; such grudgings, complainings, dissolvings, spiritual enforcings, gives hint to the civil power to compel while it beholds them, but a little more spiritually, compelling one another. Let all church-rights, privileges, bound-days, be reformed, all heresy and schism by the rule rebuked, but in all spiritual meekness and wisdom, and [let us] not call heretic and schismatic too suddenly neither. See we do not so.

Spiritual Principles drawn Forth [a]

Gospel Truth is One and the Same

That which is only in some parts of it warrantable by the Word is not purely nor in a scripture way warrantable. For there is not any will-worship but it hath something from the pattern of the true. * * * But truth must be all one and the same and homogeneal; not in parts so, but all so. There is but one Lord, one faith, &c.

Prudence and Consequences are the great Engines of Will-Worship

Things of prudence merely are not to be admitted into the spiritual way and gospel design. Prelacy had its prudence for every new additional in worship and government. And once let prudence open a door and then will more of man crowd in than the law of God can keep out. Nor is that to be admitted which is so received a maxim, 'though not directly, yet not repugnant to the Word.' Christ's rule is not such; he opposes any tradition [added] to the commandments of God. Not direct from scripture is indirect and repugnant, though not to the very letter of such words, yet to the form and analogy of truth, to the general scripture law, viz., the will of God that nothing shall be added nor diminished. * * * Nothing but God's power and will can make a thing truth. His power creates it, and his will creates it such a truth. Nothing is agreeable to the will of Christ but the very will of Christ. The will of Christ is the only legislative power in the Gospel. * * * And everything is repugnant to his will but what he wills. * * * And whatsoever is devised by prudence, though upon scripture materials, yet being not the work of this will nor having the stamp or image upon it, is none of Christ's, but as repugnant as any other tradition or invention of men. * * *

The People are Brethren and Saints in Christ's Church, but in Antichrist's, Parishioners and Servants

What kind of government is marked out in scriptures for sitting on the waters or people? Christ governs by the people ministerially, not over the people authoritatively only; and the people being once in his church way, lose their old capacity for a new, and are raised up from people to brethren, to churches. * * * The interest of the people in Christ's kingdom is not only an interest of compliancy and obedience and submission, but of consultation, of debating, counselling, prophesying, voting, &c. And let us *stand fast in that liberty wherewith Christ hath made us free.* * * *

None to be forced under Christ's Kingdom as in the Kingdoms of the World

In a spiritual government the ignorance of people which some would have for expedition that they may practically know it, is no scripture way of knowing. In practical godliness things must be known before practically known, and practice is to begin from faith, and faith from knowledge; else the obedience can be but blind, mixed, and popish. Indeed in things civil or moral, practice may bring in knowledge: habits may be acquired and gotten by acts; a man may grow temperate by practising temperance, and civilly obedient by practising civil obedience. But it is not so in spirituals: there habits go before acts, spiritual infusions before practices.

Indeed the laws of states and kingdoms and civil policy teach men best by ruling them practically, but it is not so in the church. Men are not to be forced into Christ's kingdom as into the kingdoms of the world. *The kings of the nations exercise their dominion; it shall not be so among you.*

The Power of a Formal Reformation in a Government makes it not Christ's Government

A government, though not purely Christ's, may be made up of such scripture and prudential materials as may much reform the outward man, even as a mere prudential civil government may do if severely executed. * * * In many civil states, merely from their wholesome policy and administration, excellent and precious flowers spring up, many moral virtues, as prudence, temperance, obedience, meekness, love, justice, fortitude. Yet all this makes not a government to be Christ's, but only that which is merely the discipline of Christ, and policy of Christ. * * *

The National and Congregational Church-covenant, both lawful, or both unlawful * * *

But covenants in their right nature were a dispensation more of the Old Testament strain. A national church had a covenant to gather them up into their national way of worship, and were under the laws of an external pedagogy, and now the spiritual dispensation being come, even the Gospel of Jesus Christ, there is a fulness of spirit let out upon the Saints and people of God which gather[s] them up more closely, spiritually, and cordially than the power of any former dispensation could. The very covenant of God himself, of which the former were typical and prophetical, comes in nakedly upon the spirits of his [people] and draws them in, and is a law upon their inward parts, sweetly compelling in the consciences with power and yet not with force, with compulsion and yet with consent. And surely where this covenant of God hath its kindly and spiritual operation there would need no such external supplement as before; but because of the hardness of our hearts it is thus. From the beginning it was not so; the Spirit tied up thousands together then.

Let states then have any prudential security, any design of sound wisdom to consonate people together, but let the church only be gathered up by a law of a more glorious and transcendent nature, by the pure covenant of God himself with the souls of his. * * *

All Covenanters are bound to contribute to religion as well as state * * *

The liberty of the subject is that of soul as well as body, and that of soul more *dear, precious, glorious : the liberty wherein Christ hath made us free. Be not ye then the servants of men in the things of God.* * * *

From J[ohn] G[oodwin], *Independency God's Verity* (1647) [a]

THE NECESSITY OF TOLERATION

Presbytery is the rival of Episcopacy. But Independency is of another strain, and admitteth not of human prudence in church government. For the Church is [b] a spiritual building, framed of such lively stones as are not of the world, nor [is it] of the wisdom of the world, but founded only upon the wisdom of God, revealed in the word by his Spirit, [which] is sufficient to constitute and maintain a church without any assistance from the kingdoms of the world—whose power they leave entire to itself. For the bishops and presbyters, by their church policy, stand competitors with the magistrate; to whom we leave all save only the kingdom of Christ, which (himself hath said) is not of this world, and so can be no trouble to it, unless it be first troubled by it.

But as the case stands now at present, Independency is the only lint that can stanch our wounds, the only dam that can stay the inundation of blood, which is else likely to overwhelm us. For the very name of Presbytery is hateful to the people, and it were too strange a relapse to give them again their Bishops and their liturgy, and if either of the other be permitted, there can be nothing expected but murmurings and clashings, if not open mutinyings. But if a toleration were allowed, it would take away all occasions of tumults and garboils. For when every man is permitted to use his conscience according as he is persuaded in himself, they will esteem their burdens not half so heavy as before and be encouraged to yield obedience to those injunctions imposed on them by their rulers, which otherwise is not to be expected from them; so that it is not only convenient, but also very necessary, that there be a toleration.

Again, any man the least enlightened will dispense with any compulsive ordinance more tamely than when he is constrained in point of religion. And we know well that the original of our late war was the Bishops' assuming to themselves that power which Christ never gave them, to wit, of compelling men to yield obedience to whatever they imposed. And men now are grown more various in their opinions than ever before, and will be as easily persuaded to forsake their meat as to relinquish their tenets. And moreover, it is come to that pass—but by what means I will not question—that every man esteemeth it as properly his own, as any immunity contained in Magna Charta, to use his conscience without control; and when they shall be debarred of what they have so long enjoyed, and so much covet to keep, what they may attempt let the wise judge. Therefore there is not only a reason, but also a necessity, of toleration.

II. THE LAW OF NATURE

From William Ames, *Conscience* (1639) [a]

The word *jus*, signifying right, is derived from the Latin word *jussus*, because it implies a power of some authority, commanding this or that to be done.

It is therefore taken: First, for the Law commanding. Secondly, for the object and effect of justice, or for the action itself, prescribed and required by law; and in this sense we are said to give every man his right. * * * Fourthly, for the power which any man hath to do this or that according to law, in which sense we usually say, *Such a man stands upon his right.* And not unlike to this accep[ta]tion is the applying of the same word to denote some particular privilege granted to any man, either by law or just authority. * * *

This word *right* in its largest acceptation is divided into: *divine*, of which God is the author; *human*, of which man is the contriver.

Divine right is divided into right natural, and right positive.

Right natural is that which is apprehended to be fit to be done or avoided, out of the natural instinct of natural light; or that which is at least deduced from that natural light by evident consequence. So that this right partly consists of practic[al] principles known by nature, and partly of conclusions deduced from those principles.

The divine positive right is a right added to the natural by some special revelation of God.

The right natural, or natural law, is the same which usually is called the eternal law. But it is called eternal in relation to God, as it is from eternity in him. It is called natural as it is engrafted and imprinted in the nature of man by the God of nature.

That positive right was in the mind of God from eternity, as well as the natural. But in respect it is not so easily apprehended by human reason, therefore it is not usually termed the law eternal.

The natural and positive divine right differ in this: that the positive is mutable and various according to God's good pleasure (for that which was heretofore in the Judaical church is different from that which is in the Christian church); but the right natural is always the same and like itself, and for this reason also it is called the law eternal. * * *

Quest[ion] 3: Whether it be rightly said by lawyers, that the right natural, or the law of nature is that which nature hath taught all living creatures?

In brute creatures the true nature of right or law hath no more place than it hath in plants or things inanimate. For neither is there a reason distinguishing between good and evil, neither a will or choice of one thing before another; nor, lastly, any justice at all in brutes more than in things without all life. Nevertheless, in all things there is an inclination, a power and operation, which is guided by certain reason forasmuch as concerns their nature and end. And in this respect all things created are said to have a law prescribed unto them, so that in respect to themselves it is only by similitude and some proportion termed a law or right (Psalm 148. 6; Job 38. 10–12; Jer. 33. 20, 25). * * *

Ques[tion] 4: Whether the Law of Nations be the same with the Law of Nature?

The law of nations, as it is taken for the law which all nations use, comprehends under it not only the law of nature but also the positive law. So servitude is by lawyers said to be by the law of nations, and yet [it] is evident that servitude was brought in by custom and the positive law. And the same is the reason in division of possessions, and the like.

If the law of nations ᵃ be taken for that law which is introduced by the common consent and custom of all nations, it then participates a certain middle nature between the law natural and that positive law which is peculiar to this or that nation. It hath thus much common with the natural law, that it is everywhere received without any certain authority or promulgation, and wheresoever anything is done contrary it is censured of all men to be ill done. And it hath thus much common with the positive law, that it may be changed or abrogated by the common consent of them whom it may concern. A division of things is by the law of nations. Nevertheless, by the common consent it may, upon just grounds, be somewhere enacted that almost all possessions should be in common. * * *

Ques[tion] 5: Whether the precepts of the Law of Nature be rightly stated: To live honestly; not to hurt another; to give every man his due?

This enumeration is somewhat confused and imperfect. For first, here is nothing mentioned of the worshipping of God, which nevertheless is a principle of the law of nature. * * *

Ques[tion] 6: Whether that precept be of the Law of Nature: What you would have done to yourself, do that to another . . . ?

This precept is natural, and indeed divine (Matt. 7. 12; Luke 6.

31). Yet in this it is to be observed: First, that this law doth not
include the whole compass of the natural law in general, but that
part only in which our duty between man and man is comprehended; secondly, that *our will whatsoever it be*, may not be the
square and rule of the performance of our duty to others . . .,
but *our natural will being well disposed*, and not tainted with any
passion or perturbation, by which we truly and *considerately* wish
good unto ourselves. * * *

Quest[ion] 7 : What proportion the Civil Law holds with the
Law of Nature?

The civil law is that which every city or society of men enacts
current for itself.   And such a kind of law is not only peculiar to
the Romans, but also to the Athenians, English, or any else who
have no respect to the Roman law.

This civil law inasmuch as it is right is derived from the law of
nature; for that is not law which is not just and right, and that in
morality is called right which accords with right practical reason,
and right practical is the law of nature.

This civil law therefore is derived from the law of nature, either
as a special conclusion inferred from a general proposition or as a
special determination and application of a general axiom.

That law which is derived from the natural law only by way of
conclusion, if the consequence be good, hath its whole strength
from the law of nature, as the conclusion hath its force from the
premised propositions; but that which is derived from the law of
nature by way of determination and application, is in part a new
constitution, even as every species hath its own proper form and
essence besides that which is actually comprehended in the genus.

Seeing then that, as well in conclusions as determinations, the
reason of man can only imperfectly judge—nay, and is often
therein cozened—hence it must needs follow that all human constitutions are of necessity liable to imperfection, error, and injustice.   This the authors of the Roman law confess of their own
laws: 'It is impossible that a reason should be given of all things
that are enacted—not to all men, nor of all the laws—and it is
proved in innumerable cases that there are many things received
in the civil law for the public good, which are somewhat contrary
to a disputative reason' (*Ad leg. Aquil.* f. 51).

The imperfection of the best civil law consisteth in this. First,
in regard it contains not in its compass the whole law of nature,
but so much of it only as such or such men have approved and
thought appliable to their own manners; secondly, in respect it
hath no eye at all upon the inward affections, but only upon the

outward actions; for it doth not suppress absolutely all vices, but those only which may seem likely to disturb the peace and quiet of the commonwealth, neither doth it enjoin all acts of all virtues, but those only which are opposite to the inconvenient vices; thirdly, in that it doth not principally make good men, but only good subjects or citizens; fourthly, in that upon occasion it may admit in many things of addition, detraction, or correction.

Quest[ion] 8: What proportion the Moral Law bears to the Law of Nature?

All the precepts of the Moral Law are out of the law of nature, except the determination of the sabbath day in the Fourth Commandment, which is from the positive law.

For first, we meet with nothing in them which concerneth not all nations at all times, so that these precepts do not respect any particular sort of men, but even nature itself. Secondly, nothing is contained in them which is not very necessary to human nature for the attaining of its end. Thirdly, there is nothing in them which is not so grounded upon right reason but it may be solidly defended and maintained by human discourse; nothing but what may be well enjoined from clear reason. Fourthly, all things contained in them are for the substance approved, even of the more understanding sort of the heathen. Fifthly, they all much conduce to the benefit of mankind in this present life; insomuch that if all these precepts were duly answered, there would be no need of any other human laws or constitutions. * * *

Object[ion]: But it may be objected that if the Moral [Law] were the same with the law of nature, it had no need to be promulgated either by voice or writing, for it would have been writ in the hearts of all men by nature.

A[nswer]: That to nature upright, *i.e.,* as it was in the state of innocency, there was no need of such a promulgation. But ever since the corruption of our nature, such is the blindness of our understanding and perverseness of our will and disorder of our affections, that there are only some relics of that law remaining in our hearts, like to some dim aged picture, and therefore by the voice and power of God it ought to be renewed as with a fresh pencil. Therefore is there nowhere found any true right practical reason, pure and complete in all parts, but in the written law of God (Psalm 119. 66).

Quest[ion] 9: What proportion the Judicial Law bears to the Natural?

That is properly termed the Judicial which is about judgments or any politic matters thereto belonging, as that was called the

Ceremonial Law which was about ceremonies, and that the Moral Law which was about manners and civil duties. That Judicial Law which was given by Moses to the Israelites as proper only to them, was a most exact determination and accommodation of the law of nature unto them, according to the particular condition of that people. To the Israelites therefore in respect of the use, it was of like nature with other good civil laws among other nations; but in respect of authority, which from God, the immediate giver, it received, it was of much more perfection than any. This law belongeth not to Christians under the title of a law especially obliging them, but only by way of doctrine, inasmuch as in its general nature, or in its due proportion to it, it doth always exhibit unto us the best determination of the law of nature. * * *

Those laws were properly termed Judicial, which being not ceremonial, had some singular respect to the people of the Jews, so that the whole reason and ground of them was constituted in some particular condition of that nation. But it is no certain rule (which is given by some) that wheresoever the reason of the law is moral, there the law itself is moral (as is seen in Lev. 11. 44), for any special determination of a law may be confirmed by a general reason. . . . But where the special intrinsical and proper reason of the law is moral, there it always follows that the law itself must needs be moral. Those laws, therefore, which are usually reckoned among the judicial, and yet in their nature bear no singular respect to the condition of the Jews more than of any other people, those are all of the moral and natural laws which are common to all nations.

III. RELIGIOUS PRINCIPLES OF RESISTANCE
CHRISTIAN OBEDIENCE AND ITS LIMITS

From Calvin's *Institution of Christian Religion* (Thomas Norton's translation) [a]

For when they hear that liberty is promised by the Gospel, which acknowledgeth among men no king and no magistrate but hath regard to Christ alone, they think that they can take no fruit of their liberty so long as they see any power to have pre-eminence over them. Therefore they think that nothing shall be safe, unless the whole world be reformed into a new fashion, where may neither be judgments nor laws nor magistrates, nor any such thing which they think to withstand their liberty. But whosoever can put difference between the body and the soul, between this present and transitory life and that life to come and eternal, he shall not hardly understand that the spiritual kingdom of Christ and the civil government are things far asunder. Since therefore that is a Jewish vanity, to seek and enclose the kingdom of Christ under the elements of the world, let us rather (thinking, as the scripture plainly teacheth, that it is a spiritual fruit which is gathered of the benefit of Christ) remember to keep within the bonds thereof this whole liberty which is promised and offered us in him (Gal. 5. 1; 1 Cor. 7. 21). For what is the cause why the same Apostle which biddeth us to stand, and not to be made subject to the yoke of bondage, in another place forbiddeth bond-servants to be careful of their state, but because spiritual liberty may very well agree with civil bondage? * * *

But as we have even now given warning that this kind of government is several from that spiritual and inward kingdom of Christ, so it is also to be known that they nothing disagree together. For the civil government doth now begin in us upon earth certain beginnings of the heavenly kingdom, and in this mortal and vanishing life doth, as it were, enter upon an immortal and incorruptible blessedness. But the intent of his spiritual government is, so long as we shall live among men, to cherish and maintain the outward worshipping of God, to defend the sound doctrine of godliness and the state of the Church, to frame our life to the fellowship of men, to fashion our manners to civil righteousness, to procure us into friendship one with another, to nourish common peace and quietness. All which I grant to be superfluous if the kingdom of God, such as it is now among us, do destroy this present life. But if the will of God be so that we, while we long toward the heavenly country, should be wayfaring from home upon the earth, and sith the use of such wayfaring needeth such helps, they which take them from man do take from him his very nature of man. For whereas they allege that there is so great perfection in the Church of God that her own moderate government sufficeth it for a law, they themselves do foolishly imagine that perfection which can never be found in the common fellowship of men. * * *

[The civil state] tendeth not only hereunto, . . . that men may breathe, eat, drink, and be cherished . . ., but also that idolatry, sacrilege against the name of God, blasphemies against his truth, and other offences of religion, may not rise up and be scattered among the people, that common quiet be not troubled, that every man may keep his own safe and unappaired, that men may use their affairs together without hurt, that honesty and modesty be kept among them; finally that among Christians may be a common show of religion, and among men may be manlike civility. Neither let any man be moved, for that I do now refer the care of stablishing of religion to the policy of men, which I seemed before to have set without the judgment of men. For I do no more here than I did before give men leave after their own will to make laws concerning religion and the worshipping of God, when I allow the ordinance of policy which endeavoureth hereunto, that the true religion which is contained in the Law of God, be not openly and with public sacrileges freely broken and defiled. * * *

The Lord hath not only testified that the office of magistrates is allowed and acceptable to him, but also setting out the dignity thereof with most honourable titles, he hath marvellously commended it unto us. * * * Wherefore none ought now to doubt that the civil power is a vocation not only holy and lawful before God, but also the most holy, and the most honest, of all other in the whole life of men. * * *

And . . . it were very vain that it should be disputed of private men which should be the best state of policy in the place where they live; for whom it is not lawful to consult of the framing of any commonweal. And also the same could not be simply determined without rashness, forasmuch as a great part of the order of this question consisteth in circumstances. * * * Truly, if those three forms of governments which the philosophers set out, be considered in themselves, I will not deny that either the government of the chiefest men or a state tempered of it and common government far excelleth all other. Not of itself, but because it most seldom chanceth that kings so temper themselves that their will never swerveth from that which is just and right; again, that they be furnished with so great sharpness of judgment and wisdom that every one of them seeth so much as is sufficient. Therefore the fault or default of men maketh that it is safer and more tolerable that many should have the government, that they may mutually one help another, one teach and admonish another, and if any advance himself higher than is meet, there may be overseers and masters to restrain his wilfulness. This both hath alway been approved by experience, and the Lord also hath confirmed it with his authority, when he ordained among the Israelites a government of the best men, very near unto common government, at such time as he minded to have them in best estate, till he brought forth an image of Christ in David. And as I willingly grant that no kind of government is more blessed than this, where liberty is framed to such moderation as it ought to be, and is orderly stablished to continuance, so I count them also most blessed, that may enjoy this estate. And if they stoutly and constantly travail in preserving and retaining it, I grant that they do nothing against their duty. Yea, and the magistrates ought with most great diligence to bend themselves hereunto, that they suffer not the liberty of the people of which they are appointed governors, to be in any part minished, much less to be dissolved. If they be negligent and little careful therein, they are false faith-breakers in their office, and betrayers of their country. But if they would bring this kind to themselves, to whom the Lord hath appointed another form of government, so that thereby they be moved to desire a change, the very thinking thereof shall not only be foolish and superfluous, but also hurtful. * * *

Now the office of magistrates is in this place to be declared by the way, of what sort it is described by the word of God, and in what things it consisteth. If the scripture did not teach that it extendeth to both the Tables of the Law, we might learn it out of the profane writers. For none hath entreated of the duty of magistrates, of making of laws and of public weal, that hath not begun at religion and the worshipping of God. And so have they all confessed that no policy can be happily framed unless the first care be of godliness, and that those laws be preposterous which, neglecting the right of God, 'do provide only for men. * * * And we have already showed that this duty is specially enjoined them of God; as it is meet that they should employ their travail to defend and maintain his honour, whose vicegerents they be, and by whose benefit they govern. For this cause also chiefly are the holy kings praised in scripture, for that they restored the worship of God, being corrupted or overthrown, or took care of religion, that it might flourish pure and safe under them. * * *

Next to the magistrate in civil states are laws the most strong sinews of commonwealths. * * * There be some that deny that a commonweal is well ordered, which, neglecting the civil laws of Moses, is governed by the common laws of nations. How dangerous and troublesome this sentence is, let other men consider; it shall be enough for me to have showed that it is false and foolish. That common division is to be kept, which divideth the whole Law of God published, into Moral, Ceremonial, and Judicial Laws; and all the parts are to be severally considered, that we may know what of them pertaineth to us, and what not. Neither in the meantime let any man be cumbered with this doubt, that judicials and ceremonials also pertain to the moral laws. For although the old writers which have taught this division were not ignorant that these two latter parts had their use about manners, yet because they might be changed and abrogate, the morals remaining safe, they did not call them morals. They called that first part peculiarly by that name, without which cannot stand the true holiness of manners and the unchangeable rule of living rightly.

Therefore the Moral Law . . ., sith it is contained in two chief points, of which the one commandeth simply to worship God with pure faith and godliness, and the other to embrace men with unfeigned love, is the true and eternal rule of righteousness prescribed to the men of all ages and times that will . . . frame their life to the will of God. For this is his eternal and unchangeable will, that he himself should be worshipped of us all, and that we should mutually love one another. The Ceremonial Law was the schooling of the Jews, wherewith it pleased the Lord to exercise the certain childhood of that people, till that time of fulness came, wherein he would to the full manifestly show his wisdom to the earth, and deliver the truth of those things which then were shadowed with figures. The Judicial Law, given to them for an order of civil state, gave certain rules of equity and righteousness, by which they might behave themselves harmlessly and quietly together. And as that exercise of ceremonies properly pertained indeed to the doctrine of godliness (namely which kept the church of the Jews in the worship and religion of God), yet it might be distinguished from godliness itself, so this form of judicial orders (although it tended to no other end but how the self-same charity might be best kept which is commanded by the eternal Law of God), yet had a certain thing differing from the very commandment of loving. As therefore the ceremonies might be abrogate, godliness remaining safe and undestroyed, so these judicial ordinances also being taken away, the perpetual duties and commandments of charity may continue. If this be true, verily there is liberty left to every nation to make such laws as they shall foresee to be profitable for them; which yet must be framed after the perpetual rule of charity, that they may indeed vary in form, but have the same reason. * * *

This which I have said shall be plain, if in all laws we behold these two things as we ought, the making and the equity of the law, upon the reason whereof the making itself is founded and stayeth. Equity, because it is natural, can be but one, of all laws. And therefore one law, according to the kind of matter, ought to

be the propounded end to all laws. * * * Now sith it is certain
that the Law of God which we call moral is nothing else but a
testimony of the natural law, and of that conscience which is
engraven of God in the minds of men, the whole rule of this equity
whereof we now speak is set forth therein. Therefore it alone
also must be both the mark and rule and end of all laws. Whatsoever laws shall be framed after that rule, directed to that mark,
and limited in that end, there is no cause why we should disallow
them, however they otherwise differ from the Jewish law or one
from another. * * *

The first duty of subjects toward their magistrates is to think
most honourably of their office, namely, which they acknowledge
to be a jurisdiction committed of God, and therefore to esteem
them and reverence them as the ministers and deputies of God.
* * * Of this then also followeth another thing: that with minds
bent to the honouring of them, they declare their obedience in
proof to them; whether it be to obey their proclamations, or to pay
tribute, or to take in hand public offices and charges that serve for
common defence, or to do any other of their commandments. Let
every soul (saith Paul) be subject to the higher powers (Rom. 13. 1).
For he that resisteth the power, resisteth the ordinance of God. * * *

But if we look to the word of God, it will lead us further, that
we be subject not only to the government of those princes which
execute their office toward us well, and with such faithfulness as
they ought, but also of all them which (by what means soever it
be) have the dominion in possession, although they perform
nothing less than that which pertaineth to the duty of princes.
For though the Lord testifieth that the magistrate's is a special
great gift of his liberality for preserving of the safety of men, and
appointeth to magistrates themselves their bounds, yet he doth
therewithal declare that, of what sort soever they be, they have
not their authority but from him; that those indeed which rule
for benefit of the commonweal are true exemplars and patterns
of his bountifulness; that they that rule unjustly and wilfully are
raised up by him to punish the wickedness of the people; that
all equally have that majesty wherewith he hath furnished a lawful
power. * * *

But (thou wilt say) rulers owe mutual duties to their subjects.
That I have already confessed. But if thou thereupon conclude
that obediences ought to be rendered to none but just governors,
thou art a foolish reasoner. For husbands are also bound to their
wives, and parents to their children, with mutual duties. Let
parents and husbands depart from their duty . . .; shall yet

therefore either children be less obedient to their parents, or wives to their husbands? But they are subjects both to evil parents and husbands and such as do not their duty. * * * Wherefore, if we be unmercifully tormented of a cruel prince, if we be ravenously spoiled of a covetous or riotous prince, if we be neglected of a slothful prince, finally if we be vexed for godliness' sake of a wicked and ungodly prince, let us first call to mind the remembrance of our sins, which undoubtedly are chastised with such scourges of the Lord. Thereby our humility shall bridle our impatience. Let us then also call to mind this thought: that it pertaineth not to us to remedy such evils; but this only is left for us, that we crave the help of the Lord, in whose hands are the hearts of kings and the bowings of kingdoms. * * *

And here both his marvellous goodness and power and providence showeth itself; for sometime of his servants he raiseth up open avengers and furnisheth them with his commandment to take vengeance of their unjust government, and to deliver his people, many ways oppressed, out of miserable distress; sometime he directeth to the same end the rage of men that intend and go about another thing. * * * For the first sort of men, when they were by the lawful calling of God sent to do such acts in taking armour against kings, they did not violate that majesty which is planted in kings by the ordinance of God; but, being armed from heaven, they subdued the lesser power with the greater, like as it is lawful for kings to punish their lords under them. But these latter sort, although they were directed by the hand of God whither it pleased him, and they unwittingly did work, yet proposed in their mind nothing but mischief. * * *

Though the correcting of unbridled government be the revengement of the Lord, let us not by and by think that it is committed to us to whom there is given no other commandment but to obey and suffer. I speak alway of private men. For if there be at this time any magistrates for the behalf of the people (such as in old time were the *Ephori* that were set against the kings of Lacedemonia, or the Tribunes of the people against the Roman consuls, or the *Demarchi* against the senate of Athens, and the same power also which peradventure, as things are now, the three estates have in every realm when they hold their principal assemblies), I do so not forbid them, according to their office, to withstand the outraging licentiousness of kings, that I affirm that if they wink at kings' wilfully ranging over and treading down the poor commonalty, their dissembling is not without wicked breach of faith because they deceitfully betray the liberty of the people where they know themselves to be appointed protectors by the ordinance of God.

But in that obedience which we have determined to be due to the authorities of governors, that is always to be excepted, yea chiefly to be observed, that it do not lead us away from obeying of him to whose will the desires of all kings ought to be subject, to whose decrees all their commandments ought to yield, to whose majesty their maces ought to be submitted.   And truly how unorderly were it, for the satisfying of men, to run into his displeasure for whom men themselves are obeyed?   The Lord therefore is the King of Kings, who, when he hath opened his holy mouth, is to be heard alone for all together and above all.   Next to him we be subject to those men that are set over us; but no otherwise than in him.   If they command anything against him, let it have no place and let no account be made of it.   Neither let us herein anything stay upon all that dignity wherewith the magistrates excel, to which there is no wrong done when it is brought into order of subjection in comparison of that singular and truly sovereign power of God.   After this reason Daniel denieth (Dan. 6. 22) that he had anything offended against the king, when he obeyed not his wicked proclamation; because the king had passed his bounds, and had not only been a wrong-doer to men, but in lifting up his horns against God he had taken away power from himself.   On the other side the Israelites are condemned because they were too much obedient to the wicked commandment of the king (Hos. 5. 13).   For when Jeroboam had made golden calves, they, forsaking the Temple of God, did for his pleasure turn to new superstitions (1 Kings 12. 30). * * *   I know how great and how present peril hangeth over this constancy, because kings do most displeasantly suffer themselves to be despised, whose displeasure (saith Solomon) is the messenger of death.   But sith this decree is proclaimed by the heavenly herald Peter, that we ought to obey God rather than men (Acts 5. 29), let us comfort ourselves with this thought, that we then perform that obedience which the Lord requireth, when we suffer anything rather, whatsoever it be, than swerve from godliness.   And that our courage should not faint, Paul putteth also another spur to us: that we were therefore redeemed of Christ with so great a price as our redemption cost him (1 Cor. 7. 13), that we should not yield ourselves in thraldom to obey the perverse desires of men, but much less should be bound to ungodliness.

PRESBYTERIAN PRINCIPLES OF RESISTANCE

From [Samuel Rutherford], *Lex, Rex* (1644) [a]

Who [b] doubteth (Christian reader) but innocency must be under the courtesy and mercy of malice, and that it is a real martyrdom to be brought under the lawless inquisition of the bloody tongue? Christ, the Prophets and Apostles of our Lord went to heaven with the note of traitors, seditious men, and such as turned the world upside down. Calumnies of treason to Caesar were an ingredient in Christ's cup, and therefore the author is the more willing to drink of that cup that touched his lip, who is our glorious forerunner. What if conscience toward God and credit with men cannot both go to heaven with the Saints? The author is satisfied with the former companion and is willing to dismiss the other. Truth to Christ cannot be treason to Caesar, and for his choice he judgeth truth to have a nearer relation to Christ Jesus than the transcendent and boundless power of a mortal prince.

He considered that popery and defection had made a large step in Britain, and that arbitrary government had over-swelled all banks of law. . . . And the naked truth is: prelates, a wild and pushing cattle to the lambs and flock of Christ, had made a hideous noise; the wheels of their chariot did run an equal pace with the bloodthirsty mind of the daughter of Babel. * * * And now judgment presseth the kingdoms, and of all the heaviest judgments, the sword. . . . I hope this war shall be Christ's triumph; Babylon's ruin. * * *

I have not time to examine the p[roud] prelate's preface.[1] Only I give a taste of his gall.* * * 'Do they not (Puritans) magisterially determine that kings are not of God's creation by authoritative commission but only by permission extorted by importunity, and way given that they may be a scourge to a sinful people?' *Ans*[*wer*]*:* Any unclean spirit from hell could not speak a blacker lie. We hold that the king, by office, is the Church's nurse father, a sacred ordinance, the deputed power of God. * * *

[The Presbyterians] hold (I believe with warrant of God's word): if the king refuse to reform religion, the inferior judges and assembly of godly pastors and other church officers may reform; if the king will not . . . do his duty in purging the House of the Lord, may not Eli[j]ah and the people do their duty and cast out

---

[1] *Lex, Rex*, is an answer to the *Sacrosancta regum majestas* (1644) of John Maxwell, Bishop of Killala and Achonry, afterwards Archbishop of Tuam.

Baal's priests? Reformation of religion is a personal act that belongeth to all, even to any one private person according to his place. * * *

All the forged inconsistency betwixt presbyteries and monarchies is an opposition with absolute monarchy, and concludeth with a like strength against parliaments and all synods of either side, against the Law and Gospel preached, to which kings and kingdoms are subordinate. Lord, establish peace and truth. * * *

[Passages selected from Questions I–XLI]

[I] What is warranted by the direction of nature's light is warranted by the law of nature, and consequently by a divine law; for who can deny the law of nature to be a divine law?

That power of government in general must be from God, I make good: Because (Rom. 13) there is no power but of God; the powers that be, are ordained of God. God commandeth obedience, and so subjection of conscience to powers: (Rom. 13. 5) *Wherefore we must be subject not only for wrath* (or civil punishment) *but for conscience' sake;* (1 Pet. 2. 13) *Submit yourselves to every ordinance of man for the Lord's sake, whether it be to the king as supreme, &c.* Now God only by a divine law can lay a band of subjection on the conscience, tying men to guilt and punishment if they transgress.

Conclus[ion]: All civil power is immediately from God in its root. In that God hath made man a social creature, and one who inclineth to be governed by man; then certainly he must have put this power in man's nature. So are we by good reason taught by Aristotle, God and nature intendeth the policy and peace of mankind. Then must God and nature have given to mankind a power to compass this end; and this must be a power of government.

[II] As domestic society is by nature's instinct, so is civil society natural *in radice,* in the root, and voluntary *in modo,* in the manner of coalescing. * * *

We are to distinguish betwixt a power of government, and a power of government by magistracy. That we defend ourselves from violence by violence, is a consequent of unbroken and sinless nature; but that we defend ourselves by devolving our power over in the hands of one or more rulers, seemeth rather positively moral than natural, except that it is natural for the child to expect help against violence, from his father. For which cause I judge . . . that princedom, empire, kingdom, or jurisdiction hath its rise from

a positive and secondary law of nations, and not from the law of
pure nature. The law saith, there is no law of nature agreeing to
all living creatures for superiority; for by no reason in nature hath
a boar dominion over a boar, a lion over a lion, a dragon over a
dragon, a bull over a bull. And if all men be born equally free
(as I hope to prove), there is no reason in nature why one man
should be king and lord over another; therefore . . . I conceive
all jurisdiction of man over man to be, as it were, artificial and
positive, and that it inferreth some servitude whereof nature from
the womb hath freed us, if you except that subjection of children
to parents, and the wife to the husband. And the law saith, *De
jure gentium secundarius est omnis principatus.* This also the scripture proveth, whileas the exalting of Saul or David above their
brethren to be kings, and captains of the Lord's people, is ascribed,
not to nature (for king and beggar spring of one clay-metal), but
to an act of divine bounty and grace above nature. So Psalm 78.
70-1: *He took David from following the ewes, and made him king
and feeder of his people.* * * *

If we once lay the supposition that God hath immediately by
the law of nature appointed there should be a government, and
mediately defined, by the dictate of natural light in a community,
that there shall be one or many rulers to govern the community;
then the scripture's arguments may well be drawn out of the school
of nature.

[III] But some object: If the kingly power be of divine institution, then shall any other government be unlawful and contrary
to a divine institution, and so we condemn aristocracy and democracy as unlawful. *Ans[wer]:* This consequence were good if
aristocracy and democracy were not also of divine institution, as
all my arguments prove; for I judge they are not governments
different in nature if we speak morally and theologically, only they
differ politically and positively. Nor is aristocracy anything but
diffused and enlarged monarchy, and monarchy is nothing but
contracted aristocracy. . . . And wherever God appointed a king,
he never appointed him absolute and a sole independent agent,[a]
but joined always with him judges, who were no less to judge
according to the Law of God (2 Chron. 19. 6) than the king (Deut.
17. 15). And in an obligation moral of judging righteously, the
conscience of the monarch and the conscience of the inferior judges
are equal, with an immediate subjection under the King of Kings,
for there is here a co-ordination of consciences, and no subordination, for it is not in the power of the inferior judge to judge,

quoad specificationem as the king commandeth him, because the judgment is neither the king's nor any mortal man's, but the Lord's (2 Chron. 19. 6–7).

Hence all the three forms are from God. But let no man say, if they be all indifferent and equally of God societies and kingdoms are left in the dark, and know not which of the three they shall pitch upon because God hath given to them no special direction for one rather than for another. But this is easily answered, that a republic appoint rulers to govern them is not an action indifferent, but a moral action, because to set no rulers over themselves, I conceive, were a breach of the Fifth Commandment, which commandeth government to be one or other. It is not in men's free will that they have government or no government, because it is not in their free will to obey or not to obey the acts of the court of nature, which is God's court, and this court enacteth that societies suffer not mankind to perish, which must necessarily follow if they appoint no government. Also it is proved elsewhere that no moral acts in their exercises and use are left indifferent to us. So then the aptitude and temper of every commonwealth to monarchy, rather than to democracy or aristocracy, is God's warrant and nearest call to determine the wills and liberty of people to pitch upon a monarchy *hic et nunc*, rather than any other form of government, though all the three be from God, even as single life and marriage are both the lawful ordinances of God, and the constitution and temper of the body is a calling to either of the two. Nor are we to think that aristocracy and democracy are either unlawful ordinances or men's inventions, or that those societies which want monarchy do therefore live in sins.

[IV] *Whether the king be only and immediately from God, and not from the people?* * * *

But the question is concerning the designation of the person: whence is that this man rather than this man is crowned king . . .; is it from God immediately and only . . . or is it from the people also, and their free choice? For the pastor and the doctor's office is from Christ only; but that John rather than Thomas be the doctor or the pastor is from the will and choice of men, the presbyters and people.

The royal power is three ways in the people: (1) Radically and virtually, as in the first subject; (2) *Collative vel communicative*, by way of free donation, they giving it to this man, not to this man, that he may rule over them; (3) *Limitate*, they giving it so as these three acts remain with the people: that they may measure out by ounce weights so much royal power and no more and no less, so as they may limit, moderate, and set banks and marches to the exercise; that they give it out *conditionate*, upon this and this condition, that they may take again to themselves what they gave out upon condition if the condition be violated. The first I conceive is clear: (1) Because if every living creature have radically in them a power of self-preservation to defend themselves from violence (as we see lions have paws, some beasts have horns, some claws), men, being reasonable creatures, united in society, must have power in a more reasonable and honourable way, to put this power of warding off violence in the hands of one or more rulers, to defend themselves by magistrates. (2) If all men be born, as concerning civil power, alike (for no man cometh out of the womb with a diadem on his head, or a sceptre in his hand), and yet men united in a society may give crown and sceptre to this man, and not to this man, then this power was in this united society. But it was not in them formally, for they should then all have been one king. . . . Therefore this power must have been virtually in them, because neither man nor community of men can give that which they neither have formally nor virtually in them. (3) Royalists cannot deny but cities have power to choose and create inferior magistrates. *Ergo* many cities united have power to create a higher ruler; for royal power is but the united and superlative power of inferior judges in one greater judge, whom they call a king.

[IX] *Whether or no sovereignty is so from the people that it remaineth in them in some part, so as they may in case of necessity resume it?* ✳ ✳ ✳

For the subject of royal power, we affirm the first, the ultimate, and native subject of all power is the community, as reasonable men naturally inclining to a society; but the ethical and political subject, or the legal and positive receptacle, of this power is various, according to the various constitutions of the policy. In Scotland and England it is the three estates of Parliament, in other nations some other judges or peers of the land. ✳ ✳ ✳

No society hath liberty to be without all government, for God hath given to every society . . . a faculty of preserving themselves, and warding off violence and injuries; and this they could not do except they gave their power to one or many rulers. ✳ ✳ ✳ We teach that government is natural, not voluntary; but the way and manner of government is voluntary. ✳ ✳ ✳

[XII] *Whether or not a kingdom may lawfully be purchased by the sole title of conquest?* * * *

Mere conquest by the sword, without the consent of the people, is no just title to the crown, because the lawful title that God's word holdeth forth to us, beside the Lord's choosing and calling of a man to the crown, is the people's election (Deut. 17. 15). All that had any lawful calling to the crown in God's word, as Saul, David, Solomon, &c., were called by the people, and the first lawful calling is to us a rule and pattern to all lawful callings. * * *

And that any other extraordinary impulsion ᵃ be as lawful a call to the throne as the people's free election, we know not from God's word; and we have but the naked word of our adversaries that William the Conqueror, without the people's consent, made himself by blood the lawful king of England, and also of all their posterity, and that King Fergus conquered Scotland. * * * And truly they deserve no wages who thus defend the king's prerogative royal. For if the sword be a lawful title to the crown, suppose the two generals of both kingdoms should conquer the most and the chiefest of the kingdom now when they have so many forces in the field, by this wicked reason the one should have a lawful call of God to be king of England, and the other to be king of Scotland; which is absurd.

Either conquest, as conquest, is a just title to the crown, or as a *just* conquest. If as conquest, then all conquests are just titles to a crown. * * * But strength as strength victorious, is not law nor reason. It were then reason that Herod behead John Baptist, and the Roman emperors kill the witnesses of Christ Jesus. If conquest, as just, be the title and lawful claim before God's court to a crown, then certainly a stronger king for pregnant national injuries may lawfully subdue and reign over an innocent posterity not yet born. But what word of God can warrant a posterity not born, and so accessory to no offence against the conqueror (but only sin original), to be under a conqueror against their will, and who hath no right to reign over them but the bloody sword? * * *

[*Objection*]: But the fathers may engage the posterity by an oath to surrender themselves as loyal subjects to the man who justly and deservedly made the fathers vassals by the title of the sword of justice. I answer: The fathers may indeed dispose of the inheritance of their children, because that inheritance belongeth to the father as well as to the son; but because the liberty of the son being born with the son, all men being born free from all civil subjection, the father hath no more power to resign the liberty of his children than their lives. * * *

It is objected that the people of God by their sword conquered seven nations of the Canaanites; David conquered the Ammonites for the disgrace done to his ambassadors. * * * *A facto ad jus non valet'consequentia.* God, to whom belongeth the world and the fulness thereof, disponed to Abraham and his seed the land of Canaan for their inheritance, and ordained that they should use their bow and their sword for the actual possession thereof; and the like divine right had David to the Edomites and Ammonites, though the occasion of David's taking possession of these kingdoms by his sword did arise from particular and occasional exigences and injuries. But it followeth in no sort that therefore kings, now wanting any word of promise, and so of divine right to any lands, may ascend to the thrones of other kingdoms than their own by no better title than the bloody sword. * * * I doubt not to say if Joshua and David had had no better title than their bloody sword, though provoked by injuries, they could have had no right to any kingly power over these kingdoms. And if only success by the sword be a right of providence, it is no right of precept. God's providence, as providence, without precept or promise, can conclude a thing is done, or may be done, but cannot conclude a thing is lawfully and warrantably done; else you might say the selling of Joseph, the crucifying of Christ, the spoiling of Job were lawfully done.

[XIII] *Whether or no royal dignity have its spring from nature; and how that is true, 'Every man is born free'; and how servitude is contrary to nature?* * * *
There is a subjection in respect of natural being, as the effect to the cause. So though Adam had never sinned, this morality of the Fifth Command should have stood in vigour, that the son by nature without any positive law should have been subject to the father because from him he hath his being, as from a second cause. But I much doubt if the relation of a father as a father, doth necessarily infer a royal or kingly authority of the father over the son, or by nature's law that the father hath power of life and death over or above his children. And the reasons I give are: (1) Because power of life and death is by a positive law, presupposing sin and the fall of man . . .; (2) I judge that the power royal and the fatherly power of a father over his children shall be found to be different, and the one is founded on the law of nature, the other, to wit, royal power, on a mere positive law. The second degree or order of subjection natural, is a subjection in respect of gifts, or age. So Aristotle saith that some are by nature servants. His meaning is good, that some gifts of nature,

as wisdom natural, or aptitude to govern, hath made some men of gold, fitter to command, and some of iron, and clay, fitter to be servants and slaves.   But I judge this [no] title to make a king by birth, seeing Saul whom God by supervenient gifts made a king, seemeth to owe small thanks to the womb or nature that he was a king, for his cruelty to the Lord's priests speaketh nothing but natural baseness.   It 's possible Plato had a good meaning . . ., who made six orders here: (i) That fathers command their sons; (ii) the noble the ignoble; (iii) the elder the younger; (iv) the masters the servants; (v) the stronger the weaker; (vi) the wiser the ignorant. (3) Aquinas . . . [and] Driedo . . . following Aristotle, hold, though man had never sinned, there should have been a sort of dominion of the more gifted and wiser above the less wise and weaker, not antecedent from nature properly, but consequent, for the utility and good of the weaker in so far as it is good for the weaker to be guided by the stronger; which cannot be denied to have some ground in nature.   But there is no ground for kings by nature here. * * *

As a man cometh into the world a member of a politic society, he is by consequence born subject to the laws of that society; but this maketh him not from the womb and by nature subject to a king, as by nature he is subject to his father who begat him (no more than by nature a lion is born subject to another king-lion); for it is by accident that he is born of parents under subjection to a monarch, or to either democratical or aristocratical governors, for Cain and Abel were born under none of these forms of government properly; and if he had been born in a new-planted colony in a wilderness where no government were yet established, he should be under no such government. * * *

Every man by nature is a free man born, that is, by nature no man cometh out of the womb under any civil subjection to king, prince, or judge, to master, captain, conqueror, teacher, &c., because freedom is natural to all, except freedom from subjection to parents; and subjection politic is merely accidental, coming from some positive laws of men as they are in a politic society, whereas they might have been born with all concomitants of nature, though born in a single family, the only natural and first society in the world. * * *   Man by nature is born free and as free as beasts. * * *   If any reply that the freedom natural of beasts and birds who never sinned cannot be one with the natural freedom of men who are now under sin, and so under bondage for sin, my answer is: that . . . he who is supposed to be the man born free from subjection politic, even the king born a king, is under the same state of sin, and so by reason of sin, of which he hath a

share equally with all other men by nature, he must be by nature
born under as great subjection penal for sin . . . as other men;
ergo he is not born freer by nature than other men. * * * For
things that agree to men by nature agree to all men equally. * * *
If men be not by nature free from politic subjection, then must
some, by the law of relation, by nature be kings.   But none are by
nature kings, because none have by nature these things which
essentially constitute kings, for they have neither by nature the
calling of God, nor gifts for the throne, nor the free election of the
people, nor conquest.   And if there be none a king by nature,
there can be none a subject by nature.   And the law saith, *Omnes
sumus natura liberi, nullius ditioni subjecti.* * * * We are all by
nature free. * * * As domestic society is natural, being grounded
upon nature's instinct, so politic society is voluntary, being
grounded on the consent of men.   And so politic society is natural
in radice, in the root, and voluntary and free *in modo*, in the manner
of their union; and the scripture cleareth to us that a king is made
by the free consent of the people (Deut. 17. 15), and so not by
nature.   What is from the womb, and so natural, is eternal, and
agreeth to all societies of men; but a monarchy agreeth not to
all societies of men; for many hundred years *de facto* there was not
a king, till Nimrod's time the world being governed by families,
and till Moses his time we find no institution for kings (Gen. 7).
And the numerous multiplication of mankind did occasion
monarchies.   Otherwise fatherly government being the first, and
measure of the rest, must be the best.

[XIV] *Whether or no the people make a person their king con-
ditionally or absolutely?   And whether there be such a thing as a
covenant tying the king no less than his subjects?* * * *
   There is an oath betwixt the king and his people, laying on, by
reciprocation of bands, mutual civil obligation upon the king to
the people, and the people to the king.   2 Sam. 5. 3: *So all the
elders of Israel came to the king to Hebron, and King David made a
covenant with them in Hebron before the Lord, and they anointed
David king over Israel.*   1 Chron. 11. 3: *And David made a
covenant with them before the Lord, and they anointed David king
over Israel, according to the word of the Lord by Samuel.*   2 Chron.
23. 2–[3]:. . . *And all the congregation made a covenant with the
king, Joash, in the house of God.* * * * The covenant betwixt the
king and the people is clearly differenced from the king's covenant
with the Lord (2 Kings 11. 17). * * * It is expressly a covenant
that was between Joash the king and his people.   And David made

a covenant at his coronation with the princes and elders of Israel; therefore the people gave the crown to David covenant-wise, and upon condition that he should perform such and such duties to them. And this is clear by all covenants in the word of God, even the covenant between God and man is so mutual: *I will be your God, and ye shall be my people.* The covenant is so mutual that if the people break the covenant, God is loosed from his part of the covenant (Zech. 11. 10). The covenant giveth to the believer a sort of action of law, and *jus quoddam*, to plead with God in respect of his fidelity to stand to that covenant that bindeth Him by reason of his fidelity (Isa. 43. 26; 63. 16; Dan. 9. 4–5). And far more a covenant giveth ground of a civil action and claim to a people, and the free estates, against a king, seduced by wicked counsel to make war against the land, whereas he did swear by the most high God that he should be a father and protector of the Church of God. * * * There be no mutual contract made upon certain conditions, but if the conditions be not fulfilled the party injured is loosed from the contract. * * *

[XIV] As the king is obliged to God for the maintenance of true religion, so are the people and princes no less in their place obliged to maintain true religion. * * * But when the judges decline from God's way and corrupt the law, we find the people punished and rebuked for it (Jer. 15. 4). * * * 1 Sam. 12. 24–[5]: *Only fear the Lord. But if ye do still wickedly, ye shall be consumed, both ye and your king.* And this case, I grant, is extraordinary, yet so as Junius Brutus proveth well and strongly that religion is not given only to the king that he only should keep it, but to all the inferior judges and people also in their kind.

[XVI] I presuppose that the division of goods doth not necessarily flow from the law of nature, for God made man before the fall lord of creatures indefinitely. . . . But supposing man's sin: though the light of the sun and air be common to all, and religious places be proper to none, yet it is morally impossible that there should not be a distinction between *meum* and *tuum* . . .; and the Decalogue forbidding theft and coveting the wife of another man (yet is she the wife of Peter, not of Thomas, by free election, not by an act of nature) doth evidence to us that the division of things is so far forth (men now being in the state of sin) of the law of nature, that it hath evident ground in the law of nations, and thus far natural, that the heat that I have from my own coat and cloak, and the nourishment from my own meat, are physically incommunicable to any. * * * [But] it is clear, men are just owners of

their own goods by all good order both of nature and time before
there be any such thing as a king or magistrate. * * * The law of
nations, founded upon the law of nature, hath brought in *meum*
and *tuum*, mine and thine, and the introduction of kings cannot
overturn nature's foundation. Neither civility nor grace destroyeth, but perfiteth nature.

[XIX] There is a dignity material in the people scattered, they
being many representations of God and his image, which is in the
king also, and formally more as king, he being endued with formal
magistratical and public royal authority. In the former regard
this or that man is inferior to the king, because the king hath that
same remainder [a] of the image of God that any private man hath,
and something more, he hath a politic resemblance of the King of
Heavens, being a little God, and so is above any one man. * * *
But simply and absolutely the people is above, and more excellent
than the king, and the king in dignity inferior to the people; and
that upon these reasons: (1) Because he is the mean ordained for
the people as for the end that he may save them . . .; (2) The
pilot is less than the whole passengers, the general less than the
whole army; * * * (3) A Christian people especially is the portion
of the Lord's inheritance (Deut. 32. 9), the sheep of his pasture,
his redeemed ones, for whom God gave his blood (Acts 20. 28);
and the killing of a man is to violate the image of God (Gen. 9. 6),
and therefore the death and destruction of a church, and of thousand thousands of men, is a sadder and a more heavy matter than
the death of a king, who is but one man. * * * If God give kings
to be a ransom for his Church, and if he slay great kings for their
sake, as Pharaoh, king of Egypt (Isa. 43. 3), and Sihon, king of
the Amorites, and Og, king of Bashan (Psalm 136. 18–20); . . .
if he make Babylon and her king a threshing-floor, for the violence
done to the inhabitants of Zion (Jer. 51. 33–5); then his people as
his people must be so much dearer and more precious in the
Lord's eyes than kings because they are kings, by how much more
his justice is active to destroy the one, and his mercy to save the
other. * * *
For nature doth not ascertain us there must be kings to the
world's end, because the essence of governors is kept safe in aristocracy and democracy though there were no kings. And that
kings should necessarily have been in the world if man had never
fallen in sin, I am not by any cogent argument induced to believe.
I conceive there should have been no government but these of
fathers and children, husband and wife, and (which is improperly

government) some more gifted with supervenient additions to nature, as gifts and excellencies of engines.

[XXIV] If then any cast off the nature of a king, and become habitually a tyrant, in so far he is not from God nor any ordinance which God doth own. If the office of a tyrant (to speak so) be contrary to a king's offices, it is not from God, and so neither is the power from God. Yea, laws (which are no less from God than the kings are), when they begin to be hurtful, *cessant materialiter*, they leave off to be laws, because they oblige *non secundum vim verborum, sed in vim sensus*, not according to the force of words, but according to sense. . . . But who (saith the Royalist) shall be judge betwixt the king and the people, when the people allege that the king is a tyrant?

Answ[er] : There is a court of necessity, no less than a court of justice; and the fundamental laws must then speak, and it is with the people in this extremity as if they had no ruler.

Obj[ection] : But if the law be doubtsome, as all human, all civil, all municipal laws may endure great dispute, the peremptory person exponing the law must be the supreme judge. This cannot be the people; *ergo* it must be the king.

Answ[er] : As the scriptures in all fundamentals are clear and expone themselves, and *actu primo* condemn heresies, so all laws of men in their fundamentals, which are the law of nature and of nations, are clear. And tyranny is more visible and intelligible than heresy, and it 's soon discerned. * * * The people have a natural throne of policy in their conscience to give warning, and materially sentence, against the king as a tyrant, and so by nature are to defend themselves. Where tyranny is more obscure, and the thread [so] small that it escape the eye of men, the king keepeth possession; but I deny that tyranny can be obscure long.

[XXVII] This is the difference between God's will and the will of the king or any mortal creature. Things are just and good because God willeth them, especially things positively good (though I conceive it hold[s] in all things), and God doth not will things because they are good and just. But the creature, be he king or any never so eminent, do[th] will things because they are good and just. And the king's willing of a thing maketh it not good and just; for only God's will, not the creature's will, can be the cause why things are good and just. * * * Nay, give me leave to doubt if Omnipotency can make a just law to have an unjust and bloody sense, *aut contra*, because it involveth a contradiction, the true meaning of a law being the essential form of the law.

[XXVIII] For the lawfulness of resistance in the matter of the king's unjust invasion of life and religion, we offer these arguments. That power which is obliged to command and rule justly and religiously for the good of the subjects, and is only set over the people on these conditions, and not absolutely, cannot tie the people to subjection without resistance, when the power is abused to the destruction of laws, religion, and the subjects. But all power of the law is thus obliged (Rom. 13. 4; Deut. 17. 18–20; 2 Chron. 19. 6; Psalm 132. 11–12; 89. 30–1; 2 Sam. 7. 12; Jer. 17. 24–5), and hath, and may be abused by kings to the destruction of laws, religion, and subjects. * * * There is not a stricter obligation moral betwixt king and people than betwixt parents and children, master and servant, patron and clients, husband and wife, the lord and the vassal; between the pilot of a ship and the passengers, the physician and the sick, the doctor and the scholars; but the law granteth, if these betray their trust committed to them, they may be resisted. * * * Every tyrant is a furious man, and is morally distracted, as Althusius saith. * * *

That which is inconsistent with the care and providence of God in giving a king to his Church, is not to be taught.

[XXX] Much is built to commend patient suffering of ill, and condemn all resistance of superiors, by Royalists, on the place (1 Pet. 2. 18) where we are commanded, being servants, to suffer buffets, not only for ill-doing, of good masters, but also undeservedly. . . . But it is clear, the place is nothing against resistance. * * * One act of grace and virtue is not contrary to another. Resistance is in the children of God an innocent act of self-preservation, as is patient suffering, and therefore they may well subsist in one. * * * If it be natural to one man to defend himself against the personal invasion of a prince, then it is natural and warrantable to ten thousand, and to a whole kingdom; and what reason to defraud a kingdom of the benefit of self-defence more than one man? Neither grace nor policy destroyeth nature. And how shall ten or twenty thousand be defended against cannons and muskets that kill [a] afar off, except they keep towns against the king, . . . except they be armed to offend with weapons of the like nature, to kill rather than be killed, as the law of nature teacheth?

[XXXI] Self-preservation in all creatures in which is nature, is in the creatures suitable to their nature. * * * So men, and Christian men, do naturally defend themselves; but the manner of self-defence in a rational creature is rational, and not always merely natural. Therefore a politic community, being a combination of many natures (as neither grace, far less can policy, destroy nature), then must these many natures be allowed of God to use a natural self-defence.

[XL] A contract, the conditions whereof are violated by neither side, cannot be dissolved but by the joint consent of both; and in buying and selling, and in all contracts unviolated, the sole will of neither side can violate the contract; of this speaketh the law. * * * We hold that the law saith with us that vassals lose their farm if they pay not what is due. Now what are kings but vassals to the state, who, if they turn tyrants, fall from their right? * * * Let Royalists show us any act of God making David king, save this act of the people making him formally king at Hebron, and therefore the people as God's instrument transferred the power, and God by them in the same act transferred the power, and in the same they chose the person. * * * This power is the people's, radically, naturally. * * * And God hath revealed (in Deut. 17. 14–15) the way of regulating the act of choosing governors and kings, which is a special mean of defending and protecting themselves; and the people is as principally the subject and fountain of royal power, as a fountain is of water. I shall not contend if you call a fountain God's instrument to give water, as all creatures are his instruments.

[XLI] It is no error of Gerson, that believers have a spiritual right to their civil possessions, but by scripture (1 Cor. 4. 21; Rev. 21. 4).

Independent Principles of Resistance

From John Goodwin, *Right and Might Well Met* (1649) [a]

Though some other things have been of late acted by the Army,[1] wherein many pretendingly complain of want of conscience and justice; yet I suppose they have done nothing either more obnoxious to the clamorous tongues and pens of their adversaries, or more questionable in the judgments and consciences of their friends, than that late garbling of the Parliament, wherein they sifted out much of the dross and soil of that heap, intending to reduce this body, upon the regular motion whereof the wellbeing, indeed the civil life, of the whole kingdom depends, to such

---

[1] The pamphlet is a defence of Pride's purge.

members who had not manifestly turned head upon their trust, nor given the right hand of fellowship to that most barbarous, inhumane, and bloody faction amongst us, who for many years last past have with restless endeavours procured the deep trouble, and attempted the absolute enslaving (which is, being interpreted, the utter undoing), of the nation. So that if this action of theirs shall approve itself, and appear to be regular and conformable to such laws and rules of justice which all considering and disengaged men conclude ought to be followed and observed in such cases as that which lay before them; especially if it shall appear to have been the legitimate issue of true worth and Christianity; I presume, all their other actions of like tenor and import will partake of the same justification and honour with it. * * *

The first-born of the strength of those who condemn the said act of the Army as unlawful, lieth in this: that the actors had no sufficient authority to do what they did therein, but acted out of their sphere, and so became transgressors of that law which commandeth every man to keep order, and within the compass of his calling.

To this I answer: . . . as our Saviour saith (Matt. 2. 27) that the sabbath was made for man (*i.e.*, for the benefit of man), and not man for the sabbath, so certain it is, that callings were made for men, and not men for callings. Therefore the law of the sabbath, though enacted by God, was of right, and according to the intention of the great Lawgiver himself, to give place to the necessary accommodations of men, and ought not to be pleaded in bar hereunto; in like manner, if the law of callings at any time opposeth, or lieth cross to, the necessary conveniences of men, during the time of this opposition it suffereth a total eclipse of the binding power of it. * * *

Nor did they stretch themselves beyond the line of their callings, to act therein as they did. Their calling and commission was to act in the capacity of soldiers, for the peace, liberties, and safety of the kingdom. What doth this import but a calling to prevent or suppress by force all such persons and designs whose faces were set to disturb or destroy them? * * *

If the calling which the Parliament itself had to levy forces against the King and his party, to suppress them and their proceedings as destructive to the peace, liberties, and safety of the kingdom, was warrantable and good, then was the calling of the Army to act as they did in the business under debate, warrantable and good also. * * *

Now then, supposing the same proportion to the peace, benefit,

and safety of the kingdom, in what the Army did in purging the
Parliament and in what the Parliament itself did in opposing the
King by force (which is a point of easy demonstration, and is
ex superabundanti proved in the large *Remonstrance of the Army* [1]
lately published), let us consider whether the call of the Army to
act for the kingdom as they did, be not as authentic, clear, and full,
as that of the Parliament to act as they did in reference to the
same end.

First, the authority and power of the people (or rather the
present exercise and execution of this power) to act for their own
preservation and well-being in every kind, was as well formally,[a]
and according to the ceremony of the law, as really, and according
to the true intentions and desires of the people, vested in the
Parliament. So that the Parliament by virtue of this investiture,
and during the same, had the same right of power to raise an army,
and to give unto it what commission they judged meet in order
to the benefit of the people, or to act any other thing of like tendency, which the people themselves had to choose for themselves
a parliament. Therefore whatsoever lieth within the verge of
the Army's commission derived from the Parliament, relating to
the kingdom's good, they have as full and formal a call or warrant
to act and put in execution as the Parliament itself had either to
raise an army or to do any other act whatsoever. If then first, the
tenor of their commission stood towards any such point as this
(which I presume is no way questionable), *viz.*, to suppress by
strong hand all such persons whom upon rational grounds they
should judge enemies to the peace and welfare of the kingdom;
and secondly, that those Parliament-members whom now they
have cut off from that body were upon such grounds judged such
by them (of the truth whereof they have given a sufficient account
in their said late *Remonstrance*), it is as clear as the sun, that their
calling to act as they did in cutting off these members is every whit
as legitimate and formal as that of the Parliament itself is to act
anything whatsoever as a parliament. * * *

Secondly, suppose the Army had not a call to act as they did in
the case under debate, every ways as full of formality as the call
of the Parliament to act as they did in opposition to the King, yet
might their call be (and indeed was) as material, as weighty, as
considerable, and as justifiable in the sight of God, and of all un-
prejudiced intelligent men, as the other. * * *

When the pilot or master of a ship at sea be either so far overcome and distempered with drink or otherwise disabled, as through

[1] See Appendix, pp. 456–65.

a phrenetical passion or sickness of any kind, so that he is incapable of acting the exigencies of his place for the preservation of the ship, being now in present danger either of running upon a quick sand or splitting against a rock, &c., any one or more of the inferior mariners, having skill, may, in order to the saving of the ship and of the lives of all that are in it, very lawfully assume, and act according to, the interest of a pilot or master, and give orders and directions to those with them in the ship accordingly, who stand bound, at the peril of their lives, in this case to obey them. By such a comparison as this, Master Prynne himself demonstrates how regular and lawful it is for parliaments, yea and for particular men, to turn kings—I mean, to assume that interest and power which the law appropriates to the office, and vesteth only in the person of a king—when the king steereth a course in manifest opposition to the peace and safety of the kingdom. * * *

But two things (it is like) will be here objected. First, that the Parliament were judges lawfully constituted, of the King's delinquency against the kingdom, but the Army were no judges of such a constitution, of the miscarriages of the Parliament. Therefore there is not the same consideration in point of lawfulness in the proceedings of the Army against the Parliament, which is of the Parliament's proceeding against the King. There is the same difference likewise between the act of a client and pupil, wherein the one dischargeth his advocate and the other his guardian, and the act of the Army in dethroning the Parliament-men. To this I answer:

First, that whether we place the lawfulness of a parliamentary judicature in respect of the King's delinquency either in their election by the people or in the conformity of this their election unto the laws of the land, certain it is that the Army were judges of every whit as competent and lawful a constitution, of their delinquencies in the same kind. For . . . if we measure the lawfulness of parliamentary judicature by the call of the people thereunto, the Army (as was formerly proved) hath every whit as lawful a constitution to judge who are enemies to the peace and safety of the kingdom as the Parliament itself hath. Nor doth it at all argue any illegality in their judgments about the Parliament-men, that they had not the explicit and express consent of the people therein, or that they had no call by them so to judge; no more than it proveth an illegality in many votes and ordinances of Parliament, that they were both made and published, not only without the particular and express consent, but even contrary to the mind and desires of the people, or at least of the major part of them. Besides it is a ridiculous thing to pretend a want of a call from the people against the lawfulness of such an act which is of that sovereign necessity for their benefit and good, which the actings of the Army were; especially at such a time when there is no possibility of obtaining or receiving a formal call from the people, without running an imminent ᵃ hazard of losing the opportunity for doing that excellent service unto them which the providence of God in a peculiar juncture of circumstances exhibits for the present unto us. Men's consents unto all acts manifestly tending to their relief are sufficiently expressed in their wants and necessities.

If it be yet said, 'But the people do not judge the proceedings of the Army against the Parliament-men as tending to their relief or welfare in any kind, but as contrary unto both, nor do they give so much as their subsequent consents thereunto'; I answer (besides what was lately said to the nullifying of this pretence) that physicians, called to the care and cure of persons under distempers, need not much stand upon the consents of such patients, either subsequent or antecedent, about what they administer unto them. If the people be incapable in themselves of the things of their peace, it is an act of so much the more goodness and mercy in those who, being fully capable of them, will engage themselves accordingly to make provision for them. It is a deed of charity and Christianity, to save the life of a lunatic or distracted person even against his will. Besides, it is a ruled case amongst wise men, 'that if a people be depraved and corrupt, so as to confer places of powe: and trust upon wicked and undeserving men, they forfeit their power in this behalf unto those that are good, though but a few.' So that nothing pretended from a non-concurrence of the people with the Army will hold water.

Or, secondly, if we estimate the lawfulness of that judicature by the conformity of their elections thereunto, to the laws of the land, the investiture of the Army into that judicature which they have exercised in the case in question, is conform unto a law of far greater authority than any one, yea than all the laws of the land put together; I mean, the law of nature, necessity, and of love to their country and nation, which, being the law of God himself, written in the fleshly tables of men's hearts, hath an authoritative jurisdiction over all human laws and constitutions whatsoever, a prerogative right of power to overrule them and to suspend their obliging influences in all cases appropriate to itself. Yea, many of the laws of God themselves think it no disparagement unto them, to give place to their elder sister, the law of necessity, and to surrender their authority into her hand when she speaketh. So that whatsoever is necessary is somewhat more than lawful—more (I mean) in point of warrantableness. If then the Army stood bound by the law of nature and necessity to judge the Parliament-men as they did, *viz.*, as men worthy to be secluded from their fellows in parliamentary interest, this judiciary power was vested in them by a law of greater authority than the laws of the land; and consequently the legality or lawfulness of it was greater than of that in the Parliament, which derives its legality only from a conformity to the established laws of the land. Yea, the truth is that the law of necessity, by which the Army were constituted judges of those parliamentary delinquents we speak of, cannot (in propriety of speech) be denied to be one of the laws of the land, being the law of nature, and consequently the law of all lands and nations whatsoever, established in this and in all the rest by a better and more indubitable legislative authority than reside[s] in any parliament or community of men whatsoever. * * *

Another thing that, it 's like, will be objected upon and against what hath been answered to the second main objection, is this: That the Parliament-men, disturbed in their way by the Army, at least many of them, were religious and conscientious men, voted and acted as they did conscientiously, really judging the course they steered to be the safest and most direct for bringing the great ship of the commonwealth into the harbour of rest and peace. And is it not contrary as well to principles of reason as religion, that such men, upon so fair an account as this, should be so foully handled? To this I answer: * * * When men are religious only to a mediocrity, and withal servile in their judgments to some principles which are commonly and with great confidence and importunity obtruded upon the consciences of professors for sacred truths, and yet are extremely discouraging and full of enmity to a thorough, stable, and quiet dependence upon God; by being religious upon such terms as these they become twofold more the children of fear than otherwise they were like to be, and consequently so much the more capable and receptive of sad and dismal impressions from the world upon all occasions. And it is not more commonly than truly said, that fear is a bad counsellor. . . . When religious men sin against the common interest and liberties of a free-born nation and make one purse with the known and thrice-declared enemies of their land and people, whether they do it with or against their judgments and consciences, the law of nature and necessity cannot (for the present) stand to make either a scrupulous inquiry after such a difference or a regular assignment of favour to the qualifying circumstances of demerit, but calls, yea and cries out immediately, and commands all men without exception that have a prize in their hand, to give it for the redemption of their nation out of the hand of oppression and tyranny.   And when this law hath been obeyed to the securing of the nation, she presently resigneth, and this freely and willingly, all her authority and command into the hand of positive and standing laws, calculated for the ordinary posture and state of things, until there be another cry of like danger in her ears.   When these standing laws come to resume their authority and power, there will be an opportunity to inquire, if it shall be thought con- venient, who sinned with, and who against, their consciences; and their assessments which were uniformly rated by the law of necessity, may be reduced to terms of more equity by those other laws. . . . According to the notion of that maxim in natural philo- sophy, that the corruption of the best is worst, so are the mis- carriages and errors of the best men of worst consequence in many cases.   The digressions of men religious are many times worse than the thorough discourses of other men.   When conscience and concupiscence meet (as oft they do in religious men), the con- junction is very fiery.   It was the saying of Gregory long since, 'When men conceive of sin under the notion of a duty, there it is committed with an high hand and without fear' (Greg., *de Pastor. cur.* 1. 3. 1).   Nor ever was (nor is ever like to be) the persecution of the Saints more grievous than when those that shall persecute them and put them to death, shall think that therein they do God service (John 16. 2).   So that whereas the objection in hand pleads on behalf of those Parliament-men who were religious, that they followed the light and dictate of their judgments and consciences in complying with the King and his complices, the truth is that though it may reasonably be thought so much the less sinful in them if they did it upon such terms, yet was it a ground so much the more justifiable for the Army to proceed upon to the disin- teresting of them, as they did.   For when religious men break out of the way of righteousness and truth, with the renitency and obmurmuration of their judgments and consciences, it is a sign that their judgments and consciences are yet at liberty and in con- dition to reduce them; but when these are confederate with their lust, there is little hope of their repentance. * * *

A fourth objection in the mouths of some, against which they conceive the Army cannot be justified in the business in question, is that all such actions are contrary unto, and condemned by, the laws of the land.   But to this objection, at least to the weight and substance of it, we have already answered over and over, and particularly have asserted and proved, first, that all human laws and constitutions are but of a like structure and frame with the Ceremonial Laws of old made by God himself, which were all made with knees to bend to the law of nature and necessity. Secondly, that it is to be presumed that the intent of all law-givers amongst men is, notwithstanding any or all their laws seemingly commanded the contrary, to leave an effectual door always open for the common good, and in cases of necessity to be provided for by any person or persons whatsoever. Thirdly, that all laws bind only according to the regular and due intentions of the law-makers. Fourthly, that the laws of nature and necessity are as well the laws of the land as those commonly so called. Fifthly, that when any two laws encounter one the other in any such exigent or strait of time that both of them cannot be obeyed, the law of inferior consequence ought to give place to that of superior, and the duty enjoined in this to be done though that required in the other be left undone. We now add:

First, that we charitably suppose that there is no such law of the land, which prohibiteth or restraineth any man or sort of men from being benefactors to the public; especially from preserving the public liberties in cases of necessity when they stand *in extrema regula* and are in imminent danger of being oppressed forever, there being no likelihood of relief from any other hand. And if there be no such law as this, there is none that reacheth the case of the Army—no, not in the critical or characteristical circumstance of it.

Secondly, that in case there be any such law as this, that it is a mere nullity, and the matter of it no more capable of the form of a law (*i.e.*, of an obliging power) than timber or stone is capable of information by a reasonable soul, which, according to vulgar philosophy rather than the truth, is the proper form of a man. The laws of nature and of common equity are the foundation of all laws (truly and properly so called) and whatsoever venditateth itself under the name or notion of a law, being built besides this foundation, wanteth the essence and true nature of a law, and so can be but equivocally such. * * *

I know nothing of moment that can be opposed against the lawfulness of the action hitherto apologized and justified in these papers, beyond what hath been already bought and sold (I mean urged and answered) at sufficient rates. The lawfulness of the action we speak of, being supposed, the honour and worth of it are of much more easy demonstration. For what better favour can a Christianly-heroic spirit spread abroad of itself than when men shall put their lives in their hand, and in this posture stand up to take lions by the beards when they are ready to tear in pieces and devour the sheep of the fold, to attempt the wresting of an iron sceptre out of those hands which were now lifting it up to break a poor nation in pieces like a potter's vessel? What the Army hath done in this behalf calleth to mind the unparallelable example of the Lord Jesus Christ, blessed for ever, who descended into the lower parts of the earth, went down into the chambers of death, from thence to bring up with him a lost world. It was the saying of Plato that 'to do good to as many as we can, is to be like unto God.' But to do good to as many as we can, as well enemies as friends, by an exposal of our own lives unto death for the accomplishment of it, is a lineament of that face of divine goodness, which Plato (it is like) never saw. It was the manner of almost all nations (as the Roman orator observeth) to place the assertors of their countries' liberties next to the immortal gods themselves at the table of honour. And I make no question but when the inhabitants of this nation shall have drank awhile of the sweet waters of that well of liberty which the Army have digged and opened with their swords, after it had been for a long time stopped and filled up with earth by the Philistines, they will generally recover of that malignant fever which now distempereth many of them, and be in a good posture of sobriety and strength to rise up early and call their benefactors blessed. However, the good will of him that dwelt in the bush be upon the head of such warriors, who pursue that blessed victory of overcoming evil by doing good, and, according to the method of the warfare of heaven, seek to reconcile a nation unto themselves by not imputing their unthankfulness or other their evil entreaties unto them, but in the midst of their own sufferings from them set themselves with heart and soul to set them at liberty from their oppressors.

IV. THE LAW AND THE GOSPEL: CHRISTIAN LIBERTY

From Luther's *Commentary upon Galatians* (edition of 1644) [a]

[1] For there be divers sorts of righteousness. There is a political or civil righteousness, which emperors, princes of the world, philosophers, and lawyers deal withal. There is also a ceremonial righteousness, which the traditions of men do teach. * * * Besides these, there is another righteousness, which is called the righteousness of the Law, or of the Ten Commandments, which Moses teacheth. This do we also teach after the doctrine of faith. There is yet another righteousness, which is above all these: to wit, the righteousness of faith or Christian righteousness, the which we must diligently discern from the other afore rehearsed. * * * But this most excellent righteousness, of faith I mean, which God through Christ, without works, imputeth unto us, is neither political nor ceremonial, nor the righteousness of God's Law, nor consisteth in works, but is clean contrary; that is to say, a mere passive righteousness, as the other above is active. For in this we work nothing, we render nothing unto God, but only we receive and suffer another to work in us—that is to say, God. Therefore it seemeth good unto me to call this righteousness of faith or Christian righteousness, the passive righteousness. * * *

The world understandeth not this doctrine, and therefore it neither will nor can abide it, but condemneth it as heretical and wicked. It braggeth of free will, of the light of reason, of the soundness of the powers and qualities of nature, and of good works as means whereby it could deserve and attain grace and peace, that is to say, forgiveness of sins and a quiet conscience. But it is impossible that the conscience should be quiet and joyful unless it have peace through grace, that is to say, through the forgiveness of sins promised in Christ. * * *

But because they mingle the Law with the Gospel they must needs be perverters of the Gospel. For either Christ must remain and the Law perish, or the Law must remain and Christ perish. For Christ and the Law can by no means agree and reign together in the conscience. Where the righteousness of the Law ruleth, there cannot the righteousness of Grace rule. And again, where the righteousness of Grace reigneth, there cannot the righteousness of the Law reign; for one of them must needs give place unto the other. * * *

[2] Neither do we seek the favour of men by our doctrine. For

we teach that all men are wicked by nature, and the children of wrath. We condemn man's free will, his strength, wisdom and righteousness, and all religions of man's own devising. And to be short, we say that there is nothing in us that is able to deserve grace and the forgiveness of sins: but we preach, that we obtain this grace by the free mercy of God only for Christ's sake. * * * This is not to preach for the favour of men out of the world. For the world can abide nothing less than to hear his wisdom, righteousness, religion, and power condemned. * * *

[3] For we must diligently mark this distinction, that in matters of divinity we must speak far otherwise than in matters of policy. In matters of policy (as I have said) God will have us to honour and reverence these outward veils or persons as his instruments, by whom he governeth and preserveth the world. But when the question is as touching religion, conscience, the fear of God, faith, and the service of God, we must not fear these outward persons, we must put no trust in them, look for no comfort from them, or hope for deliverance by them either corporally or spiritually. * * *

For in the cause of religion and the word of God, there must be no respect of persons. But in matters of policy we must have regard to the person; for otherwise there must needs follow a contempt of all reverence and order. In this world God will have an order, a reverence and a difference of persons. For else the child, the servant, the subject would say: I am a Christian as well as my father, my schoolmaster, my master, my prince; why then should I reverence him? Before God then there is no respect of persons, neither of Grecian nor of Jew, but all are one in Christ, although not so before the world. * * *

But be it far from us that we should here humble ourselves, since they would take from us our glory, even God himself that hath created us and given us all things, and Jesus Christ who hath redeemed us with his blood. Let this be then the conclusion of all together, that we will suffer our goods to be taken away, our name, our life, and all that we have; but the Gospel, our Faith, Jesus Christ, we will never suffer to be wrested from us. And cursed be that humility which here abaseth and submitteth itself. Nay rather let every Christian man here be proud and spare not, except he will deny Christ. * * *

[4] Whoso then can rightly judge between the Law and the Gospel, let him thank God, and know that he is a right divine. * * * Now the way to discern the one from the other, is to place the Gospel in heaven and the Law on the earth: to call the righteousness of the Gospel heavenly, and the righteousness of the Law

earthly, and to put as great difference between the righteousness of the Gospel and of the Law, as God hath made between heaven and earth, between light and darkness, between day and night. * * * Wherefore if the question be concerning the matter of faith or conscience, let us utterly exclude the Law and leave it on the earth. * * * Contrariwise, in civil policy obedience to the Law must be severely required. There, nothing must be known as concerning the Gospel, conscience, grace, remission of sins, heavenly righteousness, or Christ himself; but Moses only with the Law and the works thereof. If we mark well this distinction, neither the one nor the other shall pass his bounds, but the Law shall abide without heaven, that is, without the heart and conscience, and contrariwise the liberty of the Gospel shall abide without the earth, that is to say, without the body and members thereof. * * *

[5. Gal. 2. 21: *For if righteousness come by the Law, then Christ died in vain.*]

Paul, here disputing of righteousness, hath no civil matter in hand, that is, he speaketh not of civil righteousness (which God, notwithstanding, alloweth and requireth, and giveth rewards thereunto accordingly; which also reason is able in some part to perform); but he entreateth here of the righteousness that availeth before God, whereby we are delivered from the Law, sin, death and all evils, and are made partakers of grace, righteousness, and everlasting life, and finally are now become lords of heaven and earth, and of all other creatures. This righteousness neither man's law neither the Law of God is able to perform. * * *

[6] The first use then of the Law is to bridle the wicked: For the devil reigneth throughout the whole world, and enforceth men to all kinds of horrible wickedness. Therefore God hath ordained magistrates, parents, ministers, laws, bonds, and all civil ordinances, that if they can do no more, yet at least they may bind the devil's hands, that he rage not in his bondslaves after his own lust. * * * This civil restraint is very necessary and appointed of God, as well for public peace as also for the preservation of all things, but especially lest the course of the Gospel should be hindered by the tumults and seditions of wicked, outrageous, and proud men. But Paul entreateth not here of this civil use and office of the Law. It is indeed very necessary, but it justifieth not. * * *

Another use of the Law is divine and spiritual, which is (as Paul saith) to increase transgressions; that is to say, to reveal unto a man his sin, his blindness, his misery, his impiety, ignorance, hatred, and contempt of God, death, hell, the judgment and deserved wrath of God. Of this use the Apostle entreateth notably in the seventh to the Romans. * * *

[7] The school doctors, speaking of the abolishment of the Law, say that the Judicial and the Ceremonial Laws are pernicious and deadly since the coming of Christ, and therefore they are abolished; but not the Moral Law. These blind doctors knew not what they said. But if thou wilt speak of the abolishment of the Law, talk of it as it is in his own proper use and office, and as it is spiritually taken; and comprehend withal the whole Law, making no distinction at all between the Judicial, Ceremonial, and Moral Law. For when Paul saith that we are delivered from the curse of the Law by Christ, he speaketh of the whole Law, and principally of the Moral Law, which only accuseth, curseth and condemneth the conscience, which the other two do not. Wherefore we say that the Moral Law or the Law of the Ten Commandments hath no power to accuse and terrify the conscience in which Jesus Christ reigneth by his grace, for he hath abolished the power thereof. * * *

There is also another abolishment of the Law which is outward: to wit, that the politic laws of Moses do nothing belong unto us. Wherefore we ought not to call them back again, nor superstitiously bind ourselves unto them, as some went about to do in times past, being ignorant of this liberty. Now although the Gospel make us not subject to the judicial laws of Moses, yet notwithstanding it doth not exempt us from the obedience of all politic laws, but maketh us subject in this corporal life to the laws of that government wherein we live, that is to say, it commandeth every one to obey his magistrate and laws, not only because of wrath, but also for conscience' sake (1 Pet. 2; Rom. 13). * * *

[8. Gal. 4. 31: *Then, brethren, we are not children of the servant, but of the woman.*]

Whereupon he taketh occasion to reason of Christian liberty; the knowledge whereof is very necessary, for the Pope hath in a manner quite overthrown it, and made the Church subject to man's traditions and ceremonies, and to a most miserable and filthy bondage. That liberty which is purchased by Christ, is unto us at this day a most strong fort and munition whereby we may defend ourselves against the tyranny of the Pope. Wherefore we must diligently consider this doctrine of Christian liberty, as well to confirm the doctrine of justification, as also to raise up and comfort weak consciences against so many troubles and offences, which our adversaries do impute unto the Gospel. Now

Christian liberty is a very spiritual thing which the carnal man doth not understand. * * * It seemeth to reason that it is a matter of small importance.* * *

[Gal. 5. 2: *Stand fast therefore in the liberty wherewith Christ hath made us free.*]

In what liberty? Not in that wherewith the Emperor hath made us free, but in that wherewith Christ hath made us free.* * * This is also a liberty, but it is a civil liberty. . . . Moreover, there is a fleshly, or rather a devilish liberty, whereby the devil chiefly reigneth throughout the whole world. For they that enjoy this liberty obey neither God nor laws, but do what they list. This liberty the people seek and embrace at this day; and so do the sectaries, which will be at liberty in their opinions and in all their doings, to the end they may teach and do whatsoever they dream to be good and sound, without reprehension. These stand in that liberty wherein the devil hath made them free. But we speak not here of this liberty, albeit the whole world seeketh no other liberty. Neither do we speak of the civil liberty, but of a far other manner of liberty which the devil hateth and resisteth with all his power.

This is that liberty whereby Christ hath made us free: not from an earthly bondage . . . but from God's everlasting wrath. And where is this done? In the conscience. There resteth our liberty, and goeth no farther. For Christ hath made us free, not civilly, nor carnally, but divinely; that is to say, we are made free in such sort that our conscience is now free and quiet, not fearing the wrath of God to come. This is that true and inestimable liberty, to the excellency and majesty whereof if we compare the other, they are but as one drop of water in respect of the whole sea. * * *

To the end . . . that Christians should not abuse this liberty (as I have said) the Apostle layeth a yoke and a bondage upon their flesh by the law of mutual love. Wherefore let the godly remember that in conscience before God they be free from the curse of the Law, from sin and from death, for Christ's sake; but as touching the body they are servants and must serve one another through charity, according to this commandment of Paul: Let every man therefore endeavour to do his duty diligently in his calling, and to help his neighbour to the uttermost of his power. This is it which Paul here requireth of us: *Serve ye one another through love.* Which words do not set the Christians at liberty, but shut them under bondage as touching the flesh.

MILTON ON CHRISTIAN LIBERTY

From *Of Civil Power in Ecclesiastical Causes* (1659)

Many are the ministers of God, and their offices no less many. None more different than state and church government. * * *

The main plea [of those who assert the contrary] is . . . that of the kings of Judah. . . .

But to this I return . . .: that the state of religion under the Gospel is far differing from what it was under the Law. Then was the state of rigour, childhood, bondage, and works; to all which force was not unbefitting. Now is the state of grace, manhood, freedom, and faith; to all which belongs willingness and reason, not force. The Law was then written on tables of stone, and to be performed according to the letter, willingly or unwillingly; the Gospel, our new covenant, upon the heart of every believer, to be interpreted only by the sense of charity and inward persuasion. The Law had no distinct government or governors of church and commonwealth, but the priests and Levites judged in all causes, not ecclesiastical only, but civil (Deut. 17. 8, &c.); which under the Gospel is forbidden to all church ministers, as a thing which Christ their master in his ministry disclaimed (Luke 12. 14), as a thing beneath them (1 Cor. 6. 4), and by many other statutes, as to them who have a peculiar and far-differing government of their own. * * *

I have shown that the civil power neither hath right nor can do right by forcing religious things. I will now show the wrong it doth by violating the fundamental privilege of the Gospel, the new birthright of every true believer, Christian liberty. 2 Cor. 3. 17: *Where the Spirit of the Lord is, there is liberty.* Gal. 4. 26: *Jerusalem which is above is free; which is the mother of us all*; and [verse] 31: *We are not children of the bondwoman, but of the free.* It will be sufficient in this place to say no more of Christian liberty than that it sets us free not only from the bondage of those ceremonies, but also from the forcible imposition of those circumstances, place and time in the worship of God, which though by him commanded in the old Law, yet in respect of that verity and freedom which is evangelical, St. Paul comprehends—both kinds alike, that is to say, both ceremony and circumstance—under one and the same contemptuous name of *weak and beggarly rudiments* (Gal. 4. 3, 9, 10; Col. 2. 8 with 16), conformable to what our Saviour himself taught (John 4. 21, 23): *Neither in this mountain,* *nor yet at Jerusalem. In spirit and in truth; for the Father seeketh such to worship him.* * * *

They who would seem more knowing, confess that these things are indifferent, but for that very cause by the magistrate may be commanded. As if God of his special grace in the Gospel had to this end freed us from his own commandments in these things, that our freedom should subject us to a more grievous yoke, the commandments of men! As well may the magistrate call that common or unclean which God hath cleansed . . .; as well may he loosen that which God hath straitened or straiten that which God hath loosened, as he may enjoin those things in religion which God hath left free, and lay on that yoke which God hath taken off. For he hath not only given us this gift as a special privilege and excellence of the free Gospel above the servile Law, but strictly also hath commanded us to keep it and enjoy it. Gal. 5. 13: *You are called to liberty.* 1 Cor. 7. 23: *Be not made the servants of men.* Gal. 5. 1: *Stand fast therefore in the liberty wherewith Christ hath made us free; and be not entangled again with the yoke of bondage.*

Neither is this a mere command, but for the most part in these forecited places, accompanied with the very weightiest and inmost reasons of Christian religion. Rom. 14. 9, 10: *For to this end Christ both died and rose and revived, that he might be Lord both of the dead and living. But why dost thou judge thy brother? &c.* How presumest thou to be his lord, to be whose only Lord, at least in these things, Christ both died and rose and lived again? *We shall all stand before the judgment-seat of Christ.* Why then dost thou not only judge, but persecute in these things for which we are to be accountable to the tribunal of Christ only, our Lord and law-giver? 1 Cor. 7. 23: *Ye are bought with a price: be not made the servants of men.* Some trivial price belike, and for some frivolous pretences paid in their opinion, if—bought and by him redeemed, who is God, from what was once the service of God— we shall be enthralled again and forced by men to what now is but the service of men! Gal. 4. 31, with 5. 1: *We are not children of the bondwoman, &c. Stand fast therefore, &c.* Col. 2. 8: *Beware lest any man spoil you, &c., after the rudiments of the world, and not after Christ.* Solid reasons whereof are continued through the whole chapter. Verse 10: *Ye are complete in him, which is the head of all principality and power.* Not completed therefore, or made the more religious, by those ordinances of civil power from which Christ their head hath discharged us, *blotting out the hand-writing of ordinances that was against us, which was contrary to us, and took it out of the way, nailing it to his cross* (verse 14). Blotting out ordinances written by God himself, much more those so boldly written over again by men! Ordinances which were against us, that is, against our frailty, much more those which are against our conscience! *Let no man therefore judge you in respect of, &c.* (verse 16). Gal. 4. 3, *&c.: Even so we, when we were children, were in bondage under the rudiments of the world. But when the fulness of time was come, God sent forth his Son, &c., to redeem them that were under the Law, that we might receive the adoption of sons, &c. Wherefore thou art no more a servant, but a son, &c. But now, &c., how turn ye again to the weak and beggarly rudiments, whereunto ye desire again to be in bondage? Ye observe days, &c.* Hence it plainly appears, that if we be not free, we are not sons, but still servants unadopted; and if we turn again to those weak and beggarly rudiments, we are not free—yea, though willingly, and with a misguided conscience, we desire to be in bondage to them. How much more then, if unwillingly and against our conscience?

Ill was our condition charged from legal to evangelical, and small advantage gotten by the Gospel, if for the spirit of adoption to freedom promised us, we receive again the spirit of bondage to fear; if our fear, which was then servile towards God only, must be now servile in religion towards men. Strange also and pre-posterous fear, if when and wherein it hath attained by the re-demption of our Saviour to be filial only towards God, it must be now servile towards the magistrate. Who, by subjecting us to his punishment in these things, brings back into religion that law of terror and satisfaction belonging now only to civil crimes; and thereby in effect abolishes the Gospel, by establishing again the Law to a far worse yoke of servitude upon us than before. It will therefore not misbecome the meanest Christian to put in mind Christian magistrates, and so much the more freely by how much the more they desire to be thought Christian—for they will be thereby, as they ought to be in these things, the more our brethren and the less our lords—that they meddle not rashly with Christian liberty, the birthright and outward testimony of our adoption; lest while they little think it—nay, think they do God service—they themselves, like the sons of that bondwoman, be found persecuting them who are freeborn of the Spirit, and by a sacrilege of not the least aggravation, bereaving them of that sacred liberty which our Saviour with his own blood purchased for them. ***

From *Pro Populo Anglicano Defensio* (1651)[a]

Having proved sufficiently, that the kings of the Jews were sub-jected to the same laws that the people were; that there are no exceptions made in their favour in scripture; that it is a most false assertion, grounded upon no reason, nor warranted by any authority, to say . . . that God has exempted them from punishment by the people, and reserved them to his own tribunal only; let us now consider whether the Gospel preach up any such doctrine, and enjoin that blind obedience which the Law was so far from doing, that it commanded the contrary. Let us consider whether or no the Gospel, that heavenly promulgation, as it were, of Christian liberty, reduce us to a condition of slavery to kings and tyrants, from whose imperious rule even the old Law, that mistress of slavery, discharged the people of God, when it obtained. Your first argument you take from the person of Christ himself. But, alas! who does not know, that he put himself into the condition, not of a subject only, but even of a servant, that we might be free? Nor is this to be understood of some internal liberty only, as opposed to civil liberty; how inconsistent else would that song of his mother's be with the design of his coming into the world: *He hath scattered the proud in the imagination of their heart. He hath put down the mighty from their seat, and hath exalted the humble and meek!* How ill-suited to their occasion would these expressions be, if the coming of Christ rather established and strengthened a tyrannical government, and made a blind subjection the duty of all Christians! He himself having been born, and lived, and died under a tyrannical government, has purchased all due liberty for us. And as he gives us his grace to submit patiently to a condition of slavery, if there be a necessity of it, so if by any honest ways and means we can rid ourselves, and obtain our liberty, he is so far from restraining us, that he encourages us so to do. Hence it is that St. Paul not only of an evangelical, but also of a civil liberty, pronounces (1 Cor. 7. 21): *Art thou called, being a servant? Care not for it; but if thou mayst be made free, use it rather. You are bought with a price; be not ye servants of men.* So that you are very impertinent in endeavouring to argue us into slavery by the example of our Saviour, who, by submitting to such a condition himself, has confirmed even our civil liberties. He took upon him indeed in our stead the form of a servant, but he always retained his purpose of being a deliverer; and thence it was, that he taught us a quite different notion of the right of kings than this that you endeavour to make good: you, I say, that preach up not kingship, but tyranny, and that in a commonwealth, by enjoining not only a necessary, but a religious subjection to whatever tyrant gets into the chair, whether he come to it by succession or by conquest, or chance, or anyhow. * * * It is evident that our

Saviour's principles concerning government were not agreeable to the humour of princes. * * * He asked for the tribute-money. 'Whose image and superscription is it?' says he. They tell him it was Caesar's. *Give then to Caesar*, says he, *the things that are Caesar's.* * * * Our liberty is not Caesar's. It is a blessing we have received from God himself. It is what we are born to. To lay this down at Caesar's feet, which we derive not from him, which we are not beholden to him for, were an unworthy action, and a degrading of our very nature. If one should consider attentively the countenance of a man, and inquire after whose image so noble a creature were framed, would not any one that did so presently make answer that he was made after the image of God himself? Being therefore peculiarly God's own, that is, truly free, we are consequently to be subjected to him alone, and cannot, without the greatest sacrilege imaginable, be reduced into a condition of slavery to any man, especially to a wicked, unjust, cruel tyrant. * * * Absolute lordship and Christianity are inconsistent. * * *

From *Defensio Secunda* (1654) [a]

To these men,[1] whose talents are so splendid, and whose worth has been so thoroughly tried, you would without doubt do right to commit the protection of our liberties. * * * Then I trust that you will leave the Church to its own government . . . and no longer suffer two powers (so different as the civil and the ecclesiastical) . . . by their mutual and delusive aids in appearance to strengthen, but in reality to weaken and finally to subvert each other. * * * Then, since there are often in a state men who have the same itch for making a multiplicity of laws as some poetasters have for making many verses, and since laws are usually worse in proportion as they are more numerous, I trust that you will not enact so many new laws as you abrogate old ones which do not operate so much as warnings against evil but rather as impediments in the way of good; and that you will retain only those which are necessary, which do not confound the distinctions of good and evil, and which, while they prevent the frauds of the wicked, do not prohibit the innocent freedoms of the good, which punish crimes without interdicting those things which are lawful, only on account of the abuses to which they may occasionally be exposed. For the intention of laws is to check the commission of vice; but liberty

---

[1] Milton is here addressing Cromwell and urging him to rely upon the leaders of the Independent party.

is the best school of virtue, and affords the strongest encourage-
ments to its practice. Then, I trust that you will make a better
provision for the education of our youth . . .; that you will prevent
the promiscuous instruction of the docile and the indocile, of the
idle and the diligent, at the public cost, and reserve the rewards of
learning for the learned, and of merit for the meritorious. I trust
that you will permit the free discussion of truth without any
hazard to the author, or any subjection to the caprice of an individual, which is the best way to make truth flourish and knowledge
abound. * * * If there be any one who thinks that this is not
liberty enough, he appears to me to be rather inflamed with the
lust of ambition, or of anarchy, than with the love of a genuine and
well-regulated liberty. . . .

It is of no little consequence, O citizens, by what principles you
are governed, either in acquiring liberty or in retaining it when
acquired. * * * For who would vindicate your right of unre-
strained suffrage, or of choosing what representatives you liked
best, merely that you might elect the creatures of your own faction
whoever they might be, or him, however small might be his
worth, who would give you the most lavish feasts, and enable you
to drink to the greatest excess? Thus not wisdom and authority,
but turbulence and gluttony, would soon exalt the vilest mis-
creants from our taverns and our brothels, from our towns and
villages, to the rank and dignity of senators. * * * Who could
believe that the masters and the patrons of a banditti could be the
proper guardians of liberty? * * * Among such persons, who
would be willing either to fight for liberty or to encounter the
least peril in its defence? It is not agreeable to the nature of
things that such persons ever should be free. However much
they may brawl about liberty, they are slaves both at home and
abroad, but without perceiving it; and when they do perceive it,
like unruly horses that are impatient of the bit, they will endeavour
to throw off the yoke, not from the love of genuine liberty (which
a good man only loves and knows how to obtain), but from the
impulses of pride and little passions. But though they often
attempt it by arms, they will make no advances to the execution;
they may change their masters, but will never be able to get rid
of their servitude. * * * Instead of resentment, or thinking that
you can lay the blame on anyone but yourselves, know that to be
free is the same as to be pious, to be wise, to be temperate and just,
to be frugal with your own goods, and abstinent from another's,
and, lastly, to be magnanimous and brave; so to be the opposite
of all these is the same as to be a slave. * * *

You, therefore, who wish to remain free, either instantly be wise, or as soon as possible cease to be fools; if you think slavery an intolerable evil, learn obedience to right reason and the rule of yourselves; and finally bid adieu to your dissensions, your jealousies, your superstitions, your outrages, your rapine, your lusts. Unless you will spare no pains to effect this, you must be judged, by God, man, and your very deliverers, unfit to be entrusted with the possession of liberty and the administration of the government. * * *

V. THE PRIVILEGES OF THE SAINTS

The Elect and the Reprobate

From William Prynne, *Anti-Arminianism* (1630) [a]

The Anti-Arminian orthodox assertions, now in controversy (which I shall here evince to be the ancient, the undoubted, the established doctrine of the Church of England) contract themselves into these seven dogmatical conclusions:

1. That God from all eternity hath, by his immutable purpose and decree, predestinated unto life, not all men, not any indefinite or undetermined, but only a certain select number of particular men (commonly called the Elect, invisible true Church of Christ), which number can neither be augmented nor diminished; others hath he eternally and perpetually reprobated unto death.

2. That the only moving or efficient cause of election, of predestination unto life, is the mere good pleasure, love, free grace, and mercy of God; not the preconsideration of any foreseen faith, perseverance, good works, good will, good endeavours, or any other pre-required quality or condition whatsoever, in the persons elected.

3. That though sin be the only cause of damnation, yet the sole, the primary cause of reprobation or non-election (that is, why God doth not elect those men that perish, or why he doth pass by this man rather than another, as he rejected Esau when he elected Jacob) is the mere free will and pleasure of God, not the prevision, the pre-consideration of any actual sin, infidelity, or final impenitency in the persons rejected.

4. That there is not any such free will, any such universal or sufficient grace communicated unto all men, whereby they may repent, believe, or be saved if they will themselves.

5. That Christ Jesus died sufficiently for all men (his death being of sufficient intrinsical merit in itself, though not in God's intention, or his Spirit's application, to redeem and save even all mankind), but primarily, really, and effectually for none but the Elect, for whom alone he hath actually impetrated, effectually obtained remission of sins, and life eternal.

6. That the Elect do always constantly obey, neither do they, or can they, finally or totally resist the inward powerful and effectual call or working of God's Spirit in their hearts, in the very act of their conversion: neither is it in their own power to convert or not convert themselves, at that very instant time when they were converted.

7. That true justifying, saving faith is proper and peculiar to the Elect alone, who after they are once truly regenerated and engrafted into Christ by faith, do always constantly persevere unto the end; and though they sometimes fall through infirmity into grievous sins, yet they never fall totally nor finally from the habits, seeds, and state of grace.

The Millennium at Hand

[Hanserd Knollys],[1] *A Glimpse of Sion's Glory* (1641) [a]

Rev. 19. 6: *And I heard as it were the voice of a great multitude, and as the voice of many waters, and as the voice of mighty thunderings, saying: Hallelujah, for the Lord God Omnipotent reigneth.*

At the pouring forth of the first vial, there was a voice saying: *Babylon is fallen, it is fallen.* At the pouring forth of the sixth, John hears a voice as the voice of many waters, and as the voice of thunderings, saying: *Hallelujah, the Lord God Omnipotent reigneth*, immediately following the other. Babylon's falling is Sion's raising. Babylon's destruction is Jerusalem's salvation. The fourth vial was poured upon the sun, which is yet doing, namely upon the Emperor and that house of Austria, and will be till that house be destroyed. * * * This is the work that is in hand. As soon as ever this is done, that Antichrist is down, Babylon fallen, then comes in Jesus Christ reigning gloriously; then comes in this *Hallelujah, the Lord God Omnipotent reigneth.* * * * It is the work of the day to cry down Babylon, that it may fall more and more; and it is the work of the day to give God no rest till he sets up Jerusalem as the praise of the whole world. Blessed is he that dasheth the brats of Babylon against the stones. Blessed is he

[1] *D.N.B.* 31. 280; see further W. Haller, *The Rise of Puritanism* (1938), 270–1. Also ascribed to William Kiffin.

that hath any hand in pulling down Babylon. And beautiful likewise are the feet of them that bring glad tidings unto Jerusalem, unto Zion, saying, *The Lord God Omnipotent reigneth.* This is the work of this exercise: to show unto you how, upon the destruction of Babylon, Christ shall reign gloriously, and how we are to further it.[1] * * *

From whence came this hallelujah? *I heard as it were the voice of a great multitude, and as the voice of many waters.* By waters we are to understand people: the voice of many waters, of many people. * * *

The voice, of Jesus Christ reigning in his Church, comes first from the multitude, the common people. The voice is heard from them first, before it is heard from any others. God uses the common people and the multitude to proclaim that the Lord God Omnipotent reigneth. As when Christ came at first the poor receive[d] the Gospel—not many wise, not many noble, not many rich, but the poor—so in the reformation of religion, after Antichrist began to be discovered, it was the common people that first came to look after Christ. * * * The business, brethren, concerning the Scots, it is a business in the issue whereof we hope there will be great things. Where began it? At the very feet, at the very soles of the feet. You that are of the meaner rank, common people, be not discouraged; for God intends to make use of the common people in the great work of proclaiming the kingdom of his Son: *The Lord God Omnipotent reigneth.* The voice that will come of Christ's reigning is like to begin from those that are the multitude, that are so contemptible, especially in the eyes and account of Antichrist's spirits and the prelacy: the vulgar multitude, the common people—what more contemned in their mouths than they? * * *

Though the voice of Christ's reign came first from the multitude; yet it comes but in a confused manner, as the noise of many waters. Though the multitude may begin a thing, and their intention may be good in it, yet it is not for them to bring it to perfection: that which they do commonly is mixed with much confusion and a great deal of disorder. * * * The people had a hint of something: Down with Antichrist, down with popery. Not understanding distinctly what they did, their voice was but as the voice of many waters. Therefore it follows: *and as the voice of mighty thunderings.* * * * After the beginning of this con-

---

[1] Querying how an hallelujah is suitable to a fast, the preacher answers that it is 'suitable . . . because we are by faith to speak of things as if they were done.'

fused noise among the multitude, God moves the hearts of great ones, of noble, of learned ones; and they come in to the work, and their voice is as the voice of mighty thundering, a voice that strikes terror, and hath a majesty in it to prevail. * * * This is the work of the day, for us to lift up our voice to heaven, that it might be mighty to bring forth more and more the voice of our Parliament as a voice of thunder, a terrible voice to the Antichristian party, that they may say, *The Lord God Omnipotent reigneth.* And let us not be discouraged, for our prayers, though they be poor and mean, and scattered, they may further the voice of thunderings. * * *

Though Christ's kingdom be for a while darkened, Christ shall reign gloriously. That is implied. It is revealed to John as a great wonder, as a glorious thing. Why, did not Christ reign before? Yes, but not in that manner that now he is to reign: the kingdom of Christ hath been exceedingly darkened in the world: though it now begins to appear a little more brightly, it hath been exceedingly darkened. * * *

It may be, it is to be a stumbling block to wicked and ungodly men in his just judgment, that they should see and not understand. And it was upon this ground that God suffered his kingdom to be darkened hitherto, that Antichrist might prevail: because of much glory that he is intending a to bring out of the prevailing of Antichrist in the world, therefore in his providence he hath so permitted it as that the kingdom of his Son for many years should be darkened. And (my brethren) if the kingdom of Christ had been kept in congregations in that way that we and some other churches are in, it had been impossible that Antichrist should have got head. But God in his providence, because he would permit Antichrist to rise and to rule for a long time—and he had many things to bring out of the kingdom of Antichrist, to work for his glory—therefore God hath left this truth to be so dark: the setting up of Christ in his kingly office. Thirdly, because God would exercise the faith and other graces of his Spirit in his children, that they might believe in, and love Jesus Christ for his spiritual beauty, though there appears nothing but spiritual beauty, though no outward beauty, no outward kingdom doth appear, but he be as a spiritual king only. * * * And the less Christ doth reign outwardly in the world, the less glorious his kingdom doth appear outwardly, the more let us labour to bring our hearts under his spiritual reign. * * * For yet the voice is not heard much, that the Lord God Omnipotent reigneth, abroad in the world, though lately some noise we have heard. But blessed be God, in our congregations amongst us we may hear that the Lord God Omnipotent reigneth. It is through our wretched wickedness if his kingly power be not fully set up amongst us in all his ordinances. And that we should have an opportunity to set up his kingly power amongst us here, while it is so much opposed and so little known in the world, it is a great mercy. * * *

But though it be dark for a while, certainly he shall reign, and the voice will be glorious and distinct one day, saying, *Hallelujah, the Lord God Omnipotent reigneth.* He shall reign first personally; secondly, in his Saints.

First, personally. We will not fully determine of the manner of his personal reigning. But thus far we may see there is . . . a probability, in his person, God and Man, he shall reign upon the earth, here in this world, before that great and solemn day. There are divers scriptures that have somewhat of this in them. We cannot give the distinct voice of those scriptures, but many of God's Saints, they do hear something, and when a thing grows nearer and nearer God will reveal it more distinct. Zech. 12. 10: *They shall look upon him whom they have pierced, and shall mourn for him as one mourneth for his only son.* It is usually understood either of a spiritual looking by the eye of faith or beholding Christ at the day of judgment. But why should we take it for a spiritual looking, and looking at the day of judgment? That [the] place doth not hold out; that is not the thing intended. They shall mourn every one apart: this is not like the setting forth of the mourning at the day of judgment. And take but this one rule: that all texts are to be understood literally, except they make against some other scriptures, or except the very coherence and dependence of the scripture shows it otherwise, or it makes against the analogy of faith. Now there is nothing against this, but it may be so. A second scripture that seems to hold out somewhat is that in the 26th of Matthew, 29: *I will not henceforth drink of the fruit of the vine, until that day when I drink it new with you in my Father's kingdom.* It is true, this is likewise interpreted in a mystical sense; but there is no reason why we may not take it literally. Not in the kingdom of his Father in heaven; but in that kingdom that he shall come in here, to drink the fruit of the vine, to have communion with his Saints in this world. 2 Thess. 2. 8: *Antichrist shall be destroyed by the brightness of Christ's coming, the brightness of his personal coming.* And that place (Rev. 20) where it is said, *The Saints shall reign with him a thousand years,* which cannot be meant reigning with him in heaven. It is made as a proper peculiar benefit unto such as had refused Antichrist's

government, especially to the Christian Church. It is likely divers
of the prophets and patriarchs may come in, but especially it
belongs to the Christian Church. Now the reigning with Christ
a thousand years is not meant reigning with him in heaven. For
after these thousand years there shall be many enemies raised
against the Church; Gog and Magog shall gather themselves
together. If it were meant of heaven, that could not be; and
therefore it must be meant of Jesus Christ coming and reigning
here gloriously for a thousand years. And although this may
seem to be strange, yet heretofore it hath not been accounted so.
It hath been a truth received in the primitive times. Justin
Martyr, that lived presently after John, he spake of this as a thing
that all Christians acknowledged; and likewise Lactantius hath
such expressions in divers places of his seventh book. * * *
God intends to honour Christ and the Saints before the world.
* * * And God is pleased to raise the hearts of his people to
expect it; and those that are most humble, most godly, most
gracious, most spiritual, searching into the scriptures, have their
hearts most raised in expectation of this. And it is not like, that
that work of the Spirit of theirs shall be in vain. But God is beginning to clear it up more and more. God is beginning to stir
in the world, and to do great things in the world, the issue whereof
(I hope) will come to that we speak of. * * *
The first thing wherein the happiness of the Church consists is
this: that it shall be delivered from all the enemies of it, and from
all molesting troubles, and so be in a most blessed safety and
security. The God of peace shall tread down Satan shortly, and
all that are of Satan. Christ is described in this Rev. 19, with his
garment dyed in blood, when he doth appear to come and take the
kingdom. And he appeared with many crowns on his head; that
notes his many victories, and his name was King of Kings and
Lord of Lords. And the Saints appeared triumphing with him,
clothed with white linen and set upon white horses. Is that a
clothing for soldiers? Yes, for the army of Christ, that rather
comes to triumph than for to fight. Christ fighteth and van-
quisheth all these enemies; and they come triumphing in white.
* * * And this city that is described in the Revelation shall have
the gates always open, in regard of the security that is there—no
danger at all of any enemy.
Secondly, there shall be a wonderful confluence of people to
this church: both Jew and Gentile shall join together to flow to the
beautifulness of the Lord. Dan. 2. 35: Christ is compared to the
stone that shall break the image and shall become a mountain, and

fill the whole heaven.   Isa. 60. [8]: *They shall come as doves to the windows.*   And when John came to measure the city, the Church, it was a great and mighty city.

Thirdly, because where there is much confluence, there useth to be a contraction of much filthiness; therefore, in the third place, it shall be most pure—a pure church, yea, in great part, if not altogether; nay, we may almost affirm, altogether to be delivered from hypocrites.   *Without there shall be dogs, and whosoever shall work or make a lie.*   Not without, in hell; but without the church. Hypocrites shall be discovered and cast out from the church. Though many get into the church now; then the righteous nation shall enter in.   In the 44th of Ezekiel, 9, there is a description of the Church under the Gospel; and he shows that none uncircumcised in heart shall enter in there.   But the fulfilling of the prophecies of those chapters in the latter end of Ezekiel will not be till this time; and then no uncircumcised in heart shall enter. Rev. 21. 27: *There shall in no wise enter into it anything that defileth, &c.* * * *   It is a most pure church, and therefore is described: the walls to be precious stones, the city to be as clear as glass, and the pavement to be pure gold.

Fourthly, there shall be abundance of glorious prophecies fulfilled, and glorious promises accomplished.   When you read the Prophets, you have prophecies of many glorious things; and the knowledge of this truth will help to understand those prophecies. * * *

Fifthly, abundance of hidden mysteries of godliness will be cleared then, that now are exceeding dark. * * *   Rev. 11. 19: *There was seen the Ark of the Testament;* whereas the Ark stood before in the Holy of Holies that was shut up, that none was to come into it but the High Priest.   But now it is opened to all.   In the Ark were [a] the secrets, a type of the secrets that shall be opened at this time, that were shut up before.   Glorious truths shall be revealed, and above all the mystery of the Gospel and the righteousness of faith shall be discovered.   Before, what a little of the mystery of the Gospel and the righteousness of faith was discovered!   But this will grow brighter and brighter till that time, which is the great design of God for his glory to all eternity.

Sixthly, the gift of the Saints shall be abundantly raised.   He that is weak shall be as David; and he that is strong, as the Angel of the Lord (Zech. 12. 8).   And then shall be accomplished that promise that *God will pour his Spirit on them; and their young men shall see visions, and their old men shall dream dreams.*   It was fulfilled in part upon the Apostles, but the full is not till that time knowledge shall be increased.

Seventhly, the graces of the Saints shall be wonderfully enlarged, even in a manner glorified; though not so full as afterwards in the highest heaven, but mightily raised. The Saints shall be all clothed in white linen, which is the righteousness of the Saints; that is, the righteousness they have by Christ, whereby they shall be righteous before God, and holy before men. Holiness shall be written upon their pots, and upon their bridles: upon every thing their graces shall shine forth exceedingly to the glory of God. * * *

The people of God have been, and are, a despised people. But their reproach shall be for ever taken away, and they shall not be ashamed of religion, for it shall be glorified before the sons of men. * * * There are notable texts of scripture to show the great honour that shall be in the ways of religion. Isa. 49. 23: *Kings shall be thy nursing fathers, and queens thy nursing mothers; they shall bow down to thee, and lick up the dust of thy feet.* What a high expression is this for the honour of godliness! * * * The second place is in Zech. 12. 5: *The governors of Judah shall say in their hearts: The inhabitants of Jerusalem shall be my strength in the Lord of Hosts, their God.* We know that now in many places the governors of Judah, the great ones of the country, their spirits have been set against the Saints of God. We know what reproachful names they have put upon them, and how they have discountenanced them. Though the governors of Judah have counted them factious, and schismatics, and Puritans, there is a time coming when the governors of Judah shall be convinced of the excellency of God's people, so convinced as to say in their hearts that the inhabitants of Jerusalem, that is, the Saints of God gathered together in a church, are the best commonwealth's men: not seditious men, not factious, not disturbers of the state. * * * This shall be when the Lord God Omnipotent reigneth in his Church. And through God's mercy we see light peeping out this way. * * *

In the ninth place, the presence of Jesus Christ and of God shall be exceeding glorious in the Church: then the name of it shall be called Jehovah Shammah, *The Lord is there.* They shall follow the Lamb wheresoever he goeth; they shall see the King in his beauty and glory. And such a presence of Christ will be there as it is questionable whether there shall be need of ordinances, at least in that way that now there is. And therefore some interpret that place so: *They shall be all taught of God, and shall not need to teach one another.* * * * The presence of Christ shall be there and supply all kind of ordinances. * * *

In the tenth place, . . . many of the worthies of God, that have lived in former times, shall rise again. * * *

The eleventh is this: there shall be most blessed union of all the churches of the world. * * * Blessed will the time be when all dissensions shall be taken away; and when there shall be a perfect union of all, and not any distinction of Calvinists or Lutherans, or the like, but all shall come and serve God and be called by one name.

The twelfth is the resurrection of the creatures of the world: and so in that regard there shall be abundance of outward glory and prosperity. * * * When the fulness of the glory of the adoption of the sons of God shall come, the creatures shall be delivered to them. The whole world is purchased by Christ, and purchased for the Saints, that is Christ's aim. *All is yours*, says the Apostle, *the whole world*; and therefore (Rev. 21. 7) it is said, *The Saints shall inherit all things*. You see that the Saints have little now in the world; now they are the poorest and the meanest of all; but then when the adoption of the sons of God shall come in the fulness of it, the world shall be theirs; for the world is purchased for them by Jesus Christ. *Not only heaven shall be your kingdom, but this world bodily.* * * *

But you will say, Are these things true? To that we answer: For the truth of them I will go no further than this chapter, verse 9, *These are the true sayings of God.* * * *

But how can they be? Zech. 8. 9: *If it be marvellous in your eyes, should it also be marvellous in my eyes? saith the Lord of Hosts.* * * * It is God Omnipotent that shall do these things, by that power, *whereby he is able to subdue all things unto himself.* Mountains shall be made plain, and he shall come skipping over mountains and over difficulties. Nothing shall hinder him. * * *

But when shall these things be? Truly, brethren, we hope it is not long before they shall be; and the nearer the time comes, the more clearly these things shall be revealed. * * * No place in scripture gives us so much light to know when this shall be as Dan. 12. 11. *And from the time that the daily sacrifices shall be taken away, and the abomination that maketh desolate set up, there shall be a thousand, two hundred and ninety days.* What is the meaning of this? The light that I have from this, I acknowledge to be from that worthy instrument of God, Mr. Brightman. A day is usually taken for a year, and so many days as were set, so many years it should be. All the question is about the beginning of the time. This abomination of desolation was in Julian's time, in 360, because then Julian would set up the Temple again (that was destroyed), in despite of the Christians, and would set up the Jewish religion again. That was the abomination of desolation, says he; and the whole Jewish religion was not consumed till that time. Now reckon so many years according to the number of the days, it comes to 1650; and it is now 1641, and that place for the abomination of desolation is like to be it as any that can be named. But it is said, *Blessed is he that comes to another number : 1335 days;* that is 45 years more added. That is, says he, in 1650 they shall begin; but it shall be 45 years before it comes to full head, and blessed is he that comes to this day. And he hath hit right in other things, as never the like, in making Sardis to be the church of Germany, and foretold from thence how things would fall out, and we see now are. Now we have also a voice from the multitude as from the waters, and it begins to come from the thunderings. * * *

If God hath such an intention to glorify his Church, and that in this world, oh, let every one say to his own heart: What manner of persons ought we to be? * * * Because you are beginning this despised work, gathering a church together, which way God will honour. Certainly, the communion of Saints, and independency of congregations, God will honour. And this work is a foundation of abundance of glory that God shall have, and will continue till the coming of Christ. And blessed are they that are now content to keep the word of God's patience. And do you keep the word of God's patience though you suffer for it, as you now do. * * * Take heed that you lose not this opportunity; certainly if there should fall out any just cause amongst you of scandal in regard of divisions, or any other way, you may do more hurt to hinder this glorious work than all the persecutors could do. For you will persuade the consciences of men that this is not the way of Christ —persecutors cannot do so—so that the governors of Judah will not say, *Our strength is in the inhabitants of Jerusalem, those that profess themselves to be the people of Jerusalem.*

The Rule of the Saints [1]

Certain Queries Presented by many Christian People (1649) [a]

To his Excellency, Thomas Lord Fairfax, Lord General of the Army, and to the General Council of War: * * *

And because the great design of God in the falls and overthrows of worldly powers that have opposed the kingdom of his Son, is by making Christ's foes his footstool to lift up him on high, far above

[1] See also Collier's sermon, Appendix, pp. 390-6.

all principality and power and might and dominion, and every name that is named in this world, that he may be Prince of the kings of the earth, and all nations may serve and obey him, as you shall quickly see if you make the scriptures your counsellors. . . .[1]

Therefore our daily prayer shall be for yourselves and your noble Army, that you may never stumble at the stumbling stone, nor take that honour to yourselves, that is due to Christ, nor be instrumental for the setting up of a mere natural and worldly government, like that of heathen Rome and Athens (as too many late overtures have caused us to fear), whereby the public interest of Jesus Christ will be utterly banished the kingdom in the conclusion. But that you (whom God hath honoured so highly as to begin the great work of smiting the image on the feet) may show yourselves thankful to him that hath given you victory through our Lord Jesus Christ, may honour his Son, and comfort his Saints, in whom he reigns spiritually, and by whom he will reign visibly over all nations of the world, as these scriptures declare, with others: Dan. 2. 44, 55; and 7. 22, 27; Mic. 5. 4, 5, 6; Rev. 2. 26, 27; and 5. 9, 10; and 12. 9, 10, 11.

To which end we humbly crave, that yourselves would take into your serious and grave consideration and debate, the particulars in the papers herewith humbly offered to you, and also present them to the Honourable Parliament, that they may be improved so far as found agreeable to the will and word of God; which done, we doubt not but God shall have much glory, the godly party shall be comforted, natural men (enjoying their estates) will be at rest also and much satisfied; and this commonwealth will be exalted to be both an habitation of justice and mountain of holiness, even such a people as God will bless (Jer. 31. 23). * * *

1st Query: Whether there is not a kingdom and dominion of the Church, or of Christ and the Saints, to be expected upon earth? Dan. 7. 27, and 2. 44; Isa. 2. 2, 3, and 60. 12, &c. Rev. 11. 15; Rev. 5. 10.

2nd Q[uery]: Whether this kingdom (though more spiritual in the administration thereof, yet) be not external and visible in the world, yea, extend not to all persons and things universally? Isa. 60. 12, 14; Zech. 14. 16, 17; 1 Cor. 6. 2, 3; Eph. 1. 21, 22.

For this end consider: 1. How this fifth kingdom or monarchy

---

[1] Cited as representative examples: Psalms 2. 9–12; 72; 93; 110. 1–6; Isa. 2. 11–12; 11. 4–5; 32. 1–2; 52. 13–15; 53. 12; Jer. 33. 15–17; Ezek. 34. 22–4; Dan. 2. 34–5, 44–5; 7. 26–7; Mic. 5. 4–6; Zech. 9. 10; Luke 1. 32–3; Rev. 1. 5, &c.; 17. 14; Phil. 2. 9–11; Eph. 1. 20–2.

comes in the place of the fourth, visibly succeeding it; 2. How the main scope of the prophecies is to show the outward visible administration of the government of the world, under the several kingdoms successively, as under the first three monarchies, then under the fourth (by the Roman emperors first, then by Antichrist and the ten horns), and then how the Church comes to have the outward and visible government of the world (see Daniel and Revelation).

3rd Q[uery] : Whether this kingdom is not proper to Christ as Mediator, specifically distinct from the essential kingdom of God, and from all worldly kingdoms, and so to be administered by such laws and officers as Christ (as Mediator) hath appointed in his kingdom, and therefore not set up when magistrates become Christian, seeing they rule not then as Christian, nor as Christ's officers, nor by his law, but as worldly governors; the magistrates being officers set up by God in that essential kingdom, not in this mediatory kingdom of Christ?

4th Q[uery] : Whether the kingdoms of the world and powers thereof, as kings, yea parliaments also, and magistrates (so far as appertains to the present worldly constitution of them) must not be put down, before this kingdom can be erected? 1 Cor. 15. 24, 25; Dan. 2. 35, 44, 45.

1st Object[ion]: But these powers are not inconsistent with the kingdom of Christ. Both may stand together. *Kings shall be thy nursing fathers.*

R[eply]: The persons betrusted with these powers may befriend it. Such as rule in the kingdoms of the world may be subjects of Christ. But the question here is of the government itself, which relates to the great image (Dan. 2), and so must be broken down.

2nd Obj[ection]: But worldly government, as worldly or civil, appertains not to the fourth monarchy, nor to the image, but as opposing Christ's kingdom.

1st R[eply]: The ten toes, horns or kingdoms, are parts of the image.

2nd: They oppose Christ's kingdom as worldly or civil, because they let it (not to speak now of other opposition) as the Roman heathen empire letted Antichrist (2 Thess. 2. 7).

5th Q[uery] : Whether this be not the time (or near upon it) of putting down that worldly government, and erecting this new kingdom?

For this end consider: This kingdom is to succeed the fourth monarchy immediately, the first part whereof, the heathenish empire, is long since expired, and the second part, the Antichristian empire, is about the expiration, the time allotted (1,260 years) being about to finish.

Obj[ection]: But Christ saith, *My kingdom is not of this world.* How then can it now be expected?

R[eply]: But he doth not say, It shall not be upon the earth, nor while the earth remains (see the contrary, Rev. 5. 10). But *world* is taken for the time of continuance of that worldly government: the world is put for the Roman monarchy (Luke 2. 1). When the fifth monarchy begins, shall be those new heavens and new earth spoken of (Heb. 2. 5). The Church is called the world to come (as some expound that place, 2 Esdras 6. 9). Esau is the ending of the old world, and Jacob the beginning of the new. That is, the reign of the wicked, Esau's progeny, terminates the old world; and the reign of Jacob, of the Saints (to whom the promise of dominion is made), begins the new world.

6th Q[uery]: Whether the kingdom is not to be set up without hands (Dan. 2. 45), without human power and authority (Zech. 4. 6), but by the Spirit of Christ, calling and gathering people into less families, churches and corporations, till they thus multiply exceedingly? Thus all worldly political kingdoms arise and grow; and thus the spiritual kingdom of the Church.

7th Q[uery]: Whether these churches and corporations, thus gathered and multiplied exceedingly, shall not join together in general assemblies and church-parliaments, choosing and delegating such officers of Christ, and representatives of the churches, as may rule nations and kingdoms; and so the kingdoms of the world be the churches?

This kingdom must either be monarchical, as when Christ the Head and King appears visibly, or parliamentary, as in the meantime, when Christ's officers and the churches' representatives rule.

The Brief Resolution of the Queries

(1) There is a kingdom and dominion which the Church is to exercise on the earth. (2) That extends to all persons and things universally, which is to be externally and visibly administered, (3) by such laws and officers as Jesus Christ our Mediator hath appointed in his kingdom. (4) It shall put down all worldly rule and authority (so far as relates to the worldly constitution thereof),

though in the hands of Christians; (5) and is to be expected about this time we live in. (6) This kingdom shall not be erected by human power and authority, but Christ by his Spirit shall call and gather a people, and form them into several less families, churches, and corporations; and when they are multiplied, (7) they shall rule the world by general assemblies, or church-parliaments, of such officers of Christ, and representatives of the churches, as they shall choose and delegate; which they shall do till Christ come in person.

Q[uery]: What then is the present interest of the Saints and people of God?

R[eply]: To associate together into several church-societies and corporations (according to the Congregational way), till being increased and multiplied, they may combine into general assemblies or church-parliaments (according to the Presbyterian way); and then shall God give them authority and rule over the nations and kingdoms of the world.

For the present to lay aside all differences and divisions amongst themselves, and combine together against the Antichristian powers of the world (Rev. 15. 2, &c.), whom they may expect to combine against them universally (Rev. 17. 13, 14).

An Humble Advice concerning the Government of the Kingdom, according to the former Platform or Model

[1.] That you would stir up godly ministers and people throughout the kingdom, to associate or incorporate into church-societies (as is before expressed) and grant them your special favour, provision, and protection; so shall you be the Saints' nursing fathers.

2. That you would please to satisfy the godly dissenting brethren, both of Presbytery and Independency, by such ways and means as your wisdoms shall find out, how both their interests may meet herein, that so they may concur with one heart in the work.

3. That sister-churches oversee such incorporations and embodyings, that only such as be of approved godliness may have the right hand of fellowship given to them.

4. That such churches, where more of them are thus collected and embodied in any division, circuit, province, &c., may choose and send out some delegates, members, officers, to meet in one session, lesser parliament, presbytery, or assembly, for ordering all such affairs as there occur, according to the Word, if appertaining alone to that division.

5. That all such churches, and the members thereof, have voices in elections of such as are to sit in general assemblies or church-parliaments (so often as occasion is); and those elected, to sit there as Christ's officers and the churches' representatives, and to determine all things by the Word, as that law that God will exalt alone and make honourable.

6. That you take special care to send out and encourage godly preachers, that may go into the rest of the kingdom to preach the Gospel, that so, when others are converted and the Son of God makes them free, they may enjoy the former freedoms with the rest of the Saints.

Additional Considerations for the Improvement of the former Model

1. Consider whether it be not a far greater honour for parliaments, magistrates, &c., to rule as Christ's officers and the churches' representatives than as officers of a worldly kingdom and representatives of a mere natural and worldly people?

2. What right or claim mere natural and worldly men have to rule and government, that want a sanctified claim to the least outward blessings?

3. How can the kingdom be the Saints' when the ungodly are electors, and elected to govern?

4. Whether it be not a straitening of the Church's power, to limit it only to spiritual matters?

5. We expect new heavens and a new earth, according to his promise. How then can it be lawful to patch up the old worldly government, especially being lapsed, for its maladministration, according to its own natural principles?

6. Whether to repair the broken image that the stone hath smitten upon the feet, be not to fall upon the stone?

7. Whether all powers falling upon that stone have not deserved to be broken in pieces?

8. What a sin it would be to set up the dim light of nature for our law, when God hath given the light of the scriptures, a better law.

9. How unbeseeming it were for the followers of the Lamb to comply in the least with the powers of the world in setting up their worldly kingdoms.

10. How dangerous it is to keep out Christ from his throne when he hath exalted you and given you an opportunity to exalt him.

11. What facility appears in settling the kingdom in the hands

of the Saints, and difficulty to settle it any other way [1] and not destroy the interest of the Saints.

12. What advantage of reconciling the godly this way, and suppressing the enemies of godliness for ever.

These, and many other considerations of like nature hereby hinted, we humbly offer to your wisdoms, desiring the assistance of God's Spirit in all your counsels for the improvement of them.

VI. LIBERTY OF CONSCIENCE

INDEPENDENT POSITION

From *The Ancient Bounds* (1645) [a]

[1] [b] There are two things contended for in this liberty of conscience: first to instate every Christian in his right of free, yet modest, judging and accepting what he holds; secondly, to vindicate a necessary advantage to the truth, and this is the main end and respect of this liberty.   I contend not for variety of opinions; I know there is but one truth.   But this truth cannot be so easily brought forth without this liberty; and a general restraint, though intended but for errors, yet through the unskilfulness of men, may fall upon the truth.   And better many errors of some kind suffered than one useful truth be obstructed or destroyed. * * * Moses permitted divorce to the Jews, notwithstanding the hardness of their hearts; so must this liberty be granted to men (within certain bounds) though it may be abused to wanton opinions more than were to be wished.

[2] [c] Christ Jesus, whose is the kingdom, the power, and the glory, both in nature and in grace, hath given several maps and schemes of his dominions . . .: both of his great kingdom, the world, his dominions at large which he hath committed to men to be administered in truth and righteousness, in a various form as they please . . .; and also of his special and peculiar kingdom, the kingdom of grace.   Which kingdoms, though they differ essentially or formally, yet they agree in one common subject-matter, man and societies of men, though under a diverse consideration.   And not only man in society, but every man individually

---

[1] As subscriptions, &c. [This brief marginal note refers to, and repudiates, the method of settlement by an Agreement of the People.]

is an epitome, either of one only or of both these dominions. Of one only, so every natural man (who in a natural consideration is called *microcosmus*, an epitome of the world) in whose conscience God hath his throne, ruling him by the light of nature to a civil outward good and end. Of both, so every believer who, besides this natural conscience and rule, hath an enlightened conscience, carrying a more bright and lively stamp of the kingly place and power of the Lord Jesus, swaying him by the light of faith or scripture; and such a man may be called *microchristus*, the epitome of Christ mystical.

This is conscience, and this its division. And of this conscience is the question, or rather of the person that hath this conscience, and the things he holds or practises conscientiously. For the power of conscience itself, as it will not be beholden to any man for its liberty so neither is it capable of outward restraint: they must be moral or spiritual instruments that can work upon conscience. But the exercise or practice of conscience, or the person so exercising, is properly the object of outward restraint in question.

Now then, if we keep but to this term conscience, first, all vicious and scandalous practices, contrary to the light of nature or manifest good of societies, are cut off not to trouble us in this matter, as deriving themselves not from conscience, but a malignant will and unconscienced spirit. Nor yet may all principles that derive themselves from conscience have the benefit of this plea of liberty, so as to save their owners. As first, if they shall be found of a disabling nature, or wanting in their due proportion of benevolence to public peace, liberties, societies; . . . as for instance, scruple of conscience cannot exempt a man from any civil duty he owes to the state or the government thereof, but it may well beseem a state to force men to contribute to their own and the public good and safety. And though God can have no glory by a forced religion, yet the state may have benefit by a forced service. Again, the service of the state is outward, civil, bodily, and is perfect as to its end without the will and conscience of that person from whom it is extorted; so is not the service of God, which is inward and spiritual, yea it must be in spirit and in truth. Then much less may any such principles find favour in this discourse, as, besides the former deficiency, shall be found pregnant with positive malignity (and that in a high nature and consequence too perhaps) to societies, as the doctrines of the Papists. * * *

And of principles thus allayed and qualified, the question is not whether there be not a power to deal with them, and a force

to be applied to them, yea to conscience itself, the source of them;
for we all agree in this, that there is, *viz.*, Christ's power, and a
spiritual force. But the question is, whether outward force be to
be applied. * * *

[3] [a] Though it be easier to say what the magistrate may not
do than what he may [and though] we are never more out than
when we go about to make forms and systems and be definitive,
comprehensive doctors . . . (especially in things of this nature
which may better be perceived and discerned upon occasion from
time to time by the humble and godly than digested into a few
rules or canons)—this premised, we acknowledge that the duty of
a Christian magistrate is somewhat more than of another magistrate. Civil protection is that which all magistrates owe, whether
Christian or not Christian, to all quiet livers within their dominions, whether Christian or not Christian, as being founded upon
such politic considerations and conditions (setting aside religion)
as, being performed on the subjects' part, it cannot with justice be
denied them. But a Christian magistrate owes something more
to the truth he professes, and to those that profess the same with
him; which duty of his differs only in degree, not in kind, from
the duty of another Christian that is no magistrate. For it is the
duty of every Christian to improve every talent and advantage
entrusted with him, for the honour of Christ and good of the body
to the utmost in a lawful way. So a Christian magistrate, if he
have (as he hath by virtue of his magistracy) a talent and advantage
above other men, he is bound to improve it [in] all lawful ways to
the aforesaid purpose. To which he is to direct even all the
common acts and parts of his government; for though all do
equally share in the outward benefits of magistracy (*viz.*, peace
and plenty, *&c.*), yet ought Christian magistrates principally *ex
intentione* to direct their whole government to the good of the
churches, and the glory of God therein, forasmuch as all things
are the churches', and for the churches. And doubtless magistracy, though an ordinance of man, yet is a most glorious ordinance, and of singular use and service, if rightly applied, to the
Church; as I shall show gradually in these steps.

First, magistrates do prepare by a good government for the
Gospel. Civility, not rested in nor mistaken for godliness, makes
men in a more proximous[b] outward capacity for, and disposition
towards, religion, inasmuch as they are thereby restrained from
gross profaneness and insolent opposition of the truth, whereby
the Word may come amongst them with safety to the persons of
those that bring it; according to which part Chrysostom says well

that the magistrate helps the ministry, viz., by taking cognizance of all moral vices, and it is their part not to commend only, but to command a good moral conversation of their subjects, at least negative. In which case again Chrysostom says well *that good princes make virtue easy while they both urge it with their example and drive men to it by fear and punishments.*

But now for supernatural gifts, as illumination, special or common: to make a man of this or that judgment or opinion or faith, to make a man of this or that practice in religion, may not be required by the civil sword; it may be persuaded, induced by exhortation, example, or such means, and that 's all. * * * And by the way, wherefore hath it the denomination or distinction of *civil* power but that (*ex vi vocis*) civility is the next, most proper, immediate and almost utmost care and extent of this power? For though the Christian magistrate well discharging his place, doth promote the spiritual good and edification of the churches, yet not immediately and directly, but by and through a politic good, as he procures rest and safety to them, and so they are edified (Acts 9. 31). Which is a very considerable and needful service while the public worship and the churches in the exercise thereof, though according to their being and beauty in the Spirit they transcend the understanding and principles of the world, yet are circumstanced and habited with such outward relations and considerations as need such a worldly provision. * * * And is not here a great deal of work, and enough to take up a whole man; and may not very acceptable service be done to God herein, and much good redound to the Church, while not only the Church hath hereby fairer quarter in the world, but a rude preparation is made for the Gospel?

Thus we have committed to the magistrate the charge of the Second Table; *viz.*, materially, that is, he is not to see God dishonoured by the manifest breach thereof, or any part thereof. But is that all? No, surely. He may enter the vault even of those abominations of the First Table, and ferret the devils and devil-worship out of their holes and dens, so far as nature carries the candle before him. Therefore it seems to me that polytheism and atheistical doctrines (which are sins against the First Table and [First] Commandment), and idolatry (which is against the Second Commandment), such as may be convinced by natural light, or [by] the letter of the command where the scriptures are received, as the worshipping of images, and the breaden-god, the grossest idolatry of all:—these, so far forth as they break out and discover themselves, ought to be restrained [and] exploded by the

Christian magistrate; for 'tis that which a heathen's light should not tolerate, nature carrying so far (Rom. 1). And also blasphemy (which is against the Third Commandment, and is a common nuisance to mankind), and the insolent profanation of the Lord's day (though the keeping of it be not obvious to nature's light) ought not to be suffered by the Christian magistrate. For herein (as in the former) no man's liberty is infringed, no man's conscience enthralled, truth not at all prejudiced or obstructed, while only manifest impiety and profaneness is excluded, and the peace of those that are better disposed procured, and scandal avoided by these negatives. And thus far the magistrate is *custos utriusque tabulæ*, not to require the positive so much as to restrain the negative. And all this nature teaches hitherto.

But thirdly, as belonging to the Third Commandment, the Christian magistrate may not only require a conversation and practice, moralized according to the principles and light of nature where they run lowest (as among the heathen), but as they are improved and raised by the Gospel through the common irradiation thereof. For *consuetudo est altera natura*: custom or education is another nature. And look what notions fall upon every understanding that is so situated, or look what impressions are made upon every natural conscience by the Gospel, which ripens and meliorates nature in some degree, and hath at least some fruit and success wherever it comes, though it do not change and sanctify:—I say these fruits, *tales quales*, the magistrate is God's titheman or officer to gather them in for him, and to require a demeanour suitable to such an acknowledged light, at least negatively; that is, to restrain the contrary, that so the name of God be not taken in vain. As to instance, though it be not eruable[1] by the light of nature, the article of the Trinity, or the person and office of Jesus Christ, yet sure to teach doctrine that denies either of these where the Gospel hath sounded, is not tolerable; or to deny the Resurrection, or a Judgment Day, &c. I say, the Christian magistrate ought not to tolerate the teaching of such contradictions (in an instructed commonwealth) to received principles and manifest impressions upon all hearts that have lived under the Gospel within his dominions. And the reason is, because these principles fall into the same rank and order and consideration with natural principles (1 Cor. 11. 14), inasmuch as they are not only habituated unto men as natural, but attested unto within by a divinely-impressed conscience, though but natural and in a common way. And although in treating hereof I have reflected

[1] Evidently coined from *eruo* (dig, or search, out).

much upon the principles and light of nature and the outward good and consisting of societies, yet I make not these the only grounds authorizing the magistrate that is Christian (of whom this chapter speaks) to the premises, nor the ultimate end and scope he is to aim at therein.   For though the light of nature be God's law in the hearts of men, not to be violated, and the preservation of societies one end thereof, not to be despised, yet certainly the Christian magistrate, as he hath his authority from God, so he is to take the rise of exercising it from him who hath not committed to him the sword in vain.   And he is to aim at the glory of God (the preventing or redressing his dishonour) in every act thereof, and to punish evil out of that consideration that it is evil, though God hath given him that rule to proceed by, and to make out the evil of evil to the world, even the contrariety thereof to the light of nature and the good of societies.   Wherein also God hath admirably showed his wisdom and goodness, both in twisting and combining so the interests of his glory (in this sense we speak which is negative) and the happiness of societies, that this latter cannot be without the former, and in laying no other burden on the Christian magistrate for the material than what is within every man's cognizance and the light of nature will lead him to. * * *

Fourthly, the Christian magistrate owes a duty about the external peace and order of the churches, to look to that.   For though the magistrate take not cognizance of several forms and opinions in religion, yet of the outward manner and order he doth and ought, and to bound and rectify that is his place, and to punish disorder.   And all this (whatever noise it makes) is but a civil thing.   For there are these two things go to religion: the thing itself, and the managing of it.   Though conscience is not to be forced to or from the thing, yet the manner of the practice is to be regulated according to peace and comeliness by the civil magistrate.

But all this yet is but extrinsical to religion.   May the Christian magistrate come no nearer?   Yes, doubtless.   He may and ought to do all that he is able and hath opportunity to do in the behalf of the truth, so that he keep on this side of force; as for instance, he ought to be exemplary in the profession of the truth, as Joshua was (Josh. 24. 15: *As for me and my house, we will serve the Lord*). Wherein (as also in his exhortation of the people) he is without all scruple imitable by all in eminent place or authority.   Though the faith of their subjects or tenants is not to be pinned upon their sleeve, yet if their example, countenance, interest, exhortations will gain any credit to the truth, it is an honest way to make use thereof. * * * They may and ought to propose the truth to all, to apply means for the reclaiming of those that err, and to send forth teachers into blind and ignorant places where they are not capable of the care of their own souls, and to call synods or assemblies to confer their light in relation to a work of reformation, or to the solving of some particular difficulties. In a word, he may do anything for the truth, so that, when he have done, he leave men to their consciences that are of a different mind from him, and manage that difference without offence.

Sixthly, and lastly, the Christian magistrate ought to be a nursing father to the Church, to nourish the truth and godliness. The begetting father he is not; that is Christ, the everlasting Father by the seed of the Word. But the magistrate is to conserve and maintain the churches' peace and liberty in the exercise of their consciences and worshipping of God, in all his ordinances according to their light; and so he is to exercise a defensive power for religion both at home and abroad.

And this respect he is to bear to all equally, whom he judges to be the children of truth in the main, though scabby or itchy children through some odd differences. In which things though he be not to further them or edify them, wherein he apprehends them alien from the truth, by any compliance, but to leave those opinions to themselves to stand or fall; yet (notwithstanding them) he is to afford to them his civil protection, they managing their differences in a lawful, peaceable manner (as hath been noted before). I say, this provided, these differences ought not to impair or prejudice them at all in the interest they have in common justice and protection; but if any assault them in an unquiet way, they are to be defended, the assailants punished. So that with this difference is the magistrate to carry himself towards the acknowledged truth and the reputed errors (I mean so reputed by him): he may and ought to do all he can to promote and enlarge the truth he owns; he is not to do aught against the other in controversy, nor suffer any to do aught against them, save to apply spiritual means, to preach, write, discourse, dispute, exhort against them, which kind of fighting is allowable among brethren, so it be with right spirits. * * *

And my judgment herein for the magistrate's intermeddling thus far, is founded upon this reason or principle: It is lawful for every man (and so for the magistrate), nay, it is his duty, to do all he can for the truth; but it is unlawful to do the least thing against the truth. Now because by earnest invitations, hearty recommendations, exemplary profession, general tuition—in a word, by offering and proposing, not magisterially forcing, commanding, imposing, much and great and certain service may be, will be, done for the truth, and nothing against; and because by the other way of forcing, prohibiting, censuring, punishing (impeached in this discourse), though something may light for the truth, and sometimes (as in Austin's days is noted in the case of the Donatists), yet much more prejudice is much more probably like to redound to the truth (many a truth snibbed, kept low, or quite kept out; men confirmed in obstinacy if in errors, and more prejudiced against the right ways through the force that hangs over them); therefore that is lawful, and this is unlawful. * * *

[4] ᵃ That this public determining, binding cognizance belongs not to him appears:

[i] Because it belongs to another charge, *viz.*, to the Church, properly and peculiarly to try the spirits, and judge of doctrines; therefore it is usurpation of the Church's power and interest to take this out of her hands (1 Tim. 3. 15). * * *

[ii] Christ is the judge of controversies, and the interpreter of Holy Scripture . . .; that is, Christ by his Word and Spirit, in the true ministry of the Church, not in the Pope's sentence, nor in the commentaries of the Fathers, or the votes of synods, or the interpretations of national assemblies (though much help may be had by them). . . . Now to give the magistrate this cognizance of differences in religion, were to set up him (after we have pulled down these) as judge of controversies and interpreter of scripture.

[iii] This were also to commit unto the magistrate the better part of the ministry, whose office it is to declare the whole counsel of God, and to be the boundsmen between truth and error. . . . Nay, it is to give them a greater power and office than the ministry, who are only to propose doctrines, not to impose them. * * *

[iv] If the determining of religion, and differences therein, belong to the magistrate, *quatenus* a magistrate: then to all magistrates, or to the magistracy of every country, then to the great Turk, and pagan kings and governors. But how uncapable of such an interest they are who are aliens from the true God, and his commonwealth of Israel, I need not say. The consequence is good, for *quatenus* and *ad omne* are terms adequate and convertible. That which belongs to a man as a man, belongs to every man. If you say therefore that it belongs not to the magistrate, *quatenus* a magistrate, but *quatenus* a Christian magistrate, and so make it a flower that Christianity sticks in his crown, I answer: that Christianity being altogether accidental and extrinsical to a magistrate, adds nothing of power over others in religion, to him more than

to another man, but only personal privilege; for Christianity is the same in all, and why should one man by virtue of his Christianity (for 'tis denied to be by virtue of his magistracy) have power over judgments and consciences in matters of religion, more than another that hath equal and perhaps more Christianity? But the word of God adds nothing of that nature to a Christian magistrate; and let that suffice. For it adds nothing in the same kind, *viz.* of civil power; therefore it much less adds anything of another kind, as namely, ecclesiastical power. For the same subjection, and degree of subjection, is required of servants and subjects to masters and governors, without distinction of good and bad, Christian and pagan, nay though they be cruel and froward (1 Pet. 2. 18). By Christianity Christ hath settled no advantage of power on the head of the magistrate, though thereby he commend the yoke to the subject with an advantage of sweetness (1 Tim. 6. 1). * * *

[v] The object or matter about which magistracy is conversant, which they punish or reward, is not faith but facts, not doctrines but deeds. * * *

[vi] This practice of magistracy, to be the dictator of truth, and to moderate with the sword, lays an unhappy caution, and too effectual an obstruction, in the way of truth, which comes not in always at the same end of the town—not always by the learned and eminent in parts or power (John 7. 48: *Have any of the rulers or Pharisees believed on him?*) but even by the people oftentimes. * * * Ought not this to be considered, that truth be not prevented, by shutting the door she often chooses to come in at, and opening a stately door which she delights not always in?

[vii] The just care that Christ showed, to maintain the due distinction between magistracy and ministry, the office politic and ecclesiastic, doth likewise impeach this cognizance of the magistrate. * * * If Christ would not judge in civil things (Luke 12. 13), magistrates as such ought not to judge in the things of Christ. * * *

[5] ª The immunity and impunity of differing opinions in religion, as in relation to the civil magistrate, may seem to be a principle in nature, founded upon the light of reason, seeing [that] many of the ingenuous heathen practised it, as in that instance of Paul's case, who was impeached by the Jews of greater heresy than any differing brethren in these days can charge one another withal. For he pulled down the old religion, established by God himself, and preached a new doctrine. Yet see what pleads for Paul in the consciences of his judges, who had nothing in them but what they sucked in with their mother's milk. You have the story,

Acts 23, where I shall not comment upon the deeds of Lysias. * * *
And of the same mind in the same case is Festus, chap. 25. 18,
where declaring Paul's cause to King Agrippa, he uses these
words: *Against whom, when the accusers stood up, they brought none
accusation of such things as I supposed, but had certain questions
against him of their own superstition, and of one Jesus which was
dead, whom Paul affirmed to be alive. And because I doubted of
such manner of questions, &c.* Observe here the ingenuity of an
heathen, that will not by a secular sword cut in sunder those knots
in religion which he cannot untie by a theological resolution. * * *
See the moderation of a heathen and the stability of his resolution
against the importunity of multitudes. He is not so zealous of
his gods but he will let a Christian live; nay, he will save him
from any that would hurt him; justice so constrains him that he
disdains the solicitations of the multitude. * * * And when Paul
had declared his own cause before King Agrippa, Festus and
Bernice, and the whole council, they saw no reason to be of any
other mind (chap. 26. 31), . . . saying, *This man doth nothing
worthy of death, or of bonds.* An instance which Christians in
these days may look upon and blush, who think an inconvenient
expression deserves a prison. * * * They look[ed] for deeds, evil
deeds, and thought it unreasonable to punish him for his different
opinions. Now to enervate the force of this instance and argument, some men perhaps will represent my inference thus: These
heathens did *de facto* permit differences of opinion, and remit
those that were accused of them, *ergo* Christian magistrates must
be as careless *de jure.* But I urge it not as a fact only, but as
flowing from a principle of reason and justice, that did glow in the
hearts of these heathen, and so argues strongly from them to Christians. And let any prove it was from a principle of heathenism.

To employ the magistrate in this kind of compulsion, is a prejudice to the Lord Jesus, and the provision he hath made for the
propagation of the Church and truth. Christ hath a sword for
the vindicating of truth, for the propulsing of errors, for the con-
quering of enemies. And what is that? Why; the sword of the
Spirit, the Word of God. * * * And the Apostle cries up not only
the sufficiency, but the mightiness of this means (2 Cor. 10. 4):
*The weapons of our warfare are not carnal, but spiritual, and mighty
through God.* 'Tis through God indeed, and through him they
are so mighty that Christ will not be beholding to king or magistrate for their power to convert men by, though he may use them
to correct insolent enemies, and shelter the profession of the truth,
as was noted before. * * *

It is contrary to the nature of Christ's kingdom, to have the ministry of these carnal means; for 'tis a spiritual kingdom. * * * Christ's kingdom is not of this world nor served by this world. And as the manner of this world is contrary to him, so he delights to walk contrary to the manner of this world, who make their party as strong as they can. But Christ hath chosen (mark, 'tis upon choice, not of necessity) the weak things of the world, even babes, to show forth his praise and strength. * * *

If pastors and teachers, nay the Apostles themselves, be not lords of the people's faith (in a way humanly authoritative) to impose doctrine or practice upon them, then much less magistrates. * * *

It will be granted on all hands, that if religion be the magistrate's charge, yet as it is not his only, so neither his first charge (for though it be the highest charge, it follows not that it must be the proper charge of magistracy). But magistracy immediately and directly respects the good of men, their persons and outward being, and religion only obliquely and collaterally; for such an end must be assigned to magistracy as doth *competere omni*, hold among all, and to level magistracy at a higher and further end than God hath, or its own principle will carry, is vain. Now this will press after the other, to be admitted likewise, that the first charge must be first looked to, and attended upon, and the latter doth not disoblige from the former, much less contra-oblige the former. That is, differing opinions in religion, being of a secondary and remote consideration to the outward well-being of men, doth not oblige to destroy, or to expose to destruction by mulcts, bonds, or banishment, the persons of men; for whom, and in relation to whose preservation, magistracy was erected. For this is a rule: The law of nature supersedes institutions. Men have a natural being before they come to have a spiritual being; they are men before they are Christians. Now therefore for faultiness in Christianity, you must not destroy the man.

'Tis also certain there ought to be a proportion between the fault and the punishment, as that wherein justice mainly consists. Now this proportion is not, nor cannot be observed, when you go out of that nature and capacity in which a man hath offended, and punish him in another, as the magistrate doth when he punishes for such opinions in religion. As for instance, a man is capable of a threefold notion, according to a threefold capacity, *viz.*, natural, politic, religious. He sins or offends in his religious capacity, and hath some heterodox opinions; yet a good subject and fellow-subject, a good father to his family, *&c.* Why now, such may his errors be, that he may forfeit his religious notion, and ought to be rejected, as the Apostle says, after once or twice admonished in vain. But now to come upon his politic being or privileges, is to punish him in that notion and capacity wherein he hath not at all offended—except he have disturbed the public peace by the turbulent managing of his opinion, and then no man may excuse him. * * *

[6] [a] In policy 'tis the worst way in the world and will prove the least successful, to extirpate errors by force. For this multiplies them rather, even as the Bishops' tyrannies did drive men to extremities, and we may thank their strict urging conformity and uniformity, as the instrumental cause and means of those extremities of absolute separation and Anabaptism, which many honest and tender hearts, thinking they could never run far enough from the Bishops, did run into. As the Antinomians likewise have stumbled at our churlish exacting preachers of the Law, *who made empty the soul of the hungry, and caused the drink of the thirsty to fail* (Isa. 32. 6). And who knows but—if force were removed, and a league made, and 'free trading of truth set on foot, and liberty given to try all things—straying brethren on the right hand might be reduced? Forasmuch as we know that as sin takes occasion by the Commandment, so do errors by proscription, and to forbid them, is to sow them, and no readier way to make men fond of them than to restrain them by force; for . . . we love to be prying into a closed ark. . . . Our first parents were easily induced by the devil to believe there was more in that forbidden tree than in all the trees of the Garden; and men are not so wise as not to deliver themselves of such a sophistry unto this day.

The Apostle requires us (1 Thess. 5) *to prove all things.* * * * And this is the dignity, as well as the duty, of a spiritual man, that he judges all things, and is not concluded by the former judgment of any. And this liberty is as worthy the vindication as any in these exonerating times, this liberty of judging.[1] And 'tis established upon very good reason, for it makes much to the advantage of truth, both to the getting and holding of it. . . . The Bereans for searching into Paul's doctrine and examining it

---

[1] The margin quotes Charron, *Of Wisdom*: 'What monster is this, for a man to desire to have all things free, his body, his members, his goods, and not his spirit, which, nevertheless, is only born unto liberty? A man will willingly make benefit of whatsoever is in the world that comes from the east or the west, for the good and service, nourishment, health, ornament of his body, and accommodate it all unto his use, but not for the culture, benefit, and enriching of his spirit, giving his body the liberty of the fields, and holding his spirit in close prison.'

by the Word, are recorded by an epithet unusual for the Holy Ghost to give to men: they were *more noble*, it 's said.

Now this liberty of trying and judging is in vain if there be not a liberty of profession; and to hinder this were a most tyrannical usurpation over that connection which God hath made between the act of the understanding and the will, whereby *voluntas sequitur dictamen intellectus*, and to put asunder what God hath joined together, and indeed to violate the law of God and nature. A man cannot will contrary to the precedent act of judgment; he wills weakly without an act of judgment preceding. To force a man to a profession or practice which he wills not, nay, which he nills, is to offer unto God a sacrifice of violence on the part of the compulsor, and an unreasonable service on the part of the compelled, and therefore necessarily unacceptable. * * *

Who art thou, says the Apostle, *that judgest another man's servant ?* (Rom. 14. 4). Man in a natural or politic consideration, is the servant of men, of his prince, and the republic; but man in a religious consideration, is only the servant of God, and he stands or falls to his own master. He is the servant of men to their edification by holding forth his light and conscience before them; but he receives neither his law nor his judgment from man. God accepts perhaps whom man rejects. * * *

Many shall run to and fro, and knowledge shall be increased (Dan. 12. 4). As a dog doth in following the scent, so do men in following the truth; and they that will not give this liberty, must not expect they should discreetly follow the track. We have a proverb, that they that will find must as well seek where a thing is not as where it is. Let us look upon the truth as God's, and not ours, and let us look upon ourselves in all our discourses as hunting after it; every one acting and seeking for himself and for his part only, acknowledging that God must lead every man by a sense and instinct. So shall we give God his due glory, and save ourselves much unprofitable vexation. And this liberty of free disquisition is as great a means to keep the truth as to find it. The running water keeps pure and clear, when the standing pool corrupts. * * * The true temper and proper employment of a Christian is always to be working like the sea, and purging ignorance out of his understanding, and exchanging notions and apprehensions imperfect for more perfect, and forgetting things behind to press forward. * * *

The practice of forcing straitens men in their liberty they have as they are men and reasonable creatures, who are born with this privilege and prerogative, to be led forth always under the conduct of their own reason. Which liberty is much enlarged by being Christians. Therefore the Apostle says, *The spiritual man judgeth all things*, which is not only the clergyman, but (as Alsted glosses well) *spiritualis homo*, i.e., *vere Christianus*. And to the test and trial of such doth Paul submit his doctrine, 1 Cor. 10. 15: *I speak as unto wise men; judge ye what I say*. And 1 Cor. 14. 29: *Let the prophets speak two or three, and let the rest judge.* * * * To this argument I will add the words of a late, and (for aught I know) yet living author:

The true office of a man, his most proper and natural exercise, his worthiest profession, is to judge. Why is he a man, discoursing, reasoning, understanding? Why hath he a spirit? To build (as they say) castles in the air, and to feed himself with fooleries and vanities, as the greatest part of the world doth? * * * No, doubtless; but to understand, to judge of all things. * * * To go about to deprive him of this right is to make him no more a man, but a beast. If not to judge hurts the simple and proper nature of man, what shall it do to a wise man, who is far above the common sort of men? * * * It is strange that so many men . . . deprive themselves willingly of this right and authority so natural, so just and excellent, who, without the examining or judging of anything, receive and approve whatsoever is presented, either because it hath a fair semblance and appearance or because it is in authority, credit, and practice. Yea, they think it is not lawful to examine or doubt of anything; in such sort do they debase and degrade themselves. They are forward and glorious in other things, but in this they are fearful and submiss, though it do justly appertain unto them and with so much reason. Since there are a thousand lies for one truth, a thousand opinions of one and the same thing, and but one that is true, why should not I examine with the instrument of reason, which is the better, the truer, the more reasonable, honest, and profitable? It is to play the part of profane men and beasts, to suffer ourselves to be led like oxen. What can a wise or holy man have above a profane if he must have his spirit, his mind, his principal and heroical part, a slave to the vulgar sort? Why should it not be as lawful for one to doubt and consider of things as doubtful, as 'tis for others to affirm them? How should we be capable to know more, if we grow resolute in our opinions, settle and repose ourselves in certain things, and in such manner that we seek no farther, nor examine any more, that which we think we hold? They know not that there is a kind of ignorance and doubt, more learned and certain, more noble and generous, than all their science and certainty. * * * It is a very sweet, peaceable, and pleasant sojourn, or delay, where a man feareth not to fail or miscount himself, where a man is in the calm under covert, and out of danger of participating so many errors (produced by the fantasy of man, and whereof the world is full), of entangling himself in complaints, divisions, disputes, of offending divers parts, of belying and gainsaying his own belief, of changing, repenting, and readvising himself. For how often hath time made us see that we have been deceived in our thoughts, and hath enforced us to change our opinions! * * * There is an universality of spirit in a wise man, whereby he takes a view, and enters into the consideration of the whole universe. Like Socrates, who contained in his affection all human kind, he walketh through all as if they were near unto him; he seeth, like the sun with an equal and settled regard, as from an high watch-tower, all the changes and interchangeable courses of things; which is a livery of the Divinity, and a high privilege of a wise man, who is the image of God upon earth. * * * The most beautiful and greatest spirits are the more universal, as the more base and blunt are the more particular. Every man calleth that barbarous that agreeth not with his palate and custom; and it seemeth that we have no other touch of truth and reason than the example and the idea of the opinions and customs of that place or country where we live. These kind of people judge of nothing, neither can they: they are slaves to that they hold; a strong prevention and anticipation of opinions doth wholly possess them &c.

Thus Charron, of Wisdom (second book, chap. 2), which he speaks of in general as a disposition to wisdom. But who knows but he might intend it in the nature of the woman of Tekoah's parable, as an advantage to Divine truth? However, I bring it not as an authority, but as reason.

[7] Furthermore, are there not several statures in Christ, and that in knowledge as well as in other graces, as there are several kinds of metals in the earth, some more precious and better concocted than other? And doth not one star differ from another star in glory? Even so do men, and so will they (do we what we can), in the accurateness of their knowledge, and in the clearness of their apprehensions. Some can only see a rule of discipline in the scripture confusedly and indistinctly, like the purblind man that saw men like trees walking (and in truth 'tis most proper for them to cry for a toleration, and he had a hard heart that would deny it them). Others see more clearly the perfect draft, and all the lineaments thereof, not through the excelling of their own wit, but the teaching of Christ's Spirit, yet not assuming to themselves a greater measure of it than the other, who perhaps in other things may see more than they by the same Spirit (1 Cor. 12. 8, &c.).

Lastly, I shall conclude the positive part of this discourse with opening, in some measure, the design of Christ in establishing no other more specious, better satisfying order and means for the

propagation of the truth, and in excluding force and power and
authority human, from ministering in his kingdom in this particular—leaving this, and all that hath been said, to spiritual men
to judge, who can compare spiritual things with spiritual.

It is in this matter as 'tis in the government of particular
churches: the adversary carries it the same way, and turns upon
the same common hinge of human reason, and must be answered
the same way in both.   They diffide the sufficiency of a particular
church to manage its own affairs, and why?   Because they have
so few officers, and in some churches perhaps but one, and he
none of the greatest scholars, and the brethren a company of
illiterate men; and a good mess of government these are like
to make!   This error proceeds now from not considering where
the strength and sufficiency of this poor flock doth lie, which is
not in themselves (were they as eloquent as Apollo, as logical as
Paul), but in Christ their head, who is by his special promise
present with them (Matt. 18): *Where two or three are gathered
together in his name* [*&c.*].   *The Lord is in the midst of her; therefore
she cannot be moved* (Psalm 46).   And the government is upon
his shoulder (Isa. 9. 6).   Now hence (I say) is the mistake, through
not considering that the government of the Church by officers
is but ministerial, and that they are guided and acted by Christ,
and he puts wisdom into their hearts, and right words into their
mouths. * * * He doth fill carefully all his own institutions with
force and efficacy; and they do not wisely that judge of them
according to their appearance, for so, they are the most contemptible, unlikely things in the world.   But could you see the
virtue and power that Christ conveys secretly under them, you
would fall down before them.   So I say now in this matter of
suppressing errors (as before qualified), which we say must be
only by the ministry of the Spirit, by the word of God (which in
the hand of the Spirit is quick and powerful), by brotherly
admonitions and earnest exhortations, and holding forth the
contrary light, doctrinally and practically, *&c*.   Now alas, say
our carnal hearts, what are these like to do?   'Tis true, look upon
them in the outward appearance only and they promise little;
but men do not consider that these are but the veil and covering
of that arm and power which must do the deed.   For *God himself
is judge* (Psalm 50. 6).   Christ Jesus is the Prince of Light and
Truth, the decider of controversies, dictator to his Church, and
in the observation of Gospel rules he discovers himself unto his
people, and, by and through his people, to those that err.   The
Oracle in the Temple spake not—'twas but a form or image; but

God spake in the Oracle. The scriptures themselves are but a sealed book except Christ by his Spirit speak in them, and by them, to our understandings and hearts. What matter is it what the form be if God fill it ? * * * We forget that Christ will have his Church in all their ordinances, affairs, and administrations to show forth his death, that all things and persons in the Church must bear a suitableness and correspondency to Christ crucified, the head of the Church. * * * *And I, brethren, came not*, says Paul (who could have afforded it as soon as any man), *with excellency of speech, or of wisdom, &c. For I determined not to know anything among you, save Jesus Christ and him crucified* (1 Cor. 2). Mark here the ground and root of the whole matter (I mean of the simplicity of Christ's ways and ordinances): 'tis Christ crucified. Christ's death is thus avenged upon the glory of the world, whilst the power and greatness of this world is reprobated and rejected from the most noble uses and honourable services, namely, from ministering in his kingdom. Go, says Christ to man's wisdom and human eloquence, I will have none of thee in preaching my Gospel; and return into the scabbard, says he to the magistrate's sword, I will have none of thee to cut the way for my truth, through woods and rocks and mountains, through stony hearts and implicated reasonings. *Not by might, nor by power, but by my Spirit, saith the Lord.* Thus Christ reprobates parts and learning, and the most specious and likely means. Shall he be crucified, and shall these be in their flower and blossom ? And he brings down the mighty things of the world by the weak, and things that are, by things that are not, *that no flesh may glory in his presence, but he that glorieth, let him glory in the Lord*; that neither our faith, nor the ordinance's success, should stand in the wisdom of men, nor in the likeliness of the means, approving themselves so to man's understanding, but in the power of God. These, and such-like, are the reasons rendered in the first and second chapters of the First Epistle to the Corinthians; and these are enough, I conceive, to satisfy a moderate understanding. For my own part, I must profess it is the clue of thread that carries me through this labyrinth; 'tis the pole-star by which I steer my judgment, and by which my doubts are resolved satisfactorily. I see reason enough for that slender and abject provision which Christ hath made (in the world's account) for the propulsing of errors, and for that mean form and guise wherein all Christ's ordinances appear unto us, when I look upon the death of Christ, or upon Christ crucified. * * *

[8] ᵃ And what reformation this kingdom had in the late

days, it did consist in the incoaction or spontaneousness of
it in the Parliament, whatsoever it did in the people, as one
reports of it: [1]

Nam in senatu, ut fertur, patuit omnibus ad dicendum locus, nec
ulli hominum generi potestas contradicendi, suamq; fidem profitendi
interclusa est; imo integrum fuit cuiq; liberis velitari ac pugnare
sententiis in quo summa elucet aequitas & moderatio principum qui
allicere, ducere, persuadere; non cogere, trahere, jubere voluerunt; ut
impudens mendacium sit, si quis jam dixerit, authoritatem vicisse, non
veritatem. Illud etiam constat, liberum fuisse adversariae parti in
publica disputatione suas partes tueri, arbitris adhibitis incorruptiori-
bus, sive voce sive calamo certare, sive opponere sive respondere
maluissent.

I quote the words because if they had never been realized, yet the
idea of such a carriage when men are seeking out the truth is
lovely as being very equal and rational. * * *

[9 ᵃ Regarding the main objection, the example of the kings
of Judah]: Whatsoever they did rightly . . . yet cannot be
drawn into precedent by us. . . .

First, those were the times of the Old Testament, these of the
New; therefore 'tis not a sound way of arguing from them to
us in everything. * * * However it was that their service was
compulsorily required from them, we have a word that ours
should be free (Psalm 110): *Thy people shall be willing in the day
of thy power.* * * *

Secondly, their worship was carnal, bodily, outward, consisting
much in the conformity of the outward man and practice to certain
worldly ordinances (Heb. 9). . . . But the worship of the New
Testament is chiefly in the heart and hidden man, in spirit
and in truth (John 4), which is at the beck of no human force
or power. Therefore it is no good argument from that worship
to this.

Thirdly, the kings of Judah (as it is generally received) had a
peculiar notion from kings now. Therefore 'tis no good argument from them to these. * * * They were types of Christ, the
King of the Church, and did bear visibly, and execute typically,
his kingly office (even as priests and prophets did his other two
offices). * * * Our kings are only the ministers of God in the
world, ruling indeed *for* the Church, not *in* the Church and *over*
it as then. * * *

---

[1] Humfred. *de vera Relig. &c.* [i.e., Laurence Humphrey's *De religionis
conservatione et reformatione vera* (Basle, 1559), pp. 31-2]. For translation see Introduction, pp. [77-8].

Fourthly and lastly, the people of the Jews were interchangeably a church and a nation (so that he who was head of the state, was so also of the Church in a typical way; as he that was a member of the commonwealth, was by that a member of the Church, and *vice versa*), which no people ever since were. Therefore the argument will not hold from Israel to England, or any other nation. * * * Now though I know a national church in one sense is the apple of some men's eye . . . ; yet in this sense they will none of them hold it: that as in Israel, so in England, so in Scotland, the nation is holy, and all that are born in it are of the Church *ipso facto*, or *ipso natu*. And if not so, then may not Christ's kingly sceptre, which relates only to his Church, be swayed over them all generally. Therefore kings or magistrates may not now as then compel men to religion; but that which those kings did in a typical way, Christ, the King of his Church, doth in a spiritual, antitypical way of accomplishment. * * *

[10] Now if there be light in the things that have been brought and that they conclude for a greater liberty than some brethren want, I hope you will save them the labour of asking their liberty at your hand. * * * We never go before the throne of grace but we carry you in our hearts and prayers along with us . . . and are full of hope that God, who hath concurred with you thus far and acted you to so many worthy and memorable degrees of service to him and his Son Jesus Christ, hath not conceived that displeasure against both you and us as to reserve your further counsels, to shut the door of Christian liberty that was first opened to us by your means. And let it not be imputed to us as arrogance if in the day wherein ourselves are but probationers our principles speak for others as well as ourselves. * * * We shall bless God if he shall so far clear us and our way in your thoughts, but our peace and liberty will not fall with that rich and full contentment into our bosoms except all who walk conscientiously and inoffensively may enjoy the same with us. * * *

From Roger Williams, *The Bloody Tenent of Persecution* [1] (1644) [a]

[*Summary of Contents and Contentions*] [b]

* * * Pregnant scriptures and arguments are throughout the work proposed against the doctrine of persecution for cause of conscience. * * * All civil states with their officers of justice, in their respective constitutions and administrations, are proved essentially civil, and therefore not judges, governors, or defenders of the spiritual, or Christian, state and worship. It is the will and command of God that, since the coming of his Son the Lord Jesus, a permission of the most paganish, Jewish, Turkish, or Antichristian consciences and worships be granted to all men in all nations and countries; and they are only to be fought against with that sword which is only, in soul matters, able to conquer, to wit, the sword of God's Spirit, the word of God. The state of the land of Israel (the kings and people thereof, in peace and war) is proved figurative and ceremonial, and no pattern nor precedent for any kingdom or civil state in the world to follow. God requireth not an uniformity of religion to be enacted and enforced in any civil state; which enforced uniformity, sooner or later, is the greatest occasion of civil war, ravishing of conscience, persecution of Christ Jesus in his servants, and of the hypocrisy and destruction of millions of souls. * * * An enforced uniformity of religion throughout a nation or civil state confounds the civil and religious, denies the principles of Christianity and civility, and that Jesus Christ is come in the flesh. The permission of other consciences and worships than a state professeth only can, according to God, procure a firm and lasting peace; good assurance being taken, according to the wisdom of the civil state, for uniformity of civil obedience from all sorts. True civility and Christianity may both flourish in a state or kingdom, not withstanding the permission of divers and contrary consciences, either of Jew or Gentile. * * *

[*Religion and the Civil Peace*] [c]

Truth: * * * First for civil peace, what is it but *pax civitatis*, the peace of the city? . . . Thus it pleased the Father of Lights

---

[1] Though the dispute with Cotton originated in New England, Williams wrote in England, and with frequent reference to the situation there.

to define it. Jer. 29. 7: *Pray for the peace of the city.* Which
peace of the city, or citizens so compacted in a civil way of union,
may be entire, unbroken, safe, *&c.*, notwithstanding so many
thousands of God's people, the Jews, were there in bondage and
would neither be constrained to the worship of the city Babel,
nor restrained from so much of the worship of the true God as
they then could practise, as is plain in the practice of the three
worthies, Shadrach, Meshach, and Abednego, as also of Daniel
(Dan. 3; and 6)—the peace of the city or kingdom being a far
different peace from the peace of the religion, or spiritual worship,
maintained and professed of the citizens. This peace of their
worship (which worship also in some cities being various) being
a false peace, God's people were and ought to be nonconformi-
tants, not daring either to be restrained from the true or constrained to false worship; and yet without breach of the civil or
city peace, properly so called.

Peace: Hence it is that so many glorious and flourishing cities
of the world maintain their civil peace; yea, the very Americans
and wildest pagans keep the peace of their towns or cities, though
neither in one nor the other can any man prove a true church of
God in those places, and consequently no spiritual and heavenly
peace—the peace spiritual, whether true or false, being of a
higher and far different nature from the peace of the place or
people, [that] being merely and essentially civil and human.

Truth: * * * To illustrate this. The church, or company of
worshippers, whether true or false, is like unto a body or college of
physicians in a city, like unto a corporation, society, or company
of East India or Turkey merchants, or any other society or company in London; which companies may hold their courts, keep
their records, hold disputations, and in matters concerning their
society may dissent, divide, break into schisms and factions, sue
and implead each other at the law, yea, wholly break up and dissolve into pieces and nothing, and yet the peace of the city not be
in the least measure impaired or disturbed; because the essence or
being of the city, and so the well-being and peace thereof, is
essentially distinct from those particular societies; the city courts,
city laws, city punishments, distinct from theirs. The city was
before them, and stands absolute and entire when such a corporation or society is taken down. For instance further. The city
or civil state of Ephesus was essentially distinct from the worship
of Diana in the city, or of the whole city. Again the church of
Christ in Ephesus, which were God's people, converted and called
out from the worship of that city unto Christianity or worship of

God in Christ, was distinct from both. Now suppose that God remove the candlestick from Ephesus, yea, though the whole worship of the city of Ephesus should be altered; yet, if men be true and honestly ingenuous to city covenants, combinations, and principles, all this might be without the least impeachment or infringement of the peace of the city of Ephesus. * * *

[*Parable of the Tares* (Matt. 13. 24–30) *Interpreted*] [a]

[*Truth :*] I shall make it evident, that by these tares in this parable are meant persons in respect of their religion and way of worship, open and visible professors, as bad as briars and thorns,[1] not only suspected foxes, but as bad as those greedy wolves which Paul speaks of (Acts 20. [29]), who with perverse and evil doctrines labour spiritually to devour the flock, and to draw away disciples after them, whose mouths must be stopped, and yet no carnal force or weapon to be used against them; but their mischief to be resisted with those mighty weapons of the holy armoury of the Lord Jesus, wherein there hangs a thousand shields (Cant. 4. [4]).

That the Lord Jesus intendeth not doctrines, or practices, by the tares in this parable, is clear. For . . . the Lord Jesus expressly interpreteth the good seed to be persons, and those the children of the kingdom; and the tares also to signify men, and those the children of the wicked one (ver. 38). * * *

Again, hypocrites were not intended by the Lord Jesus in this famous parable.

First, the original word ζιζάνια, signifying all those weeds which spring up with the corn, as cockle, darnel, tares, &c., seems to imply such a kind of people as commonly and generally are known to be manifestly different from, and opposite to, the true worshippers of God, here called the children of the kingdom: as these weeds, tares, cockle, darnel, &c., are commonly and presently known by every husbandman to differ from the wheat, and to be opposite, and contrary, and hurtful unto it. * * *

The second reason why these tares cannot signify hypocrites in the church, I take from the Lord Jesus his own interpretation of the field in which both wheat and tares are sown, which, saith he, *is the world*, out of which God chooseth and calleth his Church.

The world lies in wickedness, is like a wilderness, or a sea of

---

[1] 'Briars and thorns' signify for Williams *natural* or unconverted persons; 'tares' signify heretics and false worshippers. Both groups are to be tolerated in the world (so long as they do not infringe the civil peace); neither is to be tolerated in the church.

wild beasts innumerable, fornicators, covetous, idolaters, &c.; with whom God's people may lawfully converse and cohabit in cities, towns, &c., else must they not live in the world, but go out of it. In which world, as soon as ever the Lord Jesus had sown the good seed, the children of the kingdom, true Christianity, or the true Church, the enemy Satan presently . . . sowed also these tares, which are Antichristians or false Christians. These strange professors of the name of Jesus the ministers and prophets of God beholding, they are ready to run to heaven to fetch fiery judgments from thence to consume these strange Christians, and to pluck them by the roots out of the world. But the Son of Man, the meek Lamb of God—for the Elect's sake which must be gathered out of Jew and Gentile, pagan, Antichristian—commands a permission of them in the world, until the time of the end of the world, when the goats and sheep, the tares and wheat, shall be eternally separated each from other. * * *

Such, then, are the good seed, good wheat, children of the kingdom as are the disciples, members, and subjects of the Lord Jesus Christ, his Church and kingdom; and therefore, consequently, such are the tares as are opposite to these, idolaters, will-worshippers, not truly but falsely submitting to Jesus, and in especial, the children of the wicked one, visibly so appearing. * * *

Secondly, it is manifest that the Lord Jesus in this parable intends no other sort of sinners, of ᵃ whom he saith, *Let them alone*, in church or state; for then he should contradict other holy and blessed ordinances for the punishment of offenders, both in Christian and civil state.

First in civil state. From the beginning of the world, God hath armed fathers, masters, magistrates, to punish evil-doers; that is, such, of whose actions fathers, masters, magistrates are to judge, and accordingly to punish such sinners as transgress against the good and peace of their civil state, families, towns, cities, kingdoms —their states, governments, governors, laws, punishments, and weapons being all of a civil nature; and therefore neither disobedience to parents or magistrates, nor murder, nor quarrelling, uncleanness nor lasciviousness, stealing nor extortion, neither aught of that kind, ought to be let alone either in lesser or greater families, towns, cities, kingdoms (Rom. 13), but seasonably to be suppressed, as may best conduce to the public safety.

Again, secondly, in the kingdom of Christ Jesus, whose kingdom, officers, laws, punishments, weapons, are spiritual and of a soul nature, he will not have Antichristian idolaters, extortioners, covetous, &c., to be let alone; but the unclean and lepers to be thrust forth, the old leaven purged out, the obstinate in sin spiritually stoned to death, and put away from Israel; and this by many degrees of gentle admonition in private and public, as the case requires.

Therefore, if neither offenders against the civil laws, state, and peace ought to be let alone, nor the spiritual estate, the Church of Jesus Christ, ought to bear with them that are evil (Rev. 2. [2]), I conclude that these are sinners of another nature—idolaters, false worshippers, Antichristians, who without discouragement to true Christians must be let alone and permitted *in the world* to grow and fill up the measure of their sins, after the image of him that hath sown them, until the great harvest shall make the difference. * * *

Now if any imagine that the time or date is long, that in the mean season they may do a world of mischief before the world's end, as by infection, *&c.*; a first, I answer that as the civil state keeps itself with a civil guard, in case these tares shall attempt aught against the peace and welfare of it, let such civil offences be punished; and yet, as tares, opposite to Christ's kingdom, let their worship and consciences be tolerated. Secondly, the Church, or spiritual state, city or kingdom, hath laws and orders and armouries, . . . weapons and ammunition, able to break down the strongest holds (2 b Cor. 10. [4]), and so to defend itself against the very gates of earth or hell. Thirdly, the Lord himself knows who are his, and his foundation remaineth sure; his elect or chosen cannot perish nor be finally deceived.

Lastly, the Lord Jesus here, in this parable, lays down two reasons, able to content and satisfy our hearts to bear patiently this their contradiction and Antichristianity, and to permit or let them alone.

First, lest the good wheat be plucked up and rooted up also out of this field of the world. If such combustions and fightings were as to pluck up all the false professors of the name of Christ, the good wheat also would enjoy little peace, but be in danger to be plucked up and torn out of this world by such bloody storms and tempests. And, therefore, as God's people are commanded (Jer. 29. [7]) to pray for the peace of material Babel, wherein they were captivated, and (1 Tim. 2. [1, 2]) to pray for all men, and specially [for] kings and governors, that in the peace of the civil state they may have peace: so, contrary to the opinion and practice of most, drunk with the cup of the Whore's fornication, yea, and of God's own people fast asleep in Antichristian Delilah's lap, obedience to the command of Christ to let the tares alone will prove the only means to preserve their civil peace, and [a] without obedience to this command of Christ, it is impossible (without great transgression against the Lord in carnal policy, which will not long hold out) to preserve the civil peace. Beside, God's people, the good wheat, are generally plucked up and persecuted, as well as the vilest idolaters, whether Jews or Antichristians; which the Lord Jesus seems in this parable to foretell.

The second reason noted in the parable, which may satisfy any man from wondering at the patience of God, is this. When the world is ripe in sin, in the sins of Antichristianism (as the Lord spake of the sins of the Amorites, Gen. 15.[b] [16]), then those holy and mighty officers and executioners, the angels, with their sharp and cutting sickles of eternal vengeance, shall down with them, and bundle them up for the everlasting burnings. Then shall that man of sin (2 Thess. 2. [8]) be consumed by the breath of the mouth of the Lord Jesus; and all that worship the Beast and his picture, and receive his mark into their forehead or their hands, *shall drink of the wine of the wrath of God; which is poured out without mixture into the cup of his indignation, and he shall be tormented with fire and brimstone in the presence of the holy angels, and in the presence of the Lamb. And the smoke of their torment shall ascend up for ever and ever* (Rev. 14. 10, 11). * * *

I conceive this charge of the Lord Jesus to his messengers, the preachers and proclaimers of his mind, is a sufficient declaration of the mind of the Lord Jesus if any civil magistrate should make question what were his duty concerning spiritual things.

The Apostles, and in them all that succeed them, being commanded not to pluck up the tares, but let them alone, received from the Lord Jesus a threefold charge. First, to let them alone, and not to pluck them up by prayer to God for their present temporal destruction. * * * Secondly, God's messengers are herein commanded not to prophesy, or denounce, a present destruction or extirpation of all false professors of the name of Christ, which are whole towns, cities, and kingdoms full. * * * Thirdly, I conceive God's messengers are charged to let them alone, and not pluck them up by exciting and stirring up civil magistrates, kings, emperors, governors, parliaments, or general courts or assemblies, to punish and persecute all such persons out of their dominions and territories as worship not the true God according to the revealed will of God in Christ Jesus. * * * And therefore saith Paul expressly (1 Cor. 5. 10), we must go out of the world in case we may not company in civil converse with idolaters, *&c.* * * *

I shall conclude this controversy about this parable, in this brief sum and recapitulation of what hath been said.

I hope, by the evident demonstration of God's Spirit to the conscience, I have proved, negatively: . . . that the tares in this parable cannot signify doctrines or practices, as was affirmed, but persons; . . . the tares cannot signify hypocrites in the church, either undiscovered or discovered; . . . the tares here cannot signify scandalous offenders in the church, . . . nor scandalous offenders in life and conversation against the civil state; . . . the field in which these tares are sown is not the church.

Again, affirmatively: . . . The field is properly the world, the civil state or commonwealth; . . . the tares here intended by the Lord Jesus are Antichristian idolaters, opposite to the good seed of the kingdom, true Christians; . . . the ministers or messengers of the Lord Jesus ought to let them alone to live in the world, and neither seek by prayer or prophecy to pluck them up before the harvest; . . . this permission or suffering of them in the field of the world is not for hurt, but for common good, even for the good of the good wheat, the people of God. Lastly, the patience of God is that, that the patience of men ought to be exercised toward them; and yet notwithstanding, their doom is fearful at the harvest, even gathering, bundling, and everlasting burnings, by the mighty hand of the angels in the end of the world. * * *

[The Blind Pharisee, Matt. 15. 14] [a]

Truth: * * * Beside, let it be seriously considered by such as plead for present corporal punishment, as conceiving that such sinners though they break not civil peace, should not escape unpunished—I say, let it be considered, though for the present their punishment is deferred, yet the punishment inflicted on them will be found to amount to a higher pitch than any corporal punishment in the world beside. . . . First by just judgment from God, false teachers are stark blind. God's sword hath struck out the right eye of their mind and spiritual understanding, ten thousand times a greater punishment than if the magistrate should command both the right and left eye of their bodies to be bored or plucked out. . . . Secondly, how fearful is that wound that no balm in Gilead can cure! How dreadful is that blindness which for ever to all eye-salve is incurable! For if persons be wilfully and desperately obstinate, after light shining forth, Let them alone, saith the Lord. * * * Thirdly, their end is the

ditch, that bottomless pit of everlasting separation from the holy
and sweet presence of the Father of Lights, Goodness, and Mercy
itself—endless, easeless, in extremity, universality, and eternity
of torments. * * * Fourthly, of those that fall into this dreadful
ditch, both leader and followers, how deplorable in more especial
manner is the leader's case, upon whose neck the followers tumble
—the ruin not only of his own soul being horrible, but also the
ruin of the followers' souls eternally galling and tormenting.

Peace : Some will say, these things are indeed full of horror; yet
such is the state of all sinners, and of many malefactors, whom yet
the state is bound to punish; and sometimes by death itself.

Truth : I answer, the civil magistrate beareth not the sword in
vain, but to cut off civil offences, yea, and the offenders too in
case. But what is this to a blind Pharisee, resisting the doctrine
of Christ, who haply may be as good a subject, and as peaceable
and profitable to the civil state as any? And for his spiritual
offence against the Lord Jesus in denying him to be the true
Christ, he suffereth the vengeance of a dreadful judgment, both
present and eternal, as before.

Peace : Yea, but it is said that the blind Pharisees, misguiding
the subjects of a civil state, greatly sin against a civil state, and
therefore justly suffer civil punishment;.for shall the civil magistrate take care of outsides only, to wit, of the bodies of men, and
not of souls, in labouring to procure their everlasting welfare ?

Truth : I answer, it is a truth. The mischief of a blind Pharisee's
blind guidance is greater than if he acted treasons, murders, &c.;
and the loss of one soul by his seduction is a greater mischief
than if he blew up parliaments, and cut a the throats of kings or
emperors; so precious is that invaluable jewel of a soul above all
the present lives and bodies of all the men in the world! And
therefore I affirm that justice, calling for eye for eye, tooth for
tooth, life for life, calls also [for] soul for soul; which the blind-
guiding, seducing Pharisee shall surely pay in that dreadful ditch
which the Lord Jesus speaks of. But this sentence against him
the Lord Jesus only pronounceth in his Church, his spiritual
judicature, and executes this sentence in part at present, and
hereafter to all eternity. Such a sentence no civil judge can pass;
such a death no civil sword can inflict.

I answer, secondly, dead men cannot be infected. The civil
state, the world, being in a natural state, dead in sin (whatever
be the state-religion unto which persons are forced), it is impossible it should be infected. Indeed the living, the believing,
the Church and spiritual state, that and that only is capable of

infection; for whose help we shall presently see what preservatives and remedies the Lord Jesus hath appointed.

Moreover, as we see in a common plague or infection the names are taken how many are to die, and not one more shall be struck than the destroying angel hath the names of: so here, whatever be the soul-infection breathed out from the lying lips of a plague-sick Pharisee, yet the names are taken; not one elect or chosen of God shall perish. God's sheep are safe in his eternal hand and counsel, and he that knows his material, knows also his mystical stars, their numbers, and calls them every one by name. None fall into the ditch on the blind Pharisee's back but such as were ordained to that condemnation, both guide and followers (1 Pet. 2. 8; Jude 4). The vessels of wrath shall break and split, and only they—to the praise of God's eternal justice (Rom. 9. 22).* * *

[Romans 13. Examined] a

Peace : The next scripture produced against such persecution is 2 Cor. 10. 4: *The weapons of our warfare are not carnal, but mighty through God to the pulling down of strongholds; casting down imaginations, and every high thing that exalteth itself against the knowledge of God, and bringing into captivity every thought to the obedience of Christ.* * * *

Truth : I acknowledge that herein the spirit of God denieth not civil weapons of justice to the civil magistrate, which . . . Rom[ans] 13. abundantly testifie[s]. * * *

I . . . observe that there being in this scripture [2 Cor. 10. 4] held forth a twofold state, a civil state and a spiritual, civil officers and spiritual, civil weapons and spiritual weapons, civil vengeance and punishment and a spiritual vengeance and punishment— although the Spirit speaks not here expressly of civil magistrates and their civil weapons—yet, these states being of different natures and considerations, as far differing as spirit from flesh, I . . . observe that civil weapons are most improper and unfitting in matters of the spiritual state and kingdom, though in the civil state most proper and suitable. * * *

Peace : Now, in the second place, concerning that scripture (Rom[ans] 13.) . . . my humble request . . . is for your care . . . to enlighten and clear this scripture.

Truth : First, then, upon the serious examination of this whole scripture it will appear that from the ninth verse of the twelfth chapter to the end of this whole thirteenth chapter, the Spirit handles the duties of the Saints in the careful observation of the

Second Table in their civil conversation or walking towards men, and speaks not at all of any point or matter of the First Table concerning the kingdom of the Lord Jesus. For having in the whole Epistle handled that great point of free justification by the free grace of God in Christ, in the beginning of the twelfth chapter he exhorts the believers to give and dedicate themselves unto the Lord both in soul and body; and unto the ninth verse of the twelfth chapter he expressly mentioneth their conversation in the kingdom or body of Christ Jesus, together with the several officers thereof. And from the ninth verse to the end of the thirteenth [chapter], he plainly discourseth of their civil conversation and walking one toward another, and with all men, from whence he hath fair occasion to speak largely concerning their subjection to magistrates in the thirteenth chapter.

Hence it is that [at] verse 7 of this thirteenth chapter, Paul exhorts to performance of love to all men, magistrates and subjects . . . : *Render, therefore, to all their due; tribute to whom tribute is due; custom to whom custom; fear to whom fear; honour to whom honour.* * * *

The Spirit of God here commands subjection and obedience to higher powers, even to the Roman emperors and all subordinate magistrates; and yet the emperors and governors under them were strangers from the life of God in Christ, yea, most averse and opposite, yea, cruel and bloody persecutors of the name and followers of Jesus: and yet unto these is this subjection and obedience commanded. * * * Now then, I argue, if the Apostle should have commanded this subjection unto the Roman emperors and Roman magistrates in spiritual causes . . .: I say, if Paul should have, in this scripture, put this work upon these Roman governors and commanded the churches of Christ to have yielded subjection in any such matters, he must, in the judgment of all men, have put out the eye of faith and reason and sense, at once. * * *

I dispute from the nature of the magistrate's weapons (ver. 4). He hath a sword, which he bears not in vain, delivered to him, as I acknowledge, from God's appointment in the free consent and choice of the subjects for common good.

We must distinguish of swords. We find four sorts of swords mentioned in the New Testament: First, the sword of persecution . . .; secondly, the sword of God's Spirit, expressly said to be the word of God (Eph. 6. [17]), a sword of two edges . . . piercing . . . between the soul and the spirit (Heb. 4. [12]); thirdly, the great sword of war and destruction, given to him that rides that terrible red horse of war, so that he takes peace from the earth, and men kill one another, as is most lamentably true in the slaughter of so many hundred thousand souls within these few years in several parts of Europe, our own and others. None of these three swords are intended in this scripture. Therefore, fourthly, there is a civil sword, called the sword of civil justice, which being of a material, civil nature, for the defence of persons, estates, families, liberties of a city or civil state, and the suppressing of uncivil or injurious persons or actions by such civil punishment, it cannot, according to its utmost reach and capacity, now under Christ when all nations are merely civil, without any such typical, holy respect upon them as was upon Israel, a national church—I say, [it] cannot extend to spiritual and soul-causes, spiritual and soul-punishment, which belongs to that spiritual sword with two edges, the soul-piercing (in soul-saving, or soul-killing), the word of God. * * *

Lastly, that the Spirit of God never intended to direct or warrant the magistrate to use his power in spiritual affairs and religious worship, I argue from the term or title it pleaseth the wisdom of God to give such civil officers, to wit (ver. 6) *God's ministers*.

Now at the very first blush, no man denies a double ministry. The one appointed by Christ Jesus in his Church, to gather, to govern, receive in, cast out, and order all the affairs of the Church, the house, city, or kingdom of God (Eph. 4; 1 Cor. 12). Secondly, a civil ministry or office, merely human and civil, which men agree to constitute, called therefore a human creation (1 Pet. 2. [13]), and is as true and lawful in those nations, cities, kingdoms, &c., which never heard of the true God, nor his holy Son Jesus, as in any part of the world beside, where the name of Jesus is most taken up.

From all which premises, *viz.*, that the scope of the Spirit of God in this chapter is to handle the matters of the Second Table (having handled the matters of the First in the twelfth); since the magistrates of whom Paul wrote were natural, ungodly, persecuting, and yet lawful magistrates, and to be obeyed in all lawful civil things; since all magistrates are God's ministers, essentially civil, bounded to a civil work, with civil weapons or instruments, and paid or rewarded with civil rewards;—from all which, I say, I undeniably collect that this scripture is generally mistaken, and wrested from the scope of God's Spirit and the nature of the place, and cannot truly be alleged by any for the power of the civil magistrate to be exercised in spiritual and soul-matters. * * *

Peace: Against this, I know, many object, out of the fourth verse of this chapter, that the magistrate is to avenge or punish evil: from whence is gathered that heresy, false Christs, false churches, false ministries, false seals, being evil, ought to be punished civilly, &c.

Truth : I answer, that the word κακὸν is generally opposed to civil goodness or virtue in a commonwealth, and not to spiritual good or religion in the Church.

Secondly, I have proved from the scope of the place, that here is not intended evil against the spiritual or Christian estate handled in the twelfth chapter, but evil against the civil state in this thirteenth, properly falling under the cognizance of the civil minister of God, the magistrate, and punishable by that civil sword of his, as an incivility, disorder, or breach of that civil order, peace, and civility, unto which all the inhabitants of a city, town, or kingdom, oblige themselves. * * *

['*Christ Jesus the deepest politician that ever was*'] [a]

Truth : * * * It is evil, saith he [Cotton], to tolerate notorious evil-doers, seducing teachers, scandalous livers. In which speech I observe two evils.

First, that this proposition is too large and general, because the rule admits of exception, and that according to the will of God. (1) It is true that evil cannot alter its nature but it is alway evil, as darkness is alway darkness; yet (2) it must be remembered that it is one thing to command, to conceal, to counsel, to approve evil, and another thing to permit and suffer evil with protestation against it or dislike of it—at least without approbation of it. Lastly, this sufferance or permission of evil is not for its own sake, but for the sake of good, which puts a respect of goodness upon such permission.

Hence it is that for God's own glory's sake, which is the·highest good, he endures (that is, permits or suffers) the vessels of wrath (Rom. 9. [22]). And therefore, although he be of pure eyes and can behold no iniquity, yet his pure eye [b] patiently and quietly beholds and permits all the idolatries and profanations, all the thefts and rapines, all the whoredoms and abominations, all the murders and poisonings; and yet, I say, for his glory's sake he is patient and long permits.

Hence for his people's sake (which is the next good, in his Son), he is oftentimes pleased to permit and suffer the wicked to enjoy a longer reprieve. * * *

Peace : It may be said, this is no pattern for us, because God is above law, and an absolute sovereign.

Truth : I answer, although we find him sometime dispensing with his law, yet we never find him deny himself, or utter a falsehood. And therefore, when it crosseth not an absolute rule, to permit and tolerate—as in the case of the permission of the souls and consciences of all men in the world, I have shown, and shall show further, it doth not—it will not hinder our being holy as he is holy, in all manner of conversation. * * *

This ground, to wit, for a common good of the whole, is the same with that of the Lord Jesus' commanding the tares to be permitted in the world because, otherwise, the good wheat should be endangered to be rooted up out of the field or world also, as well as the tares. And therefore, for the good' sake, the tares, which are indeed evil, were to be permitted: yea, and for the general good of the whole world, the field itself, which, for want of this obedience to that command of Christ, hath been and is laid waste and desolate with the fury and rage of civil war, professedly raised and maintained, as all states profess, for the maintenance of one true religion—after the pattern of that typical land of Canaan—and to suppress and pluck up these tares of false prophets and false professors, Antichristians, heretics, &c., out of the world.

Hence *illae lachrymae*: hence Germany's, Ireland's, and now England's tears and dreadful desolations, which ought to have been, and may be for the future, by obedience to the command of the Lord Jesus concerning the permission of tares to live in the world, though not in the Church—I say, ought to have been, and may be, mercifully prevented.

Peace : I pray descend now to the second evil which you observe in the answerer's position, *viz.*, that it would be evil to tolerate notorious evil-doers, seducing teachers, &c.

Truth : I say, the evil is that he most improperly and confusedly joins and couples seducing teachers with scandalous livers. * * *

First, it is not an homogeneal (as we speak), but an heterogeneal commixture or joining together of things most different in kinds and natures, as if they were both of one consideration. For who knows not but that many seducing teachers, either of the paganish, Jewish, Turkish, or Antichristian religion, may be clear and free from scandalous offences in their life, as also from disobedience to the civil laws of a state? * * * Again, who knows not that a seducing teacher properly sins against a church or spiritual estate and laws of it, and therefore ought most properly and only to be dealt withal in such a way, and by such weapons, as the Lord Jesus himself hath appointed; gainsayers, opposites, and disobedients

—either within his Church or without—to be convinced, repelled, resisted, and slain withal? Whereas scandalous offence [a] against parents, against magistrates in the Fifth Command[ment], and so against the life, chastity, goods, or good name in the rest, is properly transgression against the civil state and commonweal, or the worldly state of men. And therefore, consequently, if the world or civil state ought to be preserved by civil government or governors, such scandalous offenders ought not to be tolerated, but suppressed according to the wisdom and prudence of the said government.

Secondly, as there is a fallacious conjoining and confounding together persons of several kinds and natures, differing as much as spirit and flesh, heaven and earth, each from other: so is there a silent and implicit justification to all the unrighteous and cruel proceedings of Jews and Gentiles against all the prophets of God, the Lord Jesus himself, and all his messengers and witnesses, whom their accusers have ever so coupled and mixed with notorious evil-doers and scandalous livers. * * *

Peace : Yea, but he produceth scriptures against such toleration, and for persecuting men for the cause of conscience: 'Christ,' saith he, 'had something against the angel of the church of Pergamos, for tolerating them that held the doctrine of Balaam, and against the church of Thyatira, for tolerating Jezebel to teach and seduce (Rev. 2. 14, 20).'

Truth : * * * From this perverse wresting of what is writ to the church and the officers thereof, as if it were written to the civil state and officers thereof, all may see how, since the apostasy of Antichrist, the Christian world (so-called) hath swallowed up Christianity; how the church and civil state, that is, the Church and the world, are now become one flock of Jesus Christ. Christ's sheep, and the pastors or shepherds of them, all one with the several unconverted, wild, or tame beasts and cattle of the world, and the civil and earthly governors of them: the Christian Church, or kingdom of the Saints, that stone cut out of the mountain without hands (Dan. 2. [45]) now made all one with the mountain or civil state, the Roman empire, from whence it is cut or taken; Christ's lilies, garden, and love, all one with the thorns, the daughters and wilderness of the world, out of which the spouse or church of Christ is called—and amongst whom in civil things, for a while here below, she must necessarily be mingled and have converse, unless she will go out of the world before Christ Jesus, her Lord and husband, send for her home into the heavens (1 Cor. 5. 10). * * *

I affirm that the state-policy and state-necessity, which, for the peace of the state and preventing of rivers of civil blood, permits the consciences of men, will be found to agree most punctually with the rules of the best politician that ever the world saw, the King of kings, the Lord of lords, in comparison of whom Solomon himself had but a drop of wisdom compared to Christ's ocean, and was but a farthing candle compared with the all- and ever-glorious Sun of Righteousness. That absolute rule of this great politician for the peace of the field which is the world, and for the good and peace of the Saints who must have a civil being in the world, I have discoursed of in his command of permitting the tares, that is, Antichristians, or false Christians, to be in the field of the world, growing up together with the true wheat, true Christians. * * *

[*Toleration for Roman Catholics*] a

Peace: 'As for the testimony of the popish book,' saith he [Cotton], 'we weigh it not, as knowing whatever they speak for toleration of religion where themselves are under hatches, when they come to sit at stern they judge and practise quite contrary, as both their writings and judicial proceedings have testified to the world these many years.'

Truth: I answer, although both writings and practices have been such, yet the scriptures and expressions of truth alleged and uttered by them, speak loud and fully for them when they are under the hatches, that for their conscience and religion they should not there be choked and smothered, but suffered to breathe and walk upon the decks, in the air of civil liberty and conversation in the ship of the commonwealth, upon good assurance given of civil obedience to the civil state.

Again, if this practice be so abominable in his eyes from the papists, *viz.*, that they are so partial as to persecute when they sit at helm, and yet cry out against persecution when they are under the hatches, I shall beseech the Righteous Judge of the whole world to present, as in a water or glass where face answereth to face, the faces of the Papist to the Protestant, answering to each other in the sameness of partiality, both of this doctrine and practice. When Mr. Cotton and others have formerly been under hatches, what sad and true complaints have they abundantly poured forth against persecution! How have they opened that heavenly scripture (Cant. 4. 8) where Christ Jesus calls his tender wife and spouse from the fellowship with persecutors in their dens of lions and mountains of leopards! But coming to the helm, as he speaks of the papists, how, both by preaching, writing, printing, practice, do they themselves—I hope in their persons lambs—unnaturally and partially express towards others the cruel nature of such lions and leopards! Oh that the God of Heaven might please to tell them how abominable in his eyes are a weight and a weight, a stone and a stone, in the bag of weights—one weight for themselves when they are under hatches, and another for others when they come to helm! Nor shall their confidence of their being in the truth, which they judge the papists and others are not in—no, nor the truth itself—privilege them to persecute others, and to exempt themselves from persecution. * * *

['*A Model of Church and Civil Power*' *Examined*]

[I] ª *Truth:* . . . I observe that although the kingdom of Christ, the Church, and the civil kingdom or government be not inconsistent, but that both may stand together; yet that they are independent according to that scripture [*My kingdom is not of this world* (John 18. 36)]; and that therefore there may be, as formerly I have proved, flourishing commonweals and societies of men where no church of Christ abideth. And secondly, the commonweal may be in perfect peace and quiet, notwithstanding the Church, the commonweal of Christ, be in distractions and spiritual oppositions, both against their religions and sometimes amongst themselves (as the church of Christ in Corinth, troubled with divisions, contentions, &c.).

Secondly, I observe, it is true, the Church helpeth forward the prosperity of the commonweal by spiritual means (Jer. 29. 7). The prayers of God's people procure the peace of the city where they abide; yet that Christ's ordinances and administrations of worship are appointed and given by Christ to any civil state, town, or city, as is implied by the instance of Geneva, *that* I confidently deny.

The ordinances and discipline of Christ Jesus, though wrongfully and profanely applied to natural and unregenerate men, may cast a blush of civility and morality upon them, as in Geneva and other places—for the shining brightness of the very shadow of Christ's ordinances casts a shame upon barbarism and incivility —yet withal I affirm that the misapplication of ordinances to unregenerate and unrepentant persons hardens up their souls in a dreadful sleep and dream of their own blessed estate and sends millions of souls to hell in a secure expectation of a false salvation. * * *

[II] ª *Truth :* * * * If the powers of the world or civil state are bound to propose *external peace in all godliness* for their end, and the end of the Church be to preserve *internal peace in all godliness,* I demand, if their end (godliness) be the same, is not their power and state the same also; unless they make the Church subordinate to the commonwealth's end, or the commonweal subordinate to the Church's end, which—being the governor and setter-up of it, and so consequently the judge of it—it cannot be? * * *

I ask further, what is this internal peace in all godliness? Whether intend they internal, within the soul, which only the eye of God can see, opposed to external or visible, which man also can discern? Or else, whether they mean internal, that is spiritual soul-matters, matters of God's worship? And then I say, *that* peace, to wit, of godliness or God's worship, they had before granted to the civil state.

Peace : The truth is, as I now perceive, the best and most godly of that judgment declare themselves never to have seen a true difference between the Church and the world, and the spiritual and civil state; and howsoever these worthy authors seem to make a kind of separation from the world, and profess that the Church must consist of spiritual and living stones, Saints, regenerate persons, and so make some peculiar enclosed ordinances, as the Supper of the Lord, which none, say they, but godly persons must taste of; yet by compelling all within their jurisdiction to an outward conformity of the church worship, of the word and prayer, and maintenance of the ministry thereof, they evidently declare that they still lodge and dwell in the confused mixtures of the unclean and clean, of the flock of Christ and herds of the world together—I mean, in spiritual and religious worship. * * *

Truth : I confess that without godliness, or a true worshipping of God with an upright heart according to God's ordinances, neither subjects nor magistrates can please God in Christ Jesus, and so be spiritually or Christianly good. Which, few magistrates and few men either come to, or are ordained unto, God having chosen a little flock out of the world, and those generally poor and mean (1 Cor. 1. [26]; James 2. [5]).

Yet this I must remember you of: that when the most high God created all things of nothing, he saw and acknowledged divers sorts of goodness, which must still be acknowledged in their distinct kinds—a good air, a good ground, a good tree, a good sheep, *&c.* I say the same in artificials, a good garment, a good house, a good sword, a good ship.   I also add, a good city, a good company or corporation, a good husband, father, master.   Hence also we say, a good physician, a good lawyer, a good seaman, a good merchant, a good pilot for such or such a shore or harbour; that is, morally, civilly, good in their several civil respects and employments.

Hence (Psalm 122 [a]) the Church, or city of God, is compared to a city compact within itself; which compactness may be found in many towns and cities of the world where yet hath not shined any spiritual or supernatural goodness.   Hence the Lord Jesus (Matt. 12 [25]) describes an ill state of an house or kingdom, *viz.*, to be divided against itself, which cannot stand.

These I observe to prove that a subject, a magistrate, may be a good subject, a good magistrate, in respect of civil or moral goodness (which thousands want, and where it is it is commendable and beautiful), though godliness, which is more beautiful, be wanting, and which is only proper to the Christian state, the commonweal of Israel, the true Church, the holy nation (Eph. 2; 1 Pet. 2). * * *

[III] [b] *Truth:* * * * Whereas they say that the civil power may erect and establish what form of civil government may seem in wisdom most meet, I acknowledge the proposition to be most true, both in itself, and also considered with the end of it, that a civil government is an ordinance of God to conserve the civil peace of people so far as concerns their bodies and goods, as formerly hath been said.

But from this grant I infer, as before hath been touched, that the sovereign original and foundation of civil power lies in the people, whom they must needs mean by the civil power distinct from the government set up.   And if so, that a people may erect and establish what form of government seems to them most meet for their civil condition.   It is evident that such governments as are by them erected and established, have no more power, nor for no longer time, than the civil power, or people consenting and agreeing, shall betrust them with.   This is clear not only in reason, but in the experience of all commonweals where the people are not deprived of their natural freedom by the power of tyrants.

And if so—that the magistrates receive their power of governing the Church from the people—undeniably it follows that a people as a people, naturally considered—of what nature or nation soever, in Europe, Asia, Africa, or America—have fundamentally and originally as men, a power to govern the Church, to see her do her duty, to correct her, to redress, reform, establish, *&c.*   And if

this be not to pull God and Christ and Spirit out of heaven, and
subject them unto natural, sinful, inconstant men, and so consequently to Satan himself, by whom all peoples naturally are
guided, let heaven and earth judge!

Peace: It cannot, by their own grant, be denied but that the
wildest Indians in America ought (and in their kind and several
degrees do) to agree upon some forms of government, some more
civil compact in towns, &c., some less; as also, that their civil
and earthly governments be as lawful and true as any governments
in the world. And therefore, consequently, their governors are
keepers of the Church, or both Tables, if any church of Christ
should arise or be amongst them. And therefore, lastly, if Christ
have betrusted and charged the civil power with his Church, they
must judge according to their Indian or American consciences,
for other consciences it cannot be supposed they should have.

Truth: Again, whereas they say that outward civil peace cannot
stand where religion is corrupted (and quote for it 2 Chron. 15.
3, 5, 6; and Judges 8), I answer with admiration how such excellent spirits as these authors are furnished with, not only in heavenly but earthly affairs, should so forget and be so fast asleep in
things so palpably evident, as to say that outward civil peace cannot
stand where religion is corrupt, when so many stately kingdoms
and governments in the world have long and long enjoyed civil
peace and quiet, notwithstanding their religion is so corrupt as
that there is not the very name of Jesus Christ amongst them.
And this every historian, merchant, traveller in Europe, Asia,
Africa, America, can testify. For so spake the Lord Jesus himself
(John 16. [20]): *The world shall sing and rejoice.*

Secondly, for that scripture, 2 Chron. 15. 3, &c., relating the
miseries of Israel and Judah, and God's plagues upon that people
for corruption of their religion, it must still have reference to that
peculiar state unto which God called the seed of one man, Abraham, in a figure, dealing so with them as he dealt not with any
nation in the world (Psalm 147 [a]; Rom. 9). The antitype to this
state I have proved to be the Christian Church, which consequently
hath been and is afflicted with spiritual plagues, desolations, and
captivities, for corrupting of that religion which hath been revealed
unto them. This appears by the seven churches, and [by] the
people of God, now so many hundred years in woeful bondage
and slavery to the mystical Babel, until the time of their joyful
deliverance. * * *

[IV] [b] *Peace:* Their fifth head is concerning the magistrates'
power in making of laws.

'First, they have power to publish and apply such civil laws in a state as either are expressed in the word of God in Moses' judicials—to wit, so far as they are of general and moral equity, and so binding all nations in all ages—[or are] to be deduced ᵃ by way of general consequence and proportion from the word of God. For in a free state no magistrate hath power over the bodies, goods, lands, liberties of a free people but by their free consents. And because free men are not free lords of their own estates, but are only stewards under God, therefore they may not give their free consents to any magistrate to dispose of their bodies, goods, lands, liberties at large, as themselves please, but as God, the sovereign Lord of all, alone. And because the Word is a perfect rule, as well of righteousness as of holiness, it will be therefore necessary that neither the people give consent nor that the magistrate take power to dispose of the bodies, goods, lands, liberties of the people, but according to the laws and rules of the word of God.

'Secondly, in making laws about civil and indifferent things about the commonweal: first, he hath no power given him of God to make what laws he please, either in restraining from or constraining to the use of indifferent things; because that which is indifferent in its nature, may sometimes be inexpedient in its use, and consequently unlawful (1 Cor. 2. 5), it having been long since defended upon good ground, *Quicquid non expedit, quatenus non expedit, non licet.* Secondly, he hath no power to make any such laws about indifferent things wherein nothing good or evil is shown to the people, but only or principally the mere authority or will of the imposer, for the observance of them (Col. 2. 21, 22; 1 Cor. 7. 23, compared with Eph. 6. 6).

'It is a prerogative proper to God, to require obedience of the sons of men because of his authority and will. The will of no man is *regula recti*, unless first it be *regula recta*. It is an evil speech of some, that in some things the will of the law, not the *ratio* of it, must be the rule of conscience to walk by; and that princes may forbid men to seek any other reason but their authority, yea, when they command *frivola et dura*. And therefore it is the duty of the magistrate, in all laws about indifferent things, to show the reasons, not only the will; to show the expediency as well as the indifferency of things of that nature. For, we conceive, in laws of this nature it is not the will of the lawgiver only, but the reason of the law, which binds. *Ratio est rex legis, et lex est rex regis.* ✶ ✶ ✶'

Truth: In this passage these worthy men lay down such a ground as the gates of hell are not able to shake, concerning the magistrates' walking in indifferent things; and upon which ground that tower of Lebanon may be raised, whereon there hang a thousand shields and bucklers (Cant. 4. [4]), to wit, that invincible truth, that no man is to be persecuted for cause of conscience. The ground is this: 'The magistrate hath not power to make what laws he please, either in restraining [from] or constraining to the use of indifferent things.' * * *

Hence I argue, if the civil magistrate have no power to restrain or constrain his [a] subjects in things in their own nature indifferent, as in eating of meats, wearing this or that garment, using this or that gesture, but that they are bound to try and examine his commands, and satisfy their own reason, conscience, and judgment before the Lord, and that they shall sin if they follow the magistrate's command, not being persuaded in their own soul and conscience that his commands are according to God: it will be much more unlawful and heinous in the magistrate to compel the subjects unto that which according to their consciences' persuasion is simply unlawful, as unto a falsely constituted church, ministry, worship, administration, and they shall not escape the ditch by being led blindfold by the magistrate. * * *

[V] [b] *Truth* [in the course of proving in great detail that Israel is merely a prophetic type of the Christian Church, and not a model for the Christian state, explains that 'the dispute lies not concerning the monarchical power of the Lord Jesus ... but concerning a deputed and ministerial power,' and proceeds]: There are three great competitors for this deputed or ministerial power of the Lord Jesus.

First, the arch-vicar of [c] Satan, the pretended vicar of Christ on earth, who sits as God over the temple of God, exalting himself not only above all that is called God, but over the souls and consciences of all his vassals. * * *

The second great competitor to this crown of the Lord Jesus is the civil magistrate, whether emperors, kings, or other inferior officers of state, who are made to believe by the false prophets of the world that they are the antitypes of the kings of Israel and Judah, and wear the crown of Christ.

Under the wing of the civil magistrate do three great factions shelter themselves, and mutually oppose each other, striving as for life who shall sit down under the shadow of that arm of flesh.

First, the Prelacy: who, though some extravagants of late have inclined to waive the king, and to creep under the wings of the pope, yet so far depends upon the king that it is justly said they are the king's bishops.

Secondly, the Presbytery: who, though in truth they ascribe not so much to the civil magistrate as some too grossly do, yet they give so much to the civil magistrate as to make him absolutely the head of the church. For if they make him the reformer of the church, the suppressor of schismatics and heretics, the protector and defender of the church, &c., what is this in true plain English but to make him the judge of the true and false church, judge of what is truth and what error, who is schismatical, who heretical? Unless they make him only an executioner, as the pope doth in his punishing of heretics.

I doubt not but the aristocratical government of Presbyterians may well subsist in a monarchy, not only regulated but also tyrannical; yet doth it more naturally delight in the element of an aristocratical government of state, and so may properly be said to be (as the prelates the king's, so these) the state's bishops.

The third (though not so great, yet growing) faction is that so-called Independent. (I prejudice not the personal worth of any of the three sorts.) This latter, as I believe this discourse hath manifested, jumps with the Prelates, and, though not more fully, yet more explicitly than the Presbyterians, cast[s] down the crown of the Lord Jesus at the feet of the civil magistrate. And although they pretend to receive their ministry from the choice of two or three private persons in church-covenant, yet would they fain persuade the mother,[a] Old England, to imitate her daughter New England's practice, viz. to keep out the Presbyterians, and only to embrace themselves both as the state's and the people's bishops.

The third competition for this crown and power of the Lord Jesus is of those that separate both from one and the other, yet divided also amongst themselves into many several professions. Of these, they that go furthest profess they must yet come nearer to the ways of the Son of God. And doubtless so far as they have gone, they bid the most and make the fairest plea for the purity and power of Christ Jesus—let the rest of the inhabitants of the world be judges. Let all the former well be viewed in their external state, pomp, riches, conformity to the world, &c. And on the other side, let the latter be considered in their more thorough departure from sin and sinful worship, their condescending (generally) to the lowest and meanest contentments of this life, their exposing of themselves for Christ to greater sufferings, and their desiring no civil sword nor arm of flesh, but the two-edged sword of God's Spirit to try out the matter by. And then let the inhabitants of the world judge which come nearest to the doctrine, holiness, poverty, patience, and practice of the Lord Jesus Christ; and whether or no these latter deserve not so much of humanity and the subjects' liberty, as (not offending the civil state) in the freedom of their souls to enjoy the common air to breathe in. * * *

But to your last proposition, whether the kings of Israel and Judah were not types of civil magistrates? Now I suppose by what hath been already spoken, these things will be evident.

First, that those former types of the land, of the people, of their worships, were types and figures of a spiritual land, spiritual people and spiritual worship under Christ. Therefore consequently their saviours, redeemers, deliverers, judges, kings, must also have their spiritual antitypes, and so consequently [be] not civil but spiritual governors and rulers, lest the very essential nature of types, figures and shadows be overthrown.

Secondly, although the magistrate by a civil sword might well compel that national church, to the external exercise of their national a worship; yet it is not possible, according to the rule of the New Testament, to compel whole nations to true repentance and regeneration, without which (so far as may be discerned true) the worship and holy name of God is profaned and blasphemed. An arm of flesh and sword of steel cannot reach to cut the darkness of the mind, the hardness and unbelief of the heart, and kindly operate upon the soul's affections to forsake a long-continued father's worship, and to embrace a new, though the best and truest. This work performs alone that sword out of the mouth of Christ, with two edges (Rev. 1; and 3).

Thirdly, we have not one tittle in the New Testament of Christ Jesus, concerning such a parallel, neither from himself nor from his ministers with whom he conversed forty days after his resurrection, instructing them in the matters of his kingdom (Acts 1. [3]). Neither find we any such commission or direction given to the civil magistrate to this purpose, nor to the Saints for their submission in matters spiritual, but the contrary (Acts 4; and 5; 1 Cor. 7. 23; Col. 2. 18).

Fourthly, we have formerly viewed the very matter and essence of a civil magistrate, and find it the same in all parts of the world, wherever people live upon the face of the earth, agreeing together in towns, cities, provinces, kingdoms—I say the same, essentially civil, both from (1) the rise and fountain whence it springs, to wit, the people's choice and free consent, [and] (2) the object of it, viz., the common weal or safety of such a people in their bodies and goods, as the authors of this model have themselves confessed. This civil nature of the magistrate we have proved to receive no addition of power from the magistrate being a Christian, no more than it receives diminution from his not being a Christian, even as the commonweal is a true commonweal although it have not heard of Christianity; and Christianity professed in it, as in Pergamos, Ephesus, &c., makes it ne'er the [a] more a commonweal; and Christianity taken away, and the candlestick removed, makes it ne'er the less a commonweal.

Fifthly, the Spirit of God expressly relates the work of the civil magistrate under the Gospel (Rom. 13), expressly mentioning as the magistrates' object, the duties of the Second Table concerning the bodies and goods of the subject. * * *

Sixthly, since the civil magistrate[s], whether kings or parliaments, states and governors, can receive no more in justice than what the people give, and are therefore but the eyes and hands and instruments of the people, simply considered, without respect to this or that religion, it must inevitably follow, as formerly I have touched, that if magistrates have received their power from the people, then the greatest number of the people of every land have received from Christ Jesus a power to establish, correct, reform his Saints and servants, his wife and spouse, the Church. And she that, by the express word of the Lord (Psalm 149. [8]), binds kings in chains and nobles in links of iron, must herself be subject to the changeable pleasures of the people of the world, which lies in wickedness (1 John 5. [19]), even in matters of heavenly and spiritual nature. Hence, therefore, in all controversies concerning the church, ministry and worship, the last appeal must come to the bar of the people or commonweal, where all may personally meet, as in some commonweals of small number, or in greater, by their representatives. Hence, then, no person esteemed a believer, and added to the church; no officer chosen and ordained; no person cast forth and excommunicated: but as the commonweal and people please. And in conclusion, no Church of Christ in this land or world, and consequently no visible Christ the head of it; yea, yet higher, consequently no God in the world worshipped according to the institutions of Christ Jesus: except the several peoples of the nations of the world shall give allowance. * * *

I may, therefore, here seasonably add a seventh, which is a necessary consequence of all the former arguments, and an argument itself: viz., we find expressly a spiritual power of Christ Jesus in the hands of his Saints, ministers, and churches, to be the true antitype of those former figures in all the prophecies concerning Christ his spiritual power (Isa. 9; Dan. 7; Mic. 4; &c.,

compared with Luke 1. 32; Acts 2. 30; 1 Cor. 5; Matt. 18; Mark 13. 34, &c.) * * *

Secondly, concerning the laws themselves: it is true the Second Table contains the law of nature, the law moral and civil; yet such a law was also given to this people as never to any people in the world. Such was the law of worship (Psalm 147) peculiarly given to Jacob, and God did not deal so with other nations; which laws for the matter of the worship . . . were never to be paralleled by any other nation, but only by the true Christian Israel established by Jesus Christ amongst Jews and Gentiles throughout the world.

Thirdly, the law of the ten words (Deut. 10), the epitome of all the rest, it pleased the most high God to frame and pen twice with his own most holy and dreadful finger, upon Mount Sinai, which he never did to any other nation before or since, but only to that spiritual Israel, the people and the Church of God, in whose hearts of flesh he writes his laws, according to Jer. 31; Heb. 8 and 10.* * *

In the fifth place, consider we the punishments and rewards annexed to the breach or observation of these laws.

First, those which were of a temporal and present consideration, of this life: blessings and curses of all sorts, opened at large (Lev. 26; and Deut. 28), which cannot possibly be made good in any state, country, or kingdom, but in a spiritual sense in the Church and kingdom of Christ. The reason is this. Such a temporal prosperity of outward peace and plenty of all things, of increase of children, of cattle, of honour, of health, of success, of victory, suits not temporally with the afflicted and persecuted estate of God's people now; and therefore spiritual and soul-blessedness must be the antitype: . . . in the midst of revilings and all manner of evil speeches for Christ's sake, soul-blessedness, in the midst of afflictions and persecutions, soul-blessedness (Matt. 5; and Luke 6); and yet herein the Israel of God should enjoy their spiritual peace (Gal. 6. 16).

Out of that blessed temporal estate to be cast or carried captive, was their excommunication or casting out of God's sight (2 Kings 17. 23). Therefore was the blasphemer, the false prophet, the idolater, to be cast out or cut off from this holy land; which punishment cannot be paralleled by the punishment of any state or kingdom in the world, but only by the excommunicating or out-casting of person or church from the fellowship of the Saints and churches of Christ Jesus in the Gospel. And therefore, as before I have noted, the putting away of the false prophet by stoning him to death (Deut. 13) is fitly answered, and that in the very same words, in the antitype: when, by the general consent or stoning of the whole assembly, any wicked person is put away from amongst them; that is, spiritually cut off out of the land of the spiritually living, the people or Church of God (1 Cor. 5; Gal. 5).

Lastly, the great and high reward or punishment of the keeping or breach of these laws to Israel, was such as cannot suit with any state or kingdom in the world beside. The reward of the observation was life, eternal life; the breach of any one of these laws was death, eternal death, or damnation from the presence of the Lord (so Rom. 10; James 2). Such a covenant God made not before nor since with any state or people in the world. For *Christ is the end of the Law for righteousness to every one that believeth* (Rom. 10. 4). And *he that believeth in that Son of God, hath eternal life; he that believeth not hath not life, but is condemned already* (John 3; and 1 John 5). * * *

What state, what kingdom, what wars and combats, victories and deliverances, can parallel this people but the spiritual and mystical Israel of God in every nation and country of the world, typed out by that small typical handful in that little spot of ground, the land of Canaan? The Israel of God now, men and women, fight under the great Lord-General, the Lord Jesus Christ: their weapons, armour, and artillery are [a] like themselves, spiritual, set forth from top to toe (Eph. 6), so mighty and so potent that they break down the strongest holds and castles, yea in the very souls of men, and carry into captivity the very thoughts of men, subjecting them to Christ Jesus. * * *

This glorious army of white troopers, horses and harness—Christ Jesus and his true Israel [b]—gloriously conquer and overcome the Beast, the false prophet, and the kings of the earth, up in arms against them (Rev. 19). And lastly, reigning with Christ a thousand years, they conquer the devil himself, and the numberless armies, like the sand on the sea-shore, of Gog and Magog. And yet not a tittle of mention of any sword, helmet, breastplate, shield, or horse, but what is spiritual and of a heavenly nature. All which wars of Israel have been, may be, and shall be, fulfilled mystically and spiritually. * * *

I have in part, and might further discover that, from the king and his throne to the very beasts, . . . their civils, morals, and naturals were carried on in types. And however I acknowledge that what was simply moral, civil, and natural in Israel's state, in their constitutions, laws, punishments, may be imitated and followed by the states, countries, cities, and kingdoms of the world; yet who can question the lawfulness of other forms of government, laws and punishments, which differ—since civil constitutions are men's ordinances or creation (2 Pet. 2. 13), unto which God's people are commanded even for the Lord's sake to submit themselves, which if they were unlawful they ought not to do? * * *

I dare not assent to that assertion, that even original sin remotely hurts the civil state.   'Tis true some do, as inclinations to murder, theft, whoredom, slander, disobedience to parents and magistrates; but blindness of mind, hardness of heart, inclination to choose or worship this or that God, this or that Christ, beside the true, these hurt not remotely the civil state, as not concerning it, but the spiritual. * * *

But to wind up all. As it is most true that magistracy in general is of God (Rom. 13) for the preservation of mankind in civil order and peace—the world otherwise would be like the sea wherein men, like fishes, would hunt and devour each other, and the greater devour the less—so also it is true that magistracy in special, for the several kinds of it, is of man (1 Pet. 2. 13). Now what kind of magistrate soever the people shall agree to set up, whether he receive Christianity before he be set in office, or whether he receive Christianity after, he receives no more power of magistracy than a magistrate that hath received no Christianity. For neither of them both can receive more than the commonweal, the body of people and civil state, as men, communicate unto them and betrust with them. All lawful magistrates in the world, both before the coming of Christ Jesus and since, excepting those unparalleled typical magistrates of the church of Israel, are but derivatives and agents, immediately derived and employed as eyes and hands, serving for the good of the whole. Hence they have and can have no more power than fundamentally lies in the bodies or fountains themselves, which power, might or authority is not religious, Christian, &c., but natural, human, and civil. * * *

VII. MODELS OF A FREE CHURCH

THE POWER OF THE PEOPLE

From Thomas Goodwin and Philip Nye's Introduction to John Cotton's *The Keys of the Kingdom of Heaven* (1644) [a]

THE greatest commotions in kingdoms have for the most part been raised and maintained for and about power and liberties of the rulers and the ruled, together with the due bounds and limits of either. And the like hath fallen out in churches, and is continued to this day in the sharpest contentions (though now the seat of the war is changed) who should be the first adequate and complete subject of that church-power which Christ hath left on earth; how bounded, and to whom committed. This controversy is in a special manner the lot of these present times. And now that most parties (that can pretend anything towards it) have in several ages had their turns and vicissitudes of so long a possession of it, and their pleas for their several pretences have been so much and so long heard, it may well be hoped it is near determining, and that Christ will shortly settle this power upon the right heirs, to whom he primitively did bequeath it.

In those former darker times, this golden ball was thrown up by the clergy (so called) alone to run for among themselves. * * * This royal donation, bestowed by Christ upon his Church, was taken up and placed in so high thrones of bishops, popes, general councils, &c. . . . in so great a remoteness from the people that the least right or interest therein was not so much as suspected to belong to them. But . . . it hath now in these our days been brought so near unto the people, that they also have begun to plead and sue for a portion and legacy bequeathed them in it. The Saints (in these knowing times) finding that the key of knowledge hath so far opened their hearts that they see with their own eyes into the substantials of godliness, and that, through the instruction and guidance of their teachers, they are enabled to understand for themselves such other things as they are to join in the practice of, they do therefore further (many of them) begin more than to suspect that some share in the key of power should likewise appertain unto them.

It was the unhappiness of those who first in these latter times revived this plea of the people's right, to err on the other extreme (as it hath ever been the fate of truth when it first ariseth in the Church from under that long night of darkness which Antichristianism had brought upon the world, to have a long shadow of error to accompany it) by laying the plea and claim on their behalf unto the whole power, and that the elders set over them did but exercise that power for them which was properly theirs, and which Christ had (as they contended) radically and originally estated in the people only.

But after that all titles have been pleaded of those that are content with nothing but the whole, the final judgment and sentence may (possibly) fall to be a suitable and due-proportioned distribution and dispersion of this power into several interests, and the whole to neither part. In commonwealths it is a dispersion of several portions of power and rights into several hands, jointly to concur and agree in acts and process of weight and moment, which causeth that healthful κρᾶσις and constitution of them, which makes them lasting and preserves their peace, when none of all sorts find they are excluded; but as they have a share of concernment, so ᵃ a fit measure of power or privilege is left and betrusted to them. And accordingly the wisdom of the first constitutors of commonwealths is most seen in such a just balancing of power and privileges, and besides also in setting the exact limits of that which is committed unto each, yea, and is more admired by us in this than in their other laws. And in experience, a clear and distinct definement and confinement of all such parcels of power, both for the kind and extent of them, is judged to be as essentially necessary, if not more than whatever other statutes that set out the kinds and degrees of crimes or penalties.

So in that polity or government by which Christ would have his churches ordered, the right disposal of the power therein (we humbly suppose) may lie in a due and proportioned allotment and dispersion (though not in the same measure and degree) into divers hands, according unto the several concernments and interests that each rank in his Church may have rather than in an entire and sole trust committed to any one man, though never so able, or any one sort or kind of men or officers, although diversified into never so many subordinations under one another. And in like manner we cannot but imagine that Christ hath been as exact in setting forth the true bounds and limits of whatever portion of power he hath imparted unto any (if we of this age could attain rightly to discern it) as he hath been in ordering what kind of censures, and for what sins, and what degrees of proceedings unto these censures; which we find he hath been punctual in.

Now the scope which this grave and judicious author in this his

treatise doth pursue, is to lay forth the just lines and terriers of
this division of church-power, unto all the several subjects of it,
to the end to allay the contentions now on foot about it.   And in
general he lays this fundamental maxim that holds in common
true of all the particulars to whom any portion of power can be
supposed to be committed: that, look, whatever power or right
any of the possessors and subjects thereof may have, they have it
each alike immediately . . . from Christ, and so are each the first
subjects of that power that is allotted to them.   And for the
particular subjects themselves, he follows that division . . .
which the controversy itself hath made unto his hands; to wit:
(1) What power each single congregation (which is endowed with a
charter to be a body politic to Christ) hath granted to it to exercise
within itself; and (2) What measure, or rather kind, of power
Christ hath placed in neighbour-churches without it, and in
association with it.

. For the first: as he supposeth each congregation such as to have
the privilege of enjoying a presbytery or company of more or less
elders, proper unto itself, so . . . he asserteth this incorporate body
or society to be the first and primary subject of a complete and
entire power within itself over its own members, yea, and the sole
native subject of the power of ordination and excommunication
(which is the highest censure).   And whereas this corporation
consisteth both of elders and brethren (for as for women and
children, there is a special exception by a statute-law of Christ
against their enjoyment of any part of this public power), his scope
is to demonstrate a distinct and several share and interest of
power in matters of common concernment vouchsafed to each of
these, and dispersed among both, by charter from the Lord; as
in some of our towns corporate, to a company of aldermen (the
rulers) and a common council (a body of the people) there useth
to be the like.   He giving unto the elders or presbytery a binding
power of rule and authority, proper and peculiar unto them, and
unto the brethren, distinct and apart, an interest of power and
privilege to concur with them, and that such affairs should not
be transacted but with the joint agreement of both, though out of
a different right; so that as a church of brethren only could not
proceed to any public censures without they have elders over
them, so nor in the church have the elders power to censure
without the concurrence of the people; and likewise so as each
alone hath not power of excommunicating the whole of either,
though together they have power over any particular person or
persons in each.

And because these particular congregations, both elders and people, may disagree and miscarry, and abuse this power committed to them, he therefore, secondly, asserteth an association or communion of churches, sending their elders and messengers into a synod, . . . and acknowledgeth that it is an ordinance of Christ, unto whom Christ hath . . . committed a due and just measure of power . . . and furnished them not only with ability to give counsel and advice, but further . . . with a ministerial power and authority to determine, declare, and enjoin such things as may tend to the reducing such congregations to right order and peace. * * * And . . . for the extent of this power in such assemblies and association of churches, he limits and confines that also unto cases, and with cautions (which will appear in the discourse), to wit: that they should not entrench or impair the privilege of entire jurisdiction committed unto to each congregation (as a liberty purchased them by Christ's blood), but to leave them free to the exercise and use thereof until they abuse that power. . . .

As for ourselves, we are yet neither afraid nor ashamed to make profession (in the midst of all the high waves on both sides dashing on us) that the substance of this brief extract from the author's larger discourse is that very middle-way, which in our *Apology* [1] we did in the general intimate and intend, between that which is called Brownism and the Presbyterial government as it is practised; whereof the one doth in effect put the chief (if not the whole) of the rule and government into the hands of the people and drowns the elders' votes (who are but a few) in the major part of theirs, and the other, taking the chief and principal parts of that rule (which we conceive is the due of each congregation, the elders and brethren) into this jurisdiction of a common presbytery of several congregations, doth thereby in like manner swallow up not only the interests of the people, but even the votes of the elders of that congregation concerned in the major part thereof. * * *

Only we crave leave . . . to declare that we assent not to all expressions scattered up and down, or all and every assertion interwoven in it, yea, nor to all the grounds or allegations of scriptures; nor should we in all things perhaps have used the same terms to express the same materials by. For instance, we humbly conceive prophesying (as the scripture terms it) or speaking to the edification of the whole church, may sometimes be performed by brethren gifted, though not in office as elders of the church.* * *

We conceive the elders and brethren in each congregation,

[1] *An Apologetical Narration* (1644).

as they are usually in the New Testament thus mentioned distinctly apart, and this when their meeting together is spoken of, so they make in each congregation two distinct interests though meeting in one assembly (as the interest of the common council or body of the people, in some corporations, is distinct from that of the company of aldermen); so as without the consent and concurrence of both nothing is esteemed as a church act, but so as in this company of elders this power is properly authority, but in the people is a privilege or power. * * *

The like difference would appear if we had seen a government tempered of an aristocracy and democracy; in which, suppose the people have a share, and their actual consent is necessary to all laws and sentences, whereas a few nobles that are set over them (whose concernment is less general) in whom the formal sanction of all should lie, in these it were rule and authority, in that multitude but power and interest. * * *

And in this distribution of power, Christ hath had a suitable and due regard unto the estate and condition of his Church, as now under the New Testament he hath qualified and dignified it. Under the Old Testament it was in its infancy, but it is comparatively come forth of its nonage, and grown up to a riper age (both as the tenure of the Covenant of Grace, in difference from the old, runs in the Prophets, and as Paul to the Galatians expresseth it). They are therefore more generally able, if visible Saints (which is to be the subject-matter of churches under the New Testament) to join with their guides and leaders in judging and discerning what concerns their own and their brethren's consciences, and therefore Christ hath not now lodged the sole power of all church matters solely and entirely in the Church's tutors and governors, as of old, when it was under age, he did. But yet because of their weakness and unskilfulness (for the generality of them) in comparison to those whom he hath ascended to give gifts unto, on purpose for their guidance and the government of them, he hath therefore placed a rule and authority in those officers over them, not directing only, but binding; so as not only nothing in an ordinary way of church-government should be done without them, but not esteemed validly done unless done by them. And thus by means of this due and golden balancing and poising of power and interest, authority and privilege, in elders and the brethren, this government might neither degenerate into lordliness and oppression in rulers over the flock, as not having all power in their hands alone, nor yet into anarchy and confusion in the flock among themselves; and so as all things belonging to

men's consciences might be transacted to common edification
and satisfaction. * * *

Neither let it seem strange that the power of this censure, of
cutting men off and delivering them to Satan . . ., should be in-
separably linked by Christ unto a particular congregation, as the
proper native privilege hereof, so as that no assembly or company
of elders, justly presumed and granted to be more wise and judicious, should assume it to themselves or sever the formal power
thereof from the particular congregations.   For though it be hard
to give the reason of Christ's institutions, yet there is usually in
the ways of human wisdom and reason something analogous
thereunto, which may serve to illustrate, if not to justify, this
dispersion of interests.   And so (if we mistake not) there may be
found even of this in the wisdom of our ancestors, in the constitutions of this kingdom.   The sentencing to death of any subject in
the kingdom, as it is the highest civil punishment, so of all other
the nearest and exactest parallel to this in spirituals, of cutting a
soul off and delivering it to Satan; yet the power of this high
judgment is not put into the hands of an assembly of lawyers only,
no, not of all the judges themselves, men selected for wisdom,
faithfulness, and gravity, who yet are by office designed to have an
interest herein.   But when they upon any special cause of difficulty, for counsel and direction in such judgments do all meet
(as sometimes they do), yet they have not power to pronounce
this sentence of death upon any man without the concurrence of a
jury of his peers, which are of his own rank, and, in corporations,
of such as are inhabitants of the same place.   And with a jury of
these (men, of themselves, not supposed to be so skilful in the laws,
&c.), two judges, yea one . . . hath power to adjudge and pronounce that which all of them, and all the lawyers in this kingdom
together, have not, without a jury.   And we of this nation use to
admire the care and wisdom of our ancestors herein, and do esteem
this privilege of the subject in this particular (peculiar to our
nation) as one of the glories of our laws, and do make boast of it
as such a liberty and security to each person's life as (we think)
no nation about us can show the like.   And what should be the
reason of such a constitution but this (which in the beginning we
insisted on), the dispersion of power into several hands, which in
capital matters every man's trial should run through, whereof
the one should have the tie of like common interest to oblige them
unto faithfulness, as the other should have skill and wisdom to
guide them and direct the rein. * * *

The Church Covenant

From [Richard Mather], *An Apology for Church Covenant* (1643)[a]

The Church Covenant may be proved from the New Testament. . . . But suppose there were not pregnant places for it in the New Testament, yet it is not enough to prove the same unlawful. For whatsoever ordinance of the Old Testament is not repealed in the New Testament, as peculiar to the Jewish pedagogy, but was of moral and perpetual equity, the same binds us in these days, and is to be accounted the revealed will of God in all ages, though it be not particularly and expressly mentioned in the writings of the New Testament. Else . . . how shall we prove it warrantable and necessary for magistrates to punish sabbath-breaking, blasphemy, and idolatry? * * * For the scriptures of the New Testament do speak little in these cases; only the scriptures of the Old Testament do give direction and light about them . . ., and the New Testament hath nothing to the contrary, and they are all according to moral equity and reason, and therefore they are to be observed from the scriptures of the Old Testament as the revealed will of God, though there were nothing expressly for them in the New. And the same we say for the particular in hand. For that a company should be combined together into one body, in way of government and subjection, by way of mutual free covenant, as men do when they enter into church estate, nothing is more natural or agreeable to moral equity; nay, it implieth a contradiction in the very name of liberty or freedom that free men should take upon them authority or power over free men without their free consent and voluntary and mutual covenant or engagement. And therefore seeing this covenant is not repealed in the scriptures of the New Testament, the scriptures of the Old are sufficient warrant for it. * * *

We speak of voluntary relation; for there are natural relations, as between parents and children, and these need no covenant. There is no covenant to make a man a parent, or a child. There are also violent relations, as between conqueror and captives, and in these there is no covenant neither. But others are voluntary, and these always imply a covenant, and are founded therein, whether they be moral or civil, as between husband and wife (Prov. 2. 17); between master and servants (Luke 15. 15); between prince and subject; between partners in trade (2 Chron. 20. 35-7), where the covenant or agreement is that men shall bear such a share of charges, and receive such a share of profits; or religious, as between minister and people, between the church and the members. All these are done by way of covenant. * * * If men be united into a body politic or incorporate, a man cannot be said to be joined to them by mere hearty affection, unless withal he joins himself unto them by some contract or covenant. Now of this nature is every particular church, a body incorporate (1 Cor. 12. 27: *Ye are the body of Christ, &c.*), and hath power to cast-out (1 Cor. 5. 13), and to forgive and receive-in penitents (2 Cor. 7, 8), as a body incorporate; and therefore he that will join unto them must do it by way of covenant or agreement. * * * All voluntary relations, all relations which are neither natural nor violent, are entered into by way of covenant. * * *

Churches have no power over such as have not engaged themselves by covenant, and committed power unto them by professing to be subject to all the ordinances of Christ amongst them.

The truth whereof may appear by two reasons: First, because all Christians have power and right, *jure divino*, to choose their own officers to whom they commit their souls (Acts 6. 1; and 14. 23). * * * And as they have power to choose their officers, so likewise to choose their brethren according to God (Rom. 14. 1). Now if they have power to choose their officers and brethren, then none can have power over them as officers and brethren without their own consent, and whom they never chose, nor promised by any covenant or engagement to be subject to [in] the Lord.

Secondly, if the church should exercise any act of church-power over such a man as never entered into covenant with them (suppose to excommunicate him for whoredom or drunkenness, or the like) the man might protest against their act, and their sentence, as *coram non judice*, and they could not justify their proceedings if indeed there have passed no covenant or engagement between him and them. * * *

From *The Saints' Apology* (1644) [a]

First, I conceive a visible ministering church under the Gospel to be a company of believers, joining themselves together in the name of Christ, for the enjoyment of such ordinances, and exercise of such spiritual government, as the Lord hath appointed for his worship and honour, and their mutual edification. * * *

I add 'under the Gospel' because the constitution under the Law was national, the officers, ordinances and places of worship, all fitted to such a frame, and typical; which under the Gospel was changed, as appeareth both by Christ's institution (Matt. 18) and all the Apostles' practice throughout in all places, who best understood our Saviour's intention and meaning for the constitution of churches evangelical, being by him instructed and left authorized there[in].

Secondly, the matter of this church is a company of Saints, such whom as the Apostle, so the church that admits them or joins with them, ought to think it meet to judge of every one of them that Christ hath begun a good work in them and will finish it. The Apostles always style them Saints and faithful brethren, or the church of such a place, which is in God the Father and in the Lord Jesus Christ, Saints by calling, sanctified in Christ Jesus, the church elected together with them, and such-like titles applyable only unto men sanctified. That they ought to be such in profession, will not be denied; that they ought to be what they profess, is as evident. The power of the church, and the exercise of that power commanded by our Saviour, is for this end, that offences may be taken away, when men shall appear to be other than they make profession to be, and that they may be prevented, so far as man can judge, by keeping out false brethren, that they creep not in privily. The unruly are to be admonished, and if upon admonition they will not reform, Christ directeth what course shall be taken with them. And he who is to be cast out when he is known, ought not to be admitted could he be known to be other than a Saint by the church before he was received.

Thirdly, the form of such a visible church, I conceive to be the relation which by their mutual consent is raised between them for spiritual ends, by which it is that they have power of jurisdiction and may and ought to judge those that are within (1 Cor. 5. 12).

Which jurisdiction no man can lawfully be subjected unto but by his own agreement. The superiority of jurisdiction either in things spiritual or temporal (if it be not natural as the paternal) must be voluntarily subjected unto, or it is usurped and tyrannical. Therefore to raise this relation which gives a power of judging, there must be a voluntary submission of themselves one to another testified by some act, whether you will call it a covenant, or consent, or agreement between fit members for such ends.

This consent and agreement ought to be explicit [f]or the *well-being*, but not necessarily to the *being*, of a true church. For it may be implied by such constant and frequent acts of communion performed by a company of Saints joined together by cohabitation in towns and villages, as that the falling in of their spirits into this brotherly fellowship and communion in things spiritual is acted unto the true being of it; but for the want of the clear and full expression thereof among themselves, the relation it raises, the power it gives them one over another, the duty it obligeth them unto in the exercise of that power, is obscurely and little apprehended, and less practised. * * *

A Spiritual Church

From William Dell, *The Way of True Peace and Unity* [1] [a]

Now, that he that reads may understand, it is necessary for me, speaking of the unity and peace of the Church, to tell you now, at first, that I intend not to propound any way of peace either between the Church and the world, or . . . between the carnal and spiritual children of the Church, as having learned no such thing out of the word of God.

First, not between the Church and the world: for the Lord never

---

[1] Dedicated to Fairfax, Cromwell, and the Council of War, who 'through the renewing of the . . . presence of God . . . after a manifest withdrawing of it, and . . . through a blessed necessity,' are 'now doing that work of God, which once' they 'had little mind to: . . . the procuring the peace of the kingdom by subduing the great enemies of peace, and removing all the enmity against peace that was enwrapped in our very laws and degenerated constitution . . .': 'And now here . . . shall you see a better peace and agreement than you are striving for . . ., of which Christ himself is the immediate author and prince, which he communicates not to the world, but to them he chooses out of the world . . ., which hath its foundation in Christ, and its influence into each of the communion of Saints all the world over. And this peace can no more be brought about by your sword than by the magistrate's sceptre. And therefore take heed lest you now, having power in your hands to another purpose, should so far forget yourselves as to do that yourselves which you have condemned in others. Therefore suffer the Word only to be both sceptre and sword in the kingdom of God, and let the true Church remain free in the freedom which Christ hath conferred upon it; or else the Lord, whose own the Church is, will as certainly, in his due time, take the sword out of your hands as he hath done the sceptre out of the magistrate's, and throw you into one destruction with him. But I am persuaded better things of you, though I thus speak, and even such things as are suitable to the light of the Gospel and to the virtues and graces of Christ and his Spirit, which have been hitherto (and I hope, will yet still be) very manifest, not only in you honourable ones who have the chief conduct, but also in very many of the Council and Army besides. And upon such a gathering together of God's people and Saints (let the world, if it please, still laugh at that word), who can but think he hath some choice and singular work in hand for his own glory? * * * For hath not that day of the Lord of Hosts dawned, which is upon every one that is proud and lofty, and upon every one that is lifted up, and he is to be brought low, and the Lord alone is, and must be, exalted in this day.'

intended any reconciliation and agreement between these in the spiritual and eternal things of the kingdom of God. For these are two distinct seeds and sorts of people; the one from beneath, the other from above; the one the seed of the woman, the other the seed of the serpent; and between these two God hath put such an enmity that no man can take away. Wherefore they, who never minding these two different seeds between whom God hath put such irreconcilable enmity, would make all the people of one or more whole kingdoms a church at once, and would reconcile all of them together in the things of God, and in the ways of his worship, according to devices and methods of their own: *these men* know not what they do, for they walk in the darkness of their own hearts, and not in the light of the Word; which shows us clearly that it is as possible to reconcile Michael and the devil, as the angels of both.

Neither, secondly, do I find any way in the Word to reconcile all those together, who are commonly called the Visible Church, seeing even among these there are two distinct sorts of children, as Paul teacheth us: one sort of those that are born after the flesh, as Ishmael and Esau, and another of those who are born after the Spirit, as Isaac and Jacob; and there is as great enmity between these in the church as between the former in the world; for they that are born after the flesh, are always persecuting them that are born after the Spirit, but never agreeing with them. * * *

The right Church then is not the whole multitude of the people whether good or bad, that join together in an outward form or way of worship. * * * And therefore I shall not speak of this church. But the church I shall speak of is the true Church of the New Testament, which, I say, is not any outward or visible society, gathered together into the consent or use of outward things, forms, ceremonies, worship, as the churches of men are; neither is it known by seeing or feeling, or the help of any outward sense, as the society of mercers or drapers, or the like; but it is a spiritual and invisible fellowship, gathered together in the unity of faith, hope, and love, and so into the unity of the Son, and of the Father by the Spirit; wherefore it is wholly hid from carnal eyes, neither hath the world any knowledge or judgment of it.

This true Church is the communion of Saints, which is the communion believers have with one another; not in the things of the world, or in the things of man, but in the things of God. For as believers have their union in the Son, and in the Father, so in them also they have their communion; and the communion they have with one another in God cannot be in their own things, but in God's things, even in his light, life, righteousness, wisdom, truth, love, power, peace, joy, &c.   This is the true communion of Saints, and this communion of Saints is the true Church of God.

Now this true Church of God differs from the churches of men in very many particulars, as follows. * * *

In the churches of men members are admitted through an outward confession of doctrine; but none are admitted into this true Church but through a new birth from God and his Spirit.   John 3. [3]: *Except a man be born again, he cannot enter into the kingdom of God*, which is the right Church of the New Testament. * * *

The churches of men knit themselves together into such societies by some outward covenant or agreement among themselves.   But the true Church is knit into their society among themselves by being first knit unto Christ, their head; and as soon as ever they are one with him, they are also one with one another in him; and are not first one among themselves, and then after one with Christ.   So that the true Church is a spiritual society knit unto Christ by faith, and knit to one another in Christ by the Spirit and love; and this makes them infinitely more one than any outward covenant they can engage themselves in, the union wherein God makes us one, passing all the unions wherein we can make ourselves one.   And so when some believers perceive the grace that is given to others, they presently fall into one communion, without any more ado.   Wherefore they that are of the Church, the body, cannot deny communion to them that are in true union with Christ, the head, when they do perceive this grace.   For this is considerable in this matter, that we are not first one with the Church, and then after one with Christ; but we are first one with Christ, and then one with the Church, and our union with the Church flows from our union with Christ, and not our union with Christ, from our union with the Church.   Christ (John 17. [21]) prays, *That they all* (that is, believers) *may be one in us*; so that our union is not first among ourselves, and then with the Son, and with the Father, but it is first with the Son, and with the Father, and then with one another in them.   And Christ is the door through which we enter into the Church, and not the Church the door through which we enter into Christ. For men may join themselves to believers in the use of all outward ordinances, and yet never be joined to Christ, nor to that communion which believers have in Christ; but a man cannot be joined to Christ but he is joined to all believers in the world, in the communion they have with Christ and with one another in him;

which upon all occasions he enjoys with them wherever he meets with them. So that the true Church is knit up together into one body and society by one faith and Spirit; the churches of men by an outward covenant or agreement only.

The churches of men have human officers, who act in the strength of natural or acquisite parts, who do all by the help of study, learning, and the like. But in the true Church, Christ and the Spirit are the only officers, and men only so far as Christ and the Spirit dwell and manifest themselves in them. And so when they do anything in the Church, it is not they that do it, but Christ and his Spirit in them. * * *

The churches of men have the government of them laid on men's shoulders. . . . But the true Church hath its government laid only on Christ's shoulders. . . . For if the Church be gathered together in Christ, as the true Church is, Christ is always in the midst of them, and if Christ is ever present with them, his own self, how cometh it to pass that Christ may not reign immediately over them? Wherefore the true Church reckons it sufficient authority that they have Christ and his word for the ground of their practice; and whatever they find in the Word, they presently set upon the practice of it, and never ask leave either of civil or ecclesiastical powers. But the churches of men will do nothing without the authority of the magistrate or assembly, though it be never so clear in the word of God. For in their religion they regard the authority of men more than the authority of God.

The churches of men are still setting themselves one above another, but the assemblies of the true Church are all equal, having Christ and the Spirit equally present with them and in them. And therefore the believers of one congregation cannot say they have power over the believers of another congregation, seeing all congregations have Christ and his Spirit alike among them, and Christ hath not anywhere promised that he will be more with one than with another. And so Christ and the Spirit in one congregation do not subject, neither are subjected to Christ and the Spirit in another congregation, as if Christ and the Spirit in several places should be above and under themselves. But Christ in each assembly of the faithful is their head, and this head they dare not leave, and set up a fleshly head to themselves whether it consist of one or many men, seeing Antichrist doth as strongly invade Christ's headship in many as in one man, in a council, as in a pope. * * *

And thus having declared what the true Church of Christ is,

and rectified some ancient and general mistakes touching it, I shall now proceed to make known from the clear and evident word, the true and only bonds of the Church's union, peace, and agreement, as the Apostle hath delivered them to us by the Spirit. Ephes. 4. 4: *There is one body and one Spirit, even as ye are called in one hope of your calling; one Lord, one Faith, one Baptism; one God and Father of all, who is above all, and through all, and in you all.* Where note, in general, that among all these bonds of the Church's unity, the Apostle makes not so much as any mention of uniformity. * * * But it will appear . . . by the Apostle's doctrine, that no conformity or uniformity are any bonds of the true Church's peace and union, seeing the Church is such a kingdom as is not preserved in its peace by any outward forms and orders, as the kingdoms of the world are, but by inward principles. * * *

In this true Church or one body of Christ, notwithstanding diversity of members and offices, there is still an equality among them all, seeing all alike make up one body. In which regard one member is as necessary to the body as another; and no member can say to another,[a] I contribute more to the making up of the body than thou. The most honourable members cannot say thus to the most mean—not the Apostles themselves to believers among the Gentiles; for we are the body of Christ as well as they, and they are the body of Christ no more than we. Wherefore no member, for diversity of office, is to lift up himself above another member who is as necessary as itself to the making up the body, and also is every whit as useful in its place. * * *

They that do content themselves in joining to some outward and visible society and corporation of men, though called a church, and think that by being knit to them in ways of outward worship and ordinances, they live in the unity of the Church, when as yet all this while they live out of that one body that is born of the Spirit, which is the only true Church and body of Christ. He that lives out of this spiritual body, though he live in the most excellent society in the world, yet he breaks the unity of the Church, not living in one body with it. And thus many break the Church's unity, that never think on it.

Again they break this bond of the Church's unity that live in this one body, but not as members. And such are they who, having got the advantage of the magistrate's power, will needs lift themselves up above their fellow-members, and exercise authoritative, coercive, domineering power over them; whereas the very Apostles themselves were not lords of the Church, but fellow members with the faithful, living in one body and under one head with them, and so did all by love and persuasion, and nothing by force and violence. * * *

They that labour to join men into one body with the Church that are not one spirit with it, do mar the peace of it. For as unity of spirit in the Church is the bond of peace, so diversity of spirit is the breach of peace, and therefore to preserve the peace of the Church, none are to join themselves to this one body that are not of this one spirit. * * *

As all believers are called by one calling (which is the inward and effectual voice of God to the soul, by his Spirit through the Gospel), so they are called into one blessed hope of obtaining the kingdom and glory of God. And no one is called to this hope more than another, or hath more interest or share in it than another. Fishes that live in the sea, though some be greater and some less, yet none hath more interest or share in it than another, but all, being alike produced in it, enjoy it alike. The creatures that live on the earth, though some be greater and some less, yet all enjoy the sun and air alike. * * *

Now the government of the Church is twofold. (1) There is that government which God exercises *immediately* by himself; and (2) that government which he exercises *mediately* and by the faithful. The first of these again, that is God's immediate government, is twofold: (1) the government of his special providence; (2) the government of his spiritual presence. * * *

Now besides this immediate government of God, there is another sort of government of the Church, which Christ exercises mediately by the Church. And this also is Christ's government, and not man's; and men who have not known nor understood the former government of Christ, have mistaken this also through the same unbelief. Wherefore they, not so much as minding the former government of Christ, which is immediate and by himself, have made this mediate government of the Church by man, to be all. And this also I say, they have understood most grossly and carnally, and not according to the Word, but according to their own ignorant and seduced hearts. * * *

This mediate government then of Christ in the true Church (which, it may be, may better be called order and decency than government) I conceive to be nothing but this, Christ's ordering all things by the faithful, among the faithful, in reference to the communion of Saints. * * *

The first thing then is: to whom Christ hath committed the power of ordering and managing all things in the true Church, in reference to the communion of Saints. I answer, he hath given it to the true Church itself, as formerly described, even to each and all the members of it. For as natural power belongs to all natural men alike, so spiritual power (which is the true church-power) to all spiritual men alike. Christ in a believer is the root of true church-power; and because Christ dwells in all believers alike, through unity of faith, therefore all believers partake alike of spiritual and supernatural power; and no one partakes of this power more than another, any more than he partakes of Christ more than another; but Christ in them all is the self-same power of God to do all things that are to be done in the kingdom of God. * * *

But what are these *keys* about which there hath been so great ado in the Church? I answer, they are not any outward ecclesiastical power whatever, that men have devised to serve their own turns withal. But to pass by the many false conceits, wherewith many former and present writers have and do still trouble the Church, John doth tell us plainly (John 20. 22) what Matthew means by the keys of the Church. Christ (saith he) appearing to his Disciples after his resurrection, breathing on them, said, *Receive the Holy Spirit* (here are the keys of the kingdom of Heaven), and then adds, *Whose sins ye remit, they are remitted, and whose sins ye retain, they are retained.* That is, when ye have received the Spirit, then you have received the keys, to bind and to loose, to remit and retain sin, and that not according to your wills, but wholly according to the mind and will and direction of the Spirit. * * *

What is the extent of this true church-power? I answer that this power extends itself full as far as the Church, but no further. For what hath the Church to do with those that are not of the Church? *What have we to do* (saith Paul) *with them that are without?* For church-power, which is spiritual, is no more suitable to the world than worldly power, which is fleshly, is suitable to the Church. The power of the Church, which is Christ's power, only reaches so far as Christ's kingdom; that is, the people that are born of God and his Spirit. True church-government reaches as far as Christ's and the Spirit's effectual influence and operation, but no further; that is to all that are willing, but to none that are unwilling. As nothing hath more troubled the Church than to govern it and give it laws, after the manner of the world, by secular force and power; so nothing hath more troubled the world than to govern it and give it laws after the manner of the Church, by the aforesaid compulsion. Wherefore as the govern-

ment of the world is not to be spread over the Church, so neither
is the government of the Church to be spread over the world.
But as the world and the Church are distinct things in themselves,
so they are to be contented with their distinct governments.

What is the outward instrument of this power? I answer, the
Word only, which is the only sceptre and sword of Christ's kingdom, to govern his people and subdue his enemies. * * * And so
the true Church doth all in itself only by the Gospel; by the
Gospel it bindeth and looseth; by the Gospel it remits and retains
sin, by the Gospel it quickens to life and wounds to death; by the
Gospel it receives in, and casts out; by the Gospel it works faith,
renews the life, acts, orders, guides and governs all things. * * *

What the true Church can do by virtue of this power.

Now the true Church by the power it hath received from Christ
can gather itself together when, and as often as, it pleaseth. The
company of believers have power to gather themselves together
for their mutual good, instruction, preservation, edification, and
for the avoiding or preventing of evil, and that without the
consent or authority of any extrinsical and foreign power whatever; else Christ were not a sufficient founder of his Church.
And if every free society, not subjected to tyranny, hath power in
itself to congregate and come together as conveniency and necessity shall require, as is evident in all civil corporations, and in all
fraternities and meetings of love; much more hath the Church of
Christ, which is the freest society in the world, power to meet
together into a communion of Saints, though it be without and
against the consent and authority of the powers of the world. * * *

As the Church of the faithful hath power from Christ to meet
together, so . . . to appoint its own outward orders. * * * And
these things each church or communion of Saints may order by
itself, according to the wisdom of the Spirit, so it observe these
rules. That they do all things in love, seeing all laws without love
are tyranny; and so whatsoever is not from, and for, love, is not
to be appointed; and if it be, it is again to be abolished; seeing no
text of the scripture itself, if it build not up love, is rightly
interpreted. They are to do all things for peace. * * * They
must appoint nothing as of necessity; for there is no more pestilent
doctrine in the Church than to make those things necessary which
are not necessary. For thus the liberty of faith is extinguished,
and the consciences of men are ensnared. * * * They may
persuade their orders (if they see cause) by the spirit of love and
meekness, but must not enforce them upon pain of secular
punishment or church-censure, as those use to do that make

themselves lords and tyrants in the Church. For these outward things the Church can order only for the willing, but not for the unwilling. ＊ ＊ ＊

Now one thing more I shall add touching the Church's power to appoint its own orders: . . . that the true Church hath power to appoint these outward orders, not for itself only, but also for its officers (which also are part of itself), and it is not to suffer its officers to frame or impose such on it. For the Church is not the officers', but the officers are the Church['s]. ＊ ＊ ＊

The true Church hath power to choose its officers, and, if there be cause, to reform them or depose them. ＊ ＊ ＊

More particularly in this matter we shall inquire after these three things: (1) What officers are to be chosen? (2) Out of whom they are to be chosen? (3) By whom they are to be chosen?

For the first, . . . Paul teaches us, . . . *they must be faithful men, apt, and able to teach others.* For as among natural men in the world, they that have most natural power and abilities, are fittest to be the officers: so among spiritual men in the Church, they are fittest to be the officers that have most spiritual power, that is, such in whom Christ and the Spirit are most manifest; and of this the faithful of all sorts are judges. Wherefore no natural parts and abilities, nor no human learning and degrees in the schools or universities, nor no ecclesiastical ordination or orders, are to be reckoned sufficient to make any man a minister, but only the teaching of God, and gifts received of Christ, by the Spirit, for the work of the ministry, which the faithful are able to discern and judge of.

Out of whom these officers are to be chosen. And that is out of the flock of Christ, and nowhere else. ＊ ＊ ＊

By whom they are to be chosen. And that is by the congregation or community of believers. For if every free society hath power to choose its own officers, much more hath the true Church this power, being (as is said) the freest society under heaven. And so the true Church is not to have officers thrust over them by others, but is to choose them itself.[1] ＊ ＊ ＊

The true Church hath power to call its councils. ＊ ＊ ＊ Now I said, the Church, *if it need a council,* may call one; because the Church of believers now seldom needs a council, seeing all things are so clear in the word of God, with which the faithful are so well acquainted. ＊ ＊ ＊ For it is not dead laws and orders, written

---

[1] Further defined below: 'The congregations of the faithful have power in themselves, according to the doctrine of the Gospel, to choose their own ministers.'

by men, will do the true Church any good; but the living Law of God, written in their hearts by the Spirit, as God hath promised to do, saying, *I will write my Law in their hearts, and put it in their inward parts.* For as the law of sin hath been written in our natures, to corrupt us, so the law of the Spirit of Life must be written also in our natures, to reform us. * * *

The Church hath power to judge of all doctrines, and that both of its officers and councils.

The clergy and ecclesiastical men have been wont to challenge to themselves the knowledge and judgment of doctrines, and have excluded ordinary Christians from it; whereas in truth, the judgment of doctrine belongeth to the people, and not to the ministers. * * * And the Apostle commands them, *to try the spirits, whether they be of God*, and hath said, *Let one or two speak, and the rest judge* (1 Cor. 14, *&c.*). By which, with many other scriptures, it is evident that the ministers are not to judge of doctrine for the people, but the people are to judge of the doctrine of the ministers, and according as they find it to be of God, or not of God, to receive it, or reject it. For every one is to be saved by his own faith, and not by another man's. * * * And Paul gives this liberty to Christians—yea, we have it from Christ himself whether Paul had allowed it or no—to try the very Apostles themselves and the very angels of heaven, whether they bring the right word or no. * * *

Among the things . . . which are to be done to procure and preserve the peace of the Church these . . . things that follow have not the least place. * * *

The true Church is to preserve itself distinct from the world, and is neither to mingle itself with the world, nor to suffer the world to mingle itself with it. For if the Church and the world be mingled together in one society, the same common laws will no more agree to them who are of such different natures, principles and ends, than the same common laws will agree to light and darkness, life and death, sin and righteousness, flesh and Spirit. * * * Wherefore it is not the way of peace to mingle the Church and the world, but to separate them, and to keep them distinct; that those that are of one nature and spirit may be of one communion among themselves. And this way of peace God himself teacheth us by Paul (2 Cor. 6. 17) saying, *Come out from among them, my people, and be ye separate.* For to separate the Church from the world, in its communion of Saints, is the only way to preserve peace in both; seeing the Church will best agree with itself, and the world with itself.

The Church being thus distinct from the world is to be contented with its own power for its own affairs, and is not to introduce or entertain any power in it that is not of it. Wherefore the true Church, being such a kingdom as is not of this world, stands in need of no worldly power, and being a spiritual and heavenly kingdom, is only to have and exercise a spiritual and heavenly power, seeing this power alone, and by itself, is able to accomplish the whole good pleasure of God in the Church, and to work all the works in it that God hath to do. * * *

The third rule is, not to bring or force men into the Church against their wills. * * *

The fourth rule is, to make void the distinction of clergy and laity among Christians. For the clergy or ecclesiastical men have all along, under the reign of Antichrist, distinguished themselves from other Christians, whom they call the laity, . . . and separated themselves from the lay in all things, and called themselves by the name of the Church, and reckoned other Christians but as common and unclean in respect of themselves; whereas in the true Church of Christ there are no distinctions, . . . nor difference of persons; no clergy or laity . . .; but they are all, as Peter describes them (1 Pet. 2. 9), *a chosen generation, a royal priesthood, a holy nation, a peculiar people, to show forth the virtues of him that called them out of darkness into his marvellous light.* And so all Christians, through the baptism of the Spirit, are made priests alike unto God; and every one hath right and power alike to speak the Word; and so there is among them no clergy or laity, but the ministers are such who are chosen by Christians from among themselves, to speak the Word to all in the name and right of all; and they have no right nor authority at all to this office but by the consent of the Church. And so presbyters and bishops, or (which is all one) elders and overseers in the Church, differ nothing from other Christians, but only in the office of the Word which is committed to them by the Church; as an alderman or common-council man in the city differs nothing from the rest of the citizens, but only in their office, which they have not of themselves neither, but by the city's choice; or as the Speaker in the House of Commons differs nothing from the rest of the Commons, but only in his office, which he hath also by the choice of the House. And thus, and no otherwise, doth a minister differ from other Christians. * * *

The fifth rule is, to keep equality between Christians. For though according to our first nativity, whereby we are born of men, there is great inequality, some being born high, some low,

some honourable, some mean, some kings, some subjects, &c.;
yet according to our new or second birth, whereby we are born of
God, there is exact equality, for here are none better or worse,
higher or lower, but all have the same faith, hope, love, the same
God, Christ, Spirit, the same divine nature, the same precious
promises, the same incorruptible crown and inheritance of Saints
in light. * * *

The sixth rule is, to keep the officers of the Church in subordination to the whole Church or community; and not to suffer
them to get head over it; seeing the very nature of ruling the
Church is not dominion, but service. * * *

Now if any say, by what means may the Church be able to keep
out error? I answer, it may certainly keep out error by these means.

Let the Church suffer none to teach among them, that are not
themselves taught of God; though they have never so great natural
parts, and never so much human learning. * * *

Let the faithful examine everything that is taught by the word
of God, and not receive doctrines upon trust from their teachers.
* * * And though through God's especial goodness the doctrine
of the Gospel be again revived among us at this present time, yet
ought we not to sit down content with the present state of things,
but to search and see if our present doctrine do not yet err from
the primitive purity and brightness of the Gospel, and that in
many considerable points, and whether some or many corruptions
do not yet remain among us, to be purged out by the light and
truth of the Apostles' doctrine. Wherefore to conclude this
thing, let us know that the Church cannot possibly keep out error
longer than it precisely keeps itself to the bare and naked word of
God, and tries all doctrines of their teachers by it.

The Church, that it may be able to keep out errors, must desire
of God, the Spirit which he hath promised; that this Spirit of
Truth may lead them into the true and spiritual knowledge of the
Word, and understanding of the mind of Christ. For no man can
make any right judgment of the Word he hears or reads, without
the teaching of the Spirit. * * * But believers must know that
the gift of the Spirit only, without all human learning, is sufficient
to teach us perfectly which is truth and which error, and to make
us able to judge of all doctrines of men and angels; and that all
human learning in the world, without the Spirit, is not able to do
this. And so a poor, plain countryman, by the Spirit which he
hath received, is better able to judge of truth and error, touching
the things of God, than the greatest philosopher, scholar, or doctor
in the world, that is destitute of it.

Another notable means to keep error out of the Church, is to restore in it that most ancient Gospel ordinance of prophesying, which, howmuchsoever it hath been out of use during the reign of Antichrist, yet is no other than the very commandment of the Lord as Paul witnesseth (1 Cor. 14. 31). * * * When one man only speaks and the doctrine he preaches proves to be erroneous . . . error is not only preached but also goes away uncontrolled, and no way is left for the restraining [of] error proportionable to that of propagating it, nobody being permitted to speak to keep the people from the poison of it. * * * But now when the right or power of prophesying is allowed to the whole Church, the minister can no sooner vent any error, but there is some believer or other, whose heart God shall move, ready to convince it by the word of God. And so error is as soon discovered and detected as it is published; and as soon destroyed as it is detected; the word of God, though from a private Christian, being more mighty to destroy error than error can be to uphold itself against the Word. * * *

If they that publish doctrine should also be judges of it, and the people be bound to subscribe to their judgment, error would not only, by this means, have opportunity to be vented, but would also be established and confirmed without the least contradiction. But now God hath appointed it otherwise in the Church; for whoever speak there, the hearers are to judge of the truth of the doctrine, and accordingly are either to receive it or reject it, having power to do either as they see occasion; and so error cannot prevail in that church where the faithful have liberty to judge of all doctrines, and do exercise that liberty. * * *

But here now a great question will be moved . . .: Whether the magistrate hath not power to suppress error by the sword, and whether the Church may not use this remedy against error as well as all those before named ?

I answer that many men of great eminency have attributed such a power to the magistrate . . . thinking that religion would soon be lost if he should not uphold it. And to make this good they have produced many scriptures of the Old Testament, which seem to arm the magistrate against the authors and spreaders of errors. But I desire the wise-hearted to consider whether as clear scriptures may not be produced out of the Old Testament to prove that temporal power in the world belongs to ecclesiastical men, as that spiritual power in the Church belongs to worldly magistrates. * * *

The putting power into the magistrate's hands to suppress

error by the sword, gives him full opportunity to destroy and slay the true children of God, if at any time he shall mistake and judge them heretics. For what power men ignorantly allow a godly magistrate against true heretics, the same power will all magistrates arrogate to themselves as their just due, against all that differ from themselves in matters of religion though their judgment be never so true. And thus the magistrate, who is a most fallible judge in these things, instead of tares may pluck up the wheat, and kill the faithful instead of heretics, at his own pleasure, till he have destroyed all the faithful in the land. * * *

If any shall yet demand whether the magistrate can do nothing at all towards the suppressing of errors; I answer, this he may do. He may and ought, and if he be a godly man he will, countenance and encourage faithful ministers (that are called of God, and anointed by the Spirit) to this work of the Gospel; and having done this, he need not trouble himself any farther, for the Word preached will do all the rest. And let it not be doubted but if the truth of God do enter the lists against error, it will be infinitely able to prevail of itself alone without calling in any power, or borrowing any weapons, from the world. * * *

Now if they be very truths wherein Christians differ, yet such wherein they may err without danger of salvation, then these rules are of use. (1) To hear them speak their judgments with freedom, and not to condemn them unheard; for thus mayst thou soon condemn the innocent and make thyself guilty. (2) To understand fully what thy adversary means before thou contend against him; lest, if thou want this wisdom and patience, thou oppose not so much his judgment as thy own conceit. * * * If thou canst but have patience to hear him relate his own mind, perhaps in the end thou shalt understand it differs little from thy own in substance. (3) Reproach not anything thy adversary speaks with this, that thou never heardst it before. For this may not so much discover his error as thy ignorance; and that which seems to thee a new error, if it be truly examined by the Word, may prove an old truth. And if thou wilt needs condemn whatever savours of novelty, how shall the truths we yet know not be brought in, or the errors that yet remain with us be purged out? (4) Be not over-confident in what thou holdest upon thy own judgment, or other men's strengthened from multitude, custom and antiquity. For men have erred most grossly, even in those things wherein they have thought themselves most certain. And therefore, *prove all things, that thou mayst hold fast that which is good*. * * * (5) In these differences make the Word the judge, and not men. The word of God is the sole and perfect judge in all the things of God. * * * Now though all have the same outward Word, yet all are not of one mind except they attain to one spirit; for Paul saith (1 Cor. 2) that *only the Spirit of God knows the things of God.* Neither doth man's sense or reason understand the things of the Spirit, *but the spiritual man judgeth all things.* And hence it follows that we can only judge aright of divine truths by the Word, and we can only judge aright of the Word if we have the Spirit to be the interpreter of it to us. * * *

Now in case the doctrine wherein we differ be such as is absolutely necessary to salvation, and without believing which men can have no interest in Christ; yet even in this case hear them speak, and be rather confident that the truth of God will prevail over their error than fearful that their error will prevail against the truth. And so strive not for secular power to shut up men's mouths and to restrain men's writings, though they speak and print things that seem never so contrary to the truth of God and doctrine of the Gospel. For . . . if men vent errors publicly, if there be as public liberty to preach the truth I doubt not the success of the truth against it at any time with all that belongs to God. And it is the only Gospel way, to conquer error by the truth, and all human, yea and devilish doctrines, by the Gospel, which is the ministration of the Spirit and therefore so mighty that all false teachers and false doctrines must needs fall down before it; seeing, *stronger is that Spirit that is in it, than that spirit that is in the world,* which is its own spirit and the devil's. * * * Now . . . if upon hearing and debating things by the Word, it shall clearly appear that our adversaries hold such things which are so false and erroneous that they cannot be reckoned believers and members of Christ, nor retain those doctrines without unavoidable damnation, then in this case the true Church hath authority from the Word to do these things: To condemn the doctrine; to excommunicate their persons. * * *

Now these things have I spoken and propounded to the faithful and churches of Christ wherever the Providence of God shall cast this book, which may travel farther on this errand than weak flesh can do, and I so propound them all as being most ready myself to hear from any what they can propound in more light and evidence of the Word. * * *

VIII. LEVELLER PRINCIPLES [1]

GOD AND MAN

From John Lilburne, *The Free-man's Freedom Vindicated* (1646)[a]

A Postscript containing a General Proposition.

God, the absolute sovereign Lord and King of all things in heaven and earth, the original fountain and cause of all causes, who is circumscribed, governed, and limited by no rules, but doth all things merely and only by his sovereign will and unlimited good pleasure, who made the world and all things therein for his own glory,[b] by his own will and pleasure gave man, his mere creature, the sovereignty (under himself) over all the rest of his creatures (Gen. 1. 26, 28, 29) and endued him with a rational soul or understanding, and thereby created him after his own image (Gen. 1. 26–7, and 9. 6). The first of which was Adam, . . . made out of the dust or clay, out of whose side was taken a rib, which by the sovereign and absolute mighty creating power of God was made a female . . . called Eve. Which two are the earthly original fountain . . . of all and every particular and individual man and woman . . . in the world since, who are, and were, by nature all equal and alike in power, dignity, authority, and majesty, none of them having by nature any authority, dominion, or magisterial power one over or above another; neither have they, or can they exercise any, but merely by institution or donation, that is to say, by mutual agreement or consent, given, derived, or assumed by mutual consent and agreement, for the good benefit and comfort each of other, and not for the mischief, hurt, or damage of any; it being unnatural, irrational, . . . wicked, and unjust, for any man or men whatsoever to part with so much of their power as shall enable any of their Parliament-men, commissioners, trustees, deputies, . . . or servants, to destroy and undo them therewith. And unnatural, irrational, sinful, wicked, unjust, devilish, and tyrannical, it is for any man whatsoever, spiritual or temporal, clergyman or layman, to appropriate and assume unto himself a power, authority and jurisdiction, to rule, govern or reign over any sort of men in the world without their free consent, and

[1] Selections from *Putney Projects*; *The Case of the Army Truly Stated*; the first *Agreement of the People*; *A Call to all the Soldiers of the Army*; various letters from the Agitators, and Lilburne's *Plea for Common Right and Freedom*, which also illustrate Leveller principles, are printed in the Appendix.

whosoever doth it . . . do thereby, as much as in them lies, endeavour to appropriate and assume unto themselves the office and sovereignty of God (who alone doth, and is to, rule by his will and pleasure), and to be like their Creator, which was the sin of the devils, who, not being content with their first station,[a] would be like God, for which sin they were thrown down into hell, reserved in everlasting chains under darkness, unto the judgment of the great day (Jude, ver. 6). And Adam's sin it was, which brought the curse upon him and all his posterity, that he was not content with the station and condition that God created him in, but did aspire unto a better and more excellent, namely to be like his Creator, which proved his ruin, yea, and indeed had been the everlasting ruin and destruction of him and all his, had not God been the more merciful unto him in the promised Messiah (Gen., chap. 3). * * *

AN APPEAL TO PARLIAMENT

From the *Large Petition of the Levellers*[1] (March 1647) [b]

But such is our misery, that after the expense of so much precious time, blood, and treasure, and the ruin of so many thousands of honest families, in recovering our liberty, we still find the nation oppressed with grievances of the same destructive nature as formerly, though under other notions, and which are so much the more grievous unto us because they are inflicted in the very time of this present Parliament, under God the hope of the oppressed.

For as then all the men and women in England were made liable to the summons, attachments, sentences, and imprisonments of the Lords of the Council-board, so we find by woeful experience, and the suffering of many particular persons, that the present Lords do assume and exercise the same power, than which nothing can be more repugnant and destructive to the Commons' just liberty.

As then the unjust power of the Star Chamber was exercised in compelling men and women to answer to interrogatories tending to accuse themselves and others, so is the same now frequently practised upon divers persons, even your cordial friends, that have

---

[1] I follow Professor Pease (*Leveller Movement*, p. 158 n.) in accepting a pamphlet acquired by Thomason on 19th September 1648 [E. 464 (19)] as presenting the text of this petition. See also *Tracts*, ed. Haller (3. 397–405), where the whole pamphlet is reproduced.

been, and still are, punished for refusing to answer questions against themselves and nearest relations.

As then the great oppression of the High Commission was most evident in molesting of godly, peaceable people for nonconformity, or different opinion or practice in religion, in judging all who were contrary-minded to themselves to be heretics, sectaries, schismatics, seditious, factious, enemies to the state and the like, and under great penalties forbidding all persons, not licensed by them, to preach or publish the Gospel: even so now at this day, the very same, if not greater, molestations are set on foot and violently prosecuted by the instigation of a clergy no more infallible than the former, to the extreme discouragement and affliction of many thousands of your faithful adherents, who are not satisfied that controversies in religion can be trusted to the compulsive regulation of any, and after the bishops were suppressed did hope never to have seen such a power assumed by any in this nation any more.

And although all new illegal patents are by you abolished, yet the oppressive monopoly of Merchant Adventurers and others do still remain, to the great abridgment of the liberty of the people, and to the extreme prejudice of all such industrious people as do depend on clothing or woollen manufacture (it being the staple commodity of this kingdom and nation), and to the great discouragement and disadvantage of all sorts of tradesmen, seafaring men, and hindrance of shipping and navigation.

Also the old tedious and chargeable way of deciding controversies or suits in law is continued to this day, to the extreme vexation and utter undoing of multitudes of families—a grievance as great and palpable as any in the world. [And] that old and most unequal punishment of malefactors is still continued, whereby men's lives and liberties are [a] liable to the law's corporal pains (as much inflicted for small as for great offences, and that most [b] unjustly) upon the testimony of one witness, contrary both to the Law of God and common equity—a grievance very great, but little regarded.

And also tithes and other enforced maintenance are still continued, though there be no ground for either under the Gospel, and though the same have occasioned multitudes of suits, quarrels, and debates both in former and latter times.

In like manner multitudes of people, poor distressed prisoners for debt, lie still unregarded in a most miserable and woeful condition throughout the land, to the great reproach of this nation. Likewise, prison-keepers or gaolers are as presumptuous as ever they were both in receiving and detaining of prisoners illegally committed, [and are] as cruel and inhumane to all, especially to such as are well-affected, as oppressive and extorting in their fees, and are attended with under-officers of such vile and unchristian demeanour as is most abominable.

Also thousands of men and women are permitted to live in beggary and wickedness all their life long, and to breed their children to the same idle and vicious course of life; and no effectual means used to reclaim either, or to reduce them to any virtue or industry.

And last, as those who found themselves aggrieved formerly at the burdens and oppressions of those times, that did not conform to the church-government then established, refused to pay ship-money or yield obedience to unjust patents, were reviled and reproached with nicknames of Puritans, heretics, schismatics, sectaries, or were termed factious or seditious, men of turbulent spirits, despisers of government, and disturbers of the public peace: even so it is at this day in all respects with those that show any sensibility of the fore-recited grievances, or move in any manner or measure for remedy thereof; all the reproaches, evils, and mischiefs that can be devised, are thought too few or too little to be laid upon them, as Roundheads, sectaries, Independents, heretics, schismatics, factious, seditious, rebellious, disturbers of the public peace, destroyers of all civil relations and subordinations. Yea, and beyond what was formerly, nonconformity is now judged a sufficient cause to disable any person (though of known fidelity) from bearing any offices of trust in the commonwealth, whiles neuters, malignant and disaffected, are admitted and countenanced. And though it be not now made a crime to mention a Parliament, yet it is little less to mention the supreme power of this honourable House. So that in all these respects this nation remains in a very sad and disconsolate condition, and the more because it is thus with us after so long a session of so powerful and so free a Parliament, and [one that] hath been so made and maintained by the abundant love, and liberal effusion of the blood, of the people. And therefore . . . we . . . do most earnestly entreat that you will stir up your affections to a zealous love and tender regard of the people who have chosen and trusted you, that you will seriously consider that the end of your trust was freedom and deliverance from all kind of grievances and oppressions.

1. And that, therefore, in the first place, you will be exceeding careful to preserve your just authority from all prejudices of a

negative voice in any person or persons whatsoever, which may disable you from making that happy return unto the people which they justly expect, and that you will not be induced to lay by your strength till you have satisfied your understandings in the undoubted security of yourselves and of those who have voluntarily and faithfully adhered to you in all your extremities, and until you have secured and settled the commonwealth in settled peace and true freedom, which is the end of the primitive institution of all government.

2. Secondly, that you will take off all sentences, fines, and imprisonments imposed on commoners by any whomsoever, without due course of law or judgment of their equals, and to give due reparations to all those who have been so injuriously dealt withal, and for preventing the like for the time to come, that you will enact all such arbitrary proceedings to be capital crimes.

3. Thirdly, that you permit no authority whatsoever to compel any person or persons to answer to any questions against themselves or nearest relations, except in cases of private interest between party and party in a legal way, and to release such as suffer by imprisonment or otherwise, for refusing to answer to such interrogatories.

4. Fourthly, that all statutes, oaths, and covenants may be repealed so far as they tend, or may be construed, to the molestation and ensnaring of religious, peaceable, and well-affected people, for nonconformity or difference of opinion or practice in religion.

5. Fifthly, that no man for preaching or publishing his opinion in religion in a peaceable way, may be punished or persecuted as heretical, by judges that are not infallible but may be mistaken as well as other men in their judgments, lest upon pretence of suppressing errors, sects, or schisms, the most necessary truths, and sincere professions thereof, may be suppressed, as upon the like pretence it hath been in all ages.

6. Sixthly, that you will for the encouragement of industrious people, dissolve that oppressive company of Merchant Adventurers, and the like, and prevent all such others by great penalties for ever.

7. Seventhly, that you will settle a just, speedy, plain, and unburdensome way for deciding of controversies and suits in law, and reduce all laws to the nearest agreement with Christianity, and publish them in the English tongue, and that all processe[s] and proceedings therein may be true, and also in English, and in the most usual character of writing without any abbreviation, that each one who can read may the better understand their own

affairs, and that the duties of all judges, officers, and practisers in the law, and of all magistrates and officers in the commonwealth, may be prescribed, their fees limited under strict penalties, and published in print to the knowledge and view of all men; by which just and equitable means this nation shall be for ever freed of an oppression more burdensome and troublesome than all the oppressions hitherto by this Parliament removed.

8. Eighthly, that the life of no person may be taken away [but] under the testimony of two witnesses at least, of honest conversation; and that in an equitable way you will proportion punishment to offences, so that no man's life be taken away, his body punished, nor his estate forfeited, but upon such weighty and considerable causes as justly deserve such punishment; and that all prisoners may have a speedy trial, that they be neither starved nor their families ruined by long and lingering imprisonment; and that imprisonment may be used only for safe custody until time of trial, and not as a punishment for offences.

9. Ninthly, that tithes and all other enforced maintenances may be for ever abolished, and nothing in place thereof imposed, but that all ministers may be paid only by those who voluntarily choose them, and contract with them for their labours.

10. Tenthly, that you will take some speedy and effectual course to relieve all such prisoners for debt as are altogether unable to pay, that they may not perish in prison through the hardheartedness of their creditors; and that all such who have any estates may be enforced to make payment accordingly, and not shelter themselves in prison to defraud their creditors.

11. Eleventhly, that none may be prison-keepers but such as are of approved honesty; and that they be prohibited under great penalties to receive or detain any person or persons without lawful warrant; that their usage of prisoners may be with gentleness and civility, their fees moderate and certain; and that they may give security for the good behaviour of their under-officers.

12. Twelfthly, that you will provide some powerful means to keep men, women, and children from begging and wickedness, that this nation may be no longer a shame to Christianity therein.

13. Thirteenthly, that you will restrain and discountenance the malice and impudency of impious persons in their reviling and reproaching the well-affected with the ignominious titles of Roundheads, factious, seditious, and the like, whereby your real friends have been a long time, and still are, exceedingly wronged, discouraged, and made obnoxious to rude and profane people; and that you will not exclude any of approved fidelity from bear-

ing office of trust in the commonwealth for nonconformity, but rather neuters, and such as manifest disaffection or opposition to common freedom, the admission and continuation of such being the chief cause of all our grievances. * * *

AN APPEAL TO THE PEOPLE

From Richard Overton, *An Appeal from the Commons to the Free People* (1647) [a]

It is confessed that our English histories and records of the actions and transactions of our predecessors, both of ancient and late times, so far as I can understand, do not afford me any example or precedent for any appeal from parliaments to people. Neither is there any such liberty provided in the letter of our law. So that by such as prefer precedents and formalities, forms and figures, before the substance, life, and spirit of all just precedents and laws, I may probably be censured and condemned for this present enterprise, as an open and desperate enemy to parliaments and magistracy, a subverter and destroyer of all national laws and government, and a reducer (to my power) of kingdoms and people into confusion. To such I shall return even the late words of our now degenerate Parliament: *that reason hath no precedent; for reason is the fountain of all just precedents.* . . . Therefore where that is, there is a sufficient and justifiable precedent.

And if this principle must be granted of, and obeyed by all (as by no rational man can be denied), then the act of appeal in this nature, if grounded upon right reason, is justifiable and warranted, even by that which gives an equitable authority, life, and being, to all just laws, precedents, and forms of government whatsoever. For reason is their very life and spirit, whereby they are all made lawful and warrantable both for settlement, administration, and obedience; which is the highest kind of justification and authority for human actions, that can be, for greater is that which gives being and justifieth than that which receiveth and is justified. All forms of laws and governments may fall and pass away, but right reason (the fountain of all justice and mercy to the creature) shall and will endure for ever. It is that by which in all our actions we must stand or fall, be justified or condemned; for neither morality nor divinity amongst men can or may transgress the limits of right reason. For whatsoever is unreasonable cannot be justly termed moral or divine, and right reason is only commensurable and discernible by the rule of merciful justice and just mercy. It is gradual in its quantity, but one in its quality. Several are its degrees, but its perfection and fulness is only in God. And its several branches and degrees are only communicable and derivated from him, as several beams and degrees of heat from the body of the sun—yet all heat. So in reason there are different degrees, as from morality to divinity, and under those two heads several subordinate degrees, all derivated and conveyed from the Creator (the original fountain) to the creature, yet all one and the same in nature—the difference only lying in the degree of the thing, not in the thing itself, as a dwarf is as much a man as a giant though not so big a man. And so [a] the gifts and graces of God are one radically, yet different in their species, and all from one and the same Spirit, which can [b] act nothing contrary to its own nature. And God is not a God of irrationality and madness, or tyranny. Therefore all his communications are reasonable and just, and what is so is of God.

And upon this principle, as upon a firm and sure foundation, all just laws and governments are founded and erected, and in particular the fundamental laws and government of this kingdom. For it is a sure and radical maxim in our law, *Nihil quod est contra rationem est licitum* (Nothing which is against reason is lawful), reason being the very life of the law of our land; so that should the law be taken away from its original reason and end, it would be made a shell without a kernel, a shadow without substance, a carcass without life, which presently turns to putrefaction. And as reason only gives it a legal being and life, so it only makes it authori[ta]tive and binding. If this be not granted, lust, will, pride (and what the devil and corruption will) may be a law. For if right reason be not the only being and bounder of the law over the corrupt nature of man (that what is rational, the which injustice and tyranny cannot be, may only and at all times be legal, and what is legal, to be simply and purely rational, the which mercy and justice must be whensoever, wheresoever, and by whomsoever it be . . .),[c] all would fall into confusion, disorder, madness, and cruelty; and so magistracy would cease, and be converted into inhumanity and tyranny.

So that it being most evident and clear to the eye of rational man that this fundamental principle may not (in being [fundamental] to magistracy itself) be expulsed the precincts of magisterial government, but must be preserved . . . entire and absolute therein . . . as a sure and safe refuge to fly to, in all straits and extremities whatsoever, for preservation, safety, removal of oppressions, &c.; or else no safety or relief from oppression, either public or private, to be lawfully attempted, pursued, or had—so that where that principle is, there legality and authority must be, and is concomitant to, and inseparable therefrom, never to be altered while the sun and the moon endures. By it kings and kingdoms have their essential legal being, without which they cease from being either kings or kingdoms. Therefore, that which doth institute, constitute, and authorize the regality of kings and kingdoms, certainly must needs be sufficiently authori-[ta]tive for a particular, as for this expedient of mine or the like, in case it be found under the protection and authority of the said principle of right reason—as I shall clearly evidence it to be.

First, then, be pleased to consider that it is a firm law and radical principle in nature, engraven in the tables of the heart by the finger of God in creation, for every living, moving thing, wherein there is the breath of life, to defend, preserve, guard,[a] and deliver itself from all things hurtful, destructive and obnoxious thereto, to the utmost of its power. Therefore from hence is conveyed to all men in general, and to every man in particular, an undoubted principle of reason: by all rational and just ways and means possibly he may, to save, defend, and deliver himself from all oppression, violence and cruelty whatsoever, and (in duty to his own safety and being) to leave no just expedient un-attempted for his delivery therefrom. And this is rational and just. To deny it is to overturn the law of nature, yea and of religion too; for the contrary lets in nothing but self-murder, violence, and cruelty. Now the unreasonable oppression of myself, my wife, brother, and children, under the arbitrary tyranny of the Westminster Lords, and the ways and means that I have used for delivery therefrom, considered and weighed in the balance of this natural radical principle of reason, this, mine attempt of appeal (though of a desperate nature) will be found the only mean wherein I may discern any probability of relief. . . .

Secondly, necessity is a law above all laws. And this principle conveyeth and issueth forth authority and power, both to general and particular cases, even to the taking up of unusual and un-exemplary courses for public and particular deliverances. . . . And upon this principle the Netherlanders made an hostile de-fence and resistance against the King of Spain, their then sovereign lord, for the recovery of their just rights and freedom. And upon the same point rose the Scotch up in arms and entered this king-dom without all formal countenance or allowance of king or parliament, and were justified for that very act by this present

Parliament. Yea, and even this Parliament upon the same principle took up arms against the King. And now, right worthy patriots of the Army, you yourselves upon the same principle, for recovery of common right and freedom, have entered upon this, your present honourable and solemn *Engagement* against the oppressing party at Westminster, and plead yourselves justifiable thereby, and tell them . . . *that the Parliament hath declared it no resistance of magistracy to side with the just principles and law of nature and nations, being that law upon which you have assisted them.* So that if I be condemned for a traitor by all or any of you, whether Scotch, Parliament, or Army, for proceeding upon the said just principles and law of nature, for common right and freedom, I tell you plainly that out of your own mouths you shall be judged no less traitors than myself, yea, allowers of that in yourselves, which for treason you condemn in others. * * *

Thirdly, the equity of the law is superior to the letter, the letter being subordinate and subject thereto. And look how much the letter transgresseth the equity, even so much it is unequal, of no validity and force. * * * And by this principle, worthy officers and soldiers, you have charged the Parliament from their own declarations, to warrant this your present expedition; . . . by[a] which principle, together with yourselves and with them, I lay claim to a title for an equal justification and protection from the letter of the law. * * *

Fourthly, all betrusted powers, if forfeit[ed], fall into the hands of the betrusters, as their proper centre.[b] And where such a forfeit is committed, there it disobligeth from obedience, and warranteth an appeal to the betrusters, without any contempt or disobedience to the powers in the least; for such an appeal in that case is not at all from the power, but from the persons; not forsaking the power, but following of it in its retreat to the fountain. For as formerly the Parliament averred, and as now this honourable Army assumeth, . . . *all authority is fundamentally seated in the office, and but ministerially in the persons.* Therefore, the persons in their ministrations degenerating from safety to tyranny, their authority ceaseth, and is only to be found in the fundamental original rise and situation thereof, which is the people, the body represented. For though it ceaseth from the hands of the betrusted, yet it doth not, neither can it, cease from its being; for kings, parliaments, &c., may fall from it, but it endureth for ever. For were not this admitted, there could be no lawful redress in extremity. Yea, magistracy itself should be transitory and fading like as is corruption—of no certain duration or moment; but it is unchangeable and certain; man perisheth, but it endureth. It always is either in the hands of the betrusted or of the betrusters. While the betrusted are dischargers of their trust it remaineth in their hands, but no sooner the betrusted betray and forfeit their trust but (as all things else in dissolution) it returneth from whence it came, even to the hands of the trusters. For all just human powers are but betrusted, conferred, and conveyed by joint and common consent; for to every individual in nature is given an individual propriety by nature, not to be invaded or usurped by any (as in mine *Arrow against Tyranny* is proved and discovered more at large); for every one as he is himself hath a self propriety—else could he not be himself—and on this no second may presume without consent; and by natural birth all men are equal, and alike born to like propriety and freedom, every man by natural instinct aiming at his own safety and weal. And so it is that there is a general communication amongst men from their several innate properties to their elected deputies for their better being, discipline, government, property, and safety. * * *

Now these premises considered, I do confidently conclude (if confidence may be derived from the just principles of nature) that the transgression of our weal by our trustees is an utter forfeiture of their trust, and cessation of their power. Therefore if I prove a forfeiture of the people's trust in the prevalent party at Westminster in Parliament assembled, then an appeal from them to the people is not anti-parliamentary, anti-magisterial; not *from* that sovereign power, but *to* that sovereign power. For the evidence whereof I shall first present a discovery of their dealings with me, relating to the public, and then their common course to the general.[1] * * *

But for brevity's sake I shall omit the several new oppressions, exactions, and burdens, wherewith the people are loaded everywhere, even till their backs are ready to break, as every man by woeful experience can witness, and shall only relate to the main and principal end of their election and session, which is for hearing

[1] Here follows an account (pp. 7–10) of Overton's arrest, on 11th August 1646, by order of the Lords, on a charge of breach of privilege; his appeal to the House of Commons; its reference of the case, with Lilburne's, to Henry Marten's committee on the Commons' liberties, which pronounced both imprisonments illegal; Overton's refusal to appear again before the Lords; his imprisonment, as a result, in Newgate, from 3rd November 1646 till the time of writing (8th July 1647); and finally the arrest of his wife and brother. From the Lords his attack turns (pp. 10–13) to the eleven members of the Commons charged with treason by the Army, and concludes with a repudiation of the authority of that House, which by its acts has forfeited the character of a true Representative.

the cries and groans of the people, redressing and easing their grievances. And as touching this matter, this is their course: instead of relief for oppression, themselves do oppress, and, which is worst, then stop the mouths of the oppressed, . . . slight, reject and crush their just and necessary petitions, which is the highest kind of tyranny in the world, shut their doors and ears against the cry of the people both of country and City, yea, though the burdens of the oppressed are so great that multitudes in a peaceable manner have attended the House daily with petitions for no other thing than for the removal of oppression and recovery of freedom, according to the fundamental laws of this kingdom, which they [have] often declared, covenanted, protested, and sworn with hands lifted up to the most high God, to perform faithfully and truly.

Yet these very men, contrary to their many oaths, covenants, declarations, vows, and protestations, call the petitioners rogues, villains, seditious, factious fellows . . .; and not only so, but imprison some of them, as Mr. Nicholas Tew, Mr. Browne, and Major Tulidah,[a] the two first of them prisoners to this hour, the third under bail. And they stay not here, but their arrogance mounts higher and higher: [they] even vote their petitions seditious breach of their privileges, and cause them to be burnt by the hand of the common hangman—even such petitions wherein was contained the liberties and freedoms of the Commons of England, and no jot of anything . . . that was not just, honest and reasonable, and their sworn duties to perform.[1] * * *

Halters and gallows is more fit for them than places in Parliament. What! will you be more fearful of them, to bring them to justice, than they were of you, to burn your laws and liberties? For shame! Never let an English spirit be taxed with that dishonour. You have Othniels, Ehuds, Baraks, and Gideons, before you, even a mighty and puissant, virtuous army, which hath most gallantly and honourably engaged for you and their own safety and protection from those unnatural tyrants and usurpers, to remove them from the seat of your authority, and to bring them to justice, that you, and your children after you, may be delivered from the fear and prejudice of their cruelties, dwell in peace and safety, enjoy the price of your labour and travail quietly and freely to yourselves, be absolute lords and possessors of your own, and [b] be made true and real freemen indeed. Fall therefore into their

---

[1] Omitted passage cites the condemnation of the soldiers' petition by the dominant Presbyterian party in the House of Commons, and the effort to gain complete control of the City militia.

assistance and protection, and trust no longer your perjured, traitorous trustees dissembled at Westminster, but save yourselves from that cursed and wicked generation. Now is the opportunity. Do not procrastinate nor delay, lest your destruction be of yourselves. * * *

Dear friends, our destruction is beyond the privilege of Parliament. It is out of the compass of that betrusted authority. While they move in the sphere of our safety, their motions are parliamentary, legal and author[it]ative, and to be obeyed, defended and maintained. But on the contrary, the contrary must be concluded; for contraries have contrary consequents. For there is a difference betwixt their parliamentary and their own personal capacity, and their actions are answerably different. Therefore the rejection, disobedience, and resistance of their personal commands, is no rejection, disobedience, or resistance of their parliament[ary] authority; so that he that doth resist their personal commands, doth not resist the Parliament. . . .

And upon this principle of justice and reason they grounded and justified their war against the King. * * * Even so may the commonalty of England reply to their Parliament-members, that they are made for the people, not the people for them, and no otherwise may they deal with the people than for their safety and weal, for no more than the people are the King's, no more are the people the Parliament's, [they] having no such propriety in the people as the people have in their goods, to do with them as they list. As they will not grant it to be the prerogative of kings, neither may we yield it to be the privilege of parliaments. For the safety of the people is the reason and end of all governments and governors. *Salus populi est suprema lex:* the safety of the people is the supreme law of all commonwealths. * * *

Therefore it is in vain for our members in Parliament to think that we will justify or tolerate the same among them which we would not endure in the King—to pluck off the garments of royalty from oppression and tyranny, to dress up the same in Parliament-robes. No, no, that was ever, and is, far from our hearts, and we shall justify or allow the same no more in the one than in the other. For to allow it in the one is to justify it in the other, for it is equally unequal in both, and in itself resistible wheresoever it is found. For were it not resistible, all defensive war whatsoever were unlawful. And upon this point we moved against the King, the equity thereof arising from an inherent principle of nature concording with the commandment of God. For were not tyranny in itself resistible, then a man might lawfully murder himself or give power to another to be his butcher. But . . . by the law of God in nature and in his word, both the one and the other is verily unlawful. * * * And upon this ground, in case we have to deal with a mighty and furious enemy, we are bound to the utmost of our power to arm and fortify ourselves for our just and necessary defence, and by force of arms to repel and beat back the invading, assaulting enemy, whether it be an enemy for the confusion and extirpation of our persons or for destruction and ruin of our laws, our freedoms and liberties. For bondage and slavery are not inferior to death, but rather to be more avoided, condemned and resisted than present destruction, by how much the more that kind of destruction is more languishing than present. * * *

And against the justice of this defensive principle no degrees, orders, or titles amongst men can or may prevail; . . . all laws, customs and manners . . . must be subject to give place and yield thereunto, and it unto none; for all degrees and titles magisterial . . . are all subservient to popular safety, . . . all instituted and ordained only for it. For without it can be no human society, cohabitation, or being; which above all earthly things must be maintained as the earthly sovereign good of mankind, let what or who will, perish or be confounded. For mankind must be preserved upon the earth, and to this preservation all the children of men have an equal title by birth, none to be deprived thereof but such as are enemies thereto. And this is the groundwork that God in nature hath laid for all commonwealths, for all governors and governments amongst men.* * * And from hence ariseth the true definition of treason. For indeed treason is no other than a destruction to human society, or actions . . . tending to the utter overthrow of public safety, cohabitation, and peace, or to the . . . thraldom of a people or country. * * *

Now in regard the body natural, for its own safety, may prune, amputate, and cut off the corrupt, putrefied members from the body representative, yea, utterly renounce . . . and dissolve all the members therein, upon total forfeiture of, and real apostasy from, the true representative capacity of Parliament; . . . it then inevitably followeth, that this natural body, by virtue of its instincted, inherent natural sovereignty, may . . . depute any . . . persons for their . . . deputies for the removal of those dead, corrupt, putrefied members from the seat and name of their formal authority, and for the suppression of injustice and tyranny, [and the] recovery of liberty and freedom. But it may be, it will be objected that, by reason of . . . confusion and disorder at

such an exigency in the body natural, such a new deputation . . .
cannot possibly be formally effected, and therefore those forementioned members, though never so corrupt and destructive,
must be continued and subjected unto. I answer that the body
natural must never be without a mean to save itself, and therefore,
by the foresaid permanent unalterable rule of necessity and safety,
any . . . persons (in discharge of their duty to God, themselves,
and their country) may warrantably rise up in the cause and
behalf of the people, to preserve them from imminent ruin and
destruction, such . . . persons doing in that act no more than
every man by nature is bound to perform. For as every man by
the very bond of nature and neighbourhood, in case his neighbour's house be on fire, is bound forthwith without any formal
or verbal deputation of the owner, to endeavour the quenching
thereof with his utmost power and ability; even so, and much more,
may the same be said a of a whole country or kingdom; for necessity in that case of extremity justifies the act of safety and preservation in any, though without any formal election . . . from
the people in general thereto. For such formalities must give
place unto the main, being but circumstances in comparison
thereof, and a kingdom or commonwealth must not be neglected
and lost for a trifle. * * * . It is not the part of the just and merciful
freemen of England to behold the politic body of this commonwealth fallen amongst a crew of thieves, as Hollis, Stapleton,b &c.,
stripped of its precious raiment of freedom and safety, wounded
and left grovelling in its blood, even half dead, and pass by on
the other side like the merciless priest and the Levite. No, now is
the time for the compassionate Samaritan to appear, to bind up
its wounds, to pour in wine and oil, to engage in the defence and
preservation of a distressed, miserable people; for greater love
and mercy cannot be amongst men than to take compassion over
the helpless and destitute.

Therefore this evangelical principle of mercy (being of the
nearest communication to the nature of God) is a warrantable
ground for the *Solemn Engagement of the Army*, like the compassionate Samaritan, to bind up the wounds of the almost murdered
laws and liberties of England. * * *   And in case they be enforced
to a defensive resistance, in so doing they will be no resisters,
despisers, condemners or oppugners of magistracy, authority or
government. For tyranny is no magistracy. Therefore the
resistance of tyrants is no resistance of magistrates, except it be
of such [as are] so nominally, but really and essentially monsters
and pests of humanity. * * *

Now magistracy in its nature, institution, and administration, is for such a kind of safety, national and general, as wherein every . . . particular person, of what sort . . . soever, may fully and freely enjoy his liberty, peace, and tranquillity, civil and human. It is an ordinance amongst men, and for men, that all men may have a human subsistence and safety, to live as men amongst men, none to be excepted from this human subsistence but the unnatural and the inhuman. It is not for this opinion or that faction, this sect or that sort, but equally and alike indifferent for all men that are not degenerated from humanity and human civility in their living and neighbourhood. And therefore the destroyers and subverters of human society, safety, cohabitation, and being, are to be corrected, expulsed, or cut off for preservation of safety and prevention of ruin, both public and private. And thus is magistracy for the praise of them that do well, and for the punishment of those that do evil.

And as for matters of conscience or opinion about religion or worship, with which human society, cohabitation, and safety may freely subsist and stand together—that doth not fall under the power of the magisterial sword, either for introduction and settlement, or for extirpation and subversion. For the limits of magistracy extend no further than humanity or human subsistence, not to spirituality or spiritual being; and no further than its own nature extends, no further may its compulsive power be stretched. And this is the true distinction, for matter of subjection, betwixt God and Caesar; and what is God's we must in the first place give unto God, and what is Caesar's, in the second place, freely and readily we must give unto Caesar. The inward man is God's prerogative; the outward man is man's prerogative. God is the immediate Lord over the inward, and mediately over the outward; but man is only lord over the outward, and though immediate thereover, yet but by deputation or commission from him who is thus both over the one and the other. And God, who only knoweth the heart and searcheth the reins, hath reserved the gubernation thereof to himself as his own prerogative. And the only means which he useth in this kind of government, that by his ministers must be dispensed, is only by the Word, not by the sword. For the sword pierceth but the flesh; it toucheth but the outward man; it cannot touch the inward. Therefore where by the Word (to wit, by doctrine or argumentation, the proper means to work upon the intellectuals and affections) a conversion is not, nor cannot be, obtained, there no human compulsive power or force is to be used, either for plantation or extirpation.

And therefore it was that Christ refused the sword for the promulgation and settlement of his doctrine; for it was spiritual, and such were the weapons he used for that warfare of his. And therefore in imitation of his pattern, and [the] practice of the Apostles, we must rather suffer for matters of faith than be enforced or enforce thereunto. But it does not therefore follow that by defensive force we may not maintain our natural human being and subsistence upon earth; for the contrary doctrine would tend to the utter confusion of humanity, the depopulation of nations, kingdoms, and countries. Though for the spiritual warfare we are confined to spiritual weapons, yet for this human, natural warfare human and natural weapons may and are to be used, each according to its kind. So that neither the one nor the other in their distinctive propriety and administration is destructive or contradictory one to another, but both may properly meet and stand together in one individual without the least encroachment or prejudice to each other's propriety. And if the magistrate should so far extend his compulsive force, under pretence of religion and conscience, to the destruction of our human subsistence or being, we may, upon the points of our ᵃ human subsistence, lawfully make our defensive resistance, for in itself it is defendable against all opposition or destruction, from whence or from whomsoever it shall be. And of this defensive resistance none in duty can be excused but in case of an utter deprivation ᵇ of power. . . .

Therefore, these premises . . . deliberately weighed, I appeal to all moderate and rational commoners to judge impartially about this matter, whether now without all check or scruple of conscience, in maintenance and pursuance of this defensive principle of resistance, we may not, every man of us, in duty to our own natures and to our native country in general, to the utmost of our lives and fortunes, be assistant and united to this faithful Army that now is, or to whomsoever shall rise up and appear in the defensive cause of this kingdom, for the recovery of our natural human rights and freedoms, that all orders, sorts, and societies of the natives of this land may freely and fully enjoy a joint and mutual neighbourhood, cohabitation, and human subsistence, one as well as another, doing unto all men as we would be done unto, it being against the radical law of nature and reason that any man should be deprived of a human subsistence, that is not an enemy thereto. He that is fit for neighbourhood, cohabitation, human society and fellowship, and will freely comply and submit thereunto, ought not to be abridged of the same in the least measure;

he that shall deny, oppose and resist this, the same is an enemy
to mankind and is guilty of the highest kind of treason that is. * * *

I shall therefore presume, most excellent General, honourable
officers, faithful Agitators,[a] and gentleman soldiers, . . . to make
my humble address and appeal unto this Army as to the natural
head of the body natural of the people at this present. * * *

Be therefore quick and active and be not demurred, protracted
and delayed, by the old, beaten, subtle foxes of Westminster, into
your own and our destruction. Can you imagine that they
intend you any good? What have they done, I pray you, as
hitherto, but fobbed, befooled, and deluded you . . ., that they
might gather time and ground? * * *

Therefore, right worthy and faithful Agitators, be advised to
preserve that power and trust, reposed in and conferred upon you
by the body of the Army, entire and absolute. And trust no man,
whether officer or soldier, how religious soever appearing, further
than he acts apparently for the good of the Army and kingdom.
Mark them which would and do bring you into delays and demurs;
let their pretences be what they will be, their counsels are destructive. I am afraid that your officers are [b] too forward to interpose
all delays. Therefore, as I dare not totally condemn them, but
honour them so far as they have dealt honourably in your *Engagement*, I only advise you to be cautious and wary, and keep up
your betrusted power and authority, and let nothing be acted . . .
or concluded without your consent and privity. For by that
means the cause in a clandestine, underhand manner may be
given away. And what do you know but there is a design amongst
you, to take the power of all agitation from the hand of the private
soldier? * * * Sure I cannot judge that you will altogether be
befooled of your power. If you do, I am sure we shall all be befooled with you. If that once be accomplished, then farewell our
hopes in the Army. For I am confident that it must be the poor,
the simple and mean things of this earth, that must confound the
mighty and the strong. Therefore your officers that seek not
themselves, and have no sinister ends nor designs in their breasts,
will be contented that your betrusted power be preserved entire
in your hands till the end of your work be accomplished, and
rather than they will any ways seem to infringe it, [they will] be
continued in their addition to your agitation only for advice and
consultation, not for control and conclusion, not desiring a negative voice any more in your agitation than they and you would
allow the King in the great council of Parliament; that so the
sense and mind of the Army may not be prevented or denied. * * *

Certain Articles for the Good of the Commonwealth, Presented to the consideration of his Excellency Sir Thomas Fairfax, and to the Officers and Soldiers under his command.[a] * * *

1. That for the future the election and expulsion of Parliament-members may be so settled in the electors, that none may be hindered . . . from serving his country under any colour or pretence whatsoever, as for refusing the Covenant or otherwise, without order first, [and] assent or concurrence of their country.

2. That for the better security of the interest and power of the people, all titles by prerogative, privilege, patent, succession, peerage, birth, or otherwise, to sit and act in the assembly of Parliament, contrary to and without the free choice and election of the people, be utterly abrogated. . . .

3. That the authority of Parliament may be preserved and secured for the future from the obstructions and prejudice of a negative voice in any person or persons whatsoever.

4. That every county may have liberty to choose some certain number amongst themselves, to inquire and present to the Parliament what be the just laws, customs and privileges of each county. And that those county commissioners be bound to receive all . . . impeachments, by any person . . . of the respective counties, against any of their own respective knights or burgesses in Parliament, for falsifying and betraying . . . their country's trust, or anywise endeavouring the introduction of an arbitrary power in this land. * * *

[5] That all courts which are not established by the just old law of the land, and all illegal offices and officers belonging to the same, and all other vexatious and unnecessary courts, be abolished by Act of Parliament. And that provision be made, that for time to come no courts or officers whatsoever may be obtruded upon the free commoners of England, either by royal grant, patent, Act of Parliament, or otherwise, contrary to the old law of the land.

[6] That according to the old law and custom of the land, long before and some time after the Conquest, there may be courts of judicature for the speedy trial and determination of all causes, whether criminal or civil, erected and established in every hundred, for the ease and benefit of the subject, to be holden according to the old custom once or twice every month, for the ending of all causes criminal and civil whatsoever, which shall happen in the respective hundreds. * * *

[7] That all such officers as, by the ancient and common laws of this nation, are eligible,[b] and to be chosen by the free Commons,

as mayors, sheriffs, justices of peace, &c., may be left to the free election of the people in their respective places, and not otherwise to be chosen. * * *

[8] That the extortions and oppressive fees of gaolers may be redressed and eased, and that strict and severe provision be made against all gaolers and their deputies, to restrain them for the future from the like extortions and cruelties, now frequent in all gaols of the land. And that there may be a strict and severe inquisition after the blood of such prisoners as have been murdered and starved by the cruelties of gaolers, that so the persons guilty thereof may have justice executed upon them.

[9] That no prisoners be put in irons, or to other pain, before conviction and condemnation.

[10] That there may be cleanly and wholesome provision made in all the gaols of England, for the lodging of prisoners at the charge and cost of the state, and that no fees for chamber-rent, for entering or deliverance, or anything in lieu thereof, be exacted or demanded, under a severe penalty.

[11] That neither the High Court of Parliament nor any other inferior court or magistrate whatsoever may commit any freeman of England to prison upon any pretended contempts, as is frequent in these days, but only for transgression and breach of the known laws of the land. * * *

[14] That all laws of the land (locked up from common capacities in the Latin or French tongues) may be translated into the English tongue. And that all records, orders, processes, writs, and other proceedings whatsoever, may be all entered and issued forth in the English tongue, and that in the most plain and common character used in the land, . . . that so the meanest English commoner that can but read written hand in his own tongue, may fully understand his own proceedings in the law.

[15] That no free commoner of England be enforced,[a] either by the High Court of Parliament or by any subordinate court, . . . to make oath or to answer to any interrogatories concerning himself in any criminal case concerning his life, liberty, goods, or freehold. * * *

[17] That neither membership in Parliament, office nor function whatsoever in the magistracy of the land, may be any protection or demur in any wise against the due process or course of the ancient and common laws of this realm, but that in all cases of treason, murder, burglary, and felony, in all actions, suits, and civil proceedings whatsoever, the greatest man . . . in the realm may be made equally liable at all times and seasons

. . . to the trial, sentence and execution of the law, with the meanest commoner.

[18] That all wicked persons that shall bear false witness against any freeman of England . . . be adjudged and condemned of their lives, liberties, and freeholds, according to that which they would have done unto their neighbours.

[19] That the cruel practice of imprisoning debtors may be provided against, and that due rights and properties may be recovered upon more merciful terms than by way of imprisonment.

[20] That according to the Law of God, and the old law of the land, matters of theft may not be punished with death, and that such malefactors may make satisfaction either by just restitution to the party wronged or by an answerable servitude, and that such offenders upon the second conviction (lawfully had) be brand-marked visibly in the most eminent part of their face, and confined to a singular habit. And upon the third lawful conviction, to be put to perpetual servitude for the benefit of the state, saving to the party wronged a competent deduction thereout for restitution according to the theft. And that upon all occasions of war, such bondmen may be taken for the military service, and the impressing of freemen on that behalf in some measure spared.

[21] That every English native who hath goods, wares, and merchandise, may have freedom to transport the same to any place beyond the seas, and there to convert them to his own profit, it being his true and proper inheritance [so] to do . . . ; and therefore to that ª end, [that] the old trade-engrossing Company of Merchants may be dissolved, and the like for the future prevented.

[22] That the grievous oppressions by tithes and forced maintenance for the ministry be removed, and that the more easy and evangelical practice of contribution be granted and confirmed, for the benefit of the subject, and his freedom therein, for prevention of the lordliness in, and the commotions, oppressions, and tyrannies that might happen by, the clergy.

[23] That all ancient donations for the maintenance and continuance of free schools, which are . . . converted to any private use, and all such free schools which are destroyed . . . , may be restored and erected again, and that all parts or counties, . . . destitute of free schools for the due nurture and education of children, may have a competent number of such schools founded, erected, and endowed at the public charges of those respective counties and places so destitute, that few or none of the freemen of England may for the future be ignorant of reading and writing.

[24] That all ancient charitable donations towards the constant relief of the poor . . . and all hospitals that are . . . vitiated from their primitive constitution and end, or . . . deprived of any of their franchise, profits or emoluments, may be restored . . . and safely preserved to the relief and maintenance of poor orphans, widows, aged and impotent persons, &c. And that there be a convenient number of hospitals . . . erected and constituted in all the counties of England and Wales, at the public charge of the respective counties, for the good education and nurture of poor fatherless or helpless children, maintenance and relief of poor widows, aged, sick, and lame persons. And to that end, that all the glebe-lands in the kingdom may be converted to the maintenance and use of those charitable houses.

[25] That all the grounds which anciently lay in common for the poor, and are now . . . enclosed . . . , may forthwith, in whose hands soever they are, be . . . laid open again to the free and common use and benefit of the poor.

[26] That strong provision be made that neither the Parliament nor any inferior court . . . may in any wise let . . . any person or persons from contriving, promoting, or presenting any petition . . . concerning their grievances [and] liberties, to the High Court of Parliament.

PARLIAMENT ONCE MORE

From the Levellers' *Petition to the House of Commons*,[1] 11th September 1648.[a]

The truth is (and we see we must either now speak [or] for ever be silent), we have long expected things of another nature from you, and such as, we are confident, would have given satisfaction to all serious people of all parties:

1. That you would have made good the supreme [authority] of the people in this honourable House from all pretences of negative voices, either in King or Lords.

2. That you would have made laws for election of Representatives yearly and of course, without writ or summons.

---

[1] This appears to be the Petition of 11th September, referred to in the *Remonstrance of the Army* (Appendix, p. 464) and in the Whitehall Debates (pp. 141–2). But the Large Petition of March 1647 (pp. 318–23) seems also to have been revived at this time, and to have been printed more than once. It is possible that the references to the Petition of 11th September are intended to cover both documents.

3. That you would have set express times for their meeting, continuance, and dissolution: as not to exceed forty or fifty days at the most, and to have fixed an expressed time for the ending of this present Parliament.

4. That you would have exempted matters of religion and God from the compulsive and restrictive power of any authority upon earth, and reserved to the supreme authority an uncompulsive power only of appointing a way for the public worship,[a] whereby abundance of misery, persecution, and heart-burning would for ever be avoided.

5. That you would have disclaimed in yourselves, and all future Representatives, a power of pressing and forcing any sort of men to serve in wars, there being nothing more opposite to freedom, nor more unreasonable in an authority empowered for raising moneys. (In all [due] occasions for war,[b] and [with] a just cause, assistants need not be doubted; the other way serving rather to maintain injustice and corrupt parties.)

6. That you would have made both kings, queens, princes, dukes, earls, lords, and all persons, alike liable to every law of the land, made or to be made, that so all persons, even the highest, might fear and stand in awe [of them], and neither violate the public peace nor [the] private right of person or estate (as hath been frequent) without being liable to accompt as other men.

7. That you would have freed all commoners from the jurisdiction of the Lords in all cases; and to have taken care that all trials should be only of twelve sworn men, and no conviction but upon two or more sufficient, known witnesses.

8. That you would have freed all men from being examined against themselves, and from being questioned or punished for doing of that against which no law hath been provided.

9. That you would have abbreviated the proceedings in law, mitigated and made certain the charge thereof in all particulars.

10. That you would have freed all trade and merchandizing from all monopolizing and engrossing by companies or otherwise.

11. That you would have abolished excise, and all kinds of taxes except subsidies, the old and only just way of England.

12. That you would have laid open all late enclosures of fens, and other commons, or have enclosed them only or chiefly to the benefit of the poor.

13. That you would have considered the many thousands that are ruined by perpetual imprisonment for debt, and provided to their enlargement.

14. That you would have ordered some effectual course to

keep people from begging and beggary in so fruitful a nation as, through God's blessing, this is.

15. That you would have proportioned punishments more equal to offences, that so men's lives and estates might not be forfeited upon trivial and slight occasions.

16. That you would have removed the tedious burden of tithes, satisfying all impropriators, and providing a more equal way of maintenance for the public ministers.

17. That you would have raised a stock of money out of those many confiscated estates you have had, for payment of those who contributed voluntarily above their abilities, before you had provided for those that disbursed out of their superfluities.

18. That you would have bound yourselves and all future Parliaments from abolishing propriety, levelling men's estates, or making all things common.

19. That you would have declared what the duty or business [a] of the kingly office is, and what not; and ascertained the revenue, past increase or diminution, that so there might never be more quarrels about the same.

20. That you would have rectified the election of public officers for the City of London, of every particular company therein, restoring the commonalty thereof to their just rights, most unjustly withheld from them to the producing and maintaining of corrupt interest[s], opposite to common freedom, and exceedingly prejudicial to the trade and manufactures of this nation.

21. That you would have made full and ample reparations to all persons that had been oppressed by sentences in High Commission, Star [b] Chamber, and Council-board, or by any kind of monopolizers or projectors, and that out of the estates of those that were authors, actors, or promoters of so intolerable mischiefs, and that without much attendance.

22. That you would have abolished all committees, and have conveyed all businesses into the true method of the usual trials of the commonwealth.

23. That you would not have followed the example of former tyrannous and superstitious Parliaments in making orders, ordinances or laws, or in appointing punishments, concerning opinions or things supernatural, styling some blasphemies, others heresies, whenas you know yourselves easily mistaken and that divine truths need no human helps to support them; such proceedings having been generally invented to divide the people amongst themselves, and to affright men from that liberty of discourse by which corruption and tyranny would be soon discovered.

24. That you would have declared what the business of the Lords [w]as, and ascertain[ed] their condition, not derogating from the liberties of other men, that so there might be an end of striving about the same.

25. That you would have done justice upon the capital authors and promoters of the former or late wars, many of them being under your power; considering that mercy to the wicked is cruelty to the innocent, and that all your lenity doth but make them the more insolent and presumptuous.

26. That you would have provided constant pay for the Army, now under the command of the Lord Gen[eral] Fairfax, and given rules to all judges, and all other public officers throughout the land, for their indemnity, and for the saving harmless all that have anyways assisted you, or that have said or done anything against the King, Queen, or any of his party since the beginning of this Parliament; without which any of his party are in a better condition than those who have served you, nothing being more frequent with them than their reviling of you and your friends; [and] the things and worthy acts which have been done and achieved by this Army and their adherents (however ungratefully suffered to be scandalized as sectaries and men of corrupt judgments) in defence of the just authority of this honourable House and of the common liberties of the nation, and in opposition to all kinds of tyranny and oppression, being so far from meriting an odious Act of Oblivion, that they rather deserve a most honourable Act of Perpetual Remembrance, to be as a pattern of public virtue, fidelity and resolution, to all posterity.

27. That you would have laid to heart all the abundance of innocent blood that hath been spilt, and the infinite spoil and havoc that hath been made of peaceable, harmless people, by express commissions from the King; and seriously to have considered whether the justice of God be likely to be satisfied, or his yet continuing wrath appeased, by an Act of Oblivion.

These, and the like, we have long time hoped you would have minded, and [would thereby] have made such an establishment for the general peace, and contentful satisfaction of all sorts of people, as should have been to the happiness of all future generations. And which we most earnestly desire you would set yourselves speedily to effect; whereby the almost dying honour of this most honourable House would be again revived, and the hearts of your petitioners, and all other well-affected people, be afresh renewed unto you, [and] the freedom of the nation (now in perpetual hazard) would be firmly established. For which you would once more be so strengthened with the love of the people, that you should not need to cast your eyes any other ways (under God) for your security. But if all this availeth nothing, God be our guide; for man showeth us not a way for our preservation. * * *

AGREEMENTS OF THE PEOPLE

THE HISTORY OF THE SECOND AGREEMENT [1]

From John Lilburne, *Legal Fundamental Liberties* (1649) [a]

And being come to London, myself and some other of my friends, by two messengers . . . , sent a message down[2] to him [Cromwell] to Pontefract,[b] to be delivered to himself, and to debate it with him and bring his express answer back again speedily. The effect of which message was: that to our knowledge God had caused him to understand the principles of a just government under which the glory of God may shine forth by an equal distribution unto all men; that the obtaining of this was the sole intended end of the war; and that the war cannot be justified upon any other account than the defence of the people's right unto that just government and their freedom under it.

His answer to which message, by Mr. Hunt, was principally directed to the Independents. Some of whom appointed a meeting at the Nag's Head Tavern by Blackwell Hall . . . , and invited Mr. Wildman and myself, &c. thither. Whither we went accordingly, and . . . met with Colonel Tichborne,[c] Col. John White, Dr. Parker, Mr. Taylor, John Price, and divers others. Where we had a large debate of things, and where the just ends of the war were as exactly laid open by Mr. Wildman as ever I heard in my life. But towards the conclusion they plainly told us the chief things first to be done by the Army was first to cut off the King's head, &c., and force and thoroughly purge, if not dissolve, the Parliament. All of which we were all against, and pressed to know the bottom of their centre and in what they would absolutely rest for a future settlement. And I plainly told them in these words or to this effect: It 's true, I look upon the King as an evil man in his actions, and divers of his party as bad, but the Army had cozened us the last year and fallen from all their promises and declarations, and therefore could not

[1] For the first *Agreement* see Appendix, pp. 443–5.
[2] Early in November 1648.

rationally any more be trusted by us, without good cautions and security. In which regard, although we should judge the King as arrant a tyrant as they supposed him, or could imagine him to be, and the Parliament as bad as they could make them; yet, there being no other balancing power in the kingdom against the Army but the King and Parliament, it was our interest to keep up one tyrant to balance another, till we certainly knew what that tyrant that pretended fairest would give us as our freedoms; that so we might have something to rest upon and not suffer the Army (so much as in us lay) to devolve all the government of the kingdom into their wills and swords (which were two things we, nor no rational man, could like), and leave no persons nor power to be a counter-balance against them. And if we should do this, our slavery for [the] future (I told them) might probably be greater than ever it was in the King's time, and so our last error would be greater than our first. And therefore I pressed very hard for an Agreement amongst the people first, utterly disclaiming the thoughts of the other till this was done. And this (I told them) was not only my opinion, but I believe[d] it to be the unanimous opinion of all my friends with whom I most constantly conversed.

At which the gentlemen Independents were some of them most desperately choleric. But, my opinion being backed with the speeches of some others of my friends, we came calmly to choose out four and four of a side to debate and conclude of some heads towards the accomplishment of an Agreement of the People, and (as I remember) their four were Colonel Tichborne, Col. White, Dr. Parker, and Jo[hn] Price; and our four were Mr. William Walwyn, Lieut.-Col. Wetton, Mr. John Wildman, and myself. But John Price sent some of the company to tell us (after we were parted and some of us drinking a cup of wine below), he would not make one if Mr. Walwyn was one, for he had a prejudice against him. Unto which I replied, Mr. Walwyn had more honesty and integrity in his little finger than John Price had in all his body, and therefore no meeting for me, seeing John Price was so base, unless Mr. Walwyn was one though we had but two of a side! But the business being much debated and expostulated, Mr. Walwyn and John Price both (for peace' sake) were at present laid aside; and according to appointment (as I remember) all the other six met the fifteenth of November 1648, being Wednesday, at the aforementioned Nag's Head, and there after some debate unanimously agreed in these words, viz.: That in our conceptions the only way of settlement is:

    1. That some persons be chosen by the Army to represent the

whole body and that the well-affected in every county (if it may be) choose some persons to represent them, and those to meet at the headquarters.

2. That those persons ought not to exercise any legislative power, but only to draw up the foundations of a just government, and to propound them to the well-affected people in every county, to be agreed to. Which agreement ought to be above law, and therefore the bounds, limits, and extent of the people's legislative deputies in parliament, contained in the Agreement, [ought] to be drawn up into a formal contract to be mutually signed by the well-affected people and their said deputies upon the days of their election respectively.

3. To prevent present confusion, the Parliament (if it be possible) may not be by force immediately dissolved, but that the day of its dissolution be inserted in that Agreement, by virtue whereof it shall be dissolved.

4. That this way of settlement (if it may be) should be mentioned in the Army's first Remonstrance.

5. That the matter of the Petition of September 11 [1] be the matter to be settled.

Which Agreement of ours (as I remember) was immediately sent away to the headquarters at St. Albans by Mr. Highland [a] of Southwark, where (as it was afterwards told us) it was very well accepted and approved of by the great ones there. Whose high and mighty declaration [2] (drawn by Ireton at Windsor when he pretended to lay down his commission) against the King, coming to our view, we made divers objections against many passages in it, but especially at divers lashes that tacitly at the beginning of it hinted at us, which, we told some of their friends, could not be put in with a spirit of peace towards us or intention of good to the nation in those good things we desired and propounded for it. But it was with many fair expressions salved up by them. Upon which we judged it requisite for some of us to go to Windsor to speak with Mr. Ireton, the steersman himself, and accordingly (as I remember) Lieut.-Col. Wetton, Mr. Petty, Mr. Wildman, and myself met there, and, having drawn up our thoughts in writing, we communicated them to Col. Tichborne, Col. White, Mr. Moyer, and divers others of the Independent Party. Who went with us to the Governor's house; where we met with Mr. Peters, the grand journey- or hackney-man of the Army, and after we had acquainted him with our minds, we delivered him a copy of

---

[1] See above pp. 338–42.
[2] The *Remonstrance of the Army* (see Appendix, pp. 456–65).

our paper containing distinctly the heads of what we desired, and entreated him to deliver them to Commissary Ireton, with whom we desired to discourse about them. Who sent us word, at such an hour he would come to our inn at the Garter, to speak with us about them. And accordingly he did, accompanied with a whole train of officers. And a large and sharp discourse we had, our principal difference lying in ª his desire in the too strict restraining liberty of conscience and in keeping a power in the Parliament to punish where no visible law is transgressed, the unreasonableness of which was much spoken against by divers of the principal officers with him, but especially by Col. Harrison, who was then extreme fair and gilded. And so little satisfaction had we at that meeting from Ireton (the Army's Alpha and Omega) that we despaired of any good from them and were in a manner resolved to come away in haste to London and acquaint our friends with our conceptions, and so improve our interests, forcibly, as much as we could, to oppose their intended designs. But Colonel Harrison coming to us again at ten o'clock according to our desire, we had a private and large discourse with him, and fully and effectually acquainted him with the most desperate mischievousness of their attempting to do these things without giving some good security to the nation for the future settlement of their liberties and freedoms, especially in frequent, free, and successive Representatives, according to their many promises, oaths, covenants and declarations—or else as soon as they had performed their intentions to destroy the King, which we fully understood they were absolutely resolved to do (yea, as they told us, though they did it by martial law), and also totally to root up the Parliament and invite so many members to come to them as would join with them to manage businesses till a new and equal Representative could by an agreement be settled, which, the chiefest of them protested before God, was the ultimate and chiefest of their designs and desires: I say, we pressed hard for security before they attempted these things in the least, lest when they were done we should be solely left to their wills and swords, by which, we told them, they might rule over us arbitrarily without declared laws as a conquered people and so deal with us as the poor slavish peasants in France are dealt with, who enjoy nothing that they can call their own. And besides we plainly told him: we would not trust their bare words in general only, for they had broke their promise once already both with us and the kingdom, and he that would break once would make no conscience of breaking twice if it served for his ends, and therefore they must come to some absolute particular compact with us, or

else, some of us told him, we would post away to London and stir
up our interest against them—yea, and spend our bloods to oppose
them. To which he replied to this effect: it was true,[a] what we
said, for he must ingenuously confess they had once broken with
us and the kingdom, and therefore acknowledged it was dangerous
trusting them upon generals again. But, saith he, we cannot stay
so long from going to London with the Army as to perfect an
Agreement, and without our speedy going we are all unavoidably
destroyed. For (saith he) we fully understand that the treaty
betwixt the King and Parliament is almost concluded upon, at
the conclusion of which we shall be commanded by King and
Parliament to disband. The which if we do, we are unavoidably
destroyed for what we have done already, and if we do not disband
they will by Act of Parliament proclaim us traitors and declare
us to be the only hinderers of settling peace in the nation. And
then (saith he) we shall never be able to fight with both the interest
of King and Parliament, so that you will be destroyed as well as
we. For we certainly understand that Major-General Browne,
&c., are underhand preparing an army against us. And therefore
I profess—I confess I know not well what to say to your reasons,
they are so strong, but—our necessities are so great that we must
speedily go or perish; and to go without giving you some content,
is hazardable too.

Well, sir, said we, we have as much cause to distrust the Parliament-men as we have to distrust you; for we know what and how
many large promises they have made to the kingdom and how
little they have performed. And we also know what a temptation
honour, power, and profit are even to those spirits that were pretty
ingenuous and honest before. And when you have done your
work and got, as you pretend, forty or fifty of the honestest members of the House to you, alas (said we), it will be a mock-power.
Yet they may find such sweetness and delight in their pretended
power that they may fly to your swords for their protection and
bid us go shake our ears for our Agreement and go look [for] it
where we can catch it. And therefore we will trust generals no
more to your forty or fifty members of Parliament than to you.
For it 's possible, if we leave the Agreement to their framing, they
may frame us such a one as will do us no good, but rather make us
slaves by our own consents if signed by us. And therefore we
pressed him that we might agree upon a final and absolute judge
of the matter and method of the Agreement, that so we might not
spend months and years in dispute about it.

And therefore we would propound this unto him: that if their

honest friends in the Parliament, as they called them, would choose
four from amongst themselves, and the Army four from amongst
themselves, and the Independents four from amongst themselves,
we that were nicknamed Levellers would choose four from among
ourselves; and these sixteen should draw up the Agreement finally
without any more appeal to any other. And we for our parts, so
far as all our interest in England extended, would be willing to
acquiesce in, and submit to, the determinations of them, [the]
sixteen, or the major part of them. And we would be willing the
Presbyterian Party should be invited and desired to choose four
more to be of equal authority with the other sixteen, provided
they did it by the first day we should appoint to meet upon.
Which proposition he approved of extraordinary well, and said,
it was as just, as rational, and as equitable, as possibly could be, and
said he doubted not but all interests would centre in it, and engaged to acquaint them with it. And so we parted very glad that
we were likely to come to some fixed agreement for the future
enjoyment of our dear-bought and hard-purchased freedoms.

And the next morning we went to the gentlemen Independents
. . ., and we acquainted them with it, who liked it very well; and
with whom we fixed a night for several distinct meetings in London,
to choose our respective trustees for this work, and also appointed
a day to meet at Windsor again about it. * * * So we went . . . to
Commissary-General Ireton's chamber to have his concurrence,
which of all sides was taken for the concurrence of the whole
Army—or at least for the powerful and governing part of it, he
being in a manner both their eyes and ears. So . . . he . . . sent us
out word by Colonel Harrison (as he averred to us) that he did
absolutely and heartily agree to the foresaid proposition, which
to avoid mistakes was again repeated. So we seemed joyful men
of all sides, and appointed a day speedily to meet at Windsor about
it, Master Holland again and again engaging for four Parliament-
men, and Colonel Harrison, with Commissary Ireton, for four of
the Army, as we Londoners had done for each of our tribe. And
so to horse we went, and I overtook upon the road the whole gang
of Independents, with whom I discoursed again, and acquainted
them all fully with the absoluteness of our agreement. Which
they acquainted their friends with in London; who chose Colonel
Tichborne, Colonel John White, Master Daniel Taylor, and
Master Price the scrivener. And for our party there was, by
unanimous consent of the agents from our friends in and about
London, at a very ᵃ large meeting, chosen Master William Walwyn,
Master Maximilian Petty, Master John Wildman, and myself.

And for the honest men of the Parliament, as they were called, they had several meetings at the Bell in Kings Street, and at Somerset House, where (as I was informed) they chose Colonel Henry Marten,[a] Colonel Alexander Rigby, Master Thomas Chaloner,[b] and Master Scot, with one or two more to supply the places of those of them that should be absent at any time about their occasions. So when we came to Windsor, the Army men had chosen Commissary-General Ireton, Sir William Constable, and (as I remember) Colonel Tomlinson, Colonel Baxter, Lieutenant-Colonel Kelsey, and Captain Parker, some two of the which last four should always make up the number. So we had a meeting in their Council Chamber at the Castle; where we were all of all sides present but only the Parliament-men, for whom only Colonel Marten appeared. And after a large discourse about the foundations of our Agreement we departed to our lodging. Where Colonel Marten and we four nicknamed Levellers locked ourselves up and went in good earnest to the consideration of our Agreement. But much was not done in it there because of their haste to London, to force and break up the Parliament—which journey at all was very much opposed by Mr. Walwyn and many reasons he gave against their march to London at all—the absolute dissolution of which their friends in the House would no ways admit of, although Ireton, Harrison, &c., commonly styled it then a parliament *that had forfeited its trust, a mock-parliament*, and [said] that if they did not totally dissolve it, but purge it, it would be but a mock-parliament and a mock-power however. For where have we, say they, either law, warrant or commission to purge it? Or can anything justify us in the doing it but the height of necessity to save the kingdom from a new war that they, with the conjunction with the King, will presently vote and declare for; and to procure a new and free Representative, and so successive and frequent free Representatives, which this present Parliament will never suffer, and without which the freedoms of the nation are lost and gone? And the doing of which can only justify before God and man our present and former extraordinary actings with and against legal authority, and so [escape rendering] all our fighting fruitless. And this was their open and common discourse, with more of the like nature, and [especially] to those that objected against their total dissolving or breaking the House and the illegality of their intended and declared trying of the King—which also was opposed by us till a new and unquestionable Representative was sitting. * * *

But to return to our acting to complete the Agreement. All parties chosen of all sides constantly met at Whitehall after the

Army came to town, saving the Parliament-men failed — only Master Marten was most commonly there. And a long and tedious tug we had with Commissary-General Ireton only, yea sometimes whole nights together, principally about liberty of conscience and the Parliament's punishing where no law provides. And very angry and lordly in his debates many times he was. But to some kind of an expedient in the first for peace' sake we condescended ᵃ to please him, and so came amongst the major part of the sixteen commissioners, according to our original agreement, to an absolute and final conclusion, and thinking all had been done as to any more debate upon it, and that it should without any more ado be promoted for subscriptions, first at the Council of War, and so in the regiments, and so all over the nation. But alas, poor fools! we were merely cheated and cozened (it being the principal unhappiness of some of us, as to the flesh, to have our eyes wide open to see things long before most honest men come to have their eyes open, and this is that which turns to our smart and reproach), and that which we commissioners feared at the first, viz., that no tie, promises, nor engagements were strong enough to [bind] the grand jugglers and leaders of the Army, was now made clearly manifest. For when it came to the Council [1] there came the General, Cromwell, and the whole gang of creature-colonels and other officers, and spent many days in taking it all in pieces, and there Ireton himself showed himself an absolute king, if not an emperor, against whose will no man must dispute. And then shuttlecock Roe, their scout, Okey, and Major Barton (where Sir Hardress Waller sat president) begun in their open council to quarrel with us by giving some of us base and unworthy language; which procured them from me a sharp retortment of their own baseness and unworthiness into their teeth, and a challenge from myself into the field besides, seeing they were like to fight with us in the room in their own garrison. Which, when Sir Hardress in my ear reproved me for it, I justified it, and gave it him again for suffering us to be so affronted. [2] And within a little time after, I took my leave of them for a pack of dissembling, juggling knaves amongst whom in consultation ever thereafter I should scorn to come (as I told some of them), for there was neither faith, truth, nor common honesty amongst them. And so away I went to those that chose and trusted me and gave publicly and effectually (at a set meeting appointed on purpose)

[1] See Whitehall Debates, above pp. 125–69. For the Levellers' protest at the time, see Appendix, pp. 472–4.
[2] Clarke MSS. contain no record of this incident.

to divers of them an exact account how they had dealt with us and cozened and deceived us, and so absolutely discharged myself for meddling or making any more with so perfidious a generation of men as the great ones of the Army were, but especially the cunningest of Machiavelians, Commissary Henry Ireton. And having an exact copy of what the greatest part of the foresaid sixteen had agreed upon, I only mended a clause in the first reserve about religion to the sense of us all but Ireton, and put an epistle to it of the 15 [1] of December 1648, and printed it of my own accord,[2] and the next day it came abroad. About which Mr. Price the scrivener and myself had a good sharp bout at Colonel Tichborne's house within two or three days after. Where I avowed the publishing of it, and also putting my epistle to it of my own head and accord. And after that I came no more amongst them, but with other of my friends prepared a complaint against their dealing with us and a kind of protest against their proceedings; which with my own hand I presented to the General's own hands at the Mews, the 28 of December 1648; . . . and which was immediately printed by Ja. and Jo. Moxon, for William Larner[3]. . . . Within two or three days of the delivery of which I went towards my journey to Newcastle. . . .

And yet in . . . a Declaration . . . appointed by His Excellency and his Council of War to be . . . published, May 22, 1649, . . . and first printed at Oxford, and then reprinted at London, May 23, 1649, I find these very words, viz.:

'The grounds and manner of the proceedings of these men that have so much pretended for the liberty of the people, have been as followeth.

'There was a paper styled the Agreement of the People framed by certain select persons and debated at a general council of officers of the Army, to be tendered to the Parliament, and to be by them commended over to the people of the nation, it being hoped that such an expedient, if assented unto at least by the honest part of the people that had appeared for this common cause to which God hath so witnessed, it would have tended much to settlement and the composing of our differences—at least have fixed honest men to such grounds of certainty as might have kept them firm and entire in opposing the common enemy, and [in] stand[ing] united to public interest.

---

[1] Epistle is dated the tenth (see below, p. 356). Another edition (McAlpin Collection, New York) is dated the fifteenth.
[2] *Foundations of Freedom* (see below, pp. 355–67).
[3] *A Plea for Common Right and Freedom* (see below, pp. 472–4).

'The General Council of the Army, and the other sorts of men going then under the name of Levellers (so baptized by yourselves at Putney), who by their last actings have made good the same which we then judged but an imputation, had, as now it appears, different ends and aims both in the matter and manner of their proceedings. That which was intended by those men was to have somewhat tendered as a test and coercion upon the people and all sorts of men and authorities in the land. That which these, to wit, the Council of the Army, aimed at was to make an humble representation of such things as were then likely to give satisfaction and unite, and might be remitted to men's judgments to be owned or disowned as men were satisfied in their consciences, and as it should please God to let men see reason for their so doing; that so it might not be only called an Agreement, but through the freedom of it be one indeed, and receive its stamp of approbation from the Parliament, to whom it was humbly submitted.

'Hereupon those other men took so much dissatisfaction that they forthwith printed and spread abroad their paper, which was different from that of the Army, using all possible means to make the same to pass—but with how little effect is very well known. And finding by the Army's application to the Parliament that they were likely, according to their duty, to stand by and own them as the supreme authority of the nation, they have by all means essayed to vilipend that authority, presenting them to the people, in printed libels and otherwise, as worse tyrants than any who were before them.'

In which passage of the General's and his Council I shall desire to observe these things . . . :

First, that they give a false and untrue narrative of the original occasion of that Agreement, to which by our importunate importunity they were necessitated, and drawn unto that little they did in it as a bear to the stake, as is truly by me before declared; and which, as the sequel shows, they undertook merely to quiet and please us (like children with rattles) till they had done their main work (viz., either in annihilating or purging the House, to make it fit for their purpose, and in destroying the King, unto both which they never had our consents in the least), that so they might have no opposition from us, but that we might be lulled asleep in a fool's paradise with thoughts of their honest intentions till all was over, and then totally lay it aside, as they have done, as being then able to do what they pleased whether we would or no. For if they ever had intended an Agreement, why do they let their own lie dormant in the pretended Parliament ever since they presented it, seeing it is obvious to every knowing English eye that from the day they presented it, to this hour, they have had as much power over their own Parliament now sitting as any schoolmaster in England ever had over his boys? But to them it was presented (who scarce ought to meddle with it) on purpose that there, without any more stir about it, it might be lodged for ever. For, alas, an Agreement of the People is not proper to come from the Parliament, because it comes from thence rather with a command than anything else; for that it 's we, and not they, that really and in good earnest say it ought not to do, but to be voluntary. Besides, that which is done by one parliament, as a parliament, may be undone by the next parliament, but an Agreement of the People, begun and ended amongst the people, can never come justly within the Parliament's cognizance to destroy; which the General (and the chief of his Council) knew well enough; and I dare safely say it upon my conscience, that an Agreement of the People upon foundations of just freedom gone through with, is a thing the General (and the chiefest of his Council) as much hates as they do honesty, justice and righteousness (which they long since abandoned), [and] against which in their own spirits they are absolutely resolved, I do verily believe, to spend their heart's blood, and not to leave a man breathing in English air, if possibly they can, that thoroughly and resolutely prosecutes it; a new and just Parliament being more dreadful to them than the great Day of Judgment spoken so much of in the scripture. And although they have beheaded the King, yet I am confidently persuaded their enmity is such at the people's liberties that they would sooner run the hazard of letting the Prince in, to reign in his father's stead, than further really a just agreement, or endure the sight of a new Parliament rightly constituted. * * *

[As his next two points, Lilburne denies that his *Foundations of Freedom* post-dated the presentation of the Agreement to the Parliament and that this presentation was the ground of the Levellers' dissatisfaction, and proceeds]:

Fourthly, they say we used all possible means to make ours pass, but with how little success, they say, is very well known. If they mean we used all possible means to make ours pass with them, it 's true; but the reason it had no better effect was because they had no mind to it; it was too honest for them. And I am sure, in the very epistle to it, it is declared that the principal reason of the printing of it is that the people might have an opportunity to consider the equity of it, and offer their reasons against anything

therein contained.   And this was all the means, after the printing
of it, we used to make it pass. * * *

Fifthly, they say, we were troubled at their doing their duty in
submitting to authority and owning the Parliament as the supreme
authority of the nation; whenas, alas, it is as visible as the sun
when it shines in its glory and splendour, that Korah, Dathan and
Abiram of old were never such rebels against authority as the
General and his Council are, nor the Anabaptists at Munster with
John of Leyden and Knipperdolling[a] were never more contemners
of authority; nor Jack Straw, nor Wat Tyler, nor all those famous
men mentioned with a black pen in our histories and called rebels
and traitors can never be put in any scale of equal balance, for all
manner of rebellions and treasons against all sorts and kinds of
magistracy, with the General and his Council. * * * For did any
or all of them forementioned ever rebel against their advancers,
promoters, and creators, as these have done two several times?
Did ever any or all of them chop off (without all shadow of law)
a king's and nobles' heads, ravish and force a parliament twice,
nay raze the foundation of a parliament to the ground, and under
the notion of performing a trust, break all oaths, covenants, protestations, and declarations, and make evidently void all the
declared ends of the war? * * *

And as for their styling this their own junto, the supreme
authority: I know the time not long since when that style to be
given to the House of Commons single was accounted an abominable wickedness in the eye of the chiefest of them.   Yea, I also
know the time . . . that they were absolutely resolved and determined to pull up this their own Parliament by the roots, and not
so much as to leave a shadow of it (frequently then calling it a
mock-power, and a mock-parliament), yea, and had done it if
we, and some in the House of our then friends, had not been the
principal instruments to hinder them, we judging it then of two
evils the least to choose rather to be governed by the shadow of a
parliament till we could get a real and true one (which with the
greatest protestations in the world they then promised and engaged
with all their might speedily to effect) than simply, solely, and only
by the wills of swordsmen, whom we had already found to be men
of no very tender consciences.   But to me it is no wonder that
they own this for the supreme power, seeing they have totally in
law, reason and justice broke the Parliament, and absolutely, by
the hands of Tho[mas] Pride, set up indeed a mock-power and a
mock-parliament, by purging out all those that they were any way
jealous of, [and that] would not vote as they would have them, and

suffering and permitting none to sit but, for the major part of them, a company of absolute schoolboys, that will, like good boys, say their lessons after them, their lords and masters, and vote as they would have them, and so be a screen . . . betwixt them and the people, with the name of parliament and the shadow and imperfect image of legal and just authority—to pick their pockets for them by assessments and taxations, and by their arbitrary and tyrannical courts and committees (the best of which is now become a perfect Star Chamber, High Commission and Councilboard) make them their perfect slaves and vassals by their constant and continual breaking and abasing of their spirits. * * *

The Cavaliers . . . were most desperate mad at me in particular about the beheading of the late King, although I were as far as Newcastle when it was done, and refused to give my consent to be one of his judges (although I was solicited so to be before I went out of London); yea, although I avowedly declared myself at Windsor against the manner and time of their intended dealing with him, arguing there very stiffly that upon their own principles, which led them to look upon all legal authority in England as now broken, they could be no better than murderers in taking away the King's life though never so guilty of the crimes they charged upon him. For as justice ought to be done, especially for blood, which they then principally charged upon him (so said I, and still say), it ought to be done justly. For in case another man murder me, and a day, a week, or a year after, my brother or friend, that is no legal magistrate, executes him therefor, yet this is murder in the eye of the law because it was done by a hand had no authority to do it. And therefore I pressed again and again, seeing themselves confessed all legal authority in England was broke, that they would stay his trial till a new and equal free Representative upon the Agreement of the well-affected people (that had not fought against their liberties, rights and freedoms) could be chosen and sit; and then either try him thereby or else by their judges sitting in the court called King's Bench. But they at Windsor asked me how by law I could have him tried. I told them: the law of England expressly saith, 'Whosoever murders or kills another shall die'; it doth not say, excepting the King . . .; and therefore where none is excepted, there all men are included in law. But the King is a man: *ergo*, he is included as well as I. Unto which it was objected, that it would hardly be proved that the King with his own hands killed a man. To which I answered: By the law of England, he that counsels or commissionates others to kill a man or men is as guilty of the fact as he or they that do it.

And besides, the advantage of trying of the King by the rules of the law would be sufficient to declare that no man is born (or justly can be made) lawless, but that even magistrates, as well as people, are subject to the penal part of the law, as well as the directive part. And besides, to try him in an extraordinary way that hath no real footsteps nor paths in our law would be a thing of extraordinary ill precedent; for why not twenty upon pretended extraordinary cases as well as one? And why not a thousand as well as twenty? And extraordinary cases are easily made and pretended by those that are uppermost, though never so unjust in themselves. And besides, to try him in an extraordinary way when the law hath provided all the essentials of justice in an ordinary way . . . will nourish and increase in men that erroneous conceit, that magistrates, by the law of God, nature, and reason, are not—nó, nor ought not to be—subject to the penal part of the laws of men, as well as the directive part of it; which is the bane, ruin, and destruction of all the commonwealths in the world. * * *

THE SECOND AGREEMENT OF THE PEOPLE (1648)

From John Lilburne, *Foundations of Freedom* a
(with variants introduced by the Council of Officers, in notes)

The Publisher to the Judicious Reader

Dear Countryman,

This Agreement having had its conception for a common good as being that which contains those foundations of freedom and rules of government, adjudged necessary to be established in this nation for the future, by which all sorts of men are to be bound, I adjudged it a just and reasonable thing to publish it to the view of the nation, to the end that all men might have an opportunity to consider the equity thereof, and offer their reasons against anything therein contained, before it be concluded. That being agreeable to that principle which we profess, *viz.*, to do unto you as we would all men should do unto us, not doubting but that the justice of it will be maintained maugre the opposition of the stoutest calumniator, especially in those clear points in the reserve so much already controverted, *viz.*, touching the magistrate's power to compel or restrain in matters of religion, and the exercise of an arbitrary power in the Representative to punish men for state offences against which no law hath provided; which two things especially are so clear to my understanding that I dare with confidence aver that no man can demand the exercise of such a power but he that intends to be a tyrant, nor no man part with them but he that resolves to be a slave. * * *[1]

AN [2] AGREEMENT OF THE PEOPLE OF ENGLAND, AND THE PLACES THEREWITH INCORPORATED, FOR A FIRM AND PRESENT PEACE UPON GROUNDS OF COMMON RIGHT AND FREEDOM.[3]

Having by our late labours and hazards made it appear to the world at how high a rate we value our just freedom, and God having so far owned our cause as to deliver the enemies thereof into our hands, we do now hold ourselves bound, in mutual duty to each other, to take the best care we can for the future, to avoid both the danger of returning into a slavish condition and the chargeable remedy of another war. For as it cannot be imagined that so many of our countrymen would have opposed us in this quarrel if they had understood their own good, so may we safely promise to ourselves, that when our common rights and liberties shall be cleared, their endeavours will be disappointed, that seek to make themselves our masters. Since therefore our former oppressions, and not-yet-ended troubles, have been occasioned either by want of frequent national meetings in council, or by the undue or unequal constitution thereof, or by rendering those meetings ineffectual, we are fully agreed and resolved [4] to provide that hereafter our Representatives be neither left for uncertainty for time, nor be unequally constituted, nor made useless to the ends for which they are intended. In order whereunto we declare and agree:

I. That to prevent the many inconveniences apparently arising from the long continuance of the same persons in [5] authority, this present Parliament be dissolved upon or before the last day of April, in the year of our Lord 1649.

II. That the people of England being at this day very unequally distributed by counties, cities, or boroughs, for the election of their representatives, be more indifferently proportioned, and to

---

[1] Dated Friday, 10th December 1648.
[2] Notes (except where specified) record the significant changes introduced by the Council of Officers (as a result of the Whitehall Debates), before presenting the Agreement to Parliament, on 20th January 1649.[a]
[3] + and safety.   [4] + God willing.   [5] + supreme.

this end, that the Representative of the whole nation shall consist of 300 persons; [7] and in each county and the places thereto subjoined there shall be chosen to make up the said Representative at all times, the several numbers hereunder mentioned. * * *

[Here follows the distribution of seats for the counties, the cities, the parliamentary boroughs, and the two universities.] [8]

III. The Manner of Elections:

1. That the electors in every division shall be natives or denizens of England,[9] such as have subscribed this Agreement,[10] not persons receiving alms, but such as are assessed ordinarily towards the relief of the poor; not servants to, or receiving wages from, any particular person. And in all elections (except for the Universities) they shall be men of one-and-twenty years old or upwards, and housekeepers, dwelling within the division for which the election is. Provided that until the end of seven years next ensuing the time herein limited for the end of this present Parliament, no person shall be admitted to, or have any hand or voice in, such elections, who* have adhered to, or assisted the King against the Parliament in any of these wars or insurrections; or who shall make or join in, or abet any forcible opposition against this Agreement; [11] and that such as shall not subscribe it before the time limited for the end of this Parliament, shall not have vote in the next election; neither if they subscribe afterwards, shall they have any voice in the election next succeeding their subscription, unless their subscription were six months before the same.[12]

[7] 400 persons, or not more.   (Clarke MS. copy reads: three or four hundred.)

[8] + Provided that the first or second Representative may . . . assign the remainder of the 400 representers . . . unto such counties as shall appear in this present distribution to have less than their due proportion. Provided also that where any city or borough . . . shall be found in a due proportion not competent . . . to elect . . . the number of representers assigned thereto, it is left to future Representatives to assign such a number of parishes or villages near adjoining . . ., to be joined therewith in elections, or [they] may make the same proportionable. . . . That the people do, of course, choose themselves a Representative once in two years and shall meet for that purpose upon the first Thursday in every second May . . .; and the Representatives so chosen, to meet upon the second Thursday in the June following . . . and to continue their sessions . . . until the second Thursday in December following, unless they shall adjourn or dissolve themselves sooner; but not to continue longer. The election of the first Representative to be on the first Thursday in May 1649; and that and all future elections to be according to the rules prescribed in this Agreement.

[9-10] Omits.   [11-12] Omits.

2. That [13] until the end of fourteen years[14] such persons, and such only, may be elected for any division, who by the rule aforesaid are to have voice in elections in one place or other; provided that of those, none shall be eligible for the first or second Representatives who have not voluntarily assisted the Parliament against the King, either in person before the fourteenth of June, 1645, or else in money, plate, horse, or arms, lent upon the propositions, before the end of May, 1643, or who have joined in, or abetted the treasonable engagement in London in the year 1647, or who declared or engaged themselves for a cessation of arms with the Scots who invaded the nation the last summer, or for compliance with the actors in any the insurrections of the same summer, or with the Prince of Wales or his accomplices in the revolted fleet.[15]

3. That whoever, being by the rules in the two next preceding articles incapable of election, or to be elected, shall assume to vote in, or be present at, such elections for the first or second Representative, or being elected, shall presume to sit or vote in either of the said Representatives, shall incur the pain of confiscation of the moiety of his estate to the use of the public, in case he have any estate visible, to the value of fifty pounds. And if he have not such an estate, then he shall incur the pain of imprisonment for three months. And if any person shall forcibly oppose, molest, or hinder the people (capable of electing as aforesaid) in their quiet and free election of their representatives; [16] then each person so offending shall incur the pain of confiscation of his whole estate, both real and personal; and if he have not an estate to the value of fifty pounds, shall suffer imprisonment during one whole year without bail or mainprize; provided that the offender in each such case be convicted within three months next after the committing of his offence.[17]

4. That for the more convenient election of representatives, each county, with the several places thereto conjoined, wherein more than three representatives are to be chosen, shall be divided by a due proportion into so many parts, as each part may elect two, and no part above three, representatives. And for the making

[13] [14] Transposes provision respecting representatives to [15] before +

[15] + And we desire and recommend it to all men, that in all times the persons to be chosen for this great trust may be men of courage, fearing God and hating covetousness; and that our Representatives would make the best provisions for that end.

[16] + for the first Representative.

[17] + And the first Representative is to make further provision for the avoiding of these evils in future elections. + VI below.

of these divisions,[18] two persons be chosen in every hundred, lathe, or wapentake, by the people therein (capable of electing as aforesaid), which people shall on the last Tuesday in February next between eleven and three of the clock, be assembled together for that end at the chief town or usual meeting place in the same hundred, lathe, or wapentake. And that the persons in every hundred, lathe, or wapentake, so chosen, or the major part of them, shall on the fourteenth day after their election meet at the common hall of the county-town, and divide the county into parts as aforesaid, and also appoint a certain place in each respective part of the division, wherein the people shall always meet for the choice of their representatives, and shall make returns of the said divisions, and certain places of meeting therein, into the Parliament records in writing under the hands and seals of the major part of them present; and also cause the same to be published in every parish in the county before the end of March now next ensuing. And for the more equal division of the City of London for the choice of its representatives, there shall one person be chosen by the people in every parish in the said City (capable of election as aforesaid) upon the last Tuesday in February aforesaid; on which day they shall assemble in each parish for the same purpose between two and four of the clock. And that the persons so chosen, or the major part of them, shall upon the fourteenth day after their election meet in the Guild Hall of the said City, and divide the same City into eight equal parts or divisions, and appoint a certain place in every division respectively, wherein the people of that division shall always meet for the choice of their representatives, and shall make return thereof, and cause the same to be published in the manner prescribed to the several counties, as in this article.

5. That for the better provision for true and certain returns of persons elected, the chief public officer in every division aforesaid, who shall be present at the beginning of the election, and in the absence of every such officer, then any person eligible as aforesaid, whom the people at that time assembled shall choose for that end, shall regulate the elections, and by poll or otherwise clearly distinguish and judge thereof,[19] and make true return

[18–19] Substitutes: so as to make the elections less subject to confusion or mistake, in order to the next Representative, Thomas Lord Grey of Groby [two knights, one gentleman, five citizens of London, also named] or any five or more of them are intrusted to nominate . . . three or more fit persons in each county, and in each city and borough . . ., to be as commissioners for the ends aforesaid. . . . Which commissioners . . . shall . . . appoint two fit and faithful persons or more in each hundred,

thereof in writing indented under the hands and seals of himself,
and of six or more of the electors, into the Parliament's records,
within one-and-twenty days after the election, and for default
thereof, or for making any false return, shall forfeit £100 to the
public use.[20]

IV. That one hundred and fifty members at least be always
present in each sitting of the Representatives at the passing of
any law, or doing of any act whereby the people are to be bound.[21]

V. That every Representative shall within twenty days after
their first meeting, appoint a Council of State for the managing of
public affairs until the first [22] day of the next Representative, and
the same council to act and proceed therein, according to such instructions and limitations as the Representatives shall give, and
not otherwise.

---

lathe, or wapentake . . . and in each ward within the City of London, to
take care for the orderly taking of all voluntary subscriptions to this
Agreement. . . . And the same commissioners . . . for the several counties,
cities, and boroughs respectively shall, where more than three representers
are to be chosen, divide such counties, as also the City of London, into
. . . such parts as are aforementioned and shall set forth the bounds of
such divisions; and shall . . . appoint one place certain wherein the people
shall meet for the choice of the representers, and some one fit person
or more . . . to be present at the time and place of election, in the nature
of sheriffs to regulate the elections . . .; and shall in every . . . parish likewise nominate . . . one trusty person or more . . ., to make a true list of
all the persons . . . who, according to the rules aforegoing, are to have
voice in the elections, and expressing who amongst them are, by the same
rules, capable of being elected, and such list . . . to bring in and return . .
unto the person appointed in the nature of sheriff. . . . Which person . . .
being present . . ., or in case of his absence by one hour after the time
limited for the people's meeting, then any person present that is eligible,
. . . whom the people, then and there assembled, shall choose for that
end, shall receive . . . the said lists and admit the persons therein contained . . . unto a vote in the said election, and, having first caused this
Agreement to be publicly read . . ., shall proceed unto, and regulate, and
keep peace and order in the elections, and by poll or otherwise openly
distinguish and judge of the same. . . .

[20] + and [he] shall also cause indentures to be made . . . betwixt himself and six or more of the said electors, on the one part, and . . . each
person elected . . ., on the other part, expressing their election of him as a
representer of them according to this Agreement, and his acceptance of
that trust, and his promise to perform the same with faithfulness, to the
best of his understanding and ability, for the glory of God and [the] good
of the people. This course is to hold for the first Representative, which
is to provide for the ascertaining of these circumstances in order to future
Representatives.

[21] + saving that the number of sixty may make a house for debates or
resolutions that are preparatory thereunto.

[22] tenth . . . unless that next Representative think fit to put an end to
that trust sooner.

VI. That to the end all officers of state may be certainly accomptable, and no factions made to maintain corrupt interests, no member of a Council of State, nor any officer of any salary forces in army or garrison, nor any treasurer or receiver of public moneys, shall (while such) be elected to be a representative; and in case any such election shall be, the same to be void; and in case any lawyer shall be chosen of any Representative or Council of State, then he shall be incapable of practice as a lawyer during that trust.

VII.[23] That the power of the People's Representatives extend (without the consent or concurrence of any other person or persons) to the enacting, altering, repealing, and declaring of laws; to the erecting and abolishing officers of courts of justice,[24] and to whatsoever is not in this Agreement excepted or reserved from them.

As particularly:[25]

1.[26] We do not empower our Representatives to continue in

[23] + That the Representatives have, and shall be understood to have, the supreme trust in order to the preservation and government of the whole.
[24]–[25] Omits.
[25] + and the highest and final judgment concerning all natural or civil things, but not concerning things spiritual or evangelical. Provided that, even in things natural and civil, these six particulars . . . are . . . understood to be excepted and reserved from our Representatives.
[26] (Lilburne admits here 'mending a clause . . . to the sense of all of us but Ireton'; above p. 350.) Reserve in religion becomes Article IX of final Agreement:

Concerning religion, we agree as followeth: (1) It is intended that the Christian religion be held forth and recommended as the public profession in this nation, which we desire may, by the grace of God, be reformed to the greatest purity in doctrine, worship, and discipline, according to the word of God; the instructing the people thereunto in a public way, so it be not compulsive, as also the maintaining of able teachers for that end, and for the confutation or discovery of heresy, error, and whatsoever is contrary to sound doctrine, is allowed to be provided for by our Representatives; the maintenance of which teachers may be out of a public treasury, and we desire, not by tithes; provided that popery or prelacy be not held forth as the public way or profession in this nation. (2) That to the public profession so held forth, none be compelled by penalties or otherwise; but only may be endeavoured to be won by sound doctrine, and the example of a good conversation. (3) That such as profess faith in God by Jesus Christ, however differing in judgment from the doctrine, worship, or discipline publicly held forth as aforesaid, shall not be restrained from, but shall be protected in, the profession of their faith and exercise of religion according to their consciences, in any place except such as shall be set apart for the public worship (where we provide not for them unless they have leave), so as they abuse not this liberty to force, or make, any laws, oaths, covenants, whereby to compel by penalties or otherwise any person to anything in or about matters of faith, religion, or God's worship, or to restrain any person [27] from the professing his faith, or exercise of religion according to his conscience in any house or place (except such as are, or shall be, set apart for the public worship); nevertheless the instruction or directing of the nation in a public way for the matters of faith, worship, or discipline (so it be not compulsive or express popery) is referred to their discretion.

2. We do not empower them to impress or constrain any person to serve in [28] war either by sea or land,[29] every man's conscience being to be satisfied in the justness of that cause wherein he hazards his life.[30]

3. That after the [31] dissolution of this present Parliament,[32] none of the people be at any time questioned for anything said or done in reference to the late wars or public differences, otherwise than in execution or pursuance of the determination of the present House of Commons against such as have adhered to the King or his interest against the people; and saving that accomptants for public moneys received, shall remain accomptable for the same.[33]

4. That in any laws hereafter to be made, no person by virtue of any tenure, grant, charter, patent, degree or birth, shall be privileged from subjection thereto, or [from] being bound thereby as well as others.

5. [34] That all privileges or exemptions of any persons from the

---

the civil injury of others, or to actual disturbance of the public peace on their parts. Nevertheless, it is not intended to be hereby provided that this liberty shall necessarily extend to popery or prelacy. (4) That all laws, ordinances, statutes, and clauses in any law, statute, or ordinance to the contrary of the liberty herein provided for in the two particulars next preceding, concerning religion, be, and are hereby, repealed and made void.

[27] (Clarke MS. + professing Christianity).

[28] + any foreign.

[29] + nor for any military service within the kingdom, save that they may take order for the forming, training and exercising of the people in a military way, to be in readiness for resisting of foreign invasions, suppressing of sudden insurrections, or for assisting in execution of the laws, and may take order for the employing and conducting of them for those ends; provided that, even in such cases, none be compelled to go out of the county he lives in, if he procure another to serve in his room.

[29-30] Omits.

[31-32] time herein limited for the commencement of the first Representative.

[33] + IX below.   [34-35] Omits.

laws, or from the ordinary course of legal proceedings, by virtue of any tenure, grant, charter, patent, degree or birth, or of any place of residence or refuge, shall be henceforth void and null, and the like not to be made nor revived again.[35]

6. That the Representatives intermeddle not with the execution of laws, or give judgment upon any man's person or estate, where no law hath been before provided, save only in calling to an accompt, and punishing public officers for abusing or failing their trust.

7. That no member of any future Representative be made either receiver, treasurer or other officer during that employment, saving to be a member of the Council of State.

8. That no Representative shall in any wise render up, or give, or take away any the foundations of common right, liberty or safety contained in this Agreement, nor shall level men's estates, destroy propriety, or make all things common.[36]

VIII. That the Council of State, in case of imminent danger or extreme necessity, may in each interval summon a Representative to be forthwith chosen and to meet, so as the sessions thereof continue not above forty [37] days, and so it dissolve two months [38] before the appointed time for the meeting of the next Representative.

IX. [39] That all securities given by the public faith of the nation shall be made good by the next and all future Representatives,[40] save that the next Representative may continue or make null, in part or in whole, all gifts of moneys [41] made by the present House of Commons to their own members, or to any of the Lords, or to any of the attendants of either of them.

X.[42] That every officer or leader of any forces in any present

[36] + and that, in all matters of such fundamental concernment, there shall be a liberty to particular members of the said Representatives to enter their dissents from the major vote.

[37] eighty.   [38] fifty days.

[39]–[40] That no securities given ... shall be made void or invalid ... except to such creditors as have ... justly forfeited the same.

[41] + lands, ... offices, or otherwise.

[42]–[43] Substitutes:

It is agreed that whosoever shall by force of arms resist the orders of the next or any future Representative (except in case where such Representative shall evidently render up, or give, or take away the foundations of common right, liberty and safety contained in this Agreement), he shall forthwith, after ... such resistance, lose the benefit and protection of the laws, and shall be punishable with death as an enemy and traitor to the nation. Of the things expressed in this Agreement: the certain ending of this Parliament, as in the first Article; the equal or proportionable distribution of the number of the representaters to be elected, or future army or garrison, that shall resist the orders of the next or any future Representative (except such Representative shall expressly violate this Agreement), shall forthwith after his or their resistance, by virtue of this Agreement, lose the benefit and protection of all the laws of the land, and die without mercy.

These things we declare to be essential to our just freedoms, and to a thorough composure of our long and woeful distractions. And therefore we are agreed and resolved to maintain these certain rules of government and all that join therein, with our utmost possibilities, against all opposition whatsoever.[43]

These following particulars were offered to be inserted in the Agreement, but adjudged fit, as the most eminent grievances, to be redressed by the next Representative:

1. It shall not be in their power to punish or cause to be punished any person or persons for refusing to answer to questions against themselves in criminal cases.

2. That it shall not be in their power to continue or constitute any proceedings in law, that shall be longer than three or four months in finally determining of any cause past all appeal, or to continue the laws (or proceedings therein) in any other language than in the English tongue.

3. It shall not be in their power to continue or make any laws to abridge any person from trading unto any parts beyond the

---

as in the second; the certainty of the people's meeting to elect for Representatives biennial, and their freedom in elections; with the certainty of meeting, sitting and ending of Representatives so elected, which are provided for in the third Article; as also the qualifications of persons to elect or be elected, as in the first and second particulars under the third Article; also the certainty of a number for passing a law or preparatory debates, provided for in the fourth Article; the matter of the fifth Article, concerning the Council of State, and of the sixth, concerning the calling, sitting and ending of the Representatives extraordinary; also the power of Representatives to be, as in the eighth Article, and limited, as in the six reserves next following the same; likewise the second and third particulars under the ninth Article, concerning religion, and the whole matter of the tenth Article; all these we do account and declare to be fundamental to our common right, liberty, and safety; and therefore do both agree thereunto, and resolve to maintain the same as God shall enable us. The rest of the matters in this Agreement we account to be useful and good for the public; and the particular circumstances of numbers, times, and places expressed in the several Articles, we account not fundamental; but we find them necessary to be here determined for the making the Agreement certain and practicable, and do hold these most convenient that are here set down; and therefore do positively agree thereunto.

seas, unto which any are allowed to trade, or to restrain trade at home.

4. It shall not be in their power to continue excise longer than twenty days after the beginning of the next Representative, nor to raise moneys by any other way except by an equal rate, proportionably to men's real or personal estates; wherein all persons not worth above thirty pound shall be exempted from bearing any part of public charge, except to the poor and other accustomary charge of the place where they dwell.

5. It shall not be in their power to make or continue any law whereby men's estates, or any part thereof, shall be exempted from payment of their debts; or to continue or make any law to imprison any man's person for debts of that nature.

6. It shall not be in their power to make or continue any law for taking away any man's life except for murder, or for endeavouring by force to destroy this Agreement; but [they] shall use their uttermost endeavour to propound punishments equal to offences, that so men's lives, limbs, liberties and estates may not as hitherto be liable to be taken away upon trivial or slight occasion; and shall have special care to keep all sorts of people from misery and beggary.

7. They shall not continue or make a law to deprive any person in case or trial from the benefit of witnesses, as well for as against him.

8. They shall not continue the grievance and oppression of tithes longer than to the end of the first Representative; in which time they shall provide for and satisfy all impropriators. Neither shall they force any person to pay toward the maintenance of the public ministers, who out of conscience cannot submit thereunto, but· shall provide for them in some other unoppressive way.

9. They shall not continue or make a law for any other ways of judgment or conviction of life, liberty, or estate, but only by twelve sworn men of the neighbourhood.

10. They shall not continue or make a law to allow any person to take above six pound per cent. for loan of money for a year.

11. They shall not disable any person from bearing any office in the commonwealth for any opinion or practice in religion, though contrary to the public way.[44]

---

[44] These particulars (together with 3 below, the election of municipal officers) are added in the Levellers' third *Agreement of the Free People of England*, issued by John Lilburne, William Walwyn, Thomas Prince, and Richard Overton, on 1st May 1649; which also contains some further provision, *e.g.*:

IV.[a] That no member of the present Parliament shall be capable of being elected of the next Representative, nor any member of any

Unto these I shall add:

1. That the next Representative be most earnestly pressed for the ridding of this kingdom of those vermin and caterpillars, the lawyers, the chief bane of this poor nation; to erect a court of justice in every hundred in the nation, for the ending of all differences arising in that hundred, by twelve men of the same hundred annually chosen by freemen of that hundred, with express and plain rules in English made by the Representative, or supreme authority of the nation, for them to guide their judgments by.

2. That for the preventing of fraud, thefts, and deceits, there be forthwith in every county or shire in England, and the Dominion of Wales, erected a county record for the perfect registering

---

Representative shall be capable of being chosen for the Representative immediately ensuing. * * *

VIII. And for the preservation of the supreme authority, in all times, entirely in the hands of such persons only as shall be chosen thereunto, we agree and declare: That the next and all future Representatives shall continue in full power for the space of one whole year; and that the people shall of course choose a Parliament once every year. . . . Also (for the same reason) that the next or any future Representative, being met, shall continue their session, day by day, without intermission for four months, and after that shall be at liberty to adjourn from two months to two months, as they shall see cause, until their year be expired; but shall sit no longer than a year upon pain of treason to every member that shall exceed that time. And in times of adjournment [they] shall not erect a Council of State, but refer the managing of affairs in the intervals to a committee of their own members, giving such instructions (and publish[ing] them) as shall in no measure contradict this Agreement. * * *

XXIV. That it shall not be in their power to impose ministers upon any the respective parishes, but [they] shall give free liberty to the parishioners . . . to choose such as themselves shall approve, and upon such terms, and for such reward, as themselves shall be willing to contribute or shall contract for. Provided none be choosers but such as are capable of electing Representatives. * * *

And forasmuch as nothing threateneth greater danger to the commonwealth than that the military power should by any means come to be superior to the civil authority: XXIX. We declare and agree that no forces shall be raised, but by the Representative for the time being; and in raising thereof that they exactly observe these rules, namely: that they allot to each particular county, city, town, and borough, the raising, furnishing, agreeing, and paying of a due proportion, according to the whole number to be levied; and shall to the electors of Representatives in each respective place give free liberty to nominate and appoint all officers appertaining to regiments, troops, and companies, and to remove them as they shall see cause, reserving to the Representative the nominating and appointing only of the general and all general officers, and the ordering, regulating, and commanding of them all upon what service shall seem to them necessary for the safety, peace, and freedom of the commonwealth.

of all conveyances, bills, and bonds, &c., upon a severe and strict penalty.

3. That in case there be any need, after the erection of hundred courts, of mayors, sheriffs, justices of the peace, deputy lieutenants, &c.; that the people capable of election of Parliamentmen in the foregoing Agreement, be restored by the Representative unto their native, just, and undoubted right by common consent, from amongst themselves annually to choose all the foresaid officers in such manner as shall be plainly and clearly described and laid down by the supreme authority of the nation; and that when any subsidies or public taxes be laid upon the nation, the freemen of every division or hundred capable of election as aforesaid, choose out persons by common consent from amongst themselves, for the equal division of their assessments.

4. That the next Representative be earnestly desired to abolish all base tenures.

THE FEMALE OF THE SPECIES

From a *Petition of Women, Affecters and Approvers of the Petition of Sept. 11, 1648* [1] (5th May 1649) [a]

Sheweth, that since we are assured of our creation in the image of God, and of an interest in Christ equal unto men, as also of a proportionable share in the freedoms of this commonwealth, we cannot but wonder and grieve that we should appear so despicable in your eyes as to be thought unworthy to petition or represent our grievances to this honourable House. Have we not an equal interest with the men of this nation in those liberties and securities contained in the *Petition of Right*, and other the good laws of the land? Are any of our lives, limbs, liberties, or goods to be taken from us more than from men, but by due process of law and conviction of twelve sworn men of the neighbourhood? And can you imagine us to be so sottish or stupid as not to perceive, or not to be sensible when daily those strong defences of our peace and welfare are broken down and trod underfoot by force and arbitrary power?

Would you have us keep at home in our houses, when men of such faithfulness and integrity as the four prisoners, our friends,

---

[1] It is improbable that this petition was actually composed by the women. Its principles are none the less interesting.

in the Tower,[1] are fetched out of their beds and forced from their houses by soldiers, to the affrighting and undoing of themselves, their wives, children, and families? Are not our husbands, o[u]r selves, our children and families, by the same rule as liable to the like unjust cruelties as they?

Shall such men as Capt. Bray be made close prisoners, and such as Mr. Sawyer snatched up and carried away, beaten and buffeted at the pleasure of some officers of the Army; and such as Mr. Blank [a] kept close prisoner, and after most barbarous usage be forced to run the gauntlet,[b] and be most slave-like and cruelly whipped? And must we keep at home in our houses, as if our lives and liberties and all were not concerned?

Nay, shall such valiant, religious men as Mr. Robert Lockyer [2] be liable to law martial, and to be judged by his adversaries, and most inhumanly shot to death? Shall the blood of war be shed in time of peace? Doth not the word of God expressly condemn it? Doth not the *Petition of Right* declare that no person ought to be judged by law martial (except in time of war) and that all commissions given to execute martial law in time of peace are contrary to the laws and statutes of the land? Doth not Sir Ed. Coke,[c] in his chapter of murder in the third part of his *Institutes*, hold it for good law (and since owned and published by this Parliament) that for a general or other officers of an army in time of peace to put any man (although a soldier) to death by colour of martial law, it is absolute murder in that general? And hath it not by this House in the case of the late Earl of Strafford been adjudged high treason? And are we Christians, and shall we sit still and keep at home, while such men as have borne continual testimony against the injustice of all times and unrighteousness of men, be picked out and be delivered up to the slaughter? And yet must we show no sense of their sufferings, no tenderness of affections, no bowels of compassion, nor bear any testimony against so abominable cruelty and injustice?

Have such men as these continually hazarded their lives, spent their estates and time, lost their liberties, and thought nothing too precious for defence of us, our lives and liberties, been as a guard by day and as a watch by night; and when for this they are in trouble and greatest danger, persecuted and hated even to the death,[d] should we be so basely ungrateful as to neglect them in the day of their affliction? No, far be it from us. Let it be accounted folly, presumption, madness, or whatsoever in. us,·

[1] Lilburne, Overton, Walwyn, and Prince.
[2] Executed on 27th April 1649.

whilst we have life and breath we will never leave them nor forsake them, nor ever cease to importune you, having yet so much hopes of you as of the unjust judge (mentioned, Luke 18), to obtain justice, if not for justice' sake, yet for importunity, or to use any other means for the enlargement and reparation of those of them that live, and for justice against such as have been the cause of Mr. Lockyer's death. * * *

And therefore again we entreat you to review our last petition in behalf of our friends above mentioned, and not to slight the things therein contained because they are presented unto you by the weak hand of women, it being a usual thing with God, by weak means to work mighty effects. For we are no whit satisfied with the answer you gave unto our husbands and friends, but do equally with them remain liable to those snares laid in your Declaration, which maketh the abetters of the book laid to our friends' charge, no less than traitors, when hardly any discourse can be touching the affairs of the present times but falls within the compass of that book; so that all liberty of discourse is thereby utterly taken away, than which there can be no greater slavery. * * *

Democracy in the City

From *London's Liberties or a Learned Argument of Law and Reason* [1] (Dec. 1650) [a]

[Wildman's Speech in Rebuttal]

May it please your Lordship and this honourable Court to give me leave to make some answers to what the learned gentlemen on the other side have pleased to object. . . . I shall not, my Lord, endeavour (as that gentleman did) *captare benevolentiam*, to take the affections of the people before I begin to debate the matter in question. I shall not tell them that I will

---

[1] The prefatory material presents the essential facts. In the course of an investigation of the City's accounts 'it was found that the chief officers had been very faulty; and thereupon it was considered how they were elected, and there arose the question about the right of electing the chief officers of the City. And it came into debate whether the Liverymen ought to be the electors, as now they are. Thereupon the Companies of London petitioned the Court that they might continue their elective power; and divers freemen of the City petitioned for the abolishing that power of the Liveries or Companies. * * * These were referred to a committee, and counsel for the Companies there heard, and Mr. Price in the behalf of the freemen. From thence it was referred to be fully debated

not insinuate into their minds anything but what will stand upon the foundation of truth, but offer my thoughts and freely submit to your judgment.   Yet I hope to answer particularly Mr. Maynard's exceptions.

He was pleased, first, to take exception at that general principle that I averred, from whence, I said, might be deduced the right of all the Wards to choose the Lord Mayor and Sheriffs by their representatives—though the gentleman might have pleased to remember I did say I would waive those principles of common right, lest he should say we intended to bring all things to an uncertainty by unravelling the bottom of government to its first principle, and therefore I insisted upon nothing but what we claim as our *written* right.   However, he might have pleased to spare quarrelling with that principle, that a just subjection ought to be founded upon an assent of the people to their governors' power; especially in this parliamentary time, wherein the Parliament hath pleased to declare that the original of all just power (under God) is from the people.   And how governors shall derive a just power from the people but by an assent of the people, I understand not.   Neither do I know how we can otherwise be a free people, as the Parliament hath declared we are.   If he had quarrelled with this in the time of the King, it had been for his interest to have said that we ought to be subject to the son and heir of a conqueror because such.   I hope better things now.

The second thing the gentleman was pleased to except against, was that which he only imagined in his own brain—misreciting my words—like a man created by his fancy to try his skill upon. For he supposed I did say that if we had the records that are now lost, we doubted not but that they would prove the assertion we maintain.   Whereas I said : If we had the records of those times, that are lost, they would show us what the rights of the people then were.   And that I conceive to be without exception.

The next thing he takes exception against is what I said con-

---

before the Lord Mayor, Court of Aldermen, and Common Council. And on Saturday the 14th of December, the Court being sat at Guild Hall, the Companies brought for their counsel Mr. Maynard, Mr. Hale, and Mr. Wilde, gentlemen most famous in the profession of the law; and the freemen (besides Mr. John Price) had prevailed, by much entreaty, with Mr. John Wildman, as I am informed, without hopes of fees or rewards, to plead their cause.' The arguments were taken down in shorthand. Though Wildman is here found in association with the Independent John Price (see above, p. 343), his speech is coloured by Leveller principles. The whole debate offers an interesting parallel in the municipal field to that in national politics carried on at Putney three years earlier.

cerning Magna Charta, and would make this Court believe that I
had thought all that great charter was unalterable.   I confess, *if*
I had thought so I would never have drawn sword against the
King.   But the gentleman was pleased to assert that the King was
by the common law; and if he agrees with Sir Edw. Coke's [a] law,
he saith that the common law is but *recta ratio*, right reason; and
I am sure the King stood not by right reason.   If he had, the
Parliament could not have justly declared his office burdensome
and unnecessary.   But the truth is, I did only say that Magna
Charta, the great charter of England, *was unalterable according to
the principles of the gentlemen of the long robe*; I only spoke it upon
their bottom.   I said, if I should believe Sir Edw. Coke [a] in what
he said upon the statute of 42 Edw. 3, I must then say that an Act
of Parliament made contrary to that part of the Great Charter
that was declarative of the common law, was null of itself; for he
said that part of it was unalterable.   Thus I gave them only their
own authority, and made it no assertion of mine absolutely.
Though, under his favour, I think a man may assert that what is
founded upon the true common law of England, as Sir Edw. Coke
saith, which is right reason, no authority whatsoever ought to
alter (I speak not of circumstances); for if we should aver that, we
should aver contradictions in the very terms, and say that right
reason of right may be altered from right reason.

I shall let pass what the gentleman was pleased to say of the
laws being edge-tools, and of men cutting themselves with them.
I believe he met with an argument for the people's right that was
an edge-tool in his way, and he was loath to break his shins over it,
and therefore he passed over the argument with a grave caution
of the sharpness of the law, that he might divert your thoughts
from it.   But the gentleman, coming a little nearer to the matter,
lays down his maxim, which is this: that ever since the 15 of
Edward the Fourth, these Liveries have had the choice.   And then
he argues thus.   Saith he, The case would be very hard to have
your titles of land, after one hundred and ninety years' possession,
to be questioned.   And is it not as hard that the right of the
Liveries to elections should now be questioned?   Under the
gentleman's favour, the case is very different.   I suppose no man
pleads for the like title to a power or authority over the people
that men have to their lands, nor upon the same grounds.   If the
titles were alike, it were just to buy and sell authority, or places of
trust and government, as we buy and sell lands, or horses in
Smithfield; and this our common law abhors.   If we speak of
people that are arrant mere vassals, like the slaves in Algiers,[b]

authority over them is indeed bought and sold—but I hope we are not to be so esteemed—and yet the justice of those bargains is not clear. But certainly men's titles to land and to a power of government are, or ought to be, of a different nature. And I shall make bold to assert that 'tis no hard case that the right of any number of men claiming a power in or about government by succession only, should after a hundred and ninety years' possession be questioned. Suppose Mr. Maynard could have made good the Liverymen's claims to the election of the chief officers of the City by custom—but then he must have more than doubled the time of the usage he spake of—yet I humbly conceive that the exercise of any power about government is not made just by continuance of time, unless it were just in the original. If long usurpation of a power in or about government could give a right to that power, all the foundations of just government were overturned, and by consequence it were not right or just to take away an usurped power if the usurpers be grown old.

Next, the gentleman is pleased, before he comes to his material arguments, to insinuate strange, huge, dreadful, monstrous consequences that would ensue in case any man shall deny his assertions. He is pleased to say, What strange consequences would ensue if we should say for a hundred and ninety years all the Lord Mayors or Sheriffs of the City of London have been unlawfully chosen! Truly, I could only answer that we might have said before the Parliament executed justice upon the King and cast off his family, What strange consequences would ensue if we should say that almost for five hundred years the people of England have been governed by them that came in unlawfully, and claimed their power successively to make the people their vassals by the sword of William the Conqueror! But the Parliament was not affrighted by such bugbear arguments to do justice upon him, and take away the power that his family claimed by conquest over us; and, I believe, Mr. Maynard will not say they did unjustly. But suppose that which he suggests, that the Mayors have been chosen unlawfully so long, 'tis time then to provide for a lawful choice. And the continuance of the unlawful will breed more of Mr. Maynard's monstrous consequences. And if it be unlawful, 'tis not forbearing to say so that will amend the consequences.

But now the gentleman comes to his position, and saith that this government that is now is lawful. The gentleman might have pleased to have spared that—I did not yet assert that the government that is now is unlawful—yet he may take some answers to his arguments, or rather authorities, for the legality of it.

The first ground he builds upon for the lawfulness of this government is the opinion of the judges, which makes a huge cry. But by the way, the question is not now concerning the government, but only concerning the choosers or electors of the governors. The government may be the same still, though the manner and way of electing these governors may be altered from what it is at present. Yet to that opinion of the judges which makes the great noise in the Court. Oh, saith he, 'tis the opinion of all the learned judges; and then he paraphrases upon the goodness, honesty, learning, and fame of the judges that were named in the book produced. It may be those gentlemen of the long-robe were black swans; yet the argument from authority is none of the strongest. 'Tis not a very good consequence, that the thing is just because good men thought so.

Yet, under favour, the opinion of the judges I take to be not the most certain or unalterable amongst men, nor the most unbiased by their own interest. I believe, if a man should go to the twelve judges he shall scarce find four or three of the twelve of the same opinion in a dubious case. Yet if there were more that agreed, the late opinion of the judges in the case of ship-money may inform us how free the judges' opinions are from the bias of private interest in such cases, and how fit 'tis for us to depend upon them. They could, many of them, agree to destroy property at once in favour of the King. But, however, the opinion of the judges produced by Mr. Maynard, I crave leave to affirm to be against him in this case—at least not for him. I desire it may be read.

The Case of Corporations, touching the election of Governors in the fourth of the Lord Coke's *Reports*, fol. 77, 78. * * *

After Mr. Maynard had produced the authority of the judges as he supposed for his clients' case, he argues from consequences. Saith he, If this present way of electing by the Liveries were not lawful, mark the consequences. Your Charter, saith he, is forfeited. This, I confess, is a big-bellied word, but how will this assertion agree with what Mr. Maynard, Mr. Hale,[a] and Mr. Wilde all affirmed: that the Charters of the City did not originally give the City those liberties that are mentioned in the Charter, but that the Charters were only declarative of the City's rights, showing what their rights were before the Charters. Now if the Charters give not the City their rights, certainly you cannot forfeit your Charters unless the learned gentlemen shall please to say, you shall forfeit the *declaration* of your rights (for the Charters are no more, by their own confession). And if your forfeiture be no more, you may enjoy your liberties still, notwithstanding such a forfeiture as they pretend. But suppose a man should say what I did not yet say, that the present way of electing the Mayor is unlawful, is it any more than this, that the citizens have suffered their right to be taken from them for many years, and others to enjoy it unlawfully? And how will this consequence be deduced from thence, that the City hath forfeited their rights? I confess I understand not, by the law, that a body politic or corporation as such is under harder laws in our nation than the members of the commonwealth severally. Now, no man in England can forfeit his rights without a legal conviction of some crime for which the law censures him to forfeit his rights. And I know no reason why the City should have such hard measure, that in case the freemen have suffered the Companies to usurp their right, that therefore all the City's rights should be forfeited. But without question this argument might have frighted you in the King's time. Then some needy projecting courtier might have frighted you with the forfeiture of your Charter to the King, and eased you of some of your bags upon pretence of soliciting the King to renew your Charter for an easy fine. But now, if you be satisfied you have erred from the rule, I believe you may return to do right and enjoy your liberties without paying a fine.

Mr. Maynard's next argument for the Liveries' elections was this. That 'tis founded upon a constant usage time out of mind, so that (saith he) the City now prescribes unto this way of electing. And yet the gentleman was pleased afterwards to confess that to make a title by prescription there must be a constant usage since Rich[ard] the First's time, and they only produce an act of a Common Council for the Liveries' electing about a hundred and seventy-four years since, and will suppose that that act of Common Council was in confirmation of what was the custom before— whereas they produce no one footstep of a record before that time to prove that it was the usage to choose by Liverymen, but (on the contrary) it hath appeared that the election hath been four hundred years since by a select number out of the several Wards, which cannot be anyway supposed to be meant of Liverymen, they not coming as men from several Wards but as men from several Companies.

The next thing the gentleman said was this: that he hoped we would grant that we did both depart from the Charter itself. For, saith he, if we found the way of electing upon the Charter, the

Charter running to the citizens indefinitely, it must be understood of all the citizens and barons. And, saith he, you grant it is impossible they should all together make the election; so we both depart from it. Under his favour I must be bold to deny it. We depart not from the Charter. For we say that, the Charter giving a right of choice to all the citizens, they may proceed in their elections either by themselves personally or their deputies; and they, finding it inconvenient to meet personally, may depute others to make their elections, and an election so made is truly said to be made by the citizens. So that in case that way of electing were admitted which the petitioners propose, it were directly agreeable to the Charter; for then indeed the citizens should choose because they choose every one of them by their deputies, as all the people of England make laws in Parliament because every man's deputy is, or ought to be, there in Parliament.

Next, Mr. Maynard answers an objection. If, saith he, it be objected that in the way of election that is by the Liverymen, all are not represented, (saith he) it is true if you take it in some sense. But (saith he) if you take it in the sense of the law, therein they are represented, and it is the City makes these elections: . . . the Law saith so, as (saith he) in case a man's hand moves, it is the man that moves, or his eye sees a colour, it is the man that sees. I hope the gentleman will please to confess a vast difference between a body natural and a body politic. Because he may truly say, if a man's hand moves all the man moves, therefore will he say that what a few, or one member of the City doth is the City's action? If so, if one in the City commit treason all the City are traitors. I believe, gentlemen, you would be loath to admit of such a law!

But to confirm this assertion the gentleman produced something out of that which he called *Articuli super Chartas*, where he saith, the King granted to the people to choose Sheriffs, and yet the people did not choose them all in general, it was the freeholders chose them. Mr. Maynard, if he pleaseth, could have told when the people in general were restrained from electing Parliament-men, and other the Sheriffs also, and upon what pretence it was put upon freeholders only, and how it served the King's ends to procure that Statute of Restriction. If I forget not the time it was in the 8 of Henry 6, chap. 7. But, however, Mr. Maynard should have proved this to be just, before he can prove the other to be just by this. * * *

His next argument against this petition is this. Saith Mr. Maynard, It will tend to popularity if this should be admitted, that the Wards should choose. And I leave it, saith he, to the

Court to judge what the consequent of that would be. All men's educations, saith he, are not such as make them fit for government, or fit to choose governors. Truly, if it please the honourable Court but to consider who they are that are now the electors, this arrow of the gentleman's returns upon himself. I could say more of it if I should not be thought to reflect—because I have a reverent respect to all kind of trades. But if I should speak of all the several Companies, the Bricklayers, Bowyers, Fletchers, Turners, Coopers, Tallow-chandlers, &c., if I should speak of the education of most of the Liverymen of forty Companies of the City, and compute their number, and tell you upon what terms most are admitted to be of the Liveries, that is, for a small sum of money; I conceive the Court would quickly judge which way of election tends most to popularity, as he calls it, and who proposeth most men that are unfit for government, to choose the Lord Mayor and Sheriffs. Will any man suppose that the educations of all the handicraftmen of the Liveries render them so able and discreet that they are fit for government? I submit it to the Court.

As for the great word Mr. Maynard was pleased to add about the ill consequents of this change that would be to other corporations, saying that this is an earthquake comes under them: I shall conceive his oratory in this to be of the earthquake's nature, a swelling vapour, unless he will be pleased to show me how the liberty of the City, or any one citizen, is undermined by what is proposed. Only I must observe to the Court that where arguments are wanting their room is commonly supplied with words and pretences of huge strange consequences that will ensue if their desires be crossed. But the arguments from a consequence, I believe they well know their strength is not of the first degree. But, however, to suppose an ill consequence may ensue upon a city or company of persons exercising their right, and thence to conclude they must not enjoy it, is a way of arguing that I understand not.

I confess Mr. Hale is pleased to deal very ingenuously in laying down those principles wherein we agreed, which was: that the liberties of the City were by prescription, and that the Charters were but declarations of what our liberties were, and that the Common Councilmen ought to have a vote in their elections. But I said not they *ought*, but that they might have their votes if they were chosen to that purpose. But he was pleased to say that the Lord Mayor, Aldermen, and Common Council were a kind of a Representative of the City, and therefore he would thence aver that there is no inconvenience to the City, seeing they have such a Representative. I shall answer Mr. Hale thus: If a man should

say the Parliament represent the commonwealth, and seeing we
have a Representative, what matter if that two hundred or three
hundred men more went into the Parliament and voted with them,
the people of England surely would not think themselves well
dealt withal, nor think those Acts so passed to be valid. Mr.
Hale is pleased also to pursue Mr. Maynard's mode of imagining
strange kind of consequences that may ensue upon this. And,
saith he, how if the people will say when you brought it to the
representatives, We will not be bound to representatives, but we
will come and choose personally? What then (saith he) would
be the consequence of this? Truly, if Mr. Hale will suppose
that the people will not be bound by any government, nor by Acts
of Parliament, he may fill his fancy with bad consequences. And
why may it not be supposed as well, that all the people in England
should say, We will go and make laws ourselves in Parliament, as
well as that the people should not be willing to be bound in their
Wards to choose the Lord Mayor and Sheriffs by their representatives? I shall let pass also what Mr. Hale was pleased to
urge concerning that principle of a just subjection of people to
governors to be founded upon an assent, because he was pleased
to confess very ingenuously that I waived those arguments that
might reduce government to an uncertainty, or to the first principles of general common right. But, saith Mr. Hale, if that
principle be allowed amongst a free people, that subjection to their
governors ought to be by mere assent, . . . we must consider there
is a personal and a virtual assent, and it shall be conceived to be a
virtual consent where there hath been an usage time out of mind
for the people to be subject to any form of government. Of
which nature he endeavoured to prove the way of electing the
Lord Mayor and Sheriffs by the Liverymen of the several
mysteries; whereas, if Mr. Hale please to remember, they do all
aver the usage of this way of electing but to have been for one
hundred and seventy-four years that they can prove. As for any
suppositions that it was before, I think there is enough answered
to that, there being no ancienter records that mention the choice
to have been by the Liverymen, who come not as sent from
Wards. And though Mr. Hale is pleased to balance the records
produced on one hand and on the other, and saith thus, that they
produce for one hundred [and] seventy-four years to show that this
hath been the way of electing which now is; but (saith he) those
records produced to prove another way of electing is but a short
time. If he please to remember, there is no footstep of mention
made of any Liverymen, or of any of the mysteries, having a

power to elect, until that 15 of Edw. 4, and we find from Edward the First, about two hundred years before, that there were twelve men in the Wards, that were electors, which we may well think to be the representers of those Wards, and chosen by them for that purpose; and no footsteps of the discontinuance of it from the time produced. But we may well say that all the records that mention the commonalty's choice are to be interpreted by the former record, until that record comes wherein mention is made of Liverymen, there being no mention made of them formerly (under that or any other name) as such. * * *

As to the arguments from the consequences. If this government were not right, then (saith Mr. Hale) all the purchases you have made since that time you altered the way of elections, is null. I must humbly crave leave not to submit to his judgment in that till he give me better reasons; for I suppose it is grounded upon that of forfeiting a Charter, which was answered before; for though the body corporate have not had their officers rightly elected, yet the body is not thereby dissolved, and therefore their purchase may be good and without fear of forfeiture. * * *

And as for Mr. Wilde's arguments concerning the danger that would ensue upon the multitude coming to elections, upon the same ground he may say the Wards must not choose their Aldermen nor Common Councilmen—if the citizens should be deprived of their right upon that ground that it is popularity—or they may be divided and fall to blows. Upon the same grounds they may take away the liberty of choosing Common Councilmen and Aldermen, and all their common freedoms. And if these fears shall affright men from the claim of their right, they may be told next that the sky may fall, and therefore they must not go abroad.

As for the last objection of Mr. Wilde's, that in this way of popularity 'tis possible a choice may be made of unfit men, I shall only offer this to the consideration of the Court: whether it is more probable that a whole Ward meeting together to choose a small number of men that should represent them in the electing their superior officers, should choose more unfit men for that election than a Company, it may be, of Coopers, Tallow-chandlers, or other manual occupations should admit to the Livery (who admit all that will give so much money to be of the Livery). Who are the likeliest men to send fittest men for the choice, I humbly refer to the honourable Court—though it is strange to me to hear that the fear of popularity, or of giving way so much to the liberty of the people, is so much insisted on. Now we are come into the way of a commonwealth, it is a little dissonant to the present constitution. * * *

IX. DIGGER PRINCIPLES

From *The True Levellers' Standard Advanced* [1] (1649) [a]

In the beginning of time, the great Creator, Reason, made the earth to be a common treasury, to preserve beasts, birds, fishes, and man, the lord that was to govern this creation. For man had domination given to him over the beasts, birds, and fishes. But not one word was spoken in the beginning, that one branch of mankind should rule over another.

And the reason is this. Every single man, male and female, is a perfect creature of himself. And the same Spirit that made the globe dwells in man to govern the globe; so that the flesh of man, being subject to Reason, his Maker, hath him to be his teacher and ruler within himself, therefore needs not run abroad after any teacher and ruler without him. . . .

But since human flesh . . . began to delight himself in the objects of the creation more than in the Spirit Reason and Righteousness, who manifests himself to be the indweller in the five senses . . .; then he fell into blindness of mind and weakness of heart, and runs abroad for a teacher and ruler, and so selfish imaginations, taking possession of the five senses, and ruling as king in the room of Reason therein, and working with covetousness, did set up one man to teach and rule over another. And thereby the Spirit was killed, and man was brought into bondage and became a greater slave to such of his own kind than the beasts of the field were to him.

And hereupon the earth, which was made to be a common treasury of relief for all, both beasts and men, was hedged into enclosures by the teachers and rulers, and the others were made servants and slaves. And that earth that is within this creation made a common storehouse for all, is bought and sold and kept in the hands of a few; whereby the great Creator is mightily dishonoured: as if he were a respecter of persons, delighting in the comfortable livelihood of some, and rejoicing in the miserable poverty and straits of others. From the beginning it was not so. * * *

But for the present state of the old world, that is running up like parchment in the fire and wearing away, we see proud imaginary flesh, which is the wise serpent, rises up in flesh and gets dominion in some to rule over others, and so forces one part of the creation, man, to be a slave to another. And thereby the

---

[1] By William Everard, Gerrard Winstanley, John Taylor, and others. For full list see 'Notes on Text.'

Spirit is killed in both.   The one looks upon himself as a teacher
and ruler, and so is lifted up in pride over his fellow creature.
The other looks upon himself as imperfect, and so is dejected in
his spirit, and looks upon his fellow creature, of his own image,
as a lord above him.

And thus Esau, the man of flesh, which is covetousness and
pride, hath killed Jacob, the spirit of meekness, and righteous
government in the light of reason, and rules over him.   And so
the earth that was made a common treasury for all to live comfortably upon, is become, through man's unrighteous actions one
over another, to be a place wherein one torments another.

Now the great Creator, who is the Spirit Reason, suffered himself thus to be rejected and trodden under foot by the covetous,
proud flesh, for a certain time limited.   Therefore saith he: *The
seed out of whom the creation did proceed, which is myself, shall bruise
this serpent's head, and restore my creation again from this curse and
bondage; and when I, the King of Righteousness, reigns in every man,
I will be the blessing of the earth, and the joy of all nations.*

And . . . the earth hath been enclosed and given to the elder
brother Esau, or man of flesh, and hath been bought and sold
from one to another; and Jacob, or the younger brother, that is to
succeed or come forth next, who is the universal spreading power
of righteousness that gives liberty to the whole creation, is made a
servant.   And this elder son, or man of bondage, hath held the
earth in bondage to himself, not by a meek law of righteousness,
but by subtle selfish counsels, and by open and violent force.   For
wherefore is it that there is such wars and rumours of wars in the
nations of the earth?   And wherefore are men so mad to destroy
one another?   But only to uphold civil propriety of honour,
dominion and riches one over another, which is the curse the
creation groans under, waiting for deliverance.

But when once the earth becomes a common treasury again—
as it must; for all the prophecies of scriptures and reason are
circled here in this community, and mankind must have the law
of righteousness once more writ in his heart, and all must be made
of one heart and one mind—then this enmity in all lands will
cease.   For none shall dare to seek a dominion over others; neither
shall any dare to kill another, nor desire more of the earth than
another.   For he that will rule over, imprison, oppress, and kill
his fellow creatures under what pretence soever, is a destroyer of
the creation and an actor of the curse, and walks contrary to the
rule of righteousness: Do as you would have others do to you;
and love your enemies, not in words, but in actions.

Therefore you powers of the earth, or Lord Esau, the elder brother, because you have appeared to rule the creation, first take notice that the power that sets you to work is selfish covetousness, and an aspiring pride to live in glory and ease over Jacob, the meek spirit; that is, the seed that lies hid in and among the poor common people, or younger brother, out of whom the blessing of deliverance is to rise and spring up to all nations. And Reason, the living King of Righteousness, doth only look on and lets thee alone, that whereas thou counts thyself an angel of light, thou shalt appear in the light of the Sun to be a devil . . . and the curse that the creation groans under. And the time is now come for thy downfall; and Jacob must rise, who is the universal spirit of love and righteousness that fills, and will fill, all the earth. * * *

[After reproaching 'the powers of England' with their failure to make 'this people a free people,' with their having indeed, through their 'self-seeking humour,' increased its bondage, the pamphlet proceeds:]

Surely thou must not do this great work of advancing the creation out of bondage; for thou art lost extremely, and drowned in the sea of covetousness, pride, and hardness of heart. *The blessing shall rise out of the dust which thou treadest under foot, even the poor despised people, and they shall hold up salvation to this land, and to all lands, and thou shalt be ashamed.* * * *

The work we are going about is this: to dig up George's Hill and the waste ground thereabouts, and to sow corn, and to eat our bread together by the sweat of our brows.[1]

And the first reason is this. That we may work in righteousness, and lay the foundation of making the earth a common treasury for all, both rich and poor. That every one that is born in the land may be fed by the earth, his mother that brought him forth, according to the reason that rules in the creation, not enclosing any part into any particular hand, but all as one man working together, and feeding together as sons of one father, members of one family; not one lording over another, but all looking upon each other as equals in the creation. So that our Maker may be glorified in the work of his own hands, and that every one may see he is no respecter of persons, but equally loves his whole creation, and hates nothing but the serpent. Which is covetousness, branching forth into selfish imagination, pride, envy,

---

[1] Clarke MSS. contain a petition of the Diggers, and a letter from Winstanley to Fairfax, on the use of soldiers against the Diggers, late in 1649; also a Diggers' Song. See *Clarke Papers*, ed. Firth, 2. 215–24.

hypocrisy, uncleanness, all seeking the ease and honour of flesh, and fighting against the Spirit Reason that made the creation. For that is the corruption, the curse, the devil, the father of lies, death and bondage—that serpent and dragon that the creation is to be delivered from.

And we are moved hereunto for that reason, and others which hath been showed us, both by vision, voice, and revelation. For it is showed us, that so long as we or any other doth own the earth to be the peculiar interest of lords and landlords, and not common to others as well as them, we own the curse that [a] holds the creation under bondage. And so long as we or any other doth own landlords and tenants, for one to call the land his, or another to hire it of him, or for one to give hire, and for another to work for hire; this is to dishonour the work of creation—as if the righteous Creator should have respect to persons, and therefore made the earth for some, and not for all. * * *

And that this civil propriety is the curse, is manifest thus. Those that buy and sell land and are landlords, have got it either by oppression or murder or theft; and all landlords live in the breach of the Seventh and Eighth Commandments, *Thou shalt not steal, nor kill.*

First by their oppression. They have, by their subtle, imaginary, and covetous wit, got the plain-hearted poor, or younger brethren, to work for them for small wages, and by their work have got a great increase; for the poor by their labour lifts up tyrants to rule over them. Or else by their covetous wit, they have outreached the plain-hearted in buying and selling, and thereby enriched themselves but impoverished others. Or else by their subtle wit, having been alifted up [b] into places of trust, [they] have enforced people to pay money for a public use, but have divided much of it into their private purses, and so have got it by oppression.

Then, secondly, for murder. They have by subtle wit and power pretended to preserve a people in safety by the power of the sword. And what by large pay, much free-quarter, and other booties which they call their own, they get much moneys, and with this they buy land and become landlords. And if once landlords, then they rise to be justices, rulers, and state governors, as experience shows. But all this is but a bloody and subtle thievery, countenanced by a law that covetousness made; and is a breach of the Seventh Commandment, *Thou shalt not kill.*

And likewise, thirdly, a breach of the Eighth Commandment, *Thou shalt not steal.* But these landlords have thus stolen the earth from their fellow creatures, that have an equal share with them by the law of reason and creation, as well as they.

And such as these rise up to be rich in the objects of the earth. Then, by their plausible words of flattery to the plain-hearted people, whom they deceive, and that lies under confusion and blindness, they are lifted up to be teachers, rulers, and law-makers over them that lifted them up; as if the earth were made peculiarly for them, and not for others' weal. If you cast your eye a little backward, you shall see that this outward teaching and ruling power is the Babylonish yoke laid upon Israel of old, under Nebuchadnezzar. And so successively from that time the con-quering enemy have still laid these yokes upon Israel, to keep Jacob down. And the last enslaving conquest which the enemy got over Israel, was the Norman over England. And from that time kings, lords, judges, justices, bailiffs, and the violent bitter people that are freeholders, are and have been successively: the Norman bastard William himself, his colonels, captains, inferior officers, and common soldiers, who still are from that time to this day in pursuit of that victory, imprisoning, robbing, and killing the poor enslaved English Israelites.

And this appears clear. For when any trustee or state officer is to be chosen, the freeholders or landlords must be the choosers, who are the Norman common soldiers spread abroad in the land. And who must be chosen but some very rich man who is the successor of the Norman colonels or high officers? And to what end have they been thus chosen but to establish that Norman power the more forcibly over the enslaved English, and to beat them down again whenas they gather heart to seek for liberty? For what are all those binding and restraining laws that have been made from one age to another since that conquest, and are still upheld by fury over the people? I say, what are they but the cords, bands, manacles, and yokes that the enslaved English, like Newgate prisoners, wears upon their hands and legs as they walk the streets; by which those Norman oppressors, and these their successors from age to age, have enslaved the poor people by, killed their younger brother, and would not suffer Jacob to arise? * * *

It is showed us, that all the prophecies, visions and revelations of scriptures, of Prophets and Apostles, concerning the calling of the Jews, the restoration of Israel, and making of that people the inheritors of the whole earth, doth all seat themselves in this work of making the earth a common treasury; as you may read: Ezek. 24. 26–7, &c.; Jer. 33. 7–12; Isa. 49. 17–18, &c.; Zech. 8.

4–12; Dan. 2. 44–5; 7. 27; Hos. 14. 5–7; Joel 2. 26–7; Amos 9. 8 to the end; Obad. 17, 18, 21; Mic. 5. 7 to the end; Hab. 2. 6, 7; 8. 13, 14; Gen. 18. 18; Rom. 11. 15; Zeph. 3. &c.; Zech. 14. 9. And when the Son of Man was gone from the Apostles, his Spirit descended upon the Apostles and Brethren as they were waiting at Jerusalem; and the rich men sold their possessions and gave part to the poor, and no man said that aught that he possessed was his own, for they had all things common (Acts 4. 32).

Now this community was suppressed by covetous, proud flesh, which was the powers that ruled the world. And the righteous Father suffered himself thus to be suppressed for a time, times and dividing of time, or for forty-two months, or for three days and an half, which are all but one and the same term of time. And the world is now come to the half day; and the Spirit of Christ, which is the Spirit of universal community and freedom, is risen, and is rising, and will rise higher and higher, till those pure waters of Shiloa, the well-springs of life and liberty to the whole creation, do overrun . . . those banks of bondage, curse, and slavery. * * *

Another voice that was heard was this: *Israel shall neither take hire nor give hire.*

And if so, then certainly none shall say, 'This is my land; work for me and I 'll give you wages.' For the earth is the Lord's; that is man's, who is lord of the creation, in every branch of mankind. For as divers members of our human bodies make but one body perfect, so every particular man is but a member or branch of mankind; and mankind, living in the light and obedience to Reason, the King of Righteousness, is thereby made a fit and complete lord of the creation. And the whole earth is this Lord's man, subject to the Spirit, and not the inheritance of covetous, proud flesh that is selfish, and enmity to the Spirit. * * *

That which does encourage us to go on in this work is this. We find the streaming out of love in our hearts towards all, to enemies as well as friends. We would have none live in beggary, poverty, or sorrow, but that every one might enjoy the benefit of his creation. We have peace in our hearts, and quiet rejoicing in our work, and [are] filled with sweet content though we have but a dish of roots and bread for our food.

And we are assured that, in the strength of this Spirit that hath manifested himself to us, we shall not be startled, neither at prison nor death, while we are about his work. And we have been made to sit down and count what it may cost us in undertaking such a work. And we know the full sum, and are resolved to give all that we have to buy this pearl which we see in the field.

For by this work, we are assured, and reason makes it appear to others, that bondage shall be removed, tears wiped away, and all poor people by their righteous labours shall be relieved and freed from poverty and straits. For in this work of restoration there will be no beggar in Israel. For surely, if there was no beggar in literal Israel, there shall be no beggar in spiritual Israel, the antitype, much more. * * *

From *The Diggers' Mirth* (1650) [a]

A hint of that Freedom which shall come,
When the Father shall reign alone in his Son.

The Father he is God alone;
    nothing beside him is.
All things are folded in that One;
    by him all things subsist.

He is our light, our life, our peace,
    whereby we our being have;
From him all things have their increase,
    the tyrant and the slave.

And when the Father seeth it good,
    and his set time is come,
He takes away the tyrant's food,
    and gives it to the Son.

Then Esau's pottage shall be eat,
    for which he sold his right;
The blessing Jacob shall obtain,
    which Esau once did slight.

And Jacob he shall then arise
    although he be but small,
Which Esau once did much despise,
    and Esau down must fall.

For there must rise a root of Jess,
    a righteous branch indeed;
Who setteth free him that 's opprest,
    and Esau down must tread.

And Esau shall the blessing seek,
    and with tears shall it crave;
Which he did sell [b] unto the meek,
    which once he made a slave.

But sing, O Jacob, for thy time
  of freedom now is come;
And thou thyself judge Esau,
  the which hath done the wrong.

For to the Son the Father hath
  all judgment given now;
And Esau shall be justly judg'd,
  [for] which Jacob's seed hath plow'd.

And thou that as a lord hast reign'd
  over God's heritage,
Thy part thou hast already play'd;
  therefore come off the stage.

For when thou think'st thyself most safe
  and riches thou hast got;
Then in the middest of thy peace,
  torment shall be thy lot.

And of this, long time thou hast been told,
  but much thou didst it slight;
Therefore, Esau, we must be bold
  now for to claim our right.

For now['s] the Father's 'pointed time,
  which he did fore-intend,
To set up Freedom, and pull down
  the man which did offend:

The time, I say, it is now come,
  in which the Lord will make
All tyrants servants to the Son,
  and he the power will take.

This worldly strength wherewith thou didst
  all times thyself repose,
Shall prove but as a broken reed,
  for thou the field shalt lose.

For there shall rise a mighty Stone,
  which without hands is cut;
Which shall thy Kingly powers break;
  he shall be free from shot.

The first at ª which this Stone shall smite,
  shall be the head of Gold;
A mortal wound he shall them give.
  Now mind, thou hast been told.

APPENDIX^a

A. THE SPIRIT OF THE NEW MODEL

1. REPORTS OF OBSERVERS

Hugh Peter writes: [1]

[T]o return to your Army: . . . two things will commend them above any army I have known, viz., their unity, and activity. I have not known the least breach among them in the least to distract or retard your affairs, though their judgments may differ in many particulars. * * * I can say, your Army is under a blessed conduct, their counsels godly and faithful. More love I have not seen, which I believe may spring from this root: that through grace we make godliness our interest, and not opinion, the which we wish were the spirit of the kingdom though we prescribe to none. Many there be who lose a real interest to maintain a floating fancy. We could desire that the choler that we find in this city, yea that black choler (I had almost said that black-coat [2] choler) were spent upon the ignorance and profaneness of the country. One thing there is most singular in this your Army: that whereas soldiers usually spend and make forfeiture even of the civility they bring into other armies; here men grow religious, and more spiritual-thriving than in any place of the kingdom, that I may a little change the old verse, and say, *Multa fides pietasque vivis, quae haec castra sequntur.* Yea, for myself, though I have been long a learner, and sometimes an unworthy teacher of others, yet have [I] more than an ordinary cause to bless God, for being a member of this Army, in reference to my spirituals.

Richard Baxter writes: [3]

The English Army, being . . . new modelled, was really in the hand of Oliver Cromwell, though seemingly under the command of Sir Thomas Fairfax. * * * We that lived quietly in Coventry did keep to our old principles, and thought all others had done so too except a very few inconsiderable persons. * * * And when the Court News-book told the world of the

---

[1] *Mr. Peter's Message* (1646), pp. 5–6. Similar testimony is borne by other chaplains: William Dell (*The Building and Glory of the Truly Christian Church*, 1646, 'To the Reader'), and Joshua Sprigge (*Anglia Rediviva*, 1647, pp. 323–4).

[2] Reference to the Presbyterian clergy's attacks on the Army's heresies.

[3] *Reliquiae Baxterianae* (1696), Part I, §§ 71, 73.

swarms of Anabaptists in our armies, we thought it had been a mere lie, because it was not so with us nor in any of the garrison or county forces about us. But when I came to the Army, among Cromwell's soldiers, I found a new face of things, which I never dreamed of. I heard the plotting heads very hot upon that which intimated their intention to subvert both church and state. Independency and Anabaptistry were most prevalent; Antinomianism and Arminianism were equally distributed; and Thomas Moor's followers (a weaver of Wisbitch and Lyn, of excellent parts) had made some shifts to join these two extremes together. Abundance of the common troopers, and many of the officers, I found to be honest, sober, orthodox men, and others tractable, ready to hear the truth, and of upright intentions. But a few proud, self-conceited, hot-headed sectaries had got into the highest places, and were Cromwell's chief favourites, and by their very heat and activity bore down the rest, or carried them along with them, and were the soul of the Army though much fewer in number than the rest (being indeed not one to twenty throughout the Army; their strength being in the General's and Whalley's and Rich's regiments of horse, and in the new-placed officers in many of the rest).

I perceived that they took the King for a tyrant and an enemy, and really intended absolutely to master him or ruin him; and that they thought, if they might fight against him, they might kill or conquer him; and if they might conquer, they were never more to trust him further than he was in their power. . . . They said, What were the Lords of England but William the Conqueror's colonels, or the Barons but his majors, or the knights but his captains? They plainly showed me that they thought God's providence would cast the trust of religion and the kingdom upon them as conquerors. They made nothing of all the most wise and godly in the armies and garrisons that were not of their way. *Per fas aut nefas*, by law or without it, they were resolved to take down not only bishops and liturgy and ceremonies, but all that did withstand their way. They were far from thinking of a moderate Episcopacy, or of any healing way between the Episcopal and the Presbyterians'. They most honoured the Separatists, Anabaptists, and Antinomians. But Cromwell and his Council took on them to join themselves to no party, but to be for the liberty of all. * * *

I found that many honest men of weak judgments and little acquaintance with such matters, had been seduced into a disputing vein, and made it too much of their religion to talk for this opinion and for that. Sometimes for state-democracy, and sometimes for church-democracy; sometimes against forms of prayer, and sometimes against infant baptism (which yet some of them did maintain); sometimes against set times of prayer, and against the tying of ourselves to any duty before the Spirit move us; and sometimes about free grace and free will, and all the points of Antinomianism and Arminianism. * * * But their most frequent and vehement disputes were for liberty of conscience, as they called it; that is, that the civil magistrate had nothing to do to determine of anything in matters of religion by constraint or restraint, but every man might not only hold, but preach and do, in matters of religion what he pleased; that the civil magistrate hath nothing to do but with civil things, to keep the peace, and protect the churches' liberties, &c.

I found that one half almost of the religious party among them were such as were either orthodox or but very lightly touched with their mistakes; and almost another half were honest men that stepped further into the contending way than they could well get out of again, but with competent help might be recovered. But a few fiery, self-conceited men among them kindled the rest and made all the noise and bustle, and carried about the Army as they pleased. For the greatest part of the common soldiers, especially of the foot, were ignorant men of little religion, abundance of them such as had been taken prisoners, or turned out of garrisons under the King, and had been soldiers in his army. And these would do anything to please their officers, and were ready instruments for the seducers, especially in their great work which was to cry down the Covenant, to vilify all parish ministers, but especially the Scots and Presbyterians. For the most of the soldiers that I spoke with never took the Covenant because it tied them to defend the King's person, and to extirpate heresy and schism.

Because I perceived that it was a few men that bore the bell, that did all the hurt among them, I . . . would be oft disputing with them in the hearing of the rest; and I found that they were men that had been in London, hatched up among the old Separatists, and had made it all the matter of their study and religion to rail against ministers and parish churches, and Presbyterians, and had little other knowledge, nor little discourse of anything about the heart or heaven, but were fierce with pride and self-conceitedness, and had gotten a very great conquest over their charity, both to the Episcopal and Presbyterians. Whereas many of those honest soldiers which were tainted but with some doubts about liberty of conscience or Independency, were men that would discourse of the points of sanctification and Christian experience very savourily.

But we so far prevailed in opening the folly of these revilers and self-conceited men, as that some of them became the laughing-stock of the soldiers before I left them; and when they preached (for great preachers they were) their weakness exposed them to contempt. A great part of the mischief they did among the soldiers was by pamphlets which they abundantly dispersed; such as R. Overton's *Martin Mar-Priest*, and more of his, and some of J. Lilburne's, who was one of them; and divers against the King, and against the ministry, and for liberty of conscience, &c. And soldiers being usually dispersed in their quarters, they had such books to read when they had none to contradict them.

2. A Sermon at Putney

From Thomas Collier, *A Discovery of the New Creation* [a] (preached at
the Headquarters, Putney, 29th Sept. 1647)
Isa. 65. 17: *Behold I create new heavens, and a new earth.* * * *

Some apprehend that Christ shall come and reign personally, subduing his enemies and exalting his people, and that this is the new
heaven and the new earth. But this is not my apprehension; but that
Christ will come in the Spirit and have a glorious kingdom in the
spirits of his people, and they shall, by the power of Christ in them,
reign over the world, and this is the new heavens and the new earth.
First, he will have a glorious kingdom in the Saints. *The kingdom
of God is within you.* Heaven is the kingdom of God, and this kingdom
is within the Saints. And this is the new creation, the new heaven:
the kingdom of heaven that is in the Saints. It 's true we have had, and
still have, exceeding low and carnal thoughts of heaven, looking on it
as a glorious place above the firmament, out of sight, and not to be
enjoyed till after this life. But God himself is the Saints' kingdom,
their enjoyment, their glory. Where God is manifesting himself, there
is his and the Saints' kingdom, and that is in the Saints. Here lieth
the great and hidden mystery of the Gospel, this new creation in the
Saints. * * *
The nature and glory of it lieth in that renovation or renewing of the
mind: an internal and spiritual change, a transformation out of the
nature of the first, into the nature of the second, Adam. This I shall
for your satisfaction confirm unto you from scripture, although I trust
I shall deliver nothing unto you but experimental truth. See 2 Cor.
5. 17: *He that is in Christ is a new creature. Old things are passed away.
Behold, all things are become new.* Here is this new creation within, a
new creature, a mind renewed by the Spirit. This is that new man
(mentioned, Ephes. 4. 23, 24) which, after God, is created in righteousness and true holiness. * * * Now what this creation or new man is,
according to what I understand—no farther I dare to speak, it is that
union which the divine nature, the Spirit, hath with and in our spirits,
by which union it transforms our spirits into its own glory, and shall in
conclusion wholly swallow up the Saints in that spiritual glory, which
will be their eternal perfection, their heaven, their kingdom, their
glory. This is the first part of both the nature and glory of this new
creation. * * *
For I do not understand by the new heavens, a new thing contrary
to what hath been formerly, but a higher measure or manifestation of
one and the same glory, as the Covenant of Grace was called a new
covenant, not because it was not in being formerly but because it should
be more gloriously manifested than formerly, it should bring forth
more glorious effects in the Saints than formerly. * * * As first, in the
times of the Law, God made himself known to his people under dark

shadows and types: there was a glory but it was such a glory which made them exceedingly to quake and tremble. Secondly, in the days [of] Christ, who put an end to those shadows, there was a higher manifestation of light and glory, wherein was more clearness of light and joy, which was the young or middle age. But thirdly, in this last time or third dispensation of God to, and in, his people, [it] will be much more glorious, much more in the spirit, and therefore called a new heaven; it shall be the light of the same dispensation begun in the Law. See this confirmed: Rev. 21. 1; 2 Pet. 3. 13; Isa. 66. 22.

Query: Wherein doth the glory of this new heaven consist more than ordinary?

Answ[er]: First in the abundance of knowledge. Isa. 11. 9: *The knowledge of God shall cover the face of the earth, as the waters cover the sea.* You may read from ver. 6, that the lion and the lamb, *&c.* shall lie down together. I shall declare by the way what I understand to be the truth intended—not that I limit it from any farther truth that any may see in it.

1. There are all these things within us in that old creation, the lion, and the wolf, *&c.*; which opposes and prevents the Saints' joy, and spiritual enjoyment of God. Now these shall be so overpowered by the glorious appearances of light, that they shall no more hurt or destroy the Saints' peace in their holy mountain, their enjoyment of God in the spirit. . . . The glorious appearings of light in the spirits of Christians will so cover that earth which is within them, that they shall be in a great measure freed from those corruptions, those distractions, which formerly were prevalent in them.

2. God will take away the nature of wicked men, that although they remain wolves, lions, and brutes still, yet they shall not hurt nor destroy in all the holy mountain of God, that is the Church; and that through the abundance of light that shall be communicated, even unto natural men; for the earth, that is earthly men, must give glory to the God of heaven; so Hab. 2. 14. * * *

As ignorance is the grand cause of so much corruption, so many mistakes in the things of God (for always the will and affection follows the understanding, whether enlightened or blinded), so it is the knowledge of God, the breakings forth of light in the spirit, that delivers souls from that corruption and darkness. * * *

Query: Wherein shall the knowledge of the Saints increase?

Answ[er]: Amongst many I shall instance in these particulars following.

First, in the knowledge of the mysteries of God, and that as he is in them, for God is a mystery (Col. 2. 2). And it is by the appearance of God in us, we come to know God who is a mystery. The truth is that we have had, and still have, low and carnal thoughts of God, judging him to be a God afar off, and not a God nigh at hand (this is that Antichrist which denies Christ to be come in the flesh). This is that mystery of which we are exceeding ignorant, God manifest in the flesh

(1 Tim. 3. 16). We have had very narrow apprehensions of Christ and the manifestation of the glory of Christ, limiting it to that one man, when the truth is that Christ and all the Saints makes up but one Christ (1 Cor. 12. 12). And God as truly manifests himself in the flesh of all his as he did in Christ, although the measure of that manifestation is different. This is a mystery which God is revealing in the spirits of his people, and is indeed the glory of this new creation. This being in some measure manifested in the spirits of Christians, produceth in the second place:

Secondly, a knowledge of their spiritual liberty in Christ.

1. Spiritual liberty and justification from all spiritual enemies, sin, law, condemnation. Whatever opposes the soul's peace, in this new heaven it 's all done away. John 8. 36: *If the Son shall make you free, then you are free indeed.* Saints shall now come to see that they are free indeed by Christ. Acts 13. 39: *By him all that believe are justified from all things, from which they could not be justified by the Law of Moses.* Gal. 5. 1: Thus Saints shall know their liberty and stand fast in it too. ✻ ✻ ✻

2. In the knowledge of their liberty from men. 1 Cor. 7. 23: *Ye are bought with a price, be ye not the servants of men!* That is, not to be subject to men in the things of God, in matters of conscience. That belongs only to God himself. It is his proper peculiar right to rule in the spirits of his people, although it 's true that there hath been, and still is, through ignorance, a principle in man not only to usurp authority to rule in and over the conscience of others, but a principle in us also, out of conscience to submit to man in such cases. Now God is discovering, and likewise delivering his people from, this spiritual bondage unto men in the things of God; and that from the knowledge of their liberty in the spirit.

3. There is a liberty in knowledge. 1 John 2. 20: *Ye have an unction from the Holy One and ye know all things;* that is, all things that the Spirit makes known. They are not tied to other men's approbation, but walk in that light the Spirit makes known in them. See 1 Cor. 2. 15.

Secondly, the glory of this new creation consists in the Saints' knowledge of their peace, and union, with God. ✻ ✻ ✻ Every man naturally is at a distance from God, but by Jesus Christ they come to enjoy reconciliation. But . . . they enjoy not only peace with God, but peace with the Saints. It is only the glorious light of this new creation that will put an end to these divisions amongst Christians. It is not magisterial power setting up uniformity, but that one Spirit of light and truth that must bring the Saints into this unity. ✻ ✻ ✻ And the truth is that nothing else will be able to put an end to these divisions but this spiritual dispensation, this new creation of God in the spirits of his people, and this is and shall be the glory of this heaven, unity and peace amongst Saints. ✻ ✻ ✻

2. The glory of this new creation consists not only in knowledge, but in spiritual enjoyment likewise. There is the abundance of spiritual

enjoyment; it does not only see and know, but it enjoys what it sees. It sees liberty and peace, and enjoys it and lives in it. It sees God in the spirit and lives in him. * * * Hence it is the Apostle saith (1 Cor. 3. 22) *All is yours, &c.* * * *

3. The glory of this new creation consists not only in being delivered from legal and fleshly actings, but likewise lives in the power of heavenly and spiritual actings: . . . first . . . in spiritual prayer and praisings; . . . secondly . . . in acts of righteousness and justice unto men. * * *

To speak more externally, by new heavens I understand to be meant a new church estate, and that in opposition unto the old, it 's said to be new:

First, in respect of matter, or members. The old heavens were all carnal and profane creatures, people for the most part without the knowledge of God. Such was the matter of the carnal church. But the matter of this spiritual church, this new heavens, shall be the Saints, such as are all taught of God: *Thy children shall be all righteousness* (Isa. 60. 21; Rev. 21. *ult.*).

2. New in opposition to the old manners and old conversation. The members of the old church were perhaps ignorant, profane, having a form of godliness without the power of it; but the members of this new heaven shall so walk with God as to honour his name. God will so gloriously appear in them as that the world shall be convinced by their godly conversation: *The remnant that are left shall do no iniquity, &c.*

3. They shall be new in respect of form, compacted together by the Spirit, not literal forms and ordinances. The old heaven or church constitution hath been formed up with external compactings, the wisdom and power of the flesh knit together by things without them, not by the bands of the Spirit, the principle and power of love, which is an everlasting band, which will occasion Saints' communion to be sweet and spiritual.

4. They shall be new in respect of ministry, not in the letter but in the spirit, not fetched out of the bottomless pit of creature-wisdom and human abilities, but the single ministration of the Spirit; pray in the Spirit, preach and prophesy in the Spirit, praise in the Spirit; that is, in the wisdom and power of that law in the Spirit which will deliver Saints from fleshly actings into the glorious liberty of spiritual actings, that they shall no more act from a legal principle to a law without them, but from a principle of light, life, liberty, and power within them. Thus God will create a new heaven, a new church estate in the Spirit, which will produce spiritual communion, spiritual joy and gladness amongst the Saints, who live in this light and glory. * * *

This informs us of the vanity and ignorance of those who seek so much to keep up the old heavens, the old church for matter and members, that will turn the world into church by a human power. They are those that must be spiritually slain. Isa. 65. 11, 12: *But ye are they that forsake the Lord, and forget my holy mountain, that prepare a table for the troop, and furnish a drink offering unto that number; therefore I will number you to the sword, and ye shall all bow down to the slaughter,* &c. Here is the vanity of such persons that seek to uphold forms, fleshly actings, and fleshly compactings, the old ministry fetched out of human abilities, the wisdom of the flesh limiting the Spirit to those human qualifications where he appears least. All these, both persons and things, must bow down to the slaughter.

Now I come to the second part of my text: *and a new earth.* In this new creation there is not only new heavens, but a new earth.

What this new earth is, it 's to be looked upon either more mystically or more literally, as the new heavens. 1. Mystically, there is an earth in the heart of every man, nay, of every Christian, flesh and fleshly corruptions, fleshly conclusions; which prevents the joy of Saints. Now the Lord will make a new earth, he will subject that old earth that is in his Saints, that it shall not so prevail in them. He will be a fire in them (Mal. 3. 3). * * *

Secondly, by earth I understand to be meant,[a] the powers of the earth, or the magisterial power, the rule and government of this earth. *It shall be an earth wherein dwelleth righteousness* (2 Pet. 13).

Query : In what respect may the earthly magistracy or earthly powers be said to be made new ?

Answ[er] : First, in respect of the persons ruling, they shall be such as are acquainted with, and have an interest in, the righteous God; that as formerly God hath many times set up wicked men to rule and govern . . . so he will give it into the hands of the Saints.

I question not but that you have heard of the personal reign of Christ. . . .

1. He will have a glorious kingdom in the spirits of his people, and this is the new heavens. And 2. He will in and by his Saints rule the world.

That this is a truth, I shall confirm unto you from scripture. Dan. 8. 27: *And the kingdom and dominion, and the greatness of the kingdom under the whole heaven, shall be given to the people of the Saints of the Most High, whose kingdom is an everlasting kingdom, and all dominions shall serve and obey him.* What more mystical truth may be in this scripture concerning the kingdom in the spirit, I shall not question. But this I believe to be a truth, that the nations shall become the nations of Christ, and the government shall be in the hands of the Saints. Isa. 60. 12, [17-18]: *The nations and kingdoms that will not serve thee* (to wit Christ in the Saints) *shall perish; yea, those nations shall utterly be wasted.* * * * *And I will make thine officers peace, and thine exactors righteousness. Violence shall no more be heard in thy streets, wasting and destruction within thy borders.* Jer. 30. 20: *Your nobles shall be of yourselves, and your governors shall proceed out of the midst of you.* God will raise up men of singular spirits and principles to govern the nations. * * *

Secondly. * * * This is the great work that God hath to effect in the latter days of the Gospel, to reduce magisterial power to its primitive institution, that you may see (Rom. 13. 1), *There is no power but is* *ordained of God, and it is ordained for the punishment of them that do evil, but for the praise of them that do well.* Although this end hath been a long time lost,[a] yet now God will reduce it to this institution. This is the great work, Right Honourable, that God calls for at your hands, whom he hath raised up for that end. * * * It is the execution of righteousness, justice and mercy, without respect of persons. It is to undo every yoke. And this being the great work in hand, and that which God calls for, and will effect, give me leave to present amongst many national grievances, some few unto you.

First, spiritual oppressions in matters of conscience. You know that a long time man hath assumed this power to himself, to rule over the consciences of their brethren: a great oppression and that which cannot be borne in souls who live in light, and that from which God will deliver his people, and punish all that oppressed them.

Secondly, in temporal oppressions I shall mind some few.

1. Tyrannical and oppressing laws, and courts of justice; hence it comes to pass many times that to seek a remedy proves destructive—the cure proves worse than the disease. * * *

2. Oppression or grievance is in writing our laws in an unknown tongue, that the most part of our national inhabitants cannot understand their own laws, that the French should be better read in our English laws than those to whom they pertain. * * *

A third oppression the kingdom groans under is a slavery to the wills of men. Although it 's that which hath been always declared against since this war [b] began, yet we never were so volved up into it as now. There is an affection to arbitrariness in the wills of almost all men, from highest to lowest; men act according to their wills whether with or against law—a burden exceeding oppressive to this kingdom.

A fourth oppression is that of tithes, and . . . the kingdom in almost all parts is sensible of it, and groans under it, with petitions for deliverance. * * *

A fifth oppression and burden of the kingdom is free-quartering of soldiers. Much need there is of provision for soldiers' pay, lest the cure seem more heavy than the disease; lest the work be either obstructed or else carried on with more difficulty.

Sixthly, and finally, I say unto you, as Paul in another case: Whatsoever things are honest, whatsoever things are of good report, &c., think on those things, that so justice and righteousness may flow down abundantly without respect of persons. Whatsoever bears but the face of oppression in it, let it be removed.

Use : If this be the new earth and the great interest to be followed, in a word then to conclude, how should this carry on those whom it concerns, who are called of God unto it, to the accomplishment of this great work, to help forwards this great work and design of God in and by you? Note:

First, policy calls for it at your hands, Right Honourable. Is it not time for you to do something for the kingdom, that may engage their hearts unto you? Is there not much division and confusion amongst us? Much expectation of taking away of burdens? Do not the people in their petitions call for it daily? Truly prudent policy calls for righteousness, and undoing of burdens, that the hearts of the people may be engaged unto you in these times of danger and distraction.

Secondly, piety calls for it. It is the great design of God at present to exalt righteousness, and certainly God calls for it at your hands. *Do justice, love mercy, walk humbly with thy God* (Mic. 6. 8). This the Lord requireth of you.

Thirdly, peace and safety calls for it, your own peace and the kingdom's peace. What is likely to produce peace in the kingdom, if not the flowing down of righteousness and justice from you, the undoing of heavy burdens, and breaking of every yoke of oppression? Your own peace and safety consists in it. Believe it, there is no safety to be expected if once you derogate from this great interest of God, the public good. * * *

B. THE ARMY ORGANIZES: MAY—JUNE 1647

3. APOLOGY OF THE SOLDIERS TO THEIR OFFICERS [1] (3rd MAY) [a]

Sirs: We your soldiers, who have served under your commands, with all readiness, to free this our native land and nation from all tyranny and oppressions whatsoever, and that by virtue and power derived from this present Parliament, given not only to his Excellency Sir Thomas Fairfax, our now present General, but likewise under all the late generals, his predecessors, under whom we, even the whole soldiery, have served both the state and you faithfully and diligently; by which means God hath been pleased to crown us with victory in dispersing our common adversaries, so that we hoped to put an end to all tyranny and oppressions, so that justice and equity, according to the law of this land, should have been done to the people, and that the meanest subject should fully enjoy his right, liberty, and properties, in all things; which the Parliament have made known to all the world in divers of their declarations, to which they have so often bound themselves, to perform, by their oaths, vows, covenants, and protestations: upon this ground of hope we have gone through all difficulties and dangers, that we might purchase to the people of this land, with ourselves, a plentiful crop and harvest of liberty and peace. But instead of it, to the great grief and saddening of our hearts, we see that oppression is as great as ever, if not greater, yea, and that upon the cordial friends to the Parliament and us, and to the just rights and liberties of this nation; that

---

[1] Added to *The Apology of the Common Soldiers*, dated 28th April 1647, and 'Printed May 3, 1647.' For some account of an earlier *Apology*, see Introduction, p. [21].

they with us are slighted, abused, beaten, and dragged to gaols, yea, to the utter ruin of their estates, and loss of their lives; yea, the best and most candid intentions and actions of theirs and ours, grossly and foully misconstrued, even to such a height as deserving no less than to be declared as troublers of, and enemies to, the state and kingdom. And such as have [been] and are now the enemies of the Parliament and kingdom are countenanced and honoured to be in places of general trust, and are made judges of them and us for our lives and estates. * * * From whence, we believe, springs all our miseries, and that so many of our fellow soldiers that have been disbanded have been so rigorously dealt withal as ª imprisoned, indicted, and hanged, for things done in time and place of war, and necessity of the Parliament's service, required in their low condition, and without which they could not have safely sat in the House of Parliament with their heads on. And the reason of all this, we judge, is because our very enemies are made our judges. Yea, such is our condition: though we be oppressed we may not cry, as it is too apparent. When of late we did in a humble and petitionary way seek to make known our grievances to our General, such was our offence as that we must presently, without being heard, be declared enemies to the state. * * *

Therefore, brave Commanders, the Lord put a spirit of courage into your hearts that you may stand fast in your integrity that you have manifested to us your soldiers; and we do declare to you that if any of you shall not, he shall be marked with a brand of infamy for ever as a traitor to his country and an enemy to this ᵇ Army. Read and consider. Was there ever such things done by a Parliament, to proclaim us enemies to the state, as they have done about the late petition? (The Lords and they could quickly agree to this, though they will be very tedious when anything is offered that is for the good of the commonwealth.) And to keep the hirelings' wages, and not to give them that which they have so dearly bought with their blood and lives, even their ᵉ pay; and not only so, but to leave them to the merciless malice of their wicked enemies!

Is it not better to die like men than to be enslaved and hanged like dogs? Which must and will be yours and our portion if not now looked into, even before our disbanding. * * *

We have been quiet and peaceable in obeying all orders and commands, yet not, we have a just cause to tell you, if we be not relieved in these our grievances. We shall be forced to that which we pray God to divert, and keep your and our hearts upright, desiring you to present these things to the General as our desires: (1) That the honour of this Army may be vindicated in every particular, especially about the late petition, and reparations given, and justice done upon the fomenters. (2) That an Act of Indemnity may be made for all things done in time and place of war. (3) That the wives and children of those that have been slain in the service, and maimed soldiers, may be provided for. (4) Our arrears, under this General, to be paid us; our arrears under other generals [a] to be audited and stated, and security given for the payment. (5) That we that have served the Parliament freely may not be pressed out of the kingdom. (6) That the liberty of the subject may be no longer enslaved, but that justice and judgment may be dealt to the meanest subject of this land according to old law.

Now unless all these humble requests be by you for us your soldiers and yourselves stood for to be granted, it had [been] better we had never been born, or at least we had never been in arms, but that we had by the sword been cut off from the misery we and you are like to undergo. So we rest in hopes of your faithfulness,

Your soldiers.

4. Advertisements for the Managing of the Counsels of the Army,[1] Walden, 4th May 1647 [b]

1. Appoint a council for the ordering the undertakings of the Army.
2. Keep a party of able pen-men at Oxford and the Army, where their presses be employed to satisfy and undeceive the people.
3. Hold correspondence with the soldiers and well-affected friends in the several counties of the kingdom, for prevention of uproars, interposition of parties, for disarming the disaffected and securing the persons of projecting parties, namely Presbyterians.
4. Do all things upon public grounds for the good of the people, and with expedition, to avoid divisions and for the prevention of bloodshed.
5. Be vigilant to keep yourselves from supplanting, secret,[c] open, or undermining enemies;[d] especially prevent the removal or surprisal of the King's person.
6. Present the General Officers with the heads of your demands in writing, and subscribed, and so agreed to by your appointed trustees in behalf of yourselves and other soldiers.
7. Desire redress of all arbitrary and exorbitant proceedings throughout the kingdom, and, according to the Covenant, call for public justice and due punishment to be inflicted upon all offenders whomsoever.
8. Give [e] some reasons for desiring reformation in civil justice, and query how the pretended and respective ends of our taking up arms hath been performed or comported with, according to the mutual provocations and declarations of Parliament put forth to engage us in blood, and, for aught we yet find, to entangle us in stronger chains, and to clap upon our necks heavier yokes or servitude.
9. Permit not the Army to be long delayed, or tampered with too much, lest resolution languish and courage grow cold.
10. Persuade the General Officers not to depart from the Army until these storms be overblown, the subject's liberty confirmed, the kingdom settled, delinquents detected and punished, the soldiers and sufferers satisfied and rewarded; in all which respects their conduct was never of more consequence, nor their interest in the Army more

[1] Ascribed by Firth to Edward Sexby (*Clarke Papers*, 1. 22).

useful, the present employment being most important, tending to the consummation of all our cares, and the good concluding by the establishment (in peace and truth) of the work of the whole war.

11. That, according to the premises, we may be speedily [satisfied] and [our several demands] respectively performed with[al]; after which the Army may be reduced, and [to] such a number of horsemen as is not inconsistent with the kingdom's safety; the rest, being justly dealt with in point of due and deserved pay, with honourable rewards for their several services, may be disbanded, after an Act of Indemnity be made, and satisfaction be given, as aforesaid, not only to this Army, but to all the well-affected soldiers and subjects throughout this kingdom.

5. FROM THE GRIEVANCES OF REGIMENTS, PRESENTED AT SAFFRON WALDEN, 13TH–14TH MAY [a]

That [b] such rigour is already exercised that we are denied the liberty which Christ hath purchased for us, and abridged of our freedom to serve God according to our proportion of faith, and like to be imprisoned, yea, beaten and persecuted, to enforce us to a human conformity never enjoined by Christ.

That [c] notwithstanding we have engaged our lives for you, ourselves, [and] posterity, that we might be free from the yoke of episcopal tyranny, yet we fear that the consciences of men shall be pressed beyond the light they have received from the rule of the Word in things appertaining to the worship of God, a thing wholly contrary to the Word of God [and] the best Reformed Churches.

That [d] the ministers in their public labour by all means do make us odious to the kingdom, that they might take off their affections from us lest the world should think too well of us, and not only so but have printed many scandalous books against us, as Mr. Edwards's *Gangraena* and Mr. Love's *Sermons*.

That [e] we who have engaged for our country's liberties and freedom, are denied the liberty to petition in case of grievance, notwithstanding the Parliament have declared (in their Declaration, 2nd November) . . . that it is the liberty of the people to petition unto them in case of grievances, and we humbly conceive that we have the liberty.

That the freemen of England are so much deprived of their liberties and freedom (as many of them are at this day) as to be imprisoned so long together for they know not what, and cannot be brought to a legal trial according to the laws of this land, for their just condemnation or justification, although both themselves and their friends have so often petitioned to the Parliament for it; which we know not how soon may be our case.

That the laws of this land, by which we are to be governed, are in an unknown tongue, so that we may be guilty of the breach of them unknown to us, and come into condemnation.

6. LETTERS TO THE AGITATORS [1]

Gentlemen,[a] My best respects. I rid hard and came to London by four this afternoon. The House hath ordered and voted the Army to be disbanded, regiment by regiment. The General's Regiment of Foot on Tuesday next to lay down their arms in Chelmsford Church, and they do intend to send you down once more Commissioners, to do it, of Lords and Commons. They will not pay more than two months' pay, and, after we be disbanded, to state our accompts and to be paid by the excise in course. This is their good vote, and their good visible security! Pray, Gentlemen, ride night and day. We will act here night and day for you. You must by all means frame a petition in the name of all the soldiers, to be presented to the General by you the Agitators, to have him, in honour, justice and honesty, to stand by you, and to tell Skippon to depart the Army, and all other officers that are not right. Be sure now be active, and send some thirty or forty horse to fetch away Jackson, Gooday, and all that are naught. And be sure to possess his soldiers: he will sell them and abuse them; for so he hath done, he engaged to sell them for eight weeks' pay. Gent., I have it from (59) and (89) that you must do this, and that you shall expel [them] out of the Army; and if you do disappoint them in the disbanding of this regiment, namely (68), you will break the neck of all their designs. This is the judgment of (59) and (89); therefore, Gent., follow it close. The (52) are about (42), which copies I send you. And let me tell you (41) and (52) in (54) are all very gallant. I pray God keep us so too. Now, my lads, if we work like men we shall do well, and that in the hands of (53). And let all the (44) be very insistent [b] that the (55) may be called to a (43), and that with speed. Delay it not. And [c] by all means be sure to stir up the Counties to petition for their rights, and [d] to make their appeal to (55) to assist them. You shall hear all I can, by the next. So till then I rest.

Yours till death,

From 51. 11° at night.   102.

Send this to 92.   May [e] 28, 11 at night.

Send to me and you shall have powder enough and that in your own quarters, five hundred barrels, and it shall not cost a penny, and on Tuesday I will inform you how and where.

Gent.,

There is seven thousand coming down to Chelmsford: on Monday night it will be there. The Earl of Warwick, the Lord Delawarr,[f]

[1] These two letters, each headed 'Letter from Lt. C. to the Agitators', are probably from Lieutenant Edmund Chillenden. Their interest is in the flashlight picture which they give, of the secret organization and activity of the Agitators and their allies. Most of the code numbers are easy to interpret.

of the Commons, Mr. Annesley, Sir Gilbert Gerrard, Sir John Potts, Mr. Grimstone, all these are to come as Commissioners for to disband us. Therefore, Gent., you know what to do. Colonel Rainborough is to go to his regiment, and it is by Oxford. And a guard of dragoons comes with the money and the Commissioners, but how many I know not. All the honest party do much rejoice here at your courage, and the other party do much threaten and speak big. Therefore I pray be careful to have horse to apprehend and seize on the money and Commissioners before they come at the foot. And if you can banish Jackson and the rest out of that regiment, you will do the work; and be sure you do what you can. Do not let Jackson be there to go to London, nor none of them of that regiment, and you will do well enough. Let two horsemen go presently to Colonel Rainborough to Oxford, and be very careful you be not overwitted. Now break the neck of this design, and you will do well. And [this] you must now do, to make a bolt or a shot and not to dally: [to have] but a good party of horse of a thousand, and to have spies with them before (to bring you intelligence), and to quarter your horse overnight, and to march in the night.

So God bless,

I rest,

Yours,

102.

7. FROM A SOLEMN ENGAGEMENT OF THE ARMY [1] (5TH JUNE) [a]

Whereas, upon the petition intended and agreed upon in the Army in March last, to have been presented to the General, for the obtaining of our due and necessary concernments as soldiers, the Honourable House of Commons being unseasonably prepossessed with a copy thereof, and (as by the sequel we suppose) with some strange misrepresentations of the carriage and intentions of the same, was induced to send down an order for suppressing the petition; and within two or three days after . . . a declaration was published in the name of both Houses highly censuring the said petition, and declaring the petitioners, if they should proceed thereupon, no less than enemies to the state and disturbers of the public peace. * * *

And whereas, by the aforesaid proceedings and the effects thereof, the soldiers of this Army (finding themselves so stopped in their due and regular way of making known their just grievances and desires, to and by their officers) were enforced to an unusual, but in that case necessary, way of correspondence and agreement amongst themselves, to choose out of the several troops and companies several men, and those out of their whole number to choose two or more for each regiment, to act in the name and behalf of the whole soldiery of the respective regiments, troops, and companies, in the prosecution of their rights and desires in the said petition; as also of their just vindication and righting [b] in reference to the aforesaid proceedings upon and against

[1] Probably the work of Ireton.

the same, who have accordingly acted and done many things to those ends; all which the soldiery ᵃ did then approve ᵇ as their own acts.[1] ＊ ＊ ＊

Now forasmuch as we know not how far the malice, injustice, and tyrannical principles of our enemies, that have already prevailed so far to abuse the Parliament and the Army, as is aforementioned in the past proceedings against the Army, may further prevail to the danger and prejudice of ourselves or any officers or soldiers of the Army, or other persons that have appeared to act anything in behalf of the Army, or how far the same may further prevail to the danger or prejudice of the kingdom, in raising a new war or otherwise: therefore for the better prevention of all such dangers, prejudices, or other inconveniences that may ensue, and withal for better satisfaction to the Parliament and kingdom concerning our desires of conforming ᶜ to the authority of the one, and providing [for] the good and quiet of the other, in the present affair of disbanding, and for a more assured way whereby that affair may come to a certain issue (to which purpose we herein humbly implore the present and continued assistance of God, the righteous judge of all), we, the officers and soldiers of the Army subscribing hereunto, do hereby declare, agree, and promise, to and with each other, and to and with the Parliament and kingdom, as followeth:

1. That we shall cheerfully and readily disband when thereunto required by the Parliament, or else shall many of us be willing, if desired, to engage in further services either in England or Ireland, having first such satisfaction to the Army in relation to our grievances and desires heretofore presented, and such security that we ᵈ ourselves, when disbanded and in the condition of private men, or other the free-born people of England (to whom the consequence of our case doth equally extend), shall not remain subject to the like oppression, injury, or abuse, as in the premises hath been attempted and put upon us while an army, by the same men's continuance in the same credit and power (especially if as our judges), who have in these past proceedings against the Army so far prevailed to abuse the Parliament and us and to endanger the kingdom; and also such security that we ourselves or any member of this Army, or others who have appeared to act anything in behalf of the Army in relation to the premises before recited, shall not after disbanding be any way questioned, prosecuted, troubled, or prejudiced, for anything so acted, or for the entering into, or necessary prosecution of, this present ᵉ agreement; we say, having first such satisfaction and security in these things as shall be agreed unto by a council to consist of those general officers of the Army who have concurred with the Army in the premises, with two commission-officers and two soldiers to be chosen for each regiment who have concurred and shall concur with us in the premises and in this agreement, and by the major part of such of them who shall meet in council for that purpose when they shall be thereunto called by the General.

---

[1] Omitted passage deals with Parliament's plan to disband the Army.

2. That without such satisfaction and security as aforesaid, we shall not willingly disband nor divide, nor suffer ourselves to be disbanded or divided. And whereas we find many strange things suggested or suspected to our great prejudice, concerning dangerous principles, interests and designs in this Army (as to the overthrow of magistracy, the suppression or hindering of Presbytery, the establishment of Independent government, or upholding of a general licentiousness in religion under pretence of liberty of conscience, and many such things), we shall very shortly tender to the Parliament a vindication of the Army [1] from all such scandals, to clear our principles in relation thereunto. And in the meantime we do disavow and disclaim all purposes or designs in our late or present proceedings, to advance or insist upon any such interest; neither would we, if we might and could, advance or set up any one particular party or interest in the kingdom, though imagined never so much our own, but should much rather study to provide, as far as may be within our sphere or power, for such an establishment of common and equal right, freedom, and safety to the whole as all might equally partake of, that do not, by denying the same to others, or otherwise, render themselves incapable thereof.

8. FROM A REPRESENTATION OF THE ARMY (14TH JUNE) [a]

That we may no longer be the dissatisfaction of our friends, the subject of our enemies' malice (to work jealousies and misrepresentations upon), and the suspicion, if not astonishment, of many in the kingdom, in our late or present transactions . . . , we shall in all faithfulness . . . declare unto you those things which have of late protracted and hindered our disbanding, the present grievances which possess our Army and are yet unremedied, with our desires as to the complete settlement of the liberties and peace of the kingdom. Which is that blessing of God than which, of all worldly things, nothing is more dear unto us or more precious in our thoughts, we having hitherto thought all our present enjoyments (whether of life, or livelihood, or nearest relations) a price but sufficient to the purchase of so rich a blessing, that we and all the free-born people of this nation may sit down in quiet under our vines, and under the glorious administration of justice and righteousness, and in full possession of those fundamental rights and liberties without which we can have little hopes, as to human considerations, to enjoy either any comfort of life or so much as life itself, but at the pleasures of some men ruling merely according to will and power.[2] * * *

Nor will it now, we hope, seem strange or unseasonable to rational and honest men, . . . if . . . we shall, before disbanding, proceed

[1] See No. 8, also the work of Ireton.
[2] Omitted passage contains a brief and forceful statement of the particular grievances and demands of the Army.

in our own and the kingdom's behalf to propound and plead for some provision for our and the kingdom's satisfaction and future security. . . . Especially considering that we were not a mere mercenary army, hired to serve any arbitrary power of a state, but called forth and conjured by the several declarations of Parliament to the defence of our own and the people's just rights and liberties. And so we took up arms in judgment and conscience to those ends, and have so continued them, and are resolved according to your [1] first just desires in your declarations, and such principles as we have received from your frequent informations, and our own common sense, concerning these our fundamental rights and liberties, to assert and vindicate the just power and rights of this kingdom in Parliament for those common ends premised, against all arbitrary power, violence and oppression, and all particular parties and interests whatsoever; the said declarations still directing us to the equitable sense of all laws and constitutions, as dispensing with the very letter of the same and being supreme to it when the safety and preservation of all is concerned, and assuring us that all authority is fundamentally seated in the office, and but ministerially in the persons. Neither do or will these our proceedings, as we are fully and in conscience persuaded, amount to anything unwarrantable before God and men; being thus far much short of the common proceedings in other nations, to things of an higher nature than we have yet appeared to. And we cannot but be sensible of the great complaints that have been made to us generally in the kingdom from the people where we march, of arbitrariness and injustice to their great and insupportable oppressions.

And truly such kingdoms as have, according both to the law of nature and nations, appeared to the vindications and defences of their just rights and liberties, have proceeded much higher; as our brethren of Scotland, who in the first beginning of these late differences associated in covenant from the very same principles and grounds, having no visible form either of Parliament or King to countenance them—and as they were therein justified and protected by their own and this kingdom also, so we justly shall expect to be. (We need not mention the States of the Netherlands, the Portugals, and others, all proceeding upon the same principles of right and freedom.) And accordingly the Parliament hath declared it no resistance of magistracy to side with the just principles of law, nature, and nations, being that law upon which we have assisted you, and that the soldiery may lawfully hold the hands of that general who will turn his cannon against his army on purpose to destroy them, the seamen the hands of that pilot who wilfully runs the ship upon the rock (as our brethren of Scotland argued). And such were the proceedings of our ancestors of famous memory, to the purchasing of such rights and liberties as they have enjoyed through the price of their blood, and [such rights and liberties as] we, both by

---

[1] The *Representation* is addressed to the Parliament.

that and the later blood of our dear friends and fellow soldiers, with the hazard of our own, do now lay claim unto.

Nor is that supreme end, the glory of God, wanting in these cases to set a price upon all such proceedings of righteousness and justice; it being one witness of God in the world, to carry on a testimony against the injustice and unrighteousness of men, and against the miscarriages of government[s] when corrupted or declining from their primitive and original glory.

These things we mention but to compare proceedings, and to show that we are so much the more justifiable and warranted in what we do, by how much we come short of that height and measure of proceedings which the people in free kingdoms and nations have formerly practised.

Now, having thus far cleared our way in this business, we shall proceed to propound such things as we do humbly desire for the settling and securing of our own and the kingdom's right, freedom, peace, and safety, as followeth:

I. That the Houses may be speedily purged of such members as for their delinquency, or for corruption, or abuse to the state, or undue election, ought not to sit there. . . .

II. That those persons who have, in the late unjust and high proceedings against the Army, appeared to have the will, the confidence, credit, and power to abuse the Parliament and the Army, and endanger the kingdom in carrying on such things against us while an army, may be some way speedily disabled from doing the like or worse to us, when disbanded and dispersed, and in the condition of private men, or to other the free-born people of England in the same condition with us. * * *

But because neither the granting of this alone would be sufficient to secure our own and the kingdom's rights, liberties, and safety, either for the present age or posterity, nor would the proposal of this, singly, be free from the scandal and appearance of faction, or [of] design only to suppress one party under the notion of unjust or oppressive, that we may advance another, which may be imagined more our own: we therefore declare that indeed we cannot but wish that such men, and such only, might be preferred to the great power and trust of the commonwealth, as are approved at least for moral righteousness, and of such we cannot but in our wishes prefer those that appear acted thereunto by a principle of conscience and religion in them; and accordingly we do and ever shall bless God for those many worthies who, through his providence, have been chosen into this Parliament; and to such men's endeavours, under God, we cannot but attribute that vindication in part of the people's rights and liberties, and those beginnings of a just reformation, which the proceedings of the beginnings of this Parliament appeared to have driven at and tended to, though of late obstructed, or rather diverted to other ends and interests, by the prevailing of other persons of other principles and conditions.

But we are so far from designing or complying to have any absolute

arbitrary power fixed or settled for continuance in any persons whatsoever as that, if we might be sure to obtain it, we cannot wish to have
it so in the persons of any who[m] we might best confide in, or who
should appear most of our own opinions or principles, or whom we
might have most personal assurance of, or interest in; but we do and
shall much rather wish that the authority of this kingdom in the Parliaments rightly constituted, free, equally and successively chosen,
according to its original intention, may ever stand and have its course.
And therefore we shall apply our desires chiefly to such things as (by
having parliaments settled in such a right constitution) may give more
hopes of justice and righteousness to flow down equally to all in that
its ancient channel, without any overture tending either to overthrow
that foundation either of order or government in this kingdom, or to
engross that power, for perpetuity, into the hands of any particular
person or party whatsoever. * * *

We . . . humbly conceive that (of two inconveniences the less being
to be chosen) the main thing to be intended . . . (and beyond which
human providence cannot reach as to any assurance of positive good)
seems to be this, *viz.*: To provide that however unjust or corrupt
persons of Parliament, in present or future, may prove, or whatever it
be they may do to particular parties, or to the whole in particular
things, during their respective terms or periods; yet they shall not
have the temptation or advantage of an unlimited power fixed in them
during their own pleasure, whereby to perpetuate injustice and oppression upon any, without end or remedy, or to advance and uphold any
one particular party, faction, or interest whatsoever, to the oppression
or prejudice of the community and the enslaving of the kingdom unto
all posterity; but that the people may have an equal hope or possibility,
if they have [made] an ill choice at one time, to mend it in another,
and [the members] themselves may be in a capacity to taste of subjection as well as rule, and may be so inclined to consider of other men's
cases as what may come to be their own. This we speak of in relation
to the House of Commons, as being entrusted on the people's behalf
for their interest in that great and supreme power of the commonwealth (*viz.*, the legislative power, with the power of final judgments),
which, being in its own nature so arbitrary, and in a manner unlimited
unless in point of time, is most unfit and dangerous, as to the people's
interest, to be fixed in the persons of the same men * during life or their
own pleasure. Neither by the original constitution of this state was
it, or ought it to continue so. Nor doth it, wherever it is and continues so, render that state any better than a mere tyranny, or the people
subjected to it any better than vassals. But in all states where there is
any face of common freedom, and particularly in this state of England
(as is most evident both by many positive laws and ancient constant
custom), the people have a right to new and successive elections unto
that great and supreme trust, at certain periods of time; which is so
essential and fundamental to their freedom as it cannot or ought not

to be denied them,[a] or withheld from them, and [b] without which the House of Commons is of very little concernment to the interest of the Commons of England. Yet in this we would not be misunderstood to blame those worthies of both Houses, whose zeal to vindicate the liberties of this nation did procure that act for [the] continuance of [this] Parliament, whereby it was secured from being dissolved at the King's pleasure, as former Parliaments have been, and reduced to such a certainty as might enable them the better to assist and vindicate the liberties of this nation (immediately before so highly invaded, and then also so much endangered). * * *

And therefore upon all the grounds premised we further humbly desire as followeth:

III. That some determinate period of time may be set for the continuance of this and future Parliaments, beyond which none shall continue, and upon which new writs may of course issue out, and new elections successively take place, according to the intent of the Bill for Triennial Parliaments. * * *

IV. That secure provision may be made for the continuance of future Parliaments, so as they may not be adjournable or dissolvable at the King's pleasure, or any other ways than by their own consent during their respective periods; but [at] those periods each Parliament to determine of course, as before. This we desire may be now provided for, if it may be, so as to put it out of all dispute for [the] future, though we think of right it ought not to have been otherwise before.

And [1] because the present distribution of elections for Parliament-members is so very unequal, and the multitude of burgesses for decayed or inconsiderable towns (whose interest in the kingdom would in many not exceed, or in others not equal, ordinary villages) doth give too much and too evident opportunity for men of power to frame parties in Parliament to serve particular interest[s], and thereby the common interest of the whole is not so minded, or not so equally provided for, we therefore further desire:

V. That some provision may be now made for such distribution of elections for future Parliaments as may stand with some rule of equality or proportion as near as may be, to render the Parliament a more equal representative of the whole, as, for instance, that all counties or divisions and parts of the kingdom (involving inconsiderable towns) may have a number of Parliament-men allowed to their choice proportionable to the respective rates they bear in the common charges and burdens of the kingdom, and not to have more, or some other such-like rule.

And thus a firm foundation being laid in the authority and constitution of Parliament for the hopes, at least, of common and equal right and freedom to ourselves and all the free-born people of this land, we shall, for our parts, freely and cheerfully commit our stock

[1] This and the following paragraph occur only in the Cambridge edition.

or share of interest in this kingdom into this common bottom of Parliament[s]; and though it may, for our particulars, go ill with us in one voyage, yet we shall thus hope, if right be with us, to fare better in another.

These things we desire may be provided for by bill or ordinance of Parliament, to which the Royal Assent may be desired. And when His Majesty (in these things, and what else shall be proposed by the Parliament, necessary for securing the rights and liberties of the people, and for settling the militia and peace of the kingdom) shall have given his concurrence to put them past dispute, we shall then desire that the rights of His Majesty and his posterity may be considered of and settled in all things, so far as may consist with the right and freedom of the subject and with the security of the same for [the] future.

VI. We desire that the right and freedom of the people to represent to the Parliament, by way of humble petition, their grievances in such things as cannot otherwise be remedied than by Parliament, may be cleared and vindicated; that all such grievances of the people may be freely received and admitted into consideration, and put into an equitable and speedy way to be heard, examined, and redressed, if they appear real; and that in such things for which men have remedy by law they may be freely left to the benefit of [the] law, and the regulated course of justice, without interruption or check from the Parliament, except in case of things done upon the exigency of war, or for the service and benefit of the Parliament and kingdom in relation to the war, or otherwise in due pursuance and execution of ordinances or orders of Parliament.

More particularly, under this head we cannot but desire that all such as are imprisoned for any pretended misdemeanour may be put into a speedy way for a just hearing and trial; and such as shall appear to have been unjustly and unduly imprisoned, may, with their liberty, have some reasonable reparation according to their sufferings and the demerit of their oppressors.[1] * * *

IX. That public justice being first satisfied by some few examples to posterity out of the worst of excepted persons, and other delinquents having passed their compositions, some course may be taken by a general act of oblivion, or otherwise, whereby the seeds of future war or feuds, either to the present age or posterity, may the better be taken away, by easing that sense of present, and satisfying those fears of future, ruin or undoing to persons or families, which may drive men into any desperate ways for self-preservation and remedy, and by taking away the private remembrances and distinctions of parties, as far as may stand with safety to the rights and liberties we have hitherto fought for.

There are, besides these, many particular things which we could wish to be done, and some to be undone, all in order still to the same

---

[1] VII deals with the limiting of the regional powers given during the war to committees and deputy lieutenants; VIII, with the auditing of Parliament's accounts.

end of common right, freedom, peace, and safety; but these proposals aforegoing being the principal things we bottom and insist upon, we shall, as we have said before, for our parts acquiesce for other particulars in the wisdom and justice of Parliament. And whereas it hath been suggested, or suspected, that in our late or present proceedings our design is to overthrow Presbytery, or hinder the settlement thereof, and to have the Independent government set up, we do clearly disclaim and disavow any such design. We only desire that, according to the declarations promising a privilege for tender consciences, there may be some effectual course taken, according to the intent thereof, and that such who upon conscientious grounds may differ from the established forms, may not for that be debarred from the common rights, liberties, or benefits belonging equally to all as men and members of the commonwealth, while they live soberly, honestly, inoffensively towards others, and peacefully and faithfully towards the state. * * *

C. THE READING DEBATES

9. SUMMARY, WITH SELECTIONS, OF THE DEBATE IN THE GENERAL COUNCIL OF THE ARMY, AT READING, 16TH JULY 1647, ON THE PROPOSALS OF THE AGITATORS FOR FIVE POINTS TO BE INSISTED ON BY THE ARMY AND ENFORCED BY A MARCH ON LONDON [a]

The Agitators petitioned Fairfax in part as follows:

'That your petitioners out of their deep sense of the sad and heavy pressures, great distractions, continual fears, and imminent [b] dangers, under which this poor and bleeding kingdom groans, expecting to be delivered and eased (whose peace, safety, and freedom from oppression, violence, and tyranny, we tenderly and earnestly desire, even above our own lives) are enforced to present these our humble requests, in the name of the whole Army, as their sense and desire, unto your Excellency and this Honourable Council, to be considered of, (if need be) corrected, and forthwith exhibited to the Parliament. And that for the reasons annexed to these ensuing desires, the Army may be immediately marched to or near London, thereby to enable and assist the Parliament acting for the kingdom's ease and preservation, and to oppose all those that shall act the contrary.

'For the accomplishment whereof we are fully resolved (by the assistance of God and his strength, with your Excellency and your Council of War's concurrence) to put a speedy period to these present distractions.

'1st. That by order of the House the eleven Members by his Excellency and his Army impeached, and charged of high misdemeanours, be forthwith sequestered, and disabled [c] from sitting in the House.

'2ly. That the militia of the City of London be immediately returned into the hands of those in whom it lately was, who did approve themselves faithful to the kingdom and City in times of greatest dangers. An answer whereof we expect within two days.

'3ly. That there be an effectual declaration forthwith published to the whole kingdom against the inviting or coming in of foreign, or raising of intestine, forces, under any pretence whatsoever, except such as shall,ᵃ by the Parliament's appointment, receive their commissions from, and be ᵇ at the disposal and command of, his Excellency Sir Thomas Fairfax, upon pain of being proceeded against as enemies and traitors to the state, disturbers of the public peace, and invaders of this kingdom.

'4ly. That all prisoners who have been illegally committed in any part of the kingdom of England or dominion of Wales, may be forthwith set at liberty, and reparation given them for their false imprisonment, as namely: Lieutenant-Colonel John Lilburne, Mr. Musgrave, Mr. Overton's wife and brother, Mr. Larner, his two lieutenants, Mr. Tew, Mr. Prest, and all others which have been in like manner wrongfully imprisoned; and for a more speedy effecting thereof there may be a declaration published . . . commanding all judges of assizes . . . and all other officers and ministers of state whatsoever (upon pain of severest punishment if they shall neglect to put the same in execution) for the freeing of such as are in prison, and preventing the like for the future upon the meanest subjects of the kingdom.

'5ly. That we may be speedily paid up equal with the deserters of the Army, according to the Parliament's former votes, whereby the Army may not be so burdensome and oppressive to the country.' * * * [1]

'Additional Reasons more fully explaining our desires for a speedy march towards London.'

'1st. The Army's removal to this distance from London hath given liberty and opportunity to an adverse party in that city to scandalize our persons and actions by pamphlets and otherwise, whereby they prejudice the spirits of many against us, they being deprived of opportunities to understand personally from ourselves both our actions and intentions, by reason of our distance from them.

'2ly. Our adversaries by our removal far from them have taken advantage to induce many thousands to list themselves (under such new commanders as the new Committee for the Militia hath judged fit to prosecute their ends) under pretence of being auxiliary forces to the Trained Bands. And though [the] pretences may be specious, yet, considering that the principles of the actors have a natural tendency to oppose the Army, and that those whose principles did not concur with theirs were displaced in order to these proceedings, who can

[1] The petition is signed not by the Agitators, but by three officers: Major Daniel Abbott, and Captains John Clarke and Edmund Rolfe.

imagine any reason of such preparations, when no visible power appears against them, unless their thoughts and intentions be to oppose the Army? And indeed some lately have boasted that they have many thousands ready to fight with this Army, if they were commanded.

'3ly. Upon the Army's drawing back from the City, the Parliament's proceedings for the good of the people and Army hath been slacked. Whilst the Army was drawing near, the excise was lessened and eased, the injuries done to the Army considered, some moneys provided for them. But since its drawing back, no moneys have been allowed them to pay their quarters for the people's ease and the Army's content; there hath been no care to prevent the scandalizing of us, no discountenance of those that by pamphlets asperse us with mutinying, treason, and rebellion. And whether these neglects of us may not proceed from their confidence in those pretended auxiliaries, we leave to your wisdom to judge.

'4ly. The votes of Parliament, whereupon we drew back, appear to have been intended to delude us. * * *

'[5ly.] The removal of the Army to this distance necessitates such delays as give further opportunity to the adverse party to make overtures of plausible advantage to the King's party, and also to insinuate that our principles are against civil government. * * * '

After some disagreement as to the subjects to be debated, Major *Tulidah* observes: 'All centre in one thing: that all the proposals [will] be of no effect without a march to London.' *Cromwell* replies: 'Marching up to London is a single proposal; yet it does not drop from Jupiter, as that it should be presently received and debated without considering our reasons. For I hope this [temper] will ever be in the Agitators—I would be very sorry to flatter them—I hope they will be willing that nothing should be done but with the best reason, and with the best and most unanimous concurrence.' *Ireton* objects: 'We act as if we did [intend only to] get the power into our own hands. To give the kingdom satisfaction is the thing that we desire. It is not the getting power into one man's hands more than another, but it is the settling and securing their liberties in order to a peace. * * * Before we do bring ourselves into scandal and dishonour by putting it upon new punctilios and quarrelling more, [many things are to be considered; and] one is what it is that we intend to do with that power when we have it.' *Cromwell* supports Ireton, urges time to consider so momentous a decision, and suggests that the Heads of the Proposals, the plan of settlement now being prepared, should be first discussed: 'I desire we may withdraw and consider. Discourses of this nature will, I see, put power into the hands of [m]any that cannot tell how to use it, [instead of, as it is now, in the hands] of those that are like to use it ill. I wish it with all my heart in better hands, and I shall be glad to contribute to get it into better hands. * * * And whereas the Commissary does offer that these things were desired before satisfaction [could] be given [as] to the [Army's scheme for the] public settlement, there may be a convenience of bringing in that [matter] to the Council of War next sitting, if it be ready, and thought fit to be brought in.' The Agitators, *Allen* and *Lockyer*, oppose this delay. Prior to the duty of propounding schemes of settlement is that of removing power from the hands of those who seek only to augment their own power, who will use it to destroy Army and kingdom, and whose possession of it is 'the great dissatisfaction of all the well-affected in the kingdom.' *Ireton* insists: '[We should give the kingdom first] some real taste of that which we intend for the satisfaction of the kingdom, and what we would do with that power if we had it in our hands [after] the putting of it out of so many hands. I have moved it, and so must again.' *Joyce* replies: 'The Commissary-General speaks of things which he gives as laws to the kingdom. It is too hard for us to give out laws before the kingdom is in a possibility of being settled, and it is a great disadvantage for us to prescribe laws when we know not whether ever [we shall be able] to accomplish [a settlement].' The brief morning session closes with the naming of committees by *Harrison* to prepare subjects for debate, and *Rainborough* voices his sense of the futility of all talk when action is what is needed: 'For my part, I shall be weary of the meeting.'

At the resumed session *Cromwell* explains that two of the five points raised by the Agitators have not been previously offered to the Parliament (the matter of the London militia, and the release of prisoners); but all the points are (or by addition may be) handled in a paper about to be sent by the Parliamentary Commissioners,[1] drawn up by Cromwell himself and Lambert, and submitted to the General 'at our meeting in the inner room'; this paper, in response to an earlier demand, deals with the matter of the London militia; it shall be read; it omits nothing but the suspension of the eleven Members and the release of prisoners. He proceeds: 'We are now endeavouring as the main of our work to make a preparation of somewhat that may tend to a general settlement of the peace of the kingdom, and of the rights of the subject, that justice and righteousness may peaceably flow out upon us. That's the main of our business. These things are but preparatory things to that that is the main.' It is hoped to gain all the points raised, in the treaty now being negotiated, or rather as satisfaction demanded preliminary to a treaty; and they must be gained without undue delay or the fruit of a treaty will be lost; 'it's dangerous to be deluded by a treaty.' A sense of that no doubt prompted the suggestion of a march on London. 'Truly I think that possibly that may be that that we shall be necessitated to do [in the end]. Possibly it may be so; but yet I think it will be for our honour and our honesty, to do what we can to accomplish this work in the way of a treaty. * * * For certainly that

[1] 'An Answer of the Commissioners of the Army,' *Army Declarations* (1647), p. 77.

is the most desirable way, and the other a way of necessity, and not to be done but in [a] way of necessity. And truly, instead of all reasons let this [one] serve: that whatsoever we get by a treaty, whatsoever comes to be settled upon us in that way, it will be firm and durable.. * * * We shall avoid that great objection that will lie against us, that we have got things of the Parliament by force; and we know what it is to have that stain lie upon us. Things, though never so good, obtained in that way, it will exceedingly weaken the things, both to ourselves and to all posterity; and therefore I say, upon that consideration, I wish we may be well advised what to do.' The Army's Commissioners should insist on the granting of satisfaction in all the five points within the time set in the Agitators' proposal. If this fails, the course advocated by them can still be taken. The Commissary-General will give some account of the scheme for settling the kingdom, the Heads of the Proposals.

Captain *Clarke* objects that to proceed by way of treaty in these urgent matters will be 'more dilatory and wanting of that virtue and vigour' possessed by direct demands made by the Army as a whole. And may not the coupling with it of a scheme for settling the rights and liberties of the subject prove an obstacle in our present design, for the kingdom may not be immediately satisfied in what we propose? 'For my own part I conceive thus much, that we have very good and wholesome laws already, if we had but good and wholesome executors of them. And that 's the thing we insist upon, to remove such persons that are most corrupt out of power and trust, and that such persons as are of known integrity may be placed in their rooms. And whereas the Lieutenant-General was pleased to move that it was the best way to compose the differences between the Parliament and Army by way of treaty, I presume to say in the name of these gentlemen, they likewise wish it might be so. But truly, sir, we have great fears and jealousies that these treaties, managed by a power so [adverse] to us, will prove rather destructive and delusive to us than anyways certain for our security and [for] the settlement of the kingdom. If your Excellency please we are very desirous that the paper presented to you might be represented [to Parliament] as immediately from us and from this honourable Council, and by the Agitators, which we conceive will put vigour and strength to the business, and we hope effect that which [is] so earnestly desired.'

Allen expresses the complete confidence of the Army in the General and Council, who 'have travailed hard in transacting and managing of things in order to the weal both of the kingdom and Army. . . . But truly we cannot be so fully satisfied in the apprehension of your care in the managing and transacting of things for us, but we are as much sadd[en]ed that those with whom you are transacting and endeavouring to manage these great affairs for us are taking so little care of us while you in transacting are so careful of them—so little care either to save your expense [of labour] or ours.' The Lieutenant-General urges that it is more honourable to proceed by way of treaty. 'It hath been our thoughts so too, and therefore [we] have waited long that we might, if possible, have things ended in such a way; but truly we have waited so long that ᵃ our patience is expended. The Lieutenant-General hath expressed that if things be not ended in such a way, then there is a ground to go on in some other way. How far that way hath fallen short, and how far that has ᵇ presented us with a clear ground to proceed in further, I shall leave it to this honourable Council to judge. And truly it is . . . in most of our thoughts, that those who have been treating with us are not intended to conclude things in such a way.ᶜ When we see God so carrying ʰ forth, or so suffering the spirits of men to be acted [upon], that they shall refuse those peaceable things desired,ᵈ that is the great thing [to be] observed by us; ᵉ and [we must ask] whether or no [this being] once proved,ᶠ [God] hath not pointed out some other way to us. I think it is [in] most of our thoughts that he has.' For that reason, and because 'now we see delays prove so dangerous that they are almost every day expected to run into confusion, which [it] is the desire of you and us to prevent,ᵍ we have named those things that they may be offered to the House, and that we may march in order to a speedy procuring of an answer to them.'

Cromwell explains that what he said of a treaty referred to the general scheme of settlement proposed by the Army; the Agitators' five points are to be demanded of Parliament (through its Commissioners) as *preliminary to the treaty*. It must not be forgotten that there is an honest party in the House of Commons. To aid, and not to embarrass it, should be the Army's aim: 'Give me leave to say this to you. For my own part, perhaps, I have as few extravagant thoughts, overweening [thoughts] of obtaining great things from the Parliament, as any man; yet it hath been in most of our thoughts, that this Parliament might be a reformed and purged Parliament, that we might see [there] men looking at public and common interests only. This was the great principle we had gone upon, and certainly this is the principle we did march upon when we were at Uxbridge, and when we were at St. Albans,¹ and surely the thing was wise, and honourable, and just, and we see that Providence hath led us into that way. [*In reply to an interruption :*] It's thought that the Parliament does not mend—what's the meaning of that? That is to say, that company of men that sits there does not mean well to us? There is a party there that have been faithful from the sitting of the Parliament to this very day; and we know their interests, and [how] they have ventured their lives through so many hazards—they came not to the House but under the apprehension of having their throats cut every day. If we well

¹ Cromwell refers to the advance first to St. Albans (whence the *Representation* was issued), and then (24th–25th June) to Uxbridge.

consider what difficulties they have passed ᵃ we may not run into that
extreme of thinking too hardly of the [whole] Parliament. ✱ ✱ ✱ To-day
that which we desire is that which they have struggled for as for life,
and sometimes they have been able to carry it, others not, and yet
daily they get ground. If we [wish to] see a purged Parliament, I
pray let me persuade every man that he would be a little apt to hope
the best. And I speak this to you as out of a clear conscience before
the Lord: I do think that [that part of] the Parliament is upon the
gaining hand, and that this work that we are now upon tends to make
them gain more. And I would wish that we might remember this
always, that [what] we and they gaïn in a free way, it is better than
twice so much in a forced, and will be more truly ours and our posterity's. And therefore I desire not to persuade any man to be of my
mind, but I wish that every man would seriously weigh these things.'

Allen disagrees with Cromwell's reading of the facts, and is forced
to abandon his hopes: 'Truly they are the same thoughts and hopes
that we have long had, and are loath to lay down or to deviate from,
did not too visible testimony take us off, [f]or we would willingly see,ᵇ
and it would be the rejoicing of our spirits to see (as possibly might be),ᶜ
a Parliament so reformed as [that it] might back this present power,
and that power and authority might go hand in hand to carry on that
great work in order to the kingdom's welfare. . . . Your Honour is
pleased to tell us (I suppose speaking your hopes therein) that the
[honest party in] Parliament [is] the prevailing part of it, or ᵈ is a
gaining part, and like to gain more. Truly I could wish we could say
so too; but so far as we are able to judge (of ourselves) we must speak
our fears, that we conceive they are a losing party, and losers rather
than gainers. ✱ ✱ ✱ [And we ask ourselves] whether our marching
towards London may not conduce to such an end, namely to the
quelling of the spirits of those who are acting as much as in them lies
to make them and us and the kingdom be losers.'

Ireton agrees with Cromwell that the honest party in the House
is rather gaining than losing. At least he has heard no reason for
the contrary view save that the Parliament 'did not so fully nor so
wholly comply with this Army in all the things that they desire [as we
think they ought to do].' For his part, he adds: 'I cannot blame
[them], nor cannot see [how] any man [can], that walks by that rule of
doing to another as he would be done to, which is the only rule of
justice. I do not understand how we can think that of necessity they
must satisfy us in all these things we desire, and those [things] tending
still to put power into our hands, and to put all power too out of
any other hands; I cannot expect it reasonably from men. For what
reason have I to expect that other men should trust [to] me more than
I should trust to them?' As to the five points, they should be delivered
directly to the Parliament (not to the Commissioners) as a paper agreed
upon by the General, the Council of War, and all the Agitators; it

cannot but be more effectual thus. As to the treaty, if there has been undue delay the fault cannot be fairly ascribed to the Parliamentary Commissioners (or perhaps to any person), but to the Army's reluctance to proceed in it 'till some other things for present security were satisfied,' and to a mistaken effort 'to present all things for the settlement of the kingdom together.' 'For my own part I expect no great matter [from], nor [do I desire] to put much upon the way of, the treaty. I should rather desire to shorten the work . . . [and] think of another way to draw out all things [for the settlement of the kingdom] out of our own proposals.' 'We do think that the [only effective] settlement of peace is by having a settlement of it in our own hands. If ever it do come to settle[ment] it must be by setting down something that may be a rule to lay a foundation for common rights and liberties of the people and for an established peace in the nation.' The 'preparation of an entire proposal of particulars' has been undertaken, and it has been urged that 'any man that had leisure and freedom and a mind to further the work would think of any particulars to give in to myself and another [1] that was . . . set apart for that work.' The Agitators, and others so sensible of delay, have handed in nothing. As to the proposed march towards London, in any case 'I should be against it altogether unless we had [already] proposed those things for settling the peace of the kingdom and did [a] find a professed preparation against us.' [b] The particular demand regarding the militia is certainly no fit occasion for marching. While 'I am concluded by the Council so far as not to speak anything against it . . . , I wish, when we do it, we should have a more reasonable thing [to do it for] than for that.' One should weigh seriously 'the consequence of seeking to gain such things as these are by force.' The only example of a threat of force so far in the papers of the Army was on the occasion of the march towards London (in June). 'And I say yet, my ground then was that this Army stood, as it were, proscribed. You stood but as outlaws. All that were amongst you were invited to come away from you. And you were put out of protection,[c] nobody owning of you as their Army. That was one reason. Another reason [was that those] who were the professed, open, known enemies of the Army, who had, according to those things we have impeached them for, endeavoured to engage in a war, they had place in Parliament and . . . in all committees of Parliament. . . . Truly from that time [we have] seen an alteration; . . . they are withdrawn from the House and . . . are not suffered to appear, that I can hear of, upon action as members of the House. There is nothing wanting but a positive order for the sequestering of them the House, and that I think there is a great deal of justice to demand, and to demand with a further enforcement.' But the good grounds for marching, then present, are now absent.

Allen observes: 'The Commissary-General's discourse hath been

---

[1] Colonel Lambert.

large, and truly my memory (and the time) is something short. I shall
not speak but only to one particular. * * *   I do confess we are owned
in name, but I doubt not in nature, to be the Parliament's Army. * * *
Merely the reason is, if we were they would never suffer us to be
traduced, reviled, and railed upon both in pulpits and presses continually as we are, but it would be a little laid to heart by a Parliament
owning us as their Army, and it would reflect upon their honour as
well as ours.'   As to the impeached Members, 'I fear yet they are in a
capacity of doing too much [harm].'   If we are to wait to present a
full scheme of settlement in order to have sufficient ground 'to get
swords out of men's hands that will cut our throats with them,' what if
someone interposes before that for our destruction?   What, again, if
the kingdom, that we would satisfy, is not satisfied by our proposals
and rather says, '"This is not that which we expected; and [now] we
know what they do intend, we'll seek to help ourselves in another
[way]"?   And so the other and the other way; and truly if you have no
power in your hands [then] . . . , of what a consequence such a thing
may be, I leave it to you to judge.'

Cromwell intervenes to rebuke self-assertiveness, and urges union
in the Army at all costs, with the prudence of making the most of the
fact that Parliament *has* owned the Army, and the necessity of gaining
the five points without the use of force if possible: 'This I wish in ᵃ
general that we may all of us so demean ourselves in this business that
we speak those things that tend to the uniting of us, and that we do
none of us exercise our parts to strain things, and to let in things to a
long dispute, or to unnecessary contradictions, or to the stirring up of
any such seed of dissatisfaction in one another's minds as may in the
least render us unsatisfied one in another.   I do not speak this [to
assert] that anybody does do it.   But I say, this ought to become both
you and me, that we so speak and act as that the end may be union and
a right understanding one with another. * * *   To say or to think [of
the Parliament's owning of the Army], "It is but a titular thing that,
and but in name only that they do own [us]," I think is a very great
mistake.   For really it did at that time lay the best foundation [that]
could be expected for the preventing an absolute confusion in this kingdom; and I think if we had not been satisfied in that, we should not
have been satisfied in anything.   And [it is a very great mistake] to
think that this is any weighty argument, "It is but titular, because they
suffer scandalous books [against us to] flock up and down."   I would
not look [that] they should love us better than they love themselves,
and how many scandalous books go out, of them!   We have given . . .
the Parliament more to do than attend [to] scandalous books.   I hope
that will not weigh with any man. . . . They have given us so ᵇ real
a testimony that they cannot give more.   They cannot disown us without the losing of all rational and honest people in the kingdom; and
therefore let us take it as a very great and high owning of us; let not

us disown that owning. * * * Really, really, have what you will have, that you have by force I look upon it as nothing. I do not know that force is to be used, except we cannot get what is for the good of the kingdom without force. All the arguments [that are of any weight] must tend to this, that it is necessary to use force, to march up with the Army, and not to tarry four days. * * * [I counsel, to] expect a speedy answer [to that] which hath been offered, and to make that critical to us whether they own us or intend to perfect the settlement as we expect. The kingdom would be saved [even] if we do not march within four days, if we had these things granted to us. If these things be granted to us we may march to York.'

Tulidah answers: 'The Lieutenant-General hath put it to a good issue, for the weight of the business lies here.' But settlement of differences is no further advanced than when the Army marched to Uxbridge—'nay not so far, and the same things press ᵃ upon us [still].' It has been said, that we should not expect from them more than they are able to accomplish. We did not then force the Parliament; rather 'our advancing to Uxbridge put them into such a way that they had liberty to speak . . . [and] nothing will [so] expedite them and ᵇ put them into the same [way] of speaking boldly for the kingdom's interest [as our advancing] towards the City.' 'We seem to be startled at the expression of forcing things.' Suppose it be granted that we do use force, why is it 'but that with [once] forcing there should be no more forcing, [but] that by the sword we may take the sword out of those hands that are enemies to justice, to equity'? The matter of the City militia alone would justify the march. 'We cannot have anything unless by the way of advancing to London.'

Cromwell replies: 'Truly the words spoken by Major Tulidah were [spoken] with affection. But we are rational [men]. I would fain know with what reason or colour of reason he did urge any reason, but only with affirmation of earnest words. For that declaration of the Parliament, the Parliament hath owned us, and taken off that that any man can loyally or rationally charge us with. [Is it rational] if upon his apprehensions, or any man's else, we shall quarrel with every dog in the street that barks at us, and suffer the kingdom to be lost with such a fantastical thing? I desire that nothing of heat or earnestness may carry us here, nor nothing of affirmation . . . may lead us, but [only] that which is truly reason, and that which hath life and argument in it.' For the effect of our marching to Uxbridge, 'this is not to be answered with reason, but this is matter of fact. . . . 'Tis true there was fear . . . upon the Parliament . . .; for those eleven Members were afraid to be in the House. [But] if you will believe that which is not a fancy, they have [since our withdrawal] voted very essential things to their own purging.¹ * * * I believe there will go

---

¹ Cromwell refers to ordinances of 5th and 9th July against those who had been active Royalists, and had yet presumed to sit in Parliament.

twenty or thirty men out of the House of Commons. And if this be [not] an effect and demonstration of the happy progress [they have made], and that by use of that liberty that they have had by our [not] drawing near, I appeal to any man.[a] If they shall . . . disown us, and we give them no [other] cause to do it but [by] pressing only [for] just and honourable and honest things from them, judge what can the world think of them and of us.' But what, on the other hand, can it think if the Army, to secure a little gain for itself, wantonly resorts to force, and that through mere impatience when the honest party, and through them the Army, 'are upon the gaining hand' in the House? If the Army so acts, that party 'will not have wherewithal to answer that middle party in the House' on whose good opinion and support so much depends. And finally 'if we should move until we have[b] made these proposals to them and see[n] what answer they will give them, we shall not only disable them, but [probably] divide among ourselves; and I as much fear that as anything.[a] If we should [endeavour to] speak to your satisfactions, [so] you must [to] speak to our satisfactions, [and all of us to avoid disunion]. Though there be great fear of other[c] [things], I shall very much question the integrity of any man [who does not fear that. For my part, I fear the very word]; I would not have it spoken.'

The suspicions of the Parliament entertained by the Agitators and their friends have not been allayed. *Joyce* is not satisfied that the Parliament's owning of the Army extends to an owning of all its acts of war against the King; and *Sexby* voices his suspicion of the whole spirit of the declaration: 'To me this seems very clear, and I cannot see yet any satisfaction to it. I conceive that what the Parliament has done in reference to their declaring us their Army was . . . rather out of fear than love. My reasons are these: first, because to this day those that deserted us are [better] looked upon, [more] countenanced, and abundantly better paid, than we; secondly, because as yet they look upon us as enemies: . . . they send to treat with us; for truly parliaments or armies never treat with friends but enemies, and truly we cannot but look upon ourselves so.' Lieutenant *Scotton* and others who are convinced by Cromwell (and Desborough) and agree to await the Parliament's answer, are earnest that emphasis should be laid on the release of the prisoners: 'It does lie upon our spirits that there may be a real and effectual course taken that [the unjustly imprisoned] is [to be] freed.' Cornet *Spencer*, just returned from London, reports that the militia officers are listing the apprentices and preparing them 'to be ready at an hour's warning' to resist the Army, while the friends of the Army in London are eager for the Army's immediate march hither.

Cromwell is sceptical: 'Truly, sir, I think neither of these two things that gentleman spoke last are any great news. For the one of them, the listing of apprentices, I doubt they have listed them twice over; I am sure we have heard [it] more than twice over. For the other, [that our friends in London] would rejoice to see us come up, what if we [be] better able to consult what is for their good than themselves? It is the general good of them and all the people in the kingdom [we ought to aim at]. That 's the question, what 's for their good, not what pleases them. * * * [Even] if you be in the right, and I in the wrong, [still if you will force the issue we shall be divided, and] if we be divided I doubt we shall all be in the wrong. * * * The question is singly this: whether or no we shall not in a positive way desire the answer to these things before we march towards London, when perhaps we may have the same things in the time that we can march. Here is the strictness of the question.'

At this point Major *Tulidah* (Cromwell's rebuke still rankling) is heard to complain: 'If anything be spoken [against them], to say that it is out of zeal, and that we should abound [only] in their ᵃ sense! I humbly desire there may be liberty to speak, and that a providence may carry things, and [they will] not [go] that way.' But Colonel *Rich* calls for the question, declaring that there are but two things to decide: first, whether the paper and the five points should be forwarded to the Parliament, and, if so, how; secondly, the matter of the march to London, whether now or after an interval of four days. Lieutenant *Chillenden* professes 'great satisfaction in his spirit' with Cromwell's proposal of four days' delay, and asks only that special emphasis may be given to the matter of the release of Lilburne and the other prisoners, for 'it lies so weighty upon his spirit.' He then moves 'that that paper may go, concluding all things in it.' *Ireton* amends the motion so as to send the five points, but omit the 'Additional Reasons,' in which the proposal of the Army's march on London is contained. And the meeting concludes.

10. ACCOUNT OF THE DEBATE, IN A NEWSLETTER FROM READING,ᵇ 17TH JULY.

Yesterday there was a great council of war called; it held till twelve o'clock at night, consisting ᶜ of above one hundred officers, besides Agitators, who now in prudence we admit to debate. And it is not less ᵈ than necessary they should be [admitted], considering the influence they have upon the soldiers. . . . And I assure you, it is the singularest part of wisdom in the General and the officers so to carry themselves, considering the present temper of the Army, so as to be unanimous in councils, including the new persons into their number. It keeps a good accord, and obtains ready obedience, for to this hour never any troop or company yet mutinied. . . . It is the hand of God that doth it, I hope, for a good end. It is not proper to relate particular debates yesterday; yet accept of a word in general, and think it not strange, if it should be advised to march nearer to London, as an expedient to obtain satisfaction in those particulars which have been long desired by the Army of the Parliament, as in particular declaring against foreign forces' coming in, the putting Reformadoes out of the line, and suspending the eleven Members, but more especially to desire the Parliament to put the militia of the City of London into the same hands it was before, without which we cannot hold ourselves secure in proceeding to treat. . . . Though this was much pressed with reasons and earnestness by the Agitators, yet the General and the officers after many hours' debate so satisfied them with arguments and reasons to the contrary, that they submitted it to the General and officers, no man gainsaying it; and so it is resolved to send to the Parliament to desire these particulars, especially the militia, and receive a positive answer within four days.

11. Of the Debate of 17th July, on the not-yet-completed Heads of the Proposals, the account, in Clarke MSS., vol. 67, is fragmentary, breaking off suddenly. Two speeches on the value of General Discussion, and of Reference to a Committee, alone are significant:

Ireton: For . . . the passing those particulars here read without a further weighing or consideration, it might be inconvenient; and therefore I shall desire that, though there be no man that finds anything of exception against any part of the thing that is read,[a] yet that it may be referred to a less number that may weigh or consider all things.[b] [These particulars are offered] not for a present conclusion, but consideration; for I cannot say the things have been so considered as to satisfy myself in them.

Allen: I shall only offer one word. I think that the things in hand he names are things of great weight, having relation to the settling of a kingdom, which is a great work; truly, the work we all expect to have a share in, and desire that others may also. I suppose it is not unknown to you that we are most of us but young statesmen, and not well able to judge how strong [c] such things which we hear now read to us may be to the ends for which they are presented; and for us out of judgment to give our assents to it must take up some time that we may deliberate upon it. And therefore I shall desire that we may not only name them [i.e. a committee] now, but spend some time [in debate], when we hear things unsatisfactory to the ends for which they are proposed.

12. This is followed in Clarke MSS. by an order of Fairfax, dated 18th July, naming twelve officers, including Ireton, Lambert, Harrison, Rainborough, Rich, Sir Hardress Waller, a committee 'to meet, consult and proceed with the twelve Agitators, according to the appointment

made at the General Council of War yesterday, for the perfecting of
the Proposals then read, in order to the settling of the liberties and
peace of the kingdom . . . ; and Lieutenant-General Cromwell to be
present with the said council when he can.'

D. DOCUMENTS RELATING TO THE PUTNEY DEBATES

13. FROM THE HEADS OF THE PROPOSALS [a]

I. That, the things, hereafter proposed, being provided for by this
Parliament, a certain period may by Act of Parliament be set for the
ending of this Parliament; such period to be put within a year at most.
And in the same Act provision to be made for the succession and
constitution of Parliaments in future, as followeth:

1. That Parliaments may biennially be called and meet at a certain
day, with such provision for the certainty thereof, as in the late Act
was made for triennial Parliaments, and what further or other provision
shall be found needful by the Parliament to reduce it to more certainty;
and upon the passing of this, the said Act for triennial Parliaments to
be repealed.

2. Each biennial Parliament to sit 120 days certain (unless adjourned
or dissolved sooner by their own consent); afterwards to be adjournable
or dissolvable by the King, and no Parliament to sit past 240 days from
their first meeting, or some other limited number of days now to be
agreed on; upon the expiration whereof each Parliament to dissolve
of course, if not otherwise dissolved sooner.

3. The King, upon advice of the Council of State, in the intervals
betwixt biennial Parliaments, to call a Parliament extraordinary, provided to meet above 70 days before the next biennial day, and be dissolved at least 60 days before the same; so as the course of biennial
elections may never be interrupted.

4. That this Parliament and each succeeding biennial Parliament,
at or before adjournment or dissolution thereof, may appoint committees to continue during the interval for such purposes as are in any
of these Proposals referred to such committees.

5. That the elections of the Commons for succeeding Parliaments
may be distributed to all counties, or other parts or divisions of the
kingdom, according to some rule of equality or proportion, so as all
counties may have a number of Parliament-members allowed to their
choice, proportionable to the respective rates they bear in the common
charges and burdens of the kingdom, [or] according to some other
rule of equality or proportion, to render the House of Commons (as
near as may be) an equal representative of the whole; and in order
thereunto, that a present consideration be had to take off the elections
of burgesses for poor, decayed, or inconsiderable towns, and to give

some present addition to the number of Parliament-members for great counties that have now less than their due proportion, to bring all (at present) as near as may be to such a rule of proportion as aforesaid.

6. That effectual provision be made for future freedom of elections, and certainty of due returns.

7. That the House of Commons alone have the power from time to time to set down further orders and rules for the ends expressed in the two last preceding articles, so as to reduce the elections of members for that House to more and more perfection of equality in the distribution, freedom in the election, order in the proceeding thereto, and certainty in the returns, which orders and rules (in that case) to be as laws.

8. That there be a liberty for entering dissents in the House of Commons, with provision that no member be censurable for aught said or voted in the House further than to exclusion from that trust; and that only by the judgment of the House itself.

9. That the judicial power, or power of final judgment in the Lords and Commons, and their power of exposition and application of law, without further appeal, may be cleared; and that no officer of justice, minister of state, or other person adjudged by them, may be capable of protection or pardon from the King without their advice and consent.

10. That the right and liberty of the Commons of England may be cleared and vindicated as to a due exemption from any judgment, trial, or other proceeding against them by the House of Peers, without the concurring judgment of the House of Commons; as also from any other judgment, sentence or proceeding against them, other than by their equals, or according to the law of the land.

11. The same Act to provide that grand jurymen may be chosen by and for several parts or divisions of each county respectively, in some equal way (and not remain, as now, at the discretion of an under-sheriff to be put on or off); and that such grand jurymen for their respective counties may at each assize present the names of persons to be made justices of the peace from time to time as the country hath need for any to be added to the Commission, and at the summer assize to present the names of three persons, out of whom the King may prick one to be sheriff for the next year.

[II vests the power of the militia in the Lords and Commons in Parliament for ten years (to be administered in the intervals of Parliaments by a committee or council of their appointment); and thereafter in the King, only as he acts with their advice and consent.

III provides for a Council of State and defines its powers.

IV—X provide for a series of necessary Acts of Parliament: for appointment to the great offices of state by the Lords and Commons for ten years, and thereafter by the King from their nominees; for restraining all peers created since 21st May 1642 from parliamentary functions, unless with the consent of both Houses; for recalling all declarations against the Parliament, &c. &c.]

XI. An Act to be passed to take away all coercive power, authority, and jurisdiction of bishops and all other ecclesiastical officers whatsoever, extending to any civil penalties upon any; and to repeal all laws whereby the civil magistracy hath been or is bound, upon any ecclesiastical censure to proceed (*ex officio*) unto any civil penalties against any persons so censured.

XII. That there be a repeal of all Acts, or clauses in any Act, enjoining the use of the Book of Common Prayer and imposing any penalties for neglect thereof; as also of all Acts, or clauses in any Act, imposing any penalty for not coming to church, or for meetings elsewhere for prayer or other religious duties, exercises, or ordinances; and some other provision to be made for discovering of Papists and Popish recusants, and for disabling of them, and of all Jesuits or priests, from disturbing the state.

XIII. That the taking of the Covenant be not enforced upon any, nor any penalties imposed on the refusers, whereby men might be constrained to take it against their judgments or consciences; but all orders or ordinances tending to that purpose to be repealed.

XIV. That, the things here before proposed being provided, for settling and securing the rights, liberties, peace, and safety of the kingdom, His Majesty's person, his Queen, and royal issue, may be restored to a condition of safety, honour and freedom in this nation, without diminution to their personal rights, or further limitation to the exercise of the regal power than according to the particulars aforegoing.

[XV provides for exclusions from the Act of Oblivion, and for composition on terms not to exceed a fixed rate set forth.]

XVI. That there may be a general Act of Oblivion to extend unto all (except the persons to be continued in exception as before), to absolve from all trespasses, misdemeanours, &c., done in prosecution of the war; and from all trouble or prejudice for or concerning the same (after their compositions passed), and to restore them to all privileges, &c., belonging to other subjects, provided as in the fourth particular under the second general head aforegoing concerning security. * * *

Next to the Proposals aforesaid for the present settling of a peace, we shall desire that no time may be lost by the Parliament for dispatch of other things tending to the welfare, ease, and just satisfaction of the kingdom, and in special manner:

I. That the just and necessary liberty of the people to represent their grievances and desires by way of petition, may be cleared and vindicated, according to the fifth head in the late Representation or Declaration of the Army sent from St. Albans.

II. That (in pursuance of the same head in the said Declaration) the common grievances of the people may be speedily considered of, and effectually redressed, and in particular:

1. That the excise may be taken off from such commodities whereon the poor people of the land do ordinarily live, and a certain time to be limited for taking off the whole;

2. That the oppressions and encroachments of forest laws may be prevented for the future;

3. All monopolies, old or new, and restraints to the freedom of trade to be taken off;

4. That a course may be taken, and commissioners appointed, to remedy and rectify the inequality of rates lying upon several counties, and several parts of each county in respect of others, and to settle the proportions for land-rates to more equality throughout the kingdoms; in order to which we shall offer some further particulars, which we hope may be useful;

5. The present unequal troublesome and contentious way of ministers' maintenance by tithes to be considered of, and some remedy applied;

6. That the rules and course of law, and the officers of it, may be so reduced and reformed as that all suits and questions of right may be more clear and certain in the issues, and not so tedious nor chargeable in the proceedings as now; in order to which we shall offer some further particulars hereafter;

7. That prisoners for debt or other creditors (who have estates to discharge them) may not by embracing imprisonment, or any other ways, have advantage to defraud their creditors, but that the estates of all men may be some way made liable to their debts (as well as tradesmen are by commissions of bankrupt), whether they be imprisoned for it or not; and that such prisoners for debt who have not wherewith to pay, or at least do yield up what they have to their creditors, may be freed from imprisonment, or some way provided for, so as neither they nor their families may perish by their imprisonments.

8. Some provision to be made, that none may be compelled by penalties, or otherwise, to answer unto questions tending to the accusing of themselves or their nearest relations in criminal causes; and no man's life to be taken away under two witnesses.

9. That consideration may be had of all statutes, and the laws or customs of corporations, imposing any oaths either to repeal or else to qualify and provide against the same, so far as they may extend or be construed to the molestation or ensnaring of religious and peaceable people, merely for nonconformity in religion.

III. That, according to the sixth head in the Declaration of the Army, the large powers given to committees or deputy-lieutenants during the late times of war and distraction, may be speedily taken into consideration, to be recalled and made void, and that such powers of that nature as shall appear necessary to be continued may be put into a regulated way, and left to as little arbitrariness as the nature and necessity of the things wherein they are conversant, will bear.

IV. That, according to the seventh head in the said Declaration, an effectual course may be taken that the kingdom may be righted, and satisfied in point of accounts for the vast sums that have been levied.

V. That provision may be made for payment of arrears to the Army, and the rest of the soldiers of the kingdom who have concurred with the Army in the late desires and proceedings thereof; and in the next place for payment of the public debts and damages of the kingdom; and that to be performed first to such persons whose debts or damages (upon the public account) are great, and their estates small, so as they are thereby reduced to a difficulty of subsistence. In order to all which, and to the fourth particular last preceding, we shall speedily offer some further particulars (in the nature of rules), which we hope will be of good use towards public satisfaction.[1] * * *

14. The Levellers' Discontent with the Heads of the Proposals
From [John Wildman], *Putney Projects* [a]

But . . . I must not . . . beguile you . . . by styling them *The Army's Proposals.* * * * I scarce believe they passed a General Council before they were published. But that's not all; for they last of all passed the King's eye, and therefore it is no wonder that he moved for a personal treaty upon those Proposals. * * *

When the Proposals were first composed there was a small restriction of the King's negative voice: it was agreed to be proposed that whatsoever bill should be propounded by two immediate succeeding Parliaments should stand in full force and effect as any other law, though the King should refuse to consent. By this the people should not have been absolutely vassals to the King's will: they should have been under some possibility of relief under any growing oppressions. But this entrenched too much upon the King's interest to be insisted upon. * * *

In that rough draft it was proposed that all who have been in hostility against the Parliament be incapable of bearing office of power or public trust for ten years, without consent of Parliament. But in further favour of the King's interest, these ten years of excluding delinquents from power or trust, were changed to five years.

It was further added, after this intercourse with the King, that the Council of State should have power to admit such delinquents to any office of power or trust before those five years were expired; and thus by the King's insinuations to that council (if any such should be constituted), and their own relations', the greatest delinquents in England would be in the greatest trust before twelve months' end.

In the composure of the Proposals it was desired that an act for the extirpation of bishops might be passed by the King. But if there should be none to preach up the King's interest, and by flattering, seducing

[1] Dated 1st August 1647.

words to beguile the people, and foster high imaginations and superstitious conceits of the King in their hearts under the rude and general
notion of authority, his lordliness and tyranny would be soon distasted.
And therefore this proposal was so moderated that the office and
function of the bishops might be continued; and it is now only proposed
that the coercive power and jurisdiction of bishops, extending to any
civil penalties upon any, be abolished.

After this treaty with the King, the proposal for passing an Act to
confirm the sale of bishops' lands was wholly obliterated; and though
the Army afterwards desired the Parliament to proceed in the sale and
alienation of those lands, yet that was none of their proposals in order
to a peace with the King. But according to their proposals for a settled
peace, the King was first to be established on his throne with his usurped
power of a negative voice to all laws or determinations of Parliament,
and then they knew that the King might be at his choice whether he
would permit an alienation of these lands. * * *

You have seen the stream of power declared to proceed from a false
fountain, the King's will; the right to command your persons in the
exercise of the militia, given away to the capital enemy; and a respect
of persons allowed in the execution of the laws. Yet . . . I have not
searched all your wounds received from your pretended friends. Let
me search two or three more.

First, by the Proposals the people are made to depend upon the King's
absolute will for the redress of all the grievances and oppressions under
which they have groaned so many years. It is proposed, that the King
be restored to the exercise of the regal power, part whereof, in the
King['s] and their interpretation, is his negative voice, before the least
common grievance be redressed, a burden removed. Compare the
fourteenth proposal with the thirteen preceding. By this whenever
the Parliament shall remember their duty to study redress for the
people's grievances, they shall but sow the wind and reap the whirlwind, unless they gain the concurrence of the King's will. Then in
case the brutish vassalage under unknown laws, and worse than Turkish
manner of their execution, should be laid to heart, and redress prepared;
if it should be endeavoured to cut off those excretions of nature, the
great lawyers, which grow up out of the ruins and decays of the natural
members of the body politic; if the oppressions by unjust judges,
justices and other officers, by illegal imprisonments during pleasure,
by examining upon interrogatories, and those other oppressions by
forced oaths, tithes, monopolies, forest laws, &c., should have suitable
remedy contrived: yet the people's good of all such labours shall
depend solely upon the King's will. Though the degrees of oppression,
injustice, and cruelty are the turning stairs by which he ascends to his
absolute stately majesty and greatness; yet he must be depended upon
to remove oppressions. * * * Cleanliness must come forth out of
uncleanness in the abstract. And seeing this is the order wherein
the Army proposed the people's grievances to be redressed, I know no

other use of those Proposals than to support the tottering reputation of the grand officers in the minds of such as shall not discern their vanity.

Secondly, by the Proposals all the Commons of England are made to depend upon the King's absolute creatures for freedom. Although the Lords are the very offspring of the King's corrupt will, and were never so honoured by the people as to have a trust committed to them to represent any county, yet those Proposals invest them with the highest authority, only because of the King's patent:

1. The Proposals allow them a power over the militia, co-ordinate and co-equal to the Representative of all the nation, the Commons in Parliament. * * *

2. A judicial power in exposition and application of law (in no degree subordinate to the Commons) is estated in the Lords, by the ninth particular of the first proposal; so that any sentence of the Commons, representing all England, may be contradicted by five or six Lords, by virtue of the King's patent. And likewise they are invested by the fourth proposal with a power equal to the Commons in the disposing all the offices of power and trust in the nation; and the third particular of the second proposal allows them the same power in raising of money for the public service. And a restriction to their usurpation of a negative voice to all the resolutions of the Commons, is not once named or intimated, although Ireton himself hath confessed in their councils that the King by his oath is obliged to confirm such laws as the Commons should choose—the word *vulgus* in the King's oath, signifying people or folk, excludes the Lords totally from any right to intermeddle in making laws. And further the Proposals connive at least (in the tenth particular of the first proposal) at the Lords' constant treasonable subversion of the fundamental laws of England, by molesting, summoning, attaching, and imprisoning the Commons, over whom by the known laws they have no original jurisdiction.

Indeed it is offered that the Commons' liberty may be cleared as to an exemption from any judgment of the Peers, without the concurring judgment of the House of Commons. But the Lords' barbarous cruelty in vexing and imprisoning the Commons at their pleasure, and during their pleasure, is not motioned to be restrained: but it is rather insinuated that the Lords may pass upon the Commons and then desire the Commons' concurrence. Thus they indulge the Lords in their most palpable injustice and open violation of the ancient English liberties contained in Magna Charta, and lately confirmed in the Petition of Right.

And does not this practice run parallel with this proposal? Has not Cromwell suffered that gallant champion for English freedom, Lieutenant-Colonel John Lilburne, to consume in prison by that usurped lordly power? Yea, though Cromwell first engaged him against the lordly usurpation and tyranny, by impeaching the Earl of Manchester for his treachery; yet hath he not unworthily deserted both the prosecution of justice against him, and left his implored assistant alone to maintain the hazardous contest or to be crushed to pieces by their potency? * * *

15. From [John Wildman], THE CASE OF THE ARMY TRULY STATED [a]
15TH OCT.

Whereas the grievances, dissatisfactions and desires of the Army, both as Commoners and soldiers, hath been many months since represented to the Parliament, and the Army hath waited with much patience to see their common grievances redressed and the rights and freedoms of the nation cleared and secured; yet upon a most serious and conscientious view of our Narratives, Representations, Engagement, Declarations, Remonstrances, and comparing with those the present state of the Army and kingdom, and the present manner of actings of many at the Headquarters, we not only apprehend nothing to have been done effectually, either for the Army or the poor oppressed people of the nation, but we also conceive that there is little probability of any good without some more speedy and vigorous actings.

In respect of the Army, there hath been hitherto no public vindication thereof about their first Petition, answerable to the ignominy of [b] declaring them enemies to the state and disturbers of the peace; no public clearing nor repairing of the credit of the officers, sent for about that petition as delinquents; no provision for apprentices, widows, orphans, or maimed soldiers, answerable to our reasonable addresses propounded in their behalf; no such indemnity as provideth security for the quiet, ease or safety of the soldiers disbanded or to be disbanded; no security for our arrears, or provision for present pay to enable the Army to subsist without burdening the distressed country.

And in respect to the rights and freedoms of ourselves and the people, that we declared we would insist upon, we conceive there is no kind or degree of satisfaction given. There is no determinate period of time set when the Parliament shall certainly end. The House is in no measure purged, either from persons unduly elected or from delinquents that appeared to be such at the Army's last insisting upon their rights, or since; the honour of the Parliamentary authority not cleared and vindicated from the most horrid injustice of that declaration against the Army for petitioning, nor of suppressing and burning petitions, abusing and imprisoning petitioners. But those strange precedents remain upon record to the infamy of Parliamentary authority and the danger of our own and the people's freedoms. The people are not righted nor satisfied in point of accounts, for the vast sums of money disbursed by them. None of the public burdens or oppressions by arbitrary committees, injustice in the law, tithes, monopolies and restraint of free trade, burdensome oaths, inequality of assessments, excise (and otherwise), are removed or lightened. The rights of the people in their Parliaments, concerning the nature and extent of that power, are not cleared and declared. So that we apprehend our own and the people's case, little (if in any measure) better since the Army last hazarded themselves for their own and the people's rights and freedoms. Nay, to the grief of our hearts we must declare that we conceive the people and the Army's case much impaired since the first rendezvous at Newmarket when that *Solemn Engagement* [1] was entered into. * * *

In the Engagement, . . . the Army promised, every member thereof, each to other and to the Parliament and kingdom, that they would neither disband nor divide, nor suffer themselves to be disbanded or divided, until satisfaction should be given to the Army in relation to their grievances and desires, and security that neither the Army nor the free-born people of England should remain subject to such injuries, oppression and abuse, as the corrupt party in the Parliament then had attempted against them.

Secondly, the train of artillery is now to be disbanded before satisfaction or security is given to the whole Army in relation to themselves or other the free-born people, either in respect to their grievances or desires. And when the strength or sinews of the Army be broken, what effectual good can be secured for themselves or the people in case of opposition?

Thirdly, the Army is divided into quarters so far distant that one part is in no capability to give timely assistance to another if any design should be to disband any part by violence suddenly. . . . And as we conceive this dividing of the Army before satisfaction or security (as aforesaid) to be contrary to the Army's intention in their engagement at the said rendezvous, so we conceive it hath from that time given all the advantage to the enemies to band and design against the Army, whereby not only pay hath been kept from the soldiers, and security for arrears prevented, but the kingdom was endangered to have been embroiled in blood, and the settlement of the peace and freedom of the nation hath been thus long delayed.

The whole intent of the Engagement, and the equitable sense of it, hath been perverted openly by affirming, and by sinister means making seeming determinations in the Council, that the Army was not to insist upon, or demand any security for, any of their own or other the free-born people's freedoms or rights, though they might propound anything to the Parliament's consideration. And according to that high breach of their engagement their actions have been regulated, and nothing that was declared formerly to be insisted upon hath been resolvedly adhered to, or claimed as the Army's or the people's due. And we conceive it hath been by this means that the soldier hath had no pay constantly provided, nor any security for arrears given them, and that hitherto they could not obtain so much as to be paid up equally with those that did desert the Army. . . .

Fourthly, in the prosecution of this breach there hath been many discouragements of the Agitators of the regiments in consulting about the most effectual means for procuring the speedy redress of the

[1] Above, pp. 401–3.

people's grievances, and clearing and securing the native rights of the Army and all others the free Commons.

It hath been instilled into them that they ought not to intermeddle with those matters, thereby to induce them to betray the trust the regiments reposed in them. And for that purpose the endeavours of some hath been to persuade the soldier that their Agitators have meddled with more than concerned them. In the Declaration of June 14,[1] . . . it was declared that the Army would adhere to their desires of full and equal satisfaction to the whole soldiery of the kingdom (in arrears, indemnity, and all other things mentioned in the papers that contained the grievances, dissatisfactions and desires), who did then, or should afterward, concur with this Army in these desires. * * *

Sixthly, in the same declaration . . . it is declared that the Army took up arms in judgment and conscience for the people's just rights and liberties, and not as mercenary soldiers, hired to serve an arbitrary power of the state, and that in the same manner it continued in arms at that time. And . . . it was declared that they proceeded upon the principles of right and freedom, and upon the law of nature and nations. But the strength of the endeavours of many hath been and are now spent to persuade the soldiers and Agitators that they stand as soldiers only to serve the state, and may not as free Commons claim their right and freedom as due to them, as those ends for which they have hazarded their lives, and that the ground of their refusing to disband was only the want of arrears and indemnity. * * *

Eighthly, in the Declaration of June 14 . . . (as in all other remonstrances and declarations) it was desired that the rights and liberties of the people might be secured before the King's business should be considered. But now the grievances of the people are propounded to be considered after the restoring him to the regal power, and that in such a way according to the *Proposals*,[2] *viz.*, with a negative voice, that the people that have purchased by blood what was their right, of which the King endeavoured to deprive them, should yet solely depend on his will for their relief in their grievances and oppressions; and in like manner the security for the Army's arrears is proposed to be considered after the business of the King be determined, so that there is a total declension since the method formerly desired in the settling the peace of the nation. * * *

Tenthly, when imminent ruin to the whole nation was apprehended by means of the multitudes of corrupted members of Parliament, diverting and obstructing all good proceedings, then the purging of the House in part, from one kind of delinquents, was again insisted upon, and a solemn protestation was passed in the Remonstrance from Kingston . . .,[3] that the Army would not permit those to sit in the House, that usurped the name and power of Parliamentary authority

---

[1] Above, pp. 403-9.
[2] The *Heads of the Proposals* (above, pp. 422-6).
[3] *A Remonstrance of the Army*, 18th August 1647.

when the Parliament was by violence suspended, and endeavoured to raise a war to destroy the Parliament and Army, but that they would take some effectual course to restrain them from sitting there, that the people might be concluded only by those members that are free from such apparent treacherous breaches of their trust.

But hitherto this engagement for purging the House from those delinquents, whose interest engages them to be designing mischief against the people and Army, is declined and broken, to the black reproach and foulest infamy of the Army; and now these strong cords are cut in sunder and so forgotten that there are no visible endeavours or intentions to preserve the honour of the Army in its faithfulness to its engagement and protestation.

Thus all promises of the Army to the people that petitioned his Excellency and the Army to stand for the national interest, freedoms, and rights, are hitherto wholly declined, and the law of nature and nations now refused by many to be the rule by which their proceedings should be regulated. They now strip themselves of the interest of Englishmen, which was so ill resented when it was attempted by the malice of the enemies. And thus the people's expectations that were much greatened, and their hopes of relief in their miseries and oppressions, which were so much heightened, are like to be frustrate, and while you look for peace and freedom the flood-gates of slavery, oppression and misery are opened upon the nation. . . .

The mischiefs, evils and dangers which are and will be the necessary consequence of the Army's declining or delaying the effectual fulfilling of its first engagement, promises and declarations, or of its neglect to insist positively upon its first principles of common right and freedom. * * *

Now we cannot but declare that these sad apprehensions of mischiefs, dangers and confusion gaping to devour the Army, hath filled our hearts with troubles, that we never did, nor do regard the worst of evils or mischiefs that can befall ourselves in comparison to the consequence of them to the poor nation, or to the security of common right and freedom. We could not but, in real (not formal, feigned) trouble of heart for the poor nation and oppressed people, break forth and cry, 'O our bowels! our bowels! we are troubled at the very heart to hear the people's doleful groans.' And yet their expected deliverers will not hear or consider. They have run to and fro, and sighed or even wept forth, their sorrows and miseries in petitions, first to the King, then to the Parliament, and then to the Army; yet they have all been like broken reeds, even the Army itself, upon whom they leaned, have pierced their hands. Their eyes even fail with looking for peace and freedom, but behold nothing but distraction, oppression, and trouble; and could we hope that help is intended, yet the people perish by delays. We wish therefore that the bowels of compassion in the

whole Army might yearn towards their distressed brethren, and
that they might with one consent ask each to other: 'Come let us join
together speedily, to demand present redress for the people's grievances
and security for all their and our own rights and freedoms as soldiers
and Commoners. Let us never divide each from other till those just
demands be answered really and effectually, that so for the people's
ease as many forces as are not absolutely necessary may be speedily
disbanded and our honour may be preserved unspotted, when they shall
see that we minded not our own interest, but the good, freedom, and
welfare of the whole nation.' Now to all that shall thus appear we
propound:

[1] a That whatsoever was proposed to be insisted on either in the
Declaration of June the fourteenth, or the Remonstrance [of] June 23,
and in the Remon[strance] from Kingston, August 18, be adhered
to resolvedly, so as not to recede from those desires until they be
thoroughly and effectually answered. More particularly, . . . whereas it appears by positive laws and ancient just customs that the people
have right to new successive elections for Parliaments at certain periods
of time, and that it ought not to be denied them, being so essential to
their freedom that without it they are no better than slaves (the nature
of that legislative power being arbitrary), . . . that therefore it be
insisted on so positively and resolvedly, as not to recede from it.

[2] That a determined period of time be forthwith set wherein this
Parliament shall certainly be dissolved, provided also that the said
period be within nine or ten months next ensuing, that so there may be
sufficient time for settling of peace and freedom.[1] * * *

5. Whereas Parliaments rightly constituted are the foundation of
hopes of right and freedom to this people, and whereas the people
have been prevented of Parliaments, though many positive laws have
been made for a constant succession of Parliaments, that therefore it
be positively and resolvedly insisted upon that a law paramount be
made, enacting it to be unalterable by Parliaments, that the people
shall of course meet without any warrants or writs once in every two
years upon an appointed day in their respective countries, for the election of the representers in Parliament, and that all the free-born at the
age of twenty-one years and upwards be the electors, excepting those
that have or shall deprive themselves of that their freedom, either
for some years or wholly, by delinquency, and that the Parliament so
elected and called may have a certain period of time set, wherein
they shall of course determine, and that before the same period they
may not be adjournable and dissolvable by the King, or any other except
themselves.

[6] Whereas all power is originally and essentially in the whole body
of the people of this nation, and whereas their free choice or consent by their representers is the only original or foundation of all just

[1] Third demand is for a purge of the existing Parliament; fourth, for
Parliament's formal approval of the Army's Declarations.

government, and the reason and end of the choice of all just governors whatsoever is their apprehension of safety and good by them, that it be insisted upon positively, that the supreme power of the people's representers, or Commons assembled in Parliament, be forthwith clearly declared: as their power to make laws, or repeal laws (which are not or ought not to be unalterable), as also their power to call to an account all officers in this nation whatsoever, for their neglect or treacheries in their trust for the people's good, and to continue or displace and remove them from their offices, dignities or trust, according to their demerits by their faithfulness or treachery in the business or matters wherewith they are entrusted.   And further that this power to constitute any kind of governors or officers that they shall judge to be for the people's good be declared, and that, upon the aforesaid considerations, it be insisted upon, that all obstructions to the freedom and equality of the people's choice of their representers, either by patents, charters, or usurpations by pretended customs, be removed by these present Commons in Parliament, and that such a freedom of choice be provided for, as the people may be equally represented.   This power of Commons in Parliament is the thing against which the King hath contended, and the people have defended with their lives, and therefore ought now be demanded as the price of their blood.

[7] That all the oppressions of the poor by excise upon beer, cloth stuffs, and all manufactories and English commodities, be forthwith taken off, and that all excise be better regulated, and imposed upon foreign commodities, and a time set wherein it shall certainly end, if there be a necessity of its present continuance on such commodities. * * *

And it is further offered, that because the people are under much oppression and misery it be forthwith the whole work of the Parliament to hear, consider of, and study effectually redress for, all common grievances and oppressions, and for the securing all other the people's rights and freedoms, besides all these aforementioned; and in particular . . . that all the orders, votes, ordinances, or declarations, that have passed either to discountenance petitions, suppress, prevent, or burn petitions, imprison or declare against petitioners, being dangerous precedents against the freedom of the people, may be forthwith expunged out of the Journal-books, and the injustice of them clearly declared to all the people, and that in such a declaration the soldiery be vindicated as to the right and equity of their first petition. * * *

And it is further offered: . . . whereas millions of money have been kept in dead stocks in the City of London, the halls and companies, and the freemen of the City could never obtain any account thereof according to their right, that therefore a just and strict account may be forthwith given to all the freemen of any those dead stocks; and . . . whereas there hath been nothing paid out of those, nor for the lands pertaining to the City, whiles the estates of others have been much wasted by continual payments, that therefore proportionable sums to what other estates have paid may be taken out of those dead stocks and lands, which would amount to such vast sums as would pay much of the soldiers' arrears without burdening the oppressed people.

And it is further offered, that forest lands, and deans' and chapters' lands be immediately set apart for the arrears of the Army, and that the revenue of these, and the residue of bishops' lands unsold, till the time of sale may be forthwith appointed to be paid into our treasury, to be reserved for the soldiers' constant pay. And it is to be wished that only such part of the aforesaid lands be sold as necessity requires to satisfy the soldiery for arrears, and that the residue be reserved and improved for a constant revenue for the state, that the people may not be burdened, and that out of the revenues public debts may be paid. . . .

And it 's further offered for the people's ease, that the arrears of all former assessments be duly collected from those who have sufficient estates, and have not been impoverished by the war.

And whereas it 's conceived that the fees of receivers of customs and excise, if they were justly computed, would amount to near as much as the Army's pay, it is therefore offered that speedy consideration be had of the multitude of those officers and their excessive fees and profits. . . .

And for the ease and satisfaction of the people it 's further to be insisted on, that the charge of all the forces, to be kept up in the kingdom by sea or land, be particularly computed and published, and that all taxes that shall be necessary, may be wholly proportioned according to that charge; and that there be an equal rate propounded throughout the kingdom in all assessments, that so one town may not bear double the proportion of another of the same value.[1] * * *

---

[1] The proposals were also separately issued, in condensed form, as *Propositions from the Agitators of Five Regiments*, 18th Oct. 1647. The rest are similar to those found in the Leveller documents printed above — Overton's *Appeal*, the Petitions of March 1647, and 11th September 1648, Lilburne's *Foundations of Freedom* (pp. 318–67). But their presence adds to the significance of *The Case of the Army*, and demands brief summary: (1) 'That all monopolies be forthwith removed, and no persons whatsoever may be permitted to restrain others from free trade.' (2) The reform of legal procedure, including the abolition of imprisonment for debt, provision for speedy trial in criminal cases, the abolition of oaths and interrogatories of prisoners in criminal cases, the appointment of 'a committee of conscientious persons . . . to consider the intolerable oppressions by unjust proceedings in the law, that withal the laws might be reduced to a smaller number, to be comprised in one volume in the English tongue . . .; that courts might be in the respective counties or hundreds, that proceedings might become short and speedy, and that the numberless grievances in the law and lawyers might be redressed as soon as possible.' (3) The abolition of all statutes enforcing uniformity in religion and attendance at church, 'whereby many religious and conscientious people are daily vexed and oppressed,' and all statutes against conventicles, 'under pretence of which religious people are vexed for private meetings about the worship of God'; the abolition of tithes, and of enforced oaths, such as the oath of supremacy, which are 'burdens and snares to conscientious people.' (4) The abolition of 'all

These things propounded are no more than what we conceived should have been thoroughly done long since, being as to the principle [a] of them but the [b] substance and equitable sense of the former Declarations, Remonstrances, and Representations. And therefore, though our restless desires of the people's good and of the welfare of the Army have constrained us thus publicly to state our case and the remedy, according to the best improvement of the small talent of understanding that God hath given freely to us; yet let not the matter be prejudged because of the unworthy authors, neither let it be thought presumption. It may be remembered that the father's danger made a dumb child to speak, and the Army's, yea all the people's, dangers and miseries have wrested open our mouths, who had otherwise been silent in this kind to the grave.

And let it not be thought that we intend the division of the Army. We profess we are deeply sensible and desire all our fellow soldiers to consider it: in case the union of the Army should be broken (which the enemy wait for) ruin and destruction will break in upon us like a roaring sea. But we are much confident that the adhering to those desires and to that speedy way of attaining our just ends for which we first engaged, cannot be interpreted to be a desire of division, but the strongest vigorous endeavours after union. And though many whom we did betrust have been guilty of most supine [c] negligence, yet we expect that the same instruction of judgment and conscience that (we have all professed) did command us forth at first for the people's freedom, will be again so effectual that all will unanimously concur with us; so that a demand of the people's and Army's rights shall be made by the whole Army as by one man; that then all the enemies to, or obstructors of, the happy settlement of common right, peace and freedom, may hear of our union and resolution, and their hands may be weak, and their hearts may fail them; and so this Army that God hath clothed with honour in subduing the common enemy, may yet be more honourable in the people's eyes when they shall be called the repairers of their breaches, and the restorers of their peace, right, and freedom. [1] * * *

---

privileges and protections above the law.' (5) The restoration to the service of the poor of all enclosed commons, and all ancient rights and donations (almshouses, &c.), 'in whose hands soever they be detained.' The Agents add (in the hope of 'healing differences as far as possible' in the nation at large, since 'mercy and justice are the foundations of a lasting peace') that the sequestration of estates should be speedily discharged, and 'compositions be so moderate as none may exceed two years' revenue.'

[1] *The Case of the Army* is signed by Robert Everard and ten other Agents (here described as 'Agitators'), and is followed by a letter of self-justification to Fairfax, signed by seven of the same and four different Agents (and not by Everard). The Agents declare themselves to have acted from

'obligations upon our consciences (written naturally by the finger of God in our hearts). * * * For God hath given no man a talent to be

16. A Letter from the Agents to the Whole Soldiery

From *Two Letters from the Agents of the Five Regiments* (28th Oct.) [a]

But it may be some would affright you from owning your case as it's now offered, by suggesting that it's irregular and disorderly for the soldiers to join in anything before their officers, or that it's contrary to law for you to demand your rights, or that it's a resisting of authority, but we desire that our Declaration of June 14 . . . might be reviewed, wherein it appears that the Parliament hath declared that the equitable sense of the law is supreme to the letter, and doth dispense with it when a people's safety is concerned; and that all authority is fundamentally seated in the office, and but ministerially in the persons; and that therefore it's no resisting of authority or magistracy to side with the just principles and law of nature and nations, to preserve a people from perishing. And let it be remembered, that if you had not joined together at first, and chose your Agents to act for you when your officers thought it not safe for them to appear, you had been now in no capacity to plead for your own or the people's freedom. And let it be considered that Scotland associated in covenant, and so by consent composed an army to stand upon principles of right and freedom when they had no visible form either of Parliament or King to countenance them, and they were therein justified and protected by their own and this nation, and may not this Army expect justly to be in like manner protected and justified in their joining together to insist upon the settlement of those freedoms which they have purchased with their blood out of the hands of the common enemy, which God hath subdued by them?

But if any envious tongues shall be blasting us with anarchy, clamouring that we intend to destroy government in the kingdom and Army and bring all into confusion, we suppose the assertion itself is so irrational that it will rather give you the true character of every such

wrapped up in a napkin and not improved, but the meanest vassal (in the eye of the world) is equally obliged, and accomptable to God, with the greatest prince or commander under the sun in and for the use of that talent betrusted unto him. * * * For, Sir, should you—yea should the whole Parliament or kingdom—exempt us from this service, or . . . command our silence or forbearance, yet could not they nor you discharge us of our duties to God or to our own natures. * * * And if by any one your Excellency shall be suborned that we are transgressors of all order and form, and in that sense to look upon us, we desire to mind your Excellency that the law of nature and nations, attested in our public declarations and papers, may be an answer to such for the justification of our present expedient. For all forms are but as shadows, and subject to the end. And the safety of the people is above all forms, customs, &c.; and the equity of popular safety is the thing which justifieth all forms, or the change of forms, for the accomplishment thereof; and no forms are lawful longer than they preserve or accomplish the same.'

asperser than reflect upon us to our prejudice. Let it be observed that the chief foundation for all our rights and freedoms, which we are resolved most absolutely to insist upon, is a certainty of a constant Parliament every two years, and a certain time for their sitting and ending; and a sure establishment of the just power that the people betrust to those their representatives in their election, that they may make laws and repeal laws, place and displace all magistrates, and exercise all other power according to their trust, without the consent or concurrence of any other person or persons whatsoever. And we appeal to all rational men, whether in this we strive not for the freedom that we first engaged to maintain. * * *

Now it may be when the justice of our endeavours shall shine through all other reproaches, some will be muttering that we have designed to divide the Army, or the soldiers from the officers. But we appeal to your own consciences, whether persuasions to be faithful in observing our declarations, promises, and engagement, wherein we joined unanimously, tend to division. Is not this the sum of all that we have offered, *viz.*, that your own and the people's necessities, and the imminent danger of ruin, or at least slavery, to you and them, calls you to renew your union in the former desires, and in insisting upon suitable answers speedily, lest you and the people be confounded and perish by delays? And is this to divide? And as for rending from officers, let it be remembered that though the soldiers acted without them at first, yet those who were faithful did afterward concur with them. * * * [1]

17. LETTER OF JOHN SALTMARSH TO THE COUNCIL OF WAR (28TH OCT.) [a]

Honourable: Not to repeat to ye the sad outcries of a poor nation for justice and righteousness, the departure of the hearts of many Christians generally from you, the late testimonies of some in your own bowels, the withdrawing of that glory the Lord formerly clothed ye withal. But this I know: ye have not discharged yourselves to the people in such things as they justly expected from ye, and for which ye had that spirit of righteousness first put upon ye by an Almighty Power, and which carried you on upon a conquering wing. The wisdom of the flesh hath deceived and enticed, and that glorious principle of Christian liberty which we advanced in at first (I speak as to Christians) hath been managed too much in the flesh.

Now if the Lord hath opened to any of ye the unsoundness of any principle then, or in the management of them, I hope he will show ye a better course and path to walk in. And now ye are met in council, the Lord make ye to hearken to one another from the highest to the meanest, that the voice of God, wheresoever it speaks, may not be despised. And think it no shame to pass over into more righteous

---

[1] The letters are signed by Robert Everard and eleven others.

engagements. That wisdom which is from above is easy to be entreated. Look over your first Engagements, and compare them with your proceedings, that you may see what you have done, what you must do. I know it is unsavoury to nature to be accused or taxed, but I hope there will be found that spirit in you, that will esteem the wounds of a friend better than the kisses of an enemy. I write, I know, to such who in their first love were a people loving God and his appearances in the meanest Christian, and such as pursued the good and happiness of the kingdom cordially. And if the Lord hath not thought to take off the spirit of righteousness from ye and put it upon another people, he will give you to discern this last temptation wherein Satan hath desired to winnow ye, and ye shall be a diadem once more in the hands of the Lord. For myself, as I am myself, there is neither wisdom nor counsel in me; but if the Lord hath breathed on my weakness for your sakes, I shall rejoice in that mercy and grace of his. I rest,

Yours in all righteous Engagements,

JOHN SALTMARSH.

Laystreet, Octob. 28, [1647].

18. FROM A CALL TO ALL THE SOLDIERS OF THE ARMY BY THE FREE PEOPLE OF ENGLAND [1] (29TH Oct.) [a]

Take [2] heed of crafty politicians and subtle Machiavelians,[3] and be sure to trust no man's painted words; it being high time now to see actions, yea, and those constantly upright too. If any man (by bringing forth unexpected bitter fruits) hath drawn upon himself a just suspicion, let him justly bear his own blame. * * *

One of the surest marks of deceivers is to make fair, long and eloquent speeches, but a trusty or true-hearted man studieth more to do good actions than utter deceitful orations. And one of the surest tokens of confederates in evil is not only, when one of his fellows is vehement, fiery or hot in any of their pursuits, to be patient, cold or moderate, to pacify his partner, and like deceitful lawyers before their clients to qualify matters, but sometimes seem to discord or fall out, and quarrel in counsels, reasonings and debates, and yet nevertheless in the end to agree in evil; which they do purposely to hold upright men in a charitable (though doubtful) opinion, that if such and such a man be not godly and upright, they know not whom in the world to trust, whiles in the meantime under the vizards of great professions, gilded with some religious actions, they both deceive the world and bring their wicked designs and self-interests to pass.

Those of you that use your Thursday General Councils of late might

[1] Attributed to John Wildman (*D.N.B.*, 61. 235).
[2] The first part of the pamphlet is addressed to the Five Regiments.
[3] Obviously it is Cromwell and Ireton who are being attacked. Later they are named.

have observed so much of this kind of juggling, falsehood, and double dealing, as might have served to some good use at this point of extremity. But truly most that have been there have been deluded, to our great grief, which appeareth by the unreasonable proceedings of that court, as in many things, so especially in their debates about the aforesaid *Case of the Army*,[1] now published and subscribed by you. Wherein though the General was so ingenuous as to move for the public reading thereof, yet the Commissary - General Ireton and Lieutenant-General Cromwell, yea, and most of the court, would and did proceed to censure and judge both it and the authors and promoters thereof, without reading it, and ever since do impudently boast and glory in that their victory. * * *

In the Council they held forth to you the bloody flag of threats and terrors, talked of nothing but faction, dividing principles, anarchy, of hanging, punishing, yea, and impudently maintained that your regiments were abused and the aforesaid *Case* not truly subscribed, and did appoint a Committee *ad terrorem*. And abroad they hold forth the white flag of accommodation and satisfaction, and of minding the same thing which ye mind, and to be flesh of your flesh and bone of your bone, and to invite you to their headquarters, where they hope either to work upon you as they have most lamentably done upon others, even to betray your trust, confound both your understandings and counsels, corrupt your judgments, and blast your actions. And though they should not prevail with you, yet there they keep so great a state and distance that they suppose ye will not dare to make good the things ye have published. * * *

If ye do adventure to go thither, beware that ye be not frighted by the word *anarchy*, unto a love of *monarchy*, which is but the gilded name for *tyranny*; for anarchy had never been so much as once mentioned amongst you had it not been for that wicked end. 'Tis an old threadbare trick of the profane Court and doth amongst discreet men show plainly who is for the Court and against the liberties of the people, who, whensoever they positively insist for their just freedoms, are immediately flapped in the mouths with these most malignant reproaches: 'Oh, ye are for anarchy. Ye are against all government. Ye are sectaries, seditious persons, troublers both of church and state, and so not worthy to live in a commonwealth. There shall be a speedy course taken both against you and such as you. Away with all such from Parliament-doors and Headquarters!'

And if ye can escape these delusions (as through God's assistance, we trust, ye will), and not be satisfied with half or quarter remedies, or things holding a shadow only of good without the substance, we cannot in the least doubt of your good success, being firmly resolved to stand by you and to live and die with you.

Ye had need to be well armed and fortified against the devices that

---

[1] Reference is to the unreported debate of 22nd October.

will be put upon you. Ireton (ye know) hath already scandalized *The Case of the Army* in the General Council. Where, by his own and his confederate's craft and policy, he reigneth as sole master, insomuch as those friends ye have there (which we hope ye will see in due time not to be few) find it to little purpose to show themselves active in opposing him. And as he undertook so hath he answered your *Case*; wherein he showeth himself so full of art and cunning, smooth delusion (being skilled in nothing more), and if ye did not sensibly know the things to be really and experimentally true, which ye have therein expressed and published, 'tis ten to one but he would deceive you.

This is certain. In the House of Commons both he and his father Cromwell do so earnestly and palpably carry on the King's design that your best friends there are amazed thereat, and even ready to weep for grief to see such a sudden and dangerous alteration. And this they do in the name of the whole Army, certifying the House that if they do not make further address to the King, they cannot promise that the Army will stand by them if they should find opposition. And what is this but as much in effect as in the name of the whole Army to threaten the House into a compliance with the King, your most deadly enemy, and who, if things go on thus, will deceive both you and them, yea, and all that act most for him?

To what purpose then should you either debate, confer, or treat with such false sophisters or treacherous deceivers as these, who, like the former courtiers, can always play the hypocrites without any check of conscience? To what end should ye read or spend time to consider what they either write or speak, it being so evident that as they did intend so they proceed to hold you in hand till their work be done?

But if you will show yourselves wise, stop your ears against them. *Resist the devil and he will fly from you.* Hold not parley with them, but proceed with that just work ye have so happily begun, without any more regarding one word they speak. For their consciences being at liberty to say or do anything which may advance their own ends, they have great advantage against you whose consciences will not permit you to say or do anything but what is just and true and what ye mean to perform, they having shamefully proved themselves to be large promisers, thereby to deceive both you and all the people, but the worst performers that ever lived.

And therefore, certainly, ye have no warrant from God to treat either with them or their deceitful instruments, who will be speedily (in great numbers) sent amongst you. But as ye know most of them for evil, so are ye to avoid them as the most venomous serpents, and fail not in this your just enterprise to cast yourselves chiefly upon God in the use of all the knowledge, experience, means, and power, wherewith he hath furnished you; and secondly upon the people, who will be ready with all their might and strength to assist you whilst ye are faithful and real[ly] for them. Join and be one with them in heart and hand, with all possible speed, in some substantial and firm Agreement for just freedom and common right, that this nation may no longer float upon such wavering, uncertain, and sandy foundations of government, which have been one of the greatest causes both of all your and our predecessors' miseries. * * *

Your Adjutators,[1] we hear, are esteemed but as a burden to the chief officers, which we judge to be the reason that all things now are in such a languishing condition. Our hopes die daily within us, and we fear ye will too soon give yourselves and us, with our joint and just cause, into their hands. Ye should have considered that they a long time staggered before they engaged with you, and certainly had never engaged but that they saw no other way nor means to shelter and preserve themselves from the power of Hollis and Stapleton, with their confederates. * * *

We beseech you, . . . commanders and soldiers that are yet untainted in your integrity and have not yet bowed your knees to Baal, that ye will not betray yourselves, your just cause and us, so unworthily, nor seem to distrust that power and wisdom of God by which ye have done so great and mighty works, but that now ye will be bold and courageous for your God and for his people, and for justice against all ungodliness and unrighteousness of men without respect of persons.

And before it be too late, deal plainly with Ireton, by whose cowardly or ambitious policy Cromwell is betrayed into these mischievous practices, and by whose craft the power of your Adjutators is brought to nothing, and by whose dissimulation many of them are corrupted and become treacherous unto you. None but flatterers, tale-bearers, and turn-coats are countenanced by him. Let him know ye know him and hate his courses. Your General Councils, by his imperious carriage, are like unto Star Chambers. A plain man is made an offender for a word.

And if Cromwell instantly repent not and alter his course, let him know also that ye loved and honoured just, honest, sincere, and valiant Cromwell that loved his country and the liberties of the people above his life, yea, and hated the King as a man of blood, but that Cromwell ceasing to be such, he ceaseth to be the object of your love.

And since there is no remedy, ye must begin your work anew. Ye are as ye were at Bury.[2] Ye are no strangers to the way; ye have already made a good beginning, wherein we rejoice. Ye have men amongst you as fit to govern as others to be removed. *And with a word ye can create new officers.* Necessity hath no law, and against it there is no plea. The safety of the people is above all law. And if ye be not

---

[1] The two terms *Agitator* and *Adjutator* are used indifferently. I have preserved the latter in this pamphlet, that it may be represented. This second part of the pamphlet is addressed to 'all the soldiers of the Army.'

[2] The reference is to the organization of the soldiers for their own defence prior to the *Solemn Engagement.*

very speedy, effectual, and do your work thoroughly, and not by halves
as it hath been, ye and we perish inevitably.

What your General is ye best know, but 'tis too late to live by hopes
or to run any more hazards. None can deceive you but whom ye trust
upon doubtful terms. Beware of the flattery and sophistry of men,
bargain with your officers not to court it in fine or gaudy apparel, nor
to regard titles, fine fare, or compliments. Those that do are much
more liable to temptations than other men. A good conscience is a
continual feast, and let your outside testify that ye delight not to be
soldiers longer than necessity requires.

Draw yourselves into an exact council, and get amongst you the most
judicious and truest lovers of the people ye can find to help you, and
let your end be justice without respect of persons, and peace and freedom to all sorts of peaceable people. Establish a free Parliament by
expulsion of the usurpers. Free the people from all burdens and oppressions, speedily and without delay. Take an exact account of the
public treasure, that public charges may be defrayed by subsidies,
tithes abolished, the laws, and proceedings therein, regulated, and
free-quarter abandoned.

Let nothing deter you from this, so just and necessary a work. None
will oppose you therein, or so long as ye continue sincere and uncor-
rupted. For all sorts of people have been abused: kings have abused
them, parliaments have abused them, and your chief officers have most
grossly deceived the honest party. Be confident none will oppose,
and be as confident that thousands and ten thousands are ready and
ripe to assist you.

Be strong therefore, our dear true-hearted brethren and fellow
Commoners, and be of good courage, and the Lord our God will
direct you by his wisdom, who never yet failed you in your greatest
extremities. Stay for no farther, look for no other call; for the voice
of necessity is the call of God. All other ways for your indemnity are
but delusive; and if ye trust to any other under the fairest promises,
ye will find yourselves in a snare.

Whom can ye trust, who hath not hitherto deceived you? Trust
only to justice; for God is a God of justice, and those that promote
the same shall be preserved. Free the Parliament from those in-
cendiaries with all your might. The true and just patriots (yea, all
but deceivers) therein, long for your assistance, and, that being effectually done, ye may safely put yourselves and the whole nation upon them
both for provision, indemnity, and just liberty. * * *

19. *An Agreement of the People* (PRINTED 3RD NOV.) [a]

[After a preamble, substantially the same as that of the Second Agreement (above p. 356), the *Agreement* proceeds:] In order whereunto
we declare:

I. That the people of England, being at this day very unequally distributed by counties, cities, and boroughs, for the election of their deputies in Parliament, ought to be more indifferently proportioned, according to the number of the inhabitants; the circumstances whereof, for number, place, and manner, are to be set down before the end of this present Parliament.

II. That to prevent the many inconveniences apparently arising from the long continuance of the same persons in authority, this present Parliament be dissolved upon the last day of September, which shall be in the year of our Lord 1648.

III. That the people do of course choose themselves a Parliament once in two years, viz., upon the first Thursday in every second March, after the manner as shall be prescribed before the end of this Parliament, to begin to sit upon the first Thursday in April following, at Westminster (or such other place as shall be appointed from time to time by the preceding Representatives), and to continue till the last day of September then next ensuing, and no longer.

IV. That the power of this, and all future Representatives of this nation is inferior only to theirs who choose them, and doth extend, without the consent or concurrence of any other person or persons, to the enacting, altering, and repealing of laws; to the erecting and abolishing of offices and courts; to the appointing, removing, and calling to account magistrates and officers of all degrees; to the making war and peace; to the treating with foreign states; and generally to whatsoever is not expressly or impliedly reserved by the represented to themselves.

Which are as followeth:

1. That matters of religion, and the ways of God's worship, are not at all entrusted by us to any human power, because therein we cannot remit or exceed a tittle of what our consciences dictate to be the mind of God, without wilful sin; nevertheless the public way of instructing the nation (so it be not compulsive) is referred to their discretion.

2. That the matter of impressing and constraining any of us to serve in the wars is against our freedom, and therefore we do not allow it in our representatives; the rather because money (the sinews of war) being always at their disposal, they can never want numbers of men apt enough to engage in any just cause.

3. That after the dissolution of this present Parliament, no person be at any time questioned for anything said or done in reference to the late public differences, otherwise than in execution of the judgments of the present representatives, or House of Commons.

4. That in all laws made, or to be made, every person may be bound alike, and that no tenure, estate, charter, degree, birth, or place, do confer any exemption from the ordinary course of legal proceedings, whereunto others are subjected.

5. That as the laws ought to be equal, so they must be good, and not evidently destructive to the safety and well-being of the people.

These things we declare to be our native rights, and therefore are agreed and resolved to maintain them with our utmost possibilities against all opposition whatsoever, being compelled thereunto not only by the examples of our ancestors, whose blood was often spent in vain for the recovery of their freedoms, suffering themselves, through fraudulent accommodations, to be still deluded of the fruit of their victories, but also by our own woeful experience, who, having long expected, and dearly earned, the establishment of these certain rules of government, are yet made to depend for the settlement of our peace and freedom upon him that intended our bondage and brought a cruel war upon us.

[LETTER TO THE FREE-BORN PEOPLE OF ENGLAND]

For the noble and highly honoured the free-born people of England, in their respective counties and divisions, these.

Dear Countrymen, and Fellow Commoners,

For your sakes, our friends, estates, and lives have not been dear to us. For your safety and freedom we have cheerfully endured hard labours and run most desperate hazards, and in comparison to your peace and freedom we neither do, nor ever shall, value our dearest blood. And we profess, our bowels are and have been troubled, and our hearts pained within us, in seeing and considering that you have been so long bereaved of these fruits and ends of all our labours and hazards. We cannot but sympathize with you in your miseries and oppressions. * * * And therefore upon most serious considerations that your principal right, most essential to your well-being, is the clearness, certainty, sufficiency, and freedom of your power in your representatives in Parliament, and considering that the original of most of your oppressions and miseries hath been either from the obscurity and doubtfulness of the power you have committed to your representatives in your elections or from the want of courage in those whom you have betrusted to claim and exercise their power, which might probably proceed from their uncertainty of your assistance and maintenance of their power . . ., and further minding the only effectual means to settle a just and lasting peace, to obtain remedy for all your grievances, and to prevent future oppressions, is the making clear and secure the power that you betrust to your representatives in Parliament, that they may know their trust, in the faithful execution whereof you will assist them: upon all these grounds, we propound your joining with us in the Agreement herewith sent unto you; that by virtue thereof we may have Parliaments certainly called, and have the time of their sitting and ending certain, and their power or trust clear and unquestionable, that hereafter they may remove your burdens and secure your rights, without oppositions or obstructions, and that the foundations of your peace may be so free from uncertainty that there may be no grounds for future quarrels or contentions to occasion war and bloodshed. And we desire you would consider that, as these things wherein we offer to agree with you are the fruits and ends of the victories which God hath given us, so the settlement of these are the most absolute means to preserve you and your posterity from slavery, oppression, distraction, and trouble. By this, those whom yourselves shall choose shall have power to restore you to, and secure you in, all your rights; and they shall be in a capacity to taste of subjection as well as rule, and so shall be equally concerned with yourselves in all they do. For they must equally suffer with you under any common burdens, and partake with you in any freedoms; and by this they shall be disabled [a] to defraud or wrong you when the laws shall bind all alike, without privilege or exemption. And by this your consciences shall be free from tyranny and oppression, and those occasions of endless strifes and bloody wars shall be perfectly removed without controversy. By your joining with us in this Agreement, all your particular and common grievances will be redressed forthwith without delay: the Parliament must then make your relief and common good their only study.

Now because we are earnestly desirous of the peace and good of all our countrymen, even of those that have opposed us, and would to our utmost possibility provide for perfect peace and freedom, and prevent all suits, debates, and contentions that may happen amongst you in relation to the late war; we have therefore inserted it into this Agreement that no person shall be questionable for anything done in relation to the late public differences, after the dissolution of this present Parliament, further than in execution of their judgment; that thereby all may be secure from all sufferings for what they have done, and not liable hereafter to be troubled or punished by the judgment of another Parliament, which may be to their ruin unless this Agreement be joined in, whereby any Acts of Indemnity or Oblivion shall be made unalterable, and you and your posterities be secure.

But if any shall inquire why we should desire to join in an Agreement with the people, to declare these to be our native rights, and not rather petition to the Parliament for them, the reason is evident. No Act of Parliament is, or can be, unalterable, and so cannot be sufficient security to save you or us harmless from what another Parliament may determine if it should be corrupted. And besides Parliaments are to receive the extent of their power and trust from those that betrust them, and therefore the people are to declare what their power and trust is; which is the intent of this Agreement. And it's to be observed, that though there hath formerly been many Acts of Parliament for the calling of Parliaments every year, yet you have been deprived of them, and enslaved through want of them. And therefore both necessity for your security in these freedoms that are essential to your well-being, and woeful experience of the manifold miseries and distractions that have been lengthened out since the war ended, through want of such a settlement, requires this Agreement.

And when you and we shall be joined together therein, we shall readily join with you to petition the Parliament, as they are our fellow Commoners equally concerned to join with us.

And if any shall inquire why we undertake to offer this Agreement, we must profess we are sensible that you have been so often deceived with Declarations and Remonstrances, and fed with vain hopes, that you have sufficient reason to abandon all confidence in any persons whatsoever from whom you have no other security of their intending your freedom than bare declaration.   And therefore, as our consciences witness that in simplicity and integrity of heart we have proposed lately, in *The Case of the Army Stated*, your freedom and deliverance from slavery, oppression, and all burdens, so we desire to give you satisfying assurance thereof by this Agreement, whereby the foundations of your freedoms provided in *The Case, &c.*, shall be settled unalterably. * * *

And though the malice of our enemies, and such as they delude, would blast us by scandals, aspersing us with designs of anarchy and community; yet we hope the righteous God will not only by this our present desire of settling an equal, just government, but also by directing us unto all righteous undertakings simply for public good, make our uprightness and faithfulness to the interest of all our countrymen shine forth so clearly that malice itself shall be silenced and confounded. We question not but the longing expectation of a firm peace will incite you to the most speedy joining in this Agreement: in the prosecution whereof, or of anything that you shall desire for public good, you may be confident you shall never want the assistance of

Your most faithful fellow Commoners, now in arms for your service. . . .[1]

[LETTER TO THE OFFICERS AND SOLDIERS]

For our much honoured and truly worthy fellow Commoners and soldiers, the officers and soldiers under command of his Excellency Sir Thomas Fairfax.

Gentlemen and Fellow Soldiers:

The deep sense of many dangers and mischiefs that may befall you in relation to the late war, whensoever this Parliament shall end, unless sufficient prevention be now provided, hath constrained us to study the most absolute and certain means for your security.   And upon most serious considerations we judge that no Act of Indemnity can sufficiently provide for your quiet, ease, and safety, because, as it hath formerly been, a corrupt party (chosen into the next Parliament by your enemies' means) may possibly surprise the House and make any Act of Indemnity null, seeing they cannot fail of the King's assistance and concurrence in any such actings against you that conquered him.

And by the same means your freedom from impressing also may in

---

[1] The letter is signed by Robert Everard and nine others.

a short time be taken from you, though for the present it should be granted. We apprehend no other security by which you shall be saved harmless for what you have done in the late war, than a mutual Agreement between the people and you, that no person shall be questioned by any authority whatsoever for anything done in relation to the late public differences, after the dissolution of the present House of Commons, further than in execution of their judgment, and that your native freedom from constraint to serve in war, whether domestic or foreign, shall never be subject to the power of Parliaments, or any other. And for this end we propound the Agreement that we herewith send to you, to be forthwith subscribed.

And because we are confident that in judgment and conscience ye hazarded your lives for the settlement of such a just and equal government that you and your posterities, and all the free-born people of this nation, might enjoy justice and freedom, and that you are really sensible that the distractions, oppressions, and miseries of the nation, and your want of your arrears, do proceed from the want of the establishment both of such certain rules of just government and foundations of peace as are the price of blood and the expected fruits of all the people's cost; therefore in this Agreement we have inserted the certain rules of equal government under which the nation may enjoy all its rights and freedoms securely. And as we doubt not but your love to the freedom and lasting peace of the yet-distracted country will cause you to join together in this Agreement, so we question not but every true Englishman that loves the peace and freedom of England will concur with us. And then your arrears, and constant pay (while you continue in arms), will certainly be brought in, out of the abundant love of the people to you; and then shall the mouths of those be stopped that scandalize you and us as endeavouring anarchy, or to rule by the sword; and then will so firm a union be made between the people and you that neither any homebred or foreign enemies will dare to disturb our happy peace. * * *

Postscript.

Gentlemen: We desire you may understand the reason of our extracting some principles of common freedom out of those many things proposed to you in *The Case Truly Stated*, and drawing them up into the form of an Agreement. It's chiefly because for these things we first engaged against the King. * * * Therefore these things, in the Agreement, the people are to claim as their native right and price of their blood, which you are obliged absolutely to procure for them. And these being the foundations of freedom, it is necessary that they should be settled unalterably, which can be by no means but this Agreement with the people.

And we cannot but mind you that the case of the people in all their grievances depends upon the settling those principles or rules of equal government for a free people. And were but this Agreement established, doubtless all the grievances of the Army and people would be redressed immediately, and all things propounded in your *Case Truly Stated*, to be insisted on, would be forthwith granted. * * *

We shall only add that the sum of all the Agreement which we herewith offer to you is but in order to the fulfilling of our Declaration of June 14, wherein we promised to the people that we would with our lives vindicate and clear their right and power in their Parliaments. * * * [1]

20. SUMMARY (WITH QUOTATION) OF THE REPORTS OF THE COMMITTEE ON THE ARMY'S PAPERS AND THE AGREEMENT OF THE PEOPLE [a]

[The [2] eighteen reported present include: Cromwell, Ireton, Waller, Rich, Rainborough, Goffe, Chillenden, Sexby, Allen, and the Agent Walley. The terms of reference are stated]: To consider the papers of the Army, and the paper of the People's Agreement, and to collect and prepare somewhat to be insisted upon and adhered unto for settling the kingdom, and to clear our proceedings hitherto. * * *

[I. Present Parliament to end 'on the first day of September next ensuing' (*cf. Agreement*).

II. (1) Biennial Parliament meeting 'on the first Thursday in April every second year' (*cf. Agreement*); but provision for the certainty thereof left to be settled before end of present Parliament, and Council of State to be allowed to alter place of sitting. (2) Each biennial Parliament to 'sit until the last day of September next ensuing,' and then 'dissolve of course' (*cf. Agreement*); but capable of being 'adjourned or dissolved sooner by their own consent' (*cf. Heads*). (3) Each biennial Parliament to appoint committees, and a Council of State (*cf. Heads*) on whose advice (4) the King may summon extra Parliaments (*cf. Heads*). (5) Representation to be made more equal (but no precise formula as in *Heads, Agreement*, or *Case of the Army*)]:

5. (i) That the election of members for the House of Commons in succeeding Parliaments shall be distributed to all counties, or other parts or divisions of the kingdom, according to some rule of equality of proportion, so as to render the House of Commons, as near as may be, an equal Representative of the whole body of the people that are to elect; and in order thereunto, that all obstructions to the freedom and equality of their choice, either by petitions or charters or other prerogative grants, be removed [*cf. Case of the Army*], and the circumstances of number, place, and manner for more equal distributions be set down by the Commons in this present Parliament before the end thereof; and what they shall order therein, as also what they or the Commons in succeeding Parliaments shall from time to time further order or set down for reducing the said elections to more and more

---

[1] Signed by the same Agents, with the note: 'Agents coming from other regiments unto us have subscribed the Agreement, to be proposed to their respective regiments and you.'

[2] Report of meeting of 30th October.

perfection of equality in distribution thereof, freedom in the election, order and regularity in the proceeding thereof, and certainty in the returns, shall be laws in full force to those purposes [*cf. Heads*].

(ii) That the qualifications of the people that shall have voices in the elections, as also of those that shall be capable of being elected, be determined by the Commons in this present Parliament before the end thereof, so as to give as much enlargement to common freedom as may be, with a due regard had to the equity ᵃ and end of the present constitution in that point. Wherein we desire it may be provided that all free-born Englishmen, or persons made free denizens of England, who have served the Parliament in the late war for the liberties of the kingdom, and were in the service before the 14th of June 1645, or have voluntarily assisted the Parliament in the said war with money, plate, horse, or arms, lent upon the Parliament's propositions for that purpose, brought in thereupon before the ¹ day of 1642, shall, upon such certificates thereof as by the Commons in this present Parliament shall be determined sufficient, or upon other sufficient evidence of the said service or assistance, be admitted to have voices in the said elections for the respective counties or divisions wherein they shall inhabit, although they should not in other respects be within the qualifications to be set down as aforesaid. As also that it be provided, that no person who, for delinquency in the late war or otherwise, hath forfeited or shall forfeit his said freedom, and is or shall be so adjudged by the Commons in Parliament, either by particular judgment or otherwise, or according to general rules or law for that purpose, whiles he standeth or shall stand so adjudged and not restored, shall be admitted to have any voice in the said elections or be capable of being elected. And for that purpose, that it be provided either by law or judgment in this present Parliament, that no person whatsoever who hath been in hostility against the Parliament in the late war shall be capable of having a voice or being elected in the said elections, or to vote or sit as a member or assistant in either House of Parliament, until the second biennial Parliament be past.

(iii) That no Peers made since the 21st day of May 1642, or hereafter to be made, shall be admitted or capable to sit or vote in Parliament without consent of both Houses [*cf. Heads*].

6. For clearing of the power of Parliament in future, and the interest of the people therein, resolved: ²

(i) That the power of this and all succeeding Representatives of the Commons in Parliament doth extend on the behalf, and as to the whole interest, of all the Commons of England to the enacting, altering, and repealing of laws, to the conclusive exposition and declaration of law, and to final ᵇ judgment without further appeal, and generally to

¹ [In margin:] Date of ordinance for 5th & 20th part [i.e. 29th November 1642].

² Report of meeting of 2nd November commences here. See above, p. 113, note.

all things concerning the commonwealth, whatsoever is not by the represented reserved to themselves, as is hereafter expressed. [a]

(ii) That no law shall be repealed, nor any new law or ordinance made to bind the Commons of England, nor any parliamentary judgment, trial, order, or other proceeding valid against any Commoner, without the particular concurrence and consent of the House of Commons, except in case of actual violence or affront done by a Commoner to the House of Peers as a court, and in that case no further proceeding to be valid but by the House of Commons, saving to the securing or imprisoning of the offender's person till he can be tried.

(iii) That no Commoner of England shall be exempt from, but shall be subject to, and concluded by, the power and judgment of the House of Commons, without further appeal, as also to and by all such orders, ordinances, and laws, or expositions and declarations of law, as shall be made, passed, and insisted on, by that House, except in such fundamental things as are by the people electing generally reserved to themselves, as is hereafter expressed.

(iv) That no person whatsoever being an officer of justice or minister of state shall be exempt from, but shall be accountable and subject to, the same power and judgment of the House of Commons for any maladministration of his place to the hurt or damage of the commonwealth; but the persons of Peers, otherwise than in such capacity as aforesaid, shall be tried and judged only by their peers.

(v) That no person whatsoever so adjudged by Parliament (as before) shall be capable of protection or pardon from the King, or to have their fines remitted, without the advice or consent of Parliament, nor such fines to be disposed of otherwise than [as] by the same judgment, advice, or consent shall be directed.

(vi) That in all elections of Representatives for the people these things following are by the people electing reserved to themselves, and so generally to be understood, to wit:

Matters of religion and the ways of God's worship, as to any positive compulsion there, are not entrusted to any human power.

That the matter of impressing or constraining any free Commoner of England to serve in the wars, any further or otherwise than for the immediate defence of this kingdom and keeping the peace within it, is likewise reserved.

That no Commoner be henceforth questioned for anything said or done in reference to, or prosecution of, the late war or public contests within this kingdom, otherwise than by the judgment, or with the concurrence, of the present House of Commons, or in execution or prosecution of such judgment.

That the matter and effect of the preceding articles (to wit: first, concerning the certain succession of biennial Parliaments; then the second, concerning the certainty of their sitting; likewise the matter of the sixth, and the particulars under it concerning the clearing of the power of Parliaments in future as to the interest of the people therein; and so much of the intent of the fifth as concerns the equal distributing of future representatives) are reserved by the people represented as their fundamental rights not to be given away or abrogated by their representatives [*cf. Agreement*]. * * *

21. PROCEEDINGS IN THE GENERAL COUNCIL, 4TH–9TH NOV.

From *A Letter from Several Agitators to their Regiments* (11th Nov.) [a]

Gentlemen and Fellow Soldiers:

We esteem it our duty to render you an account of the present state of our affairs with us, and at the Headquarters. We have been consulting about the most speedy and effectual settlement of your and all the people's freedoms, whereby the people may be disposed into a capacity and willingness to provide constant pay, and secure our arrears. We found by sad experience that there was no possibility of obtaining either so long as the settlement of the people's freedoms was delayed, and therefore, as well in love and real respects to you and to our dear country, we were constrained to propound the foundations of freedom to be forthwith established by a mutual Agreement between the people and you. And though we dare aver that there is nothing contained in that Agreement, or in *The Case of the Army Stated*, which is propounded to be insisted on, but what is (at least) the equitable sense of our former Declarations and Remonstrances; yet we find many at the Headquarters obstructing and opposing our proceedings.

We sent some of them to debate in love the matters and manner of the Agreement. And the first article thereof, being long debated, it was concluded by vote in the affirmative: *viz., That all soldiers and others, if they be not servants or beggars, ought to have voices in electing those which shall represent them in Parliament, although they have not forty shillings per annum in freehold land.* And there were but three voices against this your native freedom. After this they would refer all to a committee. And the next General Council our friends obtained a general rendezvous, and a letter from the Council to clear the Army from any desire or intent of constraining the Parliament to send new propositions to the King [1] (*whereby your indemnity for fighting against the King should be begged of the King*, and so the guilt of innocent blood taken upon your own heads, and your enemies should boast and insult

---

[1] The letter to the Speaker was signed by William Clarke, 'by appointment of the General Council of the Army,' and read in part: 'Whereas it is generally reported that the House was induced to make another address to the King by propositions, by reason it was represented to the House as the desire of the Army; from a tenderness to the privileges of parliamentary actings, this night the General Council of the Army declared that any such representation of their desires was [al]together groundless, and that they earnestly desire no such consideration may be admitted into the House's resolutions in that particular.' (From *Clarke Papers*, ed. Firth, 1. 440–1.)

over you, saying, you were forced to ask them to save you harmless).
At the next meeting a Declaration was offered to the Council, wherein
the King's corrupt interest was so intermixed that in short time, if he
should so come in, he would be in a capacity to destroy you and the
people. (And assure yourselves, if any power be but in the least
given to him, he will improve it to the utmost to enslave and ruin you
that conquered him, and to advance your enemies to trample upon
you.) Upon this we desired only a free debate on this question:
*Whether it were safe either for the Army or people to suffer any power to
be given to the King?* And Lieut[enant]-Gen[eral] Cromwell and the
rest professed, as before God, they would freely debate it. And
Monday last a General Council was appointed for that purpose, but
when they met they wholly refused, and instead of that, spake very
reproachfully of us and our actings, and declaimed against that which was
passed, the Council before, concerning the voices of those in elections
which have not forty shillings a year freehold; and against the letter
sent by the Council to the Parliament. And the day before, Commissary-General Ireton withdrew and protested he would act no more
with them unless they recalled that letter.

And to prevent any further debate they would have dissolved the
Council for above a fortnight, and thus our hopes of agreeing together
to settle your and the people's freedoms were then frustrate. And
though the chief of them had desired some of our friends, not above
three days before, to go on in their actings, for they might come in when
they should do us more service than at that time; yet there they
made great outcries against us and complaints of distempers in the
Army, which were nothing but endeavours after their rights and
freedoms.

The next day they still waived and refused the free debate of the
aforesaid question, and dissolved the Council for above a fortnight,
and for a time resolved they would only prepare some fair propositions
to the Army about arrears and pay, and sent to the Parliament for a
month's pay against a rendezvous. But they declared they would
divide the Army into three parts, to rendezvous severally. And all
this appears to be only to draw off the Army from joining together to
settle those clear foundations of freedom propounded to you, and to
procure your rights as you are soldiers, effectually.

Thus you may observe the strange inconstancy of those that would
obstruct our way, and the great matter wherein the difference lies, and
the candidness of our actings. But we hope it will be no discouragement to you, though your officers—yea, the greatest officers—should
oppose you. It is well known that the great officers which now opposed
did as much oppose secretly when we refused to disband according to
the Parliament's order; and at last they confessed the providence of
God was the more wonderful because those resolutions to stand for
freedom and justice began amongst the soldiers only. And yet now they
would affright you from such actings by telling you it is disobedience

to the General's command, and distempers, and mutinies. These were the words of that faction in Parliament which opposed you before. And you may consider that you had done as much service for the people by disobedience to the Parliament as ever you did by obedience, if you had fulfilled your Declarations and Engagements which you then passed.

As for the month's pay, if it come you may consider it is but your due; and yet we believe none had been procured for you unless we had thus appeared. And if any declarations or propositions about pay or arrears be offered to you, remember you have been fed with paper too long. We desire that there may be a general rendezvous, and no parting each from other till we be fully assured we shall not return to burden the country by free-quarter, and till our arrears be actually secured, and the foundations of our freedom, peace and security in the Agreement established; and likewise, until a sure way be settled for calling committees, sequestrators, and Parliament-men, to account for the country's money, that so the country may know we intend their good and freedom. We know some fair overtures will be made to you about pay, arrears, seeming freedom and security; but we hope, as you formerly rejected such overtures from the Parliament, knowing that without a settlement of freedom no constant pay or arrears will be provided—so now we are confident you will not be deceived, and hope you are all resolved for a general rendezvous, that we may all agree together in fulfilling our Declarations and Engagements to the people, that so we may not become the objects of scorn and hatred. * * * [1]

From Clarke MSS. [a]

[At the General Council] Putney, 8 November, 1647.
Cromwell spoke much to express the danger of their principles who had sought to divide the Army. That the first particular of that which they called the *Agreement of the People* did tend very much to anarchy, that all those who are in the kingdom should have a voice in electing Representatives.

Capt. [William] Bray made a long speech to take off what the Lieut[enant]-General said, and that what he called anarchy was for propriety.

Cromwell moved to put it to the question: Whether that the Officers and Agitators be sent to their quarters, yea, or no?

Resolved upon the question: that the General Council doth humbly advise his Excellency, that (in regard the General shortly intends a rendezvous of the Army, and forasmuch as many distempers are reported to be in the several regiments, whereby much dissatisfaction is given both to the Parliament and kingdom through some misrepre-

---

[1] Signed by Edward Sexby, Robert Everard, and thirteen others (Agitators and Agents).

sentations) to the end a right understanding may be had, and the soldiers quieted, in order to their obedience to his Excellency for the service of the Parliament and kingdom, it is thought fit to desire his Excellency that for a time the said Officers and Agitators resort to their several commands and regiments, to the ends aforesaid, there to reside until the said rendezvous be over, and until his Excellency shall see cause to call them together again according to the *Engagement*. * * *

[A Committee of eighteen was named, including Cromwell, Ireton, Cowling, Waller, Tichborne, Hewson, Rich, Tomlinson, Goffe, and the Agitators Allen and Lockyer.] This Committee to draw up instructions for what shall be offered to the regiments at the rendezvous, to consider of the later letter sent to the Parliament, and what shall be thought fit further to be proposed to them. [1] * * *

[At the General Council]   Putney, 9 November, 1647.

The General present.   This Committee is to take into consideration the *Engagement*, Declarations, and papers of the Army, and upon them to collect a summary of those things that concern the good of the kingdom, the liberties of the people, and interests of the Army, and further to consider *The Case of the Army Stated*, and a paper commonly called the *Agreement of the People*, and to consider how far any thing contained in the same are consistent with the said Engagements and Declarations and interests aforesaid. This summary so concluded by the major part of the Committee to be represented to the General. [2] * * * [A Committee of twenty-three is named, including Cromwell, Ireton, Cowling, Waller, Tichborne, Rich, Tomlinson, Goffe, Chillenden, and John Wildman; later eight more added, including Harrison and Rainborough. A note of its adjournment 'till Thursday come fortnight, at the Headquarters.']

[Resolution:] If any by that letter bearing date 5th of November do make any construction as if we intended that we were against the Parliament's sending propositions to the King, we do hereby declare that it was no part of our intentions in the said letter, but that the same is utterly a mistake of our intention and meaning therein, our intentions being only to assert the freedom of Parliament.

---

[1] Followed in Clarke MSS. by draft of a request to Parliament (mentioned in the Agitators' letter) for six weeks' pay for the Army, or, failing that, one month's; also recommending the raising of funds for arrears from the lands of bishops, and of deans and chapters, and objecting once more to free-quarter.

[2] Rushworth (*Collections*, 6. 868) adds: for his order to communicate the same to the several regiments at their respective rendezvous.

E. DOCUMENTS RELATING TO THE WHITEHALL DEBATES

22. PETITION OF 11TH SEPTEMBER 1648: see pp. 338–42.

23. FROM A REMONSTRANCE OF FAIRFAX AND THE COUNCIL OF OFFICERS [1] (16th November 1648) [a]

To the Right Honourable the Commons of England Assembled in Parliament. * * *

We are not ignorant that that rule of *Salus populi suprema lex* is of all others most apt to be abused or misapplied, and yet none more surely true. It is too ordinary (especially of late times) for men who, either from intentions of evil or inordinate temper of spirit, would break those bonds of law and magistracy which they find to restrain them, to frame pretences of public danger and extremity thereof, and from thence immediately to assume a liberty to break, or else neglect and fly above, the due bounds of order and government, and stir up others to the same, pleading privilege from that vast large rule of *Salus populi, &c.* From such misapplications whereof, great disturbances do oft arise and confusion is endangered; and yet we know the same may be justly pretended and followed, and that, where it is from honest public intentions and upon clear grounds, with very happy effects. We have seen in this our age several instances in both kinds, and the hand of God bearing testimony, and giving judgment for some, and yet against others where the pretensions have been the same, or so like as it was hard for human judgment to distinguish. * * * Neither wants there ground for men to make some judgment therein. For certainly he that engageth upon such pretences really for public ends, and but upon public necessity or extremity, and with a sober spirit, . . . will both try first all honest ways possible . . . whereby he may accomplish them and avoid the danger (if possible) with due regard to, and by concurrence [b] with, or [c] preservation of, the magistracy and government un[der] which God hath set him, before he will fly to ways of extremity; neither will he (when engaged therein) proceed further or longer in that way against or without the magistracy than that first necessity, or some other emergent upon the proceeding, does justly lead, and the security of the ends require: not driving that pretence of necessity further to serve or advantage himself or perpetuate those ways of extremity, but, when the necessity or danger is over and the public ends secured, will return to magistracy and order again, and meanwhile so act in all as carefully to avoid both injury to the innocent and offence to the weak, and as subjecting . . . all to an indifferent and equal judgment. . . .

For our parts, both prudential considerations and the experience we have of the danger that is in the least breaking or letting loose or

[1] The work of Ireton.

entangling the reins of order and government upon such pretences, makes us most tender of it, as that which is never otherwise to be used or admitted than as a desperate cure in a desperate case, and at the utmost peril as well of them that use it as of those for whom. And the experiences we have seen of God's righteous judgments in such cases, as it makes us not apt without trembling and fear to think of such proceedings, so much the more strict to observe all the aforesaid cautions concerning them, and yet where just occasion and a real public necessity calls thereunto, not to fear such appeals to God for any outward difficulties or dangers appearing to ourselves therein. But both from divine and human considerations, as we do and ever shall avoid the occasions by all means possible (even to utmost extremity), and do pray and hope we may never come to it: so, if ever such extremity do happen to us, we hope (through the grace of God) we shall be careful and enabled, both in the engaging and proceeding therein, so to act as before the Lord, and to approve ourselves both to God and good men, and as submitting to the judgment of both. And therefore though we are full of sad apprehensions of present dangers to the public interest, and the extremity even at hand, yet we shall first in all humbleness and soberness of mind, and with all clearness (as God shall enable us), remonstrate to you our apprehensions both of the dangers at hand and of the remedies, with our grounds in both. * * *

[After urging Parliament to adhere to its own resolution of no further addresses to the King and descanting on his untrustworthy character, the document proceeds to prove that the ends for which the struggle was undertaken cannot be guaranteed by treaty with the King.]

The sum of the public interest of a nation in relation to common right and freedom (which has been the chief subject of our contest), and in opposition to tyranny and injustice of kings or others, we take to lie in these things following:

1. That for all matters of supreme trust or concernment to the safety and welfare of the whole, they have a common and supreme council of Parliament; and that (as to the common behalf, who cannot all meet together themselves) to consist of deputies or representers freely chosen by them, with as much equality as may be, and those elections to be successive and renewed, either at times certain and stated, or at the call of some subordinate standing officer or council entrusted by them for that purpose, in the intervals of the supreme, or else at both.

2. That the power of making laws, constitutions, and offices, for the preservation and government of the whole, and of altering or repealing and abolishing the same, for the removal of any public grievance therein, and the power of final judgment concerning war or peace, the safety and welfare of the people, and all civil things whatsoever, without further appeal to any created standing power, and the supreme trust in relation to all such things, may rest in that supreme council; so as:

(i) That the ordinary ordering and government of the people may be

458 APPENDIX

by such offices and administrations, and according to such laws and rules, as by that council, or the representative body of the people therein, have been prescribed or allowed, and not otherwise.

(ii) That none of those extraordinary or arbitrary powers afore-mentioned may be exercised towards the people by any as of right, but by that supreme council, or the representative body of the people therein; nor without their advice and consent may anything be imposed upon, or taken from, the people; or if it be otherwise attempted by any, that the people be not bound thereby but free, and the attempters punishable.

(iii) That those extraordinary powers, or any of them, may be exercised by that supreme council, or by the representative body of the people therein, and where they shall see cause to assume and exercise the same in a matter which they find necessary for the safety or well-being of the people, their proceedings and determinations there-in may be binding and conclusive to the people and to all officers of justice and ministers of state whatsoever; and that it may not be left in the will of the King or any particular persons (standing in their own interest) to oppose, make void, or render ineffectual such their deter-minations or proceedings; and especially, since the having of good constitutions, and making of good laws, were of little security or null, without power to punish those that break, or go about to overthrow them. . . , that therefore the same council or representative body therein, having the supreme trust, may in all such cases where the offence or default is in public officers abusing or failing their trust, or in any person whatsoever if the offence extend to the prejudice of the public, may call such offenders to account and distribute punish-ments to them, either according to the law, where it has provided, or their own judgment, where it has not and they find the offence, though not particularly provided against by particular laws, yet against the general law of reason or nations, and the vindication of public interest to require justice; and that in such case no person whatsoever may be exempt from such account or punishment, or have power to protect others from their judgment, or (without their consent) to pardon whom they have judged. * * *

But . . . the matters aforementioned being the main parts of public interest originally contended for on your parts, and theirs that engaged with you, and thus opposed by the King for the interest of his will and power, many other more particular or special interests have occasionally fallen into the contest on each part.ª As first on the Parliament's part, to protect and countenance religious men and godliness in the power of it, to give freedom and enlargement to the Gospel for the increasing and spreading of light amongst men, to take away those corrupted forms of an outside religion and church-government, whether imposed with-out law, or rooted in the law in times of popish ignorance or idolatry, or of the Gospel's dimmer light, by means whereof snares and chains were laid upon conscientious and zealous men, and the generality of people held in darkness, superstition, and a blind reverence of persons and outward things, fit for popery and slavery; and also to take away or loosen that dependence of the clergy and ecclesiastical affairs upon the King, and that interest of the clergy in the laws and civil affairs, which the craft of both in length of time had wrought for each other. Which several things were the proper subject of the reformation endeavoured by the Parliament. Contrariwise, on the King's part the interest was to discountenance and suppress the power of godliness, or anything of conscience obliging above or against human and outward constitutions; to restrain or lessen the preaching of the Gospel and growth of light amongst men, to hold the community of men, as much as might be, in a darksome ignorance and superstition or formality in religion, with only an awful reverence of persons, offices, and outward dispensations, rendering them fit subjects for ecclesiastical and civil tyranny; and for these ends to advance and set up further forms of superstition, or at least hold fast the old which had any foundation in the laws, whereby chains and fetters might be held upon, and advantages taken against, such in whom a zeal or conscience to anything above man should break forth, and to uphold and maintain the dependence of the clergy and church-matters upon the King, and greatness of the clergy under him, and in all these things to oppose the reformation endeavoured by the Parliament. Also on the Parliament's part, their interest, as well as duty, was to discountenance irreligion, profaneness, debauchery, vanity, ambition, and time-serving, and to prefer such especially as were otherwise given, viz., conscientious, strict in manners, sober, serious, and of plain and public spirits. Contrary to these, on the King's part it was to countenance or connive at profaneness, looseness of manners, vanity and luxury of life, and prefer especially such as had a mixture of ambition and vainglory with a servile spirit, rendering them fit to serve another's power and greatness for the enjoying of some share therein to themselves; in all or most of which respects it has been the great happiness and advantage to [the] Parliamentary and public interest that it hath been made one (very much) with the interest of the godly, or (for the name whereof it has been so much derided) the Saints; as on the other side, the King's, one with their greatest opposites, by occasion whereof God hath been doubly engaged in the cause, viz., for that, and for the righteousness of it. And to this indeed, through the favour and presence of God therewith, the Parliament hath cause to own and refer the blessing and success that hath accompanied their affairs. Which, accordingly as they have held square and been kept close to this, have prospered gloriously, and wherein or so oft as this hath been thwarted, swerved from, or neglected in their manage, have suffered miserable blastings. * * *

Now if yet any shall object the Covenant as perpetually obliging to endeavour the preservation of the King's person and authority, and consequently not allowing any such way of security against him as would be to the hurt of his person or prejudice of his authority, and so concluding us under a necessity of perpetual addresses to him for security until he give it, as being the only way consistent with the preservation of his person and authority, to this we answer: that indeed the Covenant, heaping together several distinct interests (which are or possibly may come to be inconsistent, or one destructive to the other, or at least may be so made use of) and yet engaging positively for them all, without expressing clearly and unquestionably which is chief and perpetual, and . . . how far, and upon what conditions the covenanter shall be obliged to them, and what shall disoblige him, we find it is (as other promissory oaths of that kind) apt to be made a very snare, serving to draw in many of several judgments and affections, each in respect to that interest therein engaged for, which himself does most affect. And so those that make least conscience of the oath, make but an advantage of it upon all occasions to cry up that interest which themselves prefer (though to the destruction or prejudice of the rest, yea, of that which is really the main and best), while those that make most conscience of the oath, and affect the principal and honestest part in it, are oft withheld from what's just and necessary in relation thereunto, being staggered in regard of the prejudice it may be to the rest, to which jointly they seem obliged. But this Covenant as it is drawn, though it have something of that ensnaring nature, yet as to this point has not left the takers without an honest way out. Or if it had, yet through the providence of God the snare is broken and they may escape.

For the Covenant engaging to the matters of religion and public interests primarily and absolutely (without any limitation), and after that to the preservation of the King's person and authority, but with this restriction, . . . *in the preservation of the true religion and liberties of the kingdoms*; in this case, though a caviller might make it a question, yet who will not rationally resolve it, that the preceding matters of religion and the public interest are to be understood as the principal and supreme matters engaged for, and that of the King's person and authority as inferior and subordinate to the other? * * *

Yea, might it not justly be so understood, that the obligation to preserve his person and authority should be fulfilled in (as well as not extended further than) the preservation of religion and liberties? * * * Or if it might be so understood [as protecting the King's person and authority, and those of persons acting on his commission], doth it not call for explanation to clear it from being understood in so wicked a sense? Yea, if it did by the advantage of words extend to such a sense past explanation, and if so (through error in consideration, or deceit in the framing of it, or through flattery, evil custom, or unbelief and carnal policy in the passing of it) you had literally engaged yourselves, and drawn in others to be engaged, unto so wicked and mischievous a thing; did it not call for repentance when you find such wickedness in it? And rather than unnecessarily to continue yourselves, and hold others, under but a colour of obligation to a thing so evil, so full of prejudice and danger unto, and so inconsistent with the security of, so many other unquestionably good things to which in the same Covenant, as well as by immutable duty, you stand obliged, would it not call for your utmost consideration and endeavour (so far as Providence has left you any occasion, without sin or wrong) to extricate and clear yourselves and others from such a snare? * * *

Whatever, or how expressly soever, the Covenant may seem to have engaged unto . . . anything in the King's behalf, or to his only benefit, yet, as God ordered the business, it does not now oblige you at all before God or man in that matter. For first (considering it only as a covenant betwixt man and man, as for the civil parts of it), where . . . several persons joining to make a mutual covenant or agreement, do therefore covenant for some things to the good and union of themselves amongst themselves who are present and parties to it, and withal do make a covenanting clause therein for something else to the good or benefit of another person not present nor party to the agreement, . . . to the end he might join with them in the agreement, and partake the benefit thereof as well as themselves—we say, in such case, if the absent party, as he never required it, so (when 'tis tendered to him for his conjunction) shall not accept the agreement, but refuse to join in it, and (conceiving his interest prejudiced thereby) shall oppose it, and . . . multiply contests with all the covenanters about the matters contained in it; surely that person in so doing, as he keeps him free and no way obliged thereby as to what concerns the rest . . . so he excludes himself from any claim to any benefit therefrom at their hands as to what concerns himself. * * *

Secondly, considering it as an oath, the form of an oath, added to that of a covenant, makes it no other than a covenant still, but taken as in the presence of God, and only adds the calling of God to witness as to the truth of your intentions and faithfulness of your endeavours to perform what it as a covenant obligeth unto; and . . . how far it, in the nature of a covenant, as to any particular matter obligeth, so far, and no further or otherwise, doth that calling of God to witness engage him the more to avenge any falsehood in your intentions, or unfaithfulness in your endeavours to perform it. And this is all the enforcement which that form of an oath addeth to that of a covenant, without obliging to any further matter, or for any longer or more absolute continuance than it as a covenant doth oblige; and therefore wherein, and upon what supposition soever, the obligation ceaseth as a covenant, that enforcement also ceaseth as an oath; so that if as a covenant it oblige not to his benefit upon supposal of his refusal or opposal, upon the same it enforceth nought to his benefit as an oath.

Having thus endeavoured to remonstrate the danger and evil of the way you are in, and cleared the way unto what we have to propose, we shall with the same plainness and faithfulness give you our apprehensions of the remedies. . . . First, we conceive and hope that from what hath before been said, you may find abundant cause to forbear any further proceeding in this evil and most dangerous treaty, and to return to your former grounds in the votes of non-addresses, and thereupon proceed to the settling and securing of the kingdom without, and against, the King, upon such foundations as hereafter are tendered; but if, notwithstanding all the evils and dangers remonstrated to lie even in the treaty itself, you will yet proceed in such an evil way, we shall at least desire that you make sure to avoid that main venom and mischief attending it, *viz*., the King's restitution with impunity, *&c*., and that imperfect bargaining for partial justice against inferior offenders. * * *

[The *Remonstrance* proceeds to demand 'exemplary justice . . . in capital punishment upon the principal author and some prime instruments of our late wars, and thereby the blood thereof expiated, and others deterred from future attempts of the like in either capacity'; then to propound the terms on which the Prince and Duke of York may be admitted to offices of government, and other delinquents admitted to composition, *&c*., and finally to suggest the disposal of the royal revenues 'for a good number of years while the desolation and spoils of the poor people . . . may be in good measure repaired or recovered,' and, as a first charge, 'the satisfaction of arrears to the soldiery,' and reparation of losses especially of those who voluntarily engaged for, and have constantly adhered to, the common cause.']

Now . . . we proceed in order to the general satisfaction and settling of the kingdom as followeth:

I. That you [1] would set some reasonable and certain period to your own power, by which time that great and supreme trust reposed in you shall be returned into the hands of the people, from and for whom you received it; that so you may give them satisfaction and assurance that what you have contended for against the King (for which they have been put to so much trouble, cost, and loss of blood) hath been only for their liberties and common interest, and not for your own personal interest or power.

II. That (with a period to this Parliament, to be assigned as short as may be with safety to the kingdom and public interest thereof) there may be a sound settlement of the peace and future government of the kingdom, upon grounds of common right, freedom, and safety, to the effect here following:

III. That from the end of this, there may be a certain succession of future Parliaments (annual or biennial) with secure provision:

1. For the certainty of their meeting, sitting, and ending.

2. For the equal distribution of elections thereunto, to render the House of Commons, as near as may be, an equal Representative of the whole people electing.

[1] It will be remembered that the *Remonstrance* is addressed to the House of Commons.

3. For the certainty of the people's meeting (according to such distributions) to elect, and for their full freedom in elections: provided that none who have engaged, or shall engage, in war against the right of Parliament, and interest of the kingdom therein, or have adhered to the enemies thereof, may be capable of electing or being elected at least during a competent number of years; nor any other who shall oppose, or not join in agreement to, this settlement.

4. For future clearing and ascertaining the power of the said Representatives: in order to which, that it be declared that (as to the whole interest of the people of England) such Representatives have, and shall have the supreme power and trust as to the making of laws, constitutions and offices, for the ordering, preservation, and government of the whole, and as to the altering and repealing or abolishing of the same, [as to] the making of war or peace, and as to the highest and final judgment in all civil things, without further appeal to any created standing power; and that all the people of this nation, and all officers of justice and ministers of state, as such, shall in all such things be accountable and subject thereunto, and bound and concluded thereby, provided that:

(i) They may not censure or question any man, after the end of this Parliament, for anything said or done in reference to the late wars or public differences, saving in execution of such determinations of this Parliament as shall be left in force at the ending thereof, in relation to such as have served the king against the Parliament.

(ii) They may not render up, or give or take away, any the foundations of common right, liberty or safety contained in this settlement and·agreement. But that the power of these two things (last mentioned) shall be always understood to be reserved from, and not entrusted to, the said Representatives.

[5.] For liberty of entering dissents in the said Representatives: that, in case of corruption or abuse in these matters of highest trust, the people may be in capacity to know who are free thereof, and who guilty, to the end only they may avoid the further trusting of such, but without further penalty to any for their free judgments there.

[6.] That no King be hereafter admitted but upon the election of, and as upon trust from, the people by such their Representatives, nor without first disclaiming and disavowing all pretence to a negative voice against the determinations of the said Representatives, or Commons in Parliament; and that to be done in some certain form, more clear than heretofore in the coronation oath.

These matters of general settlement (viz., that concerning a period to this Parliament, and the other particulars thence following hitherto), we propound to be declared and provided by this Parliament, or by the authority of the Commons therein, and to be further established by a general contract or agreement of the people, with their subscriptions thereunto, and that withal it may be provided, that none may be capable of any benefit by the agreement, who shall not consent and subscribe thereunto; nor any King be admitted to the crown, or other person to any office or place of public trust, without express accord and subscription to the same. * * *

We shall therefore earnestly desire that these things may be minded and prosecuted effectually, and that nothing may interrupt them, save what shall be for immediate and necessary safety. And that (to avoid interruptions from such things as are not necessary, or less proper for parliamentary consideration or debates) you would leave all private matters and things of ordinary justice and right to the laws and present proper officers and administrations thereof until better can be provided, and commit all ordinary matters of state to the manage of a fit Council of State (sufficiently empowered for that purpose, and assisted with the addition of some merchants in relation to the balancing, security, and advance of trade), so as you may be the more free for the present to attend ᵃ those aforesaid considerations of public justice, and the settlement of the kingdom upon just and safe foundations of public interest, and that, when you have effectuated them or put them into a way of effect, you may (for the after-time of this Parliament's continuance) more entirely apply your counsels to such other things as are the most proper work of Parliaments, and by and for which Parliaments have had their esteem in this nation, and the kingdom most benefit by them, *viz.*: the reformation of evils or inconveniences in the present laws and administrations thereof, the redress of abuses, and supplying of defects therein, and the making of better constitutions for the well-government and prosperity of the nation, as also the due proportioning of rates, and providing of money in the most equal and least grievous ways for all necessary uses of the public, and the like. And, in order to such things, that you would in due time and place (*viz.*, after public justice, and the general settlement) consider such special overtures of that kind as have been tendered to you in the petitions of well-wishers to public good, and particularly in that Large Petition from many about London, dated the eleventh of September last, and also what shall be tendered of like kind from others, that so what is really for the remedy of common grievances, or the advancement of common good, may not be slighted or neglected, but that evils in that kind being removed, and good things ordained and provided by you for the ease, benefit, and prosperity of the people in all things possible, you may (when you come to lay down your trust) leave a good savour behind you, both to the name of Parliaments and also of men professing godliness so much as this House hath done, and therein chiefly to the honour of Almighty God, who hath in his rich grace and mercy done such wonders for you and us. And for furtherance to all these ends (since the heart of man is deceitful, and corrupt above all things, and most apt to answerable counsels and actings where it can hope to walk in the dark, undiscerned or undistinguished, though but to the eye of man), we must again desire that even from henceforth the aforesaid liberty of entering dissents, as it is in the Scotch Parliament (where lately there hath appeared a most useful effect of it), so also may be admitted amongst you, or at least that in these transactions of such high moment to the public and all honest interests, and in times so apt to deceit, defection, and apostasy, that liberty may be taken by all honest faithful members that desire to appear, as their hearts to God, so their ways to good men. Yet still we wish not, whoever should by that means be detected for corrupt counsels, that for his judgment there, any advantage should be taken withoutdoors, but only that men may avoid the further trusting of such persons, and that the innocent may not be unjustly prejudiced or suspected. * * *

And now to conclude, we hope that, in an age of so much light, mere will or resolution will not be held forth or pursued against it; but that what reason or righteousness there is in the things we have said, will be considered and followed. Nor let it find prejudice with you from any disdain towards those from whom it comes, being in the condition of an army, looked upon as servants under you, since servants may speak to their masters, and ought to be heard and regarded even when they speak for their own right only, and rather when they speak for the good and safety of them they serve, but much more when they speak of that wherein they have some joint interest with them; and yet more when (those their immediate masters being themselves also servants and trustees for the benefit of others) they speak for the interest of those for whom both are employed.

24. History of the Second Agreement of the People: see pp. 342-55.

25. From the Declaration of the Army, on the March to London, 30th November 1648 [a]

And as the incompetency of this Parliament, in its present constitution, to give an absolute and conclusive judgment for the whole (especially to be the sole judges of their own performance or breach of trust) doth make the juster way for such an appeal, so indeed we see no other way left for remedy, in regard the present unlimited continuance of this Parliament doth exclude the orderly succession of any other more equal formal judicature of men, to which we might hope in due time other ways to appeal. Thus then we apprehend ourselves in the present case, both necessitated to, and justified in, an appeal from this Parliament, in the present constitution as it stands, unto the extraordinary judgment of God and good people. And yet in the prosecution of this appeal, as we shall drive it on but to the speedy obtaining of a more orderly and equal judicature of men in a just Representative, according to our *Remonstrance*, . . . so in the present procuring of justice, with the people's ease and quiet, and in the settling of the kingdom upon a due, safe, and hopeful succession of Parliaments, it is our heart's desire, and shall be our endeavour, that so much both of the matter and form of the present parliamentary authority may be preserved, as can be safe, or will be useful to these ends, until a just and full constitution thereof, both for matter and form (suitable to the public ends it serves for) can be introduced.

And therefore, first, it should be our great rejoicing (if God saw it good), that the majority of the present House of Commons were become sensible of the evil and destructiveness of their late way, and would resolvedly and vigorously apply themselves to the speedy execution of justice, with the righting and easing of the oppressed people, and to a just and safe settlement of the kingdom upon such foundations as have been propounded by us and others for that purpose, and would, for the speedier and surer prosecution of these things, exclude from communication in their counsels all such corrupt and apostatized members as have appeared hitherto but to obstruct and hinder such matter of justice, safety, and public interest, and to pervert their counsels a contrary way, and have therein so shamefully both falsified and forfeited their trust.

But however, if God shall not see it good to vouchsafe that mercy to them and the kingdom, we shall, secondly, desire that so many of them as God hath kept upright, and shall touch with a just sense of those things, would by protestation or otherwise acquit themselves from such breach of trust, and approve their faithfulness by withdrawing from those that persist in the guilt thereof, and would apply themselves to such a posture whereby they may speedily and effectually prosecute those necessary and public ends. . . . And for so many of them, whose hearts God shall stir up thus to do, we shall therein, in this case of extremity, look upon them as persons having materially the chief trust of the kingdom remaining in them, and though not a formal standing power to be continued in them, or drawn into ordinary precedents, yet the best and most rightful that can be had as the present state and exigence of affairs now stand. And we shall, accordingly, own them, adhere to them, and be guided by them in their faithful prosecution of that trust, in order unto, and until, the introducing of a more full and formal power in a just Representative to be speed[il]y endeavoured.

Now yet further to take away all jealousies in relation to ourselves, which might withhold or [a] discourage any honest members from this course: [b] as we have the witness of God in our hearts that in these proceedings we do not seek, but even resolve we will not take, advantages to ourselves either in point of profit or power, and that if God did open unto us a way wherein with honesty and faithfulness to the public interest and good people engaged for us, we might presently be discharged, so as we might not in our present employments look on, and be accessory to, yea, supporters of, the Parliament, in the present corrupt, oppressive, and destructive proceedings, we should with rejoicing, and without more ado, embrace such a discharge rather than interpose in these things to our own vast trouble and hazard. So, if we could but obtain a rational assurance for the effectual prosecution of these things, we shall give any proportionable assurance on our parts concerning our laying down of arms, when, and as, we should be required. But for the present, as the case stands, we apprehend ourselves obliged in duty to God, this kingdom, and good men therein, to improve our utmost abilities in all honest ways for the avoiding of these great evils we have remonstrated, and for prosecution of the good things we have propounded; and also that such persons who were the inviters of the late invasion from Scotland, the instigators and encouragers of the late insurrections within this kingdom, and (those forcible ways failing) have still pursued the same wicked designs by treacherous and corrupt counsels, may be brought to public justice, according to their several demerits. For all these ends we are now drawing up with the Army to London, there to follow Providence as God shall clear our way.

26. TEXT OF THE SECOND AGREEMENT OF THE PEOPLE: see pp. 355–67.

27. SUMMARY OF THE DEBATES ON THE AGREEMENT, IN THE COUNCIL OF OFFICERS, 16TH DECEMBER–6TH JANUARY; AND OF THE EXAMINATION OF ELIZABETH POOLE ON 29TH DECEMBER AND 5TH JANUARY.[a]

December 16: Agreement VII 2 (p. 362). *Question:* 'Whether we shall present in this Agreement any reserve from the power of the Representative in point of impressing men for the war?' (Resolved in affirmative.) *Question:* 'Whether there shall be a reserve from the Representative to impress for foreign service?' (Resolved in affirmative; Hewson and Scoutmaster Roe dissenting.) Clause phrased as in Agreement presented to Parliament (VIII 2: p. 362, n. 29), but without the words: 'and may take order for the employing and conducting of them for those ends.'[1]

December 18: Agreement VII 3–6 (pp. 362–3). Third[2] Reserve was passed as in Agreement presented to Parliament (VIII 3: p. 362, n. 30). Fourth Reserve was 'laid aside.' Fifth was 'suspended as not proper to the place.' *Question:* 'Whether the Sixth Reserve (p. 363) shall be waived or not?' (Resolved in negative, 18 : 16.)[3]

December 21: Agreement VII; VII 1. 'An expedient upon the

[1] Added to the Committee on the First Reserve (in religion): Dr. Pagett, Dr. Cox, Dr. Goddard, Major Carter, Capt. Hodden.
[2] Numbering of reserves is according to the Agreement, Article VII, as printed in Lilburne's *Foundations of Freedom* (above, pp. 361–3).
[3] Added to Committee on Religion: Col. Hewson, Major Barton, Col. Okey. 'Memorandum: at the meeting to-morrow, to consider of some moderate men to meet in London at Colonel Tichborne's.' (Reference is perhaps to moderate Presbyterians to be taken into the discussion.) On 19th December, Major Coleman, Capt. Spencer, Mr. Cooly, added to Committee.

First Reserve, concerning Religion, brought in and debated.'[1] *Question:* 'Whether the particulars now debated shall be referred or no?' (Resolved in negative.) 'All but officers to go forth.' *Question:* 'Whether the word *moral* shall be in the paper now read or no?' (Resolved in negative, 27 : 17.) [2] Phrased practically as in Agreement presented to Parliament, VIII (p. 361, n. 25), but lacks emphatic phrase, 'but not concerning things spiritual and evangelical,' and the six particulars reserved in 'things natural and civil.' *Question:* 'Whether under this general article of the power of your Representatives now agreed on, there shall be any reserve subjoined concerning religion?' (Resolved in negative, 37 : 12; it is later transferred to separate article, IX.)

December 26: Agreement VII 6 (p. 363): 'The Sixth Reserve . . . read and debated. Afterwards read thus (as an expedient): That the said Representatives may not exercise the power of immediate judgment in particular questions of right and wrong between one person and another. Nor may they give immediate judgment upon any man's person or estate for any offence which does not extend immediately to the hurt or damage of the public. Nor for any such offence may they proceed to the taking away of life or limb, unless before the fact done it were so provided against by express law then in force. Nor may they inflict or award other punishment for such an offence not so provided against beforehand, save where it is clearly against the general law of human society and where the vindication or securing of the public interest does require such justice.' *First Question:* 'Whether the Sixth Reserve shall pass as it now stands or no?' (Unanimously resolved in negative.) Last part of VII 6 read (p. 363): 'That the Representative may not give judgment upon any man's person or estate where no law hath been before provided, save only in calling to account and punishing public officers failing in their trust.' *Second Question:* 'Whether this clause now read shall be put to the question as part of the reserve or no?' (Resolved in affirmative, 22 : 15.) *Third Question:* 'Whether this clause now read shall pass as of the reserve as it is?' (Resolved in affirmative, 25 : 13.)

December 29: Agreement VII 5, 7, 8; VIII, IX, VII 5 (pp. 362-3).

[1] Firth quotes from *Perfect Diurnal*, 22nd December: 'The General Council of the Army have had many large debates this week upon that reserve in the Representative in matters of religion; some Presbyterian ministers have been discoursed withal, and at last an expedient is agreed upon, which will give satisfaction. Much debate also upon the power of the Representative in civils, as how they might proceed to punish, not being directed by a known law.'

[2] In view of what follows, the question appears to be whether there should be granted to the Representative 'the highest and final judgment concerning all natural, civil, *and moral* things.' The connection with religion is in the contention that it falls within the scope of the moral law. The addition is opposed by that principle which later adds the specific phrase reserving 'things spiritual and evangelical.'

The Seventh Reserve read and passed unanimously (becoming VII). The Eighth Reserve read and passed unanimously (becoming VIII 6, and later receiving as an addition the provision for entering dissents, p. 363, n. 36). The Eighth Article read and altered practically to the form in Agreement as presented to Parliament, VI. The Ninth Article read and altered practically to the form in VIII 3. The Tenth Article read and altered to the form in first part of X (p. 363, nn. 42-3). The Fifth Reserve (formerly waived) read. *Question:* 'Whether this shall pass as a reserve or no?' (Resolved in the negative.) The [preamble?] of the Agreement read. Committee of ten officers named, including Ireton, Harrison, Rich, and Waller, 'to consider of a form of conclusion and subscription to this Agreement as to the officers of the Army.'

In strange contrast with these debates on the constitution are two fully recorded examinations of Elizabeth Poole, on 29th December and 5th January. These are also reported in: *A Vision wherein is Manifested the Disease and Cure of the Kingdom, being the sum of what was delivered to the General Council of the Army, Decemb. 29, 1648. Together with a true copy of what was delivered in writing (the fifth of the present January) to the said General Council, of divine pleasure concerning the King, in reference to his being brought to trial, what they are therein to do and what not, both concerning his office and person. By E. Poole, herein a servant to the Most High God.*

The vision [1] was of a 'woman . . . full of imperfection, crooked, weak, sickly, imperfect,' and a man, 'a member of the Army,' devoted to 'his country, to its liberty and freedom, which he should gladly be a sacrifice for.' The man (the Army) was to effect the recovery of the woman (the kingdom): ' . . . he should, before the Lord, act diligently and faithfully to employ all means which I should by the gift of God [in me] direct for her cure.' All depended on 'that Spirit of Eternal Power which had called me to believe and him to act; neither was he to be slack in action, nor I to be staggered in believing.' God had manifested his presence with the Army, and they must 'go forward and stand up for the liberty of the people as it was their liberty and God had opened the way to them.' But they must deny themselves; for ' . . . perfectly dying in the will of the Lord, you may find your resurrection in him.' [2] *Rich* highly approved this doctrine: 'I cannot but give you that impression that is upon my spirit in conjunction with that testimony which God hath manifested here by an unexpected providence. * * * The truth is: . . . [there are] many things in which we are to take a liberty, and use the liberty in reference to the men of the world that we have to deal withal; but that principle which is to carry us, as in consideration of ourselves, before God and the world, [is] after that liberty which the world doth not understand. It

---

[1] I have tried to restore the correct order of the argument by reference to the pamphlet.

[2] This quotation is from the pamphlet.

is true, we may use these arguments to satisfy such as understand no more but such [things] as the world gives testimony of; but if we have not another manner of testimony, [of] such things that God hath by his providence given us satisfaction of, I believe, as she says, the conclusion of it will be but fleshly after having begun in the spirit.   I think every man is to search his own heart, and to see what is within, and not [to look for deliverance] from himself or from men from outward means, but from that kingdom which, when it comes, will have no end.' *Mrs. Poole* declared: 'It is true, that the Lord hath a controversy with the great and mighty of the earth, with the captains and rulers.   He will contend for his own name amongst them.' *Harrison* was eager to know what prescription she had by the gift of God, to offer for the Army's cure of the kingdom: 'Whether anything was given to you more particularly to express than before?' She replied: 'No, sir. For it was presented to me as the Church; . . . by the gift and faith of the Church you shall be guided, which spirit is in you, which shall direct you.' *Ireton* could 'see nothing in her but those [things] that are the fruits of the Spirit of God . . . because it comes with such a spirit that does . . . hold forth humility and self-denial. . . .'

On January 5, *Elizabeth Poole* said: 'I have heard [that] some of you [are busied] upon that which is called the Agreement of the People. 'Tis very evident to me that the kingly power is fallen into your hands and you are entrusted with it that you might be as the head to the body.   Now . . . if you shall take that up as an Agreement of the People . . . , it seems to me . . . that you shall give power out of your hands, whereas God hath entrusted it with you and will require it of you, how it is improved. * * * Betray not you your trust.'   She then delivered a paper against the King's execution. *Ireton* asked: 'What would you hold forth to us as the demonstration . . . that this that you have delivered to us to be read is from God, from him given in to you, and from you to be delivered to us?' She replied that the paper would 'bear witness for itself,' and added: ' . . . Kings are set in [their places] for government, though I do not speak this to favour the tyranny or bloodthirstiness of any.   For I do look upon the [Norman] Conquest to be of divine pleasure [whereby kings came to reign],[1] though . . . God is not the supporter of tyranny or injustice; those are things [that] he desires may be kept under.'   *Rich* asked: ' . . . whether that which is the will of God is not [always] concordant with natural reason; . . . whether it be the will of God that anything in point of government should be inconsistent with the most essential being for which it was ordained?   Now, if . . . any outward thing, and [any] state and power and trust [may be forfeited if it is abused, I would know] if it be not the will or the mind of God that if any man, empowered or entrusted for the public good, for the government's sake, should be tyrannous to the governed (for the well-being of which he was set in the chair)—then whether for the highest breach of [that]

[1] This phrase is from the pamphlet.

trust there cannot be such an outward forfeiture of life . . . as [there is] of the trust itself?' Lt.-Col. *Kelsey* pointed out that 'God doth not send a messenger but that there may be an impression upon their hearts [that are] to receive it.' Such a communication as Mrs. Poole's 'either . . . must be from God . . . or else there must be something of argument and reason to demonstrate it to us. Now there is nothing of reason in it. And if it be from God the Council would be glad to hear what outgoings there are in that particular.' The meeting evidently disapproved of Mrs. Poole's declaration against the punishment of Charles by death, and was sceptical of its divine origin.

January 6 : '*Debate concerning the setting a period to this Parliament by the last of April*' (*Agreement I*, p. 356). *Ireton* argues that the dissolution of the present Parliament by the Agreement 'will be a greater security in case the Army should be forced to remove, when the ill-affected party may [otherwise] come in again. It will give much satisfaction to the people in regard of their expressing their desires [for the Army] not to set up themselves, but [rather] their resolves for a future Representative.' *Cromwell* thinks that 'it will be more honourable and convenient for them to put a period to themselves.' *Ireton* replies: 'If the Parliament should vote a day for their dissolution *without the Agreement*, all the endeavours [imaginable] will be used for Parliaments to come in [in] the old way. But if men find there is no avoidance of this Parliament but by this Agreement, there is nothing so much likely to keep men's hands off from opposing the Agreement. * * * The people may [be taught to] think [that] if they oppose this Agreement they oppose the ending of this Parliament.' *Cromwell* asks: 'Then you are afraid they will do [that]?' *Ireton* answers: 'If the generality of [the] people could see the end of this Parliament [in any other way, they] would be for opposing anything of this kind—or would wait for the expiring of that [time], to look for a succession of new Parliaments in the old way and [the] old form of a King [and Parliament] again. Nothing [could be] of more [real] advantage to this Parliament than to end it by the Agreement with safety [to its members and] without prejudice to future Parliaments.' It was possibly at this debate [1] that *Cowling* opposed the effort to return to a constitutional mode of government, and especially an Agreement which surrendered the Army's power: 'I have heard mention, since I came, of two men, Joseph and Moses. The one was a greater provider for the well-being of the people, and the other did as much in delivering the people when they were not well [used]. I desire that, as Moses, you will not be so full of punctilios as to look upon the old constitution. . . . [The Jews observed the customs of Egypt] and the best they brought forth was a [golden] calf. Now this I should offer to you: Take heed how you stick unto that constitution without [leaving] which you are not able to form a way by which every man may enjoy his own.'

---

[1] The speech is reported under 5th January, where it appears to have no place.

28. The Levellers' Dissatisfaction with the Debates

From John Lilburne, *A Plea for Common Right and Freedom*
(28th Dec. 1648) [a]

And we were very much satisfied that your last *Remonstrance* terminated in proposing an Agreement of the People as the only proper means for quieting the long and woeful distractions of the nation, and the matter of our foresaid Petition of the eleventh of Sept[ember] as requisite to be seriously considered; both which intimated a nearer compliance with our desires than we had formerly found. But much more satisfactory it was, that you allowed us to choose out certain friends from amongst us, to be joined with you in the drawing up of an Agreement for the people, to be offered unto them for their union therein. And which (though with great expense of time and much contest) was at length effected, so that our hopes revived and our confidence was great that the work would then go on currently amongst you without stop or interruption.

But since the same hath been tendered to the consideration of your Council, the long time spent already therein and the tedious disputes and contests held thereupon, and that in things so essential unto our freedom, as without which we account the Agreement of no value! For what freedom is there to conscientious people where the magistrate shall be entrusted with a restrictive power in matters of religion, or to judge and punish in cases where no law hath been before provided? Which are the points that as yet remain in suspense, and about which most of the time hath been spent, though they are such as wherein all the cordial friends of this Army are fully satisfied, as clearly appeareth by their adhering to our foresaid Petition of the eleventh of Septemb[er]. And when we consider how many in this Council have appeared in behalf of these unreasonable powers in the magistrate; how they have been countenanced that have spoken for them, and how discountenanced that have spoken against them, and that at length; [how] interests directly opposite to freedom of conscience in point of God's worship are nevertheless called for, to receive satisfaction, whose principles and Covenant lead to no less than persecution in matters of that nature, and which (upon the least hope of power) they have eagerly practised, as in Col[onel] Leigh's committee; and since at present reproaches of Leveller, Jesuit, and the like begin afresh to be as rife as ever, which usually have forerun the destruction of good endeavours, we profess these are such manifest effects of evil influences and do so evidently demonstrate that both you and we are almost overgrown with destructive interests, and administer so much occasion to doubt the Agreement pretended is not really, or not effectually, intended in that fulness of right, freedom, and redress of grievances as all true-hearted friends expected, that we deem it afresh, worthy [of] all our fears, and of your more than ordinary intention to discover from whence those evil and dangerous effects do proceed, lest before you are aware (as it befell the well-minded members in Parliament) you be entangled in such perplexities that, when you would, it shall not be in your power to help yourselves, or to free this commonwealth from misery and bondage.

All which . . . we judged ourselves bound in conscience thus timely to advertise you of, and do most earnestly entreat that . . . , to prevent your and our being overgrown with destructive interests . . ., you will employ all your might to the speedy production of so full and ample [an] Agreement for the people as (to the restoring all true freedom and for removing of all known grievances) may deserve the stamp of so successful an Army. ✳ ✳ ✳

That to these just and necessary ends you will instantly reduce your Council into a certain method of orderly proceeding, which will much conduce to the furthering and clearing of your debates and resolutions, wherein we are now exceedingly concerned.

As first, to agree what certain number of officers, and no less, shall make a Council, which, we humbly conceive, ought not to be less than the major part of the commission[ed] officers, at the Headquarters and adjacent thereunto, not excluding of others.

2. That all persons in council may sit in a distinct orderly way, so as they may be observed by the president when they are inclined to speak.

3. That you will agree how many times any person may speak to a question.

4. That you will free your determinations from all pretences of a negative voice, and from all discountenance and check by any superior officer.

And [this] being so regulated:

1. That you will consider and resolve what is the most proper way for advance of officers, so as to preserve them entire to the interest of the people, and from a servile condition or necessary dependence upon the favour or will of any; and seriously to consider whether your Articles of Martial Law (as now they are) are not of too tyrannous a nature for an army of free-born Englishmen; and to reduce the same to reason and an equal constitution.

2. To take special care of the principles of any officer to be admitted, that they be not tainted with those of arbitrary power or of persecution for matters of religion.

3. That there be no disbanding of any sort of men but by consent of the General Council, nor admission or listing of any for horse or foot but according to provision made by the said Council, it being reported that very many of late are listed, of bad and doubtful condition.

By all which means, if consciably observed (and we trust you will not be the less sensible because we advise), the growth of any corrupt interest will be effectually prevented. And if it shall seem good or anyway useful unto you, we shall choose and appoint four of our friends always to attend and assist, though not to vote with you. Nor will these things or these desires of ours seem strange unto you if you shall consider at how high a rate we have all along valued our just liberties, and how by breaking all authority you have taken upon yourselves the care, protection, and restoration thereof. You will not only cease to wonder, but resolve that we have cause to mind you thereof and of whatsoever we observe may be prejudicial thereunto, being well assured that it highly concerns you in the condition you have put yourselves not to be strait or narrow-hearted to your friends in point of liberty, or removal of known grievances, but to be as large in both as the utmost reason of these knowing times can plead for or desire. And as less than that is not expected from you in the Agreement you have in hand, so, if less in a tittle, it will not be regarded, but very much undervalue your affection to the commonwealth, as being that without which your extraordinary proceedings in overturning all the visible supreme authority of the nation, can never be justified before God or man. * * * [1]

F. RETROSPECT

29. FROM A DECLARATION OF THE ENGLISH ARMY NOW IN SCOTLAND,[2] 1ST AUG. 1650 [a]

At the beginning of the great and wonderful workings of God in these two nations of England and Scotland, we, the under-officers and soldiers of the English Army now in Scotland, were most of us (if not all) men of private callings, and not at all interested in matters of public and state affairs; but yet very many of us, in whom the Lord had begun to reveal himself in the face of Jesus Christ, were sensible of the Antichristian tyranny that was exercised by the late King and his prelates, over the consciences, bodies, and estates of the true spiritual Church of Jesus Christ; namely, those that were born again, and united to him by his Spirit, who were then by that Antichristian crew termed Puritans, sectaries, schismatics, &c., and for not conforming to all the canons and ordinances of their national church, were frequently imprisoned, banished, and otherwise grievously molested at the pleasure of those that then ruled amongst us. Under these sad sufferings of the people of God our souls mourned, and understanding by the manifold gracious promises in the word of God, that a time of deliverance was to be expected to the Church of Christ, and destruction and ruin to Babylon, our hearts, together with all the truly godly in England, were exceedingly stirred up to pray to the Lord, even day and night,

---

[1] Signed by Lilburne, Overton, Prince, and thirteen others.

[2] The *Declaration*, dated 'From the leaguer at Muscleborough, August 1, 1650,' is in answer to a paper directed by the Scots 'To the Under-officers and Soldiers of the English Army.'

that he would arise to destroy Antichrist, and to save his people. Whilst this spirit of prayer was poured forth upon God's people in England, attempts are made upon Scotland to bring them to a conformity in religious worship, by endeavouring to impose upon them a popish service-book, which was, through the great goodness of God, by his people in Scotland, resisted [a]; which made the wrath of the late King and his prelates wax so hot against them, so as Scotland had no other way to preserve itself but by coming into England with an army. Which the godly in England did not then count an invasion to destroy England—no more than they do this our present march, for the ruin of Scotland—but rejoiced to see some appearing against that Antichristian power that had persecuted the Saints, and were assured that the Lord was come forth to answer the many prayers and tears that were then poured and pouring forth for that purpose. And therefore so far as we had [b] any opportunity [we] farthered the designs of that army, some of us hazarding our lives by spreading their book, entitled *The Scots' Intentions*, and pleading for the justness of their proceedings.

Let us remember how the Lord was pleased graciously to answer the prayers of his people at that time, in their deliverance from the army, raised by the late King and his prelates for the destruction of all the people of God in England and Scotland; insomuch that soon after Scotland sits in peace, enjoying their former liberties without being imposed upon by the Antichristian prelacy in England. And England obtains a Parliament to whom they have opportunity to complain of their grievances, and through the great goodness of God so constituted that grievances are heard, and overtures made to the late King for their redress. Which was so irksome to his oppressing, tyrannical, and bloody spirit, that he again betook himself to overthrow the Parliament by force, and to that end entertains the officers of the army that had gone forth against our brethren of Scotland. And [he] withdrawing himself from his Parliament, an appearance of a civil war begins. Which being made known to us, the inferior officers and soldiers of this Army (then in our private callings), we found our hearts extraordinarily stirred up by the Lord, to assist the Parliament against the King, being abundantly satisfied in our judgments and consciences that we were called forth by the Lord to be instrumental to bring about that which was our continual prayer to God, *viz.*, the destruction of Antichrist and the deliverance of his Church and people. And upon this simple account we engaged, not knowing the deep policies of worldly statesmen, and have ever since hazarded our lives in the high places of the field (where we have seen the wonders of the Lord) against all the opposers of this work of Jesus Christ, whom we have all along seen going with us, and making our way plain before us. And having these things singly in our eye, namely, the destruction of Antichrist, the advancement of the kingdom of Jesus Christ, the deliverance and reformation of his Church, in the establishment of his ordinances amongst them in purity according to his word, and the just civil liberties of Englishmen; we did many of us rejoice at the Covenant, because we found in it a strain towards these ends, although some, being more enlightened, did apprehend it to be so mixed with worldly interest that they justly feared the interest of Jesus Christ would be only pretended to, and the interests of this world, yea, of Antichrist himself, carried under a vizard, as we have since had abundant experience of. Which hath made us, we confess, not to idolize the Covenant (as we fear too many do), though we trust it will appear before God, angels, and men that we shall ever pursue its true and lawful ends, according to the plain and candid meaning thereof; though we do not upon every occasion urge the Covenant (as we see every party, though as far different as light and darkness, apt to do), the Lord having by his word and by his Spirit convinced us of our duty therein, though there had been no such Covenant at all entered into.

But when we saw that under pretence of the Covenant, a corrupt party in Parliament by their worldly policy, after the war was ended in England, and the late King's party subdued with the loss of thousands of the lives of Saints (whose death is precious in the sight of the Lord), did endeavour to set up the King upon his own terms, and with him to establish a national church-government, not in all things agreeable to the word of God, but [such as] is destructive to the just liberties of the true spiritual Church of Christ, which he hath by his own most precious blood purchased for them, and is now come forth to bestow upon them —which did sufficiently demonstrate itself by the dealings of the then master-builders with the churches of Jesus Christ in and about London, that were then threatened to be dissolved, and laws made to prevent the communion of Saints with one another, except only in that one public form then about to be established, to the astonishment of many of us that had lifted up our hands to God and sworn to endeavour a reformation according to the word of God; and therefore after much waiting upon God by prayer, and examining our own hearts about the ends and sincerity thereof, we were abundantly satisfied that it was not only lawful but our duty, to keep our arms in our hands till the ends before mentioned should be accomplished. And to that purpose the Army, whereof we are a part, did refuse to disband, did march up to London to propose to the Parliament a way of establishment that might be more for the carrying on of the ends of religion and liberty, though therein we were not at that time successful, yet most wonderfully and graciously preserved by the Lord, and extraordinarily convinced, after much seeking the face of God, that our failing was in endeavouring to set up the King upon any terms, he being a man of so much blood that the Lord would have no peace with him, nor any that should go about to establish him. Whereupon—after his own hard heart had hindered him from yielding to any overtures that were made to him by the Parliament (through whom all the Army's proposals were to be tendered), and a second war, more dangerous than the former, contrived by him and his son (now with you), together with those in Scotland that hated us of the Army of England under the name of sectaries, being, by the unspeakable goodness and mighty power of God, waded through, and a second testimony given from heaven to justify the proceedings of his poor servants against that bloody Antichristian brood, though with the loss of many precious Saints—we were then powerfully convinced that the Lord's purpose was to deal with the late King as a man of blood. And being persuaded in our consciences that he and his monarchy was one of the ten horns of the Beast (spoken of, Rev. 17. 12–15), and being witnesses to so much of the innocent blood of the Saints that he had shed in supporting the Beast, and considering the loud cries of the souls of the Saints under the altar, we were extraordinarily carried forth to desire justice upon the King, that man of blood, and to that purpose petitioned our superior officers and the Parliament, to bring him to justice. Which accordingly by an high hand of Providence was brought to pass, which act we are confident the Lord will own in preserving the Commonwealth of England against all kingdoms and nations that shall adventure to meddle with them upon that account. When God executes his judgments upon malefactors, let none go about to resist. When he brings forth those his enemies that will not suffer Jesus Christ to be King in the midst of his Saints, and breaks them in pieces like a potter's vessel, let not Scotland nor any other nation say, 'What dost thou?' We fear they have been too busy already. The Lord that sees the secrets of all hearts, knows the compliance of Scotland with the late King's issue (now with you) was in order to disturb the peace of England, for being God's executioners upon a bloody tyrant and a supporter of the throne of the Beast. But blessed be the Lord, the crafty are taken in their own snare; England sits in peace, whilst Scotland receives into their chief city their new King at the very hour wherein an Army that had marched three hundred miles is facing them at the very gates. We wish our brethren of Scotland, especially those that truly fear the Lord, would consider these things, and not slight the providences of God so much as they do. When Scotland chose new gods, and would have a king out of a family that God had rejected, then was war in the gates. And though we do not think providences alone a sufficient rule for God's people to walk by, yet we do know that the Lord speaks to his people by his providence, as well as by his word; and he is angry with his people that do not take notice thereof, and promiseth blessing to those that do (Psalm 107 and the latter end).

And here give us leave (not in a boasting spirit, but in meekness and fear) to tell you that we are persuaded we are poor unworthy instruments in God's hand, to break his enemies and preserve his people. * * * We value the churches of Jesus Christ, who are the lot of God's inheritance, ten thousand times above our own lives; yea, we do bless the Lord we are not only a rod of iron to dash the common enemies in pieces, but also a hedge (though very unworthy) about Christ's vineyard. * * * We desire it may be known to you, our brethren of Scotland, that we are not soldiers of fortune, we are not merely the servants of men; we have not only proclaimed Jesus Christ, the King of Saints, to be our King by profession, but desire to submit to him upon his own terms, and to admit him to the exercise of his royal authority in our hearts, and to follow him whithersoever he goeth, he having of his own good will entered into a Covenant of Grace with his poor Saints. And be assured, it is he that leadeth us into Scotland, as he hath done in England and Ireland. And therefore we do in the spirit of brotherly love, and of the fear of the Lord, beseech you to look about you, for our Lord Jesus is coming amongst you as a refiner's fire, and as fuller's soap; and blessed are those in whom the least dram of sincerity shall be found. * * *

Our quarrel is still against malignants, the root whereof is now, through the evil policy of some statesmen, become the head of Scotland. We dare not quarrel with those whose hearts are upright with Jesus Christ, and faithful and loving to England, but with those who are most treacherous and false to both; and therefore we dare not any of us, though tempted thereto by your Papers, be so carnally wise as to desert the cause and work of Jesus Christ, in which we have hitherto been so long and so miraculously carried on. Do you think we are men so weakly principled as to be persuaded, without the least strength of argument, to desert the interest of our own nation, and expose thousands of the precious Saints of Jesus Christ, to be trampled upon as the dirt in the streets, when the Lord is about to put on their beautiful garments, and to make them a praise in the earth? Or can we (think you) betray our superior officers, in whom we see so much of the sweet spirit of Jesus Christ, into your hands, whose mouths are opened wide to devour them? We pray you not to wait for such a thing. The Lord hath brought us hither by his providence, and upon him we shall with confidence depend till we see a glorious issue; which we humbly and heartily desire may be without the effusion of any more blood and (if it be the will of God) both speedy and comfortable to you and us, that we may return with joy into England, and leave Scotland rejoicing that an English army hath been amongst them. Which possibly may be the sooner effected were you and we suffered to confer and open our hearts one to another. We do believe much of the bitterness of spirit would be allayed in our brethren of Scotland, did they know how exceedingly we are slandered by the pens and tongues of many of your kirkmen concerning our religion and faith towards God, which though we may not vainly boast of, yet according to the Apostle's direction, we are ready to give an answer to the meanest Christian in Scotland, that shall ask a reason of the faith and hope that is in us, with meekness and fear. * * *

NOTES ON TEXT

The text of both sets of Debates is derived from the sole primary source, the Clarke MSS., volume 67 (Worcester College, Oxford: 65. 5. 6), compared with that printed in *The Clarke Papers*, edited by C. H. Firth (Camden Society). Everything in square brackets has been added by the present editor (or adopted by him from Firth). Spelling, capitalization, and punctuation are modernized, but with some latitude in regard to punctuation where adherence to modern usage might have obscured the sense: the complicated and often loosely-built sentences have been punctuated with attention rather to the reader's requirements in the particular sentence than to strict rule and consistency. The designation of speakers has been reduced to brevity and uniformity; title (with Christian name) is given only at the first mention or when confusion might result from its suppression. For the rest, in this edition, unlike Firth's, every departure from the MS. is recorded in the notes.

In the notes all MS. readings are printed in italics. Two other signs are used: + indicates that what follows is an accidental addition in the MS., and has been omitted in the text; tr indicates transposition in the text *from after* the following phrase. Thus: (a) *butt* = MS. reads 'butt'; (b) + *butt* = MS. adds 'butt'; tr *butt the Kinge is nott* = transposed from after 'butt the Kinge is nott.' It must be observed, that in the commoner additions (such as *and, butt, that*) a single letter has been made to do duty for a page; and that, in order not to court error by disturbing the lettering on the page, the necessary corrections in proof have been effected at a few points by omitting redundant letters, and by introducing new letters out of their alphabetical order, while preserving the alphabetical order in the notes.

1. (a) *them.*   2. (a) *for*; (b) + *labour'd to*; (c) *hath*; (d) *bee*; (e) + *to*; (f) + *and.*   3. (a) *as*; (b–c) tr *Member of the House*; (d) + *and.* 4. (a) *Rainborow* (thus throughout); (b) *where*; (c) + *to*; (d) + *in relation to the Parliament.*   5. (a) + blank; (b) + *might come*; (c) + *and.* 6. (a) *as*; (b) + *for*; (c) + *cannott*; (d–e) *to come some of them to send*; (f) + *nott*; (g) + *itt*; (h) + *and*; (i) *desiring*; (j–k) *your expectations and my engement.*; (k) + *that*; (m) + *wee heere Men on purpose* (which gives emendation above: met on purpose); (n) + *any.*   7. (a) + *butt*; (b) + *them*; (c) + *and*; (d) + *they shall.*   8. (a) *that*; (b) + *and*; (c) *and*; (e–f) tr *consider the way*; (g) + *wee.*   9. (a) *which*; (a–b) tr *betweene you and us*; (c) + *appear to bee*; (d) This necessary emendation is supplied by Wildman's statement of 'the chief weight' of Cromwell's speech [p. 10]; (e) + *to the officers*; (f) *do*; (g) + *and.*

10. (a) + *to*; (b) *itt*; (c) *or.*   11. (a) *itt*; (b) + *for*; (c–d) *uppon their persons or uppon their ptie.*; (e) *finding*; (f) + *though*; (g) *hee*; (h) + *and*; (i) + *may*; (j) + *yett.*   12. (a) + *of them*; (b) + *though*; (c) + *made them and*; (d–e) *uppon the whole matter I speake this to inforce*; (f) *uppon*; (g) + *nott.*   13. (a) *and*; (b) + *how farre they*; (c) tr *speake somethinge*; (d) + *and*; (e) + *butt*; (f) + *att least.*   14. (a) + *that*; (b) + *and that*; (c) *hath*; (d) + *that they*; (e) *for.*   15. (a) *deceit*;

(b) + *butt.* 16. (a) tr *in all the world*; (b) *did*; (c–d) *a disputable Engagemt.*; (e) + *butt*; (f) + *that.* 17. (a) + *butt*; (b) + *and*; (c–18a) *manifesting.* 18. (b) *man*; (c–d) *senses*; (e) + *that* (f) + *and.* 19. (a) *Awdeley* (thus throughout); (b–c) tr *you have nott*; (d) + *or may bee*; (e) + *they*; (f) + *as they are*; (g) + *and*; (h) + *from us.*

20. (a) + *and*; (b) + *bee instruments*; (c) tr *That wee.* 21. (a) *that*; (b–c) tr *as well may meete together*; (d–e) tr *doing of itt these ten weekes*; (f) MS. gives this speech to *Lieut.Generall.* Firth adds it to Goffe's. Cromwell is clarifying (though perhaps also somewhat modifying) Goffe's motion, as Ireton recognizes when he speaks of the motion as Goffe's [p. 22]; (g) *through*; (h) + *is that*; (i) + *and.* 22. (a) *him*; (b) *God*; (c–d) tr *that doe soe*; (e) + *and*; (f) + *either*; (g) + *though*; (h) + *that.* 23. (a) *and*; (a–b) tr *withdraw from us*; (c) + *and.* 24. (a–b) tr *therefore itt was said*; (c–e) tr *that itt was said*; (d) *should*; (f) *if*; (g) + *mee*; (h) + *that*; (i) *and*; (j) + *yett.* 25. (a–b) tr *grievances are redrest*; (c) + *because that*; (d–e) *I think if*; (f) + *neither*; (g–h) tr *engaged to are unjust*; (i) + blank. 26. (a) + *and that without which I know nothing of betwixt Man and Man.* The phrase *and that . . . nothing of* is later repeated, where apparently the whole passage belongs [see b]; (b) + *betweene man and man and that*; (c–d) tr from above [see a]; (e) + *butt*; (f) + *that*; (g–h) tr *butt heere comes*; (i–j) *what a man*; (k) + *the.* 27. (a) + *wee must keepe Covenant with itt*; (b) + *that*; (c) + *or*; (d) + *and*; (e) *ours* + blank; (f) + *If*; (g) + *and*; (g–h) tr *satisfie one another.* 28. (a) *is*; (b) *hee*; (c) *to*; (d) *unlawfull*; (e–f) *bee bound . . . nott to perform itt*; (g) *are.* 29. (a) + *and*; (b) *Extreamities*; (c) + *on this hand, As*; (d–e) *because in these cases that*; (f) *what*; Firth thinks the end of the speech 'past amending'; but with Wildman's reply the sense can be determined.

30. (a) *that*; (b) + *iff*; (c) *butt*; (d) *successe or*; (e) + *which.* 31. (a) + *itt*; (b) *in*; (c–d) tr *or an end of satisfaction*; (e) *liberty*; (f) *that they.* 'The reporter changes into *oratio obliqua* for a moment' (Firth); (g) *man.* 32. (a) tr *Army*; (b) *noe*; (c) + *without*; (d) *amongst*; (e) + *that*; (f–g) tr *if those Engagemts. were nott made*; (h) + *and.* 33. (a–b) tr *is of another nature*; (c) *man*; (d) *considerations.* Firth notes that the report at this point is 'hopelessly confused.' I have amended it in the general sense of his paraphrase; (d–e) tr *is the consideration now*; (f–g) *itt*; (h) *was*; (i) + *and*; (j) *itt is*; (k) + *clearly*; (l) *said* (inserted, another hand). 34. (a–b) tr *proved unjust*; (c) + *clearly*; (d) + *that*; (d–e) tr *were a compliance or*; and substituted for *itt.* 'The report [of this speech] is so fragmentary that it is difficult to follow Ireton's argument' (Firth); (f) *since.* 35. (a–b) tr *infallibly just and right that*; (c) *Engagemt.*; (d) *Engagemt.*; (e–f) tr *a succession of Parliaments*; (g–h) *when that*; (i) + *and*; (j) *contents*; (k–l) *their resolutions with us*; (m) *furtherance.* 36. (a) + *that*; (b) + *as*; 37. (a) *and*; (b) *hopes*; (c) *act*; (d) *formerly*; (e) *butt*; (f) *to*; (g) + *nott.* 38. (a) + *said*; (b) *does*; (c) + *wee should nott have bin*; (d) *candle*; (e) *first*; (f) *resolutions*; (g) + *that.* 39. (a) + blank; (b) + *by*; (c) *lightened*; (d) *yett*; (e) + *and.*

40. (a) *that as*; (b) + *of it*; (c) + *bee*; (d) *and that.* 42. (a) *that*; (b) + *and.* 43. (a) + *and*; (c) *as*; (d) *any*; (e) + *this morning*; (f) + *that*; (g) *that.* 44. (a) + *and*; (b) + *if we finde that*; (c) + *that*; (f) *particulars*; (g) Clause tr from this point [see h–i]; + *butt*; (h–i) tr *Much businesse will bee.* Firth believes that 'Everard's speech is ex-

tremely confused, as fragments of different sentences are mixed together'; and he adds vaguely, 'Three clauses have been moved.' I have
reverted to the order of MS. save for the transposition of one clause;
(k–l) Firth omits: *I mean doing in that kinde, doing in that sort* and *such
kinde of Action, Action of that nature.* I have restored the reading of MS.
45. (a) + *the thinges*; (b) + *which*; (c) + *with*; (d–e) *itt will*; (f) *that*;
(g) + *in itt*; (h) + *that*; (i) + *that wee might consider.*   46. (a) *and*;
(b) + *soe*; (c) + *of*; (d) *Worke.*   47. (a–b) tr *if this bee.*   48. (a) *downe*;
(b) *if*; (c) *Mr Pettus* (evidently an alternative form of the name); (d) + *in*;
(e) + *and*; (f) + *as.*   49. (a) tr *presence of God*; (b) + *&c.*; (c) + *of*;
(d) *Armies*; (e) *thoughts*; (f) + *that.*

50. (a–e) Report appears to be very much confused at this point.
I have adopted Firth's reconstruction, but have recorded its departures
from MS.; (a–b) tr *this Army deare and tender to me*; (c) Here a–b,
+ *and therefore itt is that I wish*; (d) + *(if there be any) or*; (e) + *I would
nott have this Army.*   51. (a) + *nott to*; (b) + *wee seeke*; (e) *prize*;
(f) *wheresoever* (but apparently with *whatsoever* written over it); (g)
+ *that*; (h) + *going*; (i–j) tr *sad to thinke them soe*; (k) + *first*; (l–m) tr *noe
Engagemt. can take us from itt*; (n–o) tr *though itt bee just*; (o–p) tr *matter
in them that*; (q) *yett.*   52. (a) *butt*; (b–c) MS. places in brackets in
Ireton's speech. Firth suggests, but does not adopt, the change;
(d) *moved*; (e) + *that they.*   53. (a) *that*; (b) + *and*; (d) + *that*;
(e) *I*; (f) *as*; (g) + *and those that they must thus chuse*; (h) *others.*
54. (a) + *who taken together*; (b) + *Are the Representors*; (a–b) I have
adopted Firth's reading (indicating the phrases in MS. which he silently
drops), but have added [also] in order to avoid a forced interpretation of
the phrase *to make uppe*, which must mean 'to constitute,' not 'to fill
by election.' I am not at all sure, however, that Ireton is not hinting a
distinction between the property qualification demanded of electors and
that demanded of members of Parliament [cf. pp. 65, 113 n., 114], that
he is not saying: '[It is the represented] who, taken together [with those
who have more property] and consequently are to make up the representers of this kingdom—[it is the represented] and the representers,
who, taken together, do comprehend whatever is of real or permanent
interest in the kingdom'; (c) + *otherwise*; (d) + *hee in Birth or*; (e) +
butt; (f) + *look*; (g) + *you take away*; (h) + *and*; (i) + *those is.*
55. (a) *by*; (b) + *and*; (c–d) tr *taken altogether doe comprehend the
whole*; (e) + *to.*   56. (a) + *this way*; (b) *and*; (c) tr *men have*;
(d–e) tr *a Citty to send Burgesses*; (f) + *hee*; (g) + *and.*   57. (a) +
misrepresentation of the; (b) *how*; (c) + *are*; (d–e) tr *the p[er]manent
interest.*   58. (a–b) tr *freemen of Corporations*; (c) *Constitutions*;
(d) *a*; (e) + *butt*; (f) + *hath no p[er]manent interest that*; (g)+*will.*
59. (a) + *you forgott Somethinge in my Speech*; (b) *evasion*; (c) *man*;
(d–e) tr *wee are for Anarchy*; (f) The report of Ireton's speech is extremely confused. I have in general adopted Firth's rearrangement,
but have recorded the departures from MS.; (g–60 a) tr *answer upon which
that which*; (g–h) *I desire I would nott.*

60. (b) + *and*; (c) + *that*; (c–d) tr *whatever a man may claim*; (e) + *that
which*; (f) + *great and maine*; this tr to position marked g; (g–h) *that
seem'd to bee the Answer uppon which that which hath bin said against this
rests.* Here follows first paragraph of speech [59 g–60 a], and MS.
proceeds: *Now then as I say to that which is to the maine Answer that
itt will nott make the breach of propertie, Then*; (i) + *of*; (j) + *butt.*

61. (a–b) *itt is*; (c) + *Soe*; (d) *choice*.   **62.** (a) + *the*; (b) *if* (in error for *is*); (c–d) *what the objection is, and where the Answer lies to which itt is made*; (e–f) *itt*; (g) + *that*; (h) *are*; (i) *choice*.   **63.** (a) + *hee*; (b) + *that man*; (c) *butt*; (d) *an*; (e) + *a Major pte. you may have*; (f–g) tr *those men*; (h) + *for that by which*; (i) + *and that*; (j) + *this*; (k) *mee*; (l) + *you may*.   **64.** (a) *that*; (b–c) tr *a perpetual dictator*; (c) *one*; (d) *are*; (e) + *and*; (f) + *in Stane's*; (g) *equall*.   **65.** (a) + *and*; (b–c) tr *against a fundamentall Law*; (d) *from*; (e) + *hee may*.   **66.** (a) + *nott by his owne consent*; (b) *is*; (c) Emendation supplied by Ireton's speech [p. 55].   **67.** (a) + *a*; (b) *this*; (c) *us*; (d) *in*; (e) *of*; (f) + *of*; (h–i) *a fifth pte.* Emendation supplied by Rich's speech [p. 63]; (j) + *I say*; (k) + *and*; (l) tr *where wee were*; (m) tr *what shall become*.   **68.** (a) + *them*; (b) + *butt*; (c–d) tr *there may bee a way thought of*; (e) *if*; (f) + *in*; (g) + *before*.   **69.** (a) + *nott*; (b) *itt*; (c) + *I see*; (d) + *that*.

70. (a) + *that*; (b) + *and*; (c) + *in alle*; (d) tr *I thinke every Christian*; (e) *butt*.   **71.** (a) + *as*; (b) + *wee*; (c) *men*; (d) *hee*; (e) + *supposing*; (f–h) tr *lay aside the most fundamentall Constitution*; (g) *for*; (i–j) *all the soldiers have*; (k) *shrubs*; (l) *as*.   **72.** (a) *this*; (b) *that*; (c) *this*; (d) *lie*; (e) + *and*; (f–g) tr *that hath a freedome*; (h) + *nott*.   **73.** (a) + *in a generall sense*; (b) *light*; (c) Firth thinks that ' only the first words of some sentences are given.' I find the sense much more complete, but the order of the sentences, and even the phrases, in unrelieved confusion. I have reduced them to a rational order, which is, of course, conjectural. MS. reads: *I will minde you of one thinge, that uppon the will of one Man abusing us, and soe forth: Soe that I professe to you for my pte. I hope itt is nott denied by any man, That any wise discreete Man that hath preserved England or the Governemt. of itt, I doe say still under favour there is a way to cure all this Debate, I thinke they will desire noe more Libertie if there were time to dispute itt, I thinke hee would bee satisfied & all will be satisfied, and if the safetie of the Army bee in danger for my pte. I am cleare itt should bee amended, the point of Election should bee mended*; (d) *or*; (e) *hee*; (f) *was*; (g) tr *If the thinge*; (h) *satisfying*.   **74.** (a) + *butt*; (b) *to*; (c–d) *was nott that*; (e) + *as free*; (f) + *to*.   **75.** (a) + *and*; (b) + *for my pte.*; (c) *shall*; (d) *property*; (e) *that*; (f) *see*.   **76.** (a) + *wch. is before you*; (b) *I*; (c–e) tr *I will nott give itt an ill worde*. 'The remainder of this speech is simply a chaos of detached phrases from different sentences' (Firth); (d) *in*; (f) *a*; (g) + *and*; (h) + *that wee*; (i–j) tr *love in my heart*; (k) + *a*.   **77.** (a) *doe*; (b) *by*; (c–d) *distributions of itt*; (e) tr *as itt stands*; (f) + *that*.   **78.** (a–b) tr *to consider*; (c) + *and*; (d) + *nott*; (e–f) tr *there is as much reason*; (f) + *butt*.   **79.** (a) + *is*; (b) *that 's*; (c) tr *there 's a greater*; (d) tr *you take away*; (e) + *from some Men*; (f) + *nott*.

80. (a) + *and*; (b) Speech is transposed from after Chillenden's. I do not agree with Firth that it is 'merely a second version of the speech [on p. 75], not a new speech.' It is different in phrasing, though similar in argument at one or two points, and it refers to other matters, two of which have been mentioned, since Clarke's previous speech, by Petty and Rolfe [pp. 79–80]. Since, however, 'Waller does not answer Clarke, but Chillenden,' the speech must have become misplaced, and it could hardly have stood before Rolfe's since it seems to concur with that speech in its last sentence. Hence the transposition; (c) *should*.   **81.** (a) + *to butt*; (b) + *butt*; (c) + *that*; (d–e) tr *noe finger in appointing the lawgiver*; (f) *oibq*.   **82.** (a) *that*; (b–c) *leave this*; (d–f) tr *this enlarge-*

ment of that businesse; (e) + in that; (g–h) this enlargement of that businesse.   83. (a) every; (b) + itt; (c) doe; (d) + I declar'd; (d–e) tr there
manifested in the paper I declar'd; (f) + and were; (g) + that there were
meetings; (h) I; (i) liberties; (j) and.   84. (a) + that; (b) + as; (c) + on
the other hand they told me, That; (d) disputations; (e) ingeniously; (f) +
and.   85. (a) tr with such an heart; (b–c) tr thinke itt is nott very variable;
(d–e) tr though this be nott a rule of exactnesse; (f) + if nott that; (g–h) will
nott believe you.   86. (a) + & all the Engagemts.; (b) + for satisfaction;
(c) + butt; (d) + I doe nott see; (d–e) the Authours of this paper the
subscribers; (f) + for my pte. I do nott know what disbanding is iff that;
(g–j) tr than the outcries of the authours of itt; (h) them; (i) + wee all;
(k) + if.   87. (a–b) tr endeavouring to draw the souldiers to run this way;
(c–f) tr have the managing of the businesse; (c–d) by this or that way;
(e) or; (f–h) tr that wee have declar'd [for] before; (g) + itt; (i) +that;
(j) + whether we will nott devide with such satisfaction; (k) + whether that
were a deviding; (l–m) hee may; (n–o) tr a sense that wee doe nott know of.
88. (a) + heere itt is putt according to the inhabitants; (b) + and; (c) they;
(d–e) tr that the Commons shall chuse without Lords or any body else [butt
where I see thinges] [p. 89; and see 89 d]; (f–g) wee shall.   89. (a) + is
bound att his Coronation; (d) + butt where I see thinges + transposed sentence [88 d–e]; (e) + only as; (f–g) tr destruction of the Kingdome to
throwe them out [and]; (h) and; (i) + of; (j) + and.

90. (a) + butt when they cannott act justly; (b) appear'd to bee; (c) that;
(d) the; (e) + nott; (f–g) by the Kinge; (h) + to bee.   91. (a–b) tr and
nott any ordinance of Parliament; (c) of this that; (d) to; (e) wheras; (f) butt;
(g) tr troubled with the Kinges interests; (h–i) tr if this were setled; (j) +
that; (k) for.   92. (a) tr this very Parliament may destroy wheras;
(b) see; (c) + and; (d) senses; (e) tr I feare; (f) plausible; (g) + that;
(h) of.   93. (a) + are; (b) + and then itt says there; (c) tr can bee noe
peace and have; (d) + as; (e) + and; (f) + & itt is suggested; (g) + butt;
(h) would; (i) they; (j) + them.   94. (a) + butt; (b) + and; (c) + then;
(f) that; (g) + that; (i) + by; (j) + for my pte.   95. (a) + then;
(b) + butt wheras; (c) + now; (d) + blank (4½ pp.)—perhaps left for
other speeches, which were not transcribed.   96. (a) are; (b) thinge is.
97. (a) + of; (b) itt; (c–d) which satisfies; (e) first; (f–g) and in all these
Governemts. they were happy & Contented with itt, and; (h) yett; (i) + and.
98. (a) illegal; (b–c) tr which does satisfie the Kingdome [as]; (d) + as,
followed by the transposed phrase b–c; (e) + by; (f) att; (g) any; (h)
+ that; (i) + and.   99. (a–b) spoke to was; (c) + and; (d) + that;
(e) desires; (f) + or.

100. (a) + that was; (b) of; (c) + yett; (d) then; (e) + and; (f) + Certainly.   101. (a) + and; (b) + butt when any thinge is spoken; (c) I;
(d) + butt.   102. (a) + still; (b) + and; (c) + truly; (d) them;
(e) + that.   103. (a) + Truly; (c) + and; (c–d) tr shall nott bee offended
[and]; (e) + butt; (f) + and + transposed phrase [c–d]; (g) itt; (h) tr had
bin; (i) nothing; (j) + ordinary.   104. (a) + and; (b) was + to which
you do well to take heede; (c) made; (d) hath; (e) should; (f) + that.
105. (a) + that they; (b) + and; (c) itt; (d) what; (e) apprehensions.
106. (a) + and that is this (I); (b) + them; (c) + butt; (d) + nott; (e) or.
107. (a) call'd; (b) that; (c) + that; (d) to; (e) + hee; (f) + I finde that;
(g) + which is; (h) + and.   108. (a) butt; (b) + Itt is demonstrable;
(b–c) tr that doe butt hold Compliance with them; (d) + butt; (e) + soe.
109. (a) dissent; (b–c) tr from after c–d in its original position [see below];

(c–d) tr *itt is unjust they should have that power*, and there immediately
followed by b–c; (e–f) *them*.

110. (a) + blank (one line); (b) + *is itt*; (c–d) *itt*; (e) *soe*; (e–f) I adopt
Firth's suggestion that this is an interruption by Wildman, and correct
his reading; (g–h) *that is that*.   111. (a) + *I thinke* ; (b) + *that*;
(c) + *by all that itt is apparent*; (d) + *some Relation*; (e) + *butt*; (f) There
are spaces for completion of Latin phrase; (g) *the*.   112. (a) *have*;
(b) + *itt*; (c) *thoughts*; (d) + *that*; (e) *where*; (f) + *and*; (g–h) tr *any
thinge of the Kinge's Declaration to that purpose* [*that*]; (i) + blank;
(j) *dispensation*; (k) + *soe*; (l–m) tr *for the Establishment of the Kingdome*.
113. (a–114 h) tr [see p. 113, n. 2], with some alteration of order [see
below], from after Ireton: [*That*] *if a Lord shall bee accused & by a Jury
found guilty hee will Expect to bee tryed by his Peeres* [p. 116]; (b) First
part of Wildman's speech has been transposed from this position [b] to
114 g–h and 114 b–d, because it deals with a later proposal.   114. (a) +
and; (b–d) tr [see above, 113 b]; (c–d) *the interest of the Kinge & Lords
is laid aside wch. the Lord by a Judgemt. from heaven hath given away*;
(e–f) tr *will take them uppon his Memory, and by the way*; (g–h) tr [see
above, 113 b]; (i–j) *them*.   115. (a) *them*; (b) + *that*; (c) *onely*; (d) +
have bin subject; (e) + *and*; (f) *or*; (g) + *to bee*; (h) *to*; (i) + *any*.
116. (a) + *that*; (b) Here occur the transposed speeches 113 a–114 h;
+ *Com. Ireton* before next paragraph; (c–d) tr *any other difference they
are tryed by their peeres*.   117. (a–b) tr *I did then suppose agreed uppon*;
(c) *will*; (d–e) tr *those that the Commons shall chuse*.   118. (a) + *butt*;
(b) + *and*; (c) *that*.   119. (a) tr *Kinge to itt*; (b) *included*; (c) + *they*;
(d) *take*; (e) *doth*; (f) *none*; (g) + *and*; (h–i) tr *from Constitution or from
Right* [p. 120]; (j) + *butt*.   120. (a–b) *200* (It is certainly possible that
the mistake, which is repeated, is Cowling's, but more probable that
it is the reporter's or the transcriber's); (c) *200*; (d) + *and*; (e) *of*;
(f) + *they*.   121. (a) *That* (+ blank); (b) + *wheras*; (c–d) tr *with
their estates*.   122. (a–b) tr *as just as any in the world*; (c–d) tr *yett is
bound to stand to itt*; (e–f) tr *have Established the Kinge againe*. 123. (a–b)
MS. gives to Ireton as first sentence of his speech. Firth suggests (but
does not adopt his own suggestion) that it is another interruption by
Wildman, to which Ireton's speech is a reply; (c) + *to*; (d) + *and*;
(e) + *that*; (f) *Lords*.

125. (a) For source of text, and principles adopted in editing the Whitehall Debates, see p. 479.   (b–e) This summary of the measures discussed and passed at this meeting is from Firth, 2. 71–2; where it is
printed from a second and fragmentary account of the Whitehall Debates
in Clarke MSS. vol. 16; (c) + resolutions of adjournment, &c.; (d)
Stapylton; (f) After heading (place, date, etc.), transferred to opening line
above, + *Present, Lo: Generall Fairfax* + blank (for remaining names).
For list of officers present, see *Clarke Papers*, ed. Firth, 2 270–81.
126. (a) *offers*.   127. (a) + *either than*; (b) + *and*; (c) *has*; (d) In MS.
one word written over another: the final word may be *where*.   128. (a) *itt*
(b) + *now*; (c) *exercise*; (d) + *That* + blank (half-line); (e) + *that*;
(f) *expresse*; (g) + *nott*; (h) *them*; (i) *for*.   129. (a) + *that*; (b) + *may*.

130. (a) + *butt*; (c) *by*; (d) + *that*; (e) *as*; (f) *that*; (g) + *in*; (h) *neither*;
(i) + *itt*.   131. (a–b) tr *controversies heretofore hath bin this*; (c) + *butt*;
(d) + *as*; (e) + *some*; (f) *butt*.   132. (a) + *what in matter of acting*;
(b) + *that*; (c) *hee*; (d) *saving*; (e) *to*; (f) tr *hath bin offer'd*.   133. (a) +

that; (b) + *nott*; (c) + *if hee*; (d) *Designe*; (f) *to*; (g) *him*; (h) *his*; (i) *outward*; (j) + *in itt as that*; (k–l) *to of*; (m) *hee*.   135. (a) *needinesse*;
(b) + *for*; (c) + *if so bee and*; (d) *if*; (e) *them*; (f) *this*; (g) + *and*.
136. (a) + *and itt may bee*; (b) *for*; (c) + *as*; (d) + *as are manifest in
them*; (e) + *going*; (f) + *that*; (g) *offence*; (h) + *beeing the power*; (i) tr
power.   137. (a) + *and*; (b) *incomes*; (c) + *nott*; (d) *for*; (e) *mindes*.
138. (a) *hath*; (b) + *and*; (c) + *butt*; (d) *their*; (e) *wee*; (f) *sufferinges* +
butt.   139. (a) + *that*.

140. (a) *wee*; (b) + *that*; (c) *state*; (d) + *and*; (e) + *however*; (f) +
whether; (g) + *butt*.   141. (a) + *if*; (b) + *to itt*; (c) *and*.   142. (a)
+ *indeed*; (c–d) tr *because in* [*that*] *our Remonstrance*; (e–f) tr *to matters
of Justice and of the Kingedome*; (g) *for*; (h) + *and*; (i) + *that*; (j) + *itt*;
(k) + *butt*.   143. (a) *wee*; (b) *or*; (c) *an I*.   144. (a) + *that*; (b) + *and*.
145. (a) + *for to*; (b) + *itt*; (c) + *a*; (d) + *and*; (e) + *butt*.   146. (a) *temporall*; (b) + *itt*; (c) *that*; (d–e) tr *and hee had this case of conscience*.
147. (a–b) *and whiles I am in Bonds heere you will punish mee, when I shall
come to Returne to my Spirit, Itt was nott the Saints butt God himself*:
scattered fragments whose reconstruction is purely conjectural; (c) + *and*;
(d) *to*; (e) + *itt*.   148. (a) + *that*; (b) *whole*; (c) *Hewson*; Col. Harrison
had offered a reason for referring the question of the reserve to a committee [p. 140]; Col. Tichborne had urged it without offering particular
reasons; Col. Hewson is not reported as speaking on the subject of a
committee; (d) *C. I.*   149. (a) *this*; (b) + *iff*; (c–d) *hee*; (e) + *that*;
(f) + *civill*.

150. (a) *would*; (b) + *that wch.*; (c) + *and*; (d) + blank; (e) *large*.
151. (a) *to*; (b–c) (d–e) mutually transposed; (f) + *they*; (g) + *I conceive*;
(h) + *and*; (i) + *how*; (j–k) tr *wee have pretended to*; (l–152 a) *that have
bin in the good land have bin in such a scattered time*.   152. (b) + *uppe*;
(c) + *or ought to bee*; (d) + blank (half-line), + *that*; (e–f) *a losse at a
longe time*; (g) *that*.   153. (a) *att*; (b) + *now*; (c) + *itt*; (d) + blank
(one line) + *and*; (e) + *that*; (f) + *butt*; (g–h) tr *shall nott preach though
they bee called of God*; (i) *Contests*; (j) *reasonings*.   154. (a) + *that*;
(b) *matters*; (f) *them*; (g) *hee*; (h) + *1.*; (i) *is acted*; (j) + *that they*.
155. (a) *they*; (b) + *1.*; (c) + *and*; (d) *unto*; (e) + *that they*; (f–g) tr *were
to exercise*; (h) + *that*; (i) + *may*.   156. (a–b) *as Magistrates & nott
as civill Magistrates, as Magistrates having an aucthority Civill or naturall
or as persons signifying*; (c) *by*; (d) + *only*. There follows in MS. a
fragment ascribed to Nye, which is probably the first part of his speech
on p. 159, and is transposed to that place [see 159 e–h]; (e) + blank
(half line) + *that wheras*; (f) + *that*; (g) *driven*.   157. (a) *this*; (b) +
for; (c) *contemplations*; (d) + *such a*; (e) *wch.*; (f) + *first*; (g–h) *and the
exercise of the samenesse of power for the Exercise of the Gospell under the
Law*; (i) + *First*; (j) + *itt*; (k) + *as*; (l) + *butt*.   158. (a) + *that*;
(b) Two words are indecipherable. Firth reads the second *poetically*.
It is better to mark the whole phrase as conjectural; (c) + *that they*;
(d) *that's*; (e) *him*; (f–g) *divested uppon*; (h) *was*.   159. (a) + *and*;
(b) + *now*; (c) + *if they*; (d) *Magistrates*; (e–h) tr from after Ireton's
speech [see 156 d], where it makes no sense, purporting to introduce an
argument which, in fact, is not introduced. Again, Nye is too nearly
in agreement with Ireton to be likely to reply to him. Finally (if it is
argued that the rest of Nye's speech has been omitted), Goodwin ignores
him and refers only to Ireton; (f–g) tr *suggest my thoughts this way before*;
(i) tr *to him by the people*; (j) tr *typicall*; (k) + *that*; (l) + *and if so*.

160. (a) *and*; (b) *whether*; (c) *for*; (d) + *that*; (e) + *this*; (f) + *and*; (f–g) tr *to avoide such Evills*; (h) + *the.*   161. (a) + *and*; (b) *besides*; (c) + *this, however*; (d) tr *thinges were*; (e) + *itt*; (f–g) *by whome hee is restrain'd.*   162. (a) tr *uppon Conscience*; (b) *of*; (c) + blank; (d) + *1*; (e) + *and*; (f) + *hee*; (g–h) tr *and as the Magistrate of a Kingdome or a Nation*; (h) + *and that*; (i) + *nott*; (j–k) tr *the Members of any Ecclesiasticall Society [as]*; (l) *any*; (m) + *as*; (n) *as.*   163. (a) + *that*; (b) *therof*; (c) *wee*; (d) + *they*; (e–f) *without any*; (g) + *and*; (h) + *as*; (i) *as.*   164. (a) tr *itt will bee much*; (b) *panges*; (c) *sense,* which appears to have been (indistinctly) altered to *fence*; (d–e) *the punishmt. of the Ceremoniall Law was nott of the Morall Law itt self, the punishment of the Morall Law was not of the Morall Law itt self, butt of the purity of the Jewes*; (f) *Morall*; (g) *hath*; (h) *as*; (i) *they*; (j–k) tr *often minded this day*; (l) + *that.*   165. (a–b) tr *some thinges mentioned*; (c) *that*; (d) *commands*; (e) *New*; (f) *that*; (g) *giving*; (h–j) tr *wch. was punished with death in the New* [i.e. Old] *Testament*; (i–j) *the 1. Corinthians 1. 7*; (k) + *that*; (l) *was*; (m) + *and the like.*   166. (a) + *as*; (b) + *that*; (c) + *and*; (d) + *the same*; (e) tr *I will*; (f) + *before.*   167. (a) + *and*; (b) tr *were written were all under*; (c–d) *hee*; (e–f) *they*; (g) tr *to what thinges are*; (h) + *that*; (i) *of.*   168. (a) *is*; (b) *this*; (c) tr *Nye*; (d) *Idolatry*; (e) + blank (1½ lines).   169. (a) + *because*; (b) + *nott*; (c) + *and*; (d) *which*; (e) *itts (selfe*, scored out); (f–g) tr *butt nott quatenus Magistrates*; (h) + *that*; (i) Almost illegible; possibly *tide*; (j) + *uppon the 3d. Article, the last Article, That*; (k–170 a) tr *hath revealed himself.*

170. (b) + *Debate uppon the last wordes. So as they abuse nott this Libertie*; (c) + *uppon the 4th. Article concerning religion*; (d) *ha's*; (e) *going*; (f) + *that*; (g) + *Question uppon the matter concerning Religion.*   171. (a) + *Present* (+ blank for names); (b) *did*; (c) + *butt*; (d) *Agreements.*   172. (a) *destructive*; (b) + *that*; (b–c) tr *is noe more butt*; (d) + *and*; (e) *a*; (f) + *that wee did nott enough.*   173. (a) + *I doe nott look uppon that*; (b) *this*; (c–d) *them*; (e) *would*; (f–g) tr *I doe thinke that a dozen or 24*; (h) + *they.*   174. (a) tr *nothing more*; (b–c) tr *Kinge, Lords and Commons* (d) *reserving*; (e) + *that*; (f) + *to*; (g) + *and*; (h) *and*; (i) *him*; (j) *that.*   175. (a–b) *That that all putt*; (c–d) tr *in the midst of January*; (e) + *or*; (f–g) tr *the Men att Westmr.*; (h) + *that*; (i) *other.*   176. (a) *make*; (b) + *in*; (c–d) tr *nott bee disputing amonge our selves. Some are*; (d–e) tr *the Spiritt is now to make* [i.e. break] *forth*; (f) *this*; (g) *that*; (h) + *that*; (i) + *is*; (j) + *soe*; (k) + *nott*; (l) + *itt would be*; (m) *you*; (n) *your.*   177. (a) *libertie*; (b–c) tr *the best Magistrate[s] that ever were*; (d) + *itt*; (e) *nott*; (f) *epuration* (not *edification*, as Firth, with hesitation, reads it; which yet seems required by the sense); (g) *and*; (h) *butt*; (i) + *that*; (j–k) tr *butt itt is more of God*; (l) *they.*   178. (a) + *1. That*; (b–c) tr *to answer the lusts within us*; (d) *workes*, altered to *wordes*; (e) *wordes*; (f–g) tr *and secondly to take away that reproach*; (h–i) tr *all of Argument that did come downe to itt*; (j) *this.*

179. (a) The texts of the illustrative documents, whether in Part III or the Appendix, are derived from contemporary printed sources, and (except where another library is mentioned) from a copy in the British Museum. The principles on which the selections are edited, and the notations used, are identical with those adopted in editing the Debates, but with two additional signs: three dots (. . .) for omissions of less than a sentence, three asterisks (* * *) for omissions of a sentence or more. A sufficiently full title of each book or pamphlet is given in these notes, together with a record of other omissions (or adaptations). The date

following the title is that supplied by the copy in the Thomason Collection (British Museum).

179. (b) THE SMOKE IN THE TEMPLE. WHEREIN IS A DESIGNE FOR PEACE AND RECONCILIATION OF BELIEVERS OF THE SEVERAL OPINIONS OF THESE TIMES. * * * BY JOHN SALTMARSH. . . . London, Printed by Ruth Raworth for G. Calvert . . . 1646 [Jan. 16]; (c) pp. 9–19: scripture references transferred to footnotes. **181.** (a) pp. 3–6: marginal references omitted; (b–c) tr from end of paragraph. **182.** (a) + as. **183.** (a) pp. 59–68.

186. (a) INDEPENDENCIE GODS VERITIE. OR THE NECESSITIE OF TOLERATION. * * * WRITTEN BY J. G. B. D., London, Printed for William Ley, 1647. (McAlpin Collection, Union Theological Seminary, New York.) Pp. 7–8; (b) *which is of.*

187. (a) CONSCIENCE WITH THE POWER AND CASES THEREOF. DIVIDED INTO V BOOKES. WRITTEN BY THE GODLY AND LEARNED WILLIAM AMES. . . . TRANSLATED OUT OF LATINE INTO ENGLISH FOR MORE PUBLIQUE BENEFIT. * * * Imprinted Anno MDCXXXIX. Book 5, chap. 1. **188.** (a) *nature.*

191. (a) THE INSTITUTION OF CHRISTIAN RELIGION. WRITTEN IN LATINE BY M. IOHN CALVIN. TRANSLATED INTO ENGLISH * * * BY THOMAS NORTON. Imprinted at London by Anne Griffin for Ioyce Norton and R. Whitaker, 1634. Book 4, chap. 20. Section numbers omitted; marginal scripture references incorporated, in brackets.

199. (a) LEX REX: THE LAW AND THE PRINCE. A DISPUTE FOR THE JUST PREROGATIVE OF KING AND PEOPLE. * * * London: Printed for Iohn Field . . . Octob. 7. 1644. Numbering of arguments, and. some headings, omitted; marginal scripture references incorporated, in brackets; other marginal matter omitted; (b) Preface. **201.** (a) *Angell.* **204.** (a) + *to.* **209.** (a) *remander.* **211.** (a) *killeth.*

212. (a) RIGHT AND MIGHT WELL MET. OR A BRIEFE AND UNPARTIAL ENQUIRY INTO THE LATE AND PRESENT PROCEEDINGS OF THE ARMY. . . . BY JOHN GOODWIN. [Quotes John 7. 24; Prov. 17. 15; also from Tertullian and Seneca.] London, Printed by Matthew Simmons for Henery Cripps . . . 1648 [Jan. 2, 1649]. Compared with copy in McAlpin Collection. Marginal quotations omitted; marginal references incorporated, in brackets. **214.** (a) *formerly.* **216.** (a) *eminent.*

221. (a) A COMMENTARIE OF MASTER DOCTOR MARTIN LUTHER UPON THE EPISTLE OF S. PAUL TO THE GALATHIANS. * * * London, Printed by George Miller . . . 1644 (4th edition of a translation first issued in 1575). Marginal gloss omitted; numbers in square brackets supplied.

228. (a) Translation is from Milton, *Prose Works* (Bohn edition), vol. 1, but has been somewhat revised by comparison with the Latin text printed in the *Columbia Milton* and the accompanying translation. **230.** (a) Translation is from Milton, *Prose Works*, vol. 1, but has been somewhat revised by comparison with the Latin and the improved translation in the *Columbia Milton.*

232. (a) Anti-Arminianisme. Or the Church of Englands old antithesis to new Arminianisme. * * * By William Prynne. . . . The second edition much enlarged. * * * Imprinted, 1630. Pp. 72–5. The second column, setting forth the Arminian position, has been omitted, as also the marginal scripture references.

233. (a) A Glimpse of Sions Glory: or the Churches beautie specified. Published for the good and benefit of all those whose hearts are raised up in the expectation of the glorious liberties of the Saints. [Quotes Psalm 87. 3; Isa. 40. 10, 11.] London, Printed for William Larnar . . . MDCXLI. 'To the Reader,' signed W. K. (i.e. William Kiffin), omitted.   235. (a) intended.   238. (a) where.

241. (a) Certain Qværes humbly presented in way of petition, By many Christian people dispersed abroad throughout the county of Norfolk and city of Norwich, to the serious and grave consideration and debate of his Excellency the Lord General and of the General Council of War. * * * Together with an humble advice for the settling of the kingdom, according to such a model hinted therein, offered as the sence of many Christians, who conceive themsleves ingaged (as by their prayers, so) by their councels, to help on the present work of God. . . . London, Printed for Giles Calvert . . . 1648 [Feb. 19, 1649].

247. (a) The Ancient Bounds, or Liberty of Conscience, tenderly stated, modestly asserted, and mildly vindicated. I Cor. 10. 15: I speake as to wise men, judge yee what i say. * * * Licensed and entred according to order. London, Printed by M. S. for Henry Overton . . . 1645 [June 10]. Compared with corrected copy in McAlpin Collection. Chapter numbers and marginal gloss omitted; biblical references incorporated, in brackets; Address to the Reader, preceding that headed 'A Light to the Work,' omitted; all other omissions indicated; numbers in square brackets supplied; notes thereon indicate the chapter from which the selection is taken; (b) 'A Light to the Work'; (c) Chap. 1.   249. (a) Chap. 2; (b) proximious.   254. (a) Chap. 3. 255. (a) Chap. 4.   258. (a) Chap. 6.   263. (a) Chap. 9.   264. (a) Chap. 10.

266. (a) The Bloudy Tenent of Persecution for Cause of Conscience, discussed in a conference betweene Truth and Peace. Who in all tender affection present to the High Court of Parliament . . . these, among other passages of highest consideration. Printed in the year 1644 [July 15]. Chapter numbers and marginal gloss omitted; headings, and under the last heading section numbers, supplied; (b) Numbering omitted; (c) Chap. 6.   268. (a) Chaps. 19–28.   269. (a) unto. 270. (a) + Truth; (b) 1.   271. (a) + that; (b) 12.   272. (a) Chaps. 31–3.   273. (a) cuts.   274. (a) Chaps. 44–52.   277. (a) Chaps. 53 (wrongly numbered 54)–60; heading is from chap. 60; (b) eyes.   279. (a) offenders.   280. (a) Chap. 74.   281. (a) Chap. 83.   282. (a) Chaps. 86–91.   283. (a) 133; (b) Chaps. 92–3.   284. (a) 146; (b) Chap. 94.   285. (a) deducted.   286. (a) their; (b) Chaps. 120–3, 128, 131; (c) or.   287. (a) t'other.   288. (a) natural.   289. (a) no.   291. (a) is; (b) + Rev. 19.

293. (a) THE KEYES OF THE KINGDOM OF HEAVEN, AND POWER THEREOF, ACCORDING TO THE WORD OF GOD. BY THAT LEARNED AND JUDICIOUS DIVINE, MR IOHN COTTON. * * * THE SECOND TIME IMPRINTED * * * PUBLISHED BY THO. GOODWIN, PHILIP NYE. London, Printed by M. Simmons for Henry Overton . . . 1644 [Second edition; Thomason's copy of first, dated, June 14]. 294. (a) + *that.*

299. (a) AN APOLOGIE OF THE CHURCHES IN NEW-ENGLAND FOR CHURCH-COVENANT. OR A DISCOURSE TOUCHING THE COVENANT BETWEEN GOD AND MEN, AND ESPECIALLY CONCERNING CHURCH-COVENANT. . . . SENT OVER IN ANSWER TO MASTER BERNARD, IN THE YEARE 1639. AND NOW PUBLISHED. . . . London, Printed by T. P. and M. S. for Benjamin Allen, 1643.

300. (a) THE SAINTS APOLOGIE, OR A VINDICATION OF THE CHURCHES (WHICH INDEAVOUR AFTER A PURE COMMUNION) FROM THE ODIOUS NAMES OF BROWNISTS AND SEPARATISTS, IN A LETTER SENT TO AN EMINENT DIVINE OF THE ASSEMBLY. * * * London, Printed with order, by A. C. Anno MDCXLIV [May 15].

302. (a) THE WAY OF TRUE PEACE AND UNITY AMONG THE FAITHFUL AND CHURCHES OF CHRIST, IN ALL HUMILITY AND BOWELS OF LOVE PRE-SENTED TO THEM. BY WILLIAM DELL. . . . [Quotes from Psalm 120; also from St Augustine.] London, Printed for Giles Calvert . . . 1649 [Feb. 8]. Marginal references, numbering of arguments, and some superfluous headings, omitted. 306. (a) + *that.*

317. (a) THE FREE-MANS FREEDOME VINDICATED. OR A TRUE RELATION OF THE CAUSE AND MANNER OF LIEUT. COL. IOHN LILBURNS PRESENT IMPRISONMENT IN NEWGATE. * * * [No title-page (McAlpin Collection)]; (b) + *and who.* 318. (a) + *but.*

318. (b) TO THE RIGHT HONOURABLE AND SUPREME AUTHORITY OF THIS NATION, THE COMMONS IN PARLIAMENT ASSEMBLED. THE HUMBLE PETITION OF MANY THOUSANDS, EARNESTLY DESIRING THE GLORY OF GOD, THE FREEDOME OF THE COMMON-WEALTH, AND THE PEACE OF ALL MEN [Sept. 19, 1648]. 319. (a) + *as;* (b) + *most.*

323. (a) AN APPEALE FROM THE DEGENERATE REPRESENTATIVE BODY THE COMMONS OF ENGLAND ASSEMBLED AT WESTMINSTER: TO THE BODY REPRESENTED. THE FREE PEOPLE IN GENERAL OF THE SEVERAL COUNTIES, CITIES, TOWNES, BURROUGHS, AND PLACES WITHIN THIS KINGDOME OF ENGLAND, AND DOMINION OF WALES. AND IN ESPECIALL, TO HIS EXCELLENCY, SIR THOMAS FAIRFAX (CAPTAINE GENERALL) AND TO ALL THE OFFICERS AND SOULDIERS UNDER HIS COMMAND. BY RICHARD OVER-TON, PRISONER IN THE INFAMOUS GOALE OF NEWGATE, FOR THE LIBERTIES AND FREEDOMES OF ENGLAND. [Quotes 2 Cor. 10, 16; 11, 4; and applies them to the contemporary situation of Parliament, City, and people.] London, Printed in the yeare, 1647 [July 17]. Marginal gloss omitted. 324. (a) + *though;* (b) + *not;* (c) + *or else.* 325. (a) *award.* 326. (a) to; (b) *centure.* 328. (a) *Tuliday;* (b) + *to.* 331. (a) + *as;* (b) *Stapylton.* 333. (a) *your;* (b) *depravation.* 334. (a) *adjutators* (so below; also *adjutation*); (b) + *not.* 335. (a) Appended to the *Appeal;* (b) *illegible.* 336. (a) + *to put.* 337. (a) *the.*

338. (a) To the Right Honorable, the Commons of England In Parliament Assembled. The humble petition of divers wel-affected persons inhabiting the City of London, Westminster, the Borough of Southwark, Hamblets, and places adjacent [Sept. 15, 1648] (McAlpin Collection). **339.** (a) tr *Religion and God*; (b) *which*. **340.** (a) *dusines*; (b) *state*.

342. (a) The Legall Fundamentall Liberties of the People of England Revived, Asserted, and Vindicated. Or, an epistle written the eighth day of June 1649, by Lieut. Colonel John Lilburn. * * * London, Printed in the grand yeer of hypocriticall and abominable dissimulation. 1649; (b) *Pomfret*; (c) *Tichburn* (later *Tychburn, Titchburn*). **344.** (a) *Hiland*. **345.** (a) *at*. **346.** (a) +*in*. **347.** (a) *every*. **348.** (a) *Martyn* (later *Martin*); (b) *Challiner*. **349.** (a) + *in*. **353.** (a) *Neperdullion*.

355. (a) Foundations of Freedom or an Agreement of the People: Proposed as a rule for future government in the establishment of a firm and lasting peace. Drawn up by several well-affected persons, and tendered to the consideration of the General Councel of the Army; and now offered to the consideration of all persons who are at liberty, by printing or otherwise, to give their reasons for, or against it. Unto which is annexed several grievances, by some persons offered to be inserted in the said Agreement, but adjudged only necessary to be insisted on, as fit to be removed by the next representatives. Published for the satisfaction of all honest interests. 1648 [Preface dated 10th Dec. 1648; Thomason's date, 15th Dec.]. Compared with another edition in McAlpine Collection (with same preface dated 15th Dec., and with the imprint: London, Printed for R. Smithurst, 1648). **356.** (a) Text of these passages is supplied by A Petition from . . . Fairfax and the General Council of Officers . . . to . . . the Commons of England in Parliament assembled, concerning the Draught of an Agreement of the People. . . . Together with the said Agreement presented Jan. 20. . . . Tendred to the consideration of the People. * * * London Printed for John Partridge, R. Harford, G. Calvert, and G. Whittington MDCXLIX [Jan. 22]. Compared with text in Rushworth's *Collections*. **365.** (a) Text supplied by An Agreement of the 'Free People of England. Tendered as a peace-offering to this distressed nation. By Lieutenant Colonel John Lilburne, Master William Walwyn, Master Thomas Prince, and Master Richard Overton . . . May the 1. 1649. [No title-page; colophon: London, Printed for Gyles Calvert (McAlpin Collection).]

367. (a) To the Svpreme Avthority of England the Commons assembled in Parliament. The humble petition of divers well-affected women of the Cities of London and Westminster, the Borough of Southwark, Hamblets and parts adjacent. Affecters and approvers of the Petition of Sept. 11. 1648 [May 5, 1649]. **368.** (a) *Blanck*; (b) *gantlop*; (c) *Cook*; (d) + *and*.

369. (a) London's Liberties; or a Learned Argument of Law & Reason, upon Saturday, December 14. 1650. Before the Lord Major, Court of Aldermen, and Common Councell at Guild Hall, London. Between Mr Maynard, Mr Hales & Mr Wilde of Coun-

CELL FOR THE COMPANIES OF LONDON. AND MAJOR JOHN WILDMAN AND MR JOHN PRICE OF COUNCELL FOR THE FREEMEN OF LONDON. * * * THIS DISCOURSE WAS EXACTLY TAKEN IN SHORT-HAND BY SEVERALL THAT WERE PRESENT AT THE ARGUMENT. . . . London, Printed by Ja. Cottrel for Gyles Calvert . . . 1651 [Dec. 19, 1650]. **371.** (a) *Cook* (thus throughout); (b) *Argier.* **373.** (a) *Hales* (thus throughout).

379. (a) THE TRUE LEVELLERS STANDARD ADVANCED: OR THE STATE OF COMMUNITY OPENED, AND PRESENTED TÓ THE SONS OF MEN. BY WILLIAM EVERARD, IOHN PALMER, IOHN SOUTH, IOHN COURTON, WILLIAM TAYLOR, CHRISTOPHER CLIFFORD, IOHN BARKER, FERRARD WINSTANLEY, RICHARD GOODGROOME, THOMAS STARRE, WILLIAM HOGGRILL, ROBERT SAWYER, THOMAS EDER, HENRY BICKERSTAFFE, IOHN TAYLOR, &C. BEGINNING TO PLANT AND MANURE THE WASTE LAND UPON GEORGE-HILL, IN THE PARISH OF WALTON, IN THE COUNTY OF SURREY. London, Printed in the year MDCXLIX [April 26, 1649]. Address 'To all my fellow creatures that shall view these ensuing lines,' signed John Taylor, April 20, 1649, omitted. Heading of main body of text, 'A declaration to the powers of England and to all the Powers of the World . . .' omitted. **382.** (a) *and*; (b) *a lifter up.*

385. (a) THE DIGGERS MIRTH, OR, CERTAIN VERSES COMPOSED AND FITTED TO TUNES, FOR THE DELIGHT AND RECREATION OF ALL THOSE WHO DIG, OR OWN THAT WORK, IN THE COMMONWEALTH OF ENGLAND. * * * SET FORTH BY THOSE WHO WERE THE ORIGINAL OF THAT SO RIGHTEOUS A WORK, AND CONTINUE STILL SUCCESSFULL THEREIN AT COBHAM IN SURREY. London, Printed in the Year 1650 [April 4]. Pamphlet contains a second song; neither is that copied in Clarke MSS. and printed by Firth (Clarke Papers, 2.221); (b) *set.*

387. (a) For principles on which documents in the Appendix are edited, see above, 179 (a).

389. (a) *that.*

390. (a) A DISCOVERY OF THE NEW CREATION. IN A SERMON PREACHED AT THE HEAD-QUARTERS AT PUTNEY Sept. 29. 1647. BY THOMAS COLLIER. 2 Pet. 3. 13. NEVERTHELESSE WE LOOK FOR NEW HEAVENS, AND A NEW EARTH, WHEREIN DWELLETH RIGHTEOUSNESSE. London. Printed for Giles Calvert . . . 1647 (McAlpin Collection). 'Epistle to the Reader' omitted. **394.** (a) + *1.* **395.** (a) *loosed*; (b) *was.*

396. (a) 'A Second Apologie of All the Private Souldiers in his Excellencies Sir Thomas Fairfax his Army, to their Commission Officers,' in THE APOLOGIE OF THE COMMON SOULDIERS OF HIS EXCELLENCIE SIR THO. FAIRFAXES ARMY. TO HIM THEIR NOBLE AND RENOWNED GENERALL AND TO ALL THE REST OF THE COMMISSION-OFFICERS. ABOUT WHICH APOLOGIE THE SAID ARMIES COMMISSIONERS WERE QUESTIONED, AND IMPRISONED ABOUT TWO HOURES, BY THE HOUSE OF COMMONS, THE LAST OF APRIL 1647. FOR DELIVERING THIS APOLOGIE TO THEIR GENERALL AND OTHER OF THEIR CHIEFE COMMANDERS IN LONDON. London, Printed May 3. 1647. The first Apology is dated 28th April 1647, and signed by the Agitators of eight regiments. **397.** (a) + marginal reference to instances, with a promise to prove them; (b) *his*; (c) *his.* **398.** (a) + *and.*

398. (b) Clarke MSS., vol. 41; and *Clarke Papers*, ed. Firth, 1. 22–4; (c–d) *open Enemies or undermining*; (e) *Crave*.

399. (a) Clarke MSS., vol. 41; (b) Colonel Waller's Regiment, art. 12; (c) Colonel Farley's Regiment, art. 12; (d) Colonel Lambert's Regiment, art. 13; (e) Colonel Hewson's Regiment, arts. 1, 6, 12.

400. (a) Clarke MSS., vol. 41; and *Clarke Papers*, ed. Firth, 1. 100–1; (b) *instant*; (c) tr *means*; (d) tr *petition*; (e) Clarke MSS., vol. 41; and *Clarke Papers*, ed. Firth, 1. 105–6; (f) *Dewar*.

401. (a) A SOLEMNE ENGAGEMENT OF THE ARMY UNDER THE COMMAND OF HIS EXCELLENCY SIR THOMAS FAIRFAX, WITH A DECLARATION OF THEIR RESOLUTIONS AS TO DISBANDING AND A BREIFE VINDICATION OF THEIR PRINCIPLES AND INTENTIONS. * * * SUBSCRIBED BY THE OFFICERS AND SOULDIERS OF THE SEVERALL REGIMENTS AT THE RENDEZVOUS NEARE NEW-MARKET ON FRYDAY AND SATURDAY, JUNE 4 AND 5. * * * London: Printed for George Whittington . . . 1647 [June 11]. Compared with the Cambridge edition, printed by Roger Daniel, as reprinted in *Old Parliamentary History*, 15. 424–30; (b) *writing*. **402.** (a–b) Cambridge text: *do own and approve*; (c) *confering*; (d) + *of*; (e) *necessary*; Cambridge text, *present*.

403. (a) A REPRESENTATION FROM HIS EXCELLENCIE SR. THOMAS FAIRFAX, AND THE ARMY UNDER HIS COMMAND, HUMBLY TENDERED TO THE PARLIAMENT: CONCERNING THE JUST AND FUNDAMENTALL RIGHTS AND LIBERTIES OF THEMSELVES AND THE KINGDOME, WITH SOME HUMBLE PROPOSALS AND DESIRES IN ORDER THEREUNTO, AND FOR SETTLING THE PEACE OF THE KINGDOME. ST. ALBANS, JUNE 14. 1647. * * * Cambridge: Printed by Roger Daniel, Printer to the Universitie. Compared with the London edition, printed for George Whittington, 1647, which lacks two paragraphs present in the Cambridge edition. **406.** (a) London text; Cambridge text + *now*. **407.** (a–b) London text.

409. (a) Clarke MSS., vol. 67; and *Clarke Papers*, ed. Firth, 1. 170–214 (which see for full text); (b) *eminent*; (c) *disenabled*. **410.** (a) + *bee*; (b) *are*. **414.** (a) *as*; (b) *was*; (c) + *that*; (d–e) transposed; (f) *proved one*; (g) + *and*; (h) *carried*. **415.** (a) + *that*; (b–c) transposed; (d) transposed. **416.** (a) *doe*; (b) *you*; (c) + *and*. **417.** (a) + *the*; (b) *as*. **418.** (a) *prest*; (b) *to*. **419.** (a) + *and*; (b) *had*; (c) *others*. **420.** (a) *our*; (b) *Clarke Papers* ed. Firth, 1. 215–16; (c) *consisted*; (d) *more*. **421.** (a–b) transposed; (c) *longe*.

422. (a) A DECLARATION FROM HIS EXCELLENCIE SR. THOMAS FAIRFAX, AND HIS COUNCELL OF WARRE. CONCERNING THEIR PROCEEDING IN THE PROPOSALLS, PREPARED AND AGREED ON BY THE COUNCELL OF THE ARMIE. . . . TOGETHER WITH THE HEADS OF THE SAID PROPOSALLS. * * * London: Printed for Matthew Simmons 1647 [dated Aug. 1; Thomason dates, Aug. 5].

426. (a) PUTNEY PROIECTS. OR THE OLD SERPENT IN A NEW FORME. PRESENTING TO THE VIEW OF ALL THE WELL AFFECTED IN ENGLAND, THE SERPENTINE DECEIT OF THEIR PRETENDED FRIENDS IN THE ARMIE, INDEAVOURING TO INTRODUCE TYRANNY AND SLAVERY IN A NEW METHOD. COMPOSED BY THE DILIGENT AND IMPARTIALL OBSERVATION AND CERTAIN

INTELLIGENCE OF JOHN LAWMIND. [Quotes Mic. 7, 3–5; Matt. 24, 24–5.] London, Printed in the Yeare 1647 [Dec. 30]. Marginal references omitted.

429. (a) THE CASE OF THE ARMIE TRULY STATED, TOGETHER WITH THE MISCHIEFES AND DANGERS THAT ARE IMMINENT, AND SOME SUTABLE REMEDIES, HUMBLY PROPOSED BY THE AGENTS OF FIVE REGIMENTS OF HORSE TO THEIR RESPECTIVE REGIMENTS AND THE WHOLE ARMY. AS IT WAS PRESENTED . . . OCTOBER 15. 1647 UNTO HIS EXCELLENCY SIR THOMAS FAIRFAX. * * * [Quotes Deut. 20. 8; Judges 7. 7.] London, printed in the yeare 1647 [Oct. 19]. Marginal references omitted; (b) *by*. 433. (a) Numbering has been corrected. 436. (a) *principal*; (b) *this*; (c) *sapine*.

437. (a) TWO LETTERS FROM THE AGENTS OF THE FIVE REGIMENTS OF HORSE, THE ONE TO THE WHOLE SOULDIERY OF THE ARMY, THE OTHER TO SOME WHO SENT UNTO THEM, TO RECEIVE FURTHER INFORMATION AND SATISFACTION [Oct. 28, 1647].

438. (a) ENGLANDS FRIEND RAISED FROM THE GRAVE. * * * BEING THE TRUE COPIES OF THREE LETTERS, WRITTEN BY MR JOHN SALTMARSH, A LITTLE BEFORE HIS DEATH. * * * London, Printed for Giles Calvert . . . 1649 [July 31].

439. (a) A CAL TO ALL THE SOULDIERS OF THE ARMIE, BY THE FREE PEOPLE OF ENGLAND. 1. JUSTIFYING THE PROCEEDINGS OF THE FIVE REGIMENTS. 2. MANIFESTING THE NECESSITY OF THE WHOLE ARMIES JOYNING WITH THEM, IN ALL THEIR FAITHFULL ENDEAVOURS, BOTH FOR REMOVING OF ALL TYRANNY AND OPPRESSION . . . AND ESTABLISHING THE JUST LIBERTIES AND PEACE OF THIS NATION. 3. DISCOVERING (WITHOUT ANY RESPECT OF PERSONS) THE CHIEFE AUTHORS . . . OF ALL OUR MISERIES, ESPECIALLY THE NEW RAISED HYPOCRITS BY WHOSE TREACHEROUS PRACTICES, ALL THE JUST INTENTIONS AND ACTIONS OF THE ADJUTATORS AND OTHER WELL MINDED SOULDIERS HAVE BEEN MADE FRUITLESS. [Quotes Isa. 58. 6; Matt. 23. 27–8.] Printed in the yeare 1647 [Oct. 29].

443. (a) AN AGREEMENT OF THE PEOPLE FOR A FIRME AND PRESENT PEACE, UPON GROUNDS OF COMMON-RIGHT AND FREEDOME; AS IT WAS PROPOSED BY THE AGENTS OF THE FIVE REGIMENTS OF HORSE; AND SINCE BY THE GENERALL APPROBATION OF THE ARMY, OFFERED TO THE JOYNT CONCURRENCE OF ALL THE FREE COMMONS OF ENGLAND. * * * Printed Anno Dom. 1647 [two editions, Nov. 3, and Nov. 4]. 'Letter to the Freeborn People of England' (p. 445) and 'Letter to the Officers and Soldiers' (p. 447), printed with the *Agreement*. Preamble here omitted (see p. 443). 446. (a) *disenabled*.

449. (a) Clarke MSS., vol. 67; and *Clarke Papers*, ed. Firth, 1. 363–7, 407–9. 450. (a) *equality*; (b) *small*. 451. (a) Marginal notes omitted; these indicate that clauses were passed unanimously, save (ii) where margin reads: *Major Corbett; noe*.

452. (a) A LETTER SENT FROM SEVERAL AGITATORS OF THE ARMY TO THEIR RESPECTIVE REGIMENTS. . . . WHEREIN IS DISCOVERED THE GROUND

OF THE PRESENT DIFFERENCES BETWEEN THEM AND THE GENERAL COUNCEL, CONCERNING THE KING, AND THE ESTABLISHMENT OF COMMON RIGHT AND FREEDOM FOR ALL PEOPLE IN THIS KINGDOM. WITH A TRUE ACCOUNT OF THE PROCEEDINGS OF THE GENERAL COUNCEL THEREUPON. London, Printed for John Harris. 1647 [Nov. 11] (McAlpin Collection). **454.** (a) Clarke MSS., vol. 67; and *Clarke Papers*, ed. Firth, 1. 411–6.

456. (a) A REMONSTRANCE OF HIS EXCELLENCY THOMAS LORD FAIRFAX, LORD GENERALL OF THE PARLIAMENTS FORCES, AND OF THE GENERALL COUNCELL OF OFFICERS. HELD AT ST. ALBANS THE 16. OF NOVEMBER, 1648. PRESENTED TO THE COMMONS ASSEMBLED IN PARLIAMENT, THE 20 INSTANT, AND TENDRED TO THE CONSIDERATION OF THE KINGDOME. London Printed for John Partridge and George Whittington . . . MDCXLVIII [Nov. 22]; (b–c) *or with.* **458.** (a) *party* (thus throughout, except in the phrase immediately following). **464.** (a) *intend.*

465. (a) THE DECLARATION OF HIS EXCELLENCY THE LORD GENERAL FAIRFAX, AND HIS GENERAL COUNCEL OF OFFICERS, SHEWING THE GROUNDS OF THE ARMIES ADVANCE TOWARDS THE CITY OF LONDON. * * * London, Printed by John Field for John Partridge, Novemb. 1. 1648 [Dec. 1]. **466.** (a–b) *discourse . . . from this courage.*

467. (a) Clarke MSS., vol. 67; and *Clarke Papers*, ed. Firth, 2. 133–70.

472. (a) A PLEA FOR COMMON-RIGHT AND FREEDOM. TO HIS EXCELLENCY, THE LORD GENERAL FAIRFAX, AND THE COMMISSION-OFFICERS OF THE ARMIE. OR, THE SERIOUS ADDRESSES, AND EARNEST DESIRES OF THEIR FAITHFUL FRIENDS . . . PROMOTERS AND PRESENTERS OF THE LATE LARGE-PETITION OF THE ELEVENTH OF SEPTEMBER, MDCXLVIII. AS IT WAS PRESENTED TO HIS EXCELLENCY, DECEMB. 28. 1648. BY L. C. JOHN LILBURN . . . RICHARD OVERTON . . . THO. PRINCE [thirteen others named]. London Printed by Ja. and Jo. Moxon, for Will. Larnar . . . 1648 [Dec. 29].

474. (a) A DECLARATION OF THE ENGLISH ARMY NOW IN SCOTLAND, TOUCHING THE JUSTNESS & NECESSITY OF THEIR PRESENT PROCEEDINGS IN THAT NATION. Imprimatur Joh: Rushworth. London, Printed by Edward Husband and John Field, Printers to the Parliament of England. August 12. 1650. Compared with another edition: A DECLARATION OF THE ENGLISH ARMY . . . TO THE PEOPLE OF SCOTLAND. **475.** (a) *reserted*; (b) *have.*

INDEX

Figures in parentheses refer to pages of Introduction